11.35 Russell + Russell 1-68 (Swearingen)

WAR AND DIPLOMACY
IN THE JAPANESE EMPIRE

WAR
AND DIPLOMACY
IN THE JAPANESE EMPIRE

By

TATSUJI TAKEUCHI

Professor of International Relations
Kwansei Gakuin University

Introduction by
QUINCY WRIGHT

NEW YORK / RUSSELL & RUSSELL

FIRST PUBLISHED IN 1935 BY THE UNIVERSITY OF CHICAGO
REISSUED, 1967, BY RUSSELL & RUSSELL
A DIVISION OF ATHENEUM HOUSE, INC.
L. C. CATALOG CARD NO: 66-27158
PRINTED IN THE UNITED STATES OF AMERICA

Reprinted from a copy in the collections of
The New York Public Library

Author's Preface

THIS VOLUME undertakes to examine and evaluate the processes of formulating, executing, and controlling the Japanese foreign policy since the establishment of a parliamentary system of government in 1890. The primary emphasis is placed upon procedure rather than the substance of policy. Therefore, no attempt is made in this volume to give an exhaustive treatment of the substance of policy, as it more properly belongs to a separate study on the diplomatic history of modern Japan.

Part I is devoted to a brief discussion of the structure and functions of various organs for the conduct of Japanese foreign relations. In Part II, on the other hand, detailed procedural analyses of eighteen diplomatic incidents are made in order to examine the conduct of foreign relations in practice. Part III, which comprises the last three chapters, may be said to constitute the summary and conclusions of the present study.

It is obviously impossible for a study of this nature to avoid errors in data or mistakes in judgments, particularly when dealing with recent incidents. It is the author's humble wish that the present inquiry may only serve as an incentive to further research in this important field of international relations.

It is impossible to make individual acknowledgments of all the assistance received by the author during the course of his research on this subject. However, special mention should be made of the courtesies so generously extended to the author by the heads of the following libraries: the University of Chicago libraries, Northwestern University Library, Tokyo Imperial University Library, Kwansei Gakuin University

Library, the Teikoku Toshokan (Imperial Library) at Uyeno, and the Teikoku Gikai Toshokan (Parliamentary Library) in Tokyo. He also takes this opportunity to mention his indebtedness to Dr. Tatsukichi Minobé, the late Dr. Sakuzo Yoshino, Professors Masamichi Royama and Kisaburo Yokota of the Tokyo Imperial University, and Professor Jumpei Shinobu of Waseda University. Thanks are also due to Dr. Ichiro Kiyosé, former vice-speaker of the House of Representatives, the late Marquis Kinichi Komura, former chief of the intelligence bureau of the foreign office, as well as Mr. Setsuichi Aoki, former chief of the Tokyo office of the secretariat of the League of Nations. These gentlemen and others, whose names are deliberately withheld here, read portions of the manuscript or otherwise gave invaluable assistance to the author. And finally, the author begs to mention Professor Quincy Wright, under whose guidance and inspiration the present work was executed at the University of Chicago. These gentlemen, of course, are not responsible for the general plan of the work, the conclusions reached, nor for the errors found in this volume.

TATSUJI TAKEUCHI.

Kwansei Gakuin University
Nishinomiya, Japan
June 20, 1935

CONTENTS

CONTENTS

Chapter III

Chapter IV

Chapter V

Chapter VI

Chapter VII

Chapter VIII

APPENDIX

BIBLIOGRAPHY

Introduction

THE PRESENT STUDY is part of a coöperative project for investigating the causes of war initiated by the Social Science Research Committee at the University of Chicago in 1927. While it is planned to publish a general summary of the results of the investigation, those special studies which have an independent interest, of which this is one, are published as they are completed.[1]

The project began with no theory of the causes of war but with a series of approaches suggested at several meetings by members of the departments of Political Science, Economics, History, Sociology, Anthropology, Geography, and Psychology at the University of Chicago in the spring of 1926. Certain of these suggestions were selected for detailed study by research assistants working under the direction of members of the university staff, or by members of the staff itself, but such unity as the project may eventually acquire will be a result of final synthesis rather than of initial analysis.

The studies planned included several on the internal structure and functioning of governments in making war and

---

[1]Those published to date as books or articles include the following: Frederick L. Schuman, *War and Diplomacy in the French Republic*, New York, 1931; Harold D. Lasswell, *World Politics and Personal Insecurity*, New York, 1935; Eugene Staley, *War and the Private Investor*, New York, 1935; Hazel C. Benjamin, "Official Propaganda and the French Press During the Franco Prussian War," *Journal of Modern History*, June, 1932; James T. Russell and Quincy Wright, "National Attitudes in the Far Eastern Controversy," *American Political Science Review*, August, 1933; Philip Davidson, "Whig Propagandists of the American Revolution," *American Historical Review*, April, 1934; Schuyler Foster, "How America Became Belligerent: A Quantitative Study of War News, 1914-1917," *American Journal of Sociology*, January, 1935.

conducting diplomacy. It is clear that governments of states
are immediately responsible for the initiation of most modern
wars. Governments differ from each other according to the
types of men in positions of power, and according to the
constitutional structures which more or less determine the
classes or sections of the population which shall exert influence and the degree of deliberation and breadth of participation which shall precede important decisions. One might
expect to find that the frequency of war in the foreign relations of a given state is related to the type of governing personality and constitutional structure which prevails in the
state, but before such an expectation can be tested, detailed
descriptive accounts on a somewhat common model of these
personalities and constitutional structures operating in a
number of states in the same international milieu must be
available.

In 1931, Dr. Frederick L. Schuman published a study prepared under the auspices of this committee entitled *War and
Diplomacy in the French Republic*. The present study follows a
similar model with respect to Japan. In successive parts it
discusses the constitutional structure of Japan, sets forth the
operation of this structure in the most important international
transactions from 1890 to 1934, and finally synthesizes this
material according to types of activity involved. These are
classified as treaty making, war making, and the formulation
of foreign policy. Although the outlines of the two books are
the same, Dr. Takeuchi's treatment differs from that of Dr.
Schuman in that it is more descriptive and less interpretative.
In the second part, particularly, Dr. Takeuchi gives less attention to the diplomatic background of the episodes treated
and the actual motivations of the actors. The extraordinary
detail, however, with which Dr. Takeuchi has explained the
internal workings of the Japanese government in these incidents on the basis of documents and other materials, mostly
in the Japanese language, renders it invaluable for understanding that curious combination of oriental and occidental
elements, the Japanese state.

The manuscript, with exception of Chapter XXVI, was
completed just before the Mukden incident of September,
1931. It was decided to postpone publication until an account
of this incident could be added, but the momentous inter-

national events which followed—the occupation of Manchuria,
the bombardment of Shanghai, the Japanese recognition of
Manchukuo, the censuring of Japan by the League of Nations
Assembly, Japan's withdrawal from the League, as well as
significant internal changes in Japan—succeeded each other
with such rapidity that Dr. Takeuchi found it impossible to
conclude his chapter until the last of these events had occurred
in the spring of 1933. Even then it was scarcely possible to
appraise the situation from the standpoint either of Japanese
foreign policy or of Japanese constitutional development until
another year had passed. In the meantime new events had
occurred, especially the London naval conversations and the
Japanese denunciation of the naval treaties in December,
1934. The consequences of these events, however, are still
pending, and it was decided to publish this study without
further delay, terminating it with Japan's withdrawal from
the League.

The period from the promulgation of the written Constitution of 1889 to the ratification of the London Naval Treaty
in 1930 constitutes a definite epoch in Japanese constitutional
history, an epoch in which parliamentary control of the executive began and developed, reaching its peak in the latter
episode. Since that episode, perhaps, in part, because of it,
parliament has been forced to retire into the background,
while the military and naval authorities have increased their
influence. How long this new trend will last, it is impossible
to say, but the circumstances precipitating it are described in
Chapter XXVI in more detail than in any other publication
in the English language.

Dr. Takeuchi's treatment of the Japanese participation in
the process of negotiating and ratifying the London Treaty,
written it must be recalled before the Mukden incident, is of
exceptional interest. First, because it seems to mark the triumph of the cabinet and parliament over the Privy Council
and the military and naval advisers. Second, because it discloses the reality of "dual government" between civilian and
military authorities in Japan. Third, because it seems to point
toward just such an effort of the military to reëstablish its
prestige as occurred in September, 1931. Dr. Takeuchi points
out that while the Hamaguchi cabinet was able to retain the
confidence of the Diet for its signature of the treaty, against

the advice of the naval advisers, yet in spite of its recent victory at the polls, it did not dare to state the constitutional grounds on which it assumed this responsibility. To have done so would have been to assert cabinet superiority in state affairs, not only over the naval advisers, but also over the army advisers. Such a statement would have resulted in aligning the army, even more powerful than the navy, against the cabinet, and the cabinet could not face that risk. As a final comment on this episode, Dr. Takeuchi notes that after the treaty had been ratified the foreign minister, Shidehara, was forced to retract his statement that the imperial ratification of the treaty was convincing evidence that the national defense was secure under the London Treaty. The opposition would not tolerate this shielding of what it considered a grave diplomatic blunder by dragging the throne into politics. There perhaps, also, was something ominous in the fact that Premier Hamaguchi, whose vigor had put the London Treaty through, and who had seen in its ratification evidence that the world had progressed "from the pioneer to the settlement stage," was shot six weeks after this event. As a result of the shooting he died nine months later.

Less than a year after the treaty was ratified, the Manchurian incident occurred, with consequences which Dr. Takeuchi describes in Chapter XXVI no less objectively than he has described those of the earlier period of constitutional development.

Comparison of the Japanese institutions for conducting foreign relations, with the French institutions discussed by Dr. Schuman, throws further light on the general relationship between constitutional institutions and foreign policies. In theory the two constitutions are very different. The French Constitution is based upon parliamentary sovereignty with full cabinet responsibility to the parliament and the subordination of the military to the civilian cabinet. Dr. Schuman, however, points out that in practice parliamentary control is sometimes nominal, particularly in the conduct of foreign affairs. The executive usually initiates and acts, and parliament follows. On certain occasions the military or naval authorities have taken action on their own responsibility, and the cabinet, confronted by a *fait accompli*, has had to endorse it.

In Japan constitutional theory places the Diet in a much

less important rôle. The Privy Council is the constitutional adviser of the Crown on foreign affairs, and the military and naval advisers have direct access to the Emperor on matters of imperial defense. Practically the genro, or elder statesmen, were the main advisers of the Emperor on all important matters. But with only the aged Saionji surviving of this group, its political importance is nearing an end. The dominance of the Diet over these bodies is not established in constitutional theory, nor is its dominance over the cabinet, although the parliamentary responsibility of the cabinet was gaining in recognition prior to 1931. The rôle of parliament had tended to increase during the first forty years of Japanese development under the Constitution of 1889, but Dr. Takeuchi is very cautious about predicting the continuance of this development. The theoretical position of the Privy Council and of the military and naval advisers, supported by powerful clans, has been sufficiently maintained in practice so that the triumph of parliamentarism is by no means assured. Especially in policies relating to China, Dr. Takeuchi points out, military and naval circles had a large influence since the Russo-Japanese War and dominated the situation during the Manchurian episode from 1931 to 1933.

In both France and Japan, the executive and the military have often initiated warlike activities without prior parliamentary consent, but in France they have had to reckon with the possibility of parliamentary veto, while in Japan they have been urged to act by anxiety to maintain an accepted constitutional position in the face of practical parliamentary encroachments. In both France and Japan the foreign policy of the state has in the main been determined by factors other than its constitutional organization. But in France, so far as constitutional institutions have an influence, they check warlike activities, while in Japan they more often act as a spur to such activities. It is difficult to avoid the conviction, in reading Dr. Takeuchi's detailed account, that a development of the position of parliament and cabinet in Japan beyond the possibility of constitutional challenge by the military would be in the interest of peace

QUINCY WRIGHT.

University of Chicago
September, 1935

PART I: CONSTITUTIONAL ORGANIZATION

Chapter I

THE IMPERIAL CONSTITUTION

Fundamental Characteristics of the Constitution[1]

THE CONSTITUTION of Japan represents a compromise between the old monarchical traditions and the modern constitutionalism of the West.[2] That is, the Constitution embodies in broad outline the foundations of Japanese national polity developed since the beginning of her history, colored by basic principles of modern constitutionalism. Hence, the fundamental characteristics of the Constitution may be comprehended under the following three heads: (1) monarchism, (2) constitutionalism, and (3) unitarism.[3]

The monarchical features of the Constitution are brought out most strikingly in the following four aspects: (1) amendment of the Constitution, (2) the autonomy of the imperial household, (3) limitations upon the legislative power of the Diet, and (4) independence of the supreme command.

The power to initiate the process of constitutional amendment is exclusively reserved to the throne. Therefore, the Imperial Diet is denied the power to initiate a constitutional

[1]For constitutional history of Japan prior to the promulgation of the written Constitution on Feb. 11, 1889, see Yoshino, "Draft Constitutions," *Kokka Gakkai Zasshi*, XLII (1928), 1793–1804; Prince Ito, "History of the Establishment of the Constitution," *ibid.*, XI (1897), 417–428, 529–544; Viscount Kaneko, "Prince Ito and the Drafting of the Constitution," *ibid.*, XXIV (1910), 979–1001; Count Okuma (ed.), *Fifty Years of New Japan* (Tokyo, 1910), I, 122–132; Kudo, *Teikoku Gikaishi* (Tokyo, 1901), I, 1–14; Minobe, *Kempo Satsuyo* (Tokyo, 1932), pp. 85–98.

[2]For commentaries on the Constitution, see Prince Ito, *Kempo Gikai* (Tokyo, 1889); Hozumi, "Principles of the Constitution," *Kokka Gakkai Zasshi*, III (1889), 170–177, 193–214, 274–300, 339–364, 397–410, 431–461, 505–533; Minobe, *Kempo Seigi* (Tokyo, 1928).

[3]Minobe, *Kempo Satsuyo* (1932), pp. 119–127.

amendment, while the people cannot petition for it. More-over, such important matters as those relating to the suc-cession to the throne, institution of regency, and other matters concerning the imperial household are regulated by imperial household laws, and placed outside the jurisdiction of the Diet. The legislative prerogative of the throne, to be exercised independent of the legislative branch of government, is far wider than is recognized in most monarchical states. This power of the throne is particularly noted in its prerogatives over police ordinances and foreign relations. Another point to be noted in this connection is the separation of the imperial prerogative over supreme command from other prerogatives over state affairs. The placing of this important prerogative outside the scope of cabinet responsibility and parliamentary discussion constitutes a significant feature of the Japanese Constitution.

The principles of modern constitutionalism incorporated into the Constitution by its framers represent an interesting contrast with the fundamental nature of Japanese polity. So far as compatible with those foundations of the state which are the products of history, such general principles as (1) government with the consent of the governed, (2) parlia-mentary responsibility of the ministers of state, and (3) "government of laws" were incorporated into the Constitu-tion. To carry out the principles of government with the consent of the governed, the Imperial Diet was established to represent the views of the people. To restrain the autocracy of the House of Representatives, however, the imperial prerogative to dissolve the popular chamber is recognized, and also a second chamber, the House of Peers, having equal powers, was established. Furthermore, the establishment of the Privy Council as an advisory organ to the throne on im-portant affairs of state places further restrictions upon the basic principles of popular government. The second character-istic of constitutional government is that the responsibility in the exercise of the rights of sovereignty can be definitely lo-cated, and that the people and their representatives in the Diet can question and vote upon the same. The parliamentary responsibility of cabinet ministers is an instance of this practice. The doctrine of government of laws and not of men is recognized in that the rights and duties of the subjects are defined in the Constitution and that they are modifiable only by laws and not subject to the arbitrary discretion of the executive branch of government.

The third characteristic of the Japanese Constitution is that it sets up a unitary system of government. The only two notable exceptions to this general principle are local self-government and the relatively large degree of autonomy enjoyed by colonial governments.

NATURE AND EFFECT OF THE CONSTITUTION

The supremacy of the Constitution over ordinary laws is generally recognized by jurists.[4] Thus, the Constitution cannot be modified by statutes, emergency imperial ordinances, treaties, or Imperial House Law, and all organs of the state are subject to the provisions of the Constitution.

INTERPRETATION OF THE CONSTITUTION

There is no express provision in the Constitution providing for interpretation thereof. From the general principles of separation of powers, each branch of the government is independent of the other within their respective jurisdictions, and hence each is competent to interpret the Constitution not binding upon other branches of government.[5]

AMENDMENT OF THE CONSTITUTION[6]

The power to initiate constitutional amendment is exclusively vested in the throne. Thus, a draft of a proposed constitutional amendment must be submitted to the Diet by imperial order.[7] Prince Ito, the principal drafter of the Constitution, attributes this exclusive power to the fact that the emperor is the sole author of it.[8]

[4]Minobe, Kempo Seigi, p. 24; Ichimura, Teikoku Kempo Ron, pp. 170–194; Shimizu, Kempo Hen (Tokyo, 1923), pp. 211–220.

[5]For a fuller discussion of this subject see Chap. VI, infra.

[6]Prince Ito, Kempo Gikai, pp. 134–136; Minobe, Kempo Satsuyo (1932), pp. 102–104; also his Kempo Seigi, pp. 718–726; Shimizu, Kempo Hen, pp. 192–209; Ichimura, Teikoku Kempo Ron, pp. 218–226.

[7]Constitution, Art. LXXIII, Cl. I.

[8]Prince Ito, Kempo Gikai, p. 135. Professor Minobe takes exception to Prince Ito on this point and argues that, since the coming into effect of the Constitution, Japan ceased to be an autocracy and became a constitutional monarchy, and hence

Two important restrictions upon the nature of draft amendments should be noted: (1) that it must be either a modification of, or an addition to, the Constitution, and not designed to abolish or suspend the Constitution itself;[9] and (2) that it may not conflict with the principles embodied in Article I of the Constitution that "the Empire of Japan shall be reigned over and governed by a line of emperors unbroken for ages eternal."[10]

Before submission to the Diet for deliberation and consent, a draft amendment must be referred to the Privy Council for advice.[11] Inasmuch as the amending power of the Constitution belongs to the prerogative of the throne to be exercised upon the advice of the ministers of state, a draft amendment is to be prepared by ministers of state in cabinet and petitioned to the emperor for submission to the Privy Council. In this connection, it should be noted that, although the Diet is denied the power of initiating a constitutional amendment, it would be within its constitutional powers to petition the throne for proposing a constitutional amendment.[12]

Though the Constitution provides only for submission of draft amendments to the Diet, there can be no doubt as to the necessity of obtaining parliamentary consent thereto as in the case of ordinary projects of law, since the amendment of the Constitution is a legislative function. However, the legislative power of giving consent to a project of constitutional amendment differs from its ordinary law-making power in that it is greatly limited and that greater caution is required in its deliberations.

As a natural consequence of the denial of the power of initiating the amending process, the Diet cannot take a vote on any matter other than what is contained in the project submitted thereto. That is, no amendment can be offered on

an amendment to the fundamental document which set up the constitutional system should no longer be made by the prerogative of the emperor alone but should require the consent of the Diet (*Kempo Seigi*, p. 720).

[9]Minobe, *Kempo Seigi*, pp. 62–64, 721. Dr. Shimizu concurs with Minobe on this point (*Kempo Hen*, p. 209). On the other hand, Ichimura holds that, though the Constitution may not be suspended by the emperor alone, there is nothing in legal theory to prevent its suspension, in part or in whole, under Article LXXIII of the Constitution (*Teikoku Kempo Ron*, p. 226).

[10]Minobe, *Kempo Seigi*, p. 723.

[11]*Sumitsuin Kansei*, Art. VI, Cl. II.

[12]Minobe, *Kempo Seigi*, p. 724.

matters not within the scope of the draft or new items inserted by the Diet. The power on the part of the Houses of the Diet to amend a draft submitted thereto is implied from the power of consent.[13] While in ordinary law-making process the presence of only one third of the members of the House is sufficient to open debates, and a majority of votes cast by the members present is required for its passage,[14] the quorum for deliberation upon constitutional amendment is two thirds of the whole membership of the House, and two-thirds vote is required for decision upon such a project.[15] Moreover, the Constitution cannot be amended during a period of regency.[16]

There remains an interesting question as to the fate of a draft amendment in case of its adverse vote in either House. Such jurists as Ichimura,[17] Hozumi,[18] and Minobe,[19] hold that parliamentary consent is required for valid amendment of the Constitution, while Justice Shimizu supports a contrary view.[20]

The Imperial House Law

Imperial House Law was issued for the governance of internal affairs of the Imperial Family. Minobe holds that, in so far as the provisions concern the imperial household, the Imperial House Law binds the state and the people, and calls this "a principle of the antonomy of the Imperial Court."[21] Although the *Koshitsu Tempan* was issued without the countersignature of a minister of state, the *Koshikirei* of 1907 provides that in promulgating an amendment to the Imperial House Law, ministers of state as well as the minister of the imperial household attach their signatures.[22] To amend the

[13]*Ibid.*, pp. 724–725. Ichimura denies this power of amending the draft on the ground that to admit the amendment power would be tantamount to admitting the power of initiating the amendment process (*Teikoku Kempo Ron*, p. 219). Ichimura is supported by Shimizu (*Kempo Hen*, pp. 201–202), Y. Hozumi (*Kempo Teiyo* [1910], I, 168).

[14]Constitution, Art. LXVI, LXVII.

[15]*Ibid.*, Art. LXXIII.

[16]*Ibid.*, Art. LXXV.

[17]*Teikoku Kempo Ron*, p. 222.

[18]*Kempo Teiyo*, I, 168.

[19]*Kempo Seigi*, p. 720.

[20]*Kempo Hen*, p. 205.

[21]Minobe, *Kempo Satsuyo* (1932), pp. 104–107.

[22]Imperial Ordinance No. 6, 1907, Art. IV.

Imperial House Law, a draft prepared in conference between the minister of the imperial household and the ministers of state is submitted by imperial order to the deliberation and advice of the Imperial Family Council and the Privy Council. Although no amendment to the Constitution has been made,[23] the Imperial House Law has been amended twice. Thus, eight articles were added to the Imperial House Law on February 11, 1907, and one on November 28, 1918.[24]

A question may be raised here as to the relative position of the Constitution and the Imperial House Law. A majority of jurists agree that the Constitution stands above the Imperial House Law, and in consequence, an amendment to the Imperial House Law may not affect the Constitution, whereas under Articles II, XVII, and LXXIV of the Constitution, the Imperial House Law may be radically modified. On the other hand, it is equally evident that the Imperial House Law may not be modified by ordinary laws or imperial ordinances. Hence, the Imperial House Law stands between laws and the Constitution.[25]

[23]Prince Ito, the principal drafter of the Constitution, prepared a draft amendment to the Constitution and also one for the ordinance concerning the House of Peers, in 1898, and ordered the then chief of the Legislative Bureau, Dr. Kenjiro Ume, to examine the same. But no tangible result was accomplished because of the violent opposition raised by bureaucrats and conservative members of the House of Peers (Gozo Noma, *Rippo Ichigen Ron* [Tokyo, 1927], II, 372–373).

[24]Minobe, *Kempo Seigi*, pp. 728–733.

[25]*Cf.* Ichimura, *Teikoku Kempo Ron*, pp. 253–266; also Minobe, *Kempo Satsuyo*, p. 107.

Chapter II

THE IMPERIAL THRONE, THE LORD PRIVY SEAL AND THE GENRO

THE EMPEROR AND THE THRONE

BARON HOZUMI, the late president of the Privy Council and a leading jurist, once defined the fundamental principle of Japanese constitutional system as theocratico-patriarchal constitutionalism.[1] Indeed, the most characteristic feature of her national polity is that the emperor reigns over and governs the state as the head of the vast Japanese family. This inherited power of the imperial throne is expressly confirmed in the first article of the Constitution which declares that "the Emperor of Japan shall be reigned over and governed by a line of Emperors unbroken for ages eternal."[2] The emperor, to whom the Constitution attributes sacredness and inviolability,[3] is the symbol of national unity.[4]

[1]"The Emperor holds the sovereign power, not as his own inherent right, but as an inheritance from his Divine Ancestor. The government is, therefore, *theocratical*. The Emperor rules over the country as the supreme head of the vast family of the Japanese nation. The government is, therefore, *patriarchal*. The Emperor exercises the sovereign power according to the Constitution, which is based on the most advanced principles of modern constitutionalism. The government is, therefore, *constitutional*. In other words, the fundamental principle of the Japanese government is *theocratico-patriarchal constitutionalism*" (*Ancestor-Worship and Japanese Law* [Tokyo, 1901], pp. 87–88).

[2]A leading liberal, Yukio Ozaki, M.P., aptly states this point as follows: "The sovereign has no mind of his own; the mind of the people is his mind, and on this principle our successive Emperors have acted. It implies the guiding of, as well as acting upon, the sentiments of the people" (*Voice of Japanese Democracy* [Tokyo, 1918], p. 11). *Cf.* Prince Ito, *Commentaries on the Constitution of the Empire of Japan* (Tokyo, 1889), p. 205; Minobe, *Kempo Seigi*, pp. 65–76; Y. Hozumi, *Kempo Teiyo*, I, 183–188.

[3]Constitution, Art. II. Commenting upon this article, Prince Ito says: "Not only shall there be no irreverence for the Emperor's person, but also shall He not be made a topic of derogatory comment nor one of discussion" (*Commentaries*, p. 6).

9

The distinction which exists between the king and the crown in the practice of the British Constitution applies in some measure to Japan. Thus, with the establishment of constitutional government in 1889, important restrictions have been placed upon the emperor in his exercise of the prerogatives of the throne.

THE SUCCESSION TO THE THRONE

The throne never dies. It is a hereditary institution whose order of succession is regulated by the Imperial House Law, promulgated by Emperor Meiji at the same time with the Constitution. The principle adopted is that of primogeniture.[5] Unlike the British system, the Imperial Diet is without power to participate in its amendment.

When the emperor is a minor or when he is prevented by some permanent cause from personally governing the state, a regency is instituted, with the advice of the Imperial Family Council and with that of the Privy Council, to exercise the prerogatives of the throne in the name of the emperor.[6] Here again the Diet is denied a voice.[7]

Though there is no express provision either in the Constitution or the Imperial House Law concerning temporary incapacity of the emperor to exercise his powers, on account of sickness, travel abroad, or other causes, leading jurists are

Minobe holds that this inviolability implies that: (1) no disrespectful act may be done towards him; (2) no political responsibility in the exercise of his imperial prerogatives, minister of imperial household assuming responsibility for imperial household affairs; (3) he is not accountable to laws for his private conduct; and (4) the emperor may not be dethroned under any circumstances. The only exception to this general principle of non-accountability of the emperor to ordinary laws of the state is a civil action concerning ordinary imperial property (*Kempo Seigi*, pp. 114–120). *Cf.* Ichimura, *Teikoku Kempo Ron*, pp. 290–304.

[4] *Cf.* Uyesugi, *Kempo Jutsugi* (Tokyo, 1927), pp. 97–98.

[5] Constitution, Art. II; Imperial House Law, Art. I. *Cf.* Minobe, *Kempo Satsuyo* (1932), pp. 211–221.

[6] Constitution, Art. XVII; Imperial House Law, Art. XIX. The only limitation placed upon regency is that neither the Constitution nor the Imperial House Law may be amended during the period of a regency (Constitution, Art. LXXV). For further discussion on the institution of regency, see Shimizu, *Teikoku Koho Taii* (Tokyo, 1926), pp. 116–131. *Cf.* Ichimura, *op. cit.*, pp. 326–346; Minobe, *Kempo Seigi*, pp. 315–325; Uyesugi, *Kempo Jutsugi*, pp. 125–138; Y. Hozumi, *Kempo Teiyo*, I, 250–262.

[7] Prince Ito opposed a parliamentary participation in the institution of a regency on the ground that it would tend to bring about the degradation of the Imperial Family (*Commentaries*, p. 33).

divided upon the constitutionality of entrusting to some member of the Imperial Family the exercise of the imperial prerogatives within certain limits.[8]

SOVEREIGNTY AND THE THRONE

On the constitutional position of the emperor, students of Japanese law hold two conflicting theories.[9] The question of the location of the sovereignty of the state constitutes the bone of controversy between the two schools. The conservative school, led by Prince Ito, contends for imperial absolutism, holding that the sovereignty resides in the emperor, while the liberal school argues for the limited character of the emperor's prerogatives, holding that the sovereignty of the state resides in the state and that the emperor is an organ of the state.

Thus the defenders of the conservative school maintain that the emperor granted the Constitution of 1889 as a benevolent sovereign to his subjects and not as a concession to the demands of the people, that in the exercise of his inherited powers the emperor receives no restrictions by the constitution of his own making, and that, rightly interpreted, it says nothing concerning the rights of the subjects. This school, upholding the doctrine of imperial absolutism, even denies the representative character of the Diet.[10] On the other hand, the expounders of the liberal school, led by Professor Minobe, emphasize the universality of the basic principles of constitutional government. In support of the limited character of imperial prerogatives in the exercise of the rights of sovereignty, they point out that (1) the constitutional provision

[8]Minobe (*Kempo Satsuyo*, pp. 282–284) supports its constitutionality, while Shimizu (*Kempo Hen*, pp. 623–635) and Ichimura (*Teikoku Kempo Ron*, pp. 346–350) deny it.

[9]The conservative school was founded by Professor Yatsuka Hozumi, and succeeded by Professor Shimizu, Uyesugi, and Kakei, while the liberal school was founded by Professor Minobe and supported by Professor Ichimura, Sasaki, and others. Most outstanding of the controversies on the interpretation of the Constitution was the one between Professors Uyesugi and Minobe of the Imperial University of Tokyo. For the views of Minobe, Uyesugi, Hozumi, Ichimura, Inouye, Oda, Ukita, see Hoshijima (ed.), *Saikin Kempo Ron* (Tokyo, 1927), *passim*.

[10]For instance, Dr. Y. Hozumi holds that the sovereignty which resides in the position of the emperor is inherent, absolute, complete, one, permanent, and without limitations, and that the existence of the state of Japan is dependent upon the existence of the sovereignty of the emperor, and boldly declares that "the Emperor is the State" (*Kempo Teiyo*, I, 213, 220–221).

for the exercise of imperial prerogatives with responsible
advice of ministers of state, (2) the parliamentary consent to
law, budget, and taxation, and (3) the exercise of the judicial
power through the court are the outstanding instances of express limitations placed upon the emperor in exercising the
prerogatives of the throne by the Constitution itself.[11]

The Nature and Scope of the Prerogatives of the Throne[12]

In a broad sense, the prerogatives of the throne are co-
extensive with the sovereignty of the state and include the
legislative power as well as the judicial power of the state, not
to speak of the broad executive power. However, when used in
a more limited sense, it refers to the autocratic power of the
emperor as the head of the state, and includes only those
powers to be exercised without parliamentary consent and
not delegated to independent organs. In other words, it ex-
cludes the legislative power in its formal sense and also those
powers exercised by independent organs such as the ordinary
courts of law, the Administrative Court, and the Board of
Audit.[13]

Regarding the scope of the prerogatives, distinction should
be made between the legislative, judicial, and executive
powers. In view of the constitutional stipulations for the
exercise of the legislative power with the consent of the Diet
and that of the judicial power by the courts of law, the imperial prerogatives in these two spheres should be strictly
construed. On the other hand, there is no reason to restrict
the executive prerogatives of the emperor to those enumerated
in the Constitution, since administrative acts, in the nature
of the case, are executed independent of the Diet or the
courts.[14] In exercising this broad executive power, the emperor

[11]For a systematic exposition of the functional theory of the emperor, see Minobe,
Kempo Seigi (Tokyo, 1928) *passim.*

[12]Minobe, *Kempo Seigi*, pp. 163–168. *Cf.* Y. Hozumi, *Kempo Teiyo*, II, 620–683;
Uyesugi, *Kempo Jutsugi*, pp. 605–645; Shimizu, *Kempo Hen*, pp. 1159–1178.

[13]*Cf.* Minobe, *Kempo Seigi*, pp. 163 ff.; also Sasaki, *Nihon Kempo Yoron* (1931),
pp. 323–329.

[14]Minobe, *Kempo Seigi*, pp. 167–168. Justice Shimizu places judicature and administration outside the scope of imperial prerogatives (*Kempo Hen*, p. 1170).
Uyesugi defines the prerogatives as comprehending residual powers, that is, those
powers whose modes of exercise are not expressly provided for in the Constitution
(*Kempo Jutsugi*, p. 610 ff).

always acts upon the advice of the ministers of state who assume the responsibility therefor. Consequently, it falls within the constitutional liberty of the people to comment upon and to criticize such matters.

We may discuss the prerogatives under the following five categories: (1) imperial household affairs, (2) supreme command of the army and navy, (3) ritualistic affairs, (4) conferment of honors, and (5) general affairs of state.[15]

PREROGATIVES OVER IMPERIAL HOUSEHOLD AFFAIRS[16]

The prerogatives over imperial household affairs are clearly separated from those over general affairs of state and exercised by the emperor as the patriarch of the Imperial Family with the advice of the minister of the imperial household, who is independent of the cabinet.[17] Prior to the establishment of constitutional government, however, no clear distinction was recognized between dynastic matters and general affairs of state, and consequently, the property of the Imperial Court was not separated from that of the state. With the establishment of constitutional government, however, imperial household affairs were placed beyond the reach of the Diet, and the separation was drawn between the affairs of the Court and those of the state. And yet, within the prerogatives over the imperial household are included matters which are not, strictly speaking, internal affairs of the Court but of vital concern to the people and to the state as well, such as those relating to the succession to the throne, institution of regency, and to the Imperial House Law. Over those matters bearing upon the general affairs of state, the cabinet is consulted, but the Diet has no means of questioning responsibility for such consultation.

The emperor exercises his prerogatives over imperial household affairs upon advice of the minister of the imperial household, who, unlike the cabinet, cannot be questioned or made

[15]Minobe, *Kempo Satsuyo*, pp. 221–223 ff. *Cf.* Shimizu, *Kempo Hen*, pp. 1171–1288; Ichimura, *Teikoku Kempo Ron*, pp. 790–896. Sasaki enumerates thirty-five specific prerogatives under the Constitution (*Nihon Kempo Yoron*, pp. 329–335).

[16]Minobe, *Kempo Satsuyo*, pp. 246–273.

[17]Ministers of state do not assume responsibility for imperial household affairs and refuse to make reply to interpellations in the Diet. For the well-known case of Minister Tanaka of the imperial household during the Twenty-fifth Diet, see *Teikoku Gikaishi*, VII, 11, 1175–1176, 1197–1198, 1300.

subject of parliamentary debate. The emperor is further assisted by the Imperial Family Council, the Privy Council as well as the Lord Privy Seal.

PREROGATIVES OVER THE SUPREME COMMAND[18]

The imperial prerogatives over military affairs may be divided into (1) the prerogative over supreme command of the army and navy, and (2) the prerogative over the administration of the nation's armed forces. The former prerogative is recognized in Article XI, while the latter is in Article XII of the Constitution. The *tosui taiken*, or prerogative over supreme command, comprehends the power of using the forces for the protection of the state from attack both from without and from within, and other powers directly relating to military operations. On the other hand, the *hensei taiken*, or prerogative over the organization and administration of armed forces, includes the organization of military divisions and of fleets, and all matters relating to military districts and sub-districts, to the storing up and distribution of arms, to the education of military and naval men, to inspections, to discipline, to modes of salutes, to styles of uniforms, to guards, to fortifications, to naval defenses, to naval ports and to preparations for military and naval expeditions, and also to the fixing of the number of men to be recruited each year.[19]

Though both the power of supreme military command and that of administration of the forces belong to the prerogatives of the emperor, the principle of the separation of military command from that of military administration has been recognized since the establishment of the cabinet system in 1885.[20] Under the existing system, the supreme military command is exercised by the emperor, not through the cabinet, but through the chiefs of general staffs of the army and navy, who are directly responsible to the emperor. From the time of the promulgation of the Constitution, the constitutionality of the

[18]The view propounded by Minobe that the supreme military command is a prerogative of the emperor as generalissimo and not as the head of the state is sharply challenged by Sasaki. *Cf.* articles by Minobe and Sasaki in *Kaizo*, XII, Nos. 6, 7 (June, July, 1930), pp. 19–26, 104–126.

[19]Prince Ito, *Commentaries*, p. 26.

[20]Minobe in *Kaizo*, XII, No. 6 (June, 1930), p. 21.

existing military organization had never been seriously questioned by constitutional jurists.[21]

Thus, the doctrine of the independence of the supreme command of general affairs of state has been recognized and practiced since the establishment of the general staff in 1878, and the subsequent development of political institutions, notably the establishment of the cabinet in 1885, the promulgation of the Constitution in 1889, and the gradual development of cabinet responsibility for state affairs, has not only confirmed this independence but has had the tendency even to enlarge its scope. The system finds no express sanction in the written Constitution. On the contrary, it is to be observed that the present system constitutes an important exception to, if not a violation of, the basic principles of constitutional government,[22] and that a new system of civilian control of military affairs might be instituted without amending the Constitution.[23] Moreover, the imperial prerogative over the supreme command, being outside the domain of ministerial responsibility, does not permit parliamentary interference in its exercise; and the distinction between the prerogative over the supreme command and that over the organization of the armed forces being juridical, the demarcation between them has been left to practice and tradition.

That the existing system violates the fundamental principles of responsible government, and that certain limits upon the scope of this power should be defined, goes without saying. Thus, the exercise of the prerogative over the supreme command should be confined to the command as well as the direction of military operations, the determination of internal organization of the forces, the subject of budgetary limitations, the instruction and education of those within the service as well as volunteers, and the internal discipline of the forces.[24]

In exercising this prerogative over supreme command, the

---

[21]In reply to a question asked in the Budget Committee of the House of Peers in the Fifty-sixth Diet, Prime Minister Tanaka confirmed the independence of the prerogative over supreme command of that over state affairs (*Kwampo gogai*, March 16, 1929, p. 446). Compare Ito, *Commentaries*, p. 25; Minobe, *Kempo Seigi*, pp. 250–256; Ichimura, *Teikoku Kempo Ron*, pp. 586–865.

[22]On this point see Dr. Yoshino, *Niju Seifu to Iaku Joso* (Tokyo, 1922), *passim*.

[23]Minobe, *Kempo Seigi*, p. 255; Sasaki, *Nihon Kempo Yoron*, p. 687.

[24]Minobe, *Kempo Satsuyo* (1932), pp. 325–326.

emperor is assisted by organs which are separate from, and independent of, those which advise the throne over general affairs of state. Hence, in Japanese constitutional practice, His Majesty's government and His Majesty's high command are independent of each other. Over the high command, the emperor is assisted by the minister of war, minister of navy, chief of general staff, chief of naval general staff, and the chief aid-de-camp to the emperor.[25] Moreover, as advisory organs to the emperor on important military affairs, the *Gensui-fu* (board of field marshals and fleet admirals)[26] and the *Gunji Sangiin* (supreme war council)[27] were established. In time of war, the supreme military command is concentrated in the *Senji Daihonei*, or Imperial Headquarters.[28]

The general staffs are charged with the duty of drawing up a program for national defense and military operations. Such program for national defense is reported directly to the emperor by the chief of army general staff (in case of land defense) or the chief of naval general staff (in case of naval defense). When the matter is of sufficient importance, it may be submitted to the deliberation of the Board of Field Marshals and Fleet Admirals, or to the Supreme War Council, or to both. After an imperial sanction has been given, the matter is referred to the war minister or to the navy minister for execution.[29] The *Gensui-fu*[30] and *Gunji Sangiin*[31] are both advisory organs to the emperor. Only matters of vital importance are referred to the deliberation of these bodies for advice. The Supreme War Council corresponds to the Privy Council on civil affairs and consists of (1) field marshals and fleet admirals, (2) minister of war, (3) minister of navy, (4) chief of general

[25]*Op. cit.*, p. 330. For further discussion on this point, see Chap. III, *infra*.

[26]Imperial Rescript, Jan. 20, 1898, and also Imperial Ordinance No. 5, 1898 (Jan. 20, 1898). Texts in *Genko Horei Shuran* (1927), Vol. I, Bk. III, p. 42.

[27]*Gunji Sangiin Jorei* (Imperial Ordinance No. 294, 1903). Issued on Dec. 28, 1903. Text in *ibid.*, Vol. I, Bk. III, p. 42.

[28]*Senji Daihonei Jorei* (Imperial Ordinance No. 293, 1903). Issued on Dec. 23, 1903. Text in *ibid.*, Vol. I, Bk. III, p. 42.

[29]Strictly speaking, general staffs are planning boards and not of execution or administration. However, in practice, the staffs have extended their activities into military administration.

[30]In Sept., 1929, the board consisted of one naval member and three army members (*Jiji Nenkan* [1930], p. 105).

[31]In Sept., 1929, supreme war councilors numbered thirteen, of whom eight were army members and five were naval members (*Jiji Nenkan* [1930], p. 165).

staff, (5) chief of naval general staff, and (6) specially appointed war councilors.[32]

A measure that concerns the national defense as a whole is submitted to the deliberation of this war council as a whole, but if the matter in question concerns only the naval defense, only the naval members of the Council deliberate upon it, while only army members are consulted in case of land defense. The petition to the emperor for submission of a measure to the deliberation of these bodies may be made either by the chiefs of staff, minister of war, or the navy minister. In practice, however, it is made upon agreement between the minister and the chief concerned.

PREROGATIVES OVER RITUALISTIC AFFAIRS

The rituals and worship which long constituted important activities of the government in Japan[33] are now performed by the emperor personally or by a member of the Imperial Family or by ritualistic officials. This prerogative of the emperor over ritualistic affairs is placed outside the domain of cabinet responsibility.[34]

THE THRONE, AND THE "FOUNTAIN OF HONOR"

Even under the Tokugawa régime the emperor retained this prerogative of conferring honors, and is expressly recognized in the Constitution.[35] This prerogative is exercised with the advice of either the minister of the imperial household or the director of the Bureau of Decorations[36] and placed beyond the scope of ministerial responsibility.

PREROGATIVES OVER GENERAL AFFAIRS OF STATE

We have already examined elsewhere the nature and scope of the prerogative of the throne over state affairs and have observed that it comprehends the legislative, the executive, and the judicial powers of the state.

[32]*Cf.* Minobe, *Kempo Satsuyo* (Tokyo, 1932), p. 332.

[33]*Cf.* Y. Hozumi, *Ancestor-Worship and Japanese Law*, pp. 1–76.

[34]Minobe, *Kempo Satsuyo*, pp. 240–243.

[35]Art. XV.

[36]*Koshikirei*, Arts. XVI–XXI. *Cf.* Minobe, *Kempo Seigi*, pp. 288–307; Prince Ito, *Commentaries*, pp. 29–30; Ichimura, *Teikoku Kempo Ron*, pp. 886–893.

Under the legislative prerogative, the emperor convokes, opens, closes, and prorogues the Diet, and dissolves the Lower House,[37] subject to the limitation that the Diet must be summoned at least once a year for a period of three months. Thus, the Diet is denied the power to meet upon its own initiative. Moreover, the emperor causes the cabinet to initiate bills;[38] he sanctions laws, and orders the same to be promulgated and executed.[39] His sanction, though never denied since the establishment of the Diet, is the necessary condition precedent to the making of laws.

The throne is not only an integral part in the law-making process but it possesses a large executive power, extending over the organization of various administrative establishments, appointment of civil and military officers, foreign relations, martial law, pardoning power, colonial administration, and other powers. More important of these powers shall receive our attention.

Under Article X of the Constitution, the emperor determines the organization of the different branches of the administration, the salaries of all civil and military officers, and the conditions of the service.[40] In the exercise of this organization prerogative, the emperor receives restrictions under the Constitution, the laws, and the budgetary power of the Diet. The Constitution provides for statutory determination of the organization of certain organs of government, placing them beyond the reach of the ordinance power of the emperor. Hence, the organization of the ordinary courts of law, the Administrative Court, the Board of Audit are to be determined only by laws, while the ministers of state and the Privy Council cannot be abolished or deprived of their constitutional powers. Moreover, the budgetary power of the Imperial Diet may seriously affect the operation of this prerogative. The Diet, for instance, by refusing to appropriate necessary funds, may render a new organization non-operative. In practice, therefore, when the establishment of an organization requires new appropriations, the cabinet usually seeks

[37]Constitution, Art. VII.

[38]Ibid., Art. LVII.

[39]Ibid., Art. XII.

[40]Compare the author's discussion upon the Japanese civil service in White, *The Civil Service in the Modern State* (Chicago, the University of Chicago Press, 1930), pp. 515–555.

the necessary parliamentary consent to such appropriations prior to its actual establishment. In case of an urgent necessity, however, the necessary expenditures may be provided for out of the reserve funds or other "expenditures over the budget," but by subsequent parliamentary reduction its abolition may be forced. The appointing prerogative also receives like limitations.

The broad scope of the diplomatic prerogative of the throne may be observed from the sweeping language employed in the Constitution. Thus, Article XIII of the fundamental law provides that "the Emperor declares war, makes peace and concludes treaties." Unlike the practice in other constitutional governments, no formal restrictions are placed upon the foreign relations power of the emperor. In Part II and in Part III, we shall observe in detail the nature, scope and operation of this prerogative so sweepingly stated in the organic law of the land.

The judicial prerogative of the throne is provided in the Constitution as follows: "The Judicature shall be exercised by the Courts of law according to law, in the name of the emperor."[41] We shall discuss this subject in our chapter on the judiciary.

THE LORD PRIVY SEAL

The Lord Privy Seal is an organ of the imperial household.[42] Being closest to the throne, this office becomes important in state affairs as well. Presumably, the most important function of this office is to advise the throne in the formation of a new cabinet, but in practice this is done by the genro.[43]

THE GENRO OR ELDER STATESMEN

The body of elder statesmen called genro is an extra-constitutional, extra-legal institution. This body, more or less informally constituted toward the latter part of the Meiji Era, has no status within the Constitution, laws, or ordi-

[41]Art. LVII.

[42]Baba, *Kempo Seiji no Riron to Jissai*, pp. 268–270. For the organization of the office of the Lord Privy Seal, see Imperial House Ordinance No. 4, 1907 (Nov. 1, 1907).

[43]*Cf.* Minobe, *Kempo Satsuyo* (1932), p. 312.

nances.[44] Yet there gradually developed the custom that those statesmen who played leading rôles in the Restoration of 1868 and in the early period of the constitutional history of Japan[45] are to be consulted by the emperor on matters of paramount importance, both domestic and foreign, such as the formation of a new cabinet, declaration of war, conclusion of peace, or negotiation of important international commitments.[46]

The most important function of the genro is to be consulted in the formation of a new cabinet. This practice of recommending a successor to the retiring prime minister started as early as 1892.[47] And the recommendation of the genro has always been followed by the emperor in appointing a new premier.[48] The request for opinion of the genro on the selection of a new prime minister is formally made upon the advice of the Lord Privy Seal, usually in coöperation with the minister of the imperial household, while on other matters, upon that of the cabinet.

At present,[49] Prince Saionji is the sole remaining genro. Various views are entertained as to the fate of the institution after Prince Saionji's death. The present genro is known to

[44]With the formation of Yamagata cabinet in 1898, genro as an institution began to be recognized. *The Tokyo Nichi Nichi,* in its leading article (Nov. 5, 1898), cited Ito, Yamagata, Oyama, Saigo, Kuroda, Matsukata, and Inouye as comprising the genro. *Cf. Kokka Gakkai Zasshi,* XXXVIII, No. 4 (April, 1924), p. 611.

[45]Until the formation of the Katsura cabinet in June, 1901, the office of prime minister was always occupied by a genro. *Cf. Kokka Gakkai Zasshi,* XXXVIII, No. 5 (May, 1924), p. 781; also *Taiyo,* XXXIII, No. 13 (Nov., 1927), p. 86.

[46]On several occasions, the genro was made a subject of parliamentary discussion. For instance, at the outset of the Twenty-fourth Diet (Jan. 23, 1908), Representative Sawa made a scathing attack upon the body, declaring it a useless political relic of the *régime ancien* (*Teikoku Gikaishi,* VII, 203-204). All the cabinets have uniformly denied encroachment by the genro in the administration. Thus, in reply to an interpellation in the House Budget Committee of the Thirty-third Diet (June 24, 1914), Prime Minister Okuma vigorously defended his constitutional responsibility and flatly denied any interference by the genro (*Dai Sanjusankai Teikoku Gikai Shugiin Yosan Iinkaigiroku,* pp. 18-19).

[47]The following statesmen have been included among the genro: Ito, Yamagata, Inouye, Kuroda, Yamada, Oyama, Saigo, Matsukata, Katsura, and Saionji. With the exception of Prince Saionji, all the elder statesmen belong to *Choshu* or *Satsuma* clan (*Kokka Gakkai Zasshi,* XXXVIII, No. 5 [May, 1924], p. 806).

[48]Only two instances in which a retiring prime minister recommended his successor are known in Japan. The first instance was the recommendation of Marquis Okuma by Prince Ito in June, 1898, and the last instance was that of Count Komei Kato by Marquis Okuma in Sept., 1916. The genro accepted the Ito recommendation but ignored that of Okuma. Ito (ed.), *Kato Komei,* II, 62-64.

[49]March, 1932.

favor the disappearance of this extra-legal institution. The sole function of the genro having become that of recommending a new prime minister, the establishment of a sound system of parliamentary responsibility of the ministry will render the genro a "political relic." However, under the present stage of constitutional development in Japan, political fortunes of a cabinet depending upon the wishes and whims of the Privy Council, the Peers, military and naval cliques, and other extra-parliamentary forces, it is difficult to imagine a sudden disappearance of the genro as an institution.

To abolish the genro is to place upon the shoulders of the Lord Privy Seal and of the minister of the imperial household too great a political responsibility to be consonant with the principles of constitutional government. Hence, an institution of quasi-genro is likely to be developed, and this new body may be composed of the Lord Privy Seal, the minister of the imperial household, president of the Privy Council, and the two presidents of both houses of the Diet until a parliamentary system has been more firmly established in the Island Empire.[50]

[50]Prince Ito advocated the transfer of this function to the Privy Council (Hiratsuka [ed.], *Ito Hirobumi Hiroku*, 1929, pp. 61–63).

Chapter III

THE CABINET

THE WORD "CABINET" is nowhere found in the Constitution. Yet there exists, as a matter of fact, a collective body composed of departmental ministers under the presidency of a minister president for the purpose of initiating, directing, and carrying out the general policies of the government and to serve as the channel through which the imperial prerogative over general affairs is placed in operation.[1] Established in 1885,[2] the cabinet has been the directing and guiding force in government, ensuring unity and harmony in administration.[3] An attempt is made in this chapter to inquire into the structure, functions, and operation of this deliberative body, to ascertain its exact position in the constitutional system of Japan, a thorough understanding of which is indispensable to our inquiry into the conduct of foreign relations.

ORGANIZATION OF THE CABINET

When the system was first established in 1885, the cabinet consisted of a prime minister and nine departmental minis-

[1]Minobe, *Kempo Seigi*, pp. 510–512; Moriguchi, *Kensei no Genri to sono Unyo* (Tokyo, 1929), pp. 206–235.

[2]By Dajokan Notification No. 69, 1885 (Dec. 22, 1885), *dajo daijin* and other posts were abolished and minister president of state, minister of the imperial household, minister of state for foreign affairs, finance, home affairs, war, navy, justice, education, agriculture, and commerce and communications were newly created (*Horei Zensho* [1885], p. 1044). On Dec. 23, 1885, an imperial rescript was issued by Emperor Meji establishing a cabinet system, in response to a formal memorial praying for establishing the same by Prince Sanjo, the *dajo daijin* or the chancellor of state. For the texts of the imperial rescript and the memorial see *Horei Zensho* (1885), pp. 1–3.

[3]*Cf.* Prince Sanjo's memorial to the throne (quoted in Minobe, *Kempo Seigi*, pp. 521–522).

22

ters,[4] but it has gradually been enlarged, and at present the prime minister and twelve departmental ministers comprise this body.[5] The head of the cabinet is the premier, who maintains the unity of the cabinet, advises the throne on all affairs of state, exercises general supervision and control over all branches of the administration, and represents the cabinet in public affairs.[6] Hence, with the exception of the war and navy ministers over military and naval affairs, other ministers usually advise the throne through the prime minister.[7]

FORMAL FUNCTIONS OF THE CABINET

Ministers of state, being charged with the responsibility of advising the throne on state affairs on the one hand, and of directing the administration of their respective departments on the other, the matters to be submitted to the deliberation of the cabinet include items of both categories. The ordinance concerning the organization of the cabinet stipulates the submission of following matters to the cabinet council: (1) drafts of laws, estimates, and accounts; (2) treaties and important international questions; (3) imperial ordinances concerning administrative organization or execution of regulations and laws; (4) jurisdictional disputes among departments; (5) petitions from the people which may be handed down from the throne or submitted by the Diet; (6) expenditures apart from the budget; (7) appointments, promotions, and removals of *Chokuninkan* officials and local governors; and (8) other matters coming within the domain of the business of departments, involving questions of high policy of the administration as a whole.[8] Furthermore, a minister may submit

---

[4]Ministers of state for foreign affairs, home affairs, finance, war, navy, justice, education, agriculture and commerce, and communications. Minister of the imperial household was not included (*Horei Zansho* [1885], p. 1044).

[5]In 1896, *Takushokumu-sho*, or Department of Colonial Affairs, was established, but was abolished the following year. In 1920 the Department of Railways was established; in 1925 the Department of Agriculture and Commerce was replaced by the new Department of Agriculture and Forestry, and of Commerce and Industry. In 1929 the Department of Overseas Affairs was established. At present the cabinet is composed of a prime minister and twelve departmental ministers (Minobe, *Kempo Satsuyo* [1932], p. 294).

[6]*Naikaku Kansei*, Art. II.

[7]Minobe, *Kempo Satsuyo*, pp. 295-299.

[8]*Naikaku Kansei*, Art. V.

any matter bearing upon his official functions to the minister president for consideration by the cabinet.[9]

The above enumeration should not be regarded as exhaustive and placing limitations upon matters which may come before cabinet meetings. In fact, any matter, either upon the request of cabinet ministers or upon the initiative of the prime minister, may be considered in the cabinet.[10]

The cabinet meets ordinarily once a week, while special meetings may be called at any time by the premier. The meetings are usually held at the official residence of the prime minister, but, while the Diet is in session, such meetings may be called in the cabinet chamber of the Diet Building. Moreover, informal conferences of several ministers concerned may be held before submitting a matter to a formal meeting of the cabinet.

The meetings are secret, and the members of the cabinet are bound by honor not to disclose anything that is said at the cabinet table, either in the Diet or out of it. Most of the cabinet deliberations relate to matters of general policy. Discussions are not followed by a vote save in exceptional cases. When it develops that a very wide difference of views exists among members of the cabinet, the matter is left open until some compromise is arrived at, as the cabinet must present an outward unanimity. Often the final decision is left to the premier.[11] During the early period, the emperor attended some meetings, but this practice has long been discontinued, to facilitate free discussions.

FORMATION OF A CABINET

When a ministry falls,[12] the emperor, upon recommendation of the genro, or elder statesmen, appoints a new prime

[9]*Op. cit.*, Art. VI. *Cf.* Minobe, *Kempo Seigi* (1928), pp. 524–525; also Sasaki, *Nihon Kempo Yoron* (1931), p. 392.

[10]Minobe, *Kempo Satsuyo* (1932), pp. 294–295.

[11]See the famous cabinet memorial to the throne, Dec. 24, 1889 (*Jiji Shimpo* [Jan. 16, 1890], p. 2).

[12]Professor Minobe enumerates the following six circumstances which may cause a downfall of a ministry: (1) opposition of the House of Representatives; (2) lack of harmony in the cabinet; (3) opposition of the House of Peers, Privy Council, or military or naval factions; (4) opposition of the public opinion; (5) defeat in elections, and (6) death of the prime minister (*Kempo Seigi*, p. 541). For a table showing the cabinet changes during 1885–1930, see *Jiji Nenkan* (1930), pp. 153–155.

minister and commands him to select his own cabinet, and the selection thus made is always accepted by the throne.[13]

In selecting his cabinet, the prime minister ostensibly has a free hand, but in practice his selection is restricted by practical considerations. The army and navy posts cannot be occupied by civilians, and by tradition the foreign minister has usually been selected from among career diplomats. Again he must give due considerations to various factions of his party, as well as those in the Upper House.

In the early period of Japanese parliamentary history, the prime ministers were always bureaucrats, having no organic connections with political parties. In fact, the framers of the Constitution warned against "party cabinets." However, the first few years of experience with a hostile Diet convinced the more liberal statesmen of the practical necessity of coöperation with political parties to ensure a smooth working of the administration; and immediately after the Sino-Japanese War, Prince Ito allied himself with the *Jiyuto* party.[14] This close "coöperation" between the cabinet and a major political party in the Lower House opened a way to the gradual evolution of party cabinet.

THE RESPONSIBILITY OF THE CABINET

Article LV of the Constitution declares that: "The respective Ministers of State shall give their advice to the Emperor and be held responsible for it."[15] We may inquire into the significance of this express fundamental law of the land under three heads: (1) for what are the ministers of state responsible; (2) to whom are they responsible, and (3) the nature of such responsibility.

We have seen elsewhere that the emperor is inviolable,

[13]Yamada in *Kokka Gakkai Zasshi*, XXXVIII, No. 5 (May, 1924), pp. 814–815.

[14]Kudo, *Teikoku Gikaishi*, I, 468–471.

[15]Prince Ito summarizes the Japanese cabinet system as follows: "*First*, that the Ministers of State are charged with the duty of giving advice to the Emperor, which is their proper function, and that they are not held responsible on His behalf; *secondly*, that Ministers are directly responsible to the Emperor and indirectly so to the people; *thirdly*, that it is the Sovereign and not the people that can decide as to the responsibility of Ministers, because the Sovereign possesses the rights of sovereignty of the State; *fourthly*, that the responsibility for Ministers is a political one and has no relation to criminal or civil responsibility, nor can it conflict therewith neither can the one affect the other" (*Commentaries*, p. 93).

that he cannot be held responsible for any of his acts, that he exercises his prerogatives only upon the responsible advice of competent organs of the state, and that it is only upon the advice of a minister of state that the imperial prerogative over general affairs of state may be exercised. The scope of ministerial responsibility as stipulated in this article is co-extensive with the imperial prerogative over state affairs. Accordingly, the ministers cannot evade their constitutional responsibility, even when the advice of the Privy Council or the genro has been sought by the emperor.

On the juristic significance of this article there is unanimity among constitutional jurists. They are one in holding that, in legal principles, the ministers are directly responsible to the emperor and that no other organ of the state may question their legal responsibility or remove them from office. With the gradual development of parliamentary government in Japan, however, it has come to signify primarily their responsibility to the Diet. That the ministerial responsibility provided for in the Constitution refers to the legislative control of the administration may reasonably be implied from the constitutional recognition of the means through which the Diet exercises this power as the most important organ of control of the executive through parliamentary interpellations and asking questions, passing resolutions, presenting addresses to the throne, and representations to the government, voting approbations of emergency imperial ordinance, as well as its budgetary powers. In further support of the doctrine of political responsibility we may cite the well-established practice that, when a resolution of lack of confidence is voted in the Lower House, the cabinet must either resign or dissolve the House to carry the question to the electorate.[16]

On the question of whether the ministerial responsibility as stipulated in the Constitution is collective or individual there is no unanimity among jurists nor in practice. The conservative jurists, headed by Hozumi,[17] Uyesugi,[18] and Shimizu,[19] argue for the doctrine of individual responsibility,

[16]Minobe, *Kempo Satsuyo*, pp. 304–311.
[17]*Kempo Teiyo*, II, 549–556.
[18]*Kempo Jutsugi*, pp. 646–656.
[19]*Kempo Hen*, pp. 646–649, 688–727.

holding that to recognize a contrary doctrine would be to admit the principle of parliamentary government of the British type. They contend that to admit this principle would be contrary to the spirit of the Constitution and the fundamental nature of national polity, reducing the emperor to a titular headship of the state. On the other hand, the more liberal jurists, headed by Minobe,[20] Ichimura,[21] and Baba,[22] support the collective doctrine for all matters which concern the cabinet as a whole and are submitted to its deliberations, and argue for individual responsibility only for those matters which fall within the exclusive jurisdiction of a department.[23]

Closely related to the subject of ministerial responsibility is the constitutional requirement that all laws, imperial ordinances and rescripts of whatever character that relate to the affairs of state must bear the countersignature of a minister of state.[24] A ministerial responsibility, however, does not arise from the fact of countersigning, but from that of advising the throne.[25] The scope of the countersignature is coextensive with that of ministerial responsibility, and it is an external evidence of advising the emperor.[26] It naturally follows that a minister must be free to decline his countersignature when he deems the subject matter to be contrary to the Constitution, the law, or to public interest, and that, should his advice be refused, he must be free to resign his post.[27]

[20]*Kempo Seigi*, p. 552.

[21]*Teikoku Kempo Ron*, p. 632.

[22]*Kempo Seigi no Riron to Jissai* (Tokyo, 1926), pp. 258–265.

[23]Prince Ito, the chief drafter of the Constitution, recognized the principle of collective responsibility for the general policies of the administration while upholding the doctrine of individual responsibility for matters coming within the scope of a particular department (*Commentaries*, pp. 94–96). *Cf.* Moriguchi, *op. cit.*, pp. 216–219.

[24]Constitution, Art. LV, Sec. II.

[25]Prince Ito, *Commentaries*, p. 96; Minobe, *Kempo Seigi*, p. 519; Hozumi, *Kempo Teiyo*, II, 549–556; Uyesugi, *Kempo Jutsugi*, p. 674; Moriguchi, *op. cit.*, pp. 208–210.

[26]Therefore, matters relating to purely internal affairs of the Imperial Court, supreme command, conferment of honors and decorations, ritualistic affairs, and others beyond ministerial responsibility, do not require ministerial countersignature (Shimizu, *Kempo Hen*, pp. 656–669; Minobe, *Kempo Seigi*, p. 416).

[27]Justice Shimizu, however, holds a contrary view. He argues that a minister of state is not free to decline his countersignature on the ground of unconstitutionality or its being contrary to public interest since the emperor has the supreme power of interpreting the Constitution and the law as well as the ultimate authority to

The Dual Character of the Cabinet

We have seen in foregoing pages that the chief functions of the cabinet are found in its formulation of general policies, its determination of the modes, in large measure, of the exercise of the authority vested in the throne, its formulation of legislative program, and its effective leadership in the Diet.

Probably one of the greatest obstacles against the establishment of a responsible government lies in the peculiar position the war and navy ministers enjoy in the cabinet of Japan. And the full import of this "dual cabinet" cannot be overemphasized in the workings of the Japanese constitutional system. This dualism constitutes an important exception to the general principle of collective responsibility of the cabinet.[28] Thus, the war and navy ministers play a dual rôle: one as heads of departments like other ministers, and the other which we designate under the term *iaku joso*, or direct access to the emperor without consultation or even knowledge of their cabinet colleagues.[29] Originally enjoyed only by the chiefs of general staffs of both services, it was gradually extended to these two ministers. Accordingly, under the present system, both chiefs of army and naval staffs and the war and navy ministers have direct access to the emperor on matters relating to the supreme command of the forces. The scope of this prerogative has been gradually enlarged, and now the precise demarcation between matters falling within *iaku joso* and those within state affairs is difficult to draw.[30]

judge public interest (*Kempo Hen*, pp. 670–674). Uyesugi holds a similar view. He declares that a minister has no choice in attaching his countersignature when ordered to do so. Hence, in Uyesugi's opinion, ministerial responsibility is juridically independent of his countersignature (*Kempo Jutsugi*, pp. 675–677). In this, Uyesugi supports his teacher, Dr. Y. Hozumi (*Kempo Teiyo*, II, 543–548).

[28]Article VII of the organization of the cabinet provides: "With the exception of *gunki gunrei*, or matters relating to military secrecy and command, which, having been reported directly to His Majesty the emperor, may have been submitted to the cabinet for deliberation, the ministers of state for war and navy shall report to the minister president of state."

[29]See Yoshino, *Niju Seifu to Iaku Joso*, *passim;* also Dr. Nagao Ariga, "The Armed Forces in Japan," *Kokka Gakkai Zasshi*, June, July, 1900, Supplement, pp. 21–47.

[30]As a recent case illustrating this point we may cite the conflict between the cabinet and the chief of naval general staff in connection with the so-called Reed-Matsudaira compromise at the London Naval Conference of 1930. See Chap. XXVI, *infra.*

The qualifications required of the war and navy ministers constitute another hindrance to a sound development of cabinet responsibility. Though a prime minister is free in his choice of other ministers, his selection is restricted to a general or a lieutenant general for the war portfolio and to an admiral or vice-admiral for the navy post.[31] Should the military or the naval clique decline to furnish a qualified person for any cause whatever, a prime minister is unable to form his cabinet. Hence, under the present system of dualism, military or naval clique can prevent the formation of a cabinet, or wreck it after it is once formed.[32]

[31]Appended tables to *Rikugunsho Kansei* and *Kaigunsho Kansei*. Prince Ito, president of the Privy Council, declared in his report to the emperor as early as Sept. 15, 1891, that the system whereby military and naval officers fill the posts of war and navy departments was indispensable to place the supreme military and naval command beyond parliamentary interference and party politics and to maintain the principle of constitutional monarchism and to prevent gradual decline of imperial prerogatives (Hiratsuka [ed.], *Ito Hirobumi Hiroku*, pp. 113–116).

[32]The second Saionji cabinet was pledged to a policy of retrenchment. However, General Uyehara, war minister, proposed at the cabinet meeting of Nov. 22, 1912, that two divisions be placed on garrison duty in Korea. The program of a military expansion had been adopted soon after the close of the Russo-Japanese War, and Uyehara's proposal had the firm backing of the military cliques, headed by Field Marshal Yamagata. The Saionji cabinet could not accede to the program, and at its extraordinary meeting held on Nov. 30 rejected Uyehara's program. War Minister Uyehara was received in audience by the emperor on Dec. 2, 1912, and reported to the throne the urgent necessity for army expansion, and denounced the action of the cabinet, and handed in his resignation directly to the emperor, instead of presenting it through the premier. Prince Saionji called on Yamagata for an "understanding," but to no avail. The army clique refused to supply any general or lieutenant general (in active list) for the post. Under the circumstances the Saionji cabinet had to resign, although it enjoyed the support of a majority in the Lower House (Kudo, *Taisho Kenseishi*, pp. 13–20). Saionji induced the navy minister, Admiral Saito, to resign with him. Therefore Prince Katsura could not obtain any admiral to serve as his navy minister, due to a "strike" of the naval clique. He appealed to the genro, and in desperation petitioned the emperor to issue an imperial edict to Admiral Saito to remain in post. Katsura won his navy minister, but in doing so he sacrificed his political career. His cabinet fell in less than two months (Hirota, *Naikaku Kotetsu Gojunenshi*, pp. 665–667). Popular demand for the liberalization of the qualifications for the war and navy ministers began to be heard on all sides (articles in *Chuo Koron*, No. 288, Feb., 1913, pp. 50–60, 60–67). To meet and to strike a blow at the army clique after fighting with the chief of general staff and war minister, Count Admiral Yamamoto succeeded in widening the qualifications to include those in reserve list. This resulted in the resignation of the war minister (Kudo, *Taisho Kenseishi*, p. 72). With the fall of the Yamamoto cabinet in 1914, Kiyoura was ordered by the emperor to form a cabinet, March 31, 1914. He succeeded in obtaining all cabinet ministers except the navy minister. Hence, he had to decline the task of forming a cabinet, on April 7, 1914 (*ibid.*, p. 96; *Teikoku Gikaishi*, IX, 786).

The gradual encroachment of *iaku joso* upon the scope of cabinet responsibility has led to a popular demand for abolition of the present dualism by instituting a new system of civilian control of these posts.[33] That this dualism must be abolished to insure a smooth working of the cabinet there can be no doubt. To realize this far-reaching reorganization in constitutional mechanisms, Professor Yoshino, a well-known student of constitutional government, proposes the following reforms: (1) abolition of *gunrei* or the present system of military and naval ordinances; (2) abolition of the present qualifications for the war and navy posts; (3) reorganization of the general staffs, and (4) amendment of Article VII of the Constitution.[34]

[33]The most outstanding work on this subject is Yoshino, *Niju Seifu to Iaku Joso* (Tokyo, 1922). Compare Baba, *Kempo Seiji no Riron to Jissai*, pp. 201–205; Captain Mizuno, "Liberalization of War and Navy Ministeries," *Chuo Koron*, No. 412 (Aug., 1922), pp. 84–91. For parliamentary discussions during the Forty-fifth Diet, see *Teikoku Gikaishi*, XIII, 655–660, 947–948, 1273–1283; Moriguchi, *op. cit.*, pp. 262–265.

[34]Yoshino, *op. cit.*, p. 79.

Chapter IV

THE PRIVY COUNCIL

THE PRIVY COUNCIL was established in 1888[1] for the purpose of deliberating under the presidency of Prince Ito upon the drafts of the Constitution and the Imperial House Law.[2] It was evident, however, that this organ was intended to be a permanent body under the Constitution. Thus, it received the constitutional sanction in 1889,[3] and immediately following the promulgation of the Constitution, an imperial ordinance was issued amending the original ordinance concerning the organization of the Council, or *Sumitsuin Kansei*.[4]

ORGANIZATION AND PROCEDURE[5]

The Privy Council is composed of a president, a vice-president, and twenty-four councilors, appointed by the emperor, together with a secretary general and a secretariat.[6]

[1]Imperial Ordinance No. 22, 1888 (April 30, 1888). Text of this ordinance in *Kwampo*, April 30, 1888, pp. 309–311; also in *Horei Zensho*, 1888, pp. 64–68. *Cf. Jiji Shimpo* (May 1, 1888), p. 2. For a brief account of the establishment of the Council see Shimizu, "Privy Council," *Kokka Gakkai Zasshi*, XXIII (March, 1909), 335–346.

[2]See the imperial edict issued to the Council on May 4, 1888 (quoted in Minobe, *Gendai Kensei Hyoron*, Tokyo, 1930, p. 68); also Moriguchi, *Kensei no Genri to sono Unyo* (Tokyo, 1929), pp. 278–280.

[3]Constitution, Art. LVI.

[4]Imperial Ordinance No. 216, 1890 (Oct. 8, 1890).

[5]For details see the *Sumitsuin Kansei*, or the ordinance itself. Text in *Genko Horei Shuran* (1927), Vol. I, Bk. III, 5.

[6]The original ordinance of 1888 provided for a president, a vice-president, twelve or more privy councilors, a secretary general, and several secretaries (Imperial Ordinance No. 22, 1888, Art. II). On April 30, 1888, Premier Ito was succeeded by Count Kuroda and was appointed president of the Privy Council. At the same time the following were appointed privy councilors: Count Oki (retained the presidency of the *Genroin*), Count Higashikuse (retained the vice-presidency of the *Genroin*), Count Yoshii (retained the vice-ministership of the imperial household), Admiral

Ministers of state, by virtue of their office, are entitled to sit in the Council and participate in deliberations and voting. Ministers may be represented by deputies with the right to speak but not to vote.[7]

A privy councilor is appointed by the emperor upon the recommendation of the prime minister. In this recommendation the prime minister, by tradition, consults with influential members of the Council, and particularly the president of the Council. Under these circumstances, therefore, no person not acceptable to the Council can be appointed.

When a matter is submitted to the Council by the emperor, accompanied by documents prepared by the cabinet, the secretary general makes preliminary investigations, after which the president decides whether it may be referred to a special committee of inquiry. Important matters, such as ratification of treaties, emergency imperial ordinances, and electoral bills, are usually referred to a special committee for further inquiry. The actual work of the Council is performed by this special committee thus appointed, and the cabinet ministers primarily concerned are called before this committee to explain a project under examination. When the inquiry is completed, the committee makes its formal request to the Council in plenary session usually in the presence of the emperor, and, though a debate may ensue, the Council always adopts the recommendation of its subcommittee.

The Functions of the Council

The functions of the Council at the time of its establishment in 1888 were defined as follows:

The Privy Council shall hold deliberations and report its opinions to His Majesty the emperor for his sanction upon the following matters:

Count Kawamura, Count Sasaki, Count Terashima, Count Soyejima, Viscount Fukuoka, Viscount Sano, Viscount Shinagawa (all former councilors of the imperial household), Count Katsu, and T. Kono. Ki Inouye, chief secretary of the cabinet, was appointed secretary general of the Council. Miyoji Ito and Kentaro Kaneko, private secretaries to Prime Minister Ito, were appointed secretaries of the Council and also as private secretaries to President Ito. Michitaro Tsuda, former private secretary to Premier Ito, was appointed secretary of the Council (*Kwampo gogai*, April 30, 1888; also *Jiji Shimpo*, May 1, 1888, p. 3).

[7]Princes of the Blood may attend the meetings of the Council upon reaching twenty years of age (Imperial Message, May 18, 1888).

1. Controversies concerning the interpretation of the Constitution or of laws supplementary thereto, and questions relating to the budget and other fiscal matters.
2. Draft amendments of the Constitution or of laws supplementary thereto.
3. Important imperial ordinances.
4. Drafts of new laws and those for the abolition or amendment of existing ones; international treaties; and the planning of administrative organizations.
5. In addition to those mentioned in the above clauses, other important administrative or fiscal matters which may be submitted to the Privy Council for advice by special order of the emperor, or those upon which the advice of the Privy Council is required by special stipulation of law or ordinance.[8]

Thus, under the ordinance of 1888, drafts of all laws had to be submitted to the Council for deliberation and advice. With the opening of the Imperial Diet, however, the law-making function was transferred to the Diet, and consequently an important amendment was made in 1890.[9]

Article VI as amended reads as follows:

Upon His Majesty's submission for advice, the Privy Council shall hold deliberations and report its opinions upon the following matters:

1. Matters which are under its jurisdiction according to the provisions of the *Koshitsu Tempan,* or the Imperial House Law.
2. Drafts of laws and doubtful points relating to the provisions of the Constitution and laws and ordinances supplementary thereto.
3. Proclamation of martial law under Article XIV and the imperial ordinances to be issued under Articles VIII and LXX of the Constitution, as well as all other imperial ordinances having penal provisions.

[8]Imperial Ordinance No. 22, 1888, Art. VI.

[9]Imperial Ordinance No. 216, 1890 (Oct. 8, 1890). In order to check the rising influence of political parties, the Yamagata cabinet (1898) addressed the emperor to issue an imperial message to the Council enlarging its competence without a formal amendment of the ordinance. Thus, ordinances relating to administrative establishments, civil service, governance of overseas territories, schools, as well as establishment of *Shinninkan* posts, were added to the list (Baba, *Kempo Seiji no Riron to Jissai,* p. 266; Baba in *Taiyo,* Nov., 1927, p. 95; Nagai in *Chuo Koron,* June, 1927, p. 57).

4. International treaties and agreements (*joyaku oyobi yaku-soku*).
5. Matters relating to the amendment of the organization of the Privy Council and to the rules for the conduct of its business.
6. Matters specially submitted to its deliberation for advice, in addition to those above mentioned.

The above provisions are in effect today. A careful comparison of the amended article with the original one brings out the following points: (1) Though, under the original ordinance, it was not clear whether the Council was purely advisory or competent to hold meetings of its own accord and report its opinions upon a project without imperial request for advice, its consultative character was made plain by the amendment.[10] (2) Under the original ordinance, all projects of laws and important imperial ordinances were required to be submitted, while, under the amended article, only the enumerated draft laws and ordinances require submission to the Council. (3) A stipulation was added to require the deliberation of the Council upon draft amendments of its own organization and rules for the conduct of its business.[11]

As indicated in the article cited above, the functions of the Council fall under two heads: first, as an organ of the imperial household; and second, as an organ of the state. As an organ of the imperial household, it deliberates, together with the Imperial Family Council, upon the succession to the throne and regency and other matters of importance.[12]

As an organ of the state, the functions of the Council may be comprehended under three heads. The first pertains to those functions of the Council as the "watchdog of the constitution" and include the authority to advise upon (1) draft amendments to the Constitution, (2) draft laws and ordinances supplementary to the Constitution, and (3) questions referred to the Council regarding the interpretation of the Constitution and laws and ordinances supplementary

[10]Shimizu, "Privy Council," *Kokka Gakkai Zasshi*, XLIII (1929), 707-719.

[11]Minobe, *Gendai Kensei Hyoron*, p. 71; Moriguchi, *Kensei no Genri to sono Unyo*, pp. 282-283.

[12]It should be noted here, however, that the Privy Council does not participate in purely internal affairs of the dynasty but in matters which also concern the state (Minobe, *Gendai Kensei Hyoron*, pp. 72-81).

thereto. The second category concerns the functions of the Council in lieu of the Imperial Diet. These quasi-legislative powers may be divided into two divisions, namely: (1) concerning those powers to be exercised only when the Diet is not in session, including the approval of emergency imperial ordinances under Articles VIII and LXX of the Constitution, and (2) concerning those powers to be exercised irrespective of the sitting of the Diet, including international treaties and agreements, declaration of martial law, and imperial ordinances having penal provisions. The third category includes the self-governing functions of the Council, namely, deliberations upon draft amendments to the ordinance governing the organization of the Privy Council and the rules for the conduct of its business.[13]

The functions of the Council as the guardian and interpreter of the Constitution receive our first attention. From the time of its establishment, it has been the peculiar function of this body to protect and to interpret the Constitution, thus acting as the "watchdog" of the fundamental law.

It is one of the characteristic features of the Japanese Constitution that its amendment can be undertaken only upon the initiative of the throne.[14] A draft amendment is prepared by the cabinet and submitted to the Council for advice. When such amendment is approved, the cabinet petitions the emperor to present it to the Imperial Diet.[15] And after the Diet has acted upon it, this draft is again submitted to the Council before it is formally presented to the emperor for his sanction. As to deliberations upon draft laws and ordinances supplementary to the Constitution, distinction should be made between laws and ordinances. "Laws supplementary to the Constitution" include the Law of the Houses, the Election Law, the Law concerning the Organiza-

[13]Minobe, *Kempo Seigi* (1928), pp. 561–562; also his *Gendai Kensei Hyoron*, pp. 68–107; Ichimura, *Teikoku Kempo Ron* (1926), pp. 659–660; Shimizu, *Kempo Hen* (1923), pp. 1103–1105; Sasaki, *Nihon Kempo Yoron* (1931), pp. 416–417.

[14]The Preamble to the Constitution declares: "When in the future it may become necessary to amend any of the provisions of the present Constitution, We or Our successors shall assume the initiative right, and submit a project for the same to the Imperial Diet. The Imperial Diet shall pass its vote upon it, according to the conditions imposed by the present Constitution, and in no otherwise shall Our descendants or Our subjects be permitted to attempt any alteration thereof."

[15]In drawing up an amendment, the cabinet, with imperial sanction, may establish a special committee of inquiry (Minobe, *Gendai Kensei Hyoron*, p. 83).

tion of Courts of Law, the Jury Law, the Law of Administrative Litigation, the Law of Finance, and others. Since the Diet has the power to amend a bill introduced by the government, while a bill may be initiated in either House, the significance of Council deliberation upon a bill prior to its introduction in the Diet is greatly reduced.[16] The same may be said of ordinances submitted thereto. Here the Council likewise acts as an organ to restrain the government from hasty actions and arbitrary measures.

The competence of the Council upon "drafts of laws and doubtful points relating to the provisions of the constitution, laws and ordinances supplementary thereto" should not be interpreted as vesting the Council with the authority of a court of constitutional controversies. As Professor Minobe points out, such authority may be conferred only by the Constitution and not by an imperial ordinance. Moreover, the Council does not possess the monopoly of this authority, as the cabinet, Houses of the Diet, the administrative court, the board of audits, as well as the courts of law, all interpret the Constitution, laws and ordinances, independent of each other and within their respective jurisdictions. Hence the Privy Council cannot be called a court of last resort in interpretation of the Constitution, laws and ordinances.[17]

During its existence of over forty years, only one instance may be found when a specific constitutional issue was submitted to the Council for opinion. A serious controversy arose between the two Houses of the Diet in 1892 concerning the relative powers of these Houses over the budget. To break the deadlock, the House of Peers presented an address to the throne praying for an imperial interpretation. Emperor Meiji referred the question to the Council for advice. The Council made a report upholding the contention of the Upper House, and this was incorporated in the imperial edict which the emperor sent to the Peers. This interpretation was accepted by both Houses.[18] During the forty years of parliamentary history in Japan, sharp conflicts of views arose on several occasions between the cabinet and the Houses as to

[16]The Manhood Suffrage Act of 1925 is a case in point (*ibid.*, pp. 83–88).

[17]Minobe, *Kempo Satsuyo* (1932), pp. 317–320.

[18]*Teikoku Gikaishi*, I, 1743–1744, 1750, 1777, 2157–2167, 2185, 2224–2233. Compare Kudo, *Teikoku Gikaishi*, I, 152–158.

the relative position between law and treaty, parliamentary approbation of emergency imperial ordinances, and other questions of equal importance bearing upon the Constitution, but they have always been settled without their being submitted to the Council. The pronouncements of the Council, therefore, are largely limited to the projects and questions submitted by the cabinet. Hence, though it is mandatory to submit all draft amendments to the Constitution, laws and ordinances supplementary thereto, emergency imperial ordinances and other enumerated matters, it is entirely within the discretion of the cabinet whether or not a constitutional question should be submitted to the Council for its advice.

The Privy Council acts not only as the guardian of the Constitution, but it advises the throne on ratification of treaties, or otherwise exerts large influence in the conduct of foreign relations. In most parliamentary governments, the legislature plays an important rôle in treaty-making, but under the Japanese Constitution, the foreign relations power formally resides, exclusively and without restrictions, in the emperor, to be exercised upon the advice of the cabinet. Therefore, the cabinet negotiates treaties while, by virtue of the *Sumitsuin Kansei*, the Council advises the emperor as to ratification.[19]

THE PRIVY COUNCIL AND THE PARLIAMENTARY SYSTEM

Having examined some of the more important functions of the Council, we are now in position to inquire into its political significance in the constitutional structure of Japan and to evaluate its position in the operation of her parliamentary system. We have observed that the Council possesses a wide consultative faculty in the entire field of administration, and that this "third chamber" constitutes a a stumblingblock towards the establishment of a more responsible and effective system of parliamentary government.

The outstanding feature of the working of the Council has been its ever increasing supervisory power over the executive, thus abandoning its claim to impartiality and prudence which

---

[19]The nature and extent of the influence of the Privy Council over foreign relations is fully developed in Part II and Part III of this treatise.

the framers of the Constitution attributed to this body. The prohibition against the interference with the executive has more and more been violated in recent years, in domestic as well as foreign affairs.

The Council exercises an extensive amending power. As to treaties or bills which have passed the Diet, the Council cannot recommend amendment since the text is already determined, and consequently, it can only advise approval or rejection *in toto*. On the other hand, as to those projects of laws submitted thereto before introduction in the Diet and draft ordinances, the Council may freely exercise its amending power. Demand for amendment is usually made in the sub-committee of inquiry on a measure. And here also are made informal suggestions to the cabinet to withdraw a measure which the committee does not approve. Such suggestions and demands are usually accepted by the government.

The Council's supervisory activities are by no means confined to domestic policy Thus, the more astute members of the Council often exert great influence upon foreign policy or seriously embarrass the government on foreign relations. This supervisory power of the Council over the cabinet in foreign relations is most clearly brought out in advising ratification of treaties. The Council might even go so far as to attach a reservation, as witness the ratification of the Pact of Paris. It may seriously embarrass the government in the eyes of the world by delaying examination of treaties or by demanding unwarranted documents or notes, as witness the recent battle between the Council and the cabinet over the London Naval Treaty. It may even attack the foreign policy of a ministry in the presence of the emperor and thus seriously embarrass the government, as witness the alleged remarks made by Count Miyoji Ito in 1927 and in 1929 concerning the China policy of the ministry. We shall take up these incidents elsewhere.[20]

How far can the Council go in exercising its supervisory power over the cabinet without violating the provision of the ordinance defining its competence?[21] It is difficult to draw

[20]Part II, *infra*.

[21]Article VIII of the *Sumitsuin Kansei* provides that: "Though the Privy Council is the emperor's highest resort of counsel it shall not interfere with the executive."

the border line of this power. Minobe and most other jurists interpret the provision as not denying the Council any interference with the government, but rather a prohibition against direct execution of administrative powers. In other words, they hold that, in conducting an inquiry into a project submitted thereto, the Council should not only examine its constitutionality but inquire whether or not it is for the best interest of the state as well.[22]

Here a question of far-reaching importance in the working of a constitutional government is raised, namely, "What is the legal as well as the political significance of an advice of the Council?" Upon the legal effect of such advice, there seems to be an agreement of views among jurists. According to the commonly accepted legal theory, therefore, an advice of the Council has no binding effect upon other organs of the state and the cabinet is free to petition a contrary recommendation.[23] However, as to its political import, the jurists are divided.

Thus, on the question as to whether the cabinet may advise the throne to disregard a recommendation of the Council when the ministers are outvoted by the councilors, two conflicting views are entertained among jurists and students of Japanese politics. One view holds that, if the cabinet petitions the throne to reject the Council's recommendation, in the deliberation of which the cabinet ministers have participated, on the ground that such a course would be contrary to the best interest of the state or otherwise, the responsibility for choosing between such conflicting recommendations made by the Council, the highest advisory body to the throne, and by the cabinet, charged with constitutional responsibility for advising the emperor on all state affairs, falls squarely

[22]Minobe, *Gendai Kensei Hyoron*, pp. 111–112. Dr. Minobe holds that the Council's relations with the cabinet and departmental ministers should be confined to those matters which are submitted to it for advice. As the Council possesses no supervisory power over the cabinet, it is beyond its legitimate powers to ask questions, comment, or to criticize the administrative policies of a ministry not submitted thereto for advice by the emperor (*Kempo Satsuyo* [1932], pp. 314–315). Professor Sasaki likewise argues that Article VIII of the *Sumitsuin Kansei* prohibits the Council from demanding resignation of a ministry, execution of any particular policy, or modification of a project submitted thereto for advice (*Nihon Kempo Yoron* [1931], p. 418).

[23]Minobe, *Gendai Kensei Hyoron*, p. 114; Yorozu Oda in *Taiyo*, XIX, No. 11 (Aug., 1913), 109–113; Moriguchi, *Kensei no Genri to sono Unyo*, p. 284.

upon the shoulders of the emperor. To petition the throne
against a Council recommendation is to request the adoption
of a minority opinion. Such a procedure would be contrary
to the fundamental nature of the Japanese polity, the principle of majority rule, and incompatible with the doctrine of
non-responsibility of the emperor. Under the present system,
therefore, even if a minister of state is convinced that a decision of the Council is contrary to public interest or otherwise unsound, he is compelled to conform to this decision
and assume responsibility so long as he remains in office.
Hence, in practice, the Privy Council as it operates today
may force the downfall of a ministry which enjoys the confidence of the Diet.[24] The fall of the Wakatsuki ministry in
the spring of 1927 is a case in point.[25] Other jurists and pub-
licists support a contrary view. They argue that, under such
circumstances, it would be within the constitutional competence as well as duty to advise the emperor against the
Council recommendation, for it is the cabinet and not the
Council that assumes the responsibility.[26] The practice,
however, supports the first view.

The Reform of the Council

We have seen that the Privy Council, originally established
as the "palladium of the constitution and of the law" and
as the emperor's supreme advisory organ, has tended to become more and more "the third House," supervising and
controlling the executive in domestic and foreign policies.
This rapidly changing character of the Council, owing no
political responsibility to the Diet or to the people for its
activities and yet exerting an increasing influence over the

[24]Minobe, *Gendai Kensei Hyoron*, pp. 114–118; also his *Kempo Satsuyo* (1932),
pp. 313–314.

[25]Articles on the Privy Council by Representative Nagai and Professor Yoshino
in *Chuo Koron*, No. 473 (June, 1927), 55–63, 103–117; Baba, "Elder Statesmen
and the Council," *Taiyo*, XXXIII, No. 13 (Nov., 1927), 85–97; Minobe, "The
Privy Council," *Kokka Gakkai Zasshi*, XLI (1927), 1357–1390.

[26]Yorozu Oda, "Functional Aspect of the Privy Council," *Taiyo* XIX, No. 11
(Aug., 1913), 109–113. Compare Professor Sasaki, *Nihon Kempo Yoron* (1931),
p. 418; also *Tokyo Asahi*, Oct. 16, 1930, p. 2; Dr. Shimizu, "The Privy Council,"
Kokka Gakkai Zasshi, XXIII, No. 3 (March, 1909), 345–346.

entire affairs of the state, constitutes one of the greatest barriers to the parliamentary system in Japan.[27]

Proposals for the reform of the Council may be classified under the following five heads: (1) reform of membership, (2) reform of procedure, (3) curtailment of its powers, (4) abolition, (5) development of a responsible parliamentary system.

The chief object sought in all these proposals for the reform of Council is to reduce its position in the constitutional system of Japan to one as innocuous as the British Privy Council, by radically curtailing its influence upon the ministry and by confining its functions largely to dynastic affairs.[28] The extreme difficulty of the reform, however, can well be seen from the fact that no amendment to the ordinance defining the organization and powers of the Council can be made without its own consent, and that the Imperial Diet is denied any voice in the procedure.[29] Accordingly, no further restrictions upon the powers of the Council have been placed since 1890 by an amendment of the ordinance. On the contrary, we have already observed a gradual extension of its powers in practice.

However, the function of the prime minister to make recommendation to the emperor in filling vacancies in the

[27]As a natural consequence of the non-responsibility of the Council to the Diet, it is beyond the powers of the Diet to criticize or comment upon its activities. Hence, the Council ignored a *dangaian*, or an impeachment resolution, passed in the Lower House during the Fifty-third Diet by 210:194 (*Kwampo gogai*, May 8, 1927, pp. 65–77). *Cf.* Minobe in *Teikoku Daigaku Shimbun*, May 9, 1927.

[28]Minobe, *Gendai Kensei Hyoron*, pp. 366–368. *Cf.* a symposium on the reform of the Council by Dr. Oda, Dr. Egi, Viscount Akimoto, Dr. Uzawa, Representatives Taketoshi and Ozaki, Dr. Hanai, Dr. Hayashi, and Count Kato in *Taiyo*, XIX, No. 11 (Aug., 1913), 109–128; Asai, "Privy Council," *Hogaku Kenkyn*, November, 1930, pp. 1–51; Professor Sasaki, "The Reform of the Privy Council," *Tokyo Asahi*, Oct. 14–16, 1930, p. 2.

[29]The reform of the Council has, on several occasions, been made a subject of parliamentary discussion. In the forty-fourth session of the Diet, Dr. Giichi Soyejima introduced a representation resolution in the House of Representatives calling upon the government (Hara cabinet) to amend Article VI of the *Sumitsuin Kansei* greatly reducing the powers of the Council. In his speech, Professor Soyejima made a scathing attack upon the Council as an organ obstructing the sound development of responsible government in Japan. The resolution was referred to a committee, which pigeonholed it (*Teikoku Gikaishi*, XII, 1777–1780). For his urgency question in the House of Representatives during the Forty-sixth Diet, see *Kwampo gogai*, Feb. 9, 1923, pp. 173–175.

Council may be used as an effective weapon in checking any undue encroachment of the Council upon the executive. Hence, by recommending men of unquestioned integrity but of little or no political leanings to one party or another, the personnel of the Council may be radically changed, having an important effect upon the general attitude of this body towards the cabinet.[30] Again, by threatening to recommend removal from office any privy councilor who opposes an important cabinet measure, the ministry may be able to bring the Council to terms, provided such an extreme measure is supported by the informed public. Thus, in 1913, the Yamamoto cabinet proposed to extend the list of army and navy officers eligible for the war and navy portfolios and to amend the *Bunkan Ninyo Rei*, or the ordinance concerning the appointment of civil officials, and when they were met with a strong opposition in the Council, the prime minister threatened to recommend the dismissal of the opposing councilors. This threat was sufficient to force the surrender of the Council before the cabinet.[31] The adoption of such practice, however, is opposed by many jurists like Minobe who hold that, though it is within the powers of the cabinet to take such a measure towards the councilors engaged in intrigue against the former, it would be contrary to the spirit of the Constitution to resort to such procedure merely because of their opposition to the government.[32]

[30]When Baron Hamao, president of the Council, died in 1925, Count Kato, the prime minister, strongly recommended Baron Dr. Hozumi, a noted jurist, to the presidency instead of some outstanding statesman. Prime Minister Kato's determination to reduce the prestige of the Council by appointing a non-partisan jurist as its president was supported by Prince Saionji, the sole remaining genro, Dr. Ichiki, minister of the imperial household, Count Makino, Lord Privy Seal, and others close to the Imperial Court (Ito, *Kato Komei*, II, 655–660; Baba in *Kaizo*, Oct., 1930, p. 29). For the influence of personalities upon the policies of the Council, see an excellent article by a well-known journalist, Tsunego Baba, in *Kaizo*, XII, No. 10 (Oct., 1930), pp. 27–34.

[31]Compare Nagai in *Chuo Koron*, June, 1927, pp. 59–60; also Baba in *Kaizo*, Oct., 1930, pp. 4–34. For the famous case of dismissal of Count Okuma in November, 1891, because of his conference with Count Itagaki, president of the *Jiyuto*, see Kudo, *Teikoku Gikaishi*, I, 97; Ichijima (ed.), *Okumako Hachijugonenshi* (Tokyo, 1926), II, 7–8.

[32]*Gendai Kensei Hyoron*, p. 117.

Chapter V

THE ADVISORY COUNCIL ON FOREIGN RELATIONS

THE ADVISORY COUNCIL on foreign relations (1917–1922) which was established during the World War was a novel experiment in the evolution of organs of control of foreign relations in Japan.

Viscount Miura, a privy councilor, called together in conference three political leaders, namely, Kei Hara, president of the *Seiyukai*, Ki Inukai, president of the *Kokuminto*, and Viscount Komei Kato, president of the *Doshikai*, on May 24, May 30, and June 6, 1916, to discuss ways and means of placing the contemporary questions of foreign policy and national defense above partisan politics.[1] Here the veteran statesman called the attention of the heads of the three major parties to the exigencies of the time arising out of the Japanese entry into the World War and to the necessity of presenting a united front on foreign relations. Viscount Kato, former foreign minister and now the head of the government party, expressed his agreement with the general principle. He argued, however, that the responsibility for the formulation of policies should rest primarily with the authorities charged with the conduct of foreign affairs, and that a large degree of autonomy of the cabinet should be maintained, recalling the practical necessity for immediate action by the foreign minister in consultation with the premier without even obtaining the views of the cabinet in cases of extreme urgency.

These series of conferences resulted in the issuance of a joint declaration by these three leaders of political parties

[1] *Tokyo Asahi*, June 1, 7, 1916, p. 2.

43

pledging themselves to the general principle of placing questions affecting foreign relations and the prosecution of the
war beyond the play of partisan politics.[2] Though these
political leaders issued their joint declaration in individual
capacity, the inevitable effect of such an action was to bind
their parties,[3] and the joint declaration was received with
general approval.[4]

When Count Okuma formally tendered his resignation as
prime minister on October 4, 1916, he recommended Viscount Kato as his successor.[5] The genro, however, being
dominated by Prince Yamagata, recommended General
Count Terauchi instead, holding that the cabinet should
be above parties in the conduct of domestic as well as foreign
affairs.[6] In order to carry out the general principles embodied
in the joint declaration of June, 1916, and to gain majority
support in the House of Representatives, General Count
Terauchi now sought to establish an advisory council on
foreign relations.[7] Thus, after sounding the views of influential genro, privy councilors, and others, Premier Terauchi
invited Hara, Inukai, and Kato, representing the three
major parties, on June 2, 1917, in order to solicit their
"understandings" to the proposed council. Hara and Inukai,
having been previously approached, expressed their support,[8]
while Viscount Kato of the *Kenseikai* party reserved his

[2]The two memoranda embodying the "understandings" reached were made
public by Kato, Hara, and Inukai before their respective parties on June 10 (*Tokyo
Asahi*, June 11, 1916, p. 3).

[3]Ito, *Kato Komei*, II, 64–70; Hirota, *Naikaku Kotetsu Gojunenshi*, pp. 722–723;
Kudo, *Taisho Kenseishi*, pp. 146–147; *Teikoku Gikaishi*, X, 1080.

[4]See a symposium on "A Conference of Three Party Presidents" by Uyesugi,
Yoshino, Hayashi, Oyama, and Wakamiya, in *Chuo Koron*, No. 332 (July, 1916),
pp. 53–80.

[5]Kudo, *Taisho Kenseishi*, pp. 158–167.

[6]The refusal on the part of the genro to give consideration to Okuma's recommendation of Kato was due chiefly to the disfavor and enmity the genro experienced
in Kato's refusal to listen to their advice in the conduct of foreign relations.

[7]The House of Representatives of the Thirty-eighth Diet was dissolved on Jan. 25,
1917, when the *Kokuminto* resolution of non-confidence in the Terauchi super-party
cabinet became certain of passage. The *Seiyukai* party gained 54 members as against
the loss of 76 members by the *Kenseikai* party in the general election of April 20,
1917. Thus, the *Seiyukai*, which opposed the resolution in the Diet, became the
largest party, but lacked 26 members to control the House. By including President
Inukai of the *Kokuminto* with 35 members, Terauchi ministry was able to obtain
the majority in the House (Kudo, *Taisho Kenseishi*, pp. 172–189).

[8]*Tokyo Asahi*, June 1, 2, 1917, p. 2; *ibid.*, June 3, 1917, p. 3.

reply.[9] Terauchi called an extraordinary meeting of his cabinet on June 3 (Sunday) to report to his colleagues the details of the conference held the preceding day. At this meeting, the cabinet approved the draft ordinance establishing an advisory council on foreign relations.[10] On the following day, Viscount Kato declined to become a member of this council on the ground that, desirable as it was to have a united public support in foreign relations, to establish such a body under the direct supervision of the emperor would be to place restrictions upon the cabinet in the discharge of its constitutional functions.[11] Indeed, Kato's refusal to become a member of this council was based upon his conviction that it would seriously hinder him and his party in parliamentary supervision and criticism of the Terauchi cabinet, and that the creation of such a body was an implied criticism of his own conduct of foreign relations under Okuma cabinet.[12]

During the forenoon of June 4, Prince Yamagata, president of the Privy Council. Marquis Saionji, former president of the *Seiyukai* party, and Marquis Matsukata, Lord Privy Seal, were received in audience by the emperor to advise the throne upon the proposed *Gaiko Chosakai* and other important matters. Having consulted the genro, the emperor gave his sanction to the ordinance.[13] Thus, on June 5, 1917, the *Rinji Gaiko Chosakai*, or the advisory council on foreign relations, was established. The ordinance provided for a presidency, to be filled by the prime minister, and several members, to be appointed from among the cabinet ministers, former cabinet ministers, and *Shinninkan* officials. It further provided that, in case of special necessity, temporary members might be appointed from among scholars and experienced statesmen. The function of the council was to deliberate upon important diplomatic affairs.[14] The following day, the members of the council were appointed. It was com-

[9]On Oct. 10, 1916, one half of the members of the *Chuseikai* and *Koyu* Club united with the *Doshikai* to form the *Kenseikai* with Viscount Kato as its president (Kudo, *Taisho Kenseishi*, pp. 172–175).

[10]*Tokyo Asahi*, June 4, 1917, p. 3.

[11]*Ibid.*, June 5, 1917, p. 2.

[12]Ito, *Kato Komei*, II, 260–275.

[13]*Tokyo Asahi*, June 5, 1917, p. 2.

[14]Imperial Ordinance No. 57, 1917. Text in *Kwampo*, June 6, 1917, p. 105.

posed of the prime minister as president, foreign minister
as secretary general, and navy minister, war minister, home
minister, one privy councilor, two members of the House of
Peers, and presidents of two political parties.[15]

Immediate and widespread public discussion regarding the
political significance of the council as well as its constitutionality was forthcoming upon the publication of the ordinance on June 5, 1917. It was pointed out that the real object
in the establishment of the council was to insure safe sailing
through the Diet, to prevent damaging parliamentary criticisms and interpellations by binding the party leaders
through their participation in the formulation and execution
of important diplomatic policies, and finally to prevent in
advance the usual public criticism of the forthcoming peace
conference.[16] As to the constitutionality of the council,
leading jurists united in attacking it as an encroachment
upon the constitutional powers of the cabinet ministers.[17]

During the Thirty-ninth Diet the advisory council was
made a target of parliamentary debates and interpellations.[18]

[15]The advisory council was composed of the following: General Count Terauchi
(premier), Viscount Ichiro Motono (foreign minister), Baron Shimpei Goto (home
minister), General Kenichi Oshima (war minister), Admiral Tomosaburo Kato
(navy minister), Viscount Miyoji Ito (privy councilor), Viscount Tosuke Hirata
(member of the House of Peers), Baron Shinken Makino (member of the House of
Peers), Kei Hara (member of the House of Representatives and president of the
Seiyukai party), and Ki Inukai (member of the House of Representatives and president of the Kokuminto party). Hirata, Hara, Makino, Ito, Inukai were given the
treatment as ministers of state. Vice-admiral Suzuki, Vice-Minister of Foreign
Affairs Shidehara, Lieutenant General Yamada, and Chief Secretary of the Cabinet
Kodama were appointed secretaries (Kwampo gogai, June 6, 1917). Cf. Tokyo
Asahi, June 7, 1917, p. 3. The ordinance provided that the council was to be composed of a president (always prime minister), and several members to be appointed
from among the present and former premiers, ministers of state or those to whom
such treatment had been accorded, and also the Shinninkan officials (Arts. II, III).
The secretary general was to be a minister of state, while secretaries were to be appointed from among the Kotokan officials of the cabinet and the Foreign Office
and generals and admirals of the War and Navy departments (Art. V).

[16]President Inukai admitted the improper nature of the advisory council from the
standpoint of constitutional law but approved it under the political exigencies of
the time (Jiji Shimpo, June 6, 1917, p. 3). Cf. an editorial in Tokyo Asahi, June 7,
1917, p. 3.

[17]See Soichi Sasaki, "Advisory Council on Foreign Relations and the Constitution," Kokka Gakkai Zasshi, XXXI (Aug., 1917), 1137-1169; articles by Oyama,
Kambe, Tanaka, and Yoshino in Chuo Koron, No. 345 (July, 1917), pp. 54-76;
also Matsui in ibid., No. 347 (Aug., 1917), pp. 53-57.

[18]June 23, 1917-July 15, 1917.

The attack upon the council as being contrary to the spirit of the Constitution and violative of the basic principles of responsible government was ably led by veteran parliamentarians of the *Kenseikai* party, while the Terauchi government defended the council as being within the letter and spirit of the Constitution, that its competence was in no way an encroachment upon that of the cabinet or the Privy Council, and that its establishment was designed to place diplomacy and national defense outside party politics.[19]

The climax was reached when a resolution declaring that the establishment of this advisory council on foreign relations was a gross violation of the Constitution, and an encroachment upon the fundamental principles of constitutional government was introduced on July 12 by Representative Takao Saito, a leading member of the *Kenseikai* party. The supporters of the resolution argued that the *Gaiko Chosakai* violated the Constitution, that the ordinance establishing it without having received the advice of the Privy Council was not only contrary to tradition but an encroachment upon the competence of that body. They emphasized further that the real objective lay in the cabinet's effort to weather through parliamentary criticism and debates. The opposition to the resolution, on the other hand, vigorously denied every charge thus made by the defenders of the resolution. They argued that the body in question was an advisory organ to the emperor created to meet the exigencies of the war, that the Imperial Diet possessed no power to declare war, conclude peace, or to make treaties, and finally, that the body was designed to unite the public opinion upon questions of foreign policy. After a two-day debate, the resolution failed of adoption.[20]

With the establishment of this advisory council, the For-

[19]*Teikoku Gikaishi*, X, 1187–1195, 1230–1256, 1375–1378. Prime Minister Terauchi declined to state the government's position to a hypothetical question asked by Representative Kotaro Mochizuki as to establishing a parliamentary committee on foreign relations by an amendment to the Law of the Houses (*Dai Sanjukukai Teikoku Gikai Shugiin Iinkai Giroku*, Pt. I, No. 1, p. 76).

[20]The resolution was ably defended by Saito, Morito, and Furuya, while vigorously attacked by Uyehara, Nakanishi, Tsuda, and Prime Minister Terauchi (*Teikoku Gikaishi*, X, 1403–1405, 1408–1417). The government's position upon this issue was definitely stated in the premier's reply to an interpellation made in the House (*ibid.*, X, 1375–1376, 1378). *Cf.* Dr. Somei Uzawa's defense of the council in the House of Representatives (*ibid.*, X, 1243–1245).

eign Office was reduced to a position of secondary importance in the actual formulation and execution of foreign policies. Thus, General Terauchi was able to dominate the Kasumi-gaseki during his administration, the most notable instance being the ill-fated Siberian adventure during the closing days of the World War. Hence, the main object of establishing this council was accomplished as Terauchi succeeded in shielding his ministry from parliamentary criticism and general discussion over foreign affairs. Upon the formation of the Hara *Seiyukai* ministry, however, the Foreign Office again resumed its former position, and the prestige and influence of the advisory council greatly waned. This decline in power of the council was inevitable, as the ministry was now supported by a majority party in the Lower House. In these circumstances, the commanding position of the *Gaiko Chosakai* was reduced to one of nominal existence—to be content with receiving reports on foreign relations.

Immediately after the conclusion of the Peace Treaty, Baron Shimpei Goto, in concert with Viscount Miyoji Ito and Ki Inukai, expressed his desire to resign, but Premier Hara pleaded with them to remain in office pending the solution of various diplomatic issues.[21] However, with the ratification of the Washington treaties in the summer of 1922, Baron Goto tendered his resignation to the premier, Admiral Kato.[22] Baron Goto was soon followed by Ki Inukai, and the abolition of the council now became merely a question of time.[23] After obtaining cabinet approval on September 16, the advisory council was abolished on September 18, 1922, under Admiral Kato's ministry.[24]

[21]As late as March 6, 1922, Premier Takahashi, who succeeded Hara following the latter's assassination on the eve of the Washington Conference, defended the council and refused to disclose its proceedings (*ibid.*, XIII, 1215).

[22]*Tokyo Asahi*, Aug. 13, 1922, p. 1.

[23]*Ibid.*, Aug. 30, 1922, p. 2.

[24]*Ibid.*, Sept. 17, 19, 1922, p. 1. Six years later, in the summer of 1928, General Baron Tanaka sought to repeat the experiment of his former chief, but failed, owing largely to a strong opposition on the part of the Privy Council (Yoshino, *Gendai Kensei no Unyo*, pp. 224–229).

Chapter VI

THE IMPERIAL DIET

UNDER THE CONSTITUTION, the Imperial Diet has no direct means of control over the conduct of foreign relations. It possesses no constitutional power in the declaration of war, making of peace, conclusion of treaties, recognition of new states or governments, or in the appointment of diplomatic and consular officers. With the gradual development of parliamentary system, however, the Diet has tended to exert an increasing influence, though indirect and often ineffective, over foreign policies as well as over domestic affairs, through legislation, fiscal control, parliamentary interpellations and debates, and other means at its disposal. Thus, the rapidly increasing supervisory and directive power of the Diet over the executive through the established principle of parliamentary responsibility of the ministry has extended more and more to the conduct of foreign relations, though admittedly to a less degree than in domestic affairs. An attempt is made in this chapter briefly to sketch the structure and formal powers of the legislative branch of government to ascertain the actual influence and control it may exert over the executive in foreign as well as domestic policies.

ORGANIZATION OF THE DIET

The Imperial Diet, established by the Constitution of 1889,[1] is composed of two chambers—a House of Peers and a House of Representatives.[2]

[1]Constitution, Arts. XXXIII–LIV. The first session of the Diet met in the fall of 1890.

[2]*Ibid.*, Art. XXXIII. In defending the adoption of a bicameral system, Prince Ito says, "The aim of a representative system is to draw profit from the results of public deliberations. Now, when all the political forces are united in a single House, and are left to the influence of excited passions and abandoned to one-sided movements, with no restraining and equalizing power over them, that House may in the

49

The House of Peers is composed of the following six classes of members:[3] (1) the Princes of the Blood who have reached majority;[4] (2) princes and marquises over thirty years of age;[5] (3) counts, viscounts, and barons who are elected from among their respective orders for a seven-year term;[6] (4) crown members or imperial appointees on account of meritorious services to the state or of erudition;[7] (5) four members of the Imperial Academy who are elected by the same body for a seven-year term,[8] and (6) members who are elected for a seven-year term by and from among the highest taxpayers in direct national taxes.[9]

Under the Manhood Suffrage Act of 1925, the House of Representatives is composed of representatives elected by the people for a four-year term. The membership of the House is four hundred and sixty-six.[10]

intemperance of biased excitement, overstep the limits of propriety, and, as a consequence, bring about the despotism of the majority, which may in turn lead to anarchy. Evils would be far greater under such a state of things, than they were in the days when there was no representative system at all" (*Commentaries*, p. 64).

[3] *Kizokuin Rei*, or ordinance concerning the House of Peers, Art. I.

[4] *Ibid.*, Art. II. Eighteen years of age for the Crown Prince and also for the eldest grandson of the emperor, and twenty years of age for other Princes of the Blood. By tradition, imperial princes never take part in the deliberations of the House.

[5] *Ibid.*, Art. II.

[6] *Ibid.*, Art. IV. Eighteen counts, sixty-six viscounts, and sixty-six barons.

[7] *Ibid.*, Art. V. Imperial appointees must be more than thirty years of age and appointed for life. Imperial appointees of this class cannot exceed one hundred and twenty-five. They are appointed by the emperor upon recommendation of the cabinet. Naturally, a cabinet tends to recommend those government officials, party men, or business men who have rendered most services to the party in power. In consequence, these imperial appointees tend to be divided along the party lines in the Lower House and are the most active members in the Upper House.

[8] *Ibid.*, Art. V, Sec. II.

[9] *Ibid.*, Art. VI. Members coming under the category of (2) to (6) inclusive must be over thirty years of age. At present (June, 1929), the composition of the House of Peers is as follows: 16 Princes of the Blood, 13 princes, 30 marquises, 17 counts, 65 viscounts, 66 barons, 121 imperial appointees, 4 nominees of the Imperial Academy, and 64 representatives of the highest taxpayers, making a total of 396 members (*Jiji Nenkan*, 1930, p. 119).

[10] For debates in the Lower House on the Manhood Suffrage bill in the Fiftieth Diet, see *Kwampo gogai*, Feb. 22, 1925, pp. 355–377; March 3, 1925, pp. 469–502; March 28, 1925, pp. 932–940; March 30, 1925, pp. 949–952. For debates in the House of Peers, see *Dai Gojikkai Teikoku Gikai Kizokuin Gijiroku*, Nos. 18–21 (March 4, 5, 6, 7, 1925), 373, 396–516; March 25, 1925, pp. 838–484; March 26, 1925, pp. 853–923; March 27, 1925, p. 931; March 29, 1925, pp. 973–986. For the text of the act, see *Genko Horei Shuran* (1927), I, Bk. II, 12–22. For a more detailed discussion of the organization of the Diet, see Minobe, *Kempo Satsuyo* (1932), pp. 354–393.

THE COMPETENCE OF THE DIET

Broadly stated, the legal powers of the two chambers are equal, with the following important exceptions: (1) budget bills must be laid first in the Lower House, though the amending power is the same;[11] (2) the amendment of the *Kizokuin Rei* or ordinance concerning the House of Peers is placed beyond the reach of the Lower House, while the Upper House participates in the determination of the organization of the Lower House through its law-making power; (3) the Upper House has jurisdiction over disputes concerning elections of its members, while the Lower House does not enjoy such power; (4) the Upper House is consulted by the emperor concerning the privileges of nobility, and finally (5), whereas the Lower House is subject to dissolution, the Upper House is free from it.[12]

The powers of the Diet are defined in Chapter III of the Constitution, but the enumeration of these powers should not be construed as exhaustive. The general powers of the Diet should be interpreted in the light of general principles of parliamentary government. Thus the powers of the Imperial Diet may conveniently be discussed under the following three heads: legislative power, financial power, and supervisory power.

The legislative power of the Diet embraces the power of giving consent to projects of law as well as of approval of emergency ordinances issued in lieu of laws.[13] However, the legislative power of the Diet is greatly limited in its scope in that (1) it has no power over dynastic affairs; (2) no power of initiating constitutional amendment; (3) it is denied the power to convene of its own accord, and (4) it receives further restrictions under the extended ordinance power of the emperor as well as his foreign relations power.[14]

The fiscal control by the Diet may be comprehended under

[11]For a brief account of the struggle over the budget power between the two Houses during the Third Diet, when the Peers referred the matter to the imperial decision, see Kudo, *Teikoku Gikaishi*, I, 152–158. For debates, see *Teikoku Gikaishi*, I, 1688–1699, 1727–1733, 1738–1744, 1750, 1795–1796, 2185–2224, 2227–2233.

[12]Minobe, *Kempo Seigi*, pp. 436–437. *Cf.* Sasaki, *Nihon Kempo Yoron* (1931), p. 503.

[13]Constitution, Arts. V, VIII, XXXVII.

[14]*Ibid.*, Arts. VIII, IX, XIII. *Cf.* Minobe, *Kempo Satsuyo*, pp. 396–401.

the two main heads: control before, and control after, the money has been spent. The former includes the power over taxation, budget bill, raising national loans, and contracting other liabilities to the charge of the national treasury, while the latter comprehends the power to approve expenditures not provided for in the budget, emergency financial measures taken by the government, and review of expenditures.[15]

As to revenues, the imposition of a new tax or the modification of the rates of existing ones must be determined by law.[16] Thus, in Japan, the taxes are determined by statutes, in the modification of which the Diet exercises its discretion. The revenues contained in the budget are merely estimates. However, all such administrative fees or other revenues having the nature of compensation fall outside this general category. And the raising of national loans and the contracting of other liabilities to the charge of the national treasury, excepting those provided for in the budget, require legislative consent. While taxes are determined by statutes, all expenditures of the government are laid before the Diet annually in the form of a budget by the executive.[17] The Diet has no power to initiate a budget bill, and in consequence its amending power is restricted to reducing or rejecting the estimates. Neither House may increase the budget nor insert new items, for such acts are forms of initiating budget bills. Even this power is further restricted by various exceptions to the general fiscal power of the Diet.[18]

The most notable limitation upon the fiscal power of the Diet comes from the principle of the superiority of law to the budget. Thus, the Diet cannot nullify existing laws through its budgetary powers.[19] Article LXVII of the Con-

[15]For elaborate legal discussions on the parliamentary control of the finances, see Minobe, *Kempo Seigi*, pp. 621-718; Hozumi, *Kempo Teiyo*, II, 870-910; Uyesugi, *Kempo Jutsugi*, pp. 531-575; Ichimura, *Teikoku Kempo Ron*, pp. 896-1009; Shimizu, *Kempo Hen*, pp. 1374-1446; Sasaki, *Nihon Kempo Yoron*, pp. 634-673.

[16]Constitution, Art. LXII.

[17]For a detailed treatment of the budgetary system, see Gen Nishino, *Yosan Gairon* (Tokyo, 1926), *passim*.

[18]Minobe, *Kempo Seigi*, pp. 687-688.

[19]Minobe, *Kempo Seigi*, pp. 686-693. Prince Ito comments on this point as follows: "... Therefore law has precedence over a Budget, which has no power to change a law. Were it possible for a law to be affected by a Budget, that would amount to an overstepping of the right of settling the Budget beyond proper limits" (*Commentaries*, p. 121).

stitution states this general principle in the following language:

Those already fixed expenditures based by the Constitution upon the powers appertaining to the Emperor and such expenditures as may have arisen by the effect of law, or that appertain to the legal obligations of the Government, shall be neither rejected nor reduced by the Imperial Diet, without the concurrence of the Government.

From the provision of the Constitution just cited we observe that three categories of expenditures are placed outside the scope of absolute parliamentary discretion, namely: (1) already fixed expenditures based by the Constitution upon the prerogative of the emperor; (2) such expenditures as may have arisen by the effect of law, and (3) expenditures that appertain to the legal obligations of the government.

The first category includes all the expenditures which are based upon the prerogatives of the throne as set forth in Chapter I of the Constitution, to wit: ordinary expenditures required by the organization of the different branches of the administration, and by that of the army and navy, the salaries of all civil and military officers and expenditures that may be required in consequence of international treaties and agreements.[20] Of expenditures due to treaties and agreements, two categories should be noted. When a treaty stipulates payment of money, it comes under the category of "expenditures that appertain to the legal obligations of the Government," while expenditures necessary for the execution of a treaty or an agreement are classed as "already fixed expenditures." However, the Diet has the power freely to deliberate upon new expenditures or increase of the existing ones, as until they have been provided for in the budget and approved by the Diet, they do not become "already fixed expenditures." Thus, for example, when a new administrative organization is to be established the usual procedure followed by the government is to include necessary estimates of expenditures under the proposed ordinance in the budget, and such ordinance is issued after parliamentary approval thereto has been given in the form of the budget. As such a procedure is not feasible in case of international treaties or agreements,

[20]Prince Ito, *Commentaries*, p. 128.

it is quite conceivable that the Diet may refuse necessary appropriations for the execution of obligations entered into under treaties or agreements, when resort is made to expenditures not provided for in the budget.[21] The second category of expenditures—expenditures necessary for the execution of law—includes expenditures for the operation of the Imperial Diet, courts, Board of Audit, pensions, and a host of others. Except when the amount of expenditures is expressly stipulated in the law itself, the Diet is not bound to accept the estimates by the government, but the parliamentary reduction or rejection requires the concurrence of the executive. The third category of expenditures which appertain to the legal obligations of the government include the interest on the national debt, redemption of the same, subsidies or guaranties to companies, expenses necessitated by the civil obligations of the government, compensations of all kinds (e.g., salaries, pensions, and allowances of foreign advisers and employees), are likewise free from reduction or rejection.[22]

Thus, the Diet is powerless, without the concurrence of the executive, to reduce or reject expenditures due to the exercise of the prerogatives of the throne, for the execution of the law, or the legal obligations of the government. Furthermore, the fiscal power of the Diet cannot be exercised in such a way as to have the effect of nullifying the law, and the Diet may not amend the budget in a way to render the operation of administrative organizations impossible, or seriously to hinder their operation. And the concurrence of the government must be obtained by each House separately, that is, immediately after the House of Representatives has voted upon it.[23]

[21]Minobe, *Kempo Seigi*, pp. 693–694.

[22]In defending the superiority of the Constitution and laws to the budget, Prince Ito, in his semi-official *Commentaries*, declares: "Were the Diet, in voting the Budget, to reject entirely or to reduce in amount any of the expenditures based by the Constitution upon the sovereign powers of the Emperor or any expenditures necessitated by an effect of law or for the fulfillment of legal obligations, such proceeding should be regarded as subversive of the existence of the state and contrary to the fundamental principles of the Constitution" (p. 129).

[23]A very serious conflict arose between the House of Representatives and the government in the first session of the Diet over the time of asking the executive concurrence to reduction or rejection of appropriations coming under Article LXVII

The executive is under the obligation to carry out the affairs of the State within the limits of the budget passed by the Diet.[24] However, the Constitution recognizes certain instances when the executive can go beyond the limits of the budget, subject to subsequent parliamentary approval. Hence, it may spend money beyond the appropriations set forth in the titles and paragraphs in the budget, or even for purposes other than those provided for in the budget,[25] to be paid out of the reserve funds in the budget.[26] Moreover, in case of urgent needs for the maintenance of public safety, the government may take all necessary financial measures by means of imperial ordinances provided the Diet cannot be convoked owing to the external or internal conditions of the country.[27] Though all such financial measures beyond or outside the budget must be laid before the Diet for parliamentary approval to absolve the ministry of political responsibility, the withholding of approbation by the Diet affects only the continued efficacy of the measures in question and cannot possess a retroactive effect of annulling the proceedings already taken. Accordingly, the failure of a subsequent parliamentary approbation merely raises a question of political responsibility of the government.[28]

Finally, the subordinate character of the fiscal power of

of the Constitution. The issue was whether such request should be asked immediately after one House has voted for the same or after both Houses have voted upon the measure. The cabinet (Yamagata) contended that such request must be presented to the government by each House independently. This has been accepted as precedent (Kudo, *Teikoku Gikaishi*, I, 63–71; Minobe, *Kempo Seigi*, pp. 696–699).

On the question as to whether the executive is competent to give concurrence when it has the effect of modifying existing laws or ordinances, the practices are not uniform, and jurists' views vary. *Cf. Hogaku Kyokai Zasshi*, X (1892), 191–217, 295–322, 401–436; also questions and replies by government delegates in the meeting of the House Budget Committee on March 9, 1897 (*Dai Jikkai Teikoku Gikai Shugiin Yosan Iinkai Sokkiroku*, pp. 105–108).

[24]Even here, the practice of "the working budget" often renders the Diet's power over financial affairs less effective. Thus, a cabinet, particularly a new cabinet under a different political party, "revises" the budget passed in the Diet under the previous administration. This has often raised the charge of disregarding the integrity and competence of the Diet. For questions asked and replies made by the Hamaguchi cabinet, see *Kwampo gogai*, May 8, 1930, pp. 93–95. *Cf.* Dr. Rikitaro Fujisawa, "So-called Working Budget," *Kokka Gakkai Zasshi*, XLIII (1929), 1558–1567.

[25]Constitution, Art. LXIV, Sec. II.

[26]*Ibid.*, Art. LXIX.

[27]*Ibid.*, Art. LXX.

[28]Minobe, *Kempo Seigi*, pp. 661–676, 701–707.

the Diet is expressly recognized in the constitution itself
when it declares that:

> When the Imperial Diet has not voted on the Budget, or when
> the Budget has not been brought into actual existence, the Govern-
> ment shall carry out the Budget of the preceding year.[29]

Accordingly, even if the Diet fails to vote upon the budget,
one of the Houses rejects it, or the House of Representatives
is dissolved, the revenues are assured by the budget of the
preceding year.

The Diet further possesses the power of auditing the final
accounts of the expenditures and revenues of the government
as the executive is required to submit to the Diet the final
accounts of revenues and expenditures together with the
report of verification of the Board of Audit.[30] But, this power
over fiscal accounts is merely nominal and ineffective as a
means of control of the executive.

PARLIAMENTARY CONTROL OF THE EXECUTIVE

From our brief discussion of the scope and method of the
legislative control of the governmental finance, it is evident
that the parliamentary control of the executive through the
"purse strings" is far from being effective, and that its
primary function is not concerned with the giving of "consent" to the budget drawn up by the cabinet. On the contrary, by far the most notable development in the Japanese
parliamentary system has been the increasing extent to
which the national legislature is utilized by the representatives of the people for general discussion and criticism of the
administration over both domestic and foreign affairs. Thus,
in addition to its legislative and fiscal powers, the Diet
exercises its powers of control through more formal means,
such as (1) address to the throne, (2) representation to the
government, (3) receiving petitions, (4) making inquiries,
(5) passing resolutions, (6) questioning and interpellating
the government.

[29]Art. LXI.

[30]Constitution, Art. LXXII. The Privy Council, the Administrative Court, and
the Board of Audit are outside the scope of ministerial responsibility. Hence, for
any action by the Board of Audit, ministerial responsibility may not be questioned
in the Diet. On this point, see the interesting interpellations in the Twelfth Diet
(*Teikoku Gikaishi*, IV, 787, 834).

The constitutional provision that either House may respectively present addresses to the emperor[31] was very often resorted to, in the early period of the parliamentary history of Japan, by the Lower House as a means of "impeaching the cabinet." However, as the parliamentary system is more firmly established, this power has come to be exercised mainly for ceremonial purposes. The power of making representations to the government by either House[32] is of little or no political significance because the government is under no obligation to accept them. Hence, representation resolutions are usually passed by the House without much debate, except in important instances. Moreover, both Houses may receive petitions from the subjects requesting some needed legislation or administrative measures.[33] Both Houses may establish special committees of inquiry on any matter of state, but this power is greatly limited because they lack the power to summon individuals as witnesses.[34]

The most effective formal means of control by the Diet of the executive are interpellations, questions, and resolutions.[35] An interpellation may be put to the government by a member, provided he obtains the support of not less than thirty members, on any question coming within the competence of the Diet. When such interpellation is put to the government, a cabinet minister must either reply immediately, or fix the date for making such reply, or when he declines to do so, he must state the reasons therefor.[36] The practice is that when a question is of such nature as to embarrass the government or to which the executive is not disposed to give explicit reply, a very general and often evasive reply is made during the closing days of a session. And consequently, the method which is more effectively employed and increasingly resorted to by opposition members is that of putting questions from the floor. There is no express provision, either in the Constitution or in the Law of

[31]Constitution, Art. XLIX.

[32]Ibid., Art. XL.

[33]Ibid., Art. L.

[34]Law of the Houses, Arts. LXXII–LXXV.

[35]Shitsumon, or interpellation, requires thirty supporters, while shitsugi or question may be asked by any member from the floor. In this treatise "interpellation" is conveniently used to cover both categories.

[36]Law of the Houses, Arts. XLVIII, XLIX.

the Houses, for interpellations by individual members, which almost invariably require immediate replies from the government. This method is constantly resorted to during the session of the Diet. Particularly, immediately after the prime minister, foreign minister, and the finance minister have finished their addresses on their respective fields, at the beginning of each session, questions are put to the ministry in power by the leaders of opposition parties. Such interpellations must be upon matters of parliamentary competence, namely, matters that relate to the affairs of state falling within the scope of ministerial responsibility. Though replies to these interpellations, mainly intended to embarrass the government rather than to obtain correct information, may be evasive and often disappointing to the interpellators, they serve to bring the whole field of governmental responsibility into scrutiny and criticism. Cabinet ministers may often resort to the policy of refusing to reply to specific questions thus put to them on the ground of "military secrecy" or "diplomatic secrecy," or even "contrary to public interest."

The right to pass resolutions is a right not specifically recognized either in the Constitution or in the Law of the Houses, but such power has never been questioned since the beginning of the parliamentary history. A House is thus empowered to pass a resolution on any matter falling within its competence, and resolutions of want of confidence in the cabinet or in a minister of state, or upon constitutional questions are of greatest political significance. The passage of a resolution of want of confidence in the House of Representatives results usually in the dissolution of the House followed by a general election, or resignation of the cabinet or the ministers so censured. The passage of a resolution on specific policy may have an important political significance.

The parliamentary control of the executive, through legislation, budget, and other formal means discussed in the preceding pages, is greatly restricted by executive dominance in parliamentary procedure. In the first place, the Diet is denied the power to convene on its own initiative, while each session is limited to three months which may still be shortened by repeated prorogations each not exceeding fifteen days but combined exceeding fifteen days. In the second place, the executive may at any time exercise its right to petition the throne to dissolve the House of Representatives for any reason whatever. Moreover, the constitutional provision for emergency imperial ordinances and emergency financial measures is often taken advantage of by the cabinet.[37]

In recent years, the Diet has come to be an organ not primarily to perform constitutional functions of legislation and of supervision of the executive, but one through which political parties seek to obtain the powers of the government. Hence, the parliamentary interpellations and debates center not around great questions of national policy having vital concern to the interest of the people, but often around more technical or non-consequential matters as "in the names of their respective peoples," or the question relating to the time of obtaining the consent (agreement) of the naval general staff before sending instructions to London. On the other hand, party cabinets did not call special sessions of the Diet to modify the Peace Preservation Law imposing death penalty, or to decide such important matters as lifting the gold embargo, concluding the London Naval Treaty, or undertaking a large-scale military adventure in China (1931–1932). Indeed, the attitude of the government has been to avoid parliamentary scrutiny and criticism as much as possible, rather than to seek the general trends of public opinion as reflected in the national legislature.

After forty years of parliamentary experience, the prestige and integrity of the Diet have greatly decreased. The debates and proceedings within the four walls of the Diet Building are on lower level and command less respect of the public than three decades ago. This decline in the prestige of the legislature may in a large measure be attributed to the evolution of the executive leadership and corresponding decline in legislative initiative and direction over the formulation and execution of governmental policies.[38] The forty years of parliamentary history, however, has firmly established the practice no less significant in the operation of the constitu-

[37]Military and naval expeditions are usually undertaken without previous consent of the Diet.

[38]For recent criticisms upon the Diet see Professor Royama, "Reform of the Diet," *Kaizo*, XIII, No. 5 (May, 1931), 27–39; also articles by Representatives Yamamichi and Kiyose in *Minsei*, V, No. 3 (March, 1931), 10–15, 23–28.

tional government. Thus, the cabinet is formed upon the
confidence of the most popular chamber of the Diet and no
longer can defy the representatives of the people without
fatally injuring its own power. This evolution of a parliamentary system and practice along the lines developed in
England, it is hoped, tends more and more to place the whole
range of governmental functions under the ever effective
scrutiny and criticism of the Imperial Diet.

Chapter VII

THE JUDICIARY

THE COURTS OF LAW participate in the conduct of foreign relations through their power of interpreting treaties and agreements independent of the political department of government. Under the principle of separation of powers and its accompanying doctrine of judicial independence, the courts render their judgments involving questions of treaty interpretation and enforcement, of recognition of new states or governments, and of enforcement of international law, upon their own authority and independent of the executive or the legislature. An attempt is made in this chapter to examine the organization, functions, and the operation of the judiciary, to ascertain the scope and extent to which the courts of law may exert their influence upon foreign relations.

ORGANIZATION OF THE COURTS OF LAW[1]

The judicial power of the state, like the legislative and the executive powers, belongs to the throne, but is exercised by courts of law according to law in the name of the emperor. The organization of courts of law is determined by law, and not by imperial ordinances, as in the case of administrative establishments.[2] The courts of law may be divided into four categories: one supreme court (Tokyo), seven courts of appeal (Tokyo, Osaka, Nagoya, Hiroshima, Nagasaki,

[1]For a brief history of the evolution of the judicial system in Japan, see an article by Dr. Seisho Tomii in Okuma (ed.), *Kaikoku Gojunenshi* (Tokyo, 1907), I, 383–408; Minobe, *Kempo Seigi*, pp. 578–582.
[2]Constitution, Art. LVII.

61

Miyagi, Sapporo), and one prefectural court in each prefecture, and several district courts in each prefecture.[3] In addition to these ordinary courts of law, such special courts as military and naval courts, judicial tribunals of the patent bureau, and consular courts have been established.[4] In colonies, special courts are established.

The independent character of the judges is expressly recognized in Article LVIII of the Constitution as follows:

> The judges shall be appointed from among those who possess proper qualifications according to law. No judge shall be deprived of his position, unless by way of criminal sentence or disciplinary punishment. Rules for disciplinary punishment shall be determined by law.

Hence, although the appointment, removal, disciplinary, and other regulations concerning administrative officers are provided for in various civil service ordinances, such rules and regulations regarding judicial officers of courts are determined by law. However, this constitutional guaranty of judges refers to the executive interference, and hence there is nothing to preclude such limitations by law. Accordingly, restrictions may be placed upon the conditions of appointment, removal, and disciplinary punishment of judicial officers by law. In this connection, it is to be noted that, even in this matter of position, judges are not entirely free from the executive, for, though the judges receive the negative guaranty of life tenure, their promotion depends upon the recommendation of the minister of justice. Again, the public procurator's office of each court of law is under the direction of the Department of Justice.[5] In the second place, the judges are completely independent of either the executive or the legislative branch of government in rendering judgments. However, in criminal cases, this independence receives an important limitation from the fact that it is only upon the initiative of the public procurator's office that a court of law takes cognizance of a case. In view of the fact that the public

[3] *Cf.* Minobe, *Kempo Satsuyo* (1932), pp. 558–559.

[4] *Ibid.*, pp. 572–576.

[5] Dr. Kado Hara, *Shiho Seido Kaizen no Kyumu* (Tokyo, 1921), *passim*. *Cf.* Minobe, *Gendai Kensei Hyoron*, p. 198; also Dr. Ichiro Kiyose's statement in the House of Representatives, March 8, 1922, in the Forty-fifth Diet (*Teikoku Gikaishi*, XIII, 987).

procurator's office is under the direction of the ministry of justice, and prosecution is under such direction, there is room for executive interference with criminal cases, particularly when important government officials or party leaders are concerned. Third, the effect of judicial decisions is likewise independent and carried out by judicial officers. The sole exception to this independence is the exercise of the pardoning power of the emperor.[6] And as the fourth feature in the judicial independence may be cited the judicial review.

The Judicial Review

Since the court of law is to exercise the judicial power according to law, it must first inquire into the validity of a law under review. However, the scope of judicial review differs greatly between laws and ordinances.

In regard to laws, the power of judicial review extends only to its examination of the form; namely, if a law meets all legal requirements—passage by the Diet, sanction by the emperor, and promulgation in due form—a court of law is bound to declare it valid and is denied the power to look into its constitutionality in its substantive aspect. Though there is no provision in the Constitution covering this point, the Constitution does not stipulate such doctrine of separation of powers as found in the United States. Under the Japanese Constitution, law is the highest expression of the will of the state, and the courts of law are bound thereby. It is true that a law must be in conformity with the fundamental law of the land as to whether the substance of a particular law is in conformity with the Constitution, the legislator has the supreme power of interpretation, and the courts of law have no competence to impeach such interpretation. When a law has been passed by the Diet and sanctioned by the emperor, it must be regarded that both the Diet and the government affirm its constitutionality, and such conclusion is final and binding upon the courts. Under such system, modifications of the Constitution in actual practice through statutory enactments cannot be completely prevented, and thus the observance and protection of the Constitution are left

[6]*Cf.* Minobe, *Kempo Satsuyo* (1932), pp. 554–557, 560–562, 583–586.

largely in the hands of the Diet and the executive.[7] When a statute is in conflict with the Imperial House Law, the courts sustain the latter.

An interesting question is raised when a statute comes in conflict with a treaty. Should the courts of law uphold the supremacy of treaty over statute, or should they be bound by their municipal character? Dr. Minobe expounds the generally accepted theory on this point when he argues that in such an instance the treaty should be upheld, unless the statute in question had been enacted with an express purpose of breaking such treaty, in which case the courts are bound by their national character to give effect to such conflicting statute.[8] It is to be mentioned here, however, that so far no concrete cases bearing upon this point have arisen in Japanese courts. On the other hand, the courts in practice take cognizance of treaties and enforce them as a part of the law of the land.[9]

In regard to ordinances, the power of judicial review is greatly enlarged. Thus, the courts may inquire, as to not only the form but the substance as well, whether an ordinance is in conformity with the Constitution, Imperial House Law, laws or treaties, and may refuse to enforce conflicting ordinances. When an emergency imperial ordinance receives subsequent parliamentary approval, however, it partakes of the same nature as law. The ordinance concerning the House of Peers is classed, in this respect, as law. As to ordinances— be it an emergency imperial ordinance issued under Article VIII of the Constitution or police ordinance under Article IX—the courts are not empowered to look into the necessity for such insurance but are bound to look into whether such ordinances are within the limits provided for in the Constitution; and should such ordinances go beyond the limits prescribed in the Constitution, the courts refuse to enforce the same. Therefore, imperial ordinances imposing taxes or providing for rules for the disciplinary punishment of judges or establishing corporations are null and void.

[7]As to whether the court of law has the power of looking into the constitutionality of a law, both in its formal and substantive aspects, the opinions of jurists are divided. But, the practice is that, because of the non-existence of the doctrine of judicial supremacy, the Constitution is subject to constant modification.

[8]Minobe, *Kempo Satsuyo* (1932), pp. 569–570.

[9]For further elaboration on this point, see our discussion on "Treaty-making Power" in Chap. XXVII, *infra*.

The Administrative Court

One administrative court is established to take jurisdiction over administrative disputes as provided for in Article LXI of the Constitution. Thus, the ordinary courts of law take cognizance of only civil disputes while administrative disputes come before the administrative court. However, since no court of jurisdictional dispute has been established, such disputes concerning jurisdictional controversies between ordinary courts of law and the administrative court must be left to the independent decision of the courts. Each court, the administrative court or the ordinary court of law, is to determine its own competence, and a decision rendered by one court is binding upon the other.

Chapter VIII

THE FOREIGN OFFICE AND THE FOREIGN SERVICE

THE FOREIGN OFFICE

THE CENTRAL ORGAN for the conduct of the nation's diplomatic relations is the Foreign Office, presided over by the minister of state for foreign affairs, a member of the cabinet. It not only formulates foreign policies but also executes them. It is the initiating, formulating, and executing machinery in the conduct of external relations of the state.

External relations constituted the major concern of the new government following the Restoration of 1868. Thus, in January of the first year of the new era, Princes (of the Blood) Higashifushimi and Yamanashi were appointed by Emperor Meiji to head the newly created *Gaikoku Jimu Sosai*, which was abolished the following month and replaced by a new office under the title of *Gaikoku Kyoku* headed by Prince Yamanashi, only to be followed by another office in April under the title of *Gaikokukan* headed by Governor Muneshiro Date. On July 8, 1869, the office was changed to *Gaimusho*, or Department of Foreign Affairs, the forerunner of the present organization at Kasumigaseki, headed by Senka Sawa, foreshadowing the present *gaimu daijin*.[1] On December 23, 1885, Kaoru Inouye was appointed the first

[1]Text of the *Shokuin Rei* for *Gaimusho* in *Horei Zensho*, 1869, pp. 255–256. For regulations of the Foreign Office thus created, see *ibid.*, 1869, pp. 289–291. *Cf.* Jumpei Shinobu, *Gaisei Kantoku to Gaiko Kikan* (Tokyo, 1926), p. 327; also *Gaimusho Nenkan* (1929), I, 269.

gaimu daijin, or minister of state for foreign affairs, immediately following the establishment of a cabinet system in Japan under Prince Hirobumi Ito.[2]

Several minor modifications of the organization of the Foreign Office have been made since 1885, and in July, 1893, the foundations of the present system were laid under the Ito cabinet. In pursuance of the public promise made to the Imperial Diet during the fourth session for administrative reorganization, a special committee on administrative reform was established under the cabinet in the spring of 1893, in which Kei Hara, then chief of the Commercial Bureau of the Foreign Office, represented the Department. Under this able statesman and administrator, the foundations of the present Foreign Office and foreign service were carefully laid.[3] Several amendments were made to this basic ordinance in 1898, 1913, and 1921, but without fundamentally altering the foundations laid by Hara in 1893.

Under the present *Gaimusho Kansei*,[4] for the ordinance concerning the organization of the Foreign Office, and *Gaimusho Bunka Kitei* supplementing the basic ordinance,[5] the Foreign Office is headed by a minister of state for foreign affairs who is the directing and supervising executive officer of the department. In the discharge of his functions, the foreign minister is assisted by various bureaus and sections of his department. Thus the Foreign Office comprises the following establishments: Secretariat, Asiatic Bureau, European and American Bureau, Bureau of Commerce, Bureau of Treaties and Conventions, Intelligence Bureau, and Cultural Work Bureau.

The broad scope of the functions of the foreign minister as

[2]Inouye became *gaimukyo* on Sept. 10, 1879, and his title was changed to *gaimu daijin* on Dec. 23, 1885. Iwakura, Soyejima, and Terashima served in the same office between Sawa and Inouye (Tanaka, *Hara Kei Zenshu*, Tokyo, 1929, I, 983).

[3]Kei Hara, who later became the first "commoner" premier of Japan in 1918, published a book in 1899 on the diplomatic and consular services of Japan under the title of *Gaikokan Ryojikan Seido*, in the laying of the foundations of which he played a leading rôle; it may be considered as a semi-official commentary upon the system. Reprinted in Tanaka (ed.), *Hara Kei Zenshu* (Tokyo, 1929), I, 978–1074.

[4]Imperial Ordinance No. 258, 1898. Amended several times since. Text of the present *Gaimusho Kansei* in *Genko Horei Shuran* (1927), Vol. I, Bk. III, 14.

[5]First determined in the cabinet on July 5, 1890, and amended several times since. Text of the present *Gaimusho Bunka Kitei* in *Gaimusho Nenkan*, or the yearbook of the Foreign Office, 1929, I, 5–8.

the supreme head in the conduct of foreign relations is clearly defined in the *Gaimusho Kansei* itself.[6] He may issue departmental ordinances for the execution of his functions; he may issue instructions to local governors or order suspension or even rescission of orders or measures taken by local functionaries should such orders and actions be contrary to law or to public interest. Under this broad power the foreign minister is enabled to exercise, like other cabinet ministers, strict control of the press in respect to foreign affairs.[7] The foreign minister is not only the executive head of the Foreign Office, directing and supervising various functionaries at Kasumigaseki and diplomatic and consular officers abroad, he is also a member of the cabinet. In the latter capacity he represents the entire staff of the department and explains to his colleagues the views of his department on any important matter pertaining to foreign relations. Thus the foreign minister plays a dominant rôle in formulation of foreign policies in the cabinet as well as in execution of policies and programs thus decided upon by the ministry.

The extent to which a foreign minister may exert his influence over his colleagues in the formulation of a policy depends partly upon his individual prestige and partly upon the subject matter in question. Thus, a "strong" foreign minister, with his personal prestige and influence and with a wealth of information, may easily overshadow the prime minister and his cabinet, while a minister with less prestige and standing may, with equal ease, be dominated by the premier or some more aggressive members of the cabinet. Foreign Ministers Mutsu, Komura, Kato, and Shidehara may be included in the former category; Nishi, Hayashi, and Motono in the latter. That the subject matter and particular circumstances may have a controlling influence in the conduct of foreign relations may be illustrated by the then re-

[6]Article I provides that: "The minister of state for foreign affairs shall be in charge of the execution of affairs relating to foreign countries, the protection of trade and commerce, and matters relating to Japanese residents abroad, and shall supervise and control all diplomatic and consular officers." The article further provides that he shall supervise the governor of the Kwantung leased territory, and also direct the cultural work in China.

[7]*Kakusho Kansei Tsusoku*, Art. IV, V, VI. Text in Leonard D. White, *Civil Service in the Modern State* (Chicago, 1930), p. 528.

ported "dual diplomacy" of the Foreign Office and the military authorities during the Siberian expedition of 1918,[8] and other incidents.

It would be interesting, at this point, to inquire into the relative permanency of tenure of a foreign minister with reference to a cabinet change. Since the establishment of cabinet system in 1885, there have been no less than forty-eight cabinet changes, including temporary ones due to sudden resignation, illness, or death of prime ministers.[9] During this period there were twenty-six different individual foreign ministers. Thus, whereas the average life of a ministry has been one year, that of a foreign minister has been nearly two years. Of these twenty-six foreign ministers, Shidehara served under six, Okuma under five, Kato and Uchida under four, different cabinets. Of the more successful statesmen in the Foreign Office we may cite Kaoru Inouye, who directed the delicate negotiations for treaty revision for eight consecutive years;[10] Shigenobu Okuma, for a combined period of three and a half years during the decade following Inouye;[11] Jutaro Komura, who headed the department for almost seven years under two Katsura cabinets during the critical period of 1901–1911; Komei Kato, who served under four cabinets for a combined period of a little over two years covering the important years of 1900–1901, 1906, 1913, and 1914–1915; Yasuya Uchida, who served for five years under three consecutive ministries,[12] and Baron Kijuro Shidehara, who served under six cabinets consecutively since June, 1924, excepting the Tanaka *Seiyukai* government (1927–1929).

It would be of interest to observe further that, of these twenty-six individual statesmen who headed the Foreign Office during the forty-seven years of the Japanese cabinet

[8]Chap. XVIII, *infra*.

[9]There were seven such periods during which the office of the prime minister was occupied by an acting prime minister, once by Prince Sanjo, Kuroda, Saionji, Wakatsuki, and Shidehara, and twice by Uchida. Of these, Saionji, Uchida, and Shidehara were foreign ministers prior to their appointment to acting premiership, or held a Foreign Office post during such periods.

[10]Sept., 1879 to Sept., 1887.

[11]Three and a half years, under four different cabinets during 1888–1898.

[12]Oct., 1911, to Dec., 1912 (Saionji); Sept., 1918, to Sept., 1915 (Hara, Uchida, Takahashi, Kato, and Uchida).

government, no less than ten later held the portfolio of prime
minister,[13] all of whom, with the sole exception of the late
Count Komei Kato, also headed the Foreign Office at the
same time. And Marquis Okuma (1898) and Baron Tanaka
(1927–1929) headed the Foreign Office during the entire
period of their incumbency.

With only forty-odd years of parliamentary history, it is
difficult to formulate a general theory concerning the "types"
of foreign ministers. However, an analysis of these twenty-
six statesmen who occupied the executive seat at Kasumigaseki may be attempted in order to suggest the general
trends. They may be classified into the following general
categories: statesmen, diplomats, military and naval men.
Ito, Okuma, Enomoto, Saionji, Sone, and Goto may be
regarded as falling in the first category. They had little or no
experience as diplomatic officers prior to assuming the post
in the Foreign Office. On the other hand, Inouye, Aoki,
Mutsu, Nishi, Kato, Komura, Hayashi, Uchida, Makino,
Ishii, Motono, Ijuin, Matsui, Shidehara, and Yoshizawa
may be said to fall in the second category, all having had
extended experience in diplomacy both at home and abroad.
Inouye, Mutsu, and Komura, however, are exceptions, their
diplomatic life being limited to a few years prior to assuming
the responsibility of directing the entire staff at Kasumigaseki. Finally, Generals Katsura, Terauchi, and Tanaka,
and Admiral Yamamoto represent the military and naval
men. Katsura, Terauchi, and Yamamoto occupied the post
only temporarily, pending the return of foreign ministers
from service abroad, while Tanaka chose the more ambitious
rôle of assuming the responsibilities himself. The above brief
analysis suggests the general tendency in recent years for the
office of foreign minister to be more and more occupied by an
experienced diplomat rather than by an amateur. Thus,
Komura, Kato, Ishii, Uchida, Shidehara, and Yoshizawa
represent the general trends; Goto and Tanaka, the exceptions.[14]

[13]Namely, the late Prince Ito, the late Marquis Okuma, Prince Saionji, the late
General Count Terauchi, the late Count Komei Kato, Count Uchida, the late
General Prince Katsura, Admiral Count Yamamoto, the late General Baron Ta-
naka, and Baron Shidehara.

[14]Viscount Kiyoura's attempt, in Jan., 1924, to invite Baron Yoshiro Fujimura
of the House of Peers to become his foreign minister failed because of the opposition

The chief administrative officer of the Foreign Office is the vice-minister, who is the chief adviser to the foreign minister as well as the active head of all officials in the department.[15] The title *gaimu jikan*, or vice-minister, was created in 1886, and Shuzo Aoki was appointed to the post on March 4, 1886. From 1886 to 1929 there were twenty different appointments to this office, the average tenure of office being a little over two years. It will be seen that the most significant feature of the appointment to this office is that no one individual has occupied the same post twice, whereas we have seen elsewhere that it is becoming a tradition for the same statesman to occupy the portfolio of foreign minister under several cabinets. On the contrary, the practice is that, after his service as the chief administrative head at Kasumigaseki, the vice-minister is usually sent abroad as an ambassador, later to be transferred to another court, or recalled to become the executive head of the Department in Tokyo.[16]

To prevent such frequent changes in the personnel of the Department, particularly of the vice-minister and heads of the various bureaus and sections, with the changes in ministry, two political offices, namely, parliamentary vice-minister and councilor, were created in each department in 1924 under the Kato cabinet. Obviously it was intended to follow the British practice, designed to make the distinction between political and non-political officers clearer, and to place the administrative staff of each department beyond the play of political fortunes of parties. Thus Viscount Komei Kato, whose long service as His Majesty's ambassador to London convinced him of the wisdom of the British practice, introduced the new system.[17] These newly created offices are

of the Kasumigaseki bureaucracy, and consequently he was forced to accept Baron Keishiro Matsui, a typical product of the Kasumigaseki school (Kametaro Hayashi, *Nihon Seitoshi*, Tokyo, 1927, II, 293).

[15]Article XVI of the *Kakusho Kansei Tsusoku* provides that: "A vice-minister of state shall assist the minister of the department, regulate the business of his department, and supervise the affairs of each bureau."

[16]There were thirteen different appointments to the vice-ministership during 1868–1886, under different titles. For the list of vice-ministers, see *Gaimusho Nenkan* (1929), I, 270–271. Cf. Shinobu, *Gaisei Kantoku to Gaiko Kikan*, pp. 362–366.

[17]Baron Shidehara was foreign minister at the time. Though the new system received a large share of its inspiration from him, it was by no means confined to the Foreign Office. The immediate object designed to be accomplished was to satisfy many disappointed politicians at the time of the formation of the Kato coalition cabinet in June, 1924.

almost invariably filled by members of the Diet, whose main
duties are to act as liaison officers between the departments
and the legislature.

Since 1924, the parliamentary vice-minister and the councilor of the Foreign Office have displaced the vice-minister
and bureau chiefs in explaining the estimates and answering
questions before the budget committees of both Houses and
their sub-committees in charge of the Foreign Office budget
bill.[18] Though the experiment is too short to enable us to
predict its probable future development, it seems safe to
submit that, with the firmer establishment of parliamentary
system in Japan, the office of the foreign minister will be
filled by experienced diplomats who are acceptable to the
parties in power, thus tending to cast their lot with political
parties, while vice-ministers and bureau chiefs and the staff
at home and abroad will be placed beyond the easy play of
partisan politics. Under this system, an effective and working
harmony can be maintained between the cabinet and the
Foreign Office staff through its foreign minister, parliamentary vice-minister, and councilor of the department.

The above brief survey of the evolution of the Foreign
Office is sufficient to indicate the general trends towards
differentiation between the political and non-political officers
in the department, whose coördination and integration are
indispensable to a smooth operation of the various organs
for conducting foreign relations. We are thus led to inquire
into the structure and functions of various bureaus and
sections of the Foreign Office and to ascertain the actual workings of the vast machinery of diplomacy directed and super-
vised by a foreign minister at Kasumigaseki, Tokyo.

The secretariat of the Department is subdivided into five
sections: protocol and personnel, archives, accounts, translations, and telegraphs. The section of the protocol and personnel is in charge of examination, appointment, dismissal,
and supervision of officers; matters relating to credentials,
letters of recall, full powers, commissions, exequaturs;

[18]The prime minister and more often the foreign minister answer interpellations
in the Diet and in the budget committees of both Houses. It is now a practice,
however, that the parliamentary vice-minister and councilor explain the Foreign
Office budget before the sub-committee of each House in charge of the Foreign
Office budget bill, and in only exceptional cases vice-ministers or bureau heads may
appear before parliamentary committees.

foreign diplomatic and consular officers residing in Japan;
audience and other ceremonial matters; decorations of foreigners; government students abroad; and such other matters
relating to protocol and personnel affairs of the entire service.
The section of archives, as its title indicates, is charged with
the custody of the official seals of the foreign minister and
of the department, receiving and forwarding of all documents,
the preparation of statistical reports, and the compilation
and preservation of official documents. The section of accounts has charge of all matters relating to the estimates,
accounts, and expenditures of the department, as well as the
auditing of such expenditures. The section of translations is
in charge of translating foreign documents into Japanese and
vice versa, while all telegraphic communications to and from
Kasumigaseki are brought under the jurisdiction of the
section of telegraphs.[19]

There are six bureaus in the Foreign Office: two geographic
and four functional.[20] Thus, the Asiatic Bureau is in charge
of all diplomatic affairs relating to China, Hongkong, Macao,
and Siam, including negotiating and revising treaties as well
as military affairs concerning these areas,[21] while the European and American Bureau has charge of similar matters
affecting those areas not covered by the Asiatic Bureau.[22]
The Bureau of Commerce is in charge of foreign trade,
navigation, emigration, and immigration,[23] while all matters
relating to drafting and interpreting treaties, extraterritoriality, the League of Nations, and other legal matters affecting
foreign countries, come under the functions of the Bureau of
Treaties and Conventions.[24]

The Intelligence Bureau is not only the publicity agent
of the Foreign Office but also the clearing house of information on current diplomatic questions.[25] Thus, it is through
this channel that local press correspondents as well as foreign

[19] *Kakusho Kansei Tsusoku*, Art. X; *Gaimusho Kansei*, Art. II; also *Gaimusho
Bunka Kitei*, Arts. I–VI.

[20] *Gaimusho Kansei*, Art. IV.

[21] *Ibid.*, Art. V.

[22] *Ibid.*, Art. VI.

[23] *Ibid.*, Art. VII.

[24] *Ibid.*, Art. VIII.

[25] *Ibid.*, Art. IX.

news agencies obtain official information on pending problems. The chief of the bureau speaks to the representatives of the press every day on foreign affairs, and seldom does the foreign minister give interviews to press representatives in person. When the Foreign Office gives certain information to the press and yet does not desire to be quoted, the chief of the bureau usually requests them to print the information in somewhat the following form: "It is reliably informed . . ." If a direct statement from the foreign minister on a pending question is desired, a statement or memorandum may be presented to the minister for his signature, after which it may be published with his consent. This procedure is sometimes followed by foreign correspondents. It is extremely rare that a prime minister gives an interview to the press on foreign relations.[26]

The Cultural Work Bureau is charged with the cultural work in China conducted by the partially returned Boxer indemnity funds.[27]

The chief administrative officers of the Foreign Office are the vice-minister, parliamentary vice-minister, both of whom are *Chokuninkan* officials of first grade, chiefs of the Asiatic Bureau, European and American Bureau, Bureau of Commerce, Bureau of Treaties and Conventions, Intelligence Bureau, the Cultural Work Bureau, and the councilor of the Foreign Office, all of whom are ordinarily *Chokuninkan* officials of second grade. The Foreign Office formulates its policies at joint conferences of the foreign minister, vice-minister, and bureau chiefs of the department. When other departments are affected, however, such policies are determined at joint conferences of the representatives of all the interested departments. The parliamentary vice-minister and councilor do not participate in deliberations upon purely administrative affairs of the department, in which case section heads concerned are usually consulted by the foreign minister.

THE FOREIGN SERVICE

Thus far we have examined the history of the organization and the functionings of the Foreign Office as it operates to-

[26]When the late Count Komei Kato was prime minister, he gave several interviews to the press, but his example has not been followed by his successors.

[27]*Gaimusho Kansei*, Art. X.

day. An attempt is made in the following pages to inquire briefly into the organization and workings of the vast mechanisms of diplomatic and consular services.

The establishment of the Foreign Office at Kasumigaseki under the present title of *Gaimusho* on July 8, 1869, did not provide for representatives abroad.[28] On October 2, 1870, three classes of ministers and four classes of secretaries were established; Takenobu Sameshima was appointed Japanese minister resident to Great Britain, France, and Prussia, and Yurei Mori to the United States, as the first Japanese diplomatic representatives abroad.[29] An ordinance was issued on November 5, 1871, providing for the establishment of consuls general, consuls, vice-consuls, and acting consuls, but no consulate was established until January 29, 1872, when Tadamichi Shinagawa was appointed consul at Shanghai, China.[30]

Modifications introduced into the machinery for conducting foreign relations before 1893 were not primarily designed to reorganize the diplomatic and consular services but were chiefly occasioned by reorganizations of other administrative establishments. The diplomatic and consular officers were in no way different from the ordinary administrative officers in other departments. As a result, there was no special system for the appointment of these officers; there were no special examinations for entrance into the service. Finally, a series of ordinances were issued in 1893, under the Prince Ito administration, whereby diplomatic and consular officers were confined to those who successfully passed examinations, and the system of free transfers from the ordinary civil service to the diplomatic and consular services and vice versa was abolished, thereby establishing the foundations of the present system.[31] A series of modifications was further introduced

[28] *Horei Zensho*, 1869, pp. 255–256, 289–291.

[29] Dajokan Notification No. 712, 1870 (Oct. 2, 1870). Text in *Horei Zensho*, 1870, p. 424. *Cf.* Osatake, *Kokusaiho yori mitaru Bakumatsu Gaiko Monogatari*, or diplomatic episodes during the restoration period as seen from the standpoint of international law (Tokyo, 1926), p. 166.

[30] Tanaka (ed.), *Hara Kei Zenshu*, I, 982; Shinobu, *Gaisei Kantoku to Gaiko Kikan*, pp. 327–328. *Cf.* Osatake, *op. cit.*, pp. 166–167. For the list of the names and offices in the Foreign Office and foreign service in 1871, see Shinobu, *op. cit.*, pp. 328–329.

[31] The most important ordinance was *Gaikokan Ryojikan oyobi Shokisei Ninyo Rei*, or ordinance concerning the appointment of diplomatic and consular officers

in the titles and ranks of officers, while the establishment of
an examination committee for the first time for these services
constituted an important step in the evolution of the system.
Hence, by Imperial Ordinance No. 126, 1893, a committee,
composed of the vice-minister of state for foreign affairs
(chairman), chiefs of the Political Affairs Bureau and of
the Commerce Bureau, two members of the higher civil
service examination committee, and two professors of the
Imperial University, was formed to examine candidates for
the services.

With the rise of the status of Japan in the family of nations,
and with the rapid increase in international contacts and
problems, the number of officers engaged in the Department
of Foreign Affairs, both at home and abroad, increased accordingly. Thus, the small number of thirty-four members
engaged in the services in 1871[32] passed the one thousand
mark in 1931.[33] An elaborate itemization concerning the
number of particular officers in the Foreign Office is provided
in *Gaimusho Kansei,* or the ordinance concerning the organization of the Department of Foreign Affairs itself,[34] and
similar restrictions upon the diplomatic and consular officers
are made in *Zaigai Kokan Shokuin Teiin Rei.*[35]

The diplomatic and consular officers are defined in *Gaiko-*

and chancellors (Imperial Ordinance No. 187, 1893), issued on October 30, 1893.
Text in *Horei Zensho,* 1893, Vol. I, *Chokurei,* pp. 353–355. Other related ordinances
were Imperial Ordinances Nos. 123, 124, 126, 188 (*Hara Kei Zenshu,* pp. 982–1064).
Cf. Shinobu, *op. cit.,* pp. 647–648 ff.

[32]Shinobu, *op. cit.,* pp. 328–329.

[33]According to *Gaimusho Shokuinroku* the number reached 434 for *Kotokan*
officers and 569 for *Hanninkan* officers (published on Feb. 9, 1931). The *Kotokan*
include all those diplomatic officers of higher rank, such as ambassadors, ministers,
etc., down to those appointed immediately after passing the higher civil service
examination. All the chancellors come under the *Hanninkan* class. On this point
see the author's discussion in White, *The Civil Service in the Modern State,* pp.
524–525.

[34]For the text of the ordinance see *Gaimusho Nenkan* (1929), I, 4–5.

[35]Text in *ibid.,* I, 14. No limitations are placed upon the number of ambassadors.
Limitations upon other members of the services are: (1) envoys extraordinary and
ministers plenipotentiary, councilors of embassy, commercial councilors of embassy,
and ministers resident, 29; (2) first, second, and third class secretaries of embassy
and of legation, commercial secretaries of embassy and of legation, 80; (3) consuls
general, consuls, and commercial agents, 82; (4) first and second class secretary-
interpreters of embassy and legation, 16; (5) attachés of embassy and of legations,
9; (6) vice-consuls, 68; (7) *gaikokan-ho* (attaché) and *ryojikan-ho* (élève-consul),
70; (8) chancellors and élève-interpreters, 364.

kan oyobi Ryojikan Kansei.[36] According to this ordinance providing for the organization of the diplomatic and consular officers, the Japanese diplomatic officers comprise the following: ambassador extraordinary and plenipotentiary, envoy extraordinary and minister plenipotentiary, councilor of embassy, commercial councilor of embassy, first-, second-, and third-class secretary of embassy, commercial secretary of embassy, attaché of embassy, first-, second-, and third-class secretary of legation, commercial secretary of legation, attaché of legation, and *gaikokan-ho* (attaché).[37] An ambassador extraordinary and plenipotentiary is a *Shinninkan* official, while envoy extraordinary and minister plenipotentiary, councilor of embassy, commercial councilor of embassy, and minister resident are *Chokuninkan* officials, and the remaining officers belong to the *Soninkan* class.[38] The consular service includes the following four classes of officers, namely, consul general, consul, vice consul, and *ryojikan-ho* (élève-consul.[39] Consul general is either a *Chokuninkan* or a *Soninkan* official, while the remaining consular officers are of *Soninkan* class. However, it is expressly provided in the ordinance that the number of *Chokuninkan* consuls general is limited to nine at any time.[40]

At present,[41] Japan maintains embassies in Belgium, Brazil, France, Germany, Great Britain, Italy, Turkey, United States, and U.S.S.R., and legations in Argentina (Paraguay and Uruguay), Austria (Hungary), Canada, Chile (Bolivia), China, Czecho-Slovakia, Greece, Latvia, Mexico, Netherlands, Persia, Peru, Poland, Rumania, Norway (Denmark, and Finland), and Switzerland.[42] Moreover, the directorate of the Japanese bureau of the League of Nations is filled by an envoy extraordinary and minister plenipotentiary.[43]

In addition to the regular diplomatic representatives, spe-

[36]Text in *Gaimusho Nenkan* (1929), I, 12–13.

[37]Art. I.

[38]Art. II. First-class secretary may be a *Chokuninkan* official.

[39]Art. III.

[40]Art. IV.

[41]July, 1929.

[42]*Gaimusho Nenkan* (1929), I, 64. *Cf. Jiji Nenkan* (1930), p. 186; also Takenobu (ed.), *Japan Year Book* (1930), pp. 124–126.

[43]*Kokusai Remmei Teikoku Jimukyoku Kansei*, Art. III (text of the ordinance in *Genko Horei Shuran*, 1927, Vol. I, Bk. III, 17–18). Deputy Secretary General Yotaro Sugimura is a minister in his diplomatic rank (1931).

cial missions may be sent abroad for international conferences or some other purposes. Thus, in April, 1907, an imperial ordinance was issued authorizing a dispatch of diplomatic agents as ambassadors or ministers or ministers plenipotentiary to international conferences.[44] Under this ordinance, Baron Karoku Tsukuba went to the second Hague Conference as the principal delegate of Japan. In June, 1917, the ordinance of 1907 was amended so as to permit dispatch of special representatives abroad on important missions.[45] Under this widened ordinance, Viscount Ishii was sent to the United States in 1917, his visit resulting in the conclusion of the once famous Ishii-Lansing Agreement, while Tsunetada Kato went to Siberia in 1918 to take charge of the diplomatic end of the expedition.[46] Moreover, on several important occasions, personal representatives of the prime minister or the ministry have been sent abroad, most noteworthy instances being Viscount Suyematsu to England, Viscount Kaneko to America during the Russo-Japanese War, and Kamezo Nishihara, of the Nishihara loans fame under the Terauchi cabinet during the World War,[47] to China.

The consular service is represented by 30 consulates general with their 14 branch offices, 58 consulates with their 3 branch offices, and 60 honorary consulates.[48] The predominant commercial and trade interests in China are indicated by the fact that, of the 105 consular establishments Japan maintains abroad, 14 consulates general, 24 consulates, and 13 branch offices are located in China.[49]

[44]Imperial Ordinance No. 116, 1907.

[45]Imperial Ordinance No. 64, 1917.

[46]Shinobu, *Gaisei Kantoku to Gaiko Kikan*, pp. 433–438. *Cf.* his article, "Ministers and Personal Representatives," *Gaiko Jiho*, XXX, No. 6 (Sept. 15, 1919), 529–536. In reply to a question asked in the House of Representatives, January 26, 1922, Count Uchida, foreign minister, said that the foreign relations of the Siberian expedition were in charge of the chief of the political bureau, a representative of the Foreign Office but under the supervision of the commander of the expeditionary forces (*Teikoku Gikaishi*, XIII, 583).

[47]It was reported at the time that the activities of Kamezo Nishihara, a personal representative of General Terauchi, often collided with those of the diplomatic representatives in Peking. The upshot was the negotiation of the famous Nishihara loans which have figured so high in the political and military history ever since.

[48]*Jiji Nenkan* (1930), pp. 187–188. *Cf. Gaimusho Nenkan* (1929), I, 64; also *Japan Year Book* (1930), pp. 127–128.

[49]Tabulated from the list of consular establishments in *Jiji Nenkan* (1930), pp. 187–188.

Before concluding our examination of the organization of the diplomatic and consular services our attention is directed to the military and naval attachés stationed in principal embassies and legations. Being officers of the War and Navy offices, they receive their instructions from home and subject to their superiors in Tokyo. Their reports go directly to the War and Navy departments and not to the Foreign Office. Thus it is possible that a military or naval attaché may make a report to Tokyo contradicting that of the ambassador or minister stationed in the same country. This practice of direct report of the military and naval attachés to their respective superiors in Tokyo without the knowledge of ambassadors and ministers has occasioned several parliamentary interpellations concerning the unity and harmony between the representatives of the Foreign Office and those of the military and naval authorities.[50]

THE BUDGET FOR THE MINISTRY OF FOREIGN AFFAIRS

The annual budget of the Department of Foreign Affairs is one of the smallest of the departmental budgets, being next only to that of the newly established Department of Commerce and Industry.[51] A table showing the comparative expenditures of the three departments of Foreign Affairs, Navy, and War during the past ten years is inserted on page 80.[52]

It will be observed from this table that the annual expenditures of the Department of Foreign Affairs are infinitesimal compared with the expenditures for the War and Navy departments, a point which has become a subject of increasing discussion by students of administration and political economy in Japan. An examination of the itemized

[50]The government has never admitted that this practice leads to a lack of harmony between the Foreign Office and the War and Navy departments. Thus, in reply to a question put to the government in the House Budget Committee on December 17, 1914, Foreign Minister Komei Kato admitted the practice but denied the existence of any conflict (*Dai Sanjugokai Teikoku Gikai Shugiin Iinkai Giroku*, Bk. I, No. 1, p. 112). Likewise, to a similar question, Admiral Kato's government replied in the same vein in the Forty-sixth session of the Diet, declining to comment upon a proposed inquiry into the responsibility of ambassadors and ministers for such reports (*Kwampo gogai*, March 25, 1923, p. 926).

[51]The Department of Commerce and Industry was established in April, 1925.

[52]The data taken from *Dai Shijukukai Nihon Teikoku Tokei Nenkan*, or 49th statistical yearbook of Japan, compiled by the statistical bureau of the cabinet, Dec., 1930, p. 339. The data for 1920–1928 represent the final accounts for the respective fiscal years, while the budgets are taken for 1929, 1930.

Fiscal year	Expenditures of the Department of Foreign Affairs (in yen)	Percentage of the annual budget		
		Foreign affairs	War	Navy
1920	18,563,000	1.36	18.13	29.65
1921	25,734,000	1.73	16.58	32.46
1922	25,204,000	1.76	16.17	26.17
1923	24,055,000	1.58	14.72	18.09
1924	21,006,000	1.29	12.72	15.29
1925	19,878,000	1.30	14.09	15.02
1926	19,262,000	1.22	12.47	15.03
1927	22,306,000	1.26	12.35	15.49
1928	20,712,000	1.14	12.73	14.77
1929	20,935,000	1.25	13.20	15.53
1930	19,047,000	1.18	13.10	16.35

budget for the fiscal year of 1930 offers an interesting subject of statistical analysis. The budget for the Department of Foreign Affairs for the fiscal year under examination was 15,889,000 yen in the total national budget of 1,224,037,000 yen. The budget for the entire service was divided into two general categories, namely, the expenditures for the Foreign Office and those for the diplomatic and consular service. For the fiscal year of 1930 the budget under the first category was 3,321,000 yen, and for the second category, 12,143,000 yen.[53]

[53]Op. cit., 1930, p. 341.

The distribution of the budget of the Foreign Office was as follows (in 1,000 yen):

Secret service fund	1,305
International obligations	612
Operating expenses	557
Salaries	455
Telegraphic expenses	257
Students abroad	87
Salaries of foreign employees	45
Entertainment fund	3

Likewise, the distribution for the diplomatic and consular service was as follows:

Salaries	5,563
Embassies, legations, consulates	1,959
Rentals, etc.	1,215
Traveling expenses	1,179
Supervision of residents abroad	971
Telegraphic expenses	876
Entertainment fund	214
Internment of Japanese residents	88
Salaries of foreign employees	41
Judicial and registration	39
League of Nations and its functions	340
Miscellaneous expenses	86

An examination of the budget of the Kasumigaseki office discloses that by far the largest item is the secret service fund. Thus for the fiscal year of 1930, the secret service fund amounted to almost 40 per cent of the total budget of the Foreign Office. The use of this large sum, amounting to 1,305,000 yen for 1930, is not subject to any control whatever, not even that of the Board of Audit. Thus the minister of foreign affairs is unchecked in his use of this fund. Several attempts have been made in the Diet to ascertain the probable use of this fund which looms so high in the departmental budget, but the representatives of the Foreign Office have uniformly declined to disclose the ways in which it is used.[54] The bulk of the expenditures of the diplomatic and consular service is for salaries, rentals, and operating expenditures, traveling expenses, supervision of residents abroad, and telegraphic expenses. A comparatively large item for entertainment deserves a comment at this point. An entertainment fund is placed at the disposal of ambassadors and ministers "for the discharge of their official functions," while consuls also share in the disbursement of this fund, the amount depending upon the importance of each mission.[55]

PERSONNEL ADMINISTRATION

Thus far we have examined the history and general structure of the principal mechanisms for conducting foreign relations. We have inquired into the organization and personnel of the Foreign Office, structure and scope of the diplomatic and consular services. In the following pages an attempt will be made to inquire into the differences in scope between the Foreign Office and foreign service, and to examine some of the more important problems of personnel administration, such as examination, appointment, promotion, transfer, and coördination of these services.

[54]In reply to a question by Representative Yukio Ozaki in a sub-committee of the House Budget Committee on December 7, 1891, the government delegate, the late Count Tadasu Hayashi, admitted that the increase of 20,000 yen in the secret service fund was necessitated by the increasing immigration abroad (*Shugiin Dai Nikai Yosan Iinkai Sokkiroku*, No. 22, p. 1).

[55]For instances of parliamentary interpellations on this point, see *Dai Nijugokai Teikoku Gikai Shugiin Iinkai Giroku*, Bk. I, No. 2 (Feb. 1, 1909), p. 3; also *Dai Nijuhichikai Teikoku Gikai Kizokuin Yosaniin Dai Ni Bunkakai Giji Sokkiroku* (Feb. 27, 1911), No. 3, p. 14.

The functions of diplomatic officers are nowhere defined in laws or ordinances, but left to practices and customs in international relations. On the other hand, the official functions and duties of consular officers are regulated by laws and ordinances. Consular officers are thus charged with the protection of Japanese residents abroad, with the promotion of commerce and navigation, and with such other functions ordinarily assigned to them in international practices and customs.[56]

Under the Japanese system, there exists a formal distinction between the officers of the Foreign Office and the diplomatic and consular officers abroad. In principle, therefore, only those who have passed the higher civil service examination are appointed to *Kotokan* posts at Kasumigaseki and only those who have passed the higher civil service examination for the diplomatic branch are eligible to appointment in the diplomatic and consular service. This demarcation, however, is reduced to one of practical insignificance by virtue of the stipulation that a diplomatic or consular officer may be appointed a *Kotokan* official in the Foreign Office after one year's service abroad, while a *Kotokan* official at Kasumigaseki may freely be appointed a diplomatic or consular officer abroad after serving a like time in Tokyo.[57] Hence, in practice, high officials of the Foreign Office, such as the foreign minister, vice-minister, bureau chiefs, and other functionaries, have had experience in diplomatic and consular services abroad.[58]

Excepting the foreign minister, parliamentary vice-minister, councilor of the Foreign Office, ambassadors, and ministers, the entire staff of the Ministry of Foreign Affairs at Kasumigaseki and abroad is placed on civil service. We have already observed that parliamentary vice-minister and

---

[56]A bill concerning the functions of consular officers was introduced in the Thirteenth session of the Diet (1899), following the revision of unequal treaties, and passed both Houses without much debate (*Teikoku Gikaishi*, IV, 1506–1507, 1532–1533, 2076–2077, 2113). Promulgated on March 20, 1899, as Law No. 70, 1899, and amended by Law No. 3, 1925. Text in *Genko Horei Shuran* (1927), Vol. I, Bk. III, 16. Subsequently, an imperial ordinance was issued to supplement the law just issued, defining the official functions of consular officers more in detail (Imperial Ordinance No. 153, 1899. Amended several times since. Text in *ibid.*, pp. 16–17).

[57]*Gaikokan Ryojikan oyobi Shokisei Ninyo Rei*, Art. IV.

[58]Shinobu, *Gaisei Kantoku to Gaiko Kikan*, pp. 347–548.

councilor of the Foreign Office are invariably members of the Diet and, in consequence, change with parties in power, and that the portfolio of foreign minister is usually occupied by an experienced diplomat in recent years. Thus, at present, cabinet changes have no direct effect upon diplomatic and consular officers, though a change in the office of the foreign minister often results, sooner or later, in some transfers in personnel in Tokyo and abroad. Moreover, the formal provision that ambassadors and ministers may be appointed from outside the service is practically a dead letter, as there have been only four or five instances of appointment of non-career men to ministers abroad since 1897.[59]

As provided for in *Koto Shiken Rei*, or ordinance concerning the higher civil service examination, all candidates for diplomatic and consular services are required to take written and oral examinations before they are considered for appointment abroad. The examinations are conducted by the higher civil service examination committee. The questions as well as the determination of successful candidates are left entirely to the committee.

From the very beginning of the examination system, the doctrine of legal omnipotence has been the guiding principle. This general tendency did not fail to affect the diplomatic and consular examinations.[60] However, the necessity for including other subjects has long been recognized,[61] and finally, by the amendment of 1929, larger discretion to candidates in selecting subjects has been granted, thereby some-

[59]Manjiro Inagaki to Siam, Fumio Yano to China, Tokichi Masao to Siam, Count Kinjiro Hirosawa to Spain. Honorary consuls are naturally selected without reference to civil service restrictions. On this point, see an interesting question put to the government by Representative Nagashima, and the replies by Viscount Kikujiro Ishii, vice-minister of foreign affairs, on Feb. 1, 1909 (*Dai Nijugokai Teikoku Gikai Shugiin Iinkai Giroku*, Bk. I, No. 2, pp. 1–2).

[60]Under the higher civil service examination ordinance of 1918, the compulsory subjects were constitutional law, international public law, international private law, economics, diplomatic history, and a foreign language. A candidate was allowed to choose only one subject from the following: administrative law, civil law, commercial law, criminal law, public finance, commercial science, and commercial history (Imperial Ordinance No. 7, 1918, Art. XIV).

[61]The most noted leader in the "liberalization" movement was Dr. Nagao Ariga, a well-known authority on international law. As early as 1910, he pointed out the importance of knowledge and understanding of modern economic and business affairs among diplomatic and consular officers (*Gaiko Jiho*, XIII, No. 4 [April, 1910], pp. 55–58).

what limiting the traditional principles in civil service.[62] Though the higher civil service examination is a qualification examination, the practice has always been, so far as the diplomatic branch is concerned, to pass only those who may be immediately appointed.[63] Similar provisions are made for entrance into the service as *gaimu shokisei* or chancellors.[64]

The appointment of successful candidates to the diplomatic and consular services as *gaikokan-ho* or *ryojikan-ho* is determined by the personnel board of the Foreign Office, consisting of vice-minister of foreign affairs (chairman), bureau chiefs (Asiatic, European and American, Commerce, Treaties and Conventions), and sectional chiefs of the secretariat of the Foreign Office (protocol and personnel, archives, accounts, and telegraphs).[65] Should the personnel board fail to agree upon a particular appointment, the matter is re-

[62]Imperial Ordinance No. 15, 1929 (March 27, 1929). Text in *Kwampo*, March 28, 1929, pp. 766–768. The English translation of this ordinance by the author is found in White, *Civil Service in the Modern State*, pp. 535–539. The examination for the diplomatic branch of the higher civil service is provided for in Article XIV. It provides that the written examination shall be held in compulsory and optional subjects. The compulsory subjects are constitutional law, international public law, economics, and a foreign language. A candidate must know English, German, French, Chinese, or Russian. He must designate three optional subjects from the following fields: introduction to philosophy, ethics, logic, psychology, sociology, political science, national history, political history, economic history, diplomatic history, Japanese literature and Chinese classics, civil law, commercial law, criminal law, administrative law, international private law, public finance, commercial policy, and commercial science. The oral examination for the diplomatic branch is held in a foreign language designated by the candidate, international public law, and two other subjects designated by the candidate from among those in which he has taken the written examinations.

[63]The first examination was given in September, 1894, resulting in four successful candidates. From 1894 to September, 1928, thirty-seven examinations were given, with 394 successful candidates. The World War occasioned sudden increase in those passing the examinations, reaching the highest number in 1920 and 1921, with 37 each year. For the list of the names of successful candidates in each examination, see *Gaimusho Nenkan* (1929), I, 251–252. From March, 1894, to April, 1929, twenty-nine examinations were given for government students to be sent abroad by the Foreign Office, resulting in 234 successful candidates, and 179 students actually sent abroad (*Gaimusho Nenkan*, 1929, I, 263–268).

[64]During March, 1894, and April, 1927, twenty-six examinations were held for chancellors, resulting in 313 successful candidates (*ibid.*, 1929, I, 258–263).

[65]*Gaikokan-ho* may be translated as attaché or "diplomatic probationer" and is the first title given to a diplomatic appointment immediately following the examination. *Ryojikan-ho* may likewise be translated as élève-consul or "consular probationer" and is the first title given to a consular appointment after the examination (*Gaikokan Ryojikan oyobi Shokisel Ninyo Rei*, Art. II).

ferred to the foreign minister for decision, but such an instance is almost unknown.

In the early period of her début into the family of nations, when the stationing of diplomatic and consular representatives abroad was more a matter of "prestige" than one of practical necessity, instances were not unknown in which wealthy peers, business men, as well as politicians, were appointed as Japanese representatives in foreign capitals.[66] However, with a rapid increase in international contacts and the amount of business to be transacted, appointments in total disregard of necessary qualifications have now become practically impossible.[67]

The successful candidates, after further inquiry by the personnel board, are attached to the various bureaus and sections of the Foreign Office, receive general instructions concerning the commercial and diplomatic conditions abroad, as well as general procedure followed in negotiation of treaties. After a brief training at home, giving the future diplomats opportunities to familiarize themselves with the general work at Kasumigaseki, they are sent abroad as *gaikokan-ho* or *ryojikan-ho*, as we have already noted. During the first year they are not required to take up their duties but are expected to study language, international law, diplomatic history, and other routines of diplomatic and consular services.[68]

The personnel reports are sent in by ambassadors, ministers, and consuls twice a year to the personnel section of the Foreign Office. Thus, in May and November, the head of each diplomatic and consular establishment addresses a personal report to the foreign minister concerning each member of his staff, and the reports thus made personally by these ambassadors, ministers, and consuls are kept in the archives of the section of protocol and personnel for future reference. There are no periodic transfers, but such transfers in personnel are made according to particular needs of the time. Appointments and transfers of ambassadors and ministers, however, are submitted to the cabinet by the foreign minister for formal approval.

[66]*Cf.* Osatake, *Kokusaiho yori mitaru Bakumatsu Gaiko Monogatari* (Tokyo, 1926), pp. 168–169.

[67]*Cf.* Shinobu, *Gaisei Kentoku to Gaiko Kikan*, pp. 676–680, 686–690, 710–712.

[68]Shinobu, *op. cit.*, pp. 720, 721 ff.

It is to be observed, in this connection, that appointments to posts in China are ordinarily regarded as somewhat un-flattering. Criticisms have often been made both in and out of parliamentary chambers that the representatives in the diplomatic and consular establishments in China are inefficient, that radical innovations should be introduced to rectify the situation by raising the supplementary salaries which would be commensurate with their importance, and other means taken to elevate the general morale.[69] As a result of numerous criticisms and commentaries both in and out of the service in recent years, the general morale of those in China has somewhat been restored, and a parliamentary approval (appropriations) of raising the legation to that of embassy in personnel and equipment was obtained but has not yet been put into effect. Hence, at present an ambassadorial salary is attached to the legation and a councilor of embassy is stationed there, the formal change in status from legation to embassy awaiting improvement in the internal situation in China.[70]

[69] Aoyanagi pointed out, as early as 1909, that the system of selection and appointment of diplomatic and consular officers altogether disregarded the Chinese situation and encouraged appointment of more promising young men in European and American missions. He thus advocated the application of a special ordinance to China (*Gaiko Jiho*, XII, No. 7 [July, 1909], pp. 89–92). Dr. Kako Imai pointed out in 1915 that those diplomatic and consular officers stationed in China were so anxious to be transferred to more favorable positions in Europe and America that they failed to devote their best efforts to discharging their official duties. He particularly criticized the inability of the majority of them to speak and to understand the Chinese language, and consequently, more valuable and accurate information concerning the Chinese situation could be obtained by agents of the general staff (*Kokka Gakkai Zasshi*, XXIX, No. 3 [March, 1915], 425–431). Similar charges were made in the Diet. On March 13, 1913, Representative Fujiwara bitterly complained of the frequent changes in the personnel of consulates in China, to the detriment of the entire service (*Dai Sanjikkai Teikoku Gikai Shuguiin Iinkai Giroku*, Bk. I, No. 1, p. 48). Like criticism was made in the Upper House during the same session. Thus, Count Y. Yanagiwara declared, on March 22, 1913, that the diplomatic and consular posts in China were considered as merely stepping stones to more attractive ones elsewhere, and demanded that the tenure of consuls in China should be made longer (*Dai Sanjikkai Teikoku Gikai Kizokuin Yosaniin Dai Ni Bunkakai Giji Sokkiroku*, No. I, pp. 1–2). Again in March, 1921, a searching criticism was made by Mannoshin Kamiyama in the Peers Budget Committee (Shinobu, *op. cit.*, pp. 731–732), and also in the House of Representatives by Representative Yasutaro Okamura on January 26, 1922 (*Teikoku Gikaishi*, XIII, 578–579).

[70] Thus, in the table prepared by the Foreign Office in 1931 showing the salaries, ranks, etc., of diplomatic and consular officers abroad, the ambassadorial salary (supplementary) of 26,000 yen is attached to the legation in China. *Cf.* a statement by Foreign Minister Kikujiro Ishii before the House Budget Committee on Dec. 11, 1915 (*Dai Sanjuhichikai Teikoku Gikai Shugiin Iinkai Giroku*, Bk. I, No. 1, p. 28).

Diplomatic and consular officers while in foreign service receive supplementary salaries (representation allowances) according to particular locations, in addition to their regular salaries as civil service officials.[71] Ambassadors, ministers, and consuls who head diplomatic and consular establishments are furnished with an official residence. Detailed provisions are made for trips while in service, for transfers from one post to another, and also additional allowances are provided for those who are accompanied by their wives.

Under the present system, no legal limitations are placed upon the length of service at home or abroad. They are entitled to pensions after fifteen years of service, while some retire early in the prime of life to enter political or business life. After long and successful years in diplomatic life at home and abroad, some may be promoted to peerage, given posts in the Privy Council, or other exalted positions of honor and prestige.

[71] For the scale of supplementary salaries, see *Gaimusho Nenkan* (1929), I, 64.

PART II: THE CONTROL OF FOREIGN RELATIONS IN PRACTICE

Chapter IX

THE REVISION OF UNEQUAL TREATIES

DIPLOMATIC NEGOTIATIONS BEFORE 1890

THE EARLY TREATIES of commerce, concluded in the closing period of the Shogunate régime, were subject to revision after July, 1872. The efforts of Japan to secure the revision of "unequal treaties" constituted the most important feature in her international relations during 1872–1894. The main points at issue between Japan and the treaty powers were tariff autonomy and extra-territorial jurisdiction. As soon as the task of reconstruction following the restoration of 1868 was under way, the attention of the makers of New Japan was again directed to this subject.[1]

The first official step in this direction was taken in 1871, when Lord Iwakura, recently minister of foreign affairs, headed a special mission to America and Europe.[2] The mission included such leading statesmen as Kido, Okubo, Ito, and Yamaguchi. Although the mission accomplished nothing toward the solution of the issues, it gave the future leaders of New Japan an opportunity to observe the West at first hand and aided them in their dealings with the latter in subsequent years.[3] The attempts made in 1878 and 1880 failed to bring

[1] It is beyond the scope of this chapter to discuss the diplomatic history of treaty negotiations. For a brief account of Japanese foreign relations during this period, see Osatake, *Kokusaiho yori mitaru Bakumatsu Gaiko Monogatari* (Tokyo, 1926), pp. 173–267.

[2] The mission left Japan in Dec., 1871, and returned in Sept., 1873. *Cf. Horei Zensho* (1871), pp. 370–372.

[3] Jumpei Shinobu, *Gaiko Sokumenshi Dan* (Tokyo, 1926), pp. 33–69; Hiratsuka (ed.), *Ito Hirobumi Hiroku* (Tokyo, 1929), I, 331–334; Osatake, *op. cit.*, pp. 153–165, 488–491.

any results, and in 1882 a diplomatic conference was convened in Tokyo, over which Foreign Minister Inouye presided. Although nothing tangible was accomplished, the various points that were brought out at these meetings were finally embodied in a memorandum, which served as the basis of a formal conference convened in 1886.[4]

On May 1, 1886, the foreign minister, Count Inouye, opened the conference, attended by the representatives of twelve American and European treaty powers.[5] The conference held twenty-eight sessions, and on April 22, 1887, it adjourned *sine die*. The chief discussion centered upon the question of extraterritoriality. The Japanese proposal was set aside in favor of the one drawn up by the British and German representatives, calling for a majority of foreign judges in courts dealing with foreigners, and for foreign public procurators. The plan provided for the abolition of extraterritoriality in three years, while her judicial system was to be completely reorganized according to Western standards.[6] The news of the items thus proposed leaked out, arousing bitter public indignation.[7] A vigorous opposition also developed among those high in authority. Among the most determined foes of the proposal were Privy Councilor Katsu, Minister of Agriculture and Commerce Tani, Minister of Navy Saigo, Cabinet Councilor Kuroda, M. Boissonade, a French legal adviser to the department of justice. Particularly, the long memorandum prepared by M. Boissonade and submitted to the cabinet bitterly assailing any proposal providing for the appointment of foreign judges had a great influence. Viscount Tani vigorously supported the thesis of the memorandum,[8] and failing

[4]Ito (ed.), *Kato Komei* (Tokyo, 1929), I, 204–206; Hiratsuka (ed.), *op. cit.*, I, 304–306.

[5]*Jiji Shimpo*, May 1, 7, 1886, p. 1. Compare the editorials in *Jiji Shimpo*, Feb. 19, April 22, 1886, p. 1.

[6]Nintaro Ito, *Inouyeko Zenden* (Tokyo, 1918), pp. 256–257. The press was conspicuously silent on treaty negotiations, obviously under vigorous government censorship (*cf.* editorials in *Jiji Shimpo*, June 13, 14, 1887, p. 2).

[7]In a leading article, the *Jiji Shimpo*, commenting upon the reported rumor, declared that the negotiations should be discontinued if Japan should be called upon to impair her own sovereignty in order to obtain the revision of treaties (June 24, 1887, p. 2). The daily was suspended till June 30, presumably on account of this editorial.

[8]On July 5, 1887, an important cabinet meeting was called, with Saigo and Tani, recently returned from abroad, in attendance. At this meeting Tani presented a

to win his colleagues to this position, he tendered his resignation on July 26, 1887, in protest. His determined attitude on the question added tremendous impetus to the already excited public sentiment against the proposal. As the public opposition led by such veteran leaders as Shojiro Goto and Taisuke Itagaki became so outspoken, the Ito cabinet had to notify the treaty powers of an indefinite suspension of negotiations on July 29.[9]

On August 6, 1887, the *Horitsu Torishirabedokoro* was established in the Foreign Office to investigate various codes, and was presided over by Foreign Minister Inouye himself. Count Inouye, however, tendered his resignation as foreign minister on September 17, whereupon Prime Minister Ito himself took charge of the Foreign Office.[10] On September 29, 1887, a conference of local governors was called in Tokyo to instruct them upon suppressing public discussion of treaty negotiations. Before this conference of local governors, Premier Ito declared that a successful execution of treaty revision depended largely upon internal reforms and improvement of laws, and vigorously denounced any suggestion to submit questions of diplomacy to public discussion. He pointed out to these officials that the powers over military and naval affairs as well as foreign relations were vested solely in the emperor, and declared that delegation of these powers over declaration of war, making peace, and concluding treaties and alliances to the people would constitute an impairment of the sovereignty of the throne.[11] In November, the commissioner of the metropolitan police board issued a police order greatly

long memorandum expressing a strong opposition to the reported proposal. Several cabinet meetings were subsequently held to deliberate upon the matter (*Jiji Shimpo*, July 6, 1887, p. 3; *ibid.*, July 7, p. 2; July 8, p. 3; July 12, 13, p. 3; July 19, p. 2; July 21, p. 3). The matter was also submitted to the *Genroin* (*ibid.*, July 12, 1887, p. 3). Viscount Tani was given an imperial audience on July 20 to present his views to the emperor (*ibid.*, July 22, 1887, p. 3).

[9] *Jiji Shimpo*, Aug. 4, 1887, p. 1; also *ibid.*, Aug. 6, 1887, p. 2. *Cf.* Hirota, *Naikaku Kotetsu Gojunenshi* (Tokyo, 1930), pp. 245–246; Ito, *Kato Komei*, I, 206–207; Hiratsuka, *op. cit.*, I, 31–32. *Jiji Shimpo* urged upon both the government and the opposition leaders (Goto, Itagaki, Okuma, etc.) to define their position upon the treaty revision question (Aug. 13, 1887, p. 1).

[10] *Jiji Shimpo*, Sept. 19, 1887, p. 3. The *Horitsu Torishirabedokoro* was soon transferred to the Department of Justice to be presided over by Minister of Justice Yamada.

[11] *Ibid.*, Oct. 1, 1887, p. 3. Text of the prime minister's address in *ibid.*, Oct. 6, 1887, p. 3.

restricting public meetings or demonstrations regarding treaties, but it only helped to inflame further the already widespread public indignation against the government measure. The result was the issuance of the famous *Hoan Jorei*, or regulations concerning the preservation of peace, on December 25, 1887.[12] Under the operation of this suppressive measure, 570 prominent leaders of the opposition were driven out of Tokyo.[13]

Failing to appease the popular opposition in spite of these suppressive measures, Prime Minister Ito decided to appoint Shigenobu Okuma, president of the Progressive party, who had long been out of office, to the difficult post of foreign minister. Thus, on February 1, 1888, Count Okuma succeeded Prince Ito in the conduct of foreign relations.[14] Soon afterwards Ito resigned the premiership and was succeeded by Marquis Kiyotaka Kuroda, while Okuma remained in the foreign office.[15] Unlike his predecessors, Count Okuma adopted a policy of separate negotiations for treaty revision.[16] The negotiations were conducted in strict secrecy by Foreign Minister Okuma, without cabinet consultation at each stage of the negotiations.

The publication in the London *Times* of the reported outline of the Okuma terms of treaty negotiations furnished the Japanese people the first information concerning the nature of the negotiations then in progress under Foreign Minister Okuma.[17] It aroused a new outburst of public indignation, chiefly on the ground that the stipulation for appointment of

[12]Imperial Ordinance No. 67, 1887 (*Horei Zensho*, 1887, pp. 229–232). Press and Publication Laws were made more stringent (Imperial Ordinances Nos. 75, 76, 1887. Text in *Horei Zensho*, 1887, pp. 239–249).

[13]Among those driven out of Tokyo were Hayashi, Hoshi, Kataoka, Ozaki, Suzuki, and others (*Jiji Shimpo*, Dec. 28, 1887, p. 3).

[14]Ichijima (ed.), *Okumako Hachijugonenshi* (Tokyo, 1926), II, 77–96.

[15]The resignations of Inouye and Ito were thus directly due to their failure in treaty negotiations.

[16]For comparison of the Okuma plan with that of his predecessor, see Ito, *Kato Komei*, I, 208–209; Ichijima, *op. cit.*, II, 104–107.

[17]The Tokyo dispatch "From Our Correspondent" was dated March 11, 1889, and was published in *The Times* (London), April 19, 1889, p. 6. The Japanese translation was published in *Jiji Shimpo*, May 31, June 1, 3, 1889. In this dispatch to *The Times*, its Tokyo correspondent called the attention to the changed situation in Japan, and vigorously advocated a more friendly policy on the part of Great Britain. He emphasized the importance of public opinion on this point, declaring that: "To appreciate the position, it must first be borne in mind that this treaty

foreign judges under whatever name was an unwarranted impairment of sovereignty and a gross violation of Article XIX of the Constitution.[18] The popular opposition became so widespread and powerful that a cabinet meeting was called on July 30, 1889, when it was decided to present a report of the negotiations to the emperor for his decision.[19] However, in

question has now been carried beyond the domain of diplomatic and official control. A new force, that of public opinion, which forms one of the most radical features of difference between the Japan of 20 years ago and the Japan of today, has henceforth to be reckoned with. . . ." (April 19, 1889, p. 6). As reported by this correspondent, the general outline of the contemplated treaty was chiefly commercial: concessions and guarantees relating to jurisdiction were to be embodied in diplomatic notes; revision of the tariff was to be provided for on the lines agreed to at the conference of 1886–1887; and the duration of the revised schedule was to be also as then determined, at the end of which period Japan was to become autonomous in that respect. The extraterritorial problem was to be solved as follows: (1) From a prescribed date, which would have assuredly fallen before the first session of the new Diet in the autumn of 1890, foreigners were to be freely permitted to travel, trade, reside, or own real property, in all parts of the empire outside the limits of the then existing treaty settlements, provided that in everything connected with the exercise of these privileges, they became wholly subject to Japanese jurisdiction. (2) The treaty settlements were to remain as they were for a short term of years from the date above indicated, at the end of which they were to lose their distinctive character and consular jurisdiction and to become in all respects as the rest of the Empire. (3) It was to be agreed by diplomatic notes that, prior to the opening of the country provided for in the first arrangement, a number of competent foreign judges should be appointed to sit with Japanese judges in the Supreme Court of Japan, which had appellate jurisdiction in all cases involving interests or penalties of one hundred dollars or upwards; that such foreign judges should be in a majority in all cases wherein foreigners were concerned; and that the said arrangement should hold good for a certain term of years (probably 10 or 12) after which Japan was to stand in all respects as to jurisdiction on the same footing as any European state. (4) Finally, by diplomatic notes, it was to be provided in respect to the second condition above, that the new civil codes were to be duly promulgated and put into force three years before the expiration of the time limit therein denoted for the abolition of the treaty-port system; and that authorized English translations of the said codes be published a year and a half before the said time of expiration (The Times, April 19, 1889, p. 6). The Times, in a leading article, joined the correspondent in support of a more liberal policy upon this question, not only on the broad principles of justice, but also upon the expanding British trade in the Far East. Thus it declared, on April 19, 1889: ". . . It is idle to pretend that the institutions of Japan are not sufficiently civilized to afford adequate security for the rights and interests of British subjects. . . ." Commenting upon the continued existence of extraterritoriality, it observed: "In existing circumstances they [privileges of extraterritoriality] are little short of an insult to Japan as well as a serious hindrance to the development of English commerce" (The Times, April 19, 1889, p. 7).

[18]Ichijima, op. cit., II, 119–121 ff. For suppression of the press, see Hideo Ono, Nihon Shimbun Hattatsushi (Tokyo, 1924), pp. 210–214.

[19]Jiji Shimpo, July 31, 1889, p. 2. Though Prime Minister Kuroda was reported to be in favor of Okuma's draft proposal, the cabinet was by no means unanimous in this regard (ibid., Aug. 2, 1889, p. 3).

view of the gravity of such procedure, another cabinet meeting was called on August 2, when it was decided to postpone the report to the emperor as such a course would be improper while negotiations were still in progress with the foreign minister in full charge. It was further decided to interpret "foreign judges" to mean "naturalized Japanese subjects" to quiet the doubts which had been expressed as to the constitutionality of the treaties with the United States signed in February, and with Germany in June, 1889.[20]

The opposition to the Okuma proposal came from all directions and included influential parties, newspapers, privy councilors, cabinet ministers, as well as various associations.[21] By September 30, over three hundred memorials were presented to the *Genroin*, a quasi-legislative body. Of these memorials, 185 demanded suspension of negotiations; 120, immediate execution of treaty revision.[22] On October 7, several professors presented a memorial to Home Minister Yamagata who had recently returned from abroad, while Communications Minister Goto demanded a cabinet meeting to decide the policy on the question.[23] Accordingly, on Oc-

[20]*Jiji Shimpo*, Aug. 3, 1889, p. 2; Ichijima, *op. cit.*, II, 134–142. The first treaty concluded by Japan with a foreign state on the footing of absolute equality was the treaty of amity and commerce with Mexico, signed at Washington, November 30, 1888. This treaty was ratified on Jan. 29, 1889; ratifications exchanged at Washington on June 6, and promulgated on July 17, 1889. Text in *Treaties and Conventions between the Empire of Japan and Other Powers* (Foreign Office, Tokyo, 1899), pp. 31–36. On Sept. 23, Prime Minister Kuroda wrote Foreign Minister Okuma that the emperor had called the premier's attention to the apprehension entertained by several members of the Privy Council concerning the constitutionality of the proposed draft treaties (Ichijima, *op. cit.*, II, 148).

[21]The following supported the Okuma plan for treaty revision: *Yubin Hochi Shimbun, Yomiuri, Mainichi Shimbun, Asano Shimbun, Keizai Zasshi* (press); Kuroda (prime minister), Oyama, Saigo, Yamada (later changed), Enomoto (cabinet ministers); Oki, Kono (privy councilors). The opposition side was represented by: *Tokyo Koron, Toun Shimbun, Seiron, Nippon Shimbun, Kansai Nippo, Nippon* (press); Goto, Inouye, Yamagata (cabinet ministers); Ito, Terashima, Soyejima, Kawamura, Sano, Motoda (privy councilors). The semi-official *Nichi Nichi* was mildly opposed, while *Asahi* and *Kokumin no Tomo* were noncommittal (Ichijima, *op. cit.*, II, 133; Hirota, *op. cit.*, p. 256). The *Jiji Shimpo's* news report to the effect that both the cabinet and the Privy Council were divided was ordered to be rescinded by the government (*Jiji Shimpo*, Oct. 11, 12, 1889).

[22]Ichijima, *op. cit.*, II, 145–147.

[23]Minister of Education Enomoto issued instructions to schools on Oct. 9 and to prefectural authorities on Oct. 10, calling upon those authorities to place more stringent restrictions upon freedom of speech and expression (*Jiji Shimpo*, Oct. 11, 1889, p. 3).

tober 14, a conference of six cabinet ministers (foreign, home, war, navy, finance, and justice) was held at the official residence of the foreign minister, when it was decided to request the imperial sanction to hold a cabinet meeting in His Majesty's presence the following day.[24] At this formal meeting of the cabinet held in the presence of the emperor on October 15, Foreign Minister Okuma vigorously defended his plan,[25] while Home Minister Yamagata led the opposition against the proposal.[26] The upshot was the adjournment of the meeting late in the afternoon without reaching a final decision. Privy councilors also held informal meetings on October 15 and 16, and decided to petition the emperor to call a meeting of the council upon treaty negotiations, after the cabinet determined its policy.[27] On October 16, Vice-President Terashima and Councilors Soyejima and Sasaki presented a memorial to the emperor, on behalf of the Privy Council, recommending the suspension of treaty negotiations.[28] Meanwhile, the cabinet held a series of meetings for four days, and on October 18, Count Okuma finally agreed to an indefinite suspension of treaty negotiations.[29] As he reached the foreign office at Kasumigaseki, after a stormy session of the cabinet, a fanatic hurled a bomb at the foreign minister, injuring him severely.[30] As a result, the drafts were immediately withdrawn. Kuroda and his colleagues tendered their resignations to the emperor on October 25, while Prince Ito, president of the Privy Council, sharing responsibilities with the cabinet,

[24]*Ibid.*, Oct. 15, 1889, p. 3. Several members of the *Genroin* held a meeting at the home of President Oki, while Home Minister Yamagata and War Minister Oyama were both given an imperial audience. Privy Councilors Soyejima, Torio, Higasekuse, and Sasaki were also given an imperial audience to present a memorial to the throne (*ibid.*).

[25]Okuma was supported by Prime Minister Kuroda, Justice Minister Yamada, President Oki of the *Genroin*, Privy Councilor Kono, and others (*ibid.*, Oct. 16, 1889, p. 3).

[26]Home Minister Yamagata was backed by Communications Minister Goto, Minister of Agriculture and Commerce Inouye, Vice-President Terashima of the Privy Council (President Ito having tendered his resignation), and Privy Councilors Kawamura, Torio, Soyejima, Sano, and Motoda.

[27]*Jiji Shimpo*, Oct. 19, 1889, p. 3.

[28]Hirota, *op. cit.*, pp. 257–258. General Miura also presented a direct memorial to the emperor severely criticizing the Okuma plan (Hiratsuka, *Ito Hirobumi Hiroku*, I, 140–141).

[29]Komatsu, *Meiji Shijitsu Gaiko Hiwa* (Tokyo, 1927), pp. 44–45.

[30]*Jiji Shimpo*, Oct. 19, 1889, p. 2.

likewise tendered his resignation on October 30, 1889.[31] Consequently, on December 24, the Yamagata cabinet was formed with Viscount Aoki as foreign minister.[32]

It fell to the lot of the Yamagata administration to issue various laws and ordinances in preparation for the convening of the First Diet in the fall of 1890. Thus, the regulations concerning the election of the members of the House of Representatives were issued in January, 1890, and the law concerning the organization of the courts in February of the same year. During the year, various codes (civil and commercial) were also issued, in order to avoid embarrassment and possible rejection at the hands of the coming Diet.[33]

PARLIAMENTARY DEBATES ON TREATY NEGOTIATIONS

The First Diet was convened on November 25, 1890. During the first few days both Houses were engaged in organizing committees and attending to other routine matters. However, on December 9, Representative Shogo Arai presented a long question on the progress and future of treaty negotiations.[34] In explaining the question, Representative Arai declared that the real object of the question was to find the actual status of treaty negotiations, that secret diplomacy was inconsistent with constitutional government, and that the government should conduct the negotiations in accordance with public opinion based upon adequate information.[35] Immediately following this explanatory speech on January 17, 1891, Viscount Aoki, foreign minister, spoke over two hours, reviewing in detail the history of negotiations, but deliberately declining to touch upon the then pending negotiations and the policies followed, on grounds of diplomatic secrecy.[36] Imme-

[31] *Jiji Shimpo*, Oct. 25, 26, 1889, p. 3. *Cf.* Kudo, *Teikoku Gikaishi* (Tokyo, 1901), I, 15–18; also Ito, *Kato Komei*, I, 218.

[32] *Jiji Shimpo*, Dec. 25, 1889, p. 3.

[33] Hirota, *op. cit.*, pp. 263–264. For texts of these laws and regulations, see *Horei Zensho*, 1890, *passim*.

[34] Representative Arai's written question included the following items: (1) past and present status of treaty negotiations; (2) government policy as to the time of recovery of tariff autonomy and jurisdiction over foreigners; (3) alien land ownership and unrestricted residence of foreigners in the interior, and others (*Teikoku Gikaishi*, I, 516–519).

[35] *Ibid.*, I, 529–530.

[36] *Ibid.*, I, 530–536.

diately after finishing the reply, he left the chamber and did not return in spite of the House motion demanding the presence of the foreign minister to reply to questions from the floor.[37] Several questions were put to the government by members of both Houses, but the cabinet refused to disclose the present stage of negotiations.[38]

Prime Minister Yamagata resigned on May 6, 1891, following the close of the Diet, partly because he was opposed to Aoki's plan for revising the treaties. Viscount Aoki also resigned on May 29, assuming the responsibility for the attempt made by a police officer upon the life of the visiting Russian Crown Prince at Otsu, on May 11. It was reported at the time that his resignation was prompted mainly by the opposition of Premier Matsukata (who succeeded Yamagata on May 6) to Aoki's plan for treaty revision.[39]

On December 16, 1891, Representative Mayeda introduced a representation resolution calling upon the government to demand the powers of an immediate revision of treaties and to notify them, in case of refusal, of its intention to abrogate the treaties in accordance with accepted principles of international law. In view of its diplomatic importance, this resolution was debated in executive session.[40]

Upon the rejection of the naval construction bill and the ironworks bill, the House of Representatives of the Second Diet was dissolved on December 25, 1891.[41] The subsequent general election did not result in returning an absolute majority for the government, and consequently, the Matsukata cabinet could not face a friendly Diet. Hence, in this session, a bill was passed postponing the date of execution of the civil and commercial codes from January 1, 1893, to December 31, 1896. The above bill was introduced in the House of Peers by Mr. Tamotsu Murata on May 26, 1892, and after three days of heated debate it was passed with an overwhelming majority. The supporters of the bill contended that the codes had

[37]*Ibid.*, I, 538.

[38]The first session of the Diet closed on March 8, 1891.

[39]Kudo, *Teikoku Gikaishi*, I, 92–93.

[40]*Teikoku Gikaishi*, I, 1303, 1428; also Kudo, *op. cit.*, I, 127–128. On account of a certain statement made by a member during the debate, the vote upon it was postponed. There is no way of learning the fate of this resolution from the record of the debate.

[41]*Ibid.*, I, 1547.

many defects, were contrary to the prevailing customs and practices, and consequently that their operation should be postponed for further examination and revision. The government, on the other hand, vigorously opposed the bill, insisting upon the indispensability of the codes.[42] In his desperate plea for the defeat of the bill, Viscount Enomoto, foreign minister, bluntly declared that the establishment of codes to be applicable to civilized peoples was a necessary condition precedent to the revision of imperfect treaties, and that, should the operation of the codes be postponed, the revision of unequal treaties would have to be again postponed.[43] The bill was passed in the House of Representatives, by a substantial majority, after vigorous opposition by the cabinet through the minister of justice.[44]

The Fourth Diet was opened under the Ito administration on November 29, 1892.[45] The public demand for immediate recovery of tariff autonomy and complete judicial power appeared in the form of an address to the emperor. Thus, on February 15, 1893, an address resolution was introduced in the House by Representative Shoshi Suzuki, supported by the *Jiyuto* (Liberal) and *Kaishinto* (Progressive) parties.[46] The resolution declared that diplomacy should be conducted in accordance with public opinion and that the revision of treaties could be accomplished only when backed by the united support of the people. In admitting the imperial prerogative over treaty-making, the supporters of the resolution did not fail to recall the Charter Oath issued by Emperor Meiji at the time of the Restoration, seeking knowledge and wisdom all over the world for the welfare of the people. Thus, in this direct appeal to the throne, they respectfully submitted to His Majesty's convenience that the public opinion

[42]*Op. cit.*, I, 1596–1634.

[43]*Ibid.*, I, 1607.

[44]*Ibid.*, I, 2175–2192. Viscount Tanaka, justice minister, soon tendered his resignation in protest (Kudo, *Teikoku Gikaishi*, I, 179).

[45]This Ito cabinet was popularly called a *genkun naikaku*, or "a cabinet of veteran statesmen," because it included most of the leading statesmen of the Restoration period; namely, Ito, Yamagata, Kuroda, Inouye, Oyama, Goto, Mutsu, Kono, Watanabe, and Nire (Kudo, *op. cit.*, I, 181).

[46]Neither the original text of the resolution nor debates appear in the proceedings of the House. The resolution was introduced on Dec. 7, 1892; the cabinet requested an executive session for its discussion (Dec. 13, 1892); and the debate was held on Feb. 15, 1893, from 1:56 to 5:34 P.M. (*Teikoku Gikaishi*, II, 430, 525, 904).

demanded immediate revision of the existing treaties by abolishing extraterritoriality, by recovering tariff autonomy, and by prohibiting foreign coastwise trade. As "the representatives of the people," they advocated restrictions upon residence of foreigners, and opposed their ownership and operation of land, mines, railroads, canals, and shipyards. They urged a reciprocal application of the most-favored-nation treatment in treaties. After a lively debate upon the resolution in executive session, the resolution was passed by the House by a vote of 135 to 121, and was immediately reported to the emperor by the Speaker of the House.[47]

As the revision of "unequal" treaties became the center of public discussion, the question of strict enforcement of existing treaties came to be the most heated issue of the day, and when the Fifth Diet was opened on November 28, 1893, the "representatives of the people" showered the government with questions concerning strict enforcement of existing treaties, holding that the foreigners enjoying the benefits of the unequal treaties concluded during the latter period of the Tokugawa régime must also assume responsibilities and restrictions placed upon them as to ownership of land, area of residence, business, and other matters.[48] Hence, on December 19, Representative Bankon Abei introduced a representation resolution calling upon the government to enforce all the provisions of the existing treaties, but scarcely had he begun his speech explaining the resolution when the Ito cabinet prorogued the Diet for ten days.[49] On December 29, when the House was convened after the prorogation, Foreign Minister Mutsu made a long speech vigorously denouncing the resolution as being contrary to the traditional policy since the restoration and to a speedy revision of the treaties.[50] When Representative Abei resumed his speech, the Diet was again prorogued for two weeks; and finally, on December 30, the House was dissolved.[51] Thus, the cabinet, after ruthless suppression of associations and the press prior to the opening of the Diet, resorted to the dissolution of the House of Repre-

[47]Kudo, *Teikoku Gikaishi*, I, 251–254.

[48]*Teikoku Gikaishi*, II, 1222–1224, 1301, 1331–1332.

[49]*Ibid.*, II, 1337.

[50]*Ibid.*, II, 1341–1342.

[51]*Ibid.*, II, 1342.

sentatives, after a vain effort to stop the imminent passage of the resolution, against which foreign representatives had lodged a vigorous joint protest with the *Kasumigaseki*.[52]

The general election of March 1, 1894, was held in comparative peace. The outstanding features of the election were the defeat of Representative Abei, the author of the representative resolution on treaty enforcement, and a decisive victory of the *Jiyuto* party, gaining more than twenty new members.[53] On May 16, 1894, Prime Minister Hirobumi Ito came before the Lower House and declared that the dissolution of the preceding House was largely due to its attitude upon the resolution, the passage of which would have been certain to cause serious consequences to the state. Declaring that the cabinet would assume full responsibility for the conduct of foreign relations, and assuring the legislators of an early success of treaty revision, the prime minister earnestly pleaded with the House not to force the cabinet to take another decisive measure by subjecting the nation's diplomacy to partisan politics.[54] On May 21, Dr. Kazuo Hatoyama, supported by all the opposition parties, put a written question to the government on the progress of treaty negotiations.[55] In his reply, under date of June 1, the foreign minister declined to disclose the future policy or to state the existing stage of negotiations, holding that to do so would be contrary to customary rules of international relations as well as the interest of the state.[56] A representation resolution calling upon the government to hasten the revision of treaties in accordance with the address resolution passed during the

[52]Kudo, *Teikoku Gikaishi*, I, 262–263, 278–283, 301–315. When Munemitsu Mutsu entered the second Ito cabinet as foreign minister in Aug., 1892, he adopted a new policy of pressing for conclusion of completely equal treaties and was determined not to be disturbed by domestic politics. So, on July 5, 1893, he submitted to the cabinet a new draft treaty of commerce and navigation. In order to start negotiations with the British government with this new draft treaty as the basis, he petitioned the emperor to appoint Viscount Shuzo Aoki, a former foreign minister and then His Majesty's minister to Germany, as his envoy in London, with firm determination to suppress all dissenting views at home (Hirokichi Mutsu, *Hakushaku Mutsu Munemitsu Iko* [Tokyo, 1929], pp. 367–368).

[53]Kudo, *op. cit.*, I, 317.

[54]*Teikoku Gikaishi*, II, 1501–1502.

[55]*Ibid.*, II, 1557.

[56]*Ibid.*, II, 1796. The cabinet took the same attitude toward the question put to it by Representative Sakamoto (*ibid.*, II, 1557, 1558, 1761).

fourth session of the Diet was defeated by a closely contested vote of 150:140.[57]

On May 17, an address resolution strongly condemning the Ito cabinet for domestic as well as foreign policies was introduced in the House of Representatives by ten of the foremost leaders of the day.[58] The supporters of the resolution made a stinging criticism of the administration policy on treaty revision and on the use of the name of the emperor before foreign courts in connection with the warship *Chishima* case; while the opposing speeches were made by *Jiyuto* members who contended that the dissolution of the House was imminent upon passage of the pending resolution and that the august heart of the emperor should not be disturbed.[59] After a most vigorous debate, the address resolution was defeated by 149:144.[60] In order to maintain its "face" on treaty revision, the *Jiyuto* members introduced, on May 19, an address resolution mildly rebuking the cabinet for its internal administration.[61] After a long speech of introduction, the resolution was referred to a committee of eighteen members for further consideration.[62] On May 31, 1894, Chairman Soroku Ehara made the report of the committee recommending the inclusion of foreign relations in the text of the resolution,[63] while Representative Seiyano made a minority report upholding the original resolution.[64] The minority report was rejected by 161:132, while the majority report strongly condemning the Ito cabinet for its domestic as well as foreign policies was passed by a substantial majority of 153:139.[65] On the following day (June 1), the

[57]*Ibid.*, II, 1579-1586. The defeat of the resolution was chiefly due to the opposition of the *Jiyuto* members who supported the address resolution in the Fourth Diet (Kudo, *Teikoku Gikaishi*, I, 341-342).

[58]The list included such leading figures as Ozaki, Inukai, Oi, Shimada, and Haseba (*Teikoku Gikaishi*, II, 1499).

[59]The resolution was ably defended by Haseba, Hatoyama, Arai, Oi, and Ozaki, while it was mildly opposed by Kuritani, Misaki, and Suzuki (*ibid.*, II, 1513-1527).

[60]*Ibid.*, II, 1527.

[61]*Ibid.*, II, 1547-1552.

[62]By a close vote of 138:137, it was referred to a special committee to be appointed by the Speaker of the House (*ibid.*, II, 1552).

[63]In the committee, Dr. Sanaye Takata led the majority fight for inclusion of foreign relations. The committee met on May 23, 28, and 29 (*ibid.*, II, 1755).

[64]*Ibid.*, II, 1756.

[65]*Ibid.*, II, 1755-1760. Cf. *Japan Weekly Mail*, June 2, 1894, p. 669.

Speaker of the House presented the address to the emperor through the minister of the imperial household, who informed the Speaker in the afternoon of June 2 of its rejection by the emperor. The announcement of His Majesty's refusal was followed by the dissolution of the House for the second time within six months under the same ministry.[66]

Before concluding our survey of this series of conflicts between the cabinet and the House over foreign relations, seldom surpassed in the parliamentary history of Japan, our attention is directed to a significant resolution concerning parliamentary participation in treaty-making. Thus on June 1, 1894, following the refusal of the cabinet to make any reply concerning the progress of treaty negotiations or to state its policy, a resolution regarding the power of the Diet over treaties was introduced in the Lower House, supported by all six opposition parties.[67] This unique resolution read as follows:

Although the power to conclude treaties belongs to the prerogative of the emperor, matters connected therewith that call for enactment of new laws, or modification of existing laws, or matters relating to a change of taxation, shall be submitted to the Diet for its consent, in accordance with the express provisions of Articles V, XXXVII, LXII, and LXIII of the Constitution.[68]

Dr. Kazuo Hatoyama, a well-known professor of law in the Imperial University of Tokyo, expounded the scope and object of the resolution. He contended that treaties requiring establishment of new laws, modification of existing laws, imposition of new taxes or modification thereof were within the operation of Articles V, XXXVII, LXII, and LXIII of the Constitution, and consequently necessitated parliamentary consent thereto. He referred to the constitutional provisions of France, Belgium, Holland, Germany, and Italy, and declared that parliamentary consent to those matters enumerated above did in no way conflict with the prerogative of the emperor over treaties. Professor Hatoyama defended his

[66]*Op. cit.*, II, 1761, 1792, 1796. About this time Prime Minister Ito presented a memorial to Emperor Meiji to call together the cabinet ministers and leaders of parties for a conference on treaty revision. But Ito's petition was not carried out (Hiratsuka, *Ito Hirobumi Hiroku*, I, 100–103).

[67]The resolution was signed by Suzuki, Oi, Sakamoto, Hatoyama, Inukai, and Motoda (*Teikoku Gikaishi*, II, 1761).

[68]Text of the resolution in *ibid.*, II, 1767.

thesis by saying that the exercise of the imperial prerogative is done with or without the consent of the Diet, and those coming under the provisions of the four articles above cited were instances necessitating parliamentary consent.[69] Representative Jumi Suzuki, who signed the resolution, followed Dr. Hatoyama in further elaboration upon it. He contended that the absence of a proviso in Article 13 of the Constitution should not be construed to favor the doctrine of the unrestricted prerogative of the emperor in this regard. He declared, in further elucidation of the purport of this unique resolution, that the parliamentary consent was required to an enforcement bill, and not to the treaty itself, prior to ratification.[70] Dr. Kungoro Shigeoka opposed the resolution upholding the unrestricted character of the imperial prerogative over foreign relations. He referred to the absence of any constitutional restrictions, in striking contrast with various European constitutions, and declared that the House could not arrogate to itself the power of defining the prerogative of the emperor.[71] The resolution was passed by an almost unanimous vote.[72]

From our survey of parliamentary debates, it seems safe to conclude that the dissolution of the House of Representatives on June 2, 1894, following the passage of an address resolution severely condemning the Ito cabinet for its foreign policy and the resolution concerning the treaty power of the Diet by an overwhelming majority, was forced by the determination of the Ito ministry to carry out its negotiations without parliamentary interference. The parliamentary agitations, however, greatly stimulated the cabinet to more rapid action.

Thus, on July 16, 1894, the Anglo-Japanese treaty of commerce and navigation was signed in London, providing for the abolition of consular courts and the recovery of tariff autonomy, to become operative after five years.[73] Though the treaty itself was reciprocal and terminable, it was accom-

[69]*Ibid.*, II, 1767–1768.

[70]*Ibid.*, II, 1768.

[71]*Ibid.*, II, 1769.

[72]*Ibid.* See also *Jiji Shimpo*, June 2, 1894, p. 4.

[73]Viscount Kawashima, Japanese Minister in London, was replaced by an abler statesman, Viscount Aoki, minister to Germany, in Feb., 1894, and on July 16 the treaty was signed (Hiratsuka, *op. cit.*, I, 138–141). For a brief account of treaty

panied by a protocol greatly restricting her freedom in tariff
legislation. Moreover, by an exchange of notes, the Japanese
government agreed to postpone the operation of the treaty
until the several codes which had already been promulgated
should have become effective.[74] With Great Britain, the
most affected party, leading the way, the other treaty powers
promptly followed. The treaty, successfully negotiated
under ruthless suppression of the press and after repeated
dissolutions of the House of Representatives, was rushed
through the Privy Council and proclaimed on August 27,
1894, following ratification by the emperor, after a long and
stormy period of over twenty years.[75]

On March 2, 1895, Representative Kenichi Otake and four
other members presented a long and detailed written question to the government concerning the Anglo-Japanese
Treaty of 1894.[76] He severely criticized the treaty as being
far short of a complete recovery of tariff autonomy and
judicial power, and demanded that the government explain
the reasons therefor.[77] On March 18, Foreign Minister Mutsu
declined to reply to the question, saying that the negotiations
were still in progress with other powers and that the subject
matter was closely interrelated.[78]

REVISION OF TREATIES IN 1899 AND 1911

Having fulfilled the preliminary requirements for complete
enforcement of the revised treaties, the Okuma-Itagaki

negotiations up to July 16, 1894, see Hirokichi Mutsu (ed.), *Hakushaku Mutsu
Munemitsu Iko*, "Unpublished Writings of Count Munemitsu Mutsu" (Tokyo,
1929), pp. 366–373.

[74]Text of the treaty together with accompanying protocol and notes in *Treaties
and Conventions between the Empire of Japan and Other Powers* (Tokyo, 1899), pp.
37–52.

[75]Viscount Mutsu who conducted the difficult negotiations from Tokyo attributed
his success to the extreme caution taken not to disclose the exact stage of negotiations even to his colleagues. Thus, he showed drafts and memoranda only to Prime
Minister Ito, while his predecessors distributed them to cabinet members, genro,
and privy councilors (Shinobu, *Gaiko Sokumenshi Dan*, p. 395).

[76]No interpellation was made during the short session of the Seventh Diet (Oct.
18 to Oct. 22, 1894) which was called to vote the war budget necessitated by the
outbreak of the Sino-Japanese War.

[77]*Teikoku Gikaishi*, III, 775–776, 780–781.

[78]*Ibid.*, III, 921. An identical reply was given to Prince Konoye of the House of
Peers (*ibid.*, III, 302). *Cf. Japan Weekly Mail*, March 9, 1895, pp. 277, 278; also
ibid., March 23, 1895, pp. 334, 343.

coalition cabinet notified the treaty powers in July, 1898, that the revised treaties would come into effect in July, 1899, and issued a notification to the people to extend courtesies to foreigners, such as would become the dignity of a great people.[79] Thus the Yamagata cabinet,[80] by Imperial Ordinance No. 251 (June 15, 1899), fixed the date of coming into force of new treaties at July 17, 1899, with the exception of the Franco-Japanese and Austro-Japanese treaties, which were set at August 4 of the same year.[81] On June 30, Emperor Meiji issued an imperial rescript calling upon the people to conduct themselves so as to promote better understanding among peoples.[82] On July 1, in addition to various departmental instructions, the cabinet issued instructions providing for strict observance of the obligations under the revised treaties.[83]

Under the revised treaties of 1899, Japan regained her judicial autonomy, but the complete recovery of tariff autonomy was not accomplished until 1911. On February 6, 1909, Count Jutaro Komura, foreign minister, came before the Diet and stated the government's intention of terminating the existing treaties, thus regaining her complete autonomy in the fiscal power of the state.[84] In October of 1908, a committee on treaty revision was formed under the Katsura cabinet, which formulated a draft treaty by the summer of the following year. The draft treaty embodied three essential principles: equality in obligations, reciprocity in benefits, and unconditional recovery of tariff autonomy. The draft treaty embodying the above principles received the cabinet's approval in August, 1909.[85] In early spring of 1910, negotiations were entered into with the treaty powers looking toward conclusion of new treaties to succeed the treaties to

[79]Kudo, Teikoku Gikaishi (Tokyo, 1903), II, 11. See a series of articles on "Preparations for the Execution of the New Treaties," by Kei Hara in Osaka Mainichi Shimbun, Dec. 1, 1897 to Jan. 23, 1898, and Oct. 6 to Nov. 15, 1898, reprinted in Asakichi Tanaka (ed.), Hara Kei Zenshu (Tokyo, 1927), I, 698–808, 810–876.

[80]The Okuma-Itagaki coalition cabinet fell in November, 1888, remaining in power only four months, and was succeeded by Yamagata ministry.

[81]Kudo, Teikoku Gikaishi, II, 172.

[82]Ibid.

[83]Ibid., II, 173. Cf. Japan Weekly Mail, July 8, 1899, p. 36.

[84]Teikoku Gikaishi, VII, 578–579, 797–798.

[85]Ito (ed.), Kato Komei, I, 605–608.

be terminated. Accordingly, many questions were put to the government during the Twenty-seventh Diet, which opened in December, 1910.[86] On January 24, 1911, Foreign Minister Komura, in his parliamentary address on foreign relations, declared that treaty negotiations were in progress and expressed confidence in their early completion.[87] Representative Yukio Ozaki interpellated the foreign minister concerning the reported pressure being exerted by Great Britain on tariff schedules. In his reply, Count Komura declined to state whether the tariff question was included in the proposed Anglo-Japanese treaty on the ground that the matter was still under negotiation.[88] Representative Inukai introduced a resolution in the Lower House on March 21, 1911, strongly condemning the "weak" diplomacy of the Katsura cabinet in connection with treaty revision, and particularly for the reported declaration to the United States government concerning voluntary restrictions to be placed upon Japanese immigration. The resolution failed of adoption.[89]

[86]The Twenty-seventh Diet was in session from Dec. 23, 1910, to March 23, 1911.

[87]*Teikoku Gikaishi*, VIII, 254.

[88]*Ibid.*, VIII, 254–255. For subsequent interpellations on this point, see *ibid.*, VIII, 329, 425, 675, 676.

[89]*Ibid.*, VIII, 737–742.

Chapter X

THE SINO–JAPANESE WAR

THE OUTBREAK OF THE WAR[1]

THE EARLY PERIOD of the parliamentary régime in Japan is a history of conflict between the cabinet and the Diet seldom equaled by any other period of her political history. Thus, the House of Representatives was dissolved three times during the first four years of the Diet, largely on matters of foreign relations.

During the fourth session of the Diet, which opened on November 29, 1892, the conflict between the House and the cabinet culminated in the budget debates in the House of Representatives. The House reduced the government estimate of 83,760,000 yen by 8,850,000 yen, and passed the bill with several important amendments. Among the chief items thus reduced were certain administrative expenditures and the naval estimates. The House of Representatives, by an overwhelming majority of 144:38, rejected the original bill and accepted the committee report recommending complete rejection of the naval construction estimate, as was done in the previous two sessions of the Diet.[2] Then, in accordance with Article LXVII of the Constitution, the House sought in vain to obtain the concurrence of the government to its reduction.[3] On January 23, 1893, when Representative Kono

[1] For a discussion of the negotiations preceding the outbreak of the war, see Ryoei Saito, *Kinsei Toyo Gaikoshi Josetsu* (Tokyo, 1928), pp. 283–351.

[2] For debates on the budget bill, see *Teikoku Gikaishi*, II, 591–601, 607–614, 632–646, 650–662, 671–681, 688–699, 711–746. For debates on the Navy Department estimate, see *ibid.*, II, 746–759.

[3] *Ibid.*, II, 831–852. In opposing the House rejection of the Naval Construction bill, Count Inouye, acting premier, declared that the cabinet was forced to resort to such measures allowed under the Constitution to execute the program to maintain the peace of the Orient (*ibid.*, II, 832).

was about to commence his speech introducing an address
resolution rebuking the Ito cabinet for its fiscal policy and
strongly criticizing its veiled threat to the chamber concerning
the Naval Construction bill, an imperial rescript was issued
proroguing the Diet for fifteen days.[4] On February 7, Representative Kono resumed his speech, vigorously attacking
the cabinet, while Prime Minister Ito opposed the resolution
and intimated the dissolution of the House. The resolution was passed 181:103.[5] The following day, Speaker Toru
Hoshi was given an audience by the emperor to present the
address, while Prime Minister Ito also petitioned the throne
for the dissolution of the House.[6] After consultation with the
Privy Council, an imperial rescript was issued on February
10, in which the emperor said that he would command his
ministers to make every possible reform in the administration, that he would grant 300,000 yen annually for six years
from the privy purse, and that he would also command all
civil and military officers to contribute one tenth of their
monthly salaries during the same period towards building
the imperial fleet. He concluded by calling upon both the
cabinet and the Diet to unite in assisting him to bring forth
good fruits of constitutional government.[7] As a result, the
House and the cabinet changed their attitudes and both
proceeded to arrange for a compromise. The House now rein-
serted the Naval bill.

The temporary harmony thus achieved during the fourth
session of the Diet was a forced one, and consequently the
opposition became even more vigorous and outspoken as a
result of these tactics of the government. Meanwhile, public
demand for an early revision of treaties and for more vigorous
policy towards China increased. Faced with these formidable
and incessant attacks from within, and the delicate problems
of treaty revision and Sino-Japanese negotiations from
abroad, the Ito cabinet dissolved the House twice in succession.[8] Naturally, the internal conflict in Japan greatly influ-

[4]*Op. cit.*, II, 854.

[5]*Ibid.*, II, 856–873.

[6]Kudo, *Teikoku Gikaishi* (Tokyo, 1901), I, 190.

[7]Text in *Teikoku Gikaishi*, II, 879.

[8]For a series of conflicts between the House and the cabinet over foreign relations
and internal politics, see Chap. IX, *supra*.

enced the Chinese government to maintain a strong attitude in her diplomatic negotiations over Korea.[9]

The news that the Chinese government had just decided to dispatch a large force to Korea, largely upon the reports and recommendations of her representative in Tokyo, reached the *Kasumigaseki* on June 2, 1894. Thereupon, Foreign Minister Mutsu presented the report to a meeting of the cabinet, called to determine its policy upon the House address to the throne which was passed the preceding day. At this meeting, Count Yamagata, president of the Privy Council and a leading genro, was present and suggested that the chief of general staff be invited to the meeting. Accordingly, the cabinet, in joint conference with Count Yamagata, president of the Privy Council, and Prince Arisugawa, chief of staff, decided to dissolve the House and dispatch troops to Korea.[10] The war and navy authorities became suddenly active,[11] and on June 7, both the war[12] and navy[13] offices issued departmental ordinances prohibiting any publication in the press of any matter relating to the movement of her troops and her war vessels. On June 22, the cabinet met in an extraordinary meeting, when Count Yamagata and Prince Arisugawa were also present, and decided upon the policy to be pursued toward China. Immediately after the meeting, Prime Minister Ito reported the decision of the cabinet to the emperor, who referred it to the Privy Council for advice.[14] In accordance with the report of the Council on June 23, preparations for the mobilization of her land and naval forces were started,[15] and on June 27 the final decision was made at a joint meeting, held in the presence of the emperor, of the ministers, the genro, and privy councilors.[16] Important

[9]Compare Kudo, *Teikoku Gikaishi*, I, 369–370.

[10]The dissolution of the hostile House of Representatives on June 2, 1894, left the Ito ministry absolutely free and unhampered in expediting its treaty negotiations and also making necessary preparations for the impending conflict with China.

[11]For several important conferences held among high naval and army authorities, see *Jiji Shimpo*, June 5, 6, 7, 1894, p. 3; June 8, p. 4; June 9, p. 7.

[12]Department of War Ordinance No. 9, 1894 (text in *Jiji Shimpo*, June 8, 1894, p. 2).

[13]Department of Navy Ordinance No. 3, 1894 (text in *ibid.*).

[14]*Jiji Shimpo*, June 23, 1894, p. 4.

[15]*Ibid.*, June 24, 1894, p. 4. An important joint conference of high officials of the army and navy general staffs was held on June 22 (*ibid.*, June 23, 1894, p. 4.).

[16]*Ibid.*, June 28, 1894, p. 3.

conferences among high personages of the War and Navy departments, as well as the war and navy general staffs, continued,[17] while Admiral Viscount Kabayama was appointed to head the naval general staff on July 17.[18] Late in the evening of July 16 important telegrams were received at both the general staff office and the *Kasumigaseki,* reporting the Chinese refusal to compromise;[19] thereupon, a conference of high military and naval officers was held on July 17, in His Majesty's presence, to decide upon the final details of military operations.[20] Similar conferences were held in the imperial palace on July 20[21] and July 24.[22] The emperor immediately sanctioned the decisions reached.[23]

The diplomatic events moved swiftly, and on July 31 an extraordinary meeting of the cabinet was held in the imperial palace,[24] while at the same time a meeting of all the high officials of the War and Navy departments and general staffs was also in session in the palace, to make final arrangements for commencement of war.[25] Accordingly, on August 1, 1894, the declaration of war on China was issued.[26] On the same day, an emergency ordinance was issued placing the press under strict censorship of the Home Office.[27]

The Diet and the War

That the Ito cabinet succeeded in obtaining the unity of the people and harmony between the government and the House by this declaration of war, there can be little doubt.

[17]*Op. cit.,* July 14, 1894, p. 4; *ibid.,* July 18, 1894, p. 5.

[18]*Ibid.,* July 18, 1894, p. 4.

[19]*Ibid.,* July 18, 1894, p. 5.

[20]*Ibid.* At this conference, Premier Ito, President Yamagata of the Privy Council, war and navy ministers, chiefs and vice-chiefs of war and navy general staffs, and other high military and naval officers, were present.

[21]*Ibid.,* July 21, 1894, p. 4.

[22]*Ibid.,* July 25, 1894, p. 4.

[23]Sakamoto, *Gensui Koshaku Yamagata Aritomo* (Tokyo, 1925), pp. 520–523.

[24]Saito, *op. cit.,* pp. 303–305 ff.

[25]*Jiji Shimpo,* Aug. 1, 1894, p. 4.

[26]Text of the imperial rescript on the declaration of war in *Horei Zensho,* 1894, Vol. I, *Shochoku,* pp. 11–12.

[27]Imperial Ordinance No. 134, 1894 (*ibid.,* Vol. I, *Chokurei,* p. 299). *Cf. Jiji Shimpo,* Aug. 3, 1894, p. 2.

Thus, no disturbances were reported during the general election, held on September 1; the following session of the Diet, held during the short period of October 18 to October 22, passed all the governmental measures, including the huge war budget of 150,000,000 yen, without a dissenting vote.[28] A representation resolution calling upon the government to conduct the war and foreign relations so as to ensure permanent peace in the Orient and to resist any intervention by a third party to prevent the fulfillment of the object stipulated in the declaration of war was introduced by Representative Hajime Motoda on October 20 and was passed unanimously.[29]

During the interim between the close of the Seventh session and the opening of the Eighth session of the Diet, news of victories on land and sea reached Japan, and when the Diet met in its Eighth session, political parties continued to maintain their former attitudes toward the cabinet.[30] The budget bill was passed with only slight modifications. In voting for the budget, the legislators were moved by their sense of responsibility not to embarrass the cabinet in prosecuting the war, though they lacked a genuine confidence in the ministry in power.[31] On February 1, the Suzuki resolution expressing the willingness of the House to vote for any amount of appropriations needed for the prosecution of the war was passed unanimously. Its inevitable effect was to discourage the cabinet from adopting any compromising policy toward China, and to express the determination of the House to support the ministry until complete victory had been won.[32]

[28]The absence of any criticism of the government is highly significant in view of a very slight change in party alignment as the result of the general election. For the strength of each party, see Kudo, *Teikoku Gikaishi*, I, 388.

[29]*Teikoku Gikaishi*, II, 1818–1821.

[30]The Eighth Diet was in session from December 24, 1894, to March 23, 1895.

[31]Compare Representative Ozaki's notable speech in supporting the bill (*Teikoku Gikaishi*, III, 479–480; *Japan Weekly Mail*, Jan. 26, 1895, p. 93).

[32]In voting for the resolution, Representative Kakugoro Inouye disclaimed any interference on the part of the Diet with the war power of the emperor (*ibid.*, III, 551). About this time Chinese representatives approached the Japanese government for peace, though declined by the latter because of their lack of full powers. Thus the resolution was intended to encourage the cabinet to maintain a "strong and vigorous" attitude on war (Kudo, *Teikoku Gikaishi*, I, 410).

PEACE NEGOTIATIONS

Several attempts were made in October and November of
1894 on the part of Li Hung Chang to bring about a collective
mediation, and by the middle of October, Foreign Minister
Mutsu became aware of an approaching unfriendly intervention, and consequently he was anxious to close the war
as soon as an opportunity arrived.[33] Mutsu took particular
caution not to disclose Japan's terms of peace to China,
to avoid giving other powers an opportunity to intervene.
By the beginning of January, 1895, however, Mutsu had
completed a draft treaty of peace and, after obtaining the
approval of his colleagues in Tokyo, left the capital for Hiroshima with Prime Minister Ito on January 11. On January
26, two Chinese peace commissioners left for Japan. Accordingly, on the following day, a joint conference of those
cabinet ministers and high officers of His Majesty's high
command then staying at the headquarters was held, in the
presence of the emperor, to determine the conditions of
armistice and general terms of peace.[34] At this important
meeting, Foreign Minister Mutsu presented his draft treaty
to the emperor and explained the general principles embodied
in the draft, viz., the recognition of the independence of
Korea, cession of territory and payment of indemnity,
opening of new ports for trade, etc. Following Mutsu, Prime
Minister Ito made further elaboration upon the draft and
expressed an apprehension as to the success of the forthcoming peace negotiations and strongly intimated that an
intervention was pending on the part of a third power,
though he could not foresee the exact nature or extent of such
intervention.[35] Since no objections were voiced from the
floor, the emperor gave his sanction to the draft treaty, and

[33]Saito, Kinsei Toyo Gaikoshi Josetsu, pp. 358–367. Cf. an article by an anonymous
writer in the Asahi (Japan Weekly Mail, Feb. 16, 1895, p. 182).

[34]Among those present at this conference were: General Yamagata, war minister,
Prime Minister Ito, Foreign Minister Mutsu, Navy Minister Saigo, Admiral Kabayama, chief of naval general staff, General Kawakami, vice-chief of army general
staff, and others (Hirokichi Mutsu, Hakushaku Mutsu Munemitsu Iko [Tokyo,
1929], pp. 447–449; Sakamoto, op. cit., p. 536).

[35]Mutsu, op. cit., p. 449; Hiratsuka, op. cit., II, 7–9; Tatsumi, Kyokuto Kinji
Gaikoshi (Tokyo, 1910), pp. 107–112.

on January 31, Prime Minister Ito and Foreign Minister Mutsu were appointed plenipotentiaries.[36] On February 1, 1895, the delegates from both parties met to exchange full powers; and when it was found that the Chinese representatives lacked full powers, the Japanese delegates broke off further negotiations.[37]

Finally, the Chinese plenipotentiary, Li Hung Chang, arrived at Shimonoseki on March 19, and the first meeting of plenipotentiaries was held on the following day to examine the full powers and to decide upon the conditions of armistice. Li Hung Chang demanded a general and unconditional armistice, to which the Japanese plenipotentiaries objected. On March 24, Li was attacked by a would-be assassin.[38] Thereupon, Foreign Minister Mutsu proposed to grant an unconditional armistice, in which Prime Minister Ito expressed his concurrence. But, before extending such armistice, the views of the high command had to be obtained. Accordingly, Ito immediately wired the headquarters at Hiroshima to inquire of the cabinet and military authorities their views. With the exception of War Minister Yamagata, they requested a reconsideration of Ito's proposal.[39] Thereupon, Ito left Shimonoseki for Hiroshima the midnight of March 25 to approach his colleagues in person at the headquarters.

Having won the officers of the high command, and obtained His Majesty's sanction, Ito wired Mutsu, the midnight of March 27, regarding the decision just made.[40] Accordingly, on March 30, an armistice for three weeks, extending from

---

[36] Mutsu, *op. cit.*, pp. 449-453.

[37] *Jiji Shimpo*, Feb. 5, 1895, p. 2. For further details of these negotiations, see H. Mutsu, *op. cit.*, pp. 454-466. Mr. Tadasu Hayashi, vice-minister of foreign affairs, made a report to the Diet on Feb. 4 on failure of the negotiations, together with documents exchanged concerning the full powers. The reading of the report in the House of Representatives was followed by a prolonged applause from the floor (*Teikoku Gikaishi*, III, 581). For vernacular press comment see *Japan Weekly Mail*, Feb. 9, 1895, p. 150.

[38] *Jiji Shimpo*, March 26, 1895, p. 3.

[39] Mutsu, *op. cit.*, pp. 474-480.

[40] *Ibid.*, p. 480. An important meeting of high military and civil officers was held on March 27 at the hotel room of Prince Komatsu, chief of general staff, with Ito, Yamagata, Saigo, Matsukata, Kuroda, Kabayama, Kawakami, Kodama, and others, in attendance (*Jiji Shimpo*, March 29, 1895, p. 3).

March 30 to April 20, was signed.[41] Emperor Meiji, upon
learning the news, issued an imperial rescript on March 25,
warning the officials and the subjects against any acts which
would impair the dignity of the country.[42] Li Hung Chang re-
covered from his wounds, and negotiations were resumed on
April 10. The treaty of peace was signed on April 17 and was
ratified on April 20 by the emperor. The exchange of ratifications took place on May 8, and the treaty was promulgated
as an imperial ordinance on May 10, 1895.[43]

THE THREE-POWER INTERVENTION[44]

That an unfriendly European intervention was pending to
deprive Japan of her fruits of victory was well known to Prime
Minister Ito and Foreign Minister Mutsu. Consequently,
therefore, in formulating the general provisions to be incorporated in the treaty, Mutsu insisted upon excluding any
cession of territory on the mainland, but high military and
naval officers pressed upon the cabinet to demand what they
regarded as legitimate fruits of their operations. Thus, at a
joint meeting of high civil and military officers, held in the
presence of the emperor on January 27, it was decided to include the cession of the Liaotung Peninsula in the treaty of
peace, disregarding any considerations of a third-party intervention.[45] Gravest apprehensions were entertained lest

[41]*Jiji Shimpo, gogai,* March 31, 1895. *Cf.* Hiratsuka (ed.), *Ito Hirobumi Hiroku*
(Tokyo, 1929), I, 221–226, 382–384; Kudo *Teikoku Gikaishi,* I, 454; also *Japan
Weekly Mail,* April 6, 1895, p. 405. Toyotaro Koyama, the twenty-one-year-old
would-be assassin, was promptly sentenced on March 30 to life imprisonment (*ibid.,*
April 6, 1895, pp. 404, 416).

[42]Text of the rescript in *Horei Zensho,* 1895, Vol. I, *Shochoku,* p. 1. For comment
in the vernacular press, see *Japan Weekly Mail,* March 30, 1895, p. 358.

[43]Text of the imperial rescript of April 21, 1895, on the restoration of peace in
Horei Zensho, 1895, Vol. I, *Shochoku,* pp. 3–4. Text of the Treaty of Shimonoseki
in *Treaties and Conventions between the Empire of Japan and Other Powers* (Foreign
Office, Tokyo, 1899), pp. 377–384. *Cf. Japan Weekly Mail,* May 18, 1895, p. 364.
The convention of retrocession was signed at Peking on Nov. 8, ratified by the emperor on Nov. 17, ratifications exchanged on Nov. 29, and promulgated on Dec. 3,
1895.

[44]See a detailed account by Foreign Minister Mutsu himself in Mutsu, *op. cit.,*
pp. 506–561.

[45]Hiratsuka, *op. cit.,* I, 54; Hirota, *Naikaku Kotetsu Gojunenshi* (Tokyo, 1930),
pp. 322–324. That Prime Minister Ito was long apprehensive of an approaching
intervention can be seen in his speeches and memoranda (Hiratsuka, *op. cit.,* I,
39–56). *Cf.* Shinobu, *Gaiko Sokumenshi Dan,* pp. 194–195.

such an intervention should be forthcoming during the progress of peace negotiations.[46]

On April 23, 1895, the Russian, German, and French ministers called on the foreign office and "advised" the Japanese government to return the Liaotung Peninsula to China for the "peace of the Orient."[47] On April 24, Prime Minister Ito, General Yamagata (war minister), and Admiral Saigo (navy minister) held an important conference in the presence of the emperor to deliberate upon the proposal thus made by three European powers. They tentatively decided to accept their "advice." On the following day (April 25), Ito joined Foreign Minister Mutsu, Home Minister Nomura, and Finance Minister Matsukata at Maiko. Mutsu stood for rejection of the "advice" while the other two cabinet ministers supported Ito. Mutsu finally acquiesced in the general policy already adopted. This decision received the emperor's approval.[48] Immediately, Mutsu instructed Minister Nishi (St. Petersburg) to sound out the real determination of the Russian Foreign Office, Minister Kato to see to what extent the London government was prepared to support Japan, and Minister Kurino (Washington) to request the American good offices for mediation. On April 27, Nishi reported that Russia had no intention of reconsidering her proposal and added that she was making military preparations. Kato reported the intention of Great Britain to maintain strict neutrality, while Kurino and Takahira (Rome) wired the *Kasumigaseki* office that neither the United States nor Italy was prepared to offer good offices in Japan's behalf.[49] Thereupon, on April 30, after having submitted to the Privy Council for advice,[50] Foreign Minister Mutsu sent instructions to Minister Nishi to present a memorandum to the Russian foreign minister, stating that, after maintaining her honor and dignity by exchanging the

[46]From the reports received from the Japanese ministers at St. Petersburg, Berlin, and other capitals, Mutsu was able to foresee the impending intervention (Mutsu, *op. cit.*, pp. 506–509; also Hiratsuka, *op. cit.*, II, 111–116).

[47]It appears that Count Witte was largely instrumental in bringing about the intervention (Yarmolinsky, *Memoirs of Count Witte* [London, 1921], pp. 82–85).

[48]Mutsu, *op. cit.*, pp. 509–512. On April 26, War Minister Yamagata left for Port Arthur to report to the headquarters the decision of the government and to consult the high military and naval officers in the field (*ibid.*, p. 523).

[49]*Ibid.*, pp. 512–517.

[50]*Jiji Shimpo*, May 1, 1895, p. 3.

ratifications with China, Japan would be willing to add the
following two amendments: (1) Japan was to renounce her
right of perpetual occupation of Liaotung Peninsula, except
the Kwantung Province. She was to obtain from China, however, a certain sum for the territory thus retroceded. (2) Japan was to occupy the territory in question until China
should have fulfilled her obligations under the peace treaty.
An identical memorandum was dispatched to Berlin and
Paris.[51]

Minister Nishi reported on May 3 that Russia stood firm in
her original demand that Japan should have no foothold on
the continent. China, on the other hand, proposed to delay
the exchange of ratifications. Now the time had come to carry
out the program previously determined upon. Accordingly,
at the conference of the cabinet ministers and high military
and naval officers then in Kyoto, called in the evening of May
4, it was decided to accept the European "advice" on the one
hand, and to hasten the exchange of ratifications with China
on the other. As soon as the cabinet reached this decision, it
was reported to the emperor by Prime Minister Ito for His
Majesty's sanction.[52] With the emperor's approval, the Japanese acceptance of the "advice" was transmitted to St.
Petersburg, Berlin, and Paris on May 6.[53] Three days later
their respective representatives called at the foreign office to
express their satisfaction.[54] On May 10, a joint meeting of the
cabinet and the Privy Council was held in the presence of the
emperor to deliberate upon necessary measures to be taken at
this crisis.[55] Towards the evening, an imperial rescript was issued, declaring that Japan's object in the war was accomplished, that the retrocession of the peninsula in no way reflected upon the dignity and honor of Japan, and calling upon

[51]Mutsu, *op. cit.*, p. 519.

[52]The meeting lasted till after one o'clock the following morning and was attended
by Premier Ito, Foreign Minister Mutsu, Finance Minister Matsukata, Navy
Minister Saigo, Home Minister Nomura, and Chief of Naval General Staff Kabayama (*Jiji Shimpo*, May 7, 1895, p. 9).

[53]In its editorial columns, the *Jiji Shimpo* strongly urged upon the people to maintain patience, and warned against any hasty action (May 7, 1895, p. 3).

[54]Mutsu, *op. cit.*, pp. 521–522. *Cf.* Katsusaburo Iwasaki, *Koshaku Ito Hirobumi*
(Tokyo, 1909), pp. 107–108; Kudo, *Teikoku Gikaishi*, I, 461; Ito, *Kato Komei*, I,
249–252.

[55]*Jiji Shimpo*, May 11, 1895, p. 3; *ibid.*, May 12, p. 4.

the people to restrain themselves in their actions. The rescript
was countersigned by all the ministers, indicating that the issuance of the rescript had been petitioned by the entire cabinet.[56]

PARLIAMENTARY DEBATES ON THE TREATY OF SHIMONOSEKI

An outburst of public indignation followed the conclusion
of the treaty and the acceptance of the three-power intervention. The Ito ministry resorted to the time-honored measure
of stringent suppression of news, suspension of offending
papers, and dissolution of meetings.[57] The cabinet, on the
other hand, seeing its inability to carry out the post-bellum
program without party support, succeeded in reaching an
"understanding" with the *Jiyuto* party. The *Kokumin Kyokai*
did not express confidence in the Ito cabinet, but declared
that the post-bellum measures should be approved before
raising the question of no confidence in the cabinet.[58] All
the political parties and factions united in recognizing the

[56]Text of the imperial rescript in *Horei Zensho*, 1895, Vol. I, *Shochoku*, p. 5 (*cf.*
Japan Weekly Mail, May 18, 1895, p. 565; *Jiji Shimpo*, May 14, 1895, p. 2). An
imperial ordinance promulgating the treaty was also issued (*Jiji Shimpo*, May 14,
p. 2).

[57]For comment in the vernacular press, see *Japan Weekly Mail*, April 20, 27,
May 4, 11, 18, 1895. Eight of the leading "strong foreign policy" papers in Tokyo
were suspended during the week, ending on April 20 (*Japan Weekly Mail*, April
20, 1895, p. 445). On April 25, *Nichi Nichi*, *Jiji Shimpo*, *Choya Shimbun*, and
Mezamashi were suspended because of their publication of a news dispatch from
London concerning the reported combination of Russia, France, and Germany to
prevent the annexation of a Chinese territory by Japan (*ibid.*, April 27, 1895, p.
470). In consequence, practically the sole channel of information concerning the
impending intervention was the foreign press, the most influential of which was the
Japan Daily Mail. Throughout the critical days of April and May, *Jiji Shimpo* and
Nichi Nichi mildly supported the government and called upon the people to be
cautious and to wait for future opportunity. On the other hand, *Chuo*, *Hochi*, *Jiyu*,
Kokkai, *Kokumin*, *Mainichi*, *Mezamashi*, *Nippon*, *Niroku*, and *Yorozu* led the press
onslaught upon the ministry. The following editorial comment by *Niroku* serves to
indicate the general tone of a more vigorous paper: "Can it be possible that while
the ink of Rescript was still wet, an important condition was sacrificed out of mere
trepidation about foreign interference? Should the ministers have been guilty of
any such grave mistake in the discharge of their duties, the result will be to mislead
the Emperor, on the one hand, and to deceive the people on the other" (quoted in
Japan Weekly Mail, May 11, 1895, p. 522). The paper was subsequently suspended.

[58]Iwasaki, *Koshaku Ito Hirobumi*, pp. 114–117. *Cf.* Kudo, *Teikoku Gikaishi*, I,
466–470. *Cf. Japan Weekly Mail*, July 10, 1895, p. 10; Nov. 30, pp. 576–577, 582;
Dec. 21, p. 674.

necessity for naval expansion and increase in taxation.[59]

Thus in the Ninth session of the Diet, the temporary harmony and support that had characterized the previous two sessions during the war was broken, and the old fight against clan government was renewed mainly upon the treaty just concluded and the subsequent intervention.[60] At the very outset of the session, Representative Yukio Ozaki introduced an address resolution severely rebuking the cabinet for the return of the peninsula.[61] In a brilliant speech, he took the cabinet to task for its neglect of the representation resolution passed during the Seventh session, warning against a third-party intervention, and for evading responsibility for its diplomatic blunder behind the smoke screen of post-bellum reconstruction. He denounced the ministry for petitioning the issuance of the imperial rescript of May 10 contradicting the former rescript of April 21 on the restoration of peace.[62] Representative Kawashima, in opposing the resolution, declared that he did not entertain confidence in the cabinet, nor did he deny the diplomatic blunder of the retrocession of the peninsula, but pleaded that the Diet should give consideration to the important post-bellum programs before it.[63] Representative Jumi Suzuki, a *Jiyuto* member, defended the government, contending that Japan fought the war with China in the interest of peace, and that the retrocession of the peninsula was accepted in the same spirit, since a refusal would have meant a war against three powers.[64] After an all-day debate, the resolution was defeated by an overwhelming majority of 170:103.[65]

[59]Kudo, *op. cit.*, I, 471. Cf. *Japan Weekly Mail*, May 18, 1895, pp. 555, 557.

[60]For interpellations on the treaty, see *Teikoku Gikaishi*, III, 1790–1793, 1995–1996, 1955–1958, 1961–1963. No interpellation was put to the government from the floor of the Upper House on the retrocession of the Liaotung Peninsula. For summaries of questions on the treaty, see Kudo, *op. cit.*, I, 539–542.

[61]The resolution was signed by 17 prominent leaders: Ozaki, Taguchi, Takata, Inukai, Hatoyama, Suyehiro, Otake, Minoura, Shimada, Haseba, Kudo, Kanao, Ishihara, Suzuki, Daido, Koyezuka, and Nakamura.

[62]Text of Ozaki's speech in *Teikoku Gikaishi*, III, 1437–1439.

[63]*Ibid.*, III, 1440–1442.

[64]*Ibid.*, III, 1445–1448. Viscount Ishii approved the retrocession as the wisest course possible under the circumstances (Viscount Ishii, *Gaiko Yoroku* [Tokyo, 1930], p. 22).

[65]The resolution was supported by Ozaki, Taguchi, Kanao, and Fujita, while opposed by Kawashima, Suzuki, Arai, and Kusakari (*ibid.*, III, 1436–1456).

On January 10, Prime Minister Ito came before the House of Representatives and made a brief speech on the war, and presented diplomatic documents concerning the peace negotiations and the subsequent intervention.[66]

AFTERMATH OF THE WAR

The Sino-Japanese War demonstrated the weakness of China, and within three years after the conclusion of the war and the retrocession of Liaotung Peninsula "for the peace of the Orient," European powers, headed by Russia, were engaged in a general "scramble" for leases, concessions, and "spheres of interest or influence." The diplomatic events following the close of the war are generally known, and, therefore, we need not recite them here.[67] Suffice it to say, however, that this series of European encroachments upon China and expansion of their footholds in the Orient were looked upon in Japan with general dismay; and the cabinet was again made a target of press criticism and parliamentary attacks.[68]

During the critical period of 1898 the Japanese government could not formulate a consistent and definite policy to be pursued, on account of the uncertainty prevailing in her domestic affairs. Thus, during the same year, there were three cabinet changes[69] and two consecutive dissolutions of the House of Representatives.[70] Under such changing political fortunes of cabinets at this time, the Foreign Office was unable to formulate a strong and consistent policy towards China. Moreover, there were conflicting recommendations from Japanese ministers in London and Paris, the former pressing the home government to adopt a "strong policy" towards the Russian advance in Manchuria, while the latter urged a contrary

[66]For text of the report of the prime minister on the war, together with all important diplomatic documents, imperial rescripts, and notes, see *Teikoku Gikaishi*, III, 1457–1473. On January 11, he made a similar report to the Peers (*ibid.*, III, 987–988).

[67]For a brief sketch of diplomatic history of European "scramble" in China following the war, see Saito, *Kinsei Toyo Gaikoshi Josetsu*, pp. 409–483.

[68]Kudo, *Teikoku Gikaishi*, I, 612–662. *Cf.* Hirota, *Naikaku Kotetsu Gojunenshi*, pp. 409–410.

[69]Ito, Okuma, and Yamagata cabinets were all formed during 1898.

[70]Dissolution of the House on Dec. 25, 1897, under Matsukata cabinet, and on June 10, 1898, under Ito cabinet.

policy of coöperation and harmony.[71] Under the circumstances, the hands of the foreign minister were greatly cir-
cumscribed by domestic considerations. An instance may be
cited to illustrate this situation. When the Russian minister
called on Baron Nishi on April 12, 1898, for a reply to the
memorandum of March 29 concerning the Russian lease of
Port Arthur and Dalny, the foreign minister declined it until
Russia withdrew her pretensions in Korea. Prime Minister
Ito, however, promptly repudiated the foreign minister on
April 16 by informing the Russian legation that the Japanese
government would raise no objections to such a Russian
move.[72]

Parliamentary inquiry into the conduct of foreign relations
was opened on March 21, 1898, with two written questions
to the Ito cabinet, one by the opposition (*Shimpoto*) party,
the other by the *Jiyuto* party, supporting the government.
Both asked the government to state whether it obtained a
pledge from the three powers in 1895 not to seek any occupation or lease of the Liaotung Peninsula, and what diplomatic
measures were being taken by the government concerning
the general "scramble." In reply, Ito admitted that the particular circumstances rendered impossible the obtaining of any
pledge at the time of retrocession in 1895, and declined to
state precisely what measures were being taken concerning
the contemporary developments in China.[73] Being dissatisfied
with the replies, the *Shimpoto* members[74] introduced in the
Lower House an address resolution on May 30, rebuking the
administration for failing to take effective diplomatic measures in 1895 and to preserve the balance of power in the

[71]On March 26, 1898, Minister Kato in London wrote a long memorandum urging
the home government to pursue a strong policy opposing any Russian advance in
the Far East. He recommended that, should Japan's attempt to prevent the parti-
tion of China fail, Japan should join the powers in sharing the "spoils" and obtain
a stronghold in Korea, and threatened to resign his post if his recommendations
were not accepted (Ito, *Kato, Komei*, I, 284–287, 302–306, 313–328). Kato's advocacy of anti-Russian policy and of coöperation with Great Britain was vetoed
by a majority of the genro and members of the cabinet, who were being placed in a
most delicate situation because of the enormously increased budget following the
war.

[72]Ito, *op. cit.*, I, 330–331.

[73]*Teikoku Gikaishi*, IV, 925–928, 947.

[74]The resolution was signed by eleven members, including Ozaki, Shimada,
Hatoyama, Kono, and Taguchi (*ibid.*, IV, 960).

Orient.[75] The supporters of the resolution declared that the object of this resolution was to condemn the "do-nothing" policy of the government and to make clear the will of the people to the emperor, while the opponents of the resolution argued against making a diplomatic question a partisan issue. After a brief debate the resolution was defeated by 171:116.[76]

[75]Text of the resolution in *ibid.*, IV, 988.

[76]*Ibid.*, IV, 988-999. *Jiyuto* and *Kokumin Kyokai* opposed the resolution (Kudo, *Teikoku Gikaishi*, I, 628).

Chapter XI

THE ANGLO–JAPANESE ALLIANCE

The Alliance of 1902[1]

Long before the actual conclusion of the first Anglo-Japanese Alliance of 1902, as early as the conclusion of the Treaty of Shimonoseki and the unhappy three-power intervention, there began to develop a general sentiment favoring a closer "understanding" or an alliance with Great Britain. Particularly, such sentiment was more pronounced among semi-official papers.[2] It was not, however, confined to the press. Among the more influential statesmen who advocated such an "understanding" were Representative Masami Oishi and Count Komei Kato.[3] Thus, in a long memorandum to Tokyo, written on March 26, 1898, Minister Kato in London vigorously urged the home government to open negotiations for an Anglo-Japanese understanding.[4]

At this time, the public opinion supported the continued occupation by Japan of Weihaiwei which had been under Japanese occupation since 1895, pending the full payment of the Chinese war indemnity. This was supported by both the

[1]For diplomatic negotiations, see A. M. Pooley, *Secret Memoirs of Count Tadasu Hayashi* (London, 1915), *passim.*

[2]Thus, by June, 1895, *Jiji Shimpo* openly advocated an alliance. It declared: "In order to oppose Russia, England has not hesitated to join hands even with decadent countries like Turkey and China. How much more then ought she to be willing to coöperate with Japan? To speak frankly, we do not hesitate to assert that England would derive more benefit than Japan from the proposed alliance" (quoted in *Japan Weekly Mail*, June 29, 1895, p. 719). *Cf. Japan Weekly Mail*, July 27, 1895, p. 146; A. M. Pooley, *op. cit.*, p. 82; Dr. Tsuboi, *Saikin Seiji Gaikoshi* (Tokyo, 1929), IV, 450–451.

[3]Compare Kudo, *Teikoku Gikaishi* (Tokyo, 1903), II, 449.

[4]Ito (ed.), *Kato Komei* (Tokyo, 1929), I, 284–287.

high military and naval authorities and the Foreign Office
from a strategic point of view. By February, 1898, however,
influencial genro and cabinet members were inclined to adopt
the safer policy of "an innocent onlooker in foreign relations"
because of the internal instability and anxiety for financial
rehabilitation. Accordingly, on March 22, Foreign Minister
Nishi replied to the British minister in Tokyo that the Japanese government entertained no objection to her occupation
of Weihaiwei after Japan's withdrawal.[5] Upon receipt of this
reply from Tokyo, Minister Kato wrote to the foreign minister, emphasizing the importance of expressing a more favorable attitude towards London in return for her support of the
Japanese position in Korea. The earnest and persistent recommendations on the part of Minister Kato finally won the
cabinet to his views.[6]

In the middle of April, 1901, Foreign Minister Kato instructed Minister Tadasu Hayashi to open negotiations with
Great Britain in his individual capacity.[7] The preliminaries
progressed smoothly, and on August 4 an important meeting
of the genro (Ito, Inouye, and Yamagata) and Prime Minister
Katsura was held to determine the basic principles to be embodied in the treaty.[8] A series of meetings of the cabinet was
held during the summer and fall, and finally, on October 8,
Foreign Minister Komura instructed Minister Hayashi to
proceed with full powers in the negotiations.[9]

Meanwhile, Marquis Ito, a strong supporter of a Russo-
Japanese *entente*, started on his trip abroad.[10] Yamagata and
Inouye urged upon Ito to approach the Russian government
to sound its attitude toward such an understanding, while
Prime Minister Katsura, who supported his foreign minister
in the negotiations, joined Yamagata and Inouye for a differ-

[5]*Ibid.*, I, 299–301.

[6]*Ibid.*, I, 301–309.

[7]Dr. Tsuboi, *op. cit.*, pp. 456–458.

[8]Prior to 1901, influential members of the genro, particularly Ito and Inouye,
were strongly in favor of reaching an understanding with Russia for the solution of
Far Eastern questions, and saw little prospect of an alliance with Great Britain.
Minister Hayashi in London and Minister Kurino in Paris shared the same view
(Ito, *Kato Komei*, I, 288–292).

[9]Yoshino (ed.), *Kyokuto no Gaiko* (Tokyo, 1916), p. 31.

[10]Ito left Japan on September 18, 1901, and returned home on February 25, 1902.
His primary object in going to America was to receive the degree of LL.D. from
Yale University.

ent reason. Katsura's support for Ito's trip abroad at this
time was due to his desire to have a free hand in concluding
an Anglo-Japanese understanding. This he believed would be
accelerated by the absence of Marquis Ito, a leading genro
who enjoyed the utmost confidence of the emperor and whose
advice was invariably sought by the latter in reaching any
important decision.[11] Therefore, Ito's absence from Tokyo left
the cabinet comparatively free in directing the negotiations.

The negotiations in London moved very rapidly, and on
November 6, 1901, Lord Lansdowne handed a British draft
to Minister Hayashi,[12] and on the following day Hayashi requested early instructions from Tokyo.[13] Marquis Ito, upon
learning the British draft, telegraphed Prime Minister Katsura from Paris on November 15, urging the latter to postpone a definite decision until his visit to St. Petersburg.[14] By
this time, however, the British government began to entertain some concern in the presence of a leading genro in Europe
on his way to the Russian capital; and on November 22,
Prime Minister Katsura telegraphed Ito in Berlin requesting
his early departure for Russia and calling his attention to the
advanced stages of the negotiations in London, declaring that
Japan could not retract her stand without impairing her
honor.[15] On November 25 Ito arrived in St. Petersburg, and
on the following day he requested the Tokyo views concerning the nature of his conversations. Accordingly, on November 27, Katsura reiterated his former views and requested the
genro to confine his activities to "private and personal conversations," pleading that the cabinet's attitude had been decided and that the negotiations with Great Britain could no
longer be delayed.[16]

Towards the end of November, 1901, the treaty negotiations progressed rapidly, and on November 28 an important
cabinet meeting was called at the official residence of the
foreign minister to deliberate upon the attitude of the govern-

[11]Viscount Kurino in Hiratsuka (ed.), *Ito Hirobumi Hiroku* (Tokyo, 1929), I,
349–354. *Cf.* Viscount Ishii, *Gaikō Yoroku* (Tokyo, 1930), pp. 52–55.

[12]Text of the British draft in Hiratsuka, *op. cit.*, I, Supplement, pp. 13–14.

[13]*Ibid.*, p. 14.

[14]*Ibid.*, p. 15.

[15]*Ibid.*, p. 16.

[16]*Jiji Shimpo*, Nov. 28, 1901, p. 7.

ment upon the British draft just reached. The cabinet's decision to accept the London draft was reported to the emperor by Premier Katsura the following day.[17] In view of the importance of this step, the emperor referred the matter to the genro for advice. Pending the meeting of elder statesmen on December 7, Count Inouye wired Marquis Ito, informing the latter that all the other members of the genro and the cabinet had been won to the alliance, while Ito telegraphed Premier Katsura on December 6 from Berlin suggesting further modifications of the draft.[18] On December 7, a joint meeting of the genro and the cabinet was held at the home of the premier.[19] Here the highest advisers to the throne on important affairs of the state deliberated upon the draft, and all attached their signatures thereto before reporting to the emperor.[20] The following day Prime Minister Katsura was given an audience to report the result of the deliberations. However, a telegram had already been received by the emperor from Marquis Ito requesting the postponement of signing the alliance, and consequently the matter was again referred to the genro who reaffirmed the previous action, fearing that any further delay would result in the failure of the Anglo-Japanese negotiations, and that Japan would be placed in isolation by both Great Britain and Russia.[21] Thus, there being a direct conflict of views between a leading genro enjoying the utmost confidence of the emperor and the cabinet, Foreign Minister Komura directly petitioned the emperor to give his sanction. Under the circumstances, Emperor Meiji, being satisfied with his foreign minister's explanations, and convinced that the conclusion of an alliance with Great Britain was to the interest of the state, gave his decision in favor of the cabinet.[22] His Maj-

[17]*Ibid.*, Nov. 28, 29, 1901, p. 3; Hiratsuka, *op. cit.*, I, 28.

[18]Hiratsuka, *op. cit.*, I, 28, 34-35.

[19]The genro was represented by Yamagata, Saigo, Inouye, Matsukata, and Oyama, while the cabinet was represented by Prime Minister Katsura, Foreign Minister Komura, and Navy Minister Yamamoto (Dr. Tsuboi, *op. cit.*, IV, 118-120).

[20]Count Inouye attached his signature reluctantly and only after he was reminded of Ito's presence at the meeting of the genro on Aug. 4, when the general policy was formulated. Thus, immediately after the unanimous recommendation of Dec. 7, he telegraphed Ito informing him of the decision of the genro (Hiratsuka, *op. cit.*, I, Supplement, p. 36).

[21]Katsura to Ito, Dec. 13, 1901 (*ibid.*, p. 38).

[22]Viscount Ishii, *Gaiko Yoroku*, pp. 57-60; Sakamoto, *Gensui Koshaku Yamagata Aritomo* (Tokyo, 1925), pp. 588-589; Yoshino, *Gendai Kensei no Unyo* (Tokyo,

esty's sanction having thus been given, the negotiations now moved rapidly, and on January 30 the historic document was signed in London.[23]

On the forenoon of February 12, 1902, the Prime Minister came before the House of Peers and made public the conclusion of an alliance with Great Britain, stating that it had received the imperial sanction before signature. The reading of the alliance was received amid applause, indicating general approval, and the usual interpellations were not put to the government.[24] While Premier Katsura delivered his speech to the Peers, Foreign Minister Komura made an identical report to the House of Representatives which received the news with like applause. No parliamentary comment was forthcoming following the announcement.[25] Thus the conclusion of the alliance for a period of five years was received with unanimous approval of Diet members, and it formed the corner stone of Japanese diplomacy for the next twenty years.[26]

RENEWALS OF THE ALLIANCE IN 1905 AND 1911

As the Russo-Japanese War progressed and Japan's position in eastern Asia advanced, the alliance was renewed. Under the renewed alliance, Great Britain recognized Japan's paramount political, military, and economic interests in Korea, while the scope of the alliance was extended to include India. The alliance was signed in London on August 12,[27] to continue for ten years, but was not made public till September 27, pending the peace negotiations at Portsmouth.[28] This delay was designed to allay the public criticism of the govern-

1930), pp. 203–204; Yoshino, *Kyokuto no Gaiko*, pp. 35–37; Count Soyeshima, "Dual Diplomacy," *Gaiko Jiho*, No. 391 (Feb. 15, 1921), p. 369.

[23]The Privy Council was called on Jan. 29 to deliberate upon the final draft (*Jiji Shimpo*, Jan. 30, 1902, p. 3). Undoubtedly, the activities of Marquis Ito in the Russian Court had the effect of hastening the conclusion of the alliance. For diplomatic correspondence and documents in connection with Ito's journey see Hiratsuka (ed.), *Ito Hirobumi Hiroku*, I, Supplement, pp. 1–58.

[24]*Teikoku Gikaishi*, V, 1290.

[25]*Ibid.*, V, 1600. Cf. *Jiji Shimpo*, Feb. 13, 1902, p. 4.

[26]For commentaries on the alliance, see Dr. Nagao Ariga, "Anglo-Japanese Alliance," *Gaiko Jiho*, Vol. V, No. 50 (March 20, 1902), pp. 76–82; Shintaro Inagaki, "Anglo-Japanese Alliance," *ibid.*, Vol. V, No. 59 (Dec. 20, 1902), pp. 81–88.

[27]See *Tokyo Asahi*, Aug. 8, 12, 13, 14, 1905, p. 2.

[28]On Sept. 27 a meeting of the Privy Council was held when the Katsura cabinet made a detailed report on the revised alliance (*ibid.*, Sept. 28, 1905, p. 2).

ment on account of the Treaty of Portsmouth, but to no
avail.[29]

By 1911 the general situation in the Far East had been
changed. As the Russian menace had been largely removed,
the primary object of the original alliance had disappeared.
Meanwhile, the alliance began to be looked upon as a cause of
friction and apprehension rather than of better international
relationships, and Great Britain could no longer ignore the
opinions of her dominions and the general sentiment of the
Americans towards the alliance. When it became necessary to
amend the alliance in view of the pending British-American
arbitration treaty in 1911, Ambassador Kato, being aware of
the changed sentiment, strongly advised the home government not to insist upon the inclusion of any important new
items. The third alliance was signed in London on July 13 and
made public in Tokyo and London two days later.[30] The renewed alliance was received with mixed feelings and with no
such unanimity of approval as in 1902.[31]

After completing the renewal of the alliance and the conclusion of a tariff convention with Great Britain, Ambassador
Kato came back to Japan, on October 8, on leave of absence
after four years abroad. He was particularly concerned with
preserving the Anglo-Japanese Alliance as the corner stone of
Japanese diplomacy, in spite of the Franco-Japanese and
Russo-Japanese agreements concluded within the preceding
few years.[32] Thus, immediately upon his return to Tokyo, he
called on Prime Minister Saionji to deliberate upon the most
effective means of expressing to Great Britain the preëminent
position in which the alliance was held in the conduct of the
nation's foreign relations, and suggested that an imperial
message be addressed to the British king, affirming this
principle. The proposal being unprecedented in the diplomatic history of the Empire, the opinions of the genro had to
be consulted and their approval obtained.[33] A complete agree-

[29]Kudo, *Teikoku Gikaishi* (Tokyo, 1906), III, 500–505.

[30]For internal negotiations between Foreign Minister Komura and Ambassador
Kato, see Ito (ed.), *Kato Komei*, I, 631–661.

[31]*Cf.* Dr. Nagao Ariga, "The Renewed Anglo-Japanese Alliance," *Gaiko Jiho*,
XIV, No. 8 (Aug., 1911), pp. 111–116.

[32]Ito (ed.), *op. cit.*, I, 664.

[33]*Ibid.*, I, 664–667.

ment of views between the genro and the cabinet having been arrived at, the cabinet, at its meeting on April 9, 1912, unanimously approved the proposal of Ambassador Kato and was reported to the emperor by Prime Minister Saionji on April 15. The emperor promptly approved the proposal and, on April 17, an imperial message was issued to Ambassador Kato, commanding him to convey to His Majesty the King of England that the alliance had been productive of friendly relationships and that it had been a signal success in maintaining the peace of the Orient.[34] When Ambassador Kato left Tokyo for London on April 20, he had in his pocket a formal document bearing the signatures of all the cabinet ministers, declaring the Anglo-Japanese Alliance was the corner stone of their foreign policy and instructing the ambassador to further its object.[35] Upon his arrival in London on May 5, 1912, the message was duly conveyed and the king responded to the emperor in reciprocal tone.[36]

TERMINATION OF THE ALLIANCE

The alliance of 1911 provided for its expiration at the end of ten years, and consequently, the question of renewal again occupied the attention of the public in 1921.[37] By this time, the formidable opposition raised in the British dominions and the United States was generally known, and naturally reflected in the Japanese press. Thus, there was profound skepticism as to its continued existence, though an abrupt termination of an international agreement which had so long influenced the destinies of two empires was thought inadvisable. This reluctance of taking any definite step to abruptly terminate this agreement led to the joint notification to the League of Nations on July 7, 1921, recognizing the superior obligations under the League to those under the alliance.[38]

[34]Text of the message in *ibid.*, I, 668.

[35]Text of the instructions in *ibid.*, I, 669.

[36]*Ibid.*, I, 669–671.

[37]Dr. Sakutaro Tachi, "Anglo-Japanese Alliance and the League of Nations," *Gaiko Jiho*, Vol. XXXIV, No. 3 (Aug. 1, 1921), pp. 271–280. *Cf.* Viscount Ishii, *Gaiko Yoroku*, pp. 72–74; also Yoshino in *Chuo Koron*, No. 384 (July, 1920), pp. 2–7.

[38]After consulting the two remaining genro (Saionji and Yamagata), the notification was dispatched to Geneva on July 7, 1921 (*cf. Tokyo Asahi*, July 8, 1921, p. 1). The Privy Council met in plenary session on July 11, when the government's action in regard to the alliance was explained (*ibid.*, July 12, 1921, p. 1). On the

Meanwhile, the public interest in the subject was not confined to the press. Thus, Representative Seigo Nakano, on July 14, and again on July 24, 1920, demanded that the Hara cabinet should make public its policy in regard to the alliance, but the latter declined to comply on grounds of diplomatic secrecy.[39] Again, on January 24, 1921, in reply to an interpellation by Representative Mochizuki, Foreign Minister Uchida declined to disclose the progress of negotiations concerning the alliance.[40]

The alliance was replaced by the Four Power Pact of 1921, signed in Washington. During the Forty-fifth session of the Diet, many touching interpellations were made on the termination of the alliance, and the replies made by the government were unusually detailed. Thus, in reply to an interpellation by Representative Etsujiro Uyehara (January 24, 1922), Count Uchida, foreign minister, declared that the inclusion of India within the operation of the original alliance was made upon the desire of Great Britain and was designed to meet the threatening attitudes of Russia and Germany, and that the exclusion of China from the purview of the Four Power Pact was made in deference to her susceptibilities.[41]

following day, Prime Minister Hara called a meeting of the *Gaiko Chosakai*, or advisory council on foreign relations, to explain the decision already made (*ibid.*, July 13, 1921, p. 1). Text of the notification was made public immediately afterwards (*ibid.*, July 13, 1921, p. 2).

[39] *Teikoku Gikaishi*, XII, 501, 504, 599–600.

[40] *Ibid.*, XII, 1206–1210.

[41] *Ibid.*, XIII, 556.

Chapter XII

THE RUSSO-JAPANESE WAR

DIPLOMATIC NEGOTIATIONS

D URING THE Fifteenth session of the Diet, many interpellations were addressed to the government concerning the Boxer Rebellion of 1900, and subsequent diplomatic measures taken regarding the Russian activities in Manchuria, but the government replies given were uniformly negative. The ministry declined to comment upon pending moves or upon activities of foreign governments or otherwise refused to state its policy, pleading that the subject matter belonged to "diplomatic secrets" and was "contrary to the public interest of the state."[1] The sole exception was the detailed report concerning it made by Foreign Minister Kato in the House of Representatives on February 9, 1901.[2]

The Russian activities in Manchuria following the Boxer Rebellion greatly stirred public apprehension in Japan.[3] On March 12, 1901, the foreign minister requested cabinet deliberations upon Manchurian policy and transmitted a long memorandum to his colleagues outlining three alternatives. First, Japan might present a formal protest to the Russian government against the occupation of Manchuria, and should it be ignored, be prepared to resort to arms. Second, Japan might make a declaration to take such action as necessary to

[1] *Teikoku Gikaishi*, V, 496–501, 705, 721, 804, 543–545, 723–724, 986–991, 988–990, 1001–1007, 1033–1038, 1045. Cf. Kudo, *Teikoku Gikaishi*, II, 282–298, 343–347.

[2] *Ibid.*, V, 1001–1007.

[3] For commentaries upon the completion of the Trans-Siberian Railway and the South Manchuria Railway, see articles by Sato, Tani, Soga, Oishi, and Inagaki, in *Gaiko Jiho*, May 10, 1899, pp. 619–696; also an article by Heikuro Miyamoto in *ibid.*, V (1902), 181–190, 228–238, 409–416, 469–472.

maintain the balance of power and, in self-defense, place Korea under her control. The third alternative was to present only a mild protest pending further developments.[4] An extraordinary meeting of the cabinet was held on March 14, when Kato made further elaboration upon the alternatives and requested suggestions from his colleagues. Subsequently, several meetings were held, when Kato asserted as his opinion that a strong protest should be presented to Russia and that it would be accepted by her. The cabinet authorized the foreign minister to start negotiations in order to avoid an armed conflict. Accordingly, on March 24, 1901, a note was dispatched to St. Petersburg, calling upon the Russian government to refer the whole question to a joint conference of foreign representatives in Peking. This suggestion was promptly refused.[5] Immediately, Kato drafted a note expressing "general dissatisfaction" with the Russian reply, and on March 30, he presented it to Prime Minister Ito, who declined to give it his approval on the ground that the wording of the draft was too sweeping. The following morning, Kato called on the premier to insist upon his stand, when the navy minister and the war minister joined him, in deliberation upon the draft. After more than two hours of heated discussion, the navy minister, Admiral Yamamoto, suggested that the foreign minister postpone further protest pending future developments. Opposed by the prime minister and the navy minister and in the face of a negative attitude on the part of the war minister, the foreign minister had to drop the plan of dispatching the draft he had prepared.[6]

Unsatisfied with the attitudes of the navy and war ministers, Kato made a determined effort to win the prime minister

[4]The memorandum was over fifteen thousand words in length (cf. Ito, *Kato Komei*, I, 430–437). On March 11, Prime Minister Ito invited the genro (Yamagata, Matsukata, Inouye, Saigo) to his residence to confer upon the ways and means of pacifying the hostile House of Peers (*Jiji Shimpo*, March 12, 1901, p. 3). On the following day, the genro (Yamagata, Matsukata, Inouye, Saigo), president of the Privy Council (Saionji), minister of the imperial household (Tanaka), and members of the cabinet (Ito, Watanabe, Hara) met for further conference regarding the matter (*ibid.*, March 13, 1901, p. 3). As a result, the emperor issued an imperial message to the Peers (March 13) calling upon them to coöperate with the cabinet and vote for the army and navy appropriation bills (text of the message in *ibid.*, March 14, 1901, p. 3).

[5]Ito, *op. cit.*, I, 437–441.

[6]*Ibid.*, I, 441–443.

to his side. Consequently, in the late afternoon of April 3, 1901, Prince Ito called on him at the Foreign Office and finally gave his reluctant consent to Kato's draft note by modifying the "general dissatisfaction" to "reserving future expression of its views." Thus, in the early morning of April 4, Kato called on Admiral Yamamoto at the Navy Department and obtained the latter's consent thereto.[7]

Meanwhile, during the closing days of March, 1901, a series of secret meetings of high military officers was held in the War Department, and in the early morning of April 4, a detailed report on the fighting strength of the Russian forces in Manchuria was received by the general staff from a Japanese military representative there, reporting its unfavorable position from the standpoint of military operations. An extraordinary meeting of the board of field marshals and fleet admirals was called on the morning of April 5, when Prince Komatsu, General Yamagata, General Oyama, and Admiral Saigo, the emperor's supreme advisors on military and naval affairs, deliberated upon the question from the standpoint of national defense and war operations. Foreign Minister Kato, upon request of the board, attended the meeting and made detailed explanation concerning the diplomatic negotiations in progress.[8] A meeting of the cabinet was called in the afternoon, lasting from two o'clock to nine, to deliberate upon the note drafted by the foreign minister expressing the Japanese disagreement with the Russian reply of March 25.[9] After receiving the imperial sanction, the vigorous Japanese protest against the pending conclusion of a Russo-Chinese agreement was dispatched on April 6, while the military and naval authorities in Tokyo showed unusual activity.[10] Seeing the determination of the Japanese government, the Russian minister, on April 8, called at the Foreign Office to notify her termination of negotiations with China.[11] On the following

[7]*Op. cit.*, I, 443–444. *Cf. Jiji Shimpo*, April 5, 1901, p. 3.

[8]*Jiji Shimpo*, April 6, 1901, p. 3.

[9]*Ibid.*, April 6, 1901, p. 7.

[10]*Ibid.*, April 7, 1901, p. 3. *Cf.* Ito, *op. cit.*, I, 444–445; Dr. Nagao Ariga, "The Russo-Japanese Agreement," *Gaiko Jiho*, April 10, 1901, pp. 61–68; Kudo, *Teikoku Gikaishi*, II, 290–294.

[11]*Ibid.*, April 9, 1901, p. 2. The press carried a Reuter dispatch from London to the effect that Russia, under date of April 3, notified the powers of her termination of negotiations with China (*ibid.*, April 9, 1901, p. 7).

day, the foreign minister was received in audience by the emperor to report the "great victory" just won from Russia.[12]

Throughout the negotiations, Foreign Minister Kato took the initiative in pursuing a "strong" policy toward Russia, quite contrary to the views of his chief, Prime Minister Ito, and the genro who were all inclined to a "moderate" policy. Thus, Foreign Minister Kato, unlike his predecessors in the Foreign Office, adopted the principle of the "autonomy of the *Kasumigaseki* in the conduct of foreign relations" and somewhat neglected to consult with elder statesmen who had directed previous ministers in foreign relations.

Soon after the close of the fifteenth session of the Diet, Prime Minister Ito tendered his resignation, and consequently, a new cabinet (Katsura) was formed on June 2, 1901.[13] Minister Jutaro Komura to Peking entered the cabinet on September 21 as foreign minister.

During the Sixteenth session of the Diet, convened in the winter of 1901, the Katsura government assumed the usual policy of evading parliamentary scrutiny of Russo-Japanese negotiations.[14] The announcement before the Diet, on February 12, 1902, of the conclusion of the Anglo-Japanese Alliance, however, was received with great satisfaction.[15] The Seventeenth Diet, which was convened on December 6, 1902, was characterized throughout by a conflict between the cabinet and the House of Representatives over the navy expansion bill. Thus, on December 13, Prime Minister Katsura came before the Lower House and pleaded for the passage of the bill to increase the land tax for the expansion of the navy. The foreign minister, in reply to a question, denied that there was any relation between the proposed navy expansion and the recently concluded alliance with Great Britain, while Admiral Gombei Yamamoto, navy minister, declined to state the precise purpose for the sudden expansion of the navy.[16] The committee, to which the land tax bill was referred, made its report on December 16, recommending its rejection by

[12]*Ibid.*, April 10, 1901, p. 3. See also Ito, *op. cit.*, I, 445–447; Kudo, *op. cit.*, II, 294.

[13]For discussion of the circumstances which led to the resignation of the Ito cabinet, see Kudo, *op. cit.*, II, 366–376.

[14]For summary of diplomatic interpellations, see *ibid.*, II, 452–454.

[15]*Ibid.*, II, 446–450.

[16]*Teikoku Gikaishi*, V, 1859–1865.

24:3. When the committee report was made to the House, Prime Minister Katsura, Navy Minister Yamamoto, Communications Minister Yoshikawa vigorously opposed it, pleading that the naval expansion was indispensable in view of the Far Eastern situation, and that an increase in land tax was the most effective measure to be taken. When the motion to close the debate was about to be made, an imperial rescript was read proroguing the Diet for ten days.[17] A determined effort was made by the government to break down the opposition by soliciting the sympathies of the genro and others. Seeing no result, the cabinet again prorogued the Diet for another week until December 27, 1902. The desperate efforts thus made only intensified the opposition and, on December 28, Prime Minister Katsura himself made his final plea for the bill, and dissolved the House when the defeat of the bill became certain.[18]

In spite of a determined interference in the general election of March 1, 1903, the government failed to gain any substantial majority.[19] The strong coöperation between the *Seiyukai* and the *Kensei Honto* in opposition to the increased land tax bill during the Seventeenth Diet which resulted in the dissolution, however, was broken after the general election. The cabinet ministers made a special appeal to Prince Ito, president of the *Seiyukai*, for coöperation in view of the Manchurian situation, while Prince Yamagata supported the cabinet. In consequence, on April 28, Prime Minister Katsura announced, at his official residence before the invited representatives of six factions of the House of Peers, that an agreement had been reached between the government and the *Seiyukai* party regarding the naval expansion bill.[20] Having reached an "understanding" with the president of the majority party in the Lower House, the Katsura cabinet was able to put through a large naval expansion bill in the Eighteenth session of the Diet, without damaging queries put to it from the floor either in budget committees or in plenary ses-

[17]*Op. cit.*, V, 1872–1883. *Cf.* Kudo, *Teikoku Gikaishi* (Tokyo, 1906), III, 50–61.

[18]*Ibid.*, V, 1884–1886. *Cf.* Kudo, *op. cit.*, III, 61–79.

[19]As the result of the election, parties stood as follows: *Seiyukai*, 193; *Kensei Honto*, 91; *Teikokuto*, 18; Independents and others, 74. 248 members were reëlected, 32 former members, and only 96 new members (Kudo, *op. cit.*, III, 86).

[20]*Ibid.*, III, 105–123.

sion.[21] On May 27, Representative Ki Inukai introduced in the House an address resolution rebuking the cabinet for its political manipulations in connection with the increased land tax bill. This was opposed by the *Seiyukai* and other parties "coöperating" with the cabinet on the ground that, though they agreed with the general sentiment of the resolution, it was improper to cause His Majesty's anxiety over a conflict between the Diet and the ministry at the time of a great international crisis, and that all were agreed as to the necessity for naval expansion, the difference being only as to the means of raising the necessary funds. The resolution was defeated by an overwhelming majority of 228:123.[22]

Meanwhile, the diplomatic and military developments in Manchuria were moving very rapidly. Several important interpellations were addressed to the Katsura cabinet during the session concerning the Russian evacuation of troops and the government's policy, while it steadfastly declined to disclose the nature of negotiations on grounds of "diplomatic secrecy."[23]

The Russian failure to carry out the terms of the Russo-Chinese agreement of April 8, 1902, regarding the Manchurian evacuation was reported by Minister Uchida at Peking, on April 19, 1903, who urged an early determination of the Japanese policy regarding it. Pressed with the urgent necessity for decision, Prime Minister Katsura, accompanied by Foreign Minister Komura and Prince Ito, called on Prince Yamagata on April 23 for an important conference. At this conference, it was tentatively decided that Japan was willing to grant Russia a priority right in Manchuria while she was to insist that Russia should recognize Japan's similar position in Korea.[24] After several meetings, the cabinet finally decided to lodge a strong protest with the Russian government regarding

[21]The increased land tax bill was introduced in the Eighteenth session of the Diet on May 16, 1903, and the special committee, to which the bill was referred, voted, by majority of 31:4, to recommend its rejection. The government prorogued the Diet for three days to reach a compromise. As a result, it agreed to withdraw the land tax bill and to obtain the necessary funds through administrative reorganization, issuance of national loans, and other means (*ibid.*, III, 125–150).

[22]*Teikoku Gikaishi*, V, 1938–1942.

[23]*Ibid.*, V, 1902, 1916, 1917–1922.

[24]Hirota, *Naikaku Kotetsu Gojunenshi*, p. 494. For Prince Ito's views, see Hiratsuka, *Ito Hirobumi Hiroku*, I, 2–6.

the Manchurian situation, and to resort to arms, should such negotiations fail. The cabinet decision was reported to the emperor for his sanction, and on June 23, 1903, an important meeting of the genro was called to advise the throne upon the question. At this conference in His Majesty's presence, Ito and Inouye opposed the government's firm stand, holding that the time was not ripe for risking the nation, while Yamagata and Matsukata supported the cabinet.[25] Finally, at a joint meeting of the genro and the cabinet, it was decided to advise the emperor to open negotiations.[26] About this time General Oyama, chief of general staff, presented a memorial to the emperor urging an early solution of the pending question and reporting that Japan had an advantage from a strategic point of view and that a few years' delay would place Russia in a superior position. A copy of the memorial was also submitted to the cabinet.[27]

Faced with the grave responsibility for conducting negotiations with Russia, the Katsura cabinet was seriously embarrassed by Prince Ito's remaining as the head of the *Seiyukai* party, while, at the same time, enjoying the utmost confidence of the emperor as a leading genro. On June 24, Katsura requested a private conference of Yamagata and Ito, and pleaded with Ito to choose either the headship of a political party or a genro. In desperation, Prime Minister Katsura tendered his resignation on July 1, 1903, praying that the task was too difficult for him to bear and that a leading elder statesman be appointed to discharge the affairs of the state. Yamagata and Matsukata were called to the palace by the emperor for advice, whereupon these two genro recommended that the resignation be rejected, and, at the same time, advised the throne to appoint Prince Ito to the presidency of the Privy Council.[28] Accordingly, on July 6, Em-

[25]Those summoned to the palace included Ito, Yamagata, Oyama, Matsukata, and Inouye. Prime Minister Katsura and Foreign Minister Komura were also invited to the meeting (*Jiji Shimpo*, June 24, 1903, p. 3). The cabinet also met in an all-day session on June 23 (*ibid.*).

[26]Kudo, *Teikoku Gikaishi*, III, 193; Ito, *Kato Komei*, I, 507. Cf. *Jiji Shimpo*, June 25, 1903, p. 3.

[27]Cf. an anonymous article by a general in *Gaiko Jiho*, XLIII, No. 1 (Jan. 1, 1926), pp. 37–48. On June 22, Prince Ito invited Viscount Kato, former foreign minister and a leading diplomat, to obtain the latter's opinion upon the question (Ito, *op. cit.*, I, 507).

[28]*Jiji Shimpo*, July 2, 3, 4, 1903, p. 3.

peror Meiji called Prince Ito to the palace and offered him the presidency of the Council.[29] On July 12, he accepted the appointment, and his presidency of the *Seiyukai* party was succeeded by Prince Saionji, his predecessor in the Privy Council. Prince Ito, in turn, recommended the appointment of Prince Yamagata and Marquis Matsukata in the Council.[30] This was accomplished by amending the *Sumitsuin Kansei*, increasing its membership from 25 to 28, at an extraordinary meeting of the Council called on July 13.[31] By this sudden appointment of three of the leading advisers of the emperor as privy councilors, the cabinet was able to obtain a more harmonious relationship with political parties, on the one hand, and on the other was assured of a more responsible support and counsel for its measures regarding the unprecedented situation arising in Manchuria.[32]

Meanwhile, the general public was becoming impatient with the government's failure to check the Russian activities in Manchuria. Breaking the precedents, Professor Tomizu of the Imperial University of Tokyo led the public, in the press and on the platform, in demanding a more vigorous policy toward Russia, contending that war was inevitable, and urging an immediate declaration of war on Russia.[33] The leading papers, represented by *Tokyo Asahi, Osaka Asahi, Jiji Shimpo, Osaka Mainichi*, demanded war with Russia, while *Manchoho* and *Mainichi Shimbun* opposed such a step. The *Tokyo Nichi Nichi* was non-committal.[34] On June 10, 1903, seven distinguished professors of the law school of the Imperial University of Tokyo—Seisho Tomii, Toru Terao, En Kanai, Shingo Nakamura, Kanjin Tomizu, Sakuye Takahashi, Kiheiji Onozuka—presented a memorial to the premier

[29]*Ibid.*, July 7, 1903, pp. 2, 3.

[30]*Ibid.*, July 9, 10, 11, 12, 14, 1903, p. 3.

[31]*Ibid.*, July 14, 1903, p. 3. Prince Saionji became president of the *Seiyukai* party on July 15 (*ibid.*, July 16, 1903, p. 3).

[32]Kudo, *Teikoku Gikaishi*, III, 180–189. *Cf.* Tokutomi, *Seijika to shiteno Katsurako* (Tokyo, 1913), pp. 133–138.

[33]See Professor Tomizu's articles in *Gaiko Jiho*, V, No. 50 (March 20, 1902), pp. 57–61; *ibid.*, V, No. 52, pp. 49–54; *ibid.*, VI, No. 63 (April 20, 1903), pp. 201–204; *ibid.*, VI, No. 65, pp. 239–243; *ibid.*, VI, No. 66 (July, 1903), pp. 249–252. *Cf.* Heikuro Miyamoto, "The Manchurian Question," *Gaiko Jiho*, VI, No. 63 (April 20, 1903), pp. 205–207; also Dr. Nagao Ariga in *ibid.*, VI, No. 64 (May 20, 1903), pp. 225–233.

[34]Ono, *Nihon Shimbun Hattatsushi*, p. 285.

demanding that the government should take a decisive step
regarding the pending question and pointing out the inevitableness of war. Though the nature of the memorial was kept
secret at the time, it was soon learned by the vernacular press,
and finally, on June 24, the entire contents were disclosed to
the press.[35] Thereupon the *Manchoho* suddenly changed its
attitude and now advocated war, dismissing Kanzo Uchi-
mura, Shusui Kotoku, Toshihiko Sakai, and other leading
Christian or Socialist journalists, while Saburo Shimada's
Mainichi Shimbun joined the popular cry. The *Tokyo Nichi
Nichi*, a semi-government paper, was alone in supporting a
moderate policy.[36] By November, however, the public was
united in its demand for war.[37] A powerful association, *Tairo
Doshikai*, was organized on August 9, 1903, uniting all the
advocates for speedy solution of the Russian question, irrespective of party or parliamentary affiliations.[38]

Pressed by the united public for a more decisive policy
toward Russia, on the one hand, and restrained from taking
such a policy by Prince Ito, president of the Privy Council,
on the other, the Katsura cabinet was unable to pursue a
more consistent course in Russo-Japanese negotiations.[39] On
July 28, 1903, Foreign Minister Komura instructed Minister
Kurino in St. Petersburg to open formal negotiations with the
Russian government concerning the Manchurian situation.
Receiving a favorable response from the latter, Japan formally submitted, on August 12, a proposal, mutually recognizing their special interests in Manchuria and in Korea. In
her counter proposal, Russia recognized the Japanese special
interests in Korea under certain restrictions, but placed
Manchuria and its littoral exclusively within her sphere
of interest. In counter proposal, the Japanese government
demanded mutual engagement to respect China's sovereignty
and territorial integrity in Manchuria. Russia's second counter proposal was long delayed. It reached Tokyo on December

[35]*Jiji Shimpo*, June 24, 1903, p. 4.

[36]Ono, *op. cit.*; pp. 285–287. *Cf.* an article by Toshihiko Sakai in *Chuo Koron*,
XLVI (Jan., 1931), 283–304.

[37]*Cf.* articles by Makino, Watanabe, Harada, Miyamoto, Matsumiya, Kemu-
yama, in *Gaiko Jiho*, VI, No. 70 (Nov. 5, 1903), pp. 335–390; Dr. Ariga in *ibid.*,
VI, No. 71 (Nov. 20, 1903), pp. 396–400.

[38]Kudo, *Teikoku Gikaishi*, III, 216. *Cf. Jiji Shimpo*, Aug. 10, 12, 1903, p. 3.

[39]*Ibid.*, III, 217–219.

11, but entirely omitted any reference to Manchuria, thus placing the question outside the scope of diplomatic negotiations.[40]

While diplomatic negotiations were in progress between Tokyo and St. Petersburg under strict secrecy, the public demand for war became even more insistent. Thus, on November 8, the *Tairo Doshikai* presented a memorial to the government and also to Prince Ito of the Privy Council, demanding a "strong" policy, while Prime Minister Katsura invited three leaders of the Association to his residence on November 10 and assured them of the harmony between the cabinet and the Privy Council and pleaded with them to be more cautious and prudent in expressing opinions upon pending issues.[41] The more conservative members of the Privy Council also echoed the popular sentiment and presented their opinions to the emperor.[42]

The Nineteenth session of the Diet was convened on December 10, 1903. Speaker Hironaka Kono inserted in his address memorial to the throne a sentence vigorously attacking the ministry for its conduct of domestic and foreign affairs. The House voted unanimously for this ceremonial address which had been prepared by the Speaker, amid cheers. However, immediately after it was passed, the unusual wording of the address was noticed, but too late. The Speaker refused to resubmit the resolution expunging the political section. Instead, he withdrew his membership from the *Kensei Honto*. About this time, the Russian counter proposal had reached Tokyo, and the cabinet promptly dissolved the House of Representatives on December 11, 1903. This unexpected dissolution enabled the Katsura cabinet to pursue the negotiations with Russia unhampered by parliamentary scrutiny and criticism and to proceed without parliamentary interference to take all necessary measures with the friendly coöperation of the Privy Council.[43]

[40]The correspondence regarding the negotiations was presented to the Twentieth session of the Diet, and published by the Foreign Office.

[41]Hirota, *op. cit.*, pp. 489–499.

[42]Kudo, *Teikoku Gikaishi*, III, 241.

[43]*Teikoku Gikaishi*, V, 2011–2012; Kudo, *Teikoku Gikaishi*, III, 228–239; Hirota, *Naikaku Kotetsu Gojunenshi*, p. 501; Sugiyama, *Katsura Taisho Den* (Tokyo, 1919), p. 525; Tokutomi, *op. cit.*, pp. 140–141.

The Declaration of War

By the end of December, 1903, both the military and civilian authorities were convinced of the inevitableness of war, and an emergency imperial ordinance was issued on December 28, providing for emergency military expenditures and for speedy completion of the construction of a railway between Keijo and Fuzan, Korea.[44] The ordinance concerning the wartime headquarters was amended, placing the chief of naval general staff on the same footing with the chief of army general staff under the direct control of the emperor.[45] Moreover, the Supreme War Council was established,[46] and two powerful warships were purchased from Argentina.[47]

The much delayed counter proposal was received in Tokyo on January 6, 1904.[48] On the following day a joint conference of the cabinet and the military and naval authorities was held to deliberate upon the reply just received.[49] Again, on January 11, another important conference of the genro, the cabinet, and the military and naval authorities was held at the official residence of the prime minister. At this meeting, Foreign Minister Komura expressed a strong dissatisfaction at the Russian reply and proposed to break off further negotiations. However, the naval preparations were not complete, the concentration of transport vessels at Saseho naval station having been set for January 20.[50] On the following morning, Minister of Navy Yamamoto was received in audience by the

[44]Imperial Ordinance No. 291, 1903. *Cf. Jiji Shimpo*, June 20, 1903, p. 3.

[45]Imperial Ordinance No. 293, 1903. *Cf.* an editorial, *Jiji Shimpo*, Aug. 5, 1903, p. 2.

[46]Imperial Ordinance No. 294, 1903.

[47]The *Nisshin* and *Kasuga* (Sugiyama, *Katsura Teisho Den*, pp. 523–524).

[48]*Jiji Shimpo*, Jan. 7, 1904, p. 3.

[49]The cabinet was represented by the premier, foreign minister, war minister, navy minister, and the finance minister, while the military and naval authorities were represented by chief and vice-chief of army general staff as well as those of naval general staff (*ibid.*, Jan. 8, 1904, p. 3). On Jan. 8, General Oyama, chief of general staff, and Admiral Ito, chief of naval general staff, were both received in audience by the emperor (*ibid.*, Jan. 9, 1904, p. 3).

[50]The following were present: Ito, Yamagata, Matsukata, Inouye (genro); Yamamoto (navy), Terauchi (war), Komura (foreign), Sone (finance); General Oyama (chief of general staff), General Kodama (vice-chief of general staff), Admiral Ito (chief of naval general staff), Admiral Ijuin (vice-chief of naval general staff). See *Jiji Shimpo*, Jan. 12, 1904, p. 3.

emperor to report on the conference and to request that a *gozen kaigi* be held in His Majesty's presence to make formal decision upon the question. Accordingly, in the afternoon, a meeting of the genro, the cabinet, and high military and naval authorities was called in the palace.[51] After obtaining a long imperial audience, Foreign Minister Komura called on Baron Rosen (January 13) and handed him the Japanese proposals to Russia.[52] On the same day, Komura sent instructions to Minister Kurino in St. Petersburg to convey the Japanese wishes to the Russian foreign minister and to request an early reply.[53] On January 14, members of the newly created Supreme War Council were appointed.[54] On January 24, Premier Katsura was received in audience by the emperor to report the cabinet's decision to terminate the negotiations.[55] On the following day, the Supreme War Council held its first session to deliberate upon important matters of national defense and war operations.[56] After an all-day meeting on January 26, the cabinet held a conference with Ito, Yamagata, Matsukata, and Inouye, to discuss the military and

[51]The conference was attended by Hatano (justice), Kiyoura (agriculture and commerce), Kubota (education), Komura (foreign), Yamamoto (navy), Sone (finance), Oura (communications), Kodama (vice-chief of general staff), Ito (chief of naval general staff), Ijuin (vice-chief of naval general staff), and the genro (Yamagata, Ito, Oyama, Matsukata, and Inouye). Prime Minister Katsura was unable to attend on account of illness (*ibid.*, Jan. 13, 1904, p. 3).

[52]*Ibid.*, Jan. 14, 1904, p. 3.

[53]In sending the telegram, Komura gave detailed instructions to Kurino, saying that there was an absolute harmony between civilian and military authorities, and emphasized the importance of harmony and unity between diplomatic moves and military strategy, and commanded Kurino to act always in harmony with the instructions. The foreign minister further instructed the Japanese minister not to give any verbal explanations in presenting the Japanese counter proposal without further express instructions from Tokyo, that he was not to demand a reply from the Russian foreign minister except upon instructions from Tokyo to do so. He was prohibited from expressing even his "private opinions" (Shinobu, *Gaiko Sokumenshi Dan*, p. 262).

[54]The Supreme War Council was composed of Marshal Yamagata, Marshal Oyama (chief of army general staff), Admiral Ito (chief of naval general staff) Admiral Yamamoto (navy minister), General Terauchi (war minister), and specially appointed war councilors (General Count Nozu, General Baron Kuroki, General Baron Oku, and Admiral Baron Inouye). See *Jiji Shimpo*, Jan. 15, 1904, p. 3; also Koshiro Kuroda (ed.), *Gensui Terauchi Hakushaku Den* (Tokyo, 1920), p. 255.

[55]*Ibid.*, Jan. 25, 1904, p. 3. *Cf.* Tokutomi, *op. cit.*, pp. 142–143. On Jan. 24 Marshal Oyama distributed a confidential letter to each genro and cabinet minister (*Jiji Shimpo*, Jan. 25, 1904, p. 3).

[56]*Ibid.*, Jan. 26, 1904, p. 3.

financial measures to be taken;[57] and on January 30, Prince Yamagata and Prince Ito called on Prime Minister Katsura at the latter's official residence to discuss the situation in an all-day conference.[58] As a result, Komura instructed Kurino to press for an early reply from Russia.[59]

Failing to receive any reply from Russia, an extraordinary meeting of the cabinet was called at 10 A.M., February 4, to make the final decision. At 11:50, while the cabinet was still in session, Prince Ito, president of the Privy Council and a leading genro, was given an imperial audience and requested the emperor to call a special conference of the genro and the cabinet. Accordingly, a joint conference of the genro (Ito, Yamagata, Matsukata, Oyama, Inouye) and the cabinet (premier, war, navy, foreign, finance ministers) was called in His Majesty's presence at two o'clock to deliberate upon final details. At this *gozen kaigi*, it was decided to establish the headquarters in the palace, to issue orders to the navy and army to be ready for warlike operations, and to break off diplomatic negotiations at St. Petersburg on February 6.[60] In the evening, therefore, high military and naval authorities (war and navy ministers, and chiefs and vice-chiefs of army and navy general staffs) were summoned to the palace to decide upon final details regarding war operations.[61] On the following day, Foreign Minister Komura instructed Minister Kurino to notify the Russian government of the severance of diplomatic negotiations and the intention of the Japanese government to take independent action in self-defense as well as to protect her established rights and legitimate interests.

[57]The cabinet was represented by the prime minister, finance, foreign, war, and navy ministers (*ibid.*, Jan. 27, 1904, p. 3).

[58]The cabinet was represented by Premier Katsura, Foreign Minister Komura, and Navy Minister Yamamoto (*ibid.*, Jan. 31, 1904, p. 3).

[59]Hiratsuka, *Ito Hirobumi Hiroku*, I, 233–239.

[60]*Jiji Shimpo*, Feb. 5, 1904, p. 3. Throughout the negotiations, the genro, Prince Ito, in particular, and Admiral Yamamoto stood for moderation, but they could not stand any longer (Dr. Tsuboi, *Saikin Seiji Gaikoshi* [Tokyo, 1929], IV, 616–617). As to the Russian side of the negotiations, Count Witte says: "Indeed, on our part, the negotiations were conducted in a fashion which seemed to indicate our desire to compel the Japanese to resort to armed force. While our opponents repeatedly proved their willingness to yield on several points, we were intractable. In spite of the fact that we recognized the essential justice of the Japanese demands, we kept on systematically protracting the negotiations" (*Memoirs of Count Witte*, p. 126).

[61]Sugiyama, *Katsura Taisho Den*, pp. 524–525. *Cf.* Hirota, *op. cit.*, p. 502; also *Jiji Shimpo*, Feb. 6, 1904, p. 3.

At the same time Komura notified the Russian minister, Baron Rosen, of the Japanese decision.[62] Thus, in the evening of the same day, mobilization of three divisions (Konoye, Second, and Twelfth) was ordered, under command of General Kuroki, to proceed immediately to Korea.[63] At noon, February 8, the Japanese squadron attacked Port Arthur, while in the evening, the foreign minister invited press representatives to *Kasumigaseki* to issue a *communiqué* briefly describing the unsuccessful Russo-Japanese negotiations.[64] On February 10, Emperor Meiji issued the declaration of war.[65]

THE DIET AND THE WAR

The general election held on March 1, 1904, was marked by unusual orderliness and absence of partisan disturbances due to the outbreak of the war.[66] The declaration of war and the subsequent developments silenced all partisan politics, and on March 16, on the eve of the Twentieth session of Diet, the major parties passed a resolution pledging their support to all necessary appropriations for prosecution of the war.[67] The Diet approved several emergency war measures taken under Articles 8 and 70 of the Constitution, voted a large war budget, and passed resolutions expressing satisfaction at the military and naval operations.[68]

On March 23, the prime minister, foreign minister, and the finance minister appeared before the House of Representatives and delivered the usual addresses on their respective fields. After a rather detailed account of the negotiations, Foreign Minister Jutaro Komura submitted before the House

[62]Sugiyama, *op. cit.*, p. 525. For Prince Ito's account of pre-war negotiations, see Hiratsuka, *Ito Hirobumi Hiroku* (Tokyo, 1930), II, 153–168.

[63]*Ibid.*, p. 526.

[64]*Gaiko Jiho*, VII, No. 74 (Feb. 20, 1904), p. 1465. Text of the *communiqué* in *ibid.*, pp. 1465–1471.

[65]Text of the imperial rescript declaring war upon Russia in Kudo, *Teikoku Gikaishi*, III, 251. As in the case of the imperial proclamation of war upon China in 1894, the imperial rescript was countersigned by all cabinet ministers.

[66]The parties stood as follows: *Seiyukai*, 134; *Kensei Honto*, 104; *Jiyuto*, 22; *Teikokuto*, 19; *Independents*, 100 (*ibid.*, III, 259).

[67]*Ibid.*, III, 267–271. Following the precedent set at the outbreak of the Sino-Japanese War (Seventh session) in Sept., 1894, the call for the convening of an extraordinary session on March 18 was issued on March 2, 1904 (*ibid.*, III, 272).

[68]For brief summary of the proceedings of the war Diet, see *ibid.*, III, 272–294.

the diplomatic correspondence exchanged between him and Minister Kurino during the negotiations (July 28, 1903, to February 7, 1904).[69] This presentation of diplomatic documents failed to evoke any questions from the floor. The foreign minister repeated his speech in the Upper House three days later, but likewise failed to obtain the usual response from the floor.[70]

Immediately following the addresses by the three cabinet members in the House, Representative Genichi Ogawa moved to appoint a committee of eighteen members to inquire into the charge that Representative Teisuke Akiyama, publisher and editor of the *Niroku Shimpo*, was a Russian spy. It was carried without debate.[71] After examination of evidence outside the Diet and cross-examination of the accused, Chairman Ryo Koyezuka made a report to the House on March 26, declaring that the committee failed to find sufficient evidence to convict Representative Akiyama of the charge made against him, but that the accused was guilty of an action calculated to promote his own personal interest and of Russia and against the interest of Japan. Representative Akiyama made a long speech in self-defense and denied the charge brought against him. He declared that he would not resign his seat in the parliament on the ground that he was a Russian spy, but expressed his willingness to do so assuming responsibility for the "indiscreet" statement he had made in his paper. He pleaded with his colleagues to make this distinction. Members of the House, however, approved the report of the committee with an overwhelming majority. Thereupon, Representative Ogawa again moved to refer Representative Akiyama to the House disciplinary committee, declaring that the article in question not only was an impeachment of the cabinet but an impeachment of the Japanese Empire. Representative Ikuzo Ooka, a leading member of the *Seiyukai* party, moved an amendment to Ogawa's motion. This veteran member of the House pleaded with his colleagues to bury all personal feelings

[69]*Teikoku Gikaishi*, V, 2045–2047. Text of the correspondence presented to the Diet in *ibid.*, V, 2047–2056. *Cf. Gaiko Jiho*, VII, No. 76 (April 5, 1904), pp. 79–142.

[70]*Ibid.*, V, 2018–2020.

[71]*Ibid.*, V, 2056. The charge was made in connection with an article appearing in the *Niroku Shimpo*, March 16, 1904, severely criticizing the government's policy of floating national loans, and predicting Japanese defeat because of financial exhaustion (Kudo, *op. cit.*, III, 289).

in parliamentary deliberations, to be more deliberate and dignified in discussing the status of a member of the House. Thus, he moved that Representative Akiyama should tender his resignation voluntarily for his published article in question. Accordingly, before vote upon Ooka's amendment was taken, Representative Akiyama tendered his resignation.[72]

The period between the close of the Twentieth Diet and the opening of the Twenty-first session on November 28, 1904, was marked by an unusual harmony and unity among parties for the support of the government. Both Houses passed resolutions at the very outset of the session, expressing satisfaction at the victories on both land and sea.[73] The Diet, burying party differences, passed a large war budget, approved various emergency measures taken prior to the calling of the Diet, and offered little embarrassment to the cabinet.[74]

Throughout the session of the Diet, the cabinet adopted the policy of declining to reply to parliamentary interpellations on the progress of the war or upon diplomatic measures adopted concerning the reported violations of neutrality. Thus, the foreign minister failed to deliver the traditional address on foreign relations at the beginning of the Twenty-first Diet. Moreover, he declined to disclose the diplomatic measures undertaken toward neutral powers in connection with the eastward cruise of the Russian Baltic Fleet. On December 7, in the House budget committee, Representative Kungoro Shigeoka shouted that the Russo-Japanese War was not a private war of the cabinet but the people's war. He demanded that the foreign minister should be more earnest in informing the public of the diplomatic progress of the war, and should solicit more intelligent support of the people.[75] Representative Masami Oishi echoed the same sentiment in his long interpellation, but the foreign minister refused to reply in an open meeting, and requested an executive session.[76] On De-

---

[72]Ibid., V, 2083–2087. The House voted for the amendment but failed to vote upon the original motion. Representative Ooka declared that there was no necessity to vote upon his amendment since Akiyama had just resigned, assuming responsibility for his indiscreet statement (ibid., V, 2087).

[73]Ibid., VI, 8, 185.

[74]For the proceedings of the Twenty-first session of The Diet as summarized by Dr. Kudo, see his Teikoku Gikaishi, III, 292–412.

[75]Dai Nijuikkai Teikoku Gikai Shugiin Iinkaigiroku, Pt. I, No. 1, p. 6.

[76]Ibid., pp. 7–9.

cember 5, 1904, Representative Kotaro Mochizuki interpellated the government in the House as to the facts, the progress of diplomatic negotiations, and the future policy concerning the reported violations of neutrality by certain powers, citing several reported instances. The cabinet declined to reply for over two months, and on February 25, 1905, two days before the close of the session, it admitted that diplomatic negotiations had been entered into but refused to state the nature of such negotiations.[77]

Failing to obtain satisfactory replies from the reluctant cabinet concerning the progress of war diplomacy, Representative Yoshiro Kubota introduced a representation resolution in the House on February 9, calling upon the government to make public the diplomatic documents relating to the war within such limits, at such time, and through such means, as deemed advisable. In introducing the resolution, he attacked the secret policy of the administration and declared that the foreign relations should be conducted with full support of the Imperial Diet, that the cabinet was deliberately avoiding consultation with parliamentary opinions upon foreign relations. He further recalled the parliamentary resolutions and interpellations upon revision of unequal treaties in the early period of parliamentary history.[78] In the meetings of the committee to which the resolution was referred, Representative Kubota earnestly pleaded that the cabinet should be more candid and open in informing the Diet of the progress of diplomacy; he warned that, should the government fail to conduct foreign relations to the satisfaction of the public, there would be a violent conflict between the government and the people. He charged that the authorities were failing to make full use of the press in leading the public opinion; and finally, he cited the practice in England, America, and France in support of the legislative participation in foreign relations. In reply, Enjiro Yamaza, chief of the bureau of political affairs of the Foreign Office, defended the practice and declared that the Foreign Office was ready to publish such documents

---

[77] *Teikoku Gikaishi*, VI, 205, 211–214, 463. On Jan. 24, 1905, Dr. Takuzo Hanai bitterly condemned the government's avoidance of taking the Diet into confidence, its tactics of issuing emergency imperial ordinances to avoid parliamentary participation, and its refusal to explain such emergency measures to the Diet, on grounds of the exigencies of the time (*ibid.*, VI, 283).

[78] *Ibid.*, VI, 351–352.

consistent with the public interest of the state.[79] On February 21, Chairman Fukushima made the committee report, unanimously recommending the passage of the resolution, which was adopted by the House without debate.[80]

THE PORTSMOUTH PEACE CONFERENCE

With the victorious battle of Mukden (March 10, 1905), the second period in military operations started, and the Supreme War Council voted to mobilize the forces to occupy Saghalien in the latter part of the same month, but this action was suspended due to the non-coöperation of the navy. Meanwhile, the war resources of Japan were completely exhausted by the end of March; and the country was in no position to continue the war for another year. This would have required additional 250,000 men and 1,500,000,000 yen, and there was no definite assurance that this amount was forthcoming.[81] The high military authorities were well aware of the critical situation. Thus, General Kodama, chief of staff of the Manchurian expeditionary forces, made a secret return to Tokyo soon after the battle of Mukden and told the military and civil leaders that those who started the war should know when to stop it and urged them to seek an early opportunity to terminate it.[82]

The battle of the Japan Sea of May 27, in which the Russian fleet met a decisive defeat, gave a new impetus to the situation. On May 31, Foreign Minister Komura instructed Minister Takahira to ask President Roosevelt "directly and of his own motion and initiative to invite the two belligerents to come together for the purpose of direct negotiations."[83]

[79]*Dai Nijuikkai Teikoku Gikai Shugiin Iinkaigiroku*, Pt. VI, No. 15.

[80]*Teikoku Gikaishi*, VI, 437.

[81]Marshal Yamagata (chief of staff), Marshal Oyama (commander of the Japanese expeditionary forces), and General Kodama (chief of staff of the Japanese expeditionary forces) all advocated peace. Japan had already spent 2,000,000,000 yen, of which 1,450,000 yen was raised in London and New York. No further sum was forthcoming (Komatsu, *Meiji Shijitsu Gaiko Hiwa* [Tokyo, 1927], p. 352).

[82]Shinobu, *Gaiko Sokumenshi Dan*, pp. 267–272, 293–294. *Cf.* Tokutomi, *Sanju Hichihachinen Seneki to Gaiko* (Tokyo, 1925), pp. 107–108.

[83]Foreign Minister Komura to Minister Takahira, May 31, 1905 (cited in Dennett, *Roosevelt and the Russo-Japanese War* [New York, 1925], p. 215). On May 30, Premier Katsura and Foreign Minister Komura called on Prince Ito, president of the Privy Council, after which a cabinet meeting was called (*Tokyo Asahi*, May 31, 1905, p. 2).

On June 9, 1905, President Roosevelt formally extended his good offices to Tokyo and St. Petersburg.[84] The invitation was promptly accepted by Japan on June 10,[85] and by Russia on June 12.[86]

Public opinion did not welcome the President's invitation, as it was generally believed that the time was not ripe for peace. However, with the acceptance of the good offices of the President, the public attention was directed to the terms of peace. Various individuals, associations, and organizations expressed their views concerning the approaching conference. They generally agreed upon the following: (1) war indemnity of 3,000,000,000 yen; (2) cession of the whole of Saghalien and Maritime Province; (3) transfer of the Russian leasehold in Manchuria, evacuation of troops, and renunciation of all her rights and interests there; (5) surrender of all Russian vessels then in neutral ports; (6) limitations upon Russian navy in the Pacific and the Japan Sea; (7) no cession or lease of Chinese territory without the consent of Japan; (8) no armistice before signing a peace treaty, and (9) the peace conference to be held in Japan or at a place chosen by her.[87]

The attitude of the two major political parties was very general and noncommittal as to concrete terms of peace. However, on June 28, 1905, both the *Seiyukai* and the *Kensei Honto* issued declarations in which they enumerated adequate indemnity, cession of territory, and solution of the Manchurian question as constituting the essential conditions for the conclusion of a peace treaty.[88] While the major parties refused to declare themselves definitely upon concrete demands to be presented at the conference, such non-partisan associations as *Tairo Doshikai* passed resolutions, issued manifestos, and held mass meetings throughout the country to arouse the public against "dishonorable peace" and for continuation of

[84]Dennett, *op. cit.*, pp. 224–225.

[85]*Ibid.*, pp. 225–226 (*cf. Tokyo Asahi*, June 11, 1905, p. 2). On June 8 and 9, high treasury authorities met with the premier and war minister (*Tokyo Asahi*, June 9, 11, 1905). War authorities held a meeting on June 9 to deliberate upon the invitation, and the views of the army were reported to Emperor Meiji on June 9 and 10 (*ibid.*, June 10, 1905, p. 2; *ibid.*, June 11, 1905, p. 3).

[86]Dennett, *op. cit.*, p. 226.

[87]Kudo, *Teikoku Gikaishi*, III, 442–443.

[88]*Ibid.*, III, 443; *Tokyo Asahi*, June 29, 1905, pp. 2, 3.

war until complete subjugation of the enemy had been achieved.[89]

In view of the delicate nature of the negotiations at the conference, the cabinet encountered some difficulty in selecting the plenipotentiaries. At first, Prime Minister Katsura desired to send Prince Ito, president of the Privy Council and a leading statesman, but he declined the offer on the ground that the cabinet ministers who had conducted the war should also assume the responsibility for concluding peace.[90] After numerous conferences and meetings of the genro, cabinet ministers, and high military and naval authorities, the Japanese conditions and terms of peace to be presented at the conference were finally decided at the cabinet meeting on June 30.[91] On July 3, Foreign Minister Komura and Minister Takahira were appointed plenipotentiaries.[92] On the following day, an important meeting was called at the official residence of Premier Katsura to deliberate upon final details of the negotiations. The meeting was attended by four genro (Ito, Yamagata, Inouye, Matsukata), Premier Katsura, Foreign Minister Komura, War Minister Terauchi, and Navy Minister Yamamoto.[93] After obtaining imperial sanction, the Japanese conditions and terms of peace were formally set forth in the instructions issued to Envoy Komura on July 5.[94] The party started on their unwelcome mission on July 8, 1905.[95]

While the diplomatic preliminary negotiations were being conducted between Tokyo and Washington, Prince Ito and Foreign Minister Komura were successful in winning the general staff to the occupation of Saghalien prior to the actual commencement of peace negotiations, in order to obtain a

[89]Kudo, op. cit., III, 444–445.

[90]Cf. Tokyo Asahi, June 16, 19, 25, 1905, p. 2.

[91]Ibid., June 13, 14, 16, 19, 22, 24, 25, July 1, 1905, p. 2.

[92]Ibid., July 4, 1905, p. 2.

[93]Ibid., July 5, 1905, p. 2.

[94]The Japanese terms of peace were divided into three categories. As the minimum demands, Japanese delegates were to insist upon: (1) Japanese dominance in Korea, (2) withdrawal of Russian troops from Manchuria, and (3) succession to the Russian leasehold of Kwantung Peninsula and the operation of the Chinese Eastern Railway south of Harbin. Other conditions were not considered indispensable (Tokutomi, Seijika to shiteno Katsurako [Tokyo, 1913], pp. 146–147; Dr. Tsuboi, op. cit., pp. 667–668; Shinobu, Gaiko Sokumenshi Dan, pp. 279–281).

[95]Tokyo Asahi, July 9, 1905, p. 2.

diplomatic advantage at the conference.[96] Thus, upon receiving a telegram from General Kodama, of the Manchurian expeditionary forces, strongly urging an immediate occupation of the island, General Yamagata, chief of general staff, finally agreed to the move, and on July 7 Japanese troops were landed in the island.[97] On July 8 an emergency imperial ordinance was issued for the purpose of floating a 300,000,000 yen national loan in London for war expenditure.[98]

The plenipotentiaries of both countries arrived at Portsmouth, New Hampshire, on August 5, 1905; and on August 9 they held the first meeting to agree upon the language, time, and other preliminary details of the conference. On August 10 the first formal session was held and the Japanese terms of peace were presented to the Russian plenipotentiaries.[99] Altogether twelve sessions were held, besides several private conferences between Baron Komura and Count Witte. The negotiations were largely upon two items, namely, the cession of Saghalien and payment of indemnity.[100] President Roosevelt played an important part throughout the conference, and particularly exerted a strong influence upon the Japanese government to withdraw its demand for indemnity.[101]

The so-called last meeting of the conference was held on August 26, when Count Witte continued to decline the payment of indemnity. In consequence, the meeting was postponed till August 28. Immediately after the session on August 26, Baron Komura telegraphed Tokyo, declaring that he was leaving New York should Russia refuse the last demand on August 28.[102] The report of the meeting of August

[96] For meetings of high military and naval authorities, see *ibid.*, June 13, 14, 15, 19, 20, 23, 1905, p. 2.

[97] Shinobu, *op. cit.*, pp. 272–274 (see also *Tokyo Asahi*, July 11, 1905, p. 2).

[98] Imperial Ordinance No. 194, 1905. For parliamentary debates upon this emergency measure in the Twenty-second session of the Diet, see *Teikoku Gikaishi*, VI, 573, 588, 737, 835–840. *Cf.* government explanations to political leaders in *Tokyo Asahi*, July 15, 1905, p. 2.

[99] *Tokyo Asahi*, Aug. 11, 12, 14, 1905, p. 2.

[100] For frequent meetings of the cabinet, genro, and military authorities during these days, see *ibid.*, Aug. 20, 21, 23, 24, 25, 1905, p. 2.

[101] For an account of the part President Roosevelt played during the war, see Dennett, *Roosevelt and the Russo-Japanese War* (New York, 1925). On the Portsmouth Conference, see *ibid.*, pp. 236–277.

[102] Shinobu, *Gaiko Sokumenshi Dan*, pp. 290 ff.

26 reached Tokyo about 8 P.M., August 27. Alarmed by the seriousness of the situation, a joint conference of the genro and the cabinet was immediately called at the home of Prince Ito, lasting till 1:30 the following morning;[103] and an extraordinary cabinet meeting was called early in the morning, with the genro in attendance.[104] Finally, at a joint meeting of the genro, cabinet, and high military and naval authorities, held in His Majesty's presence at two o'clock in the afternoon, it was decided to conclude peace even if Japan had to withdraw her demands for cession of Saghalien and payment of indemnity. Prime Minister Katsura (acting foreign minister in the absence of Baron Komura at the conference) immediately sent instructions in accordance with the decision thus made.[105] Meanwhile, Viscount Ishii, then chief of the commercial bureau of the Foreign Office, obtained confidential information about noon of August 27 concerning the nature of a personal interview of Ambassador Meyer with the Tsar on August 23, when the latter was reported to have intimated that the southern half of Saghalien might honorably be ceded to Japan.[106] He immediately called on the prime minister to report the information just obtained from a diplomat, and suggested that a telegram be sent immediately to Baron Komura to postpone the scheduled meeting of August 28 to the following day, to be followed by another telegram instructing the plenipotentiaries to demand the cession of the southern half of the island. Having been assured of the reliability of the information, Katsura gave consent to the move, and consequently, after reporting to Chinda, the two telegrams were dispatched to Portsmouth.[107]

Baron Komura was determined to break off the negotiations if Russia continued to be obstinate. Thus, in telegrams

[103]The following were present: Ito, Yamagata, Inouye (genro); Prime Minister Katsura (acting foreign minister), War Minister Terauchi, Navy Minister Yamamoto, Vice-minister of Foreign Affairs Chinda (*Tokyo Asahi*, Aug. 29, 1905, p. 2).

[104]Three genro (Ito, Yamagata, Inouye) attended the extraordinary meeting of the cabinet called at 8 A.M., Aug. 28. At two o'clock in the afternoon the cabinet and the genro met in the palace with chiefs of staffs of both services in attendance (*ibid.*, Aug. 29, 1905, p. 2).

[105]Viscount Ishii, *Gaiko Yoroku*, p. 82. Viscount Ishii was at this time chief of the commercial bureau and also head of the telegraphic section of the Foreign Office.

[106]Meyer to Roosevelt, Aug. 23, 1905 (cited in Dennett, *op. cit.*, p. 270).

[107]Viscount Ishii, *op. cit.*, p. 83.

dispatched to Tokyo during the night of August 29, he reported to the home government that there was no sign of Russian concession, and that there was no other course left than to break off the negotiations and to resume the war. He insisted that any other course would be humiliating to the national honor of Japan. However, high military and naval authorities at home and on the field were united in opposition to the continuation of the conflict. General Kodama, chief of staff of the Manchurian forces, wired several times from the front during the negotiations at Portsmouth, demanding that the government should make peace, while Admiral Yamamoto, navy minister, vehemently supported the general in cabinet meetings.[108] Under the circumstances, there was no choice for the Katsura cabinet but to instruct the representatives at the conference to conclude peace. Greatly disappointed, Baron Komura obeyed the instructions against his own will on August 29, 1905.[109] On September 1, a protocol concerning the armistice was signed, and on September 12, the armistice was issued by the commander-in-chief of the Manchurian forces.[110] On September 5, the treaty of peace was signed at Portsmouth between the plenipotentiaries, subject to ratification by the respective sovereigns.[111]

RATIFICATION OF THE TREATY OF PORTSMOUTH

As soon as the nature of the terms of the treaty just concluded became known, spontaneous and unanimous dissatisfaction was expressed by all the leading press, and an instantaneous popular indignation at the government was forthcoming. The bitterness of the press comment was partly due to the policy of the Japanese plenipotentiaries at the conference of avoiding press interviews and of failing to utilize their services. Thus, in the editorial columns on September 1 and 2, 1905, such leading papers as the *Tokyo Asahi, Osaka, Asahi, Nippon, Jiji Shimpo, Tokyo Nichi*

[108]*Op. cit.*, p. 86. *Cf.* Shinobu, *Gaiko Sokumenshi Dan*, p. 292; also an anonymous article in *Tokyo Asahi*, Sept. 1, 1905, p. 2.

[109]Kudo, *Teikoku Gikaishi*, III, 467. *Cf.* Dr. Nagao Ariga, "The Conclusion of Peace," *Gaiko Jiho*, VIII, No. 95 (Oct. 10, 1905), pp. 268–270; *Tokyo Asahi*, Aug. 30, 31, Sept. 1, 1905, p. 2.

[110]Kudo, *op. cit.*, p. 468.

[111]*Ibid.*

Nichi, Osaka Mainichi, Tokyo Mainichi, Hochi, Mancho, and *Miyako* vigorously criticized the terms of the treaty and advocated its rejection.[112] Only the *Chuo,* party organ of the *Seiyukai* (government party), urged restraint and caution in criticism and comment, while the *Kokumin Shimbun,* a semi-official paper, praised the treaty and expressed satisfaction with its terms, declaring that the objects of the war had been attained.[113] On the other hand, several voluntary associations and organizations began an active campaign throughout the country to arouse the public against ratification of the treaty. Most noteworthy of these was the *Kowa Mondai Rengo Doshikai,* or a joint council of anti-peace associations.[114] It issued a manifesto on August 31, strongly attacking the treaty as nullifying the fruits of victory and demanding the resignation of the cabinet and the plenipotentiaries. At the same time it sent a telegram to Baron Komura demanding his immediate resignation. It presented a memorial to the emperor requesting his rejection of the treaty in accordance with the general trend of public opinion, and recalled his refusal to ratify a revised treaty drafted by Okuma in the 1890's.[115]

On September 5, a mass meeting of the citizens of Tokyo was called at Hibiya Park, but the gates were closed by order of the Home Office and guarded by the police. The indignant public broke through the iron gates and gained admittance to the park. Here they unanimously passed resolutions approving the manifesto issued by the *Kowa Mondai Rengo Doshikai* on August 31, and demanded that the Privy Council recommend to the throne rejection of the treaty. As the evening approached, the movement took on a more violent and irresponsible character, and throughout the city many collisions took place between the guards and the people; several police stations were set on fire, while the *Kokumin Shimbun-sha,* publishers of the semi-official organ which defended the cabinet throughout the war, was destroyed by fire. The casualties amounted to about 500 police

[112]Ono, *Nihon Shimbun Hattatsushi,* pp. 297–303.

[113]*Ibid.,* pp. 303–304.

[114]Among the more influential leaders of this council, Mitsuru Toyama, Kinosuke Yamada, Hironaka Kono, Kanichi Otake, Shigeto Suzuki may be noted.

[115]Kudo, *Teikoku Gikaishi,* III, 471–472.

and 600 people, while several hundred arrests were made during the day.[116] To prevent further public demonstrations and mob violence throughout the country, an extraordinary meeting of the cabinet was held on September 6 to issue emergency imperial ordinances to meet the situation. Thus, an extraordinary meeting of the Privy Council was called late in the afternoon to pass upon two emergency imperial ordinances declaring martial law in and around Tokyo, and also placing strict censorship upon the press.[117] Immediately after the meeting of the Council, Imperial Ordinances Nos. 205 and 206 were issued.[118] Thus, for the first time since the restoration of 1868, the capital was placed under martial law, and many newspapers were suspended for attacking the government upon the terms of the treaty.[119]

On September 7, more than one hundred members of the Lower House called on the prime minister and demanded that an extraordinary session of Diet be called in order to lay before it the details of the peace negotiations and to formulate the post-war program with the people; they also demanded an immediate suspension of the martial law and restoration of the freedom of the press. The prime minister declared that the government intended to call an extra session after the ratification of the treaty and return of the plenipotentiaries.[120] The following day the cabinet invited members of both Houses and press representatives for a conference and disclosed to them the terms of the treaty which had been kept secret. This move was intended to obtain their "understanding" regarding the treaty, but failed, as the government disclosed nothing beyond what was already known through the press.[121] Soon after the "informal disclosure" of the terms of the treaty, representatives of various factions of the Upper House held a conference and decided that the

---

[116]*Tokyo Asahi*, Sept. 6, 1905, p. 2.

[117]*Ibid.*, Sept. 7, 1905, p. 2.

[118]Text of the ordinances in *Horei Zensho*, 1905, *Chokurei*, pp. 293–295. *Cf. Tokyo Asahi*, Sept. 8, 1905, p. 5. These ordinances were abolished on November 29 (*ibid.*, Nov. 30, 1905, p. 5).

[119]Kudo, *op. cit.*, III, 475–484; Hirota, *Naikaku Kotetsu Gojunenshi*, pp. 503–507. For trials of the leaders, see Dr. Takuzo Hanai, *Shotei Ronso: Kokumin Taikai Jiken* (Tokyo, 1930), pp. 1–244.

[120]Kudo, *op. cit.*, III, 488.

[121]*Ibid.*, III, 484.

government was responsible for the outbreak of riotous disturbances. Several members called on cabinet ministers demanding the resignation of the home minister and the commissioner general of the metropolitan police board.[122]

What were the attitudes of political parties towards the treaty? The *Seiyukai*, the majority party which supported the ministry, was rather noncommittal. However, at the meeting of the party on September 2, Prince Saionji, its president, lauded the Portsmouth Treaty as satisfactory and promoting the cause of peace.[123] Though some dissatisfaction was felt among members of the party, no organized objection was raised against its president's speech. On the other hand, the *Kensei Honto* made its opposition to the treaty by demanding the resignation of the cabinet but failed to go so far as to urge the rejection of the treaty. Other parties were silent upon this question.[124]

To counteract the popular dissatisfaction with the peace treaty, the government made public, on September 27, the revised Anglo-Japanese Alliance which was signed on August 12 in London, but it failed to produce any appreciable degree of favorable effect upon the public.[125] Now, the government took immediate steps to push the treaty through the Privy Council. Innumerable petitions and letters, as well as personal calls, were made upon individual councilors to defeat the treaty, and so when the treaty was submitted to the Council at its unofficial meeting, several councilors violently attacked the treaty, but they recognized that to defeat the treaty after signature would be contrary to international good faith and decided to recommend its ratification.[126] Accordingly, at its plenary session of October 4, the Privy Council promptly approved the treaty without any debate or discussion whatsoever.[127] The text of the treaty reached

[122]*Ibid.*, III, 489. The commissioner resigned on September 10, while the home minister resigned on Sept. 16.

[123]*Tokyo Asahi*, Sept. 3, 1932, p. 4.

[124]Kudo, *op. cit.*, III, 489–492. Before the end of September, 1905, several hundred declarations, resolutions, and memorials were made, of which three fourths categorically urged the rejection of the treaty, while only four admitted the inevitability of the peace as concluded (*ibid.*, III, 492).

[125]*Tokyo Asahi*, Sept. 27, 1905, p. 2. *Cf.* Kudo, *op. cit.*, III, 500–504; Dr. Hanai, *Shotei Ronso: Kokumin Taikai Jiken*, pp. 155–156.

[126]*Tokyo Asahi*, Oct. 2, 1905, p. 2.

[127]Kudo, *op. cit.*, III, 492–493. *Cf. Tokyo Asahi*, Oct. 5, 1905, p. 2.

Yokohama late at night on October 5, and Baron Komura returned to Tokyo on October 16, under heavy guard. Whereupon, the emperor issued an imperial message expressing his satisfaction with the peace treaty. The treaty was ratified on October 14 and promulgated two days later.[128]

The treaty of peace having been ratified and promulgated, the Katsura cabinet was ready to resign, and consequently, at a joint conference of the cabinet and the genro, it was decided that the cabinet should solve the problems regarding Manchuria and Korea arising out of the war before tendering its general resignation. This decision was reported to the emperor. Thus, Prince Ito, president of the Privy Council, went to Seoul to conclude a convention to insure the predominant position of Japan in Korea. A convention was signed on November 17 whereby Japan assumed the control of Korean foreign relations. This received prompt approval of the Privy Council and was promulgated on November 23, 1905. Baron Komura, the foreign minister throughout the war and the principal delegate to the Portsmouth Peace Conference, assumed the responsibility for conducting the direct negotiations in Peking to conclude a convention with China under the terms of the peace treaty. After twenty sittings, a convention was signed on December 22, and ratified by the emperor on January 10, after favorable action by the Privy Council on January 6, 1906.[129]

A telegram from Peking reporting the completion of negotiations reached Tokyo on December 18, 1905. The following day the prime minister invited Prince Saionji to meet him and informed him of his intention to resign. Katsura requested Saionji to succeed him in the premiership. After obtaining a favorable response from two of the most influential genro (Prince Ito and Prince Yamagata), Prince Saionji called on Prime Minister Katsura on December 20 and formally accepted the task. At the cabinet meeting held on December 21, the resignation was decided upon, but was postponed till the return of the foreign minister from Peking.[130] Meanwhile, on December 28, the Twenty-second

[128]Text of the treaty in *Traités et conventions entre l'empire du Japon et les puissances étrangères* (Tokyo, Foreign Office, 1908), Pt. I, pp. 585–597.

[129]*Ibid.*, pp. 504–514.

[130]*Tokyo Asahi*, Dec. 20, 21, 22, 1905, p. 2.

session of Diet was opened under the Katsura cabinet, but it soon adjourned for the New Year recess. Komura returned on January 1, and the government made public the proceedings of the Portsmouth Peace Conference on January 6. At the same time the emperor ratified the Sino-Japanese Treaty.[131]

With the ratification of the treaty with China and the publication of the proceedings of the Peace Conference, Katsura completed his task, and on the same day the cabinet resigned.[132] Thus, the long and violent conflict between the government and the people ended. Accordingly, although the record of the proceedings of the Peace Conference at Portsmouth was presented to the Diet immediately upon expiration of the recess, no parliamentary interpellations were put to the Saionji ministry from the floor of either House upon the treaty. No formal address on foreign relations was made by the incoming foreign minister, while the prime minister deliberately omitted any direct reference to the Peace Conference in his address to the Imperial Diet upon the state of the nation.[133]

[131]Text of the treaty in *Traités et conventions entre l'empire du Japon et les puissances étrangères*, Pt. I, pp. 532–534. For the published text of the proceedings, see *Teikoku Gikaishi*, VI, 502–518.

[132]Hanai, *op. cit., Supplement*, pp. 33–34.

[133]Throughout the period, no express criticism of President Roosevelt was voiced in the press. The attacks were directed against the government. On the other hand, it was evident that Roosevelt's part in the peace negotiations was highly appreciated by the cabinet and the genro (Viscount Ishii, *Gaiko Yoroku*, pp. 88–90).

Chapter XIII

THE ANNEXATION OF KOREA

THAT THE JAPANESE annexation of Korea was destined to take place was indicated as early as the Eighth session of the Diet. Thus, in reply to an interpellation made in the House of Representatives on February 22, 1895, Prime Minister Hirobumi Ito merely expressed his opinion that the powers had no objection to the continued existence of Korea as an independent state and purposely declined to commit the government upon the question of Korean independence.[1] With the express recognition of the Korean independence by China under the Treaty of Shimonoseki, the Japanese position in Korea became even stronger. Accordingly, Prime Minister Ito, during the session of the Diet immediately following the close of the war, deliberately refused to state whether the cabinet was prepared to protect the independence of Korea by resorting to arms should such independence be threatened by the powers.[2] Foreign Minister Okuma of the succeeding ministry likewise declined to commit the government on this question.[3]

During the years between the close of the Sino-Japanese War and the beginning of the Russo-Japanese War, the Japanese interests were gradually increased in Korea, and in February, 1900, both Houses of the Diet passed representation resolutions calling upon the government to take effective

[1]*Teikoku Gikaishi*, III, 766. Cf. *Japan Weekly Mail*, March 2, 1895, pp. 242, 247.
[2]*Ibid.*, III, 988, 1473–1474, 1638–1640, 1790–1791, 1995.
[3]January 22, 1897 (*Dai Jikkai Teikoku Gikai Shugiin Iinkai Sokkiroku*, p. 37).

measures to complete the construction of a railroad between Seoul and Fusan.[4]

Her political, military, and economic interests in Korea having been expressly recognized in the revised Anglo-Japanese Alliance of 1905[5] and in the Treaty of Portsmouth,[6] Japan proceeded to conclude an agreement with Korea to incorporate this new position immediately following the ratification of the peace treaty. Thus, after some preliminary negotiations through Minister Hayashi in Seoul, Prince Ito, president of the Privy Council, left Tokyo in early November, 1905, in order to be personally in charge of conducting the negotiations with Korea.[7] In his personal interview with the king on November 15, Prince Ito presented a draft agreement of protectorate. It was formally presented to the Korean government the following day. Thereupon, a meeting of the Korean cabinet was called in the afternoon in the presence of the king to deliberate upon the Japanese proposal. General Hasegawa, commander of the Japanese troops in Korea, Prince Ito, and Minister Hayashi were all present throughout the session of the meeting. It lasted until two o'clock of the following morning (November 18), when the king finally consented to sign the draft agreement prepared by Japan.[8] An extraordinary meeting of the Privy Council was called on November 22, when it promptly accepted the explanations offered by Prime Minister Katsura on the agreement.[9] With His Majesty's sanction, the agreement was immediately made public on November 23.[10] Upon his return to Tokyo on December 8, Prince Ito was received in audience by the emperor to make a detailed report of the negotiations in Seoul.[11] On December 11, a joint conference of the genro and the cabinet was held at the premier's official residence,

---

[4] *Teikoku Gikaishi*, V, 171–172, 178, 609–611.

[5] Art. 3.

[6] Art. 2.

[7] Prince Ito left Tokyo on November 5 and reached Seoul on Nov. 9, 1905 (*Tokyo Asahi*, Nov. 6, 11, 1905, p. 2).

[8] *Tokyo Asahi*, Nov. 16, 17, 18, 19, 20, 1905, p. 2.

[9] *Ibid.*, Nov. 23, 1905, p. 2.

[10] Foreign Office Notification No. 6, 1905 (Nov. 23, 1905). *Cf. Tokyo Asahi*, Nov. 25, 1905, p. 5.

[11] *Tokyo Asahi*, Dec. 9, 1905, p. 3.

when Prince Ito made a detailed report upon the agreement, and Prime Minister Katsura upon the progress of the negotiations being conducted in Peking.[12] Under this agreement the control of diplomatic relations of Korea was transferred to Tokyo.[13] Thus, on December 21, the *Tokanfu oyobi Rijicho Kansei* was issued, under which Prince Ito was appointed first resident general of Korea. On the same day, the external relations of Korea were placed under the supervision of the Foreign Office in Tokyo.[14]

The next episode which precipitated the annexation was the dispatch of a secret mission by the king to the Second Hague Conference to lay the Korean case before it and to invite the assistance of the powers to free Korea from Japanese control. The speeches and activities of this mission were first reported by Shingoro Takaishi, special correspondent of the *Osaka Mainichi* at the conference.[15] Numerous telegrams were exchanged between Prince Ito, resident general of Korea, and the home government in Tokyo, and on July 10, 1907, an important joint meeting of the genro and the cabinet was held at the official residence of the prime minister, Prince Saionji, to determine the policy to be pursued in Korea.[16] As a result of this meeting, Foreign Minister Tadasu Hayashi left Tokyo for Seoul and, on July 18, called on Prince Ito to report the decision of the government.[17] The personal journey of the foreign minister to Korea and the unusual activities of the cabinet in Tokyo greatly stirred the public, while political parties passed resolutions and

[12]*Op. cit.*, Dec. 12, 1905, p. 2.

[13]Hiratsuka, *Ito Hirobumi Hiroku*, I, 313–316, 321–324. *Cf.* Kudo, *Teikoku Gikaishi*, III, 505–508. On the foreign relations power under the agreement, see Dr. Sakutaro Tachi, "The Japanese-Korean Agreement and the Treaty-Making Power," *Kokka Gakkai Zasshi*, XXI, No. 7 (July, 1907), pp. 835–844.

[14]Imperial Ordinance No. 267, 1905 (Dec. 21, 1905). The ordinance was approved by the Privy Council on Dec. 20. On the following day, Prince Ito was appointed resident general, while his presidency of the Council was succeeded by Marshal Yamagata (*Tokyo Asahi*, Dec. 22, 1905, p. 2).

[15]Ono, *Nihon Shimbun Hattatsushi*, p. 522. The Japanese prevented the attendance of the Koreans at the conference. *Cf. Tokyo Asahi*, July 6, 9, 13, 1907, p. 2.

[16]At this conference, the genro was represented by Yamagata, Oyama, Inouye, and Matsukata, while the cabinet was represented by all its members. In addition to the genro and the cabinet members, Count Katsura was also present.

[17]*Tokyo Asahi*, July 16, 17, 18, 19, 1907, p. 2.

sent representatives to the prime minister to adopt a "decisive policy" toward Korea.[18]

The Saionji ministry left Prince Ito a free hand in meeting the situation. On July 20 the king was forced to abdicate the throne in favor of his son,[19] followed by conclusion of an agreement, on July 24, whereby the Japanese resident general became a virtual regent.[20] Under the terms of this brief agreement all matters of internal administration as well as foreign relations were brought under the complete control of the Japanese resident general in Seoul.[21] This new agreement was notified to all the treaty powers of Korea on July 25.[22] On August 30, an important conference of Resident General Ito, Marshal Yamagata (president of the Privy Council), Matsukata, Inouye, Katsura, and all the members of the Saionji cabinet was held at the official residence of the prime minister, to hear the report of Prince Ito on the Korean affair and to formulate general policies to be pursued regarding Korea.[23] Thus the dispatch of a secret mission to the Hague Conference only hastened a further dominance and control of Japan over the kingdom.[24]

[18]Haruichiro Matsumiya, "The Korean Political Upheaval," *Gaiko Jiho*, X, Nos. 9–11 (Sept.–Nov., 1907), pp. 504–518, 586–598, 654–666.

[19]*Tokyo Asahi*, July 20, 21, 22, 1907, p. 2.

[20]On July 23, a conference of Yamagata, Oyama, Inouye, Matsukata (genro), Katsura (ex-premier), Saionji, Terauchi, Saito, Sakatani, Hara, Matsuda, Yamagata, Makino, Matsuoka (cabinet members), and Chinda (vice-minister of foreign affairs) was called at the premier's residence to deliberate upon the telegrams received from Resident General Ito and General Hasegawa (commander of the Japanese troops in Korea) and to discuss the question of dispatching additional forces upon request (*ibid.*, July 24, 1907, p. 4). On the afternoon of July 24, Vice-Admiral Teragaki, commander of the Second squadron, called on Prince Ito; in the evening, all the Korean cabinet ministers called on the resident general, resulting in the signing of an agreement between the Korean prime minister and Prince Ito in the early morning of July 25 (*ibid.*, July 26, 1907, p. 2).

[21]The agreement was composed of seven articles. On September 20, an ordinance was issued greatly increasing the powers of the Japanese resident general in Korea (Imperial Ordinance No. 295, 1907. Text in *Horei Zensho*, 1907, *Chokurei*, pp. 377–379).

[22]*Tokyo Asahi*, July 26, 1907, p. 4. On July 25, a meeting of Yamagata, Oyama, Matsukata, Inouye, Katsura, and members of the Saionji cabinet was held, after which Prince Yamagata, president of the Privy Council, and Prime Minister Saionji were received in audience by the emperor (*ibid.*). On the following day an extraordinary meeting of the Privy Council was held to approve the new agreement already signed. This was promptly done (*ibid.*).

[23]*Ibid.*, Aug. 31, 1907, p. 4.

[24]Matsumiya in *Gaiko Jiho*, X, 588–598 (Oct., 1907). *Cf.* Hirota, *Naikaku Kotetsu Gojunenshi*, p. 518.

Prince Ito was disappointed at the results of his administration in Korea as resident general and, by the spring of 1909, annexation of the peninsula seemed unavoidable. Meanwhile, seeing the necessity of determining the government policy on the question, Foreign Minister Komura, with the assistance of the chief of the political affairs bureau of the Foreign Office, prepared a long memorandum on Korea strongly recommending its annexation at an early opportunity. It soon obtained the support of both Premier Katsura and Prince Ito.[25] On June 14, 1909, Prince Ito resigned his post and became president of the Privy Council, Viscount Sone succeeding in his post in Korea.[26] On July 7 the memorandum prepared by the foreign minister was placed before the cabinet for its approval, after which it was presented to the emperor for his sanction. Having received the imperial sanction to the general policy decided upon in the cabinet, Foreign Minister Komura prepared memoranda upon the form of the declaration of annexation, the fate of the king, administrative policy to be followed, foreign relations, and other matters. These were presented to the cabinet for deliberation and approval. The cabinet held several meetings upon the question and even decided upon the measures to be taken in case the annexation could not be brought about by treaty.[27]

The assassination of Prince Ito at Harbin by a Korean fanatic on October 26, 1909, produced a profound effect upon the public in Japan and in Korea.[28] A powerful association called *Taikan Doshikai* was organized by the more enthusiastic annexationists in Japan who exerted a large influence in arousing popular demand for immediate annexation, while Resident General Sone took alarm at the popular opinion so spontaneously aroused. On May 30, 1910, Viscount Sone resigned his office on the ground of ill-health, and was succeeded by General Terauchi, a leading militarist who had served as war minister in all cabinets since 1902.[29]

[25]Shinobu, *Gaiko Sokumenshi Dan*, pp. 357–361.

[26]*Chuo Koron*, No. 250 (Jan., 1910), p. 322.

[27]Shinobu, *op. cit.*, pp. 366–367. *Cf. Tokyo Asahi*, July 2, 16, 20, 23, 25, 1909, p. 2.

[28]*Tokyo Asahi*, Oct. 27, 1909, p. 2. For press views upon the assassination, see *Japan Weekly Mail*, Nov. 13, 1909, p. 605.

[29]General Terauchi retained his post of war minister. Isaburo Yamagata, adopted son of Prince Yamagata, was appointed vice-res'dent general on the same day (*Tokyo Asahi*, May 31, 1910, p. 2).

The cabinet, at its meeting of June 3, decided its general administrative policy to be pursued after annexation. On June 14, a sweeping change was made in high governmental posts, followed by a dispatch of 600 gendarmes to Korea on June 17.[30] The following day, Prime Minister Katsura announced the intended annexation of Korea to the press.[31] A few days later, a bureau of colonial affairs was established under the direct supervision of the prime minister himself.[32] Accordingly, by the end of the month, the entire kingdom was under strict control of the gendarmerie, in preparation for the final step.[33] On July 8, the cabinet finished its deliberations upon the proposed treaty of annexation, the declaration to be issued, the name of the kingdom, the status of the Korean subjects, and other details connected therewith.[34]

All important preliminary preparations having been completed, General Terauchi left Tokyo on July 15 and arrived at Seoul on July 23 under heavy guard.[35] All organs of public opinion were suspended or ruthlessly suppressed. On August 13, General Terauchi telegraphed the foreign minister, informing him that he was ready and inquiring whether the *Kasumigaseki* was prepared for opening negotiations. Upon receiving a favorable reply, Viscount Terauchi formally opened the discussion on the subject with the Korean government.[36] Several conferences were held between General Terauchi and Prime Minister Ye Wan Yong of Korea, and

[30]The newly appointed resident general of Korea, General Terauchi, held a reception party, on June 15, and invited Marshal Yamagata, Marshal Oyama, Fleet-Admiral Ito, Counts Okuma and Itagaki, all the members of the cabinet (Katsura), vice-ministers of the departments, and other high officers (*ibid.*, June 16, 1910, p. 2).

[31]An extraordinary meeting of the cabinet was called on June 18 (*ibid.*, June 19, 1910, p. 2). For suppression of the press in Seoul see *ibid.*, June 20, 1910, p. 2.

[32]On June 17, an extraordinary meeting of the Privy Council was held to deliberate on the ordinance (*ibid.*, June 18, 1910, p. 2). The ordinance was issued on June 22, and Premier Katsura and Communications Minister Shimpei Goto were appointed director and vice-director, respectively (*ibid.*, June 23, 1910, p. 3).

[33]Shinobu, *Gaiko Sokumenshi Dan*, pp. 372–374; Hirota, *op. cit.*, pp. 582–585.

[34]Shinobu, *op. cit.*, p. 373.

[35]*Ibid.*, p. 374; *Tokyo Asahi*, July 16, 24, 1910, p. 2. On July 12, Premier Katsura held a farewell reception in honor of the departing resident general. Among those present were: Yamagata, Inouye, Matsukata, ministers and vice-ministers of departments, chiefs of staffs of both services, and others (*Tokyo Asahi*, July 13, 1910, p. 2).

[36]The cabinet held extraordinary conferences on August 18 and 19 to discuss the Korean question (*ibid.*, Aug. 19, 1910, p. 3; Aug. 20, 1910, p. 2).

on the evening of August 20 the resident general telegraphed to Tokyo the final text of a draft treaty of annexation and requested that it be submitted to the emperor for his sanction. Apropos of the impending change, an extraordinary meeting of the Privy Council was held on August 22 in His Majesty's presence, when Prince Yamagata, president of the Council, Prime Minister Katsura, and all the principal councilors and ministers were present. The premier reported to the throne concerning the situation in Korea, and subsequently the foreign minister explained in detail the diplomatic negotiations so far taken and the particulars of the treaty. Immediately an extraordinary meeting of high officials of the ministry of the imperial household was held to deliberate upon the status of the Korean princes to be created. The cabinet also met the same afternoon.[37]

With His Majesty's sanction, a telegram was immediately dispatched to General Terauchi, on the same day, authorizing him to sign the treaty. The approval of the Korean king having been given, the document was signed in the afternoon of August 22 by General Terauchi and Prime Minister Ye Wan Yong of Korea.[38] The treaty was promulgated on August 29, 1910.[39]

Throughout the preparation and execution of the annexation of Korea, the Katsura cabinet adhered to the usual

[37]*Op. cit.*, Aug. 23, 1910, p. 2; *Japan Weekly Mail*, Aug. 27, 1910, p. 258.

[38]On the afternoon of Aug. 21, Yamagata (president of the Privy Council and the most influential genro after Prince Ito's death), Komura (foreign minister) and Katsura (premier) held a long conference (*Japan Weekly Mail*, Aug. 27, 1910, p. 258). On Aug. 23, a cabinet meeting was held, after which Foreign Minister Komura was given an imperial audience to report upon its proceedings (*Tokyo Asahi*, Aug. 24, 1910, p. 2).

[39]Treaty No. 4, 1910. Text in *Horei Zensho*, 1910, *Joyaku*, pp. 29–30; also in *Joyaku Isan* (Tokyo, Foreign Office, 1918), pp. 682–684. *Cf. Tokyo Asahi*, Aug. 30, 1910, p. 3; also *Japan Weekly Mail*, Sept. 3, 1910, Supplement, p. 1. For English text see *Recueil des traités et conventions conclus entre l'empire du Japon et les puissances étrangères* (Tokyo, 1918), pp. 450–451. Article 8 declared: "This Treaty, having been approved by His Majesty the Emperor of Japan and His Majesty the Emperor of Korea, shall take effect from the date of its promulgation. In faith whereof, the respective plenipotentiaries have signed this Treaty and have fixed thereto their seals." For further discussion upon this point see Shinobu, *op. cit.*, pp. 375–378; Dr. Ariga, "The Annexation of Korea," *Gaiko Jiho*, XIII, No. 9 (Sept., 1910), pp. 119–124; Matsumiya, "The Annexation of Korea," *ibid.*, pp. 479–500. For various declarations, ordinances, and other official documents issued at the time of the annexation, see *Japan Weekly Mail*, Sept. 3, 1910, Supplement, pp. 1–3.

policy of declining to disclose the policy of the government or the nature of negotiations. Thus, in reply to a parliamentary criticism made in the House of Representatives on January 22, 1910, urging upon the cabinet not to hesitate to use a "big stick" policy in regard to Korea, the ministry deliberately refused to touch on the impending question of annexation.[40] The promulgation of the treaty of annexation on August 29, 1910, was universally acclaimed as a great achievement. Its formal report to the next session of the Diet (Twenty-seventh), however, evoked some sharp parliamentary debates. This was due to a declaration made to the powers that Japan did not propose to modify the existing tariff rates or tonnage dues for a period of ten years, a step taken largely in response to the protest made by Great Britain, whose friendship under the alliance Japan desired to continue.[41] The foreign minister, however, categorically denied that any pressure had been brought upon Tokyo in this regard, and declined to state whether the tariff question was included in the pending negotiations with Great Britain then in progress in London.[42]

[40]*Teikoku Gikaishi*, VII, 1587, 1599–1604, 1935. Although a written interpellation was put to the government at the outset of the Twenty-sixth session of the Diet, no reply was forthcoming till only one day before the close of the session.

[41]Thus, in the declaration issued to Germany, the United States, Austria-Hungary, Belgium, China, Denmark, France, Great Britain, Italy, and Russia, on August 29, 1910, the Japanese government voluntarily undertook to observe important restrictions upon tariff rates and tonnage dues. The statement included:

" (2) Independently of any conventional engagements formerly existing on the subject, the Imperial Government of Japan will, for a period of ten years, levy upon goods imported into Korea from foreign countries or exported from Korea to foreign countries, and upon foreign vessels entering any of the open ports of Korea, the same import or export duties and the same tonnage dues as under the existing schedules.

"The same import or export duties and tonnage dues as those to be levied upon the aforesaid goods and vessels will also, for a period of ten years, be applied in respect of goods imported into Korea from Japan or exported from Korea to Japan, and Japanese vessels entering any of the open ports of Korea.

" (3) The Imperial Government of Japan will also permit, for a period of ten years, vessels under the flags of Powers having treaties with Japan, to engage in the coasting trade between the open ports of Korea, and between those ports and any open ports of Japan." (Text of the declaration in *Recueil des traités et conventions conclus entre l'empire du Japon et les puissances étrangères* (Tokyo, 1918), pp. 452–453.

[42]Ito, *Kato Komei*, I, 674–677. For parliamentary debates see *Teikoku Gikaishi*, VIII, 18–20, 254–264, 336–338, 589, 714, 725–726; also *Dai Nijuhichikai Teikoku Shugiin Iinkai Giroku*, Pt. I, No. 1, pp. 79–80.

Chapter XIV

JAPANESE ENTRY INTO THE WORLD WAR

The Anglo-Japanese Alliance and the World War

THE INITIATIVE for the Japanese entry into the World War was taken by the cabinet. Thus during the closing days of July, 1914, numerous exchanges of views were made between Tokyo and London regarding the steps to be taken by Japan under the stipulations of the Anglo-Japanese Alliance, should Great Britain be drawn into the war.[1] By the afternoon of August 3 (Tokyo), British entrance into the war became imminent, and immediately upon receipt of such information, an extraordinary meeting of the cabinet was called at 9 o'clock the following morning (August 4), when the foreign minister explained in detail the diplomatic situation in Europe, and the navy and war ministers made some observations. While the cabinet was still in session, the British ambassador transmitted an important telegram from London. Immediately after the meeting, the Foreign Office issued a statement, intimating that Japan might be called upon to take appropriate measures under the terms of the alliance.[2] In the afternoon of August 5 the British ambassador called on the Foreign Office and conferred with Count Kato regarding an important telegram just received from

[1]Kenkichi Ichijima (ed.), *Okumako Hachijugonenshi* (Tokyo, 1926), III, 167–168. On Aug. 2, Premier Okuma was received in audience by the emperor at the detached palace at Nikko to report on the Austro-Serbian conflict (*Tokyo Asahi*, Aug. 3, 1914, p. 3). On the following day, Foreign Minister Komei Kato sent a detailed report to the emperor on the European situation based upon the reports received from Japanese ambassadors in European capitals (*ibid.*, Aug. 4, 1914, p. 3).

[2]Seitoku Ito (ed.), *Kato Komei* (Tokyo, 1929), II, 74. *Cf. Tokyo Asahi*, Aug. 5, 1914, p. 2.

London.[3] The War and Navy departments became suddenly active, and numerous calls were exchanged among high officials of those departments and the Foreign Office.[4]

About 5 P.M., August 7, the British ambassador called on the Foreign Office and formally requested the Japanese assistance in destroying German men of war in Chinese waters.[5] Thereupon, the foreign minister called on Marquis Okuma concerning the British memorandum. Count Kato expressed his opinion that (1) Japan should enter the war, (2) that the scope of the military and naval operations should not be confined to the destruction of German war vessels in Chinese waters, and that (3) negotiations should be entered into with the British government concerning the grounds upon which Japan should join the war. The prime minister expressed his assent to Kato's views, and an extraordinary meeting of the cabinet was called at the premier's private residence on the evening of August 7.[6] At this extraordinary cabinet meeting which was called in the evening and lasted till early the next morning, the foreign minister explained in detail the diplomatic developments in Europe and the negotiations with the British government. He expressed his personal opinion regarding the Japanese entrance into the war and stated to his colleagues that, though the general conditions were not such as to impose upon Japan the duty to join the war under treaty obligations, it was the proper course to take as a voluntary expression of friendship toward Great Britain under the alliance. He welcomed it as an op-

[3] *Tokyo Asahi*, Aug. 6, 1914, p. 4.

[4] In the morning of Aug. 6, a conference of the War Department and the general staff was held (*ibid.*, Aug. 7, 1914, p. 2), while Navy Minister Yashiro called on Kato for a conference. Admiral Togo and War Minister Oka were received in audience by the emperor at Nikko on the same day (*ibid.*, Aug. 7, p. 3).

[5] British memorandum: "As some time will be needed in order that our ships of war may find and destroy German ships in Chinese waters, it is most important that the Japanese fleet should, if possible, hunt out and destroy the armed German merchant cruisers who are now attacking our commerce. If the Imperial Government would be good enough to employ some of their men of war thus, it would be of greatest advantage to His Majesty's Government. This, of course, means an act of war against Germany, but this is, in our opinion, unavoidable" (quoted in Ito, *Kato Komei*, II, 78). *Cf. Tokyo Asahi*, Aug. 9, 1914, p. 3.

[6] Ito, *op. cit.*, II, 77. A regular meeting of the cabinet was held in the morning, when Kato reported on recent developments. Though this meeting adjourned at 1:30 P.M., Foreign Minister Kato, Finance Minister Wakatsuki, and Communications Minister Taketomi remained till 3:30 P.M. (*Tokyo Asahi*, Aug. 8, 1914, p. 2).

portunity to destroy the German influence from eastern
Asia and to enhance the international position of Japan.
In view of the tremendous importance of the question, he
requested a frank exchange of views among his colleagues.
Some expressed their apprehension that Japan's attack upon
Tsingtao might result in violation of Chinese neutrality,
while some expressed an opinion that there might be a
peaceful way out without resorting to arms. Finally, by two
o'clock of the next morning, the cabinet decided to join the
war.[7]

This decision of the cabinet to enter the war on the side
of the Allies was based upon the general spirit of the
Anglo-Japanese Alliance, though not legally obliged, and for
revenge upon Germany for her part in the three-power intervention after the Sino-Japanese War of 1894–1895.[8] It was
also decided at this meeting to consult the genro before final
decision.[9] Count Kato left Tokyo for Nikko early in the
morning of August 8 to report to the throne on foreign relations and the cabinet's decision just made.[10] At the cabinet
meeting held in the evening, with the genro in attendance,[11]
Foreign Minister Kato again made his report upon diplomatic
negotiations with London. A genro stated at this meeting
that peaceful measures should be taken to preserve tranquillity in the Far East, and entertained the possibility of
German victory in the war. Finally, however, the cabinet
and the genro agreed upon the policy of entry into the war
on the side of Great Britain. Thus, the informal decision to
enter the war was arrived at within thirty-six hours after
formal request for assistance was received in Tokyo.[12]

Having decided upon the policy, the next issue was the

---

[7]Ito, op. cit., II, 78–80. Cf. Tokyo Asahi, Aug. 9, 1914, p. 4.

[8]Cf. Sakutaro Tachi, "Obligations under the Anglo-Japanese Alliance," Gaiko
Jiho, XIII, No. 2 (Jan. 15, 1916), pp. 117–138; also Shin Ninagawa and Keisuke
Shimatani on "Anglo-Japanese Alliance" in Kokka Gakkai Zasshi, XIV, No. 7
(March, 1916), pp. 573–592.

[9]Ichijima, op. cit., III, 169–170.

[10]Kato left Uyeno station at 5:30 A.M. and returned at 6 P.M. (Tokyo Asahi, Aug.
9, 1914, p. 3).

[11]Prince Yamagata, Prince Oyama, Marquis Matsukata responded to Okuma's
call, but Marquis Inouye was unable to attend the meeting on account of illness
(ibid., Aug. 9, 1914, p. 4).

[12]Ito, Kato Komei, II, 80–81; Tokyo Asahi, Aug. 9, 1914, p. 4.

precise means of carrying out the policy thus determined. Immediately after the cabinet adjourned late at night on August 8, a private conference of Count Kato (foreign minister), Mr. Reijiro Wakatsuki (finance minister), Admiral Rokuro Yashiro (navy minister) and Mr. Chozo Koike (chief of the political bureau of the Foreign Office), was called at the private residence of the foreign minister. It lasted till early next morning (August 9). At this informal meeting it was decided to give Germany one week to reply and to divide the ultimatum into two sections: the first section was to be drafted in compliance with the British request, while positive reasons for Japanese entry into the war were to be set forth in the second section. It was further decided to demand transfer of Tsingtao to Japan with eventual restoration to China on the ground that, should a direct restoration be demanded, Germany might, by a secret agreement with China, retain the territory. It was also decided that eight different routes be employed to make certain of German receipt of the ultimatum.[13]

Following the decision of the cabinet on August 8, Foreign Minister Kato made an important communication to the British government. He requested London to agree to Japanese entrance into the war under the general principles embodied in the Anglo-Japanese Alliance, and not to restrict her activities to mere destruction of German war vessels in Chinese waters.[14] In the afternoon of August 9, the British ambassador called on the Foreign Office and requested Japan to postpone her declaration of war and urged that her activities should be confined to the protection of her overseas trade. At the same time, the British foreign secretary stated to Ambassador Inouye in London that Japanese declaration of war would be certain to cause disturbances in the entire Far East and great injury to British trade, and consequently requested Japan to withhold any warlike operations until the British cabinet reached a decision on the basis of information furnished by her minister in Peking and the commander of the British fleet in Chinese waters.[15] Upon receipt of this important communication, Count Kato immediately tele-

[13]*Ibid.*, II, 82–85; Ichijima, *op. cit.*, III, 170.
[14]*Ibid.*, II, 87–88.
[15]*Ibid.*, II, 88.

graphed a long memorandum to London declaring that
Japanese entry into the war would in no way threaten the
British trade, and that she entertained no territorial ambition. He called the attention of the London government
to the fact that the decision to join the war had already been
made and the result of cabinet decision already reported to
the emperor, and consequently could not be changed except
under gravest circumstances. He emphasized that popular
demand for taking revenge for the three-power intervention
had been so persistent that further delay would lead to a
serious political situation in domestic politics.[16]

In her communication of August 11 Great Britain formally
requested Japan to reconsider the question of taking warlike
measures under the Anglo-Japanese Alliance.[17] Count Kato,
in reply, reiterated his former stand and added that public
opinion supported an immediate declaration of war on
Germany.[18] On the following morning an extraordinary
meeting of the cabinet was called, when Kato made a detailed
report upon telegrams received from abroad since August 10
and explained the negotiations in progress with diplomatic
representatives in Tokyo. War Minister Oka and Navy
Minister Yashiro made explanations regarding military and
naval matters.[19] Late in the evening (10 P.M., August 12),
the British government transmitted further observations.
Thereupon, the cabinet, after an all-day session on August
13, decided to pursue the policy already agreed upon on
August 8.[20] Under these circumstances the British government finally agreed to Japanese declaration of war on
Germany.[21]

In consenting to Japanese declaration of war, the British

[16]*Op. cit.*, II, 88–90.

[17]*Ibid.*, II, 90. *Cf. Tokyo Asahi*, Aug. 13, 1914, p. 2.

[18]*Ibid.*, II, 90–91. Premier Okuma invited pressmen to his official residence on
the afternoon of Aug. 10 and requested them to exercise moderation in their news
(*Tokyo Asahi*, Aug. 11, 1914, p. 2). Navy and war officials were not idle. Navy
Minister Yashiro, Admiral Ijuin, war councilor, Admiral Shimamura, chief of naval
general staff, Admiral Yamashita, vice-chief of staff, Admiral Suzuki, vice-minister
of navy, held a conference on Aug. 11. On the same day, General Oku, war minister,
called on Marshal Yamagata (*ibid.*, Aug. 12, 1914, p. 3).

[19]*Tokyo Asahi*, Aug. 13, 1914, p. 2.

[20]The meeting lasted from 10 A.M. to 4 P.M., Aug. 13 (*ibid.*, Aug. 14, 1914, p. 2).

[21]Ito, *op. cit.*, II, 91–92. The British ambassador called at the Foreign Office at
4:30 P.M., Aug. 13 (*Tokyo Asahi*, Aug. 14, 1914, p. 2).

government made an important proposal to Tokyo; it sought to restrain Japan from operating beyond Chinese waters. Naturally, Foreign Minister Kato took a serious exception to such a proposal on the ground that it would be incompatible with her execution of the war, that Japanese war vessels should be free to pursue German men of war wherever they might be found, and further that her trading vessels should be protected anywhere in the Pacific. Though, in its communication of August 14, the British government expressed its consent to elimination of such declaration, it did not withdraw its original stand. The British object was to preclude Japanese occupation of German possessions in the South Sea islands and her intervention in the west coast regions of the continent.[22]

No early reply to the Japanese latest counter proposal was forthcoming from London. So, on August 19, Kato instructed the Japanese ambassador in London to dispose of the matter unilaterally, by presenting the text of a speech delivered by Prime Minister Okuma before a conference of prominent business men on the evening of August 18th, in which he denied any territorial ambition on the part of Japan and declared that her warlike operations were strictly limited to the necessities of her own self-defense.[23] On the other hand, the British government, without consulting the Japanese government, issued a statement through the Press Bureau, on the evening of August 17, to the effect that the British government understood that the Japanese sphere of warlike operations did not extend, excepting the protection of Japanese trade routes in the Pacific, beyond Chinese

[22]*Ibid.*, II, 92–94.

[23]Count Okuma invited a group of representative business men from different parts of the country to his official residence on Tuesday afternoon (Aug. 18), and declared that: "Japan's object is to eliminate from the Continent of China the root of the German influence, which forms a constant menace to the peace of the Far East and thus to secure the aim of the alliance with Great Britain. She harbors no design for territorial aggrandizement and entertains no desire to promote any other selfish end. Japan's warlike operations will not, therefore, extend beyond the limits necessary for the attainment of that object and for the defence of her own legitimate interests. Accordingly, the Imperial Government have no hesitation in announcing to the world that the Imperial Government will take no such action as to give any third Power any cause of anxiety or uneasiness regarding the safety of their territories and possessions" (*Japan Weekly Mail*, Aug., 1914, *Supplement*, p. 8; *London Times*, Aug. 21, 1914, p. 7). *Cf.* Ito, *Kato Komei*, II, 95; also *Tokyo Asahi*, Aug. 19, 1914, p. 4.

waters.[24] Thus, the embarrassing subject of delimiting the Japanese sphere of warlike operations in the event of a declaration of war under the alliance was settled by unilateral declarations by both parties.[25]

While negotiations with London concerning delimitation of warlike operations were in progress through the Foreign Office, preparations to join the Allies were being pushed forward. It was originally intended that the cabinet meeting of August 10 should decide the details connected with the declaration of war, to be followed by a formal cabinet meeting in the presence of the emperor. But the Japanese decision in the cabinet was delayed on account of diplomatic negotiations with London as we have seen in the foregoing pages.[26] The British reply, consenting to the Japanese declaration of war without an accompanying declaration delimiting her warlike operations, having been received in Tokyo in the forenoon of August 14, the cabinet met in an extraordinary

[24]The Press Bureau issued the following statement on the evening of Aug. 17, 1914:

"The Governments of Great Britain and Japan, having been in communication with each other, are of opinion that it is necessary for each to take action to protect the general interest in the Far East contemplated by the Anglo-Japanese Alliance, keeping especially in view the independence and integrity of China, and provided for in that Agreement.

"It is understood that the action of Japan will not extend to the Pacific Ocean beyond the China Seas except in so far as it may be necessary to protect Japanese shipping lines in the Pacific, nor beyond Asiatic waters westward of the China Seas, nor to any foreign territory except territory in German occupation on the Continent of Eastern Asia" (London *Times*, Aug. 18, 1914, p. 6. *Cf. Japan Weekly Mail*, Aug. 22, 1914, p. 191). *The Times* (London) expressed satisfaction with the declaration above cited, and said, "Australia, reassured by the Japanese declaration, may be safely left to assist in the disposal of the German possessions in the Southern Pacific" (*ibid.*, Aug. 18, 1914, p. 7). The New York *Times*, however, believed that the Japanese entry into the war was not called for under the stipulations of the alliance, and expressed apprehension as to the future developments in China. It declared: "Japan's assurances to our Government that American interests in the Pacific will be in no way threatened by her hostile dealing with Germany are, to be sure, accepted in good faith, of course. These are reinforced by the British statement that Japan will now confine her warlike operations to the China Seas. But there is a general belief that it is the policy of Japan to assert and maintain for herself supremacy and control in the Asiatic waters of the Pacific with a view, probably, to the ultimate exclusion of the influence of Western nations" (New York *Times*, Aug. 18, 1914, p. 8).

[25]Kato invited the British ambassador to the foreign office on Aug. 22, and informed him that Japan was to regard the British statement as merely a unilateral interpretation, not binding upon the Japanese government (Ito, *op. cit.*, II, 96).

[26]*Cf. Gaiko Jiho*, XX, No. 5 (Sept. 1, 1914), pp. 521–523.

session to deliberate upon the final details. At 4:30 P.M., Yamagata, Oyama, and Matsukata joined the discussion. As a result of this meeting, which lasted till 6 P.M., it was decided to request His Majesty's presence at its formal meeting on August 15.[27] Consequently, a formal *gozen kaigi* was held at 4:30 P.M. in the palace, when the members of the cabinet, genro (Yamagata, Oyama, Matsukata), General Hasegawa (chief of army general staff), and Admiral Shimamura (chief of naval general staff) deliberated upon the question of dispatching an ultimatum to Germany. After full deliberation, the emperor gave his sanction to the measure decided upon at this conference of his highest advisers.[28] At six-thirty, Count Kato, when called on by the British ambassador, informed him of the decision of the cabinet, and then invited in the representatives of Russia, France, United States, and China, to state to them the attitude of the Japanese government. At seven o'clock, Vice-Minister Matsui called on the German ambassador and handed him the ultimatum.[29] At the same time, it was transmitted to Berlin through the Japanese *chargé d'affaires* in Berlin, Japanese ambassadors to England, Russia, Italy, and ministers to Holland, Switzerland, and Sweden. The telegram which was sent from Tokyo late at midnight of the fifteenth reached Berlin early in the morning of August 17.[30]

Having dispatched an ultimatum to Germany, the war and naval authorities now became busily engaged in making preparations for the war.[31] At 10:30 A.M., August 16, the

---

[27] *Tokyo Asahi*, Aug. 15, 1914, p. 2. This petition to the emperor was immediately transmitted to Nikko through Minister of the Imperial Household Hatano (*ibid.*, Aug. 16, 1914, p. 3).

[28] Ito, *Kato Komei*, II, 99–100; Ichijima, *op. cit.*, III, 171; Taisaku Aso (ed.), *Kato Komei Den* (Tokyo, 1928), p. 139; Sakuzo Yoshino (ed.), *Kyokuto no Gaiko* (Tokyo, 1916), p. 340; *Tokyo Asahi*, Aug. 16, 1914, p. 2.

[29] Text of the ultimatum in Ito, *op. cit.*, II, 100; also Kudo, *Taisho Kenseishi* (Tokyo, 1927), pp. 109–110. *Cf. Tokyo Asahi*, Aug. 16, 1914, p. 2.

[30] *Gaiko Jiho*, XX, No. 5 (Sept. 1, 1914), pp. 523–524; Ito, *op. cit.*, II, 100–101. For commentaries upon the ultimatum in the vernacular press see *Japan Weekly Mail*, Aug. 22, 1914, pp. 185–187.

[31] Admiral Shimamura (chief of naval staff), General Hasegawa (chief of staff), and other high military and naval officers were received in audience by the emperor in the forenoon of Aug. 16 to report on their respective fields (*Tokyo Asahi*, Aug. 17, 1914, p. 3).

emperor called the meeting of the Privy Council to deliberate upon the measures taken by the government. Premier Okuma, Foreign Minister Kato, War Minister Oka, and Navy Minister Yashiro made explanations of the action decided upon. After a few interchanges of views, the action of the cabinet was approved.[32] In the afternoon, the prime minister invited press representatives to his official residence and explained the measures just taken regarding the European War, and pleaded with them to be conservative and restrained in publishing news. The foreign minister further elaborated upon the government's attitude and made public the ultimatum to Germany. In the evening, representatives of both Houses and business men were invited to the premier's official residence, at which time Count Okuma sought to obtain a general "understanding" concerning the cabinet action.[33]

Meanwhile, preparations for the eventuality of German refusal to reply to the ultimatum were being made by the cabinet.[34] By August 21 it was obvious that a German reply was not forthcoming. Cabinet meetings were held both on the 20th and 21st of August, when the rules of war, declaration of war, instructions to be issued to local governors, convocation of extraordinary session of the Diet, and other important matters were taken up.[35] These measures were submitted to the Privy Council for approval on August 22.[36] Thereupon, another extraordinary meeting of the cabinet was called for further deliberations, and its decision was reported to the throne by Count Okuma.[37] In the forenoon of August 23, a cabinet meeting was called at the official residence of the prime minister. When a German reply failed to reach Tokyo at noon, the prime minister was received in audience by the emperor to obtain imperial sanction to the proclamation of

[32]Op. cit., Aug. 17, 1914, p. 3. Cf. Ichijima, op. cit., III, 172.

[33]Gaiko Jiho, XX, No. 5 (Sept. 1, 1914), p. 524; Ichijima, op. cit., III, 173–174; Tokyo Asahi, Aug. 17, 1914, pp. 3, 4, 5.

[34]On Aug. 19, a board of press censors was established in the War Department (Tokyo Asahi, Aug. 19, 1914, p. 3). In the evening, 98 representative business men of Tokyo, Osaka, Kyoto, Kobe, Nagoya, and Yokohama invited the cabinet members for a conference (ibid., Aug. 20, 1914, p. 4).

[35]Ibid., Aug. 22, 23, 1914, p. 2.

[36]Ibid., Aug. 23, 1914, p. 2.

[37]Ibid., Aug. 23, 1914, p. 3.

war, convening of an extraordinary session of the imperial Diet to pass the war budget, and various rules and regulations concerning prosecution of the war.[38] The declaration of war was issued on August 23, 1914.[39]

Parliamentary Interpellations

The Thirty-fourth Diet called to vote for the war budget was in session from September 4 to 9, 1914.[40] The total budget asked for at this session was 53,000,000 yen and this budget was passed in both Houses without a dissenting vote. In voting for the budget, Representative Ooka, former Speaker of the House and a leader of the *Seiyukai* (opposition) party, declared that, though he detected some defects or improprieties as to the figures and method of compilation, it was to be borne in mind that the imperial proclamation of war had already been issued and that the loyal and valiant officers and men of the imperial army and navy were face to face with the enemy.[41] The prime minister threatened to dissolve the House of Representatives should the *Seiyukai* members refuse to vote for the government measures asked for.[42]

On diplomatic questions, the Okuma cabinet pursued the traditional policy of avoidance of parliamentary scrutiny and criticism. The address on foreign relations which the foreign minister, Count Kato, delivered at the outset of the session was merely formal, without enlightening the representatives as to the precise causes and procedures taken by the government leading up to the Japanese declaration of war on Germany. Government replies to parliamentary interpellations both in the committees and on the floors of the chambers were evasive and noncommittal.[43] To a question

[38]*Ibid.*, Aug. 24, 1914, p. 2. *Cf.* Ichijima, *op. cit.*, III, 177–179.

[39]Text of the declaration of war in Ichijima, *op. cit.*, III, 179–180; Kudo, *Taisho Kenseishi*, pp. 110–112; *Tokyo Asahi*, Aug. 24, 1914, p. 2.

[40]For the proceedings of this session see *Teikoku Gikaishi*, IX, 847–879.

[41]*Ibid.*, IX, 872–873.

[42]Ichijima, *op. cit.*, III, 190. *Cf. Tokyo Asahi*, Sept. 7, 1914, p. 3. The surplus for the fiscal year of 1913 to be transferred to the surplus fund for 1914 was 130,000,000 yen, which was sufficient to meet emergencies arising out of the war (Kudo, *Taisho Kenseishi*, p. 433).

[43]For the address on foreign relations by Count Kato in the House of Representatives, see *Teikoku Gikaishi*, IX, 858–859. No diplomatic interpellations were put to the government from the floor of the House of Peers during the session.

put to the foreign minister by Dr. Tomizu in the House
budget committee on September 5, 1914, concerning the
future restoration of Kiaochaowan to China,[44] and one by
Representative Ikuzo Ooka on the same day as to Kiaochaowan and the reported delimitation upon warlike operations
in the Pacific, Foreign Minister Kato refused to reply in open
meeting and requested an executive session on the ground
that the subject in question belonged to diplomatic secrets.[45]
Representative Genji Matsuda, on September 5, 1914, in his
interpellation to the government, reminded the ministry
that, at the outset of the Russo-Japanese War, the diplomatic
correspondence concerning the outbreak of the war was published, making clear the reasons which made the war inevitable, thus evoking spontaneous and positive unity of public
opinion behind the government in prosecuting the war. He
expressed a keen disappointment at the refusal of the foreign
minister to disclose the circumstances requiring the entry of
Japan into the war on the pretext of diplomatic secrecy. He
even went further and expressed doubts as to whether Japan
was obliged to declare war on Germany under the stipulations of the Treaty of Alliance. He demanded that the
ministry make clear the circumstances that forced the
Japanese entrance into the war under the Alliance. The
foreign minister again refused to reply in open meeting, and
requested an executive session, which was granted (10:18
A.M. to 12:24 P.M.).[46]

Before we examine the proceedings of the Thirty-fifth
Diet, our attention is directed to the issuance of a departmental ordinance by the Foreign Office on September 16,
1914, immediately after the close of the extra session which
was called to vote the war budget.[47] This ordinance pro-

[44]*Dai Sanjushikai Teikoku Gikai Shugiin Yosan Iinkai Giroku*, pp. 3–4.

[45]*Teikoku Gikaishi*, IX, 860–861.

[46]*Ibid.*, IX, 861–862. When the same issue was brought up in an interpellation by
Representative Tanjiro Nishimura, in a sub-committee meeting of the House budget committee of the Thirty-seventh Diet, on Dec. 17, 1915, Viscount Kikujiro
Ishii, the foreign minister who succeeded Count Kato, admitted that the Japanese
entrance into the war was brought about by the terms of the Anglo-Japanese Alliance, but refused to state under what particular article. He declared that it was in
obedience to the general spirit of the Alliance, and not under any particular article
(*Dai Sanjuhichikai Teikoku Gikai Shugiin Iinkai Giroku*, Pt. I, No. 2, pp. 6–7).

[47]*Gaimusho Rei* No. I, 1914, was issued under Article 27 of the *Shimbunshi Ho*
("Press Law").

hibited publication of any matter which might influence foreign relations, except upon special permission by the minister for foreign affairs.[48] A board of censors, composed of seven members, was appointed and began work on the same day.[49] The issuance of this censorship order by the Foreign Office, at the very time when Kato's conduct of foreign relations began to be attacked, immediately aroused spontaneous protest on the part of the press, even by supporters of the Okuma cabinet. This protest on the part of the press against what was regarded an unwarranted restriction upon the freedom of the press became so violent that a meeting of the leaders of the *Doshikai*, of which the incumbent foreign minister was president, was called on the afternoon of September 17. After the meeting, three members of the executive committee of the party (Kono, Shimada, Minoura) called on Count Kato and on the prime minister the following day.[50] On the other hand, members of the *Kasumi* Club, comprising press correspondents in charge of foreign news, held an extraordinary meeting at Uyeno, Tokyo, on the evening of September 17 and passed a resolution denouncing the ordinance as greatly restricting the freedom of speech and contrary to the principles of "people's diplomacy."[51] Convinced of the serious consequences of such public demonstrations against a departmental ordinance, editors-in-chief of eight leading newspapers in Tokyo favorable to the Okuma ministry called on the prime minister, on September

[48]Vice-Minister of Foreign Affairs Matsui cited the following items as having important bearings upon the conduct of foreign relations: (1) news, correspondence, and commentaries contrary to the object of alliances or agreements to which Japan is a party (Anglo-Japanese alliance, Russo-Japanese agreement, Franco-Japanese agreement, American-Japanese agreement); (2) reports purporting to convey an impression that a new agreement, a secret agreement, or an alliance has been made, in addition to those mentioned above; (3) reports unfounded in fact, or radical news inflammatory in character, concerning the international relationships between Japan and China, Russia, Great Britain, United States, France, and others; (4) derogatory remarks concerning the head of a friendly power; (5) aggressive and jingoistic news concerning foreign territories (*Gaiko Jiho*, XX, No. 7 [Oct. 1, 1914], p. 758).

[49]*Tokyo Asahi*, Sept. 17, 1914, p. 3.

[50]Both the premier and foreign minister emphasized the importance of taking effective measures to ensure an advantageous position of Japan after the war. This declaration was an anticipation of the Sino-Japanese negotiations of 1915 (*ibid.*, Sept. 19, 1914, p. 4).

[51]*Ibid.*, Sept. 19, 1914, p. 3.

19, to present the press views concerning the ordinance.[52] As a result of this interview, a memorandum was issued, declaring that the ordinance would be repealed at an early date, that commentaries and criticisms of diplomatic affairs would be as free as before, thus practically nullifying the effect of the ordinance.[53] Again, on October 6, before the Committee of Eighteen, representing the *Zenkoku Domei Kisha Club*, or National Union of Newspaper Reporters, the prime minister, in conference with Dr. Egi, chief secretary of the cabinet, declared that the ordinance would be repealed immediately after the conclusion of warlike operations, the cabinet being of the opinion that the ordinance in question was prejudicial to freedom of speech, and assured the representatives of the press that, in consultation with Count Kato, instructions had been issued to the authorities in charge of the execution of the ordinance to give due respect to the freedom of expression on foreign relations.[54]

When the Thirty-fifth session of the Diet was opened on December 7, 1914, the *Seiyukai* party, having a majority in the Lower House, sought to attack the Okuma ministry on foreign relations. Although no interpellations or questions were put to the government on foreign relations from the floor of the House of Peers,[55] numerous queries were showered upon the cabinet in the Lower House, to the obvious embarrassment of the Okuma ministry.[56] The opposition attacks upon the administration were centered upon the question of the precise circumstances for the Japanese entry into the war under the alliance, and the question of the future of Kiaochaowan and German possessions in the Pacific. Thus, immediately after the usual addresses by the premier, foreign, finance, and war ministers, on their respective fields,[57] Representative Heikichi Ogawa, a veteran leader of the

[52]*Mancho, Kokumin, Yamato, Yomiuri, Miyako, Hochi, Nichi Nichi, Asahi (ibid.,* Sept. 20, 1914, p. 3).

[53]*Gaiko Jiho,* XX, No. 7 (Oct. 1, 1914), pp. 755-760. For other meetings see *Tokyo Asahi,* Sept. 20, 21, 22, 1914, p. 4.

[54]Text of this memorandum in *Tokyo Asahi,* Oct. 7, 1914, p. 2.

[55]*Teikoku Gikaishi,* IX, 882-906.

[56]For proceedings of the House of Representatives which was dissolved on Christmas Day, Dec. 25, 1914, see *ibid.,* IX, 907-1049.

[57]*Ibid.,* IX, 911-915.

Seiyukai party, led the opposition onslaught upon foreign relations. In reply to a question upon the future of Kiaochaowan, Count Kato declined to make a definite statement, but emphatically declared that Japan was not committed to any power as to the future of Kiaochaowan.[58] On this important question he declared throughout the session that Japan was under no pledge to England or any other power as to the restoration of Tsingtao,[59] and that no restrictions had been placed upon the sphere of warlike operations of the imperial army and navy, the repeated reports from abroad to the contrary notwithstanding.[60] In reply to an interpellation by Representative Sennosuke Yokota regarding the departmental ordinance restricting the freedom of the press upon foreign relations, the prime minister flatly denied giving any memorandum to press representatives on September 18 and stated that some restrictions upon the press were necessary under the present delicate international relations and that as soon as the circumstances permitted the ordinance would be repealed.[61] Representative Kokubo charged the prime minister with petitioning the emperor to issue an imperial message to Count Kato approving the conduct of war diplomacy, and cited press news in his stinging attack upon what he regarded as the shielding of diplomatic authorities against parliamentary and popular criticism.[62] Prime Minister Okuma refused to reply to this embarrassing question on the ground that he did not feel constrained to reply to such matters of the Imperial Court.[63]

Being unsuccessful in their attack upon the government on foreign relations, the *Seiyukai* members now sought to seriously embarrass the Okuma cabinet by attacking its army

[58]*Ibid.*, IX, 915–918.

[59]*Ibid.*, IX, 935.

[60]Reply to an interpellation by Representative Genji Matsuda, Dec. 9, 1914 (*ibid.*, IX, 928–930).

[61]House Budget Committee, Dec. 17, 1914 (*Dai Sanjugokai Teikoku Gikai Shugiin Yosan Iinkai Giroku*, pp. 7–9). *Cf.* an interpellation in the House of Representatives, Dec. 14, 1914 (*Teikoku Gikaishi*, IX, 991, 993–994, 1003).

[62]He cited *Kokumin Shimbun*, Dec. 2, 1914, and *Chuo Shimbun*, Dec. 4, 1914.

[63]*Teikoku Gikaishi*, IX, 923–925 (Dec. 14, 1914). In reply to a question in the House Budget Committee, Dec. 17, 1914, Count Kato refused to disclose the contents of Imperial messages from time to time (*Dai Sanjugokai Teikoku Gikai Shugiin Yosan Iinkai Giroku*, p. 96).

expansion program.[64] Representative Ikuzo Ooka, a veteran leader of the *Seiyukai* party and chairman of the House Budget Committee, made his report on December 25, 1914, recommending the rejection of the appropriations, among others, for establishing two new army divisions in Chosen, and for building eight new destroyers. After an all-day debate on the Budget bill, providing for army and navy expansion, which had already been decided upon in the council on national defense, the Army Expansion bill was defeated by 213:148, while the Navy Replenishment bill was passed by 184:177. Thus, the government Budget bill was passed only after parliamentary elimination of the important features of the cabinet program, in spite of a veiled threat made by the prime minister himself in the House of Representatives during the debates, intimating a subsequent dissolution of the Lower House.[65] This threat was made good by the dissolution of the House on December 25, 1914.[66] The general election, held on March 25, 1915, resulted in a complete victory of the *Doshikai* and other supporters of the Okuma cabinet.[67]

[64]In order to unify the defense program, the *Bomukaigi* ("Council on National Defense") was established on June 23, 1914 (Imperial Ordinance No. 125, 1914). It was composed of the premier (chairman), ministers of foreign affairs, finance, war, and of navy, as well as chiefs of army and navy general staffs. The first meeting was held on July 2, and after several meetings of the Council, the well-known eight-four naval program and establishment of two divisions in Korea were decided upon, by Oct., 1914 (Mitsuo Miyata, *Gensui Kato Tomosaburo Den* [Tokyo, 1928], p. 80). *Cf.* Ichijima, *op. cit.*, III, 150, 199; *Tokyo Asahi*, July 3, 1914, p. 2.

[65]For debate upon the Budget bill, see *Teikoku Gikaishi*, IX, 1015–1048. *Cf.* Kudo, *Taisho Kenseishi*, pp. 127–129, 438–447.

[66]*Ibid.*, IX, 1048.

[67]For the election campaign see Ichijima, *op. cit.*, III, 213–251.

Chapter XV

THE SINO–JAPANESE NEGOTIATIONS, 1915

THE EXTENSION of the period of the lease of Kwantung Peninsula and the South Manchuria Railway zone was a question of vital importance to Japan. As early as 1910, Representative Oishi, charging lack of complete unity of views between the military and diplomatic authorities in regard to Manchurian administration, requested the government to state its policy regarding the future of Manchuria. Foreign Minister Marquis Komura, however, declined to state the policy toward the question of extending the lease of the entire Manchuria Railway zone.[1]

After the annexation of Korea in 1910, the fate of the Japanese interests in Manchuria became one of paramount importance in domestic as well as foreign politics of the Island Empire. With the outbreak of the World War and the subsequent Japanese entry on the side of the allies, the question of "settling the Far Eastern problems" again became the central topic of public discussion. That the Okuma cabinet entertained a genuine desire to obtain a satisfactory solution of the future security of Japanese interests in the Orient, particularly in Manchuria and in Shantung, can be surmised from the proceedings of the two sessions of Diet convened in September and December of 1914. Without disclosing the exact position of the government, Foreign Minister Kato maintained that Japan was not bound by any agreement or pledge to return Kiaochaowan to China, insisting that the insertion of "with eventual restoration to China" was made in the same spirit in which the German

[1]Interpellation in the House Budget Committee on Jan. 31, 1910, during the 26th Diet (*Dai Nijurokkai Teikoku Gikai Shugiin Iinkai Giroku*, Pt. I, No. 2, pp. 13–14).

advice to Japan to return Liaotung Peninsula to China was made at the conclusion of the Sino-Japanese War. Again, when asked by Representative Ogawa, Count Kato declined to state the policy of the cabinet toward China on the ground that Ogawa's real purpose was left unsaid, and that he did not feel it in the interest of the state to answer such a question in an open meeting. No doubt Representative Ogawa, a veteran leader of the *Seiyukai* (opposition party), meant to urge upon the government that the time was ripe for taking a positive step to gain a firmer hold in the Far East. Throughout the stormy session of the Thirty-fifth Diet, when the government lacked a majority in the Lower House, parliamentary interpellations and criticisms were centred upon its Chinese policy, and it was evident that parliamentary opposition urged a more vigorous policy to "insure" Japan's position after the close of the war.[2]

Before leaving London to become the foreign minister in the Katsura cabinet, Ambassador Kato sought to obtain the "understanding" of the British Foreign Office to the policy Kato was going to pursue in China. Thus, in his two extended interviews with Viscount Grey on January 3 and 10, 1913, in his private capacity (emphasized by the fact that he was under no instructions from Tokyo), he declared that Japan entertained vital political and psychological concern in the Kwantung Peninsula and the concessions of the South Manchuria and Antung–Mukden Railways; he said that the Japanese people were determined to maintain a permanent occupation of the Kwantung Province. He emphasized that it was the people's determination, and consequently, no ministry could run counter to that determination. He stated to the British foreign secretary that if a "psychological moment" should arrive the Japanese government would take up the matter of extending the lease and concessions in Manchuria. Sir Edward Grey expressed the opinion that the

[2]Interpellations by Representatives Ogawa and Kokubo on Dec. 8, 9, 1914 (*Teikoku Gikaishi*, IX, 917–918). *Cf.* remarks made in the House Budget Committee meeting (*Dai Sanjugokai Teikoku Gikai Shugiin Iinkai Giroku*, Pt. I, No. 1, pp. 54, 91–95, 117–118; also *ibid.*, Pt. I, No. 2, p. 4). In reply to a question in the House Budget Committee on Sept. 6, 1914, Count Kato emphasized the fact that the term, "restoration," used in the ultimatum to Germany, did not find occasion to be employed again in subsequent events (*Dai Sanjushikai Teikoku Gikai Shugiin Iinkai Giroku*, Pt. I, No. 1, p. 12).

question of extending the lease of Kwantung Province was one to be settled between Japan and China, and one not to be intervened by a third party; while, to the extension of the concessions of the Antung–Mukden Railway and the South Manchuria Railway, the British secretary for foreign affairs did not express any opposition.[3]

On his way back to Japan, Count Kato held a private conference with Minister Ijuin at Changchun. At this meeting, Kato inquired whether the time was ripe for starting negotiations for the purpose, when he was met with a negative reply. He then instructed the minister to find an opportunity to open the negotiations.[4] Kato arrived in Tokyo on January 28, 1913, and immediately called on Prime Minister Katsura the following day to report in person the details concerning his interviews with the British foreign secretary, when Prince Katsura expressed his hearty approval of Kato's activities in London.[5] However, the Katsura cabinet tendered its resignation on February 11, on account of the parliamentary opposition to its "unconstitutional" existence.[6] In the middle of March of the same year, Count Kato requested a conference of Prime Minister Yamamoto and Foreign Minister Makino to report in detail the interviews he had before his departure for Japan in January, and to state his views concerning two important diplomatic problems: Anglo-Japanese Alliance and the solution of the so-called "Sino-Japanese question." He urged upon these two cabinet ministers the necessity of opening negotiations with China for the solution of the Kwantung leased territory and the Manchurian railways, and declared that the Japanese attitude toward the alliance should be based upon its non-applicability to the United States, holding that England would rather terminate the alliance than go to war with the United States.[7]

With the formation of the Okuma ministry on April 16,

---

[3]For Count Kato's memorandum on these two important interviews with the British foreign secretary, see Ito (ed.), *Kato Komei*, II, 132–140.

[4]*Ibid.*, II, 144. Cf. *Tokyo Asahi*, Jan. 21, 1913, p. 2.

[5]*Tokyo Asahi*, Jan. 30, 31, Feb. 1, 1913.

[6]Katsura's fall can be attributed to purely domestic cause—popular demand for "constitutional" cabinet (Kudo, *Taisho Kenseishi*, pp. 21–52).

[7]Ito, *op. cit.*, II, 145–147.

1914, Count Kato succeeded Count Makino in the Foreign Office.[8] In early summer, Kato made many important changes in personnel both at the *Kasumigaseki* and in the diplomatic and consular services abroad. In particular, the legation and consulates in China were completely reorganized in personnel, in evident anticipation of an important diplomatic move toward China under the new administration.[9] Thus, as early as August 21, 1914, the foreign minister instructed Minister Hioki to call on President Yuan Shih-kai to inform the latter of the responsibility resting upon the two powers to maintain the peace in the Orient, and to urge upon the latter to enter into a frank exchange of views concerning the subject. On August 26, immediately after the declaration of war (August 23, 1914), Minister Hioki inquired of the Foreign Office concerning the negotiation, and Kato instructed Hioki to wait for a more favorable opportunity.[10]

In their issuance of *Gaimusho Rei* No. I, 1914, on September 16, placing strict censorship upon the press on foreign affairs, and their subsequent statements thereon, both Premier Okuma and Foreign Minister Kato broadly hinted at an important diplomatic move in contemplation.[11] Subsequent days saw an interchange of frequent calls among the genro, the premier, and the foreign minister;[12] and finally, on September 24, Marshal Prince Yamagata, Marshal Prince Oyama, and Marquis Okuma held an all-day conference to come to an agreement upon general outlines of the intended negotiations.[13] It was tentatively agreed that the main object of the negotiations was to obtain a more substantial foothold in Manchuria and Inner Mongolia, and that such negotiations were to be started after the surrender of Tsingtao.[14] This decision was immediately reported to the emperor.[15]

[8]Count Kato held the portfolio of the foreign minister in three cabinets previous to this, namely, the Ito (1900–1901), Saionji (1906), and Katsura cabinets (1913).

[9]*Tokyo Asahi*, July 11, 1914, p. 2. Cf. *ibid.*, July 21, 1914, p. 4; also July 26, 1914, p. 3.

[10]Ito, *op. cit.*, II, 153–154.

[11]*Tokyo Asahi*, Sept. 19, 1914, p. 4.

[12]*Ibid.*, Sept. 22, 1914, p. 3.

[13]*Ibid.*, Sept. 25, 1914, p. 3.

[14]Ito, *op. cit.*, II, 199.

[15]Cf. *Tokyo Asahi*, Sept. 27, 1914, p. 3.

The "psychological moment" arrived with the fall of Tsingtao on November 7, 1914.[16] Thereupon, in striking contrast with the complete absence of opinions since September 16, "strong" views began to appear suddenly in the press, openly advocating a continued occupation of Kiaochaowan and extension of Japanese interests on the continent.[17] Count Kato called on Prince Yamagata and other genro to obtain their "understanding" concerning the proposed negotiations;[18] and, after obtaining the cabinet's approval to initiate the negotiations, the foreign minister telegraphed Minister Hioki to return to Tokyo for conference.[19] A series of conferences were held between Count Kato and Minister Hioki as well as the genro, the premier, and the foreign minister. And consequently, after obtaining His Majesty's approval, the foreign minister handed the instructions to Minister Hioki on December 3, 1914.[20] The minister left Tokyo the following day.

We have seen elsewhere that during the Thirty-fifth Diet, convened on December 7 and dissolved on December 25, 1914, searching questions were addressed to the government concerning the future of the German interests in Kiaochaowan and settlement of the Manchurian problem and that, on those occasions, Count Kato carefully avoided stating clearly what policy his cabinet intended to pursue, but that he did not fail to intimate that his office was seriously contemplating a decisive measure. The dissolution of the House of Representatives on Christmas Day left the foreign minister completely free from constant parliamentary criticism and interpellation on the conduct of his office. Moreover, the tones of parliamentary discussion on foreign relations did not fail to indi-

[16]*Ibid.*, Nov. 8, 1914, pp. 2, 5.

[17]*Cf.* an article by Dr. Setsurei Miyake, a well-known historian-critic, in *Tokyo Asahi*, Nov. 9, 1914, p. 3. The same paper carried a news item of an interview with an anonymous diplomat. This inspired spokesman of the Foreign Office openly advocated the Japanese succession to all the rights and concessions held by Germany in Kiaochaowan, and emphasized the importance of "solving" the Manchurian question (*ibid.*, Nov. 9, 1914, p. 2).

[18]*Ibid.*, Nov. 11, 1914, p. 3.

[19]Minister Hioki reached Moji on November 18. No account of his activities in Tokyo could be found in the press (*ibid.*, Nov. 19, 1914, p. 2).

[20]On Dec. 3, both Marquis Okuma and Count Kato were granted an imperial audience to obtain His Majesty's sanction to the instructions (*ibid.*, Dec. 4, 1914, p. 3). Text of instructions in Ito, *op. cit.*, II, 154–160.

cate the general trend of public opinion as to the "solution" of Sino-Japanese relations. Meanwhile, public opinion was raised to a state of high frenzy over Chinese demand for immediate withdrawal of Japanese forces from Tsingtao and her proclamation revoking the war zone. Thus, the "psychological moment" arrived, and, on January 18, 1915, Minister Hioki called on President Yuan Shih-kai and presented to him directly the entire text of the instructions from Tokyo.[21]

The Japanese instructions were divided into five groups. The most objectionable items were included in Group V, a full acceptance of which on the part of China would have reduced her to mere protectorate of Japan.[22] The first conference was held on February 2, and twenty-four conferences were held up to April 17, when Chinese representatives took a very firm stand. Immediately after the conference of April 17, Minister Hioki telegraphed Tokyo for final instructions, explaining in detail the necessity for presenting an ultimatum to China.[23] However, Kato sought to obtain Chinese consent to a revised list, and on April 26 a revised list was presented, adding that, should the Chinese accept the amended proposals, Japan would restore the German leased territory at the close of the war on certain conditions.[24] The Chinese reply of May 1, however, did not meet the Japanese approval.[25] On May 2, therefore, a prolonged conference of high officials at the *Kasumigaseki* was held at Count Kato's residence, when resort to an ultimatum was finally decided upon.[26]

[21]Shinobu, *Taisho Gaiko Jugonenshi* (Tokyo, 1927), pp. 46–47. *Cf.* Sakuzo Yoshino, "Sino-Japanese Negotiations," *Chuo Koron*, No. 318 (June, 1915), pp. 51–60; also a symposium on China policy by Matsui, Tagawa, Ishino, and Ogawa, in *ibid.*, No. 314 (Feb., 1915), pp. 66–74.

[22]Discussion regarding the details of the negotiations as well as the contents of the Japanese "demands" is omitted here, as such treatment is beyond the scope of this book. For brief account of the negotiations, see Ichijima, *Okumako Hachijugonenshi* (Tokyo, 1926), III, 252–306; also Ito, *op. cit.*, II, 129–226.

[23]Ito, *op. cit.*, II, 160–170. By this time the press became violent in urging upon the government to take more vigorous measures, while several associations and organizations held public meetings in advocacy of stronger policy toward China (Ichijima, *op. cit.*, III, 276).

[24]The cabinet, at its meeting of April 20, decided to press for final settlement. This firm stand was reported to Prince Yamagata, Prince Oyama, and Marquis Matsukata by Home Minister Oura (*Tokyo Asahi*, April 21, 1915, p. 2).

[25]Ito, *op. cit.*, II, 170–172. *Cf. Tokyo Asahi*, May 3, 1915, p. 2.

[26]The conference lasted from 2 P.M. till early next morning (*Tokyo Asahi*, May 4, 1915, p. 2).

Foreign Minister Kato struck out Group V from the ultimatum, leaving these demands for later negotiations. At
the cabinet meeting of May 3, the prime minister and
majority of the cabinet members were inclined to present
the whole group as demands, but Kato insisted that the
ultimatum must be such as to command the respect of
world public opinion, which point he finally won from his
colleagues.[27]

In the afternoon of May 4 a joint conference of the genro
and cabinet ministers was held. Here the genro, particularly
Prince Yamagata and Marquis Matsukata, raised a serious
objection to the ultimatum, insisting that particular caution
and moderation should be exercised not to arouse the suspicion abroad that advantage was being taken of the helpless
situation in China and of the World War.[28] The cabinet
continued its deliberations till past midnight, but could
not reach a decision.[29] Accordingly, another cabinet meeting was held on the afternoon of May 5,[30] and, after full
deliberation, it finally decided upon a draft ultimatum
prepared by the Foreign Office.[31] The second joint conference of the genro and the cabinet was held at 9:30 A.M.,
May 6, at which Prince Yamagata, as an expression of lack
of confidence in the foreign minister, suggested that Count
Kato himself should go to Peking to conduct the difficult
negotiations in person.[32] This informal meeting was followed

[27] Ito, *op. cit.*, II, 172–175. *Cf.* Ichijima, *op. cit.*, III, 282.

[28] Marquis Inouye, who was absent, also agreed with Prince Yamagata and Marquis Matsukata (*Tokyo Asahi*, May 6, 1915, p. 2).

[29] Prince Yamagata, Prince Oyama, and Marquis Matsukata represented the
genro, as Marquis Inouye could not attend the conference on account of illness.
The elder statesmen left the meeting at 6:10 P.M. (*ibid.*, May 5, 1915, p. 2).

[30] During the forenoon, Home Minister Oura called on Prince Yamagata and Marquis Matsukata and informed the genro of the tentative decision of the cabinet to
postpone the discussion of Group V to later negotiations, as further insistence upon
them might lead to a war between Japan and China and also might invite greater
suspicion from the powers. The genro expressed great satisfaction (*ibid.*). *Cf.* an
editorial, "Nature of the Genro Conference," *ibid.*, May 6, 1915, p. 3.

[31] Ito, *op. cit.*, II, 176; Ichijima, *op. cit.*, III, 284. The cabinet meeting lasted from
noon till 6:30 P.M. After the meeting, an important conference of leading officials
of the Foreign Office was held till eleven o'clock at night (*Tokyo Asahi*, May 6, 1915,
p. 2).

[32] Dr. Yoshino holds that Prince Yamagata's remarks were not directed at Count
Kato personally, but were motivated by the genro's sincere belief that Kato's
direct charge of the negotiations at Peking would greatly improve the situation
(Yoshino, *Dai San Kakumeigo no China* [Tokyo, 1921], p. 81).

by a formal joint conference of the genro, cabinet, and chiefs of general staffs of both services in the presence of the emperor to deliberate upon the draft ultimatum. After obtaining the imperial sanction to the text of the ultimatum, the final instructions were telegraphed to Peking at 3:30 P.M. following the conference, and transmitted to the Chinese government on May 7, 1915.[33] On the same day, the Foreign Office issued a long communiqué setting forth in detail the Japanese account of the negotiations.[34]

When the ultimatum was dispatched to Peking, preparations were all complete for general mobilization of her military forces.[35] China accepted the ultimatum at one o'clock on the morning of May 9, 1915.[36] Immediately upon receipt of this news, the *Kasumigaseki* informed all embassies and legations abroad of the Chinese acceptance, and, at the same time, instructed all the consular agents in China to withdraw their warnings issued already on May 3 to Japanese residents to be in readiness to leave the country upon immediate notice.[37] The foreign minister was received in audience by the emperor at 11 A.M. to report the Chinese reply, which had arrived early in the morning. Retiring from the palace, Kato hastened to inform the genro (Yamagata, Matsukata, Oyama, Inouye) of the Japanese victory at Peking.[38] Treaties were signed and notes exchanged on May 25.[39]

Reference should be made at this point to the fact that, throughout the entire negotiations, Foreign Minister Kato succeeded in maintaining his leadership. He thus maintained the autonomy of the Foreign Office in the conduct of negotia-

[33]*Tokyo Asahi*, May 7, 8, 1915, p. 2. Text of the final instructions of May 6, 1915, in Ito, *op. cit.*, II, 176–180. *Cf. Gaiko Jiho*, XXI, Nos. 7, 10, 11 (April 1, May, 15, June 1, 1915), pp. 695–701, 1039–1043, 1251–1261; Sakuzo Yoshino, "Sino-Japanese Negotiations," *Chuo Koron*, No. 318 (June, 1915), pp. 51–80; also his *Kyokuto no Gaiko* (Tokyo, 1916), pp. 353–372; Hirota, *Naikaku Kotetsu Gojunenshi* (Tokyo, 1930), pp. 717–719; Shinobu, *Taisho Gaiko Jugonenshi* (Tokyo, 1927), pp. 13–18.

[34]Text of the *communiqué* in *Gaiko Jiho*, XXI, No. 10 (May 15, 1915), pp. 1148–1160; also in *Tokyo Asahi* (May 8, 1915), p. 3.

[35]*Gaiko Jiho*, XXI, No. 11 (June 1, 1915), p. 1259; *Tokyo Asahi*, May 8, 1915, p. 4.

[36]*Tokyo Asahi*, May 10, 1915, p. 2.

[37]*Ibid.*, May 5, 10, 1915.

[38]*Ibid.*, May 10, 1915, p. 3.

[39]*Ibid.*, May 26, 1915, p. 3. For text of the treaties and notes exchanged on May 25, 1915, see Ito, *op. cit.*, II, 215–221. For a table comparing the original proposals, revised proposals of April 26, 1915, and the final text, see *ibid.*, II, 221–226.

tions against repeated encroachments by the genro, for which he incurred the lasting disfavor of the highest advisers to the throne on the formation of cabinets.[40] Moreover, he was able to prevent a large-scale military demonstration. Thus, in March, 1915, when military authorities sought to bring pressure upon China by a large-scale expedition of guards into Manchuria, Foreign Minister Kato gave his consent to dispatch troops to Hsing Ming Tsuen only under certain conditions. But General Oka, war minister, made a direct report to the emperor on the matter and obtained the imperial sanction to dispatch troops. As soon as Count Kato learned this, he lodged a strong protest with the prime minister and immediately was given an audience by the emperor to petition His Majesty's reconsideration of the war minister's report.[41]

When the Thirty-sixth Diet was opened on May 20, opposition parties subjected the Sino-Japanese diplomacy to critical analysis and made frantic attacks upon the government.[42] On May 22, 1915, the foreign minister came before the House of Representatives and made a report on the negotiations. Immediately after the speech by the finance minister which followed that of the foreign minister, Representative Hajime Motoda, a veteran leader of the *Seiyukai*, the chief opposition party in the Lower House, led the onslaught upon the government regarding the treaties. The debate lasted all day, during which those eloquent parliamentary leaders vainly sought to compel the Okuma cabinet to admit a diplomatic blunder in the negotiations. The demand for

[40]Count Kato, upon assuming the office, discontinued the unbroken tradition of over fifteen years' standing of transmitting for advice all secret diplomatic correspondence to the genro, who inevitably exerted undue pressure upon foreign relations (*ibid.*, II, 49). During the early part of April, 1915, Prince Yamagata wrote a long memorandum concerning the Sino-Japanese negotiations, but Kato did not even acknowledge its receipt. Moreover, the foreign minister rejected the proposal of Prince Matsukata that a genro be sent to Peking to conduct the negotiations. The genro's disfavor of Kato was complete when the latter ruthlessly rejected the approach of Dr. Nagao Ariga, who had been sent to Tokyo by President Yuan Shih-kai to make a direct appeal to the genro for "moderation" of Japanese proposals, and who greatly influenced Inouye and Matsukata (*ibid.*, I, 23–28). Accordingly, Kato did not receive the recommendation to form a ministry so long as any of these three genro was living (see *Tokyo Asahi*, Sept. 24, 1915, p. 2).

[41]*Ibid.*, I, 60; also *ibid.*, II, 163–165.

[42]For brief defense of the negotiations, see an article by Seiichiro Koyama in *Gaiko Jiho*, XXI, No. 11 (June 1, 1915), pp. 1197–1204.

production of diplomatic documents concerning the entire negotiations to the Diet met a flat refusal on the part of the ministry on the ground that the treaties had not yet been ratified and that, even if ratification had been made, it was not bound by law to submit such diplomatic documents to the legislature. Furthermore, the prime minister defended the several joint conferences held with the genro during the progress of the negotiations, citing precedents and declaring that whatever had been the influence of the genro on the outcome, the cabinet would assume the entire responsibility under the treaties.[43]

The foreign minister's address in the Upper House on May 22 likewise occasioned a lively interpellation by Mr. Ren Nakakoji who condemned the government for keeping Group V secret from the powers. He declared that the foreign minister should have taken personal charge of the negotiations at Peking. Mr. Nakakoji concluded his speech by requesting the government to assume a different attitude in making replies from what it was taking in the Lower House. Count Kato declared in reply that Japan was not bound to make known the proposals to Great Britain, Russia, France, or the United States, and that Group V was from the beginning considered in a different category. He defended the negotiations conducted by Minister Hioki.[44]

The climax of opposition attacks upon the Sino-Japanese negotiations took the form of a resolution of censure, introduced by the *Seiyukai* and *Kokuminto* combination.[45] It was introduced in the House of Representatives on June 3, 1915, by Representative Kei Hara, president of the *Seiyukai* party, and was ably defended by Representative Heikichi Ogawa, a leading member of the *Seiyukai*. The opposition parties attacked the government negotiations on the ground that the

[43]*Teikoku Gikaishi*, IX, 1212-1239; *Dai Sanjurokkai Teikoku Gikai Shugiin Iinkai Giroku*, Pt. I, No. 1, pp. 4-5, 78, 88; Ichijima, *op. cit.*, III, 309-316. *Cf. Tokyo Asahi*, May 23, 1915, pp. 2-3.

[44]*Ibid.*, IX, 1057-1064. The war minister, throughout the session, denied that military authorities brought any pressure upon China during the progress of negotiations (*ibid.*, IX, 1065). During interpellations in the House of Peers, it was also brought out that the government was unwilling to restore Kiaochaowan to China unless conditions were satisfactorily met by China (*ibid.*, IX, 1076). *Cf. Tokyo Asahi*, May 23, 1915, p. 2.

[45]Text of the resolution in *ibid.*, IX, 1346.

time was not proper, that military pressure was brought to bear on China, that the negotiations brought about a widespread anti-Japanese movement in China, and finally, that the declaration concerning the restoration of Kiaochaowan was a gross impairment of the prestige and interest of Japan. On the other hand, the resolution was opposed by Representative Chokuon Kataoka, Foreign Minister Kato, and, finally, by Prime Minister Okuma himself. Count Kato, in a detailed refutation point by point raised during the debate, defended his conduct of the negotiations. The prime minister himself took the floor of the House and urged the defeat of the resolution, contending that the negotiations were a great success and that such diplomatic issues should not be subjected to partisan politics. The resolution was overwhelmingly defeated by 232:133.[46]

While parliamentary discussion and criticism were occupying the public attention, the Okuma government pushed the treaties through the Privy Council with earnestness and conviction. Thus, the foreign minister led the government delegates in explaining the details of the treaties before the sub-committee of inquiry on June 4 and 5, resulting in the recommendation by the committee for ratification of the treaties by a unanimous vote.[47] At the plenary session of the Council, held on June 7, 1915, Dr. Hiroyuki Kato and Viscount Kiyoura urged upon the foreign minister to spare no efforts in developing the newly acquired concessions in Mongolia. The Privy Council unanimously recommended ratification of the treaties which, in subsequent years, occupied interesting pages in the diplomatic history of modern Japan.[48] The emperor promptly ratified the treaties on June 7, and ratifications were exchanged the following day between

[46]*Ibid.*, IX, 1346–1369; *Tokyo Asahi*, June 4, 1915, p. 2. *Cf.* Kudo, *Taisho Kenseishi*, pp. 476–478; Ito, *op. cit.*, II, 43–44.

[47]Not all members of the sub-committee were satisfied with the manner in which the negotiations were conducted or substance of the final treaties. But they could not condemn the treaties as such, and consequently, included in their report a warning against future occurrence of ambiguity or incompleteness in the treaty text. This is the first instance of a sub-committee of the Privy Council recommending ratification of a treaty with warning attached to the report (*Tokyo Asahi*, June 7, 1915, p. 2).

[48]Ito, *op. cit.*, II, 202. An interesting light might be thrown upon the parliamentary tactics in Japan when it is observed that the treaties which were so violently attacked on June 3 were not even mentioned in parliamentary interpellations and debates during the remainder of the session, which lasted till June 9, 1915.

Count Kato and the Chinese minister.[49] Accordingly, the treaties were published in the *Kwampo* on June 9, 1915.[50]

After his successful parliamentary battles in the Thirty-sixth Diet, Count Kato had to face the displeasures from the genro whose "advice" he had so ruthlessly rejected during the course of the negotiations. Thus, on June 19, less than two weeks after the close of the Diet, a conference of two genro, Yamagata and Inouye, was held,[51] followed by a call of Prime Minister Okuma upon Marquis Inouye the following day.[52] On June 23, a conference of four elder statesmen—Yamagata, Inouye, Matsukata, and Oyama—was held at the home of Marquis Inouye.[53] Again, on June 25, a secret conference of the elder statesmen and Prime Minister Okuma was held.[54] The genro, at these meetings, deliberated upon questions relating to: (1) measures to be taken toward China; (2) development of concessions in Manchuria and Mongolia; (3) substitution of the present minister to Peking by another or dispatch of a special mission; (4) prevention of an anti-Japanese boycott, and (5) the European front. The undeniable undercurrent that ran throughout the repeated conferences of the elder statesmen was directed toward removing Count Kato from the *Kasumigaseki* post, and reasserting the influence of the genro in the nation's diplomacy. Furthermore, it was made plain to the prime minister that the removal of Kato from the Foreign Office would have a favorable effect upon the strained diplomatic relations between the two countries.[55]

Thus, pressure was brought to bear upon Marquis Okuma to demand the resignation of his trusted foreign minister. On August 10, 1915, Count Komei Kato tendered his resignation, taking advantage of the exposure of a systematic parliamentary corruption made during the Thirty-fifth Diet under

[49] *Tokyo Asahi*, June 8, 1915, p. 3; *ibid.*, June 9, 1915, p. 4. President Yuan Shih-kai ratified the treaties on June 1 (*ibid.*, June 2, p. 4), and the ratification reached the Chinese legation in Tokyo on June 6 (*ibid.*, June 8, 1915, p. 3).

[50] *Cf. ibid.*, June 10, 1915, p. 4.

[51] *Ibid.*, June 20, 1915, p. 2.

[52] *Ibid.*, June 21, 1915, p. 2.

[53] *Ibid.*, June 24, 1915, p. 2.

[54] *Ibid.*, June 26, 1915, p. 2.

[55] Ito, *op. cit.*, II, 46–50. *Cf. Tokyo Asahi*, June 27, 1915, p. 2.

the direction of Viscount Oura in vain effort to secure the passage of an Army Expansion bill.[56]

[56]During the Thirty-fifth Diet, Viscount Oura, the then minister of agriculture and commerce, conducted a systematic attempt at "winning" opposition members to the passage of an Army Expansion bill. This parliamentary scandal was exposed to the public through the courts, and those guilty were punished according to law. However, Viscount Oura, since he declared his intention to retire from public office and from all honors and privileges, escaped any judicial prosecution. Therefore, when Viscount Oura tendered his resignation as home minister on July 29, 1915, the cabinet members tendered their resignation, assuming, also, collective responsibility, but their resignations were rejected by the emperor, upon advice of the genro. However, Foreign Minister Kato, Finance Minister Wakatsuki, Navy Minister Yashiro, all stood firm upon resignation. Thus Kato took this opportunity to resign from the Foreign Office, to be succeeded by Viscount Ishii in October, 1915 (Kudo, *Taisho Kenseishi*, pp. 133–137; Ichijima, *op. cit.*, III, 316–325).

Chapter XVI

ADHERENCE TO THE LONDON DECLARATION OF ALLIANCE

On AUGUST 4, 1914, the French ambassador in Tokyo called on the Foreign Office and formally proposed the conclusion of a Franco-Japanese alliance, while a Russo-Japanese alliance was proposed by the Russian government through Ambassador Motono in St. Petersburg, on August 10.[1] The genro were strongly inclined to the proposal, particularly toward a Russo-Japanese alliance, and Prime Minister Okuma was also favorably disposed. However, Count Kato, a staunch supporter of the Anglo-Japanese alliance as the corner stone of Japanese foreign policy, successfully opposed these proposals on the ground that negotiations looking to the conclusion of such important political treaties of alliance should be postponed until after the close of the war. On January 9, 1915, the French and Russian ambassadors in London called on the British foreign secretary to urge upon him the conclusion of an all-inclusive four-power alliance and, as a second proposal, suggested Japanese adherence to the Declaration of London of September 4, 1914. By this declaration, which was the basis of the alliance against the central powers, Great Britain, France, and Russia engaged not to conclude separate peace but to reach an agreement with each other on all peace demands.[2]

The attention of the Foreign Office was interrupted from January to May, 1915, on account of the Sino-Japanese negotiations. However, toward the latter part of May the move-

[1] Cf. Tokyo Asahi, Aug. 11, 1914, p. 2; ibid., Aug. 21, 25, 1914, p. 3.
[2] Text of the declaration in ibid., Sept. 10, 1914, p. 3.

ment for a Russo-Japanese alliance was revived, with two influential genro (Yamagata, Inouye) and Viscount Motono, Japanese ambassador to Russia, as chief advocates. Several conferences of the genro were held in May and June, following the elaborate memorandum signed by four genro on May 27, 1915, and addresses to the prime minister and the foreign minister, urging upon the government to take immediate steps for conclusion of an alliance. Count Kato stood firm against such an alliance on the ground that it would lessen the effect of the alliance with Great Britain. On July 29, Ambassador Motono telegraphed Tokyo that the Russian government was anxious for Japanese adherence to the Declaration of London. On August 1, and again on August 3, 1915, the British government inquired whether Japan was favorably disposed to the adherence should it be offered. The foreign minister, by this time, was more friendlily inclined to the move, and consequently he advised Marquis Okuma to accept the proposal on the ground that such a move would further insure Japanese participation at the coming peace conference, without adding any new responsibility upon the shoulders of the government. Meanwhile, a formal invitation for Japanese adherence was extended by Great Britain on August 15. Accordingly, immediately after Viscount Ishii succeeded Count Kato as foreign minister,[3] the Japanese adherence to the declaration was consummated on October 19, 1915, through an exchange of notes in London.[4]

Foreign Minister Kato came before both Houses of the Diet on September 9 to report the Declaration of London of September 4, 1914, signed by Great Britain, Russia, and France. The text of the declaration, as well as the memorandum of the British government to Tokyo, stating that the declaration did not in any way affect the obligations of the existing alliance between Japan and England, and that by

[3]Viscount Ishii became foreign minister on October 13, 1915.

[4]Text of the Japanese adherence to the London Declaration of Alliance in *Recueil des traités et conventions conclus entre l'empire du Japon et les puissances étrangères* (Tokyo, Foreign Office, 1918), pp. 465–468. The notes were published as notification of the Foreign Office on October 30, 1915 (*Gaimusho Kokuji* No. 41, 1915). *Cf.* Tadao Matsumoto, M. P., "Diplomatic History of Japan during the Early Period of the World War," *Gaiko Jiho*, No. 623 (Nov. 15, 1930), pp. 83–109; Ichijima, *Okumako Hachijugonenshi*, III, 331–334; Ito, *Kato Komei*, II, 103–118; *Tokyo Asahi*, Oct. 30, 1915, p. 2.

virtue of Article 2 of the alliance full coöperation and frank exchange of views were well protected, was made public.[5] No question was addressed to the foreign minister following his report to the Peers. However, immediately following his report in the Lower House, Representative Heikichi Ogawa inquired of Kato as to whether there existed any agreement or any exchange of views with the British government concerning the disposition of Kiaochaowan at the end of the war. Foreign Minister Kato replied that, excepting the treaty provisions of the alliance, there was no agreement as to the future of Kiaochaowan.[6] The question as to whether Japan's diplomatic position was jeopardized by refusing to adhere to the declaration was raised several times during the Thirty-sixth Diet, when the foreign minister assured the members of the Diet that the Japanese voice was fully protected under Article 2 of the Anglo-Japanese Alliance.[7]

In his address on foreign relations at the outset of the Thirty-seventh session of Diet, December 7, 1915, Viscount Kikujiro Ishii, who had succeeded Count Kato on October 13, reported the Japanese adherence to the Declaration of London on October 19, 1915, and said that the adherence was not absolutely necessary but was expedient to enhance the determination and unity of the Allied powers, and to make clear the relative position of the powers at the peace conference. He assured the Diet that no responsibilities not imposed by the Anglo-Japanese Alliance were added by this declaration. He stood firm upon this declaration against numerous parliamentary interpellations in both Houses, and declined to disclose the reported difficulties the government was encountering at the hands of the Privy Council, pleading that the proceedings of the Council were absolutely secret.[8]

The Japanese adherence to this declaration was achieved by an exchange of notes in London, without first submitting the

[5]Japanese text of the Declaration of London and the British memorandum in *Teikoku Gikaishi*, IX, 853–854. As soon as Viscount Ishii read the news of the declaration, he wired from France urging upon Count Kato to adhere to it (Viscount Ishii, *Gaiko Yoroku*, pp. 113–121).

[6]*Teikoku Gikaishi*, IX, 878.

[7]*Ibid.*, IX, 929; *Dai Sanjugokai Teikoku Gikai Shugiin Iinkai Giroku*, Pt. I, No. 2, p. 5; *Tokyo Asahi*, June 5, 1915, p. 2.

[8]For parliamentary discussion upon the adherence see *Teikoku Gikaishi*, X, 26–27, 87, 89, 226–227, 235–237, 248–251, 268–273, 295–296, 299–302.

same to the deliberation of the Privy Council for advice as in the case of a treaty requiring subsequent ratification. And when the notes were submitted to this body, after having been exchanged, the Okuma cabinet was severely censured by the Council. Moreover, this procedure followed by the government in adhering to the London Declaration was subjected to vigorous discussion in the meetings of the Peers Budget Committee.[9] In reply to a question by Baron Tanetaro Megata on January 22, 1916, Prime Minister Okuma declared that treaties requiring subsequent ratification were submitted to the Privy Council for advice before promulgation, but that the practice had not been uniform with regard to agreements concluded by exchange of notes, such as the Japanese adherence to the Declaration of London. Although he refused to disclose the issues then pending between the cabinet and the Council, he emphasized the fact that the procedure was in no way a violation of the Constitution.[10] Upon further inquiry by Baron Megata, Dr. Sakuye Takahashi, chief of the Bureau of Legislative Affairs, replied that no clear demarcation could be drawn between treaties and agreements within the meaning of Article 6 of *Sumitsuin Kansei*, or ordinance concerning the organization of the Privy Council.[11] And on January 24, Foreign Minister Ishii admitted that the adherence to the declaration was achieved by an exchange of notes without having been submitted to the Privy Council for advice on account of its urgency, and that the procedure followed in this case was in no way different from those followed in similar instances.[12] On the same day, Dr. Rentaro Mizuno, a well-known jurist, argued that the Japanese adherence to the London Declaration should come within the meaning of "treaties and agreements" as provided for in Article 6 of the *Sumitsuin Kansei*, and questioned the

[9]The controversy between the cabinet and the Council over the procedure taken in this instance never became subject of debates on the floor of the House of Peers, and when it was mentioned in the House of Representatives, the foreign minister dismissed the subject as being not subject to discussion in the House (*Teikoku Gikaishi*, X, 288, 299–302).

[10]*Dai Sanjuhichikai Teikoku Gikai Kizokuin Yosan Iinkai Giji Sokkiroku*, No. 5, p. 62. On January 24, 1916, Prime Minister Okuma denied having said that only the more important treaties requiring subsequent exchange of ratifications were to be submitted to the Privy Council (*ibid.*, No. 6, p. 77).

[11]*Ibid.*, No. 5, p. 68.

[12]*Ibid.*, No. 6, p. 71. *Cf. Tokyo Asahi*, Jan. 25, 1916, p. 3.

government as to its legal interpretation of the article in question. In reply, Viscount Ishii argued at length that the precise scope of treaties and agreements could not be stated in abstract terms, but that such interpretation depended upon concrete cases. He declared that, at the time of the establishment of the Council, there was no room for doubt as to the interpretation of the article as being confined to questions arising out of the revision of unequal treaties. He reminded the interpellator that international commitments had come to be made in numerous ways, such as exchange of notes, of memoranda, or merely verbal commitments. He expressed his regret that he could not explain further on the ground that the matter was still pending between the Council and the cabinet.[13]

[13]*Op. cit.*, No. 6, pp. 72–73. The government took a more defiant attitude toward interpellations in the House Budget Committee. The replies to interpellations were more detailed and conciliatory in the Peers Budget Committee than in the House Budget Committee (*Dai Sanjuhichikai Teikoku Gikai Shugiin Iinkai Giroku*, Pt. I, No. 1, p. 107). *Cf.* Viscount Ishii, *op. cit.*, pp. 121–126.

Chapter XVII

THE LANSING–ISHII AGREEMENT

Shortly after the United States entered the World War, the Terauchi ministry sent a special mission, headed by Viscount Kikujiro Ishii, a former minister for foreign affairs, to congratulate the United States on its decision. The object of the mission, however, was to exchange views with American diplomatic authorities concerning the Far Eastern affairs and to reach an understanding.[1]

Viscount Ishii reached Washington in the early part of September, and after a few days' sojourn in Washington he approached President Wilson concerning the possibility of reaching an understanding on the Chinese question. At the first exchange of views with the President, Mr. Wilson expressed greatest concern with the problem of maintaining the principles of open door and equal opportunity. Perceiving the possibility of reaching an agreement with the United States by accepting the Wilson proposal for abolishing the spheres of influence, and, at the same time, obtaining the acceptance by the United States of Japan's special position in China, Viscount Ishii telegraphed the Tokyo government for instruc-

[1]That a genuine apprehension was entertained concerning the Chinese situation between Japan and the United States, and that a complete mutual understanding was earnestly desired, could be easily surmised from a review of parliamentary interpellations during the thirty-ninth Diet. Thus Representative Mochizuki declared, at the meeting of the House Budget Committee on June 29, 1917, that Japan should approach the United States with a view to wiping out all causes for misunderstandings and suspicion regarding China and also the defense of the Philippines Islands, and interpellated the foreign minister, Viscount Motono, as to what precise measures the government was taking. Viscount Motono admitted the necessity but declined to state the measures contemplated (*Dai Sanjukukai Teikoku Gikai Shugiin Iinkai Giroku*, Pt. I, No. 1, p. 78).

201

tions to initiate negotiations.[2] His suggestion was laid before
the advisory council on foreign relations for deliberation,
when a majority of the members opposed any declaration
renouncing spheres of influence in China, and, in consequence, Viscount Ishii failed to receive instructions thereon.[3]
Accordingly, without waiting for instructions, he started
negotiations with Secretary Lansing with a view to arriving
at an understanding concerning China. Secretary Lansing
suggested that a joint declaration should be issued pledging
the two governments to respect the territorial integrity of
China and the principles of open door and equal opportunity.
Viscount Ishii argued that the issuance of such a declaration
would do little to clarify the situation. He contended that an
insertion of the principles with which Japan had repeatedly
expressed her full concurrence would be certain to arouse
public apprehension that the action was an admission on the
part of Japan of the violation of such principles. Thus, Viscount Ishii insisted upon inclusion of a statement recognizing
Japan's special position in China, similar to that of the
United States in regard to her Central and South American
neighbors. The main issue was the terms to be employed to
express the Japanese position. Viscount Ishii suggested the
expression, "paramount interest," which was vigorously
objected to by Secretary Lansing. Viscount Ishii called
the Secretary's attention to the use of the expression by the
Secretary of State Seward in describing the relation of the
United States to Mexico, but to no avail. Finally, Viscount
Ishii's suggestion of "special interest and influences" was
further reduced to "special interest."[4] Hence, on November
2, 1917, the so-called "Lansing-Ishii Agreement" was concluded by an exchange of notes.[5]

Soon an interesting controversy arose as to the precise
interpretation of "special interest" taken in conjunction
with the principle of "territorial propinquity." Before the
hearings of the Senate Foreign Relations Committee on
August 11, 1919, Secretary Lansing denied that the "special
interest" as used in the agreement included political interest.

[2]Viscount Ishii, *Gaiko Yoroku*, pp. 136–139.

[3]*Ibid.*, p. 140.

[4]*Ibid.*, pp. 140–146.

[5]Text of the agreement in *ibid.*, pp. 147–148.

Viscount Ishii wrote in his diary refuting Secretary Lansing's testimony concerning the interpretation of the phrase in question. He took the position that it referred primarily to "political interest" and indirectly to "economic interest," holding that to argue for special economic interest in China would have been contrary to the doctrine of the open door and equal opportunity.[6] That Viscount Ishii's position clearly embodied the sentiment of the government of Japan at the time is evident from the address on foreign relations delivered by Foreign Minister Motono, on January 23, 1917, in which he repeatedly referred to the special position of Japan in China, particularly in Manchuria and Mongolia. He declared that there could be no question as to Japan's special position in China because of her geographic, political, and economic relations.[7]

However, with the increasing criticisms raised both in the United States and in China, the short-lived agreement was terminated on April 14, 1923, by an exchange of notes between Secretary Hughes and Ambassador Hanihara.[8]

[6]*Ibid.*, pp. 151–159.

[7]*Teikoku Gikaishi*, X, 1047, 1061.

[8]Viscount Ishii says that the termination did not affect the actual position of Japan, since her special position was not based upon the discredited agreement but upon concrete realities of history and geography (*Gaiko Yoroku*, pp. 161–163).

Chapter XVIII

THE SIBERIAN EXPEDITION

Joint Expedition of 1918

AFTER THE COLLAPSE of the Russian Tsarist government and the conclusion of the Brest-Litovsk Treaty, the expedition of troops to Siberia became a subject of general discussion. By March, 1918, keen interest was manifested on all sides, but the consensus of opinion was opposed to any undertaking of an expedition to Siberia at this time.[1] As the subject assumed larger political and diplomatic importance, government censorship of the press on foreign relations became more outspoken and rigid.[2]

On the last day of the Fortieth Diet (March 26, 1918), Foreign Minister Motono came before the House of Representatives to make an address on Japan's policy toward Russia in view of the conclusion of the Brest-Litovsk Treaty, the advancing German influences toward the Far East, and the much-discussed Siberian expedition.[3] In his speech, Vis-

[1] See Yoshino, "What Is the Justification for the So-called Expedition?" *Chuo Koron*, No. 355 (April, 1918), pp. 1–30; Tetsu Izumi, "Siberian Expedition from the Standpoint of International Law," *Gaiko Jiho*, XXVII, No. 8 (April 15, 1918), pp. 862–872; Sakutaro Tachi, "Landing of Japanese Marines at Vladivostok," *ibid.*, XXVII, No. 9 (May 1, 1918), pp. 1027–1036; Fujitaro Wada, "Siberian Expedition and the United States," *ibid.*, XXVII, No. 9 (May 1, 1918), pp. 1086–1096. Dr. Sakuye Takahashi upheld the Siberian expedition should German influence become sufficient to threaten the independence of Japan (*Kokusaiho Gaiko Zasshi*, XVI, No. 6 [March, 1918], pp. 487–494).

[2] Professor Yoshino's article, "People's Wishes Concerning the Policy toward Russia," in *Chuo Koron*, No. 356 (May, 1918), pp. 42–49, was freely deleted by government censors.

[3] Breaking the tradition, Viscount Motono's address on Russian policy was first delivered in the House of Representatives, while his speech in the House of Peers was delivered at almost the last moment of the session.

count Motono categorically denied that Japan made any proposal to the powers for a Siberian expedition, or had received any formal proposal from the Allied and Associated powers in this regard. He declared that, should Japan be formally approached on this subject, the government would give it due deliberation. Then he made an important statement of policy when he declared that, should the situation in Siberia become such as to threaten the security of the Empire, or endanger her vital interests, the government was prepared to take speedy and effective measures in self-defense. He observed, moreover, that, even if Japan were compelled to take such necessary measures in Siberia, she entertained no enmity toward Russia or her people and disclaimed any territorial or aggressive intentions.[4] This address elicited several questions from the floor. Representative Yukio Ozaki and Kotaro Mochizuki expressed their satisfaction at the important address on foreign relations delivered before the adjournment of the Diet; they demanded a more definite statement of policy in view of the reported exchange of views with the powers. Viscount Motono admitted that negotiations were in progress concerning Siberian developments, but refused to divulge the nature of such negotiations.[5] In reply to the questions immediately following the foreign minister's address before the Peers, Viscount Motono maintained the similar policy of refusing to disclose the nature of negotiations then in progress with the powers.[6]

The American proposal for a joint expedition to Siberia for the purpose of assisting the eastward movement of the Czechoslovak troops across the continent was formally submitted to the Terauchi cabinet for deliberation on July 12, 1918. Under the dominant influence of Premier Terauchi and Viscount Goto, the cabinet decided not only to accept the American proposal for a joint expedition, but also to dispatch an "independent expedition" on its own initiative.[7] It soon developed, however, that Mr. Kei Hara and Baron Makino, both members of the *Gaiko Chosa Iinkai*, or the advisory

[4] *Teikoku Gikaishi*, XI, 617–618.

[5] *Ibid.*, XI, 618–622.

[6] *Ibid.*, XI, 157–160. On April 23, 1918, Viscount Motono was succeeded by Count Shimpei Goto at the *Kasumigaseki* office.

[7] *Tokyo Asahi*, July 13, 1918, p. 2.

council on foreign relations, to which the project had to be submitted for approval before final decision could be made, vigorously opposed such an undefined expedition at this time. This opposition on the part of Baron Makino and Kei Hara was solidly supported by the *Seiyukai* party, of which Hara was its president, and also by the *Kenseikai* party under Viscount Komei Kato.[8] Under these circumstances, General Terauchi now sought to bring strong pressure upon the opposition through the influence of the genro. Accordingly, Prime Minister Terauchi, Foreign Minister Goto, Marquis Saionji, Marquis Matsukata, and Prince Yamagata held a long conference (10:00 A.M. to 2:00 P.M.) in the palace on July 15 to obtain the "understanding" and approval of the elder statesmen regarding the cabinet's proposed action. After the conference, the government announced that the meeting was a success.[9]

Further pressure was brought to bear upon the president of the *Seiyukai* party by General Terauchi and Viscount Goto in person, who unsuccessfully sought to obtain Hara's·consent to a large-scale "independent expedition" to Siberia. Accordingly, after consulting Viscount Miyoji Ito, an influential member of the Privy Council and a member of the *Gaiko Chosakai*, Premier Terauchi decided with considerable reluctance to modify his original plans.[10] So, when the advisory council on foreign relations was called to order on July 16, a modified draft was submitted to the body for deliberation and approval.[11] The reply as submitted to this meeting consisted of two parts: namely, (1) Japanese acceptance of

[8]*Op. cit.*, July 16, 17, 1918, p. 2; *Jiji Shimpo*, July 19, 1918. *Cf.* Yoshino, "Siberian Expedition and the American Proposal," *Chuo Koron*, No. 360 (Aug., 1918), pp. 23–40. Many sections of Yoshino's article were deleted by government censors.

[9]Though invited, Marquis Okuma failed to attend the genro conference (*Tokyo Asahi*, July 16, 1918, p. 2). Marquis Saionji and Marquis Matsukata, representing the Satsuma clan, opposed the Yamagata adventure and indirectly suggested that the *Gaiko Chosakai* should decide the question. *Cf.* an anonymous article in *ibid.*, July 20, 1918, p. 2.

[10]*Ibid.*, July 17, 1918, p. 2.

[11]The following were present: General Count Terauchi (premier), Viscount Shimpei Goto (foreign minister), Admiral Tomosaburo Kato (navy minister), general Kenichi Oshima (war minister), Viscount Tosuke Hirata (member of the House of Peers), Baron Shinken Makino (member of the House of Peers), Viscount Miyoji Ito (privy councilor), Representative Kei Hara (president of *Seiyukai* party), and Representative Ki Inukai (president of *Kokuminto* party). Secretaries of the council were also present.

the American proposal for a joint expedition to Vladivostok, and (2) dispatching additional troops to Siberia upon her own initiative for self-protection and for police purposes. No objection was raised regarding the first point. However, both Kei Hara and Baron Makino raised a serious objection to the second proposition. They contended that no urgent necessity existed at the moment for undertaking an "independent expedition" to Siberia, particularly without consulting Great Britain or obtaining her "understanding." After an all-day session, they finally reached a compromise: Japan was to reserve the right to dispatch additional troops to Siberia in case of necessity to protect the Czechoslovak soldiers. Hence, though a large-scale expedition as originally planned had to be abandoned, freedom of action was reserved for the future, subject to the condition that such troops should be withdrawn as soon as the object of such expedition had been accomplished.[12]

The advisory council on foreign relations continued its session for three days, and finally, on July 18, it completed its deliberations.[13] Thereupon, immediately following the adjournment of the Gaiko Chosakai, Premier Terauchi was received in audience by the emperor to report the decision just reached and to request His Majesty's sanction thereto.[14] The cabinet met the following morning for a brief session to receive a formal report from the premier and the foreign minister upon the proceedings of the advisory council. Immediately afterwards, the Privy Council, held in the presence of the emperor, promptly approved the action of the Gaiko Chosakai.[15] Consequently, the Japanese reply to the American proposal was transmitted to Washington through Ambassador Ishii on the morning of July 19, accepting the American proposal for a joint expedition, while at the same time reserving to herself the right of sending additional forces in case of necessity in self-defense.[16]

General Terauchi's project for an "independent expedition" to Siberia, it was reported, was engineered by Marshal

[12]*Tokyo Asahi*, July 18, 1918, p. 2. *Cf.* Ito, *Kato Komei*, II, 289–297.
[13]Meetings were held on July 16, 17, 18, 1918.
[14]*Tokyo Asahi*, July 19, 1918, p. 2.
[15]*Ibid.*, July 20, 1918, p. 2.
[16]*Ibid.*, July 21, 1918, p. 2.

Prince Yamagata, president of the Privy Council, a leading genro, and head of the all-powerful Choshu military oligarchy, and ably supported by his faithful lieutenants, General Terauchi, then prime minister, and General Tanaka, vice-chief of general staff. Every possible pressure was brought to bear upon opposition forces to achieve this objective by utilizing the prestige and influence of a genro council, by making direct appeals, and, finally, by ruthless suppression of the freedom of speech and the press.[17]

The American reply to the Japanese communication of July 19 having been transmitted to Tokyo on July 28 through Ambassador Ishii,[18] the cabinet continued its deliberations for several days, and finally, on August 1, the question was submitted to the *Gaiko Chosakai*, which deliberated three hours upon the reply to be transmitted to Washington.[19] After obtaining the formal approval of the cabinet the following morning, Prime Minister Terauchi was granted an imperial audience at 11:30 A.M., August 2, to report the final decision of the government regarding the joint expedition to Vladivostok.[20] With His Majesty's sanction, the government issued an important statement in the afternoon. This declaration bore the signatures of all the members of the cabinet and set forth the reasons for dispatching troops to Vladivostok. It declared that the present expedition was undertaken upon American proposal, that the Japanese government entertained no political or territorial designs therein, and that the troops would be withdrawn as soon as possible, leaving wholly unimpaired the sovereignty of Russia in all its aspects, whether political or military.[21] The declaration deliberately omitted any mention of the size of the troops to be dispatched. On the other hand, in a press interview, Premier

[17]Viscount Uchida, ambassador to Russia, tendered his resignation on July 15, when it became certain that the Terauchi cabinet would embark on an expeditionary adventure, his earnest pleas to the contrary notwithstanding (*ibid.*, July 17, 1918, p. 3).

[18]Two columns of the *Tokyo Asahi* reporting the nature of the American reply were completely deleted. No news regarding activities of government officials or contents of the Washington dispatch could be found in the press. See *ibid.*, July 29, 30, 31, 1918.

[19]The proceedings of this meeting of the *Gaiko Chosakai* were not made known to the press.

[20]*Tokyo Asahi*, Aug. 3, 1918, p. 2.

[21]Text of the declaration in *Kwampo gogai*, Aug. 2, 1918. *Cf. Tokyo Asahi*, Aug. 3, 1918, p. 3; also *Gaiko Jiho*, XXVIII, No. 4 (Aug. 15, 1918), pp. 437–438.

Terauchi even intimated that additional contingents might be sent if necessity arose in the future.[22]

The significance of the Japanese policy toward the Siberian adventure may be better understood upon the assumption that the Terauchi government was well prepared for the American proposal. When Foreign Minister Motono delivered his significant address on the Russian situation on the closing day of the Fortieth Diet (March 26, 1918), intimating that Japan might be called upon to take appropriate measures in Siberia in self-defense, he had already concluded an agreement with the Chinese minister in Tokyo providing for joint defense of the Siberian border. In accordance with this agreement of March 25, 1918, military and naval authorities were dispatched to Peking to conclude additional agreements regarding technical details connected with the joint defense of the borders. Thus, under the military and naval agreements of May 16 and 19, respectively, Japan obtained the right to station guards along the northern end of the Chinese Eastern Railway.[23] Consequently, following the declaration of August 2, the Terauchi administration decided, at an extraordinary meeting of the cabinet of August 5, to station guards in the Manchuli region.[24] On August 8, Premier Terauchi invited General Otani, supreme war councilor, to his official residence and informed him of the impending expedition. General Otani's appointment as commander of the Japanese expeditionary forces was announced the following day.[25]

PARLIAMENTARY DEBATES ON THE SIBERIAN EXPEDITION

The Forty-first Diet, which was opened on December 27, 1918, found the opposition members pressing the government to state definitely the real object for continued maintenance of expeditionary forces in Siberia. Thus, immediately following the traditional address on foreign relations by Vis-

[22]*Tokyo Asahi*, Aug. 3, 1918, p. 2.

[23]Koshiro Kuroda (ed.), *Gensui Terauchi Hakushaku Den* (Tokyo, 1920), pp. 926–927.

[24]On this very day, Viscount Shimpei Goto, Japanese foreign minister, assured Ambassador Morris that Japan would not send more than 12,000 troops (Frederick L. Schuman, *American Foreign Policy toward Russia Since 1917* [London, 1928], pp. 114–117).

[25]K. Kuroda, *op. cit.*, p. 938, *Tokyo Asahi*, Aug. 9, 10, 1918, p. 2.

count Uchida, the new foreign minister under Hara *Seiyukai*
ministry,[26] Representative Kataoka, a *Kenseikai* leader, questioned the government as to why it was necessary to send ten
times as many troops as the United States and called upon
the ministry to make public its policy.[27] On the following
day (January 22, 1919), Representative Mochizuki put a long
and detailed question to the government on diplomatic affairs, in the course of which he declared that the foreign
minister under a party cabinet should take the people into
confidence in foreign affairs. Replies by Prime Minister Hara
and by Foreign Minister Uchida were general and evasive,
both declining to answer specific questions on the ground that
the matters were still in process of negotiation. It is to be
observed, in this connection, that, in the course of his interpellation, Representative Mochizuki openly condemned the
prime minister for recommending Count Terauchi and
Viscount Goto to membership in the advisory council on
foreign relations, and charged that the foreign minister had
been reduced to a position of mere clerkship in the council.[28]
On March 26, the last day of the session, General Giichi
Tanaka, war minister, came before the Lower House to report
on the military operations and activities of the Japanese
expeditionary forces in Siberia.[29] This speech by General
Tanaka provoked a sharp interpellation by Representative
Sadakichi Kato, who declared that, according to press reports, Japan recently extended an invitation to the United
States to send a joint expedition for the purpose of suppressing the radicals and was promptly declined by the latter. He
vigorously pressed the government to state the real objective
for the dispatch of 73,000 troops, and questioned the sincerity
of the declaration of the foreign minister that Japanese forces
were not interfering with the internal affairs of Siberia. The

[26]On September 29, 1918, Hara *Seiyukai* cabinet was formed, following the fall
of the Terauchi government because of the "rice riots" which took place in August.
For discussion of the formation of this first real party cabinet under a "commoner,"
see Kudo, *Taisho Kenseishi* (Tokyo, 1927), pp. 221–225.

[27]*Teikoku Gikaishi*, XI, 912–913, 917–918. The protest of the Wilson administration to Japanese military activities in northern Manchuria, lodged with Tokyo by
Secretary Lansing in Nov., 1918, and kept confidential for fourteen years, was made
public by Secretary of State Stimson on July 29, 1932.

[28]*Ibid.*, XI, 927–931.

[29]*Ibid.*, XI, 1347–1348.

foreign minister, in reply, defended the forces on the ground
that they were protecting the legitimate rights and interests
of Japanese subjects.[30]

By January, 1920, the announced object of the joint expedition was achieved through the rescue of the Czechoslovak
troops. Consequently, the United States government notified
Tokyo, on January 9, of the withdrawal of the American
forces, to which the Japanese government expressed regret
for not having been consulted prior to the decision, but expressed satisfaction at the absence of American objection to
continued maintenance of Japanese forces or even to its
necessary increase. British and French troops followed the
example of the United States.[31] On January 22, 1920, both
the war and foreign ministers spoke before the Diet on the
Siberian expeditionary forces and foreign relations, respectively.[32] In interpellating the cabinet upon the Siberian situation, Representative Kataoka condemned the government
for dispatching troops without parliamentary consent,[33] while
discussions in the Upper House centered around the reported
lack of harmony and unity between the Foreign Office and
the military authorities.[34] On January 27, Mr. Ichizo Hattori
called the attention of the government to the widespread
rumors in Europe and America that Japanese diplomacy conducted by the Foreign Office and the activities of military
authorities were often in conflict, that while the *Kasumigaseki*
diplomacy was following the accepted rules of diplomatic
procedure, the military authorities were interfering with the
internal affairs of another state or assisting one faction
against another. He declared that such rumors, if unchecked,
were highly detrimental to the honor and standing of Japan.
General Tanaka, in reply, flatly denied any interference by
military authorities with diplomatic authorities in the conduct of foreign relations.[35] Baron Shuntoku Sakamoto, in a

[30]*Ibid.*, XI, 1352–1354. General Tanaka's speech in the House of Peers, early in
the morning, did not occasion any interpellation from the floor (*ibid.*, XI, 891–892).

[31]Shinobu, *Taisho Gaiko Jugonenshi* (Tokyo, 1927), pp. 71–75.

[32]*Teikoku Gikaishi*, XI, 1380, 1591 ff.

[33]*Ibid.*, XI, 1599.

[34]See the reported clash of opinion between Count Uchida (foreign minister) and
General Tanaka (war minister) in the *Gaiko Chosakai* on Aug. 15, 1919 (*Tokyo
Asahi*, Aug. 16, 1919, p. 2).

[35]*Teikoku Gikaishi*, XI, 1423–1424.

searching interpellation on the Siberian situation, demanded
that the government state the future policy toward Siberia,
to which the prime minister declined to reply, saying that the
time was not ripe for the government to state what it intended to do with Siberia.[36] The sentiments thus expressed in
both Houses of the Diet, demanding a government declaration of its policy and opposing any increase of forces in Siberia, were widely shared by the informed public.[37]

The Hara cabinet dissolved the House of Representatives
on February 26, 1920, on the Manhood Suffrage bill, and in
the subsequent general election (May 10), the *Seiyukai* party
emerged overwhelmingly victorious, capturing 279 seats out
of the total membership of 464 in the Lower House.[38] In view
of the public opinion demanding an official declaration of
policy regarding Siberia, a statement was issued by the
Foreign Office on March 31 in which the continued maintenance of expeditionary forces in Siberia was justified on
grounds of unsettled conditions there, endangering the life
and property of Japanese residents. The declaration went on
to reiterate that Japan harbored no territorial ambition in
Russia, that her troops would be withdrawn as speedily as
possible when dangers along the Korean border were removed, safety of life and property of Japanese residents assured, and freedom of communications guaranteed.[39]

Meanwhile, the discovery, on June 3, 1920, of the massacre
of over seven hundred Japanese soldiers and civilians at
Nikolaevsk, which had taken place during March and May,
1920,[40] greatly stirred public excitement and renewed the
question of government responsibility for continued maintenance of expeditionary forces in Siberia, inviting the further
hatred and enmity of the Russians.[41] There being no recognized government in Russia to negotiate for the settlement of
the incident, the Japanese government issued a declaration

[36]*Op. cit.*, XI, 1445–1446. The interpellation was made on Feb. 4, 1920.

[37]See articles by Maida, Sugimori, Miyake, Yoshino, Ishikawa in *Chuo Koron*,
No. 379 (Feb., 1920), pp. 61–80; also an editorial in *Gaiko Jiho*, XXXI, No. 8
(April 15, 1920), pp. 679–685.

[38]Kudo, *Taisho Kenseishi*, pp. 226–233.

[39]Text of the statement issued by the Foreign Office in *ibid.*, pp. 284–285.

[40]*Jiji Shimpo*, June 4, 1920, p. 3.

[41]*Cf.* Dr. Setsurei Miyake, "The Nikolaevsk Incident," *Chuo Koron*, No. 384
(July, 1920), pp. 16–20; also an editorial, *Jiji Shimpo*, June 8, 1920, p. 3.

on July 3 to occupy certain points of the island of Saghalien, pending the establishment of a responsible government and settlement of the incident.[42]

During the entire session of the Forty-third Diet, parliamentary interpellations were centered upon the Siberian expedition and the Nikolaevsk Incident. Thus, immediately following the customary addresses by the premier, foreign minister, finance minister, and war minister, on July 3, 1920, when the foreign minister declared the intended occupation of northern Saghalien, Representative Yuko Hamaguchi led the *Kenseikai* onslaught upon the government. He succeeded in forcing a repetition in the House of Representatives, on July 6, of the statement the war minister had made in the Upper House three days previously, in reply to an interpellation by Baron Yoshiro Sakatani, that he would assume the entire responsibility for all military affairs including military operations, whether done under the general staff or otherwise. General Tanaka, however, declined to resign, holding that there had not been any official negligence in connection with the incident.[43] In the course of his interpellation on July 8, Representative Mochizuki charged the entire cabinet with official negligence in failing to take proper and prompt measures to prevent the occurrence of the massacre, citing many telegrams and dispatches, and contended that the cabinet was in possession of sufficient information at the time regarding the impending danger. He demanded that the government should make public all the facts relative to the incident and state its policy before "the representatives of the people."[44]

On July 9, 1920, a resolution was introduced in the House of Representatives by Representative Seigo Nakano, a parliamentary leader of the *Kenseikai* party, calling for the establishment of a special parliamentary committee to investigate the Nikolaevsk incident as well as other matters relating to diplomatic and military affairs.[45] Representative Sasaki sup-

[42]Shinobu, *Taisho Gaiko Jugonenshi* (Tokyo, 1927), pp. 78–80.

[43]*Teikoku Gikaishi*, XII, 15–17, 308. General Tanaka resigned from his office on June 9, 1921, when the cabinet decided to withdraw the expeditionary forces from Siberia, thus making good his indirect promise made in the Forty-third Diet (Kudo, *Taisho Kenseishi*, pp. 285–287).

[44]*Ibid.*, XII, 320–328. *Cf.* Junichiro Otsu, *Dai Nihon Kenseishi* (Tokyo, 1928), VIII, 538–571.

[45]Text of the resolution in *Teikoku Gikaishi*, XII, 344.

ported the resolution, while opposing speeches were made by Representative Fusajiro Ichinomiya and Prime Minister Kei Hara. To the proposed committee were to be presented the reports of the general staff, as well as those of diplomatic and consular officers to the Foreign Office, in order to investigate the degree of coöperation between the diplomatic and military authorities. The prime minister, in opposing the resolution, declared that it was a resolution of censure and not calculated to advance the cause of constitutional government. The resolution was defeated by a standing vote.[46]

During the Forty-first Diet, Viscount Kato, president of the *Kenseikai* party, led the opposition attack upon the Siberian policy of the Hara *Seiyukai* cabinet. In his maiden speech in the House of Peers, on January 24, 1921, this distinguished diplomat and party leader reviewed the history of the expedition and declared that he failed to see any cause for continued maintenance of expeditionary forces. The prime minister's defense of the government policy was unusually detailed and sincere.[47] On the following day, Representative Chuji Shimooka declared that the Siberian expedition had been a failure from its very inception, that the real objective for the expedition was the assistance of the "Whites" against the "Reds," and promotion of the interest of certain factions of the people.[48] Finally, in his unsuccessful resolution of February 5, Representative Nakano called upon the government to make clear the principle of non-interference in Russia and demanded immediate evacuation from Siberia. He charged the genro and military authorities with controlling the government policy from behind the scene.[49] These criticisms regarding the expedition as expressed in the Diet were fully shared by the informed public. The apparent absence of organized dissatisfaction and public criticism was largely due

[46]*Op. cit.*, XII, 344–353.

[47]*Ibid.*, XII, 722–724; Tanaka (ed.), *Hara Kei Zenshu* (Tokyo, 1929), II, 557–565. *Cf.* Ito, *Kato Komei*, II, 359–367. In October and November, preceding the opening of the Forty-fourth Diet, Viscount Kato made a tour of the country, vigorously attacking the Hara ministry for remaining in Siberia (*ibid.*, II, 357). In reply to an interpellation by Mr. Ren Nakakoji in the House of Peers on Jan. 24, 1921, Prime Minister Hara admitted that the expansion of communism could not be made a ground for expedition (*Teikoku Gikaishi*, XII, 719). On Jan. 31, Dr. Senshi Egi charged that diplomatic policies changed with cabinets (*ibid.*, XII, 803).

[48]*Ibid.*, XII, 1221–1225.

[49]*Ibid.*, XII, 1344–1348.

to the vigorous suppression of the press and of expression by the government.[50]

The bitter denunciation of the expedition, both in and out of the Diet, continued to grow; and on June 24, 1922, Admiral Kato, immediately upon formation of his ministry,[51] and after obtaining the approval of the cabinet and the advisory council on foreign relations, announced the intended evacuation of troops from Siberia at the end of October of the same year.[52] The withdrawal of expeditionary forces from Siberia was hailed by the press and the public as an admission of complete failure of the enterprise, and was urged by liberals to take this opportunity to curb the strength of military cliques. It was freely charged by the more outspoken of the critics of the expedition that the affair was engineered by military cliques and profit-seeking financiers, and consequently, it never enjoyed the support or the sympathy of the people.[53]

With the complete evacuation of troops from Siberia in October, 1922, public attention was now shifted to the question of continued occupation of Saghalien, which remained to be made a subject of public discussion,[54] until it was finally settled by treaty on January 20, 1925, concluded between Japan and the U.S.S.R.

Secret Military Funds Incident

During the Fifty-first session of the Diet, the use of secret military funds during the Siberian expedition became a subject of parliamentary scrutiny, when War Minister Ugaki denied any mismanagement of the funds by his predecessors (Generals Oshima, Tanaka, and Yamanashi), and refused to

[50]Yoshino, "From Dual Government to Dual Japan," *Chuo Koron*, No. 393 (March, 1921), pp. 91–95.

[51]The Kato cabinet was formed on June 12, 1922 (*Tokyo Asahi*, June 13, 1922, p. 2).

[52]Mitsuo Miyata (ed.), *Gensui Kato Tomosaburo Den* (Tokyo, 1928), p. 160; *Tokyo Asahi*, June 25, 1922, p. 2.

[53]See articles by Captain Kotoku Mizuno, Dr. Kiichi Horiye, Prof. Kimio Hayashi, Dr. Sakuzo Yoshino, Dr. Setsurei Miyake, and Prof. Kojiro Sugimori, in *Chuo Koron*, No. 416 (Dec., 1922), pp. 75–100.

[54]Viscount Kato put a searching question to the Admiral Kato cabinet in the House of Peers on Jan. 23, 1923, urging immediate and unconditional evacuation of troops from Saghalien Island as being most conducive to the settlement of pend-

disclose the manner in which the funds were disposed of on grounds of military secrecy and "in the best interest of the state."[55]

The public attention was again focused upon this question during the following session of the Diet.[56] Thus on March 24, 1927, Chairman Isobe of the House committee on final accounts made a report to the House, together with a summary report of the committee hearings.[57] Thereupon, Representative Ichiro Kiyose made a long speech on the military secret funds in connection with the expedition, in which he bitterly accused General Tanaka, former minister of war, of gross misappropriation of secret funds.[58] He declared that the executive could not encroach upon the legislative branch by arbitrary expenditure of certain funds under the pretext of "secret military funds" not authorized therefor, and thereby placing the same beyond the reach of the Board of Audit. He charged irregularity in expenditures and misappropriation of funds for private transactions of business. He declared, furthermore, that the final accounts of the Siberian expedition ought to have been made as soon as the withdrawal of troops therefrom was completed (October, 1922), and went on to charge that the delay was due to the anxiety on the part of the military authorities for an early public exposure of their transactions, and for disposal of 60,000,000 yen left unused on March 31, 1923.[59] He shouted to the echo of the legislative chamber that, under the constitutional system of Japan, the movement of troops, organized by national conscription and maintained by people's taxes, should never be left to the arbitrary discretion of high personages among military cir-

ing issues (Ito, *Kato Komei*, II, 416–420). When Representative Genji Matsuda called the attention of Prime Minister Kato, who formed the coalition cabinet on June 11, 1924, to the latter's speech of Jan. 23, 1923, in regard to the Saghalien question, Viscount Kato denied having ever advocated an unconditional evacuation of troops (*Kwampo gogai*, July 2, 1924, p. 21).

[55]Interpellations by Representatives Mitsuchi and Akita, both being *Seiyukai* members, on March 6 and 23, 1926 (*Kwampo gogai*, March 7, 1926, pp. 655–657; March 24, 1926, pp. 933–935).

[56]During both the Fifty-first and Fifty-second sessions of Diet, no interpellations on military secret funds in connection with the Siberian expedition were made in the House of Peers.

[57]*Kwampo gogai*, March 25, 1927, pp. 852–855.

[58]*Ibid.*, March 25, 1927, pp. 859–864.

[59]*Ibid.*, March 25, 1927, pp. 860–863.

cles, for purposes known only to themselves. He cited the
secret order of February 6, 1918, issued by War Minister
Tanaka to the military authorities in Siberia, ordering them
to maintain order by assisting the "Whites" without parliamentary knowledge; he accused General Tanaka of the expenditure of 21,110,000 yen during the period of December,
1918, to February, 1920, for his systematic assistance of
"White Russians."

When Dr. Kiyose uttered these words of condemnation of
the Tanaka administration of military funds, the House was
thrown into violent disturbance by *Seiyukai* members, and
consequently, the Speaker had to declare a recess.[60] After
a five-hour recess, the House was called to order, when Representative Sunada of the *Seiyukai* party, whose president
was so violently assailed, moved to refer Representative
Kiyose to the House disciplinary committee, declaring that
Representative Kiyose's disclosures were matters requiring
utmost secrecy and that they related to questions of fundamental policy touching upon the declarations of the Foreign
Office and the decisions of the advisory council on foreign
relations. When Representative Kiyose rose to speak
on his own behalf, the House was again thrown into
disorder, and consequently the meeting was adjourned for
the day.[61]

On March 25, he resumed his speech on point of personal
privilege; and the *Seiyukai* motion was lost.[62] In his continued
attack upon the Tanaka administration of military affairs,
Dr. Kiyose pointed out that, though General Tanaka replied
in the House of Representatives on January 22, 1920, that
the troops in Siberia numbered 26,000, the actual strength in
Siberia at the time was 56,000. This veteran jurist and student of constitutional government declared that 500,000,000
yen out of 900,000,000 yen (total expenditures for the expedition) had been wasted and lost.[63] Representative Kiyose's
open charges against the former minister of war and later
president of the *Seiyukai* party, the chief government
party during the period in question, were officially denied

[60] *Ibid.*, March 25, 1927, p. 864.
[61] *Ibid.*, March 25, 1927, pp. 864–865.
[62] *Ibid.*, March 26, 1927, pp. 880–882.
[63] *Ibid.*, March 26, 1927, p. 883.

by the war minister of the opposition party now in power.[64]

In spite of the official denials and subsequent failure of prosecution, Dr. Kiyose's bold and systematic exposure of the irregularities and misappropriations of military funds, together with the concurrent discrepancy between the Foreign Office diplomacy and the activities of the military authorities stationed in Siberia, did much to arouse public interest in the whole question of "dual diplomacy" and civilian control of military affairs.[65]

[64]*Op. cit.*

[65]For a discussion of the Kiyose incident which caused the resignation of the Speaker, Vice-Speaker, and Chief Secretary of the House, see Ichiro Kiyose, *Dai Gojuni Gikai ni okeru Yo no Kimitsuhijiken Enzetsu* (Tokyo, 1927), *passim;* also his articles in *Chuo Koron,* No. 472 (May, 1927), pp. 42–52, and in *Kaizo,* IX, No. 5 (May, 1927), pp. 47–52.

Chapter XIX

THE PARIS PEACE CONFERENCE

WITH THE ENTRY of the United States into the World War in April, 1917, issues to be settled at the peace conference at the close of the war began to be discussed more widely and concretely in Japan. Thus, immediately after the usual address on foreign affairs delivered at the beginning of the Thirty-ninth Diet (June 26, 1917) by Viscount Motono, Baron Korekiyo Takahashi rose to interpellate the government on Japan's attitude toward peace. He referred to the celebrated pronouncements of President Wilson, and corresponding declarations made by responsible spokesmen in Great Britain, France, Italy, and Russia. In reply, Viscount Motono assured the Peers that, though the government felt it unadvisable at the time to make public the aims and aspirations of Japan at the peace conference, it entertained no apprehension as to the support that would be forthcoming from the Allied powers at the conference.[1] In the afternoon of the same day Representative Kotaro Mochizuki interpellated the foreign minister as to measures undertaken to insure the fate of Kiaochaowan and German South Sea Islands now under Japanese occupation. Viscount Motono replied in the same manner as he did in the Upper House, and likewise assured the Representatives that the government had taken appropriate measures to protect the rights and interests of Japan concerning the German concessions in Shantung and future disposition of South Sea Islands, and that he was certain that there would be no opposition at the peace conference from the Allied powers to such measures as might be

[1] *Teikoku Gikaishi*, X, 1092–1094.

deemed necessary to insure the peace of the Far East.[2] To numerous demands from the floor the cabinet adopted the same attitude of refusing to state the Japanese conditions of peace or its policies at the conference.[3]

Upon conclusion of an armistice in early November, 1918, a series of conferences was held among high officials of the Foreign, War, and Navy departments to formulate the policy of the government at the approaching conference.[4] As the general outline of Japanese proposals was completed on November 12, an important meeting of the *Gaiko Chosakai* for deliberation was held the following day. Before this advisory council on foreign relations Foreign Minister Uchida explained the diplomatic negotiations then in progress and details connected with the signing of the armistice; he outlined the Japanese terms and demands to be presented at Paris. Having obtained the imperial sanction, Count Uchida dispatched important instructions to Ambassador Chinda of London and Ambassador Matsui of Paris.[5]

In view of the personal presence of President Wilson and other leading statesmen to represent the interested powers at the conference, as well as the significance of this conference to the war diplomacy of the Empire,[6] the public was unanimous in demanding the appointment of a leading statesman, whose caliber and statesmanship could be favorably compared with those of other representatives at the conference, and whose prestige and influence at home were such as to carry weight and influence with all parties concerned. Under the circumstances, Premier Hara finally succeeded in persuading Prince Saionji, his former chief as head of the *Seiyukai* party, a former premier and a leading genro, to act as Japan's principal delegate. This aged statesman accepted the post upon the condition that Baron Makino be appointed a plenipotentiary to

[2]*Op. cit.*, X, 1195, 1197.

[3]*Ibid.*, XI, 170–180.

[4]See *Tokyo Asahi*, Nov. 10, 11, 12, 13, 1918, p. 2.

[5]The following members of the council were present: Premier Hara, Foreign Minister Uchida, Navy Minister Kato, Viscount Hirata, Baron Goto, Viscount Miyoji Ito, Baron Makino, and Rep. Ki Inukai. General Count Terauchi was absent on account of illness (*ibid.*, Nov. 14, 1918, p. 2).

[6]*Cf.* Dr. Tomizu, "Japanese Policy at the Conference," *Gaiko Jiho*, XXVIII, No. 11 (Dec. 1, 1918), pp. 1115–1125; also Dr. Kambe, "Our Policy at the Conference," *ibid.*, XXIX, No. 1 (Jan. 1, 1919), pp. 23–31.

assist him in the negotiations.[7] After deliberation in the *Gaiko Chosakai*,[8] the members of the Japanese delegation to Paris were announced on December 3, 1918.[9] After further deliberations in the advisory council on December 8,[10] the Japanese claims were finally embodied in the instructions handed to Baron Makino when he left Tokyo two days later.[11]

During the Forty-first session of the Diet (December 25, 1918, to March 25, 1919), interpellations were put to the government in both Houses, demanding that the government should make public the Japanese proposals at the conference, progress of negotiations, particularly, with regard to the fate of the "racial equality" issue, former German concessions at Shantung and possessions in the South Sea Islands, the League of Nations, the Anglo-Japanese Alliance, and other leading issues of the day. The cabinet consistently declined to state specifically the policy it proposed to pursue on any of these vital issues; it refused to divulge the progress of negotiations on grounds of diplomatic secrecy.[12]

The policy of maintaining absolute secrecy regarding questions of high politics at the peace conference was not confined to the Diet. Thus the proceedings of the *Gaiko Chosakai* were, with few notable exceptions, scrupulously kept secret.[13] The advisory council on foreign relations, which, since the formation of the Hara *Seiyukai* ministry in September, 1918, had lost its former prestige and influence enjoyed under Terauchi government, met from time to time to hear and deliberate upon the progress of peace negotiations. Finally, the cabinet

[7]Views of Prince Yamagata were consulted before the appointment of Prince Saionji (*Tokyo Asahi*, Nov. 27, 1918, p. 2).

[8]At the meeting of the advisory council on December 2, the personnel of the delegation, as well as the claims at the conference, was deliberated upon (*ibid.*, Dec. 3, 1918, p. 2).

[9]The Japanese delegation consisted of Prince Saionji (ex-premier and a genro), Baron Makino (former foreign minister), Ambassadors Chinda (London) and Matsui (Paris).

[10]*Tokyo Asahi*, Dec. 9, 1918, p. 2.

[11]*Ibid.*, Dec. 11, 1918, p. 5.

[12]*Teikoku Gikaishi*, XI, 657–658, 667–671, 994, 1176–1177, 1263–1268, 1349–1352; *Dai Shijuikkai Teikoku Gikai Kizokuin Iinkai Giji Sokkiroku*, No. 2, pp. 3–4.

[13]As an exception, following the meeting of the *Chosakai* on April 30, the government let it be known to the press that it was determined to obtain the recognition of its claims regarding the Shantung question (*Tokyo Asahi*, May 1, 1919, p. 2). *Cf.* Secretary Robert Lansing's account of this episode at the conference in his *Peace Negotiations* (Boston and New York, 1920), pp. 253–256.

reported the pending signature of the peace treaty to the council on June 26,[14] and held its last deliberation upon the draft the following day.[15]

A copy of the original text of the peace treaty was brought back to Tokyo by Councilor Ogawa of the Navy Department on August 19, 1919.[16] Thereupon, detailed examination of the text of the treaty, as well as the proceedings of the conference, was undertaken by the Foreign Office and other interested departments. On September 2, an important joint conference of high officials of the *Kasumigaseki* and Navy Department was held to confer upon the report to be presented to the Privy Council when the latter would formally examine the treaty.[17] On the forenoon of September 9, Foreign Minister Uchida made a detailed report upon the treaty to his colleagues in the cabinet;[18] and in the afternoon Count Uchida made similar explanations to the *Gaiko Chosakai* regarding the text of the treaty and the report to be presented to the Privy Council. A recent communication from Washington, disclaiming any presumption that its acceptance of the Japanese claims regarding Shantung at the conference might have implied that it approved the Sino-Japanese treaties of 1915 or the agreement entered into in 1918, was transmitted to this meeting of the advisory council for comment and discussion. Though no formal action was taken, it was reported that the council was unanimous in urging the government to adopt a more consistent China policy.[19]

Having completed its preparations, the cabinet formally petitioned the throne on September 11 to submit the peace treaty to the Privy Council for deliberation and advice.[20] Thereupon an informal meeting of the Privy Council was

[14]*Tokyo Asahi*, June 27, 1919, p. 2.

[15]*Ibid.*, June 28, 1919, p. 2.

[16]*Ibid.*, Aug. 20, 1919, p. 2. Prince Saionji, chief delegate to the conference, returned to Tokyo on August 24 (*ibid.*, Aug. 25, 1919, p. 9).

[17]The *Kasumigaseki* was reported by Hanihara, chief of political affairs bureau of the Foreign Office, and Mushakoji, Aoki, Sugimura, Kawashima, all section chiefs, while Councilor Yamakawa represented the Navy Department (*ibid.*, Sept. 3, 1919, p. 2).

[18]*Ibid*, Sept. 10, 1919, p. 2.

[19]*Ibid.*, Sept. 11, 1919, p. 2.

[20]*Ibid.*, Sept. 12, 1919, p. 2.

called the following day to hear the details leading up to the submission of the treaty to the Council.[21] In view of the importance of the treaty, Prince Yamagata appointed a sub-committee of nine members, headed by Viscount Kiyoura, to examine this historic document.[22]

The sub-committee held its first meeting on September 15, when Prime Minister Kei Hara and Foreign Minister Uchida explained in detail the proceedings of the peace conference.[23] The committee held sixteen meetings up to October 24, when it completed its deliberations upon the treaty from all angles. The attention of the councilors was directed chiefly to two aspects of the treaty: (1) the League of Nations and the Japanese Constitution, and (2) the Anglo-Japanese Alliance. To the questions thus raised, the government contended that all treaties, being self-imposed restrictions upon the exercise of its sovereignty, should not be taken to impair the independence of the contracting parties, and consequently the peace treaty including the League Covenant did in no way violate the Imperial Constitution. As to the future of the Anglo-Japanese Alliance, the cabinet intimated that it intended to propose a radical modification in the near future to bring it in harmony with the letter and spirit of the Covenant of the League.[24]

The sub-committee desired to delay its report to the Privy Council, pending final action of the United States Senate. However, in view of the ratification already completed in Great Britain, France, and Italy, and the International Labor Conference scheduled to be convened at Washington at the end of the month, the Hara ministry urgently requested the committee to expedite its deliberations. In consequence, at its Sixteenth session, held on October 24, it

[21]The Privy Council was represented by Vice-President Kiyoura, President Yamagata being absent, and fourteen councilors, Secretary General Nikami, and three secretaries, while the cabinet was represented by all its members (*ibid.*, Sept. 13, 1919, p. 3).

[22]The special committee thus appointed comprised nine of the most influential members of the Council: Viscount Keigo Kiyoura (chairman), Viscount Miyoji Ito, Viscount Kentaro Kaneko, Viscount Kencho Suyematsu, Baron Nobushige Hozumi, Hanichiro Yasuhiro, Dr. Kitokuro Ichiki, Dr. Seisho Tomii, and Marquis Katsunosuke Inouye (*ibid.*)

[23]*Ibid.*, Sept. 16, 1919, p. 2.

[24]*Ibid.*, Oct. 7, 11, 22, 1919, p. 2.

voted unanimously to recommend ratification of the treaty.[25]
On October 27, the Privy Council met in a plenary session,
Prince Yamagata presiding. Viscount Kiyoura made a
lengthy report of the committee, lasting two hours, recommending ratification of the treaty without any reservation.
Premier Hara, Foreign Minister Uchida, Navy Minister
Kato, and War Minister Tanaka made explanations. As no
questions were asked from the floor, the committee report
was unanimously accepted by the Council. The decision of
the Council was immediately reported to the emperor by
Prince Yamagata, while the cabinet, at an extraordinary
meeting following the adjournment of the Council, decided
to petition the emperor for ratification.[26] Two days later,
the treaty was submitted to the *Gaiko Chosakai*, when it
promptly approved the action already taken.[27] Immediately
thereupon, the cabinet formally petitioned the emperor for
ratification of the treaty. This petition was granted on October 30, 1919.[28]

When the following session of the Diet was convened, Dr.
Senshi Yoku and Dr. Sakuye Takahashi led the opposition
interpellation in the House of Peers,[29] while in the Lower
House, the *Kenseikai* party was no less vigorous in criticizing
the Japanese failure at the conference. Thus, on January 29,
1920, Representative Nagashima introduced a resolution
calling for establishment of a special committee of inquiry on
foreign relations to investigate the peace negotiations, the
treaty, and future international relations arising out of the
peace treaty, and to report its findings to the House.[30] In his
long and eloquent speech of introducing this significant resolution, Representative Nagashima emphasized (1) that the
resolution was intended to bring all facts into light and not
to censure the cabinet; (2) that it was not intended to influence the effect of the treaty in any respect, and (3) that no
attempts were made to place restrictions upon future conduct

[25]*Op. cit.*, Oct. 26, 27, 1919, p. 2.
[26]*Ibid.*, Oct. 28, 1919, p. 2.
[27]*Ibid.*, Oct. 30, 1919, p. 2.
[28]*Ibid.*, Oct. 31, 1919, p. 2. *Cf.* Kudo, *Taisho Kenseishi* (Tokyo, 1927), p. 269.
[29]*Teikoku Gikaishi*, XI, 1383 ff.
[30]Text of the resolution in *ibid.*, XI, 1646.

of foreign relations by the government. He referred to the Senate of the United States and declared that no attempt was made to assume such a rôle; he readily admitted the complete lack of competence of the House in the actual conduct of foreign affairs. In pointing out the circumstances under which the Siberian expedition was embarked upon in 1918, and its subsequent developments, he emphasized the importance of the public character of the proposed parliamentary committee. He pointed out that, in all leading countries, the respective parliaments were well informed in the progress of negotiations and the treaty, and expressed profound regret that no report of the negotiations was ever presented to the Imperial Diet. He shouted to the cabinet ministers that it was the period of transition from bureaucracy to democracy in the conduct of foreign relations. Premier Hara, in opposing the resolution, declared that the government had been always ready to furnish any information asked for, consistent with public interest of the state, and that the resolution was designed to place restrictions upon the conduct of foreign relations. He concluded his speech by pointing out the novel character of the resolution and emphasizing the parliamentary tradition of never interfering with the imperial prerogative over treaty-making. The resolution was defeated by the *Seiyukai* majority.[31]

The Paris Peace Treaty, with the Covenant of the League of Nations, raised some interesting academic questions regarding its constitutionality under Japanese law. Leading jurists of the nation united in upholding the constitutionality of the covenant. Thus, Professor Minobe argued that it did not impair the sovereignty of the state, though it obviously placed limitations upon the imperial prerogative, and declared that, in view of its direct importance to the life of the people, it would have been in accordance with sound principles of constitutional government, had the government summoned the Diet in an extraordinary session to submit the treaty to its deliberation and criticism before petitioning ratification. Professor Minobe supported the above thesis on the ground that the Constitution did not prohibit such a proce-

[31] *Ibid.*, XI, 1646–1652.

dure.[32] Professor Makino concurred with Dr. Minobe,[33] while Dr. Yoku Egi, a leading constitutional jurist of the *Kenseikai* party, held that the League was a superstate and that the covenant was unconstitutional.[34]

[32]Minobe, "The League of Nations and the Imperial Constitution," *Kokka Gakkai Zasshi*, XXXIV, No. 1 (Jan., 1920), pp. 78–102.

[33]Makino, "The League, the Constitution, and the Treaty," *Kokusaiho Gaiko Zasshi*, XVIII, No. 4 (Dec., 1919), pp. 319–329.

[34]Cited in *ibid.*, p. 323.

Chapter XX

THE WASHINGTON CONFERENCE

Parliamentary Initiative

O N JANUARY 22, 1921, Prime Minister Hara, Foreign Minister Uchida, and Finance Minister Takahashi addressed the House of Representatives on their respective fields.[1] Immediately following the usual addresses at the beginning of the Forty-fourth session of the Diet, Representative Yuko Hamaguchi, a leading member of the *Kenseikai* (opposition) party, put a long question to the Hara government upon the reported negotiations then in progress between Washington and London for a naval conference, and requested the prime minister to state the attitude of the Japanese government upon the subject.[2] He prefaced his interpellation by calling the attention of the House to the fact that, according to the budget for the fiscal year of 1921, of the total sum of 1,560,-000,000 yen, 760,000,000 yen, namely, 48 per cent of the total budget, constituted the navy and war expenditures, being 10,000,000 yen more than the total amount raised through taxes. He then demanded specific replies upon (1) the exact extent to which the question had progressed in the United States and Great Britain; (2) the views of the prime minister concerning the probability of diplomatic realization of such a conference; (3) the views of the premier upon the armament limitation question, and (4) whether the press interview reported to have been given by Ambassador Hayashi in London the previous day had the full approval of the home government.

[1] *Teikoku Gikaishi*, XII, 1180–1184.
[2] *Ibid.*, XII, 1184–1190.

In reply to this searching interpellation presented by an opposition party, Premier Hara admitted that the subject was being widely discussed in the press but denied that it had become an international question, and declined to state the government's attitude toward the pending question on the ground that it had not yet become an international issue. As to Ambassador Hayashi's reported remarks made to the press, the prime minister declared that, though an ambassador acts under instructions when approaching the government to which he is accredited, he usually does so in his individual capacity when he speaks to the press. He admitted that he was informed that Ambassador Hayashi stated to the press in his individual capacity that the Japanese government would give due consideration to the subject when it should become an international question.[3]

Unsatisfied with the premier's reply, Representative Hamaguchi declared that, granting that an ambassador might speak in an individual capacity, there must have been instructions from the home government to the ambassador to make a statement to the press on such an important question as the limitation of armaments, that he could not have possibly made upon his own authority a statement which might be implied to mean that the Japanese government was willing to reduce her naval strength by 50 per cent by an international agreement.[4] In reply, the foreign minister, Count Uchida, admitted that a minister cannot make a statement on the attitude or policy of the home government without instructions, and declared that a minister abroad is within his authority to make a statement on any important question, provided that it is within the scope of the known attitude of the government. Count Uchida went on to say that he had a telegraphic communication from Ambassador Hayashi to the effect that he had stated to the press as his personal opinion that the Japanese government would not hesitate to give it due consideration, should the armament limitation question become an international issue. The foreign minister denied that the government had given the ambassador any instructions but declared that the government did not find

[3] *Op. cit.*, XII, 1190.
[4] *Ibid.*, XII, 1193.

any cause to repudiate the ambassador's statement or to instruct him to the contrary.[5]

On January 24, Representative Kotaro Mochizuki interpellated the government on the same question, but the replies were general and noncommittal.[6] Several additional interpellations were made to the government. Finally, on February 10, 1921, Representative Yukio Ozaki, a leading liberal and a parliamentarian of high standing, introduced a resolution in the Lower House demanding a reduction of naval armaments in concert with Great Britain and the United States, and land armaments in accordance with the provisions of the Covenant of the League of Nations.[7] In his opening speech Representative Ozaki referred to the Senate and House resolutions of the United States Congress calling upon the president to call a conference, and also made a lengthy reference to the League of Nations and its principles looking toward armament reduction. He declared that the object of the resolution was intended to express the will of the Japanese people that they were ready for a conference when invited, and that if such an invitation was not forthcoming they were ready to call one in Tokyo. The chief opposing speech was made by Representative Koreshige Tsunoda, who declared that the sentiments expressed in the resolution were ideal but too impractical to be adopted. Because of the opposition of both the *Seiyukai*, the government party, and the *Kenseikai*, the chief opposition party, the resolution met an overwhelming defeat by a majority of 285:38.[8]

DRAFTING OF THE INSTRUCTIONS

With the closing of the Diet, public attention began to be directed to questions of armament reduction. Accordingly, in striking contrast with his failure to arouse the interest of his fellow legislators, his direct appeal to the people elicited an immediate response. He made more than seventy speeches throughout the country in the interest of armament reduction to a combined audience of more than 100,000 people.

[5] *Ibid.*, XII, 1194.
[6] *Ibid.*, XII, 1206–1214.
[7] Text of the resolution in *ibid.*, XII, 1356.
[8] *Ibid.*, XII, 1356–1365.

He distributed 100,000 postcards at these meetings to regis-
ter the reaction of his hearers to his plea for armament reduction. Of the 30,000 replies received, 93 per cent supported
him while 3 per cent were noncommittal on the subject. His
direct appeal to the people received wide publicity and support from the press, while military and naval organizations
were busy in "educating" the public to the "inevitability of
a Japanese-American war."[9]

On July 11, 1921, the American chargé d'affaires called on
Foreign Minister Uchida at the *Kasumigaseki* to extend the
invitation of President Harding to a conference on naval
armaments to be held in Washington the following fall. Immediately thereupon, Count Uchida called together high
officials of his department to deliberate upon the invitation
thus informally extended.[10] The matter was referred to the
cabinet at its meeting called the following day, when, after
full deliberation, it decided to accept the American proposal.
At the same time, however, it was decided to inquire of the
Washington government as to the method of determining
the scope and agenda of the "Pacific conference."[11]

Meanwhile the government had to formulate a unified
program of action at the approaching conference. Numerous
meetings of high officials of departments concerned, as well
as joint conferences of their representatives, were called.
Finally, at its meeting of July 26, the cabinet approved a
draft communication to Washington, formally accepting the
American invitation of July 23. Accordingly, the Japanese
reply was conveyed to the American embassy in the evening,
at the same time that the communication to Ambassador
Shidehara at Washington was transmitted, emphasizing the
importance of preliminary negotiations regarding the nature
and scope of the proposed conference.[12] On July 28, Premier
Kei Hara, Admiral Kato, navy minister, and Admiral Yama-

---

[9]Yukio Ozaki, "The Armament Limitation Conference and the People," *Kokusai
Remmei*, I, No. 7 (Oct., 1921), pp. 1–5. *Cf.* an article by Premier Hara in *Gaiko Jiho*,
XXXIV, No. 6 (Sept. 15, 1921), pp. 770–782; also Viscount Kato's speech at Niigata
on Sept. 18, 1921 (*Gaiko Jiho*, Oct. 1, 1921, pp. 1010–1013). The League of Nations
Association passed several resolutions in July favoring the American invitation
(*Kokusai Remmei*, Vol. I, No. 8 [Nov., 1921], p. 93).

[10]*Tokyo Asahi*, July 12, 1921, p. 2.

[11]*Ibid.*, July 15, 1921, p. 2.

[12]*Ibid.*, July 27, 1921, p. 2.

shita, chief of naval general staff, were all received in audience by the emperor to report on the approaching conference.[13]

Having accepted the American invitation, the Hara government now had to draw up a long communication to Washington outlining in detail the Japanese understandings and policies at the conference. A joint conference of the representatives of the Foreign, Navy, and War departments was held on August 18 to confer upon a draft reply to be transmitted to Washington.[14] After further deliberation by the Foreign Office following this joint conference, the draft reply was submitted to cabinet deliberations the following day.[15] After a few changes in minor details, the draft reply was printed on the evening of August 22[16] and was submitted again to the cabinet the following morning for formal approval. In the afternoon it was referred to the *Gaiko Chosakai* for further scrutiny. At this meeting of the advisory council on foreign relations, Foreign Minister Uchida made a detailed explanation of the recent attitudes of Great Britain, France, Italy, and the United States toward the conference. After an unusually lively session, the council accepted the draft already approved by the cabinet in the forenoon.[17] Toward the evening, the Japanese reply accepting the formal invitation of the American government was handed the American embassy in Tokyo, at the same time that the communication to Ambassador Shidehara in Washington was transmitted.[18]

On September 27, 1921, Prince Tokugawa, president of the House of Peers, Admiral Baron Tomosaburo Kato, minister of navy, and Baron Shidehara, Japanese minister at Washington, were appointed Japanese plenipotentiaries.[19] During

[13]*Ibid.*, July 29, 1921, p. 1.

[14]The *Kasumigaseki* was represented by Vice-Minister Hanihara, Chief of Asiatic Bureau Yoshizawa, Chief of European and American Bureau Matsudaira, and Chief of Treaty Bureau Yamakawa, while the navy side was headed by Vice-Admiral Kanji Kato, and the military by Major General Tanaka (*ibid.*, Aug. 19, 1921, p. 2).

[15]*Ibid.*, Aug. 20, 1921, p. 2.

[16]*Ibid.*, Aug. 23, 1921, p. 2.

[17]The meeting was attended by Hara, Uchida, Ooka, Goto, Ito, Yamanashi, and Kato. Hirata and Chinda were unable to attend the meeting (*ibid.*, Aug. 24, 1921, p. 1).

[18]*Ibid.*, Aug. 24, 1921, p. 2.

[19]*Ibid.*, Sept. 28, 1921, p. 1.

the absence of Admiral Kato in Washington, Prime Minister Hara, a civilian, took charge of the navy department. This established a precedent for a civilian minister to take charge of the navy department, only after a vigorous opposition on the part of Field Marshal Yamagata, a leading genro and chief of the military clique. This arrangement was accepted upon the understanding that it could not be extended to the War Department.[20]

After full deliberations in numerous joint conferences of the Foreign, Navy, and War departments, the basic policy of the Tokyo government to be followed at the conference was finally determined upon, and its full details were set forth in the instructions to be handed the plenipotentiaries upon departure for Washington. The lengthy document setting forth the Japanese policy in full detail received a cabinet approval on October 7,[21] and the *Gaiko Chosakai* started its critical examination of this important document on October 10.[22] The advisory council on foreign relations held three sessions, on October 10, 12, and 14, when Prime Minister Hara explained the details connected with the appointment of the plenipotentiaries and policies to be pursued at the approaching naval conference. Foreign Minister Uchida made further elaborations, explaining the bearings of the conference upon the Sino-Japanese, Russo-Japanese, and America-Japanese relations. As the result of these meetings the original instructions were modified in minor detail. Immediately following the approval of the advisory council, Prime Minister Hara was received in audience by the emperor. With His Majesty's sanction, the instructions were handed the plenipotentiaries.[23]

[20]This opposition on the part of the military to Premier Hara's taking charge of the Navy Department during the conference was based upon their fear that this precedent might open the way for a civilian war or navy minister. Admiral Kato invited Fleet Admirals Togo and Inouye, and naval members of the Supreme War Council for a conference to report his appointment as a delegate and also to explain the circumstances connected with the new arrangement at the Navy Department (*ibid.*, Oct. 6, 1921, p. 3). *Cf.* Yoshino, *Niju Seifu to Iaku Joso* (Tokyo, 1922), pp. 37–38; also Nakano, *Tosuiken no Dokuritsu* (Tokyo, 1934), pp. 679–680.

[21]*Ibid.*, Oct. 8, 1921, p. 3.

[22]Chairman Hara, Secretary General Uchida, and Councilors Kato, Yamanashi, Ooka, Goto, Chinda, Ito, and Inukai were present at the meeting (*ibid.*, Oct. 11, 1921, p. 1).

[23]*Ibid.*, Oct. 11, 13, 15, 1921, p. 2.

The content of the instructions was not made public. According to the press reports, however, the instructions embodied the following basic policies of the government as
finally determined upon: (1) Japan was prepared to accept
a curtailment of her naval armaments so long as her national
security was not impaired thereby. (2) She had no establishments in her Pacific possessions which threatened the security of other powers, nor did she entertain any intention to
make such establishments in the future. Moreover, she was
prepared to conclude an agreement to abolish all the military
or naval establishments and to pledge also not to construct
such establishments anew in the Pacific islands which would
threaten the peace and security of other interested powers.
(3) Japan did not wish to terminate the Anglo-Japanese
Alliance, but was not opposed to concluding a new alliance
or agreement to replace it. (4) As to the Island of Yap, she
was ready to extend the principles of open door and equal
opportunity to other powers. (5) Regarding China, she was
prepared to renew her assurances of the well-known principles of equal opportunity and the open door. (6) As to the
Shantung question, she was determined to insist that the
matter was to be settled by direct negotiations between
Japan and China, and to oppose any attempt at discussion
in the conference.[24]

THE CONTROL OF THE DELEGATES

Throughout the conference, members of the *Gaiko Chosakai* were fully informed of the activities and policies of the
delegates at Washington. Though Admiral Baron Kato,
principal builder of the modern imperial navy, was given
practically a free hand at the conference, important decisions
were made by the cabinet always upon consultation with the
advisory council on foreign relations.

The first important meeting of the *Gaiko Chosakai* after
the opening of the naval conference was held on November
22 under the chairmanship of Premier Takahashi.[25] Here

[24]*Ibid.*, Oct. 14, 1921, p. 2.

[25]Premier Kei Hara was assassinated at Tokyo Station on Nov. 4, 1921. Foreign
Minister Count Uchida was appointed acting premier. Viscount Korekiyo Takahashi was appointed prime minister on Nov. 13, 1921 (*ibid.*, Nov. 5, 13, 1921, p. 2).

the members of the advisory council heard a detailed account of the proceedings of the conference and deliberated upon the naval ratio proposed by Secretary Hughes of the United States.[26] The meeting was resumed again on November 24, after which the cabinet decided to instruct the delegates to insist upon 70 per cent ratio, though the matter was left for Admiral Kato to exercise his discretion in his negotiations.[27] Subsequently, the council held several meetings to deliberate upon the progress of negotiations, and participated in formulating instructions to Washington regarding the acceptance of 5:5:3 ratio, Four-Power Pact, Yap question, Shantung settlement, Nine-Power Treaty, and other important decisions at the conference.[28]

THE DIET AND THE CONFERENCE

The Washington treaties occupied the major attention of the public during the Forty-fifth session of the Diet.[29] The debates in the Diet were centered around (1) the reduction of naval armaments and (2) the Four-Power Pact replacing the Anglo-Japanese Alliance, but were conspicuously silent on the Chinese question.

On January 21, 1922, Foreign Minister Uchida made his usual address on foreign relations and described in remarkable detail the proceedings at Washington.[30] On January 24, Representative Etsujiro Uyehara addressed a long question to the government on the conference. In his speech he strongly condemned the *Seiyukai* government for keeping the people ignorant of its policy at the conference, while the British and French governments were anxious to take their peoples into confidence; he recalled the *Seiyukai* opposition to the Ozaki resolution on naval and land armaments in the Forty-fourth Diet and inquired why the present *Seiyukai* cabinet was sup-

[26]*Op. cit.*, Nov. 23, 24, 1921, p. 2.

[27]*Ibid.*, Nov. 25, 1921, p. 2. In early December, prior to making his final decision on the 5:5:3 ratio, Kato cabled a long telegram to Admiral Togo, the genro of the Japanese navy, for opinion. In reply, Togo is said to have accepted the ratio as unavoidable (Ito, "Admiral Togo," *Chuo Koron* [July, 1934], pp. 188–189).

[28]*Ibid.*, Nov. 29, 30, Dec. 7, 8, 10, 11, 16, 1921, p. 2.

[29]Dec. 26, 1921, to March 25, 1922.

[30]*Teikoku Gikaishi*, XIII, 509–511.

porting the naval limitation program.[31] In reply, Count Uchida denied that the government ever opposed a limitation of naval armaments, and admitted that the Japanese acceptance of the 5:5:3 ratio was made after receiving the approval of the home government.[32] On February 18, Representative Seigo Nakano introduced a resolution in the House declaring that the government had failed in obtaining the full understanding of the people concerning the proceedings of the conference. The resolution was opposed by Dr. Kiroku Hayashi, who declared that the real meaning of the resolution was not clear and that the government took proper steps in making public the proceedings of the conference. After a brief debate, the resolution was defeated by a standing vote.[33]

During this session, a leading Seiyukai whip, Representative Ikuzo Ooka, introduced a representation resolution calling upon the administration to take appropriate measures concerning the inevitable unemployment of workers which would follow the acceptance of the Washington treaties. It was promptly passed by the House.[34] Finally, on March 16, the *Kenseikai* party introduced a resolution of want of confidence in the government, violently attacking the government's concessions at the conference. The resolution was opposed by the *Seiyukai* majority, contending that the conference was a success. It was defeated by a majority of 254: 141.[35]

The Four-Power Pact which replaced the Anglo-Japanese Alliance also received much comment in the Diet. Foreign Minister Uchida, however, declined to reply in detail to questions addressed to the government on the subject, pleading that, though the pact had been signed, it had not received the imperial ratification. He admitted that the pact signed by the plenipotentiaries should be respected but insisted that

[31] *Ibid.*, XIII, 550–555.

[32] *Ibid.*, XIII, 555. Count Uchida made the same admission on January 23 (*ibid.*, XIII, 530). For deliberations in the cabinet and the *Gaiko Chosakai* upon the acceptance of the ratio, see *Tokyo Asahi*, Dec. 11, 1921, p. 2.

[33] *Ibid.*, XIII, 730–737.

[34] *Ibid.*, XIII, 724–726, 1297. The *Kenseikai* (opposition) resolution demanding reduction in taxes was pigeonholed (*ibid.*, XIII, 1088–1090).

[35] *Ibid.*, XIII, 1116–1137. For interpellations in the House of Peers, see *ibid.*, XIII, 46–60, 90–98, 107–115.

he could not discuss the subject fully prior to its ratification.[36] In reply to a question by Dr. Egi in the Peers' Budget Committee on February 20, Count Uchida declared that the Japanese government took the position that Japan proper was excluded from the operation of the pact but declined to disclose the nature of the negotiations with the interested powers concerning the subject on the ground that the matter had been satisfactorily adjusted.[37] When pressed to state the government's interpretation of Article 2 of the pact in relation to Article 10 of the Covenant of the League of Nations, the foreign minister refused to reply, declaring that it concerned the question of treaty interpretation and that it would be given only when faced with a concrete situation.[38]

The Washington treaties were on the whole favorably commented upon in the press as relieving the international tension particularly over the Pacific and as reducing the burden of taxation.[39]

RATIFICATION OF THE TREATIES

As the Washington treaties just concluded—particularly those relating to limitation of naval armaments of five principal powers and to the defense of the Pacific—necessitated important changes in national defense, both the army and naval general staffs had to draw up a new defense program. This new program having been drafted, General Uyehara, chief of staff, and Admiral Yamashita, chief of naval general staff, were received in audience. As a result, an important meeting of the Board of Field Marshals and Fleet Admirals was called on March 31, 1922, to deliberate upon the new

[36]Op. cit., XIII, 529–530.

[37]Dai Shijugokai Teikoku Gikai Kizokuin Yosan Iinkai Giji Sokkiroku, No. 2, pp. 5–6. Cf. the interpellation on this subject in the Lower House (Teikoku Gikaishi, XIII, 529). Also Dr. Yoku Egi, "Four-Power Pact and the Senate Reservations," Gaiko Jiho, XXXV, No. 10 (May 15, 1922), pp. 1577–1587. For further details on this point, see Kin Ashida, Saikin Sekai Gaikoshi, or Recent Diplomatic History of the World (Tokyo, 1934), III, 748–755.

[38]Teikoku Gikaishi, XIII, 555.

[39]Cf. a symposium on the conference by Professor Kojiro Sugimori, Captain Kotoku Mizuno, and Dr. Setsurei Miyake in Chuo Koron, No. 405 (Feb., 1922), pp. 85–104; also on land armament question in ibid., No. 406 (March, 1922), pp. 81–96. Cf. Dr. Kiriku Hayashi, "Washington Conference and Japan," Gaiko Jiho, XXXV, No. 9 (May 1, 1922), pp. 1435–1449.

defense program. This supreme advisory organ to the throne on national defense approved the new program for naval and land defenses.[40] Thereupon, an extraordinary meeting of the Privy Council was called in the palace on April 6, with Count Keigo Kiyoura in the chair. All cabinet ministers were present. Here, Admiral Kato, minister of the navy and Japan's delegate to Washington, in his two-hour report made a detailed account of the conference.[41] In the afternoon, Admiral Kato called together at his official residence a conference of Fleet Admirals Togo and Inouye, Admirals Shimamura, Nawa, and Kato, supreme war councilors, commanders of squadrons, naval bases and stations, as well as high officers of both the naval general staff and the navy department. For seven hours, Navy Minister Kato explained in detail the proceedings of the conference, discussing the treaties from all technical angles. A free exchange of views followed his explanation. Admiral Kato succeeded in obtaining the approval of his naval colleagues regarding his activities at Washington.[42] On the following day, Admiral Kato summoned again all the commanders of squadrons, naval bases and stations to his office to explain the new policy of naval retrenchment.[43]

As the "understanding" of the navy was obtained regarding the 5:5:3 ratio and a new defense program drafted thereunder, a joint meeting of the cabinet and the *Gaiko Chosakai* was held at the official residence of Prime Minister Takahashi on April 11, when Admiral Kato made formal report of the Washington conference to the cabinet and members of the advisory council on foreign relations and explained the changes made in national defense under the treaties.[44] Hence, the treaties were formally referred to the Privy Council for advice as to ratification.

Immediately thereupon, President Keigo Kiyoura appointed a sub-committee of nine members to examine these treaties. This committee was headed by Miyoji Ito and composed of eight of the most influential members of the Coun-

[40]*Tokyo Asahi*, April 1, 8, 1922, p. 2.

[41]*Ibid.*, April 7, 1922, p. 1.

[42]*Ibid.*, pp. 1, 2.

[43]*Ibid.*, April 8, 1922, p. 2.

[44]*Ibid.*, April 12, 1922, p. 1.

cil.[45] The sub-committee held its first session on April 17, when President Kiyoura, Vice-President Hamao, Secretary General Futakami, and the entire members of the committee represented the Privy Council, while Premier Takahashi, Foreign Minister Uchida, Navy Minister Kato, and Chief Baba of the Bureau of Legislative Affairs represented the government. At this meeting, Prime Minister Takahashi made a general statement regarding the government stand, while Count Uchida and Admiral Kato made general explanations of the treaties. All the treaties were favorably reported by the sub-committee to the Privy Council. The Privy Council, in turn, merely accepted, one by one, these reports of its sub-committee. Upon favorable action by the Privy Council the Prince Regent completed his ratification of these treaties on August 5, 1922, and promulgated them on August 17, 1922.

In conclusion, it is submitted that the fact that Admiral Kato, the "father of the modern navy of Japan," had taken personal charge of the negotiations at Washington, while maintaining the strict discipline of the "Big Navy" camp at the conference and at Tokyo, contributed no small part toward this early ratification of the Washington treaties.

[45]The sub-committee consisted of Miyoji Ito (chairman), Kaneko, Hozumi, Yasuhiro, Ikki, Tomii, Hirayama, Arimatsu, and Kuratomi.

Chapter XXI

THE SINO–JAPANESE POSTAL AGREEMENT

Making of the Agreement

IN PURSUANCE of the resolution regarding foreign postal agencies in China, adopted at the Washington Conference on February 1, 1922,[1] negotiations were entered into between the Japanese and Chinese representatives in Peking in August, 1922,[2] and on December 9, 1922, the so-called Sino–Japanese Postal Agreement was signed.[3] The substance of the agreement was made public by the Foreign Office on December 11.[4]

After preliminary preparations, the text was reported to the Prince Regent for his sanction, whereupon it was referred to the Privy Council for advice on December 21.[5] Immediately, a sub-committee of inquiry was appointed to examine the matter, under the chairmanship of Count Miyoji Ito. Count Ito and his conservative colleagues in the Council who were opposed to the reversal of policy toward China now sought to reprimand the Admiral Baron Kato cabinet, particularly the foreign minister. When, during the course of the sub-committee hearings, it was brought out that the question of postal agencies in Kwantung Leased Territory

[1]Text of the resolution in *Conference on the Limitation of Armament* (Washington, 1922), p. 1646.

[2]*Cf. Tokyo Asahi*, Sept. 2, 1922, pp. 2, 3.

[3]*Ibid.*, Dec. 11, 1922, p. 1.

[4]Text of the agreement as well as the accompanying notes in *Gaiko Jiho*, XXXVII, No. 1 (Jan. 1, 1923), pp. 250–254; also in *Tokyo Asahi*, Dec. 11, 1922, p. 3.

[5]Statement made by Foreign Minister Uchida in the House of Representatives on January 25, 1923 (*Kwampo gogai*, Jan. 26, 1923, p. 79). *Cf. Tokyo Asahi*, Dec. 14, 1922, p. 2.

and the South Manchuria Railway zone was reserved for future consideration, the councilors took vigorous exception, contending that such an admission on the part of the negotiators was a usurpation of powers and constituted an independent agreement. Moreover, the Council took exception to the procedure in the conclusion of the agreement. They contended that the cabinet violated the *Sumitsuin Kansei* in submitting the document after it had been brought into effect with signature.[6] Accordingly, at its meeting of December 28, the sub-committee decided to present a memorial to the throne.[7] On the other hand, the cabinet held extraordinary meetings on December 28 and 29 to face this unprecedented situation.[8] At 4:00 P. M., December 29, an extraordinary meeting of the Privy Council was held to deliberate upon the committee report, when Chairman Miyoji Ito bitterly attacked the Postal Agreement as to both substance and procedure. Count Uchida, foreign minister, defended the particular procedure followed in this instance on grounds of necessity under the exigencies of the time. Finally, all the privy councilors, with the exception of cabinet members present, unanimously voted to approve a draft memorial to the throne, praying their inability to advise the Prince Regent on the agreement, and severely censuring the cabinet's procedure as well as the substance of the agreement.[9]

On account of its unusual nature, the memorial of the

[6]While the Washington treaties were under investigation in the sub-committee of the Privy Council in the summer of 1922, the subject of postoffices in China was a target of queries by the councilors, when the cabinet assured them that the postal agencies along the South Manchuria Railway would not become a subject of future negotiations. Accordingly, the committee recommended ratification of the treaties with an accompanying statement in its report to the plenary session of the Council that its recommendation placed confidence in the declared assurances of the ministers of state (*Gaiko Jiho*, XXXVII, No. 2 [Jan. 15, 1923], p. 418). *Cf. Tokyo Asahi*, July 2, 1922, p. 2.

[7]The following councilors were present: Miyoji Ito (chairman), Kaneko Hozumi, Ichiki, Tomii, Yasuhiro, Arimatsu, and Hirayama (*Tokyo Asahi*, Dec. 29, 1922, p. 2).

[8]*Ibid.*, Dec. 30, 1922, p. 2.

[9]An anonymous article entitled "The Truth Regarding the Memorial of the Privy Council," *Gaiko Jiho*, XXXVII, No. 2 (Jan. 15, 1923), pp. 415–423. For the reported text of the report of the Council to the throne, see the statement quoted by Representative Ichiro Kiyose in the Lower House on Feb. 3, 1923 (*Kwampo gogai*, Feb. 4, 1923, p. 151). *Cf. Tokyo Asahi*, Dec. 30, 31, 1922, p. 2.

Privy Council was referred to the cabinet by Prince Regent Hirohito, whereupon an extraordinary meeting of the cabinet was called the following afternoon to determine its attitude toward the question. As the cabinet was firmly convinced that it violated no constitutional principles in concluding the agreement, nor did it impair the interest of the state, it decided to present a counter-memorial to the throne.[10] In accordance with this decision of the cabinet, Count Uchida was received in audience by the Prince Regent the following day (December 31) to present the cabinet's counter-memorial, praying His Majesty's sanction to the agreement. This was promptly granted, whereupon the Sino-Japanese Postal Agreement was published in the *Kwampo gogai* for January 1, 1923, merely as a notification of the Foreign Office, without any statement regarding the advice of the Privy Council.[11]

Far from improving the tension between the cabinet and the Privy Council, this summary action on the part of the cabinet merely tended to make the situation more critical. Consequently, the Prince Regent requested the views of Count Tosuke Hirata, Lord Privy Seal, who, after consulting Marquis Matsukata and Prince Saionji, the two remaining genro,[12] presented his views to the throne.[13] As a result, imperial messages were issued to both the cabinet and the Council to arrive at harmony and coöperation.[14]

As the Diet was in session, Admiral Baron Kato pleaded with the councilors to postpone the discussion of differences until the close of the Diet.[15] On March 27, the day following the adjournment of the Forty-sixth Diet, Premier Kato called on Count Kiyoura, president of the Privy Council, for "understanding."[16] Accordingly, Count Kiyoura called a meeting of the sub-committee on March 29, when Admiral Kato explained in person the details connected with the conclusion of the agreement. This informal meeting of the sub-

[10]*Tokyo Asahi*, Dec. 31, 1922, p. 2.

[11]*Gaimusho Kokuji* No. 1, 1923. *Cf. Tokyo Asahi*, Jan. 1, 1923, p. 2.

[12]*Tokyo Asahi*, Jan. 16, 1923, p. 2.

[13]*Ibid.*, Jan. 23, 1923, p. 2.

[14]*Ibid.*, Jan. 24, 1923, pp. 1, 2. *Cf. Kwampo gogai*, Feb. 2, 1923, pp. 120–121.

[15]*Ibid.*, Jan. 31, 1923, p. 2; *ibid.*, Feb. 1, 2, 3, 1923, p. 3; *ibid.*, Feb. 9, 1923, p. 1.

[16]*Ibid.*, March 29, 1923, p. 2.

committee was followed, on March 31, by a plenary session of the whole Council, when Premier Kato in person succeeded in reaching a satisfactory understanding with the Council. This satisfactory solution was immediately reported to the Prince Regent by Count Kiyoura.[17] Consequently, on April 2, accompanied by Count Uchida, foreign minister, Prime Minister Kato was given an imperial audience in the palace to report the "understanding" thus reached, and the incident was closed.[18]

PARLIAMENTARY DEBATES UPON THE AGREEMENT

On January 25, 1923, Representative Fujiya Suzuki, a leading jurist of the *Kenseikai* party, put a long question to the government on the recently concluded postal agreement with China and demanded specific replies on the following four points:

(1) Was not the assumption of international obligations by signing the Sino-Japanese Postal Agreement and the accompanying protocols without having received the imperial sanction thereto a usurpation of the imperial prerogatives? And did not the negotiators go beyond powers when they signed the provisional agreement concerning the South Manchuria Railway zone?

(2) Why did the government fail to submit the draft agreement to the Privy Council prior to signature? Does the cabinet regard the submission subsequent to signature a proper procedure? Why did the government hasten to conclude this agreement prior to the coming into effect of the Nine-Power Treaty? What is the position of the Department of Communications on the subject?

(3) Why did not the government promulgate the postal agreement in accordance with Article 8 of the *Koshikirei*, or the ordinance concerning the forms of public documents? Why did the government petition the advice of the Council at all?

(4) What responsibility does the cabinet take for the anxiety felt by His Majesty because of the memorial of the Privy Council?

In his speech, Representative Suzuki declared that a treaty is a contract between states and comes into effect with signature if subsequent ratification is not reserved; he argued that the respresentatives went beyond their delegated powers

[17]*Op. cit.*, March 30, April 1, 1923, p. 2.

[18]Miyata (ed.), *Gensui Kato Tomosaburo Den* (Tokyo, 1928), pp. 164-165. See also *Tokyo Asahi*, April 3, 1923, p. 2.

when they signed the Postal Agreement concerning the excluded region of the South Manchuria Railway. Commenting upon the competence of the Council over treaties and agreements, this well-known parliamentarian-jurist declared that all international commitments, whether they require subsequent ratification or otherwise, and by whatever name they may be called—treaties, agreements, declarations, protocols —must be submitted to the Council for advice. In support of his thesis he declared that a treaty binds the contracting states and at the same time places limitations upon the rights and duties of the people, and that the externally binding effect cannot be nullified by the rejection of internal organs. Thus he argued that all treaties and agreements must be submitted to the Council in accordance with Article 8 of the *Koshikirei*, irrespective of subsequent ratification.[19]

Replies were made by four cabinet ministers. The prime minister declined to state the internal negotiations with the Council but assured the House that he would assume the political responsibility for the agreement.[20] Count Uchida made a detailed reply on all points raised. He declared that conventions concluded under direction of the department of communications, such as those relating to parcel post, are, by tradition submitted to the Council for advice prior to signature, but the Foreign Office does not follow such practice. Thus, all treaties and agreements concluded through the Foreign Office are always signed before submitting them to the Council for advice, without suspending the signature pending action by the Council. Foreign Minister Uchida vigorously defended his action, not only by precedents, but also by the urgent necessity of the circumstances, declaring that to delay the conclusion of the agreement because of an internal procedure would have been contrary to the public interest of the state, and flatly denied any usurpation of the imperial prerogatives. The government took the position that the agreement required imperial sanction prior to its completely coming into effect and consequently submitted it to the Council. He defended the publication of the agreement as a notification of the Foreign Office, holding that only those treaties requiring ratification are published as treaties with

[19] *Kwampo gogai*, Jan. 26, 1923, pp. 73–78.
[20] *Ibid.*, p. 78.

the accompanying preamble stating that the advice of the Privy Council has been obtained, and that other agreements are published as notifications of the Foreign Office, irrespective of their having received the advice of the Council. He cited the Anglo-Japanese Alliance as a notable instance of an agreement which was published not as a treaty but as a notification of the Foreign Office.[21] Justice Minister Dr. Keijiro Okano supported the foreign minister, while Viscount Toshisada Mayeda, communications minister, said that the Foreign Office took charge of all treaties and agreements arising out of the Washington Conference, that the matter was decided upon in a cabinet council, and consequently he declined to state the position of his department before the House.[22]

Unsatisfied with the replies thus given by the cabinet ministers, Representative Suzuki made a further interpellation, and demanded the precise position of the cabinet on the external and internal effect of the agreement. Suzuki contended that this agreement became effective between the parties upon signature; he held that the proper procedure was to have obtained the imperial sanction to the draft agreement prior to signature, and again after signature, prior to its proclamation as a domestic law. In reply, Foreign Minister Uchida declared that, under the highly complicated processes of contemporary international intercourse, negotiations usually continue up to the time of signature, that to suspend the negotiations for the purpose of obtaining the advice of the Council would be inexpedient and unpractical, and that the Foreign Office had not yet adopted such a procedure. Here the cabinet ministers successfully avoided answering directly the question of the external and internal effects of a treaty or an agreement.[23] The government continued to decline to comment upon the relations between the Council and the cabinet throughout the session, pleading that the proceedings of the Council were secret.[24]

[21]*Op. cit.*, pp. 78–79.

[22]*Ibid.*, p. 80. On Jan. 26, Nakakoji, Sakatani, Megata, and Egi called on Premier Admiral Kato on this issue (*Tokyo Asahi*, Jan. 27, 1923, p. 2).

[23]*Kwampo gogai*, Jan. 26, 1923, pp. 80–81.

[24]*Ibid.*, Feb. 2, 1923, pp. 120–121; *Dai Shijurokkai Teikoku Gikai Kizokuin Iinkai Giji Sokkiroku*, No. 3, pp. 8–9; *Tokyo Asahi*, Jan. 27, 1923, p. 2.

On February 3, Dr. Ichiro Kiyose introduced a resolution in the House of Representatives calling upon the government to make public the details connected with the conclusion of the Sino-Japanese Postal Agreement and subsequent memorials to the throne reported to have been presented by both the cabinet and the Council.[25] In his brilliant speech, Dr. Kiyose declared that members of the Diet should be informed of the details connected with the conduct of foreign relations, and particularly the concluding of treaties, in order to discharge their constitutional duties in deliberating upon budgets and projects of law. He admitted that, under the existing law, the Imperial Diet did not possess the power to give consent to a treaty; he argued, however, that a treaty, when concluded and promulgated, imposes upon the subjects the duty of obedience to it. Thus, he demanded that, in the interest of smooth working of the constitutional system, details regarding conclusion of treaties should be made known to the Diet though it possessed no formal power of giving consent thereto. He cited the reported text of the memorial of the Council to the throne and called upon the government to make public the internal negotiations between the cabinet and the Privy Council. Representative Kokubo of the *Seiyukai* opposed the resolution, expressing satisfaction at the premier's declaration that the agreement came into effect upon receiving the imperial sanction and not upon signature, and cited the precedent of the imperial message reported to have been issued to Foreign Minister Kato in December, 1914. Representative Seigo Nakano supported the resolution, while the prime minister, Admiral Kato, expressed the government's opposition to the pending resolution, saying that the details regarding the exchange of views between the cabinet and the Council could not be made public. The resolution met an overwhelming defeat by 211: 77.[26]

The parliamentary attack upon the cabinet on the technical question of procedure in treaty-making brought some

[25]Text of the resolution in *Kwampo gogai*, Feb. 4, 1923, p. 150. *Cf. Tokyo Asahi*, Jan. 25, 1923, p. 3.

[26]*Ibid.*, Feb. 4, 1923, pp. 150–153. In an urgency interpellation, Professor Giichi Soyejima vigorously attacked the Privy Council as interfering with the executive by criticizing the China policy of the Admiral Kato administration (*ibid.*, Feb. 9, 1923, pp. 173–175).

interesting facts into the open but failed to weaken the ministry thereby. The Privy Council had to accept the *fait accompli* and had to be satisfied with obtaining an admission that the Postal Agreement was an executive agreement rather than a treaty requiring ratification.

Chapter XXII

THE TSINAN INCIDENT

The "Positive Policy" of General Tanaka

Baron shidehara's liberal policy toward China invited a vigorous opposition from the more conservative groups in and out of the Imperial Diet. The dissatisfaction was particularly pronounced among the more conservative members of the Privy Council. This opposition on the part of the councilors to the "weak" policy toward China was partly responsible for their rejection of an emergency imperial ordinance on April 17, 1927, prepared by the Wakatsuki cabinet to rescue the Bank of Japan. The immediate effect of this action of the Council was the resignation of the *Minseito* ministry.[1]

The *Minseito* cabinet was succeeded by the more militaristic and conservative *Seiyukai* ministry under the premiership of General Baron Tanaka, a former war minister and a leading figure in the *Choshu* military oligarchy. The fact that General Tanaka personally took charge of the Foreign Office added to the well-known attitude of the *Seiyukai* party on the Chinese question indicated the general foreign policy to be pursued by the new ministry, and greatly alarmed the more liberal section of the general public. On April 22, only two days after coming into office, Prime Minister Tanaka issued a statement outlining the policies of the new administration.[2] In order to formulate a "new policy," on which a great deal of advance publicity had been given, a conference

[1] Count Miyoji Ito, chairman of the sub-committee which investigated the government draft ordinance, bitterly criticized the Chinese policy of Baron Shidehara, in the presence of the emperor, at the plenary session of the Privy Council on April 17, 1927.

[2] Text of the statement in *Gaiko Jiho*, XLV, No. 9 (May 1, 1927), pp. 161–162.

of the representatives of the Foreign, Finance, War, and
Navy departments, general staffs of both services, the Kwantung garrison, the Japanese minister and three important
consuls general in China was held at the Foreign Office under
the chairmanship of General Tanaka during June 27 and
July 7, 1927.[3] During the conference views were exchanged
among these representatives of various organs chiefly concerned with conducting foreign relations with China, and on
July 7 Prime Minister Tanaka issued "instructions" to those
representatives upon what was then reported to be the "positive policy towards China." In emphasizing the difference of
policies to be pursued towards China proper and towards
Manchuria and eastern Mongolia, he declared that Japan
possessed special interests in the latter mentioned areas, that
it was her duty to maintain peace and order there, and that
she was prepared to protect her rights and interests should
they be threatened by disturbances in those three provinces.[4]

THE TSINAN INCIDENT, MAY, 1928

By the beginning of April, 1928, the Chinese Nationalist
forces were well advanced in their march against Marshal
Chang Tso Lin, the war lord of Manchuria and reputed
friend of General Tanaka. Accordingly, Marshal Chang's position became dangerous; in fact, his withdrawal seemed certain unless some strong interference were again made by a
third party as in the spring of 1927.[5] The occupation of

[3]The Foreign Office was represented by Baron Tanaka, permanent and parliamentary vice-ministers, councilor, chiefs of the Asiatic bureau, commerce bureau,
European and American bureau, and of the intelligence bureau. The foreign service
was represented by Japanese minister to China and consuls general at Mukden,
Shanghai, and Hankow, chief of the military affairs bureau of the War Department,
vice-chief of general staff, a section chief of the staff, and commander of the Kwantung garrison. The naval authorities were represented by vice-minister, chief of the
naval affairs bureau of the Navy Department, and vice-chief of naval general staff.
Other interests were represented by chief of the finance bureau of the Finance Department, governor of the Kwantung leased territory, and chief of the police bureau
of the government general of Chosen.

[4]*Gaiko Jiho*, XLVI, No. 2 (July 15, 1927), pp. 167–174. *Cf.* the Port Arthur Conference of Aug. 15, 1927 (*ibid.*, Sept. 1, 1927, p. 173).

[5]The dispatch of a portion of the Manchuria garrison to Shantung Province for
the announced purpose of protecting the life and property of Japanese residents
there imperiled by the advancing Nationalist troops invited an immediate protest
(June 1, 1927) from the Nationalist government, while it aroused serious popular
apprehension at home (Yoshino, *Gendai Kensei no Unyo*, pp. 419–431).

Manchuria by the Nationalist forces at this time seemed detrimental to the Japanese interests; the time was ripe for the "positive policy" to find its logical expression.

In order to formulate the policy of the army regarding the rapidly moving situation in China, the war minister, General Shirakawa, invited representatives of the South Manchuria Railway Company, the War Office, and the general staff to a conference on April 9, 1928.[6] On the following day an important conference of the representatives of the *Kasumiga-seki*, War Department, and the general staff, the South Manchuria Company and the Kwantung government was held in the Foreign Office to discuss the policy of the government.[7] On April 12 General Suzuki, chief of general staff, called on Prime Minister Tanaka at the latter's official residence to confer upon the Manchurian situation.[8] Meanwhile the authorities of the Kwantung government pressed the cabinet for immediate action, while the general staff, being fully informed of the fighting situation near Tsinan, likewise demanded immediate measures. On April 17, a conference upon the situation was held between the war minister and the chief of staff; General Shirakawa reported the results of this conference to the cabinet the same day and made explanations about the Chinese battle lines to his colleagues. In view of the gravity of the situation, the cabinet decided to take an immediate measure, leaving the exact number of forces to be sent as well as the time of dispatching them to a joint conference of the Foreign, War, and Navy departments. Thus, the final decision on this important question was left in the hands of General Tanaka (premier and foreign minister), General Shirakawa (war minister), and Admiral Okada (navy minister).[9]

In the early part of the morning of April 18, the "Big Three" held a conference at the official residence of the prime minister and reached a unanimous decision to dispatch an immediate expedition to Tsinan, after which representatives

[6]The following representatives were present at this joint conference: president and vice-president of the South Manchuria Railway Company, war minister, vice-minister of war, chief of the military affairs bureau of the War Department, councilor of the War Department, and vice-chief of general staff.

[7]*Tokyo Asahi*, April 10, 1928, p. 6.

[8]*Ibid.*, April 13, 1928, p. 1.

[9]*Ibid.*, April 18, 1928, pp. 1, 6.

of the three departments met in conference at the Foreign
Office to decide upon the details.[10] Hence, this momentous
decision to dispatch troops for the announced purpose of
protecting the Japanese residents in and around Tsinan was
made in the cabinet without any civilian representative of
the Foreign Office. Officials at the *Kasumigaseki*, therefore,
had the honor of being informed of the expedition after the
matter had already been decided. Under the circumstances
they were forced to defend the decision, in the making of
which they had had little voice; they were compelled to execute the policy for the formulation of which they had but
official sympathy. This decision to dispatch troops was bitterly condemned in the editorial columns of the liberal papers
as unwarranted by the circumstances and as detrimental to
the future relations between Japan and China.[11]

An extraordinary meeting of the cabinet was called at ten
o'clock in the morning of April 19, when General Shirakawa
and Admiral Okada made their reports on the Chinese situation. After brief deliberation upon the matter, the cabinet
decided immediately to dispatch the Sixth division (Kumamoto), the Chiba railway corps, and the Nakano telegraph
corps to the threatened area. Early in the afternoon, Baron
Tanaka hurried to the Akasaka detached palace to report
the decision of the cabinet and to obtain His Majesty's sanction. The premier was immediately followed by General
Suzuki, chief of staff, who also reported the decision of the
staff and petitioned for the imperial sanction to the measure
decided upon.[12] Thereupon, the mobilization order reached
the commander of the Sixth division at Kumamoto, Kyushu,
at 1:20 P. M. of the same day.[13] In the following evening
(April 20), a statement was issued, disclaiming any intention
to interfere with the domestic affairs of the neighbor country
or to favor one faction against another, and declaring the in-

[10]*Op. cit.*, April 19, 1928, p. 6.

[11]Yoshino, *Gendai Kensei no Unyo*, pp. 444–450. *Cf.* a leading article in *Tokyo
Asahi*, April 19, 1928, p. 7.

[12]*Tokyo Asahi*, April 20, 1928, p. 1.

[13]*Ibid.*, April 20, 1928, p. 6. For several days the chiefs of staff of all divisions
throughout the land were in session. Upon receipt of the mobilization order, Lieut.
Colonel Washitsu, a high staff officer of the Japanese forces in China, and Colonel
Kuroda, chief of staff of the Sixth division, left immediately for their respective
posts (*ibid.*, p. 1).

tention of withdrawing the troops as soon as the security of the Japanese residents was assured.[14] This non-aggressive and non-interference policy was reiterated on subsequent occasions by the commander of the expeditionary forces, in Shantung.[15]

THE FIFTY-FIFTH DIET AND THE EXPEDITION

The dispatch of troops on the eve of the Fifty-fifth session of the Diet was partly intended to produce an important political effect in Japan. Apparently, therefore, the decision was intended, not only to "save" the war lord of Manchuria from an imminent danger, but also to demonstrate afresh the vaguely defined "positive policy" of General Tanaka's government.[16] The party strength of the *Seiyukai* (government) and the *Minseito* (opposition) being evenly divided, the opposition leaders made determined efforts during the short session of the Diet to embarrass the *Seiyukai* ministry, while General Tanaka and his party were equally anxious to gain popular support for their somewhat dubious policy toward China.

The first important interpellation was made by General Koichiro Shimizu in the House of Peers on April 27. He demanded that the war minister state whether the cabinet was prepared to carry out the announced policy in spite of the opposition of China and other powers. In reply, General Shirakawa assured the interpellator that the government was prepared to protect the resident nationals and denied that the dispatch of troops at this time was in any way intended to favor one faction against another.[17] Meanwhile, on May 3, Japanese troops collided with the Nationalist forces at Tsinan, resulting in several deaths and injuries to many civilians and soldiers on both sides. The following day (May 4), War Minister Shirakawa came before the House of Peers and reported the latest information concerning the Tsinan

[14]*Ibid.*, April 21, 1928, p. 2.

[15]*Cf. ibid.*, April 27, 1928, p. 7. On April 20 Minister Yoshizawa presented to the foreign minister of the Peking government a written memorandum explaining the expedition, while the latter immediately requested the withdrawal of the Japanese forces (*ibid.*, April 22, 1928, p. 6).

[16]The Fifty-fifth session of the Diet lasted from April 23 to May 7, 1928.

[17]*Kwampo gogai*, April 28, 1928, pp. 7-9.

incident.[18] On the afternoon of the same day he made similar report to the Lower House[19] and was followed by an eloquent interpellation by Representative Ryutaro Nagai, a leading member of the *Minseito* party. He charged that the sending of troops to Tsinan did not accomplish the announced purpose because it failed to protect the Japanese residents, and declared that it was a foregone conclusion that the unwelcome presence of the Japanese troops there would incite resentment and indignation on the part of the Chinese, and that Tokyo had been informed at the time that the Chinese government could be held responsible for any difficulties that might ensue. He further charged that the decision of the first dispatch of forces to Tsinan on May 28, 1927, was made against the telegram sent from the resident consul general, Saito, who protested against such a move, declaring that there was no necessity for it and that the decision of the cabinet of May 27, 1927, was based upon erroneous information presented by the war minister. Thus he openly charged the Tanaka ministry with using the expedition for political purposes. In reply, General Shirakawa denied every charge made by the veteran interpellator; and both the prime minister and the war minister declined to comment upon the question of the responsibility for the incident.[20] This was again made a subject of parliamentary discussion in both Houses of the Diet on May 5.[21]

On May 6, 1928, the last day of the session, Premier and Foreign Minister General Baron Tanaka, came before the House of Peers and made an unusually detailed report upon the latest developments in Tsinan, reading several telegrams received by the Foreign Office. War Minister Shirakawa followed his chief.[22] Baron Shozo Yabuki made a searching interpellation. He demanded a reply, among others, upon the exact nature of the cabinet decision of April 19 in connection with the dispatch of troops to Shantung Province. Baron Tanaka was evasive and noncommittal in his reply: he de-

---

[18]*Op. cit.*, May 5, 1928, pp. 39–41. No important questions were put to the war minister following his brief account in the Upper House.

[19]*Ibid.*, May 5, 1928, pp. 73–74.

[20]*Ibid.*, pp. 74–77.

[21]*Ibid.*, May 6, 1928, pp. 55–58, 89–104.

[22]*Ibid.*, May 7, 1928, pp. 63–64.

clined to disclose the nature of cabinet deliberations prior to reaching the decision. Moreover, he refused to state the policy of the government towards internal warfare in China on the ground that it depended upon future developments; he insisted that the government was unable to answer in advance.[23] Unsatisfied with the answer thus given, Baron Yabuki declared that, inasmuch as the dispatch of troops was decided in the cabinet, the ministry must assume the responsibility for the incident. The prime minister, in reply, calmly declared that the cabinet could not assume the responsibility for the blunders of this character, and that the commander of the forces was responsible for the movement of troops and operations.[24]

FURTHER DEVELOPMENTS

By May 5, 1928, the serious tension in Tsinan seemed to have subsided, but on May 7 the commander of the Sixth division sent a telegram to Tokyo, stating that he had demanded that General Chiang Kai-shek withdraw his troops to a point about seven miles from Tsinan and from either side of the Shantung Railway, and that he had demanded a reply within twelve hours. The general staff was taken by surprise, and in the evening a conference of high military authorities was called. As a result, War Minister Shirakawa proposed at the cabinet meeting of May 8 that one wartime division should be sent to the strained region, which was promptly approved. On the following day, only two days after the adjournment of the Fifty-fifth Diet, a mobilization order was issued to the Third division (Nagoya).[25] This expedition of additional contingents met a vigorous protest on the part of the Nanking government, which presented a long memorandum to the Secretariat of the League of Nations on

[23] *Ibid.*, pp. 65–67.

[24] *Ibid.*, pp. 69–70. General Shirakawa declared again in the Fifty-sixth Diet that he could be held responsible for the decision of the cabinet to dispatch troops, but not for the movement of troops in Shantung or Tsinan, as it came under the power of supreme command of the armed forces (*ibid.*, March 20, 1929, p. 841).

[25] Statement made by War Minister Shirakawa in the House of Peers on March 20, 1929, in reply to a question by G. Nagao (*ibid.*, March 21, 1929, pp. 558–559). General Shirakawa flatly denied that the cabinet purposely avoided parliamentary scrutiny by delaying its decision until after the adjournment of the Diet (*ibid.*).

May 11, while the Tokyo government likewise transmitted a memorandum defending its action in Tsinan.[26]

A storm of criticism and denunciation was showered upon this extravagantly militaristic and irresponsible measure adopted by the government.[27] The criticism was so instantaneous and so widespread that the government had to issue a public statement approving the Japanese commander. Thus on May 13, both the war minister and the chief of general staff sent messages to General Fukuda at Tsinan, commending his measures.[28] The assassination of Marshal Chang Tso Lin on June 4 at Mukden cast further apprehension upon the Tanaka government for its execution of the so-called "positive policy."[29]

Meanwhile the activities of Chang Hsueh Liang, son of the late Marshal Chang Tso Lin, became embarrassing to Tokyo. Accordingly, an important cabinet meeting was held on July 17 to decide upon an "advice" to be transmitted to young Chang regarding his policy towards the Nanking government. On the following day Consul General K. Hayashi invited the young marshal to the consulate general and advised the latter "in his individual capacity" to postpone his reported conciliation with Nanking.[30] Baron G. Hayashi, former ambassador to Great Britain (1920–1925), was also sent to Mukden to "advise" the young war lord of Manchuria.[31] A statement was issued by Prime Minister Tanaka

[26]*Gaiko Jiho*, XLVII, No. 12 (June 15, 1928), pp. 154–157.

[27]A strict censorship of the press upon the measure was ordered to suppress any unfavorable criticism of the government. For example, see an article by Nyozekan Hasegawa in *Kaizo*, X, No. 6 (June, 1928), pp. 124–132.

[28]Statement made by Representative Nagai in the House of Representatives on Jan. 22, 1929 (*Kwampo gogai*, Jan. 23, 1929, p. 17).

[29]For the untimely death of Marshal Chang Tso Lin, see Chap. XXIV, *infra*.

[30]The government's insistence that the Japanese consul general give his "advice" upon request and in his individual capacity was seriously challenged in subsequent parliamentary interpellations. Thus, Baron Shidehara, General Tanaka's predecessor in the Foreign Office, in his interpellation on this point in the House of Peers on Feb. 2, 1929, expressed his opinion that the advice so given by the Japanese consul general was evidently under instructions from Tokyo (*Kwampo gogai*, Feb. 3, 1929, p. 89). Representative R. Nagai supported Baron Shidehara in the Lower House during the same session and declared that it was unthinkable for the consul general to make such an important "advice" without instructions (*ibid.*, Jan. 23, 1929, p. 18).

[31]*Cf.* a question addressed by General Shimizu in the House of Peers on Jan. 29, 1929 (*ibid.*, Jan. 30, 1929, pp. 51–55).

on July 18 in which he set forth the following four conditions for the settlement of the Tsinan incident: (1) an apology from the Nationalist government, (2) punishment of those responsible for the incident, (3) payment of an indemnity, and (4) a guarantee of future security.

Surrounded by criticism on all sides, the Tanaka cabinet, at its meeting of July 10, finally decided to pursue a less extravagant policy and to withdraw the troops gradually.[32] On August 15 a conference was held at the official residence of the war minister, when the war minister, vice-minister of war, chief and vice-chief of general staff decided to withdraw the Sixth division from Shantung.[33] The following day, the chief of staff was given an audience by the emperor concerning the decision reached the previous day. With the imperial sanction, the order was issued to Commander Fukuda of the division.[34] Again, on October 6, General Suzuki, General Shirakawa, and General Baron Tanaka held an important conference and decided to withdraw 7,000 additional troops from Shantung.[35] This decision was submitted to the cabinet for formal approval at its meeting on October 12. The chief of staff, as well as the prime minister, was received in audience by the emperor in the afternoon to report the decision to the throne. Thereupon an order was dispatched the same day to the commander of the Shantung expeditionary forces.[36]

The way was thus cleared for the opening of the Diet in December. The Fifty-sixth session of the Diet was opened on December 26, which, after organizing itself, adjourned for the New Year recess. On the morning of January 22, 1929, General Baron Tanaka, prime minister and foreign minister, addressed the House of Peers on the state of the nation and on foreign relations. In his speech as foreign minister he dwelt at length upon his Chinese policy and boldly declared that Japan, having risked her national independence, had

[32]Dr. Sakuzo Yoshino, former professor of politics at the Imperial University of Tokyo, led the popular attack upon General Tanaka's method of protection of Japanese residents. See his articles written during this period in *Gendai Kensei no Unyo*, pp. 451–474.

[33]*Tokyo Asahi*, Aug. 16, 1928, p. 1.

[34]*Ibid.*, Aug. 17, 1928, p. 2.

[35]*Ibid.*, Oct. 7, 1928, p. 1.

[36]*Ibid.*, Oct. 13, 1928, p. 1.

the greatest concern over peace and order in Manchuria, where she possessed special rights and interests, military as well as political. No immediate interpellations were forthcoming from the floor regarding this "positive policy" so boldly expounded by General Tanaka himself.[37]

Parliamentary scrutiny of the "big stick" policy under the *Seiyukai* administration came from the *Minseito* members in the Lower House. Baron Tanaka's address on foreign relations on January 22 was followed by a long and searching question by Representative Ryutaro Nagai, a liberal leader of the *Minseito* (opposition) party. During the course of his interpellation he charged that, on April 22 and 23, 1928, the Japanese consul general at Tsinan ordered the withdrawal of the Japanese residents from the affected region and declared that the dispatch of troops at that moment was certain to invite hostility and resentment on the part of the Nationalist forces. He bitterly condemned the entire policy as incompetent and detrimental to the future relations between the two countries; he eloquently denounced the failure of the so-called "positive policy."[38] Baron Kijuro Shidehara, on the other hand, in his long and brilliant address in the Upper House, took the Tanaka policy to task and defended his own administration of foreign affairs under the Wakatsuki ministry. He took special interest in calling the attention of the Peers to the Nanking incident, when no Japanese resident was injured without dispatching a single soldier, and bitterly criticized the Tanaka diplomacy, charging the latter with conducting the China policy for partisan purposes and for domestic effect.[39] He concluded his interpellation by declaring that:

It is practically impossible to conduct foreign relations in total disregard of domestic relations and opinions; but if the domestic considerations and internal effect should be allowed to dominate and control the conduct of our foreign relations, we cannot but be apprehensive of the future of our country and of the peace of the world.[40]

[37]*Kwampo gogai*, Jan. 23, 1929, p. 6.
[38]*Ibid.*, Jan. 23, 1929, pp. 10–23.
[39]*Ibid.*, Feb. 3, 1929, pp. 87–91.
[40]*Ibid.*, p. 91.

Baron Tanaka, in reply, vigorously defended his policy, denying the charges made by his predecessor at the *Kasumigaseki*. Pressed to state whether the government was prepared to dispatch troops to Manchuria to maintain peace and order, in case the vested rights were not placed in jeopardy, General Tanaka finally admitted that peace and order itself was indispensable to the protection of the vested rights and a necessary condition for their security.[41]

The questions and replies on the Chinese policy of the government, of which the Tsinan incident was only an instance, in the Diet were somewhat disappointing to students of parliamentary government, as the operation of the Manhood Suffrage Act failed to be reflected in any way in parliamentary debates upon foreign relations. Thus, Baron Tanaka and the war minister pursued the traditional policy of avoiding embarrassing interpellations and declining to disclose information concerning foreign relations. On the other hand, Baron Shidehara's interpellation was largely confined to the defense of his own administration and failed to touch more concretely upon broad questions of policy and responsibility.[42] However, they brought into the open some of the more important aspects of the Tanaka's much-advertised Chinese policy and served as instruments of embarrassment and attack, which, though indirect, contributed to the downfall of the ministry in July of the same year.[43]

THE SETTLEMENT OF THE INCIDENT

The growing discontent and disappointment at the Chinese policy of the *Seiyukai* administration, characterized by its repeated dispatches of troops, its technical blunders in connection with the signing of the Pact of Paris, and the general apprehension aroused both at home and abroad because of the untimely assassination of Marshal Chang Tso Lin, were not confined to the opposition members in the Diet. By December, 1928, a formidable opposition to the foreign policy

[41] *Ibid.*, Feb. 3, 6, 1929, pp. 91–93, 95–98.

[42] *Cf.* a leading article entitled, "The Tanaka Diplomacy and the Shidehara Diplomacy," in *Tokyo Asahi*, Feb. 3, 1929, p. 7.

[43] The parliamentary criticism and scrutiny upon the Pact of Paris and the so-called "Grave Manchurian Incident" were partly responsible for the fall of the Tanaka cabinet on July 2, 1929, only to be succeeded by the Hamaguchi ministry with Baron Shidehara as foreign minister. Chaps. XXIII, XXIV, *infra*.

of General Tanaka had been developed among influential quarters in the House of Peers as well as among privy councilors. Under the circumstances, General Tanaka had to adopt the more liberal policy of his predecessor, and on January 30, the administration recognized the revised tariff schedules of the Nanking government.

Meanwhile, the negotiations between Minister Yoshizawa and Dr. C. T. Wang, foreign minister of the Nationalist government, progressed rapidly. Consequently, the cabinet met in an extraordinary session on February 2 in the Diet Building to formulate its policy regarding the rapidly progressing Sino-Japanese negotiations. Parliamentary Vice-Minister Mori, as well as Chief Arita of the Asiatic bureau of the Foreign Office, was invited to this meeting to give detailed reports concerning the latest developments in Shanghai. After the cabinet deliberation, instructions were issued to Minister Yoshizawa as to the next move. Likewise, on the same day, high officers of the general staff held a conference and decided to insist upon guarantee after the withdrawal of troops.[44] On February 5 it was reported from Shanghai that an agreement of views had been reached concerning the settlement of the Tsinan incident.[45] This news dispatch elicited an immediate reaction in Tokyo, and on February 7 Representative Keijiro Nakamura (Minseito) addressed an urgency question to Foreign Minister Tanaka concerning the reported settlement of the Tsinan incident. He called the attention of the House to the press report to the effect that the Japanese government abandoned its original contention that the responsibility lay wholly with the Chinese side and agreed to a reciprocal expression of regrets, and that she consented to refer the question of damages to life and property to a joint commission. Representative Nakamura demanded

[44]*Tokyo Asahi*, Feb. 3, 1929, p. 6. Though the instructions were kept secret, the *Asahi* reported the instructions to be: (1) complete withdrawal of troops to be done only after peace is restored; (2) emphasis to be placed upon future guarantee of security; (3) mutual expression of regret at the incident; (4) compensation for damages to be left to a joint expert commission; (5) Japan to insist upon the carrying out of the Sino-Japanese agreements entered into after the Washington Conference; and (6) creation of a joint commission to protect the communication system in Shantung.

[45]*Ibid.*, Feb. 6, 1929, p. 1. After the adjournment of the Lower House, Baron Tanaka called a meeting of the cabinet to report the progress of negotiations (*ibid.*, p. 6). *Cf.* Chicago *Daily News*, Feb. 6, 1929, p. 2.

whether the reported concessions were true. In reply, Baron Tanaka declined to disclose the proposals on the ground that the negotiations were still in progress.[46]

The reported agreement proved true upon rupture of the negotiations on February 8, when Minister Yoshizawa and Foreign Minister Wang came to a deadlock concerning the time of withdrawal of troops and future guarantees. Minister Yoshizawa, under new instructions, now insisted upon two months to complete evacuation, while Dr. Wang contended three weeks was sufficient; Yoshizawa sought to obtain a concrete guarantee for the security after the withdrawal of Japanese troops.[47] This sudden change of attitude on the part of the Tokyo government was largely due to the vigorous stand of the general staff, reflecting the widespread dissatisfaction of the public at the loss of national "face."[48] An extraordinary meeting of the cabinet was called at noon of the following day, when it was decided not to make any further concession.[49] Several private conferences were held between the two representatives, but no progress was made during the session of the Diet because of domestic considerations. Meanwhile the Tanaka cabinet introduced a supplementary appropriation bill of 1,253,000 yen for the stationing of troops for two additional months. On March 22 Representative Nagai questioned whether two months were sufficient for the settlement of the incident. Baron Tanaka declared, in reply, that two months were thought to be sufficient, in the absence of some unforeseen changes in the situation, thus implying an early settlement.[50]

Towards the closing days of the Diet, negotiations progressed rapidly, and on March 24, only one day before the close of the session, the representatives signed a provisional agreement.[51] After the approval of the cabinet, instructions were issued to Minister Yoshizawa to sign the agreement,

[46]*Kwampo gogai*, Feb. 8, 1929, pp. 241–244. *Cf. Tokyo Asahi*, Feb. 7, 8, 1929, p. 6. On the same day, General Shirakawa, war minister, in a sub-committee meeting of the House of Representatives, declared that the responsibility for the incident lay with China (*Tokyo Asahi*, Feb. 8, 1929, p. 6).

[47]*Tokyo Asahi*, Feb. 9, 1929, p. 6.

[48]*Ibid.*, Feb. 6, 1929, p. 1.

[49]*Ibid.*, Feb. 10, 1929, p. 7.

[50]*Kwampo gogai*, March 23, 1929, pp. 896–898.

[51]*Tokyo Asahi*, March 25, 1929, p. 3.

without obtaining the sanction of the emperor. The agreement was formally signed on March 28, two days after the adjournment of the Fifty-sixth session of the Diet, and made public simultaneously in Tokyo and Nanking.[52] The delay in formal signature of the notes until the close of the Diet was evidently intended to avoid the inevitable storm of parliamentary criticism and interpellations. On the other hand, the deliberate omission of presenting the draft agreement to the emperor for his sanction was designed thereby to avoid inquiry and scrutiny at the hands of the Privy Council. However, the settlement of this important incident by an executive agreement was immediately made a subject of stinging criticism as lacking in due observance of the proper procedure.[53] Thus, the privy councilors took the position that the government should have petitioned for His Majesty's sanction, with subsequent submission of the text to the Council for advice, before instructing Minister Yoshizawa to sign the agreement. They insisted that neither the address of the chief of staff to the emperor nor the report of Baron Tanaka to the throne regarding the details of the negotiations could be taken as obtaining His Majesty's approval.

On April 2 the prime minister was reported to have expressed an apology to the throne for failing to obtain his ratification before allowing the agreement to come into force.[54] The following day, he visited Baron Kuratomi, president of the Privy Council, to express the regret of the cabinet.[55] Several calls were made upon leading members of the Council to seek their "understanding." On April 10 the Privy Council met in plenary session in the presence of the emperor, when Prime Minister, General Baron Tanaka, explained to the councilors that the settlement of the Tsinan incident by an exchange of notes without petitioning an imperial sanction was necessary because of the urgency of the circumstances and declared that the government would be careful in the future to observe the proper procedure. The explanation thus offered did not satisfy the councilors, and Dr. Senshi Egi, Viscount I. Ishiguro, Marquis Katsunosuke Inouye took vig-

[52]*Op. cit.*, March 29, 1929, p. 1.
[53]*Ibid.*, March 30, 1929, p. 6.
[54]*Ibid.*, April 3, 1929, p. 6.
[55]*Ibid.*, April 4, 1929, p. 6.

orous exceptions to Baron Tanaka and bitterly attacked the procedure in this instance.[56] The meeting did not clarify the unfavorable atmosphere of the Council.

In accordance with the pledge given to the councilors, Baron Tanaka submitted the draft notes to be exchanged between the Japanese and the Nationalist governments concerning the settlement of the Nanking and Hankow incidents. On April 30, a special committee under the chairmanship of Viscount Kaneko, appointed to inquire into the notes drafted by the representatives, held a hearing, when Prime Minister and Foreign Minister Tanaka, accompanied by bureau and section chiefs concerned, explained the negotiations up to the signing of the provisional agreements for the settlement of these two incidents. The sub-committee, after the hearings, decided to recommend approval. Immediately after the close of the hearings, Baron Tanaka called an extraordinary meeting of the cabinet to report the proceedings of the sub-committee.[57] On May 1 the Council met in a plenary session, when Chairman Kaneko made the committee report, recommending a favorable action. Several questions were addressed to the government, to which Prime Minister Tanaka and Chief Arita of the Asiatic bureau of the Foreign Office replied. As was expected, a privy councilor put an embarrassing question to Baron Tanaka. He called the attention of the premier to the similarity in nature of the settlement of the Nanking and the Hankow incidents to that of the Tsinan incident and demanded the reason why the procedure adopted in this instance by the government was different and inquired whether it was due to the relative importance of the incidents concerned. To this embarrassing question in the presence of the emperor, Baron Tanaka was unable to give a definite answer and only replied that these two incidents were important. The Council, by a unanimous vote, approved the committee report. After obtaining the imperial sanction, instructions were sent to Minister Yoshizawa to sign the notes. Thus formal signatures were attached to the notes on May 2 and made public on May 6, 1929.[58]

[56]For deliberations of the Council see *ibid.*, April 11, 1929, p. 1.

[57]*Ibid.*, May 1, 1929, p. 1.

[58]*Ibid.*, May 2, 1929, p. 1; May 3, p. 2; May 7, p. 6. The withdrawal of troops from Shantung was completed on May 20, 1929 (*ibid.*, May 21, p. 6).

Chapter XXIII

THE PACT OF PARIS

Diplomatic Negotiations

On the afternoon of April 13, 1928, the American ambassador in Tokyo called on Baron Giichi Tanaka at the Foreign Office and formally handed him the American text of the renunciation of war pact, together with notes exchanged between the American and French governments. At this conference Baron Tanaka expressed the opinion that the Japanese government was in favor of such a pact in principle and that a detailed reply would be made after full deliberations. The text of the American draft treaty as well as notes was released to the press on the following day.[1] The French text was handed to Mr. Katsuji Debuchi, vice-minister of foreign affairs, by the French ambassador on April 21. It was immediately released to the press.[2] The press expressed slight doubts as to the efficacy of such a proposal.[3]

After careful examination of the proposal by the Foreign Office and subsequent approval by the cabinet, the Japanese government replied to the American proposal on May 26, which read, in part, as follows:

The proposal of the United States is understood to contain nothing that would refuse to independent states the right of self-

[1]*Tokyo Asahi*, April 14, 1928, p. 6. In early January, 1928, the prime minister, Baron Tanaka, admitted to newspaper correspondents that the Japanese government had been approached by the American government on this subject through Ambassador Matsudaira at Washington, but refused to state whether Tokyo would favor it or not (*ibid.*, Jan. 6, 1928, p. 6).

[2]*Ibid.* April 22, 1928, p. 7.

[3]*Cf.* a leading article in *ibid.*, April 22, 1928, p. 7.

defense, and nothing which is incompatible with the obligations of agreements guaranteeing the public peace, such as embodied in the Covenant of the League of Nations and the Treaties of Locarno. Accordingly the Imperial Government firmly believe that unanimous agreement on a mutually acceptable text for such a treaty as is contemplated is well capable of realization by discussion between the six Powers referred to, and they would be happy to collaborate with cordial good will in the discussions with the purpose of securing what they are persuaded is the common desire of all the peoples of the world—namely, the cessation of wars and the definite establishment among the nations of an era of permanent and universal peace.

The text was made public by the Foreign Office immediately.

The second formal American draft was handed the Japanese government on June 23, 1928. Immediately the phraseology, "in the names of their respective peoples," was found to be likely to arouse misunderstandings and controversies in connection with its bearing upon the provisions of the Constitution, and consequently the government asked Washington to amend the phraseology or expunge it from the text. To this, however, the Washington government expressed reluctance on the ground that such an amendment might lead to endless negotiations and endanger its success, and argued that the phraseology in question did not contain any legal meaning objected to by Japan.

While negotiations were in progress between Tokyo and Washington, it became evident that other powers were ready to sign the pact. Consequently, without pressing further on this question, the cabinet decided to agree to the text of the pact, after exchanging notes pertaining to the interpretation of the phraseology in question. Thus, on July 16, 1928, Mr. S. Sawada, chargé d'affaires of Japan at Washington, forwarded the following memorandum:

It is understood that the phrase "in the names of their respective peoples" in Article I of the draft Treaty for the Outlawry of War does not signify "as the agents of their peoples"; namely that it is not the peoples themselves who conclude this Treaty and that the phrase in question has been inserted in the Treaty for the purpose of impressing upon the peoples the importance of the renunciation of war.[4]

[4] Text in *Collection des Traités*, Collection VII, No. 9 (le 26 Août 1929), p. 8.

To this memorandum, Secretary of State Kellogg replied:

I received this morning a memorandum from the Japanese Chargé d'Affaires in which he says that it is understood that the phrase "in the names of their respective peoples" in Article I of the Treaty for the Renunciation of War does not signify that the Emperor signs "as the agent of this people." As I said in my memorandum which I gave the Japanese Chargé on July 6, 1928, the words "in the name of the people" are synonymous with "on behalf of the people." As under the Japanese Constitution the Emperor signs in his own name and not for his people, it is quite clear that this phrase cannot signify in Japan an agency of any kind. The Japanese translation will be perfectly correct interpreted as I stated above.[5]

After exchanging the memoranda above cited with reference to the interpretation of the phraseology in question, Japan formally agreed to sign the treaty on July 20.

"In the Names of Their Respective Peoples"

Immediately upon the signature of the pact at Paris, the *Minseito* party, the chief opposition party, did not fail to make capital of this phraseology. On August 29, Dr. Egi, one of the most influential members of the party and former cabinet minister, called on Count Miyoji Ito, an influential member of the Privy Council who, together with Viscount Kentaro Kaneko, played junior rôles in the drafting of the Constitution.[6]

In arousing the public opinion against the Tanaka *Seiyukai* government for signing this pact, Representative Keijiro Nakamura took a leading rôle.[7] An extraordinary meeting of the executive committee of the *Minseito* (opposition) party was called on September 15; and on September 18, it issued a manifesto, declaring that, though the party was in hearty accord with the general sentiment of the treaty, the words "in the names of their respective peoples" were clearly violative of the spirit of the Constitution, encroaching upon the *taiken* or the imperial prerogative over foreign relations, and demanded that the government should make public the dip-

[5] *Op. cit.*, p. 9.
[6] See an anonymous article in *Tokyo Asahi*, April 19, 1929, p. 6.
[7] *Ibid.*, Sept. 16, 1928, p. 2.

lomatic notes exchanged between the Japanese and American governments prior to May 26, 1928, relating to the interpretation of the phraseology.[8]

To this formal charge of violation of the Constitution the Foreign Office asserted that the phraseology in question did not purport to state the location of sovereignty and that the government had taken due means to safeguard against any misinterpretation.[9] The *Minseito* party's onslaught against ratification of the pact without reservation soon received an energetic support from certain influential members of the Privy Council, the "watchdog of the Constitution."

PARLIAMENTARY DEBATES ON THE PACT

With the opening of the Fifty-sixth session of the Imperial Diet, the *Minseito* party sought to deal a fatal blow to the *Seiyukai* ministry by vigorously attacking the objectionable phrase contained in the pact. Thus, Representative Nakamura put a lengthy question on January 23, 1929, to the Tanaka government on the pact. In the course of his speech (representing the *Minseito* party), he asked whether the administration regarded the phraseology used in the pact as proper or improper, and if improper, why the government did not offer amendment to the text when first approached by Washington on April 13, 1928. He further asked whether there existed any agreement (verbal) or any notes exchanged concerning the point in question, and if so, requested the same be made public. To this, Baron Tanaka replied that the government interpreted the phrase, "in the names of their respective peoples," to mean that the emperor declared "on behalf of the state," and flatly denied that it was in any way in conflict with the fundamental character of the national polity. He declined to comment upon the diplomatic negotiations or make public the official translation on the ground that the pact had not yet been ratified by the emperor.[10]

Among the opponents of the ratification of the pact was

[8]*Ibid.*, Sept. 19, 1928, p. 2.

[9]*Cf. ibid.*, Sept. 18, 1928, p. 2.

[10]*Kwampo gogai*, Jan. 24, 1929, pp. 50–53. In reply to a question by General Koichiro Shimizu in the House of Peers, Baron Tanaka made similar remarks (*ibid.*, Jan. 30, 1929, p. 57). *Cf.* Baron Yoshiro Sakatani's interpellation in the Upper House on March 15, 1929 (*ibid.*, March 16, 1929, pp. 463–464).

Representative Yukio Ozaki, a well-known liberal whose
forty years of parliamentary career made him a conspicuous
figure. As the cabinet failed to comply with his demand for
publication of the notes exchanged regarding the phraseology,[11] he introduced a resolution calling upon the government to take immediate steps to ratify the treaty with
reservation. In defending the resolution, this veteran statesman declared that treaties could be concluded by the
emperor only in his own name, and consequently the Pact
of Paris could not be ratified without reservation annulling
the effect of the objectionable phrase so far as Japan was
concerned. The resolution failed of adoption.[12]

Parliamentary interpellations on the pact were not confined to the constitutional issues arising out of the objectionable phraseology. Thus interpellators sought to inquire into
the government interpretation of the effect of the pact in
its relation to the doctrine of self-defense and in its bearing
upon her policy in Manchuria and Mongolia. In replying to
the Peers concerning the effect of the pact upon national defense and foreign relations, particularly in Manchuria, the
prime minister was more detailed and deliberate than in the
Lower House.[13] On January 24, Mr. Tanahashi put a direct
question to the war and navy ministers on the effect of the
pact upon national defense. He prefaced his interpellation by
referring to the overwhelming vote in the Senate of the
United States in giving advice and consent to the ratification
of the pact and declared that Japanese action in this regard
should be such as not to invite any suspicion from abroad.
He requested the war and navy ministers to state definitely,
in so far as compatible with the interest of the state and not
violative of military and naval secrets, the effect of the pact
upon the future program of national defense. To this delicate
question both the war and navy ministers merely replied that
the national defense was for the security of the nation and
disclaimed any aggression or militarism. Hence, both minis-

[11]*Op. cit.*, March 20, 1929, pp. 833–837.

[12]*Ibid.*, March 26, 1929, pp. 1026–1040.

[13]Thus, to a question by Representative Nakamura concerning the right of self-
defense under the pact, in view of the American attitude toward the Monroe Doctrine and the British exceptions to Egypt, the prime minister refused to make any
elaboration, saying that the government's position had already been made clear
(*ibid.*, Jan. 24, 1929, p. 53).

ters declined to make a direct reply to the question and failed to elucidate the House concerning the government's interpretation of the effect of the pact upon the armament policy of the Empire.[14] Again, to a direct interpellation by General Koichiro Shimizu, Baron Tanaka replied to the Peers that the government fully considered the subject and that Manchuria was within the field covered by self-defense; and declared that, should there be disturbances in Manchuria which might threaten the peace and order, Japan would be compelled to take necessary measures, and that such steps could not be charged as violating the pact.[15] Thus the premier took advantage of the interpellation to state the government's position on the effect of the pact upon her diplomacy in Manchuria.

Controversies upon the constitutionality of the pact did not end with the close of the Fifty-sixth Diet in March, 1929. Soon this question became one of public debate, and an array of learned jurists argued in the press, pamphlets, and platforms. They contended that the phraseology in question did not purport to indicate the location of sovereignty, that the pact was clearly within the letter and spirit of the Constitution, and uniformly expressed keen disappointment at the *Minseito* party for making a political football of the phraseology.[16]

The contentions of the jurists on the constitutionality of the pact were met by several distinguished ex-diplomats who argued that the pact as it stood was clearly a violation of the Constitution and contrary to the fundamental character of national polity.[17] Viscount Kikujiro Ishii, former foreign minister and now a privy councilor, declared that the pact

[14]*Ibid.*, Jan. 25, 1929, pp. 21–25.

[15]*Ibid.*, Jan. 30, 1929, pp. 49–57.

[16]For the views of Minobe, Tachi, Kamikawa, Takayanagi, and Takaki, see a pamphlet entitled, "In the Names of Their Respective Peoples," published in Tokyo, 1929. *Cf.* Minobe, *Gendai Kensei Hyoron*, pp. 290–296, 302–310; Jumpei Shinobu's article in *Gaiko Jiho*, XLVIII, No. 8 (Oct. 15, 1928), pp. 44–50, and in *Kokusai Chishiki*, IX, No. 4 (April, 1929), pp. 7–19; Takayanagi, "The Foundations of Japanese Diplomacy," *Kaizo*, XI, No. 6 (June, 1929), pp. 2–13; Professor Matsubara in an article in *Tokyo Asahi*, May 3, 1929, p. 11.

[17]Dr. Honda in his article in *Gaiko Jiho*, XLIX, No. 5 (March 1, 1929), pp. 51–68. Dr. Kumataro Honda is a former ambassador to Germany and a well-known jurist. Dr. Honda's arguments are refuted point by point by Mr. A. Kasama, former counselor of embassy, in *ibid.*, L, No. 1 (April 1, 1929), pp. 33–53.

was incompatible with the Constitution, that it was an encroachment upon the treaty-making power as well as the
war power of the emperor, and that it should not be ratified
without reservation.[18] He held that such a reservation would
be acceptable to other signatory powers, and, if refused, he
was ready to advocate withdrawal from the pact in order to
protect the basic principles of Japanese polity.[19]

SUBMISSION OF THE PACT TO THE PRIVY COUNCIL

Soon opposition parties and influential members of the
Privy Council began to express their opposition to the pact
as it stood. By this time, it became evident that the *Minseito's* opposition to the pact was largely one of party politics,
using this opportunity to embarrass the Tanaka *Seiyukai*
cabinet. Accordingly they became more violent and outspoken, which was calculated to inflame the more conservative members of the Council. The liberal press of the nation
regretted the tactics being employed by the *Minseito* party
which, in effect, was acting in accord with the more un-
scrupulous members of the "third chamber," at the hands
of which the *Minseito* ministry met with a disastrous political assassination in April, 1927. Thus the leading dailies
welcomed the fall of the Tanaka government but were disappointed at the party tactics of the opposition party in-
triguing with their common enemy. They advocated speedy
ratification of the pact with an interpretative declaration
regarding the objectionable phrase in the interest of international good faith.[20] The *Tokyo Asahi Shimbun*, a leading
liberal paper, vigorously condemned a reported move on the
part of the cabinet to petition ratification with reservation,
on the ground that it might lead to serious diplomatic complications, and urged its ratification with an interpretative
declaration that the phraseology in question had no legal
effect so far as Japan was concerned. It expressed the conviction that the government should have made a declaration
at the time of signature in Paris.[21]

[18]Viscount Ishii, *Gaiko Yoroku*, pp. 284–316.
[19]*Ibid.*, p. 309.
[20]See the editorials in *Tokyo Asahi*, April 6, 11, 26, 1929.
[21]Editorials in *ibid.*, April 26, 1929.

Following the close of the Fifty-sixth session of the Diet, the cabinet took immediate steps to determine its attitude towards the Council. Baron Tanaka called on Prince Saionji, the sole remaining genro, to report to him in detail the issues arising out of the pact;[22] he paid his visit to Baron Kuratomi, president of the Privy Council, on April 3, to inform the latter that the government would attach a reservation concerning the objectionable phrase.[23] Accordingly, Baron Tanaka ordered the *Kasumigaseki* staff to draw up a draft reservation to be presented to the cabinet. On April 12 Baron Tanaka invited his cabinet members to a conference, to which three high officials of the Foreign Office were specially invited,[24] to explain the details of the pact, the precedents as well as legal effects of such reservations. The views of the cabinet were divided. One group argued that the pact, by its very nature, could hardly be ratified with a reservation, and accordingly urged that official action should be delayed until more favorable sentiments developed among the councilors. On the other hand, some members contended that ratification with reservation was undesirable but that, since the Council would not recommend ratification without it, there was no other course than to satisfy the opposing councilors. After some deliberations, it tentatively agreed upon the text, declaring that the phrase "in the names of their respective peoples" did not have any effect so far as Japan was concerned.[25]

Having decided upon the general attitude of the cabinet on the pact, the next step was to confer with leading members of the Council in order to reach a complete agreement upon the text of the reservation to be made. In a desperate attempt to obtain a definite action by the Council, the cabinet did not hesitate to remove Representative Etsujiro Uyehara from office, because of his alleged criticism of certain councilors, in an interview with a reporter of the *Japan Advertiser*, in which he was reported to have declared that their opposition to the pact was a political intrigue against the Tanaka *Seiyu-*

[22]*Ibid.*, April 5, 1929, p. 1.

[23]*Ibid.*, April 5, 1929, p. 6.

[24]Mr. Yoshida, Vice-minister of Foreign Affairs; Mr. Hotta, chief of the European and American bureau; Mr. Matsunaga, chief of the treaty bureau.

[25]*Tokyo Asahi*, April 13, 1929, p. 6.

kai cabinet. This report invoked a sharp protest from the councilors so criticized.[26] In order to deliberate upon the exact form of the reservation, a conference of Railways Minister Ogawa, and Justice Minister Hara, and high officials of the Foreign Office was called on April 20. It was agreed at this meeting that the proposed statement was to have the form of a reservation so far as its internal effect was concerned, but a unilateral declaration externally.[27]

The general contents of the proposed reservation having thus been decided upon, after numerous interviews and calls on Dr. Nikami, chief secretary of the Privy Council, Count Miyoji Ito, leading member of the Council, President Kuratomi of the Council, and others, the cabinet tentatively approved a draft text of the reservation at its meeting of May 7, 1929,[28] and formally approved it on May 10, 1929.[29] Premier Tanaka called on Prince Saionji on May 6 to report to the genro the cabinet's position on the pact,[30] and on Count Makino, Lord Privy Seal, on May 9, to report to him on the nature of the premier's visit to the genro and also to obtain his assistance and "understanding" regarding the attitude of the cabinet.[31]

As soon as the cabinet's attitude towards the pact became definitely known, it was reported in the press that Count Kosai Uchida, a privy councilor and the Japanese plenipotentiary at Paris to sign the pact on August 27, 1928, was to resign in the event that the government should petition the throne for its ratification with reservation. Count Uchida called on Prince Saionji on May 7 to report to the genro his intention to resign from the Privy Council.[32] It was generally reported that the call of Baron Tanaka on Prince Saionji on May 6 was to appeal to the genro to persuade Count Uchida not to resign. It was generally seen that the resignation of Count Uchida would lead to a grave political situation, which

[26]*Japan Advertiser*, April 15, 16, 17, 1929; *Tokyo Asahi*, April 18, 19, 20, 1929; *Jiji Shimpo*, April 20, 1929.

[27]*Jiji Shimpo*, April 21, 1929, p. 2.

[28]*Ibid.*, May 8, 1929, p. 2; *Tokyo Asahi*, May 8, 1929, p. 6.

[29]*Tokyo Asahi*, May 11, 1929, p. 6.

[30]*Ibid.*, May 7, 1929, p. 6.

[31]*Jiji Shimpo*, May 10, 1929, p. 1.

[32]*Tokyo Asahi*, May 8, 1929, p. 6.

naturally would raise the question of the responsibility of Prime Minister Tanaka for recommending his appointment as Japan's plenipotentiary at Paris.[33] Moreover, this sudden change of stand on the part of the Tanaka ministry in the face of the opposition of the Privy Council upon its repeated declaration during the Diet just closed did not fail to arouse resentment among members of the House of Peers as an insult to the Diet.[34]

THE PRIVY COUNCIL AND THE PACT

After numerous visits to influential members of the Council, and after due deliberations by various organs concerned, all cabinet ministers attached their signatures to the draft declaration and ratification on June 9. On June 10 Baron Tanaka was granted an imperial audience to report details concerning the pact and circumstances connected with the declaration attached thereto. The phrase, "viewed in the light of the provisions of the Imperial Constitution," was inserted at the instance of Count Ito, and with the verbal understanding on the part of the president, vice-president of the Council, Count Miyoji Ito, Viscount Kentaro Kaneko, that they would refrain from raising in the plenary session of the Council the question whether the insertion of such a phrase in the declaration constituted an admission on the part of the government of the unconstitutionality of the original text.[35]

The emperor submitted the Pact of Paris to the Privy Council for its advice on the morning of June 11. Baron Kuratomi, president of the Council, immediately conferred with Dr. Kiichiro Hiranuma, vice-president, regarding the appointment of a sub-committee of inquiry. Thereupon a special committee of nine councilors was appointed on June 11 under the chairmanship of Count Ito.[36] Railways Minister Heikichi Ogawa, under instructions from the prime minister, called on Count Uchida not to resign even in the event of the approval

[33]*Ibid.*, May 7, 1929, p. 6; *Jiji Shimpo*, May 7, 1929, p. 2.

[34]*Jiji Shimpo*, May 7, 10, 1929, p. 6.

[35]*Ibid.*, June 11, 1929, p. 2.

[36]*Ibid.*, June 12, 1929, p. 2. The committee was composed of most eminent jurists in the Council, including Count Ito and Viscount Kaneko, original drafters of the Constitution, Dr. Egi, Dr. Tomii, and Viscount Ishii.

of the pact by the Council, pleading that such a step would inevitably cause a political situation of gravest character. Count Uchida refused to state what he would do, pending a definite action in the Council.[37]

The first meeting of the sub-committee was held on June 17, 1929, when the Privy Council was represented by President Kuratomi, Vice-President Hiranuma, Chairman Ito, Councilors Kaneko, Tomii, Ishiguro, Ishii, Egi, and Saito, while the government side was represented by Premier Baron Tanaka, Chief Mayeda of the Legislative Bureau, Vice-Minister of Foreign Affairs Yoshida, Chief Matsunaga of the Treaty Bureau, and Chief Hotta of the European and American Bureau. At this meeting, Baron Tanaka explained the details connected with the negotiation of this pact and said that the government signed the text after exchanging notes with the American government, interpreting that the phraseology did not purport to signify "agent of the people." He declared that, in view of the general controversies which followed, the cabinet decided to attach a declaration to prevent any further misunderstanding upon this point. His remarks were followed by searching questions by Viscount Ishii, Viscount Kaneko, Dr. Tomii, Viscount Ishiguro, Dr. Egi, and Arai. Upon interpellation by Viscount Ishiguro, Mr. Mayeda was compelled to admit that the declaration was attached in order to prevent any possibility of misunderstanding concerning the Constitution. Dr. Egi declared that it was an admission on the part of the government of the unconstitutionality of the pact.[38] The sub-committee, at its second meeting held on the following day (June 18), decided to recommend its ratification, interpreting the attached declaration as a formal reservation.[39]

A copy of the report of the committee was transmitted to each cabinet minister and privy councilor on June 22,[40] and the plenary session of the Privy Council was called on June 26, with the emperor in attendance.[41] A heated debate ensued at this plenary session, when Count Ito ably defended his re-

[37] *Op. cit.*, June 12, 1929, p. 2.
[38] *Tokyo Asahi*, June 18, 1929, p. 2.
[39] *Ibid.*, June 19, 1929, p. 2.
[40] *Ibid.*, June 23, 1929, p. 2.
[41] *Ibid.*, June 27, 1929, pp. 1, 2.

port, holding that the pact as was signed violated the Constitution, and that the reservation was necessary to defend the honor of the Japanese polity and to protect the imperial Constitution. Count Uchida, on the other hand, vigorously opposed the declaration. He argued that the pact in no way violated the letter or the spirit of the Constitution and consequently no interpretative declaration was necessary. However, Count Uchida's position was violently assailed by Chairman Ito and Viscount Ishii of the Council, while Baron Tanaka, representing the cabinet, denied that it in any way encroached upon the fundamental law of the land. After several hours of debate, the Privy Council voted to approve the sub-committee report recommending the ratification of the Pact of Paris with a declaration attached thereto.[42]

RATIFICATION AND PROCLAMATION

With this action by the Council, the emperor ratified the pact with the declaration, that:

The Imperial Government declared that the phraseology, "in the names of their respective peoples," appearing in Article I of the Treaty for the Renunciation of War, signed at Paris on August 27, 1928, viewed in the light of the provisions of the Imperial Constitution, is understood to be inapplicable in so far as Japan is concerned.

The act of ratification was deposited at Washington on July 24, and the pact was proclaimed on July 25, 1929, as a treaty in the *Kwampo*, and was also published in the treaty collection.[43] Immediately upon taking measure to deposit the act of ratification in Washington, the Japanese government telegraphed instructions to Ambassador Debuchi to call on Secretary of State Stimson to hand him a memorandum stating that the Japanese declaration did not purport to modify in any way the provisions of the treaty or to influence the

[42]*Ibid.*, June 27, 1929, p. 2. Of Vice-President Hiranuma and the twenty-one councilors who were present, nineteen members voted for the report of the committee while three members opposed the report (Uchida, Sakurai, and Yashiro). All the cabinet members voted for the committee report. *Cf. Osaka Asahi*, June 27, 1929, p. 1.

[43]*Collection des Traités*, Collection VII, No. 9 (le 26 Août, 1929).

contents thereof. No objection was raised to the Japanese declaration.

Defeated in the Council, Count Uchida, the Japanese plenipotentiary who signed the pact at Paris, tendered his resignation immediately after the meeting of the Council on June 26.[44] Naturally, this raised a grave question of the responsibility of the cabinet. Partly due to the heavy loss of prestige sustained at the hands of the Privy Council regarding this question, but more directly due to the unhappy "Grave Manchurian Incident," the Tanaka government fell on July 2 and was succeeded by the Minseito administration. Count Uchida's resignation was accepted soon following the formation of the new ministry.[45]

[44]*Tokyo Asahi*, June 27, 1929, p. 2.
[45]See Chap. XXIV, *infra*.

Chapter XXIV

A GRAVE MANCHURIAN INCIDENT

PARLIAMENTARY INQUIRY INTO THE INCIDENT

THE UNTIMELY DEATH of Marshal Chang Tso Lin, the Manchurian war lord, in the early morning of June 4, 1928, at the railroad intersection under a Japanese-controlled railway bridge in the suburb of Mukden, created a great sensation in the Far East. Though the subject was reported widely in the Chinese and foreign press, there was a notable absence of reliable news in the Japanese papers. The Home Office, through the metropolitan police board, issued a notification to the press not to print news concerning the incident which might be detrimental to the interest of the state and which might embarrass the international standing of Japan abroad.

However, it was foreseen that the incident would be made a special target of searching interpellation and criticism in the approaching session of the Diet. In order to forestall embarrassing onslaughts upon the Tanaka *Seiyukai* cabinet, unsuccessful efforts were made by the government to prevent making the incident a political issue. Thus, on January 21, 1929, Baron Tanaka (prime minister) pleaded before a group of representative members of the House of Peers not to ask questions on the incident during the approaching session of the legislature.[1] Prior to the reopening of the Diet after the New Year's recess, on January 22, 1929, Premier Tanaka requested a conference of Mr. Takejiro Tokonami, president of the *Shinto* Club, and Mr. Yuko Hamaguchi, president of the *Minseito* (chief opposition) party. At this conference he

[1] Statement made in the House of Representatives on January 23, 1929 (*Kwampo gogai*, Jan. 24, 1929, p. 33).

275

pleaded with them not to make the incident a subject of parliamentary discussion in view of its international significance and in the best interest of the state, and further stated that, even if such interpellations be made on the subject, the government would be compelled to refuse any reply on the ground that the subject was still under investigation. To this request for not putting any questions on the subject Mr. Tokonami consented, but Mr. Hamaguchi refused to commit the members of his party upon this matter. To further prevent public discussion of the incident, the metropolitan police board sent a notice on January 25 to all the publishers of papers not to print any proceedings of the House Budget Committee which were secret in character.[2]

Notwithstanding the efforts made by the administration to keep the incident from becoming a subject of public discussion and a party issue, the *Minseito* party did not fail to take full advantage of the issue to seriously embarrass the cabinet and eventually to cause the downfall of the ministry. Many eloquent members of the party demanded the publication of the report concerning the incident, to which Baron Tanaka consistently refused to respond. He divulged neither the nature of the findings nor the location of the responsibility for the incident, pleading that the matter was still under investigation.[3] As the persistent demands made during the Diet were motivated solely by an attempt to embarrass the government rather than to obtain correct information, the cabinet was likewise determined not to make any statement concerning the incident. Accordingly, it pursued the policy of "still under investigation" against the "exposure tactics" of the *Minseito* party.[4]

On January 31, representing the *Minseito* party, Representative Yamaji, a well-known parliamentarian, put a long question to the cabinet. In the course of his eloquent speech he declared that the prime minister's appeal to a representa-

---

[2]Text of the notice in *ibid.*, Jan. 27, 1929, p. 98. The meeting of the House Budget Committee is supposed to be an executive session, but newspaper correspondents are permitted to be present, while no press correspondents are admitted to the proceedings of the Peers' Budget Committee.

[3]For interpellations in the House of Representatives, see *Kwampo gogai*, Jan. 24, 1929, pp. 33–34; Jan. 27, 1929, p. 98; March 20, 1929, pp. 831–832. For interpellations in the House of Peers see *ibid.*, Jan. 25, 1929, pp. 43–47; Jan. 30, 1929, p. 46.

[4]*Tokyo Asahi*, Jan. 26, 1929, p. 1.

tive group of members of the Diet at the beginning of the session not to touch upon the incident was a request to give up the power of parliamentary interpellation; he asserted that, though the press comment upon the incident was prohibited in Japan, it was widely discussed in foreign papers in Japan and abroad, and that their remarks were highly derogatory to the prestige and dignity of the Empire. He demanded that the government should take immediate steps to give correct information on the incident in order to clear away the causes of misunderstanding and apprehension. He further asked whether the ministry ever pressed the Chinese authorities for an immediate and vigorous investigation of the incident, or whether it was withholding the publication of the report although such investigation had been completed, in view of its political significance. He declared that it was beyond his understanding that the incident was still under investigation after a lapse of almost eight months. Government replies, made by Premier Tanaka and War Minister Shirakawa, were general, being a reassertion that the matter was still under investigation.[5]

Unsatisfied with those replies, Representative Yamaji introduced a resolution calling upon the government to make public all the findings which had been made with a view to wiping out all the misunderstandings and apprehensions entertained both at home and abroad. A spirited debate followed the introduction of this resolution. Representative Tabuchi, an independent member, charged that the introduction of the resolution was motivated by party politics, that it was intended to bring about the downfall of the present Tanaka government. On behalf of the *Seiyukai* party, Representative Hata declared that the *Kenseikai* cabinet[6] had refused to make public the damages incurred during the Nanking and Hankow incidents and argued that he was opposed to the resolution, which was obviously inspired by party politics, placing the interest of the state below that of the party. Though the *Minseito* resolution was supported by the *Shinto* Club, *Kakushinto*, and by the laborites, it was defeated by 220 to 198.[7] No formal resolution was introduced in the Upper

[5] *Kwampo gogai*, Feb. 1, 1929, pp. 148-153.
[6] The *Kenseikai* party is the forerunner of the *Minseito* party.
[7] *Kwampo gogai*, Feb. 1, 1929, pp. 153-156.

House, but the sub-committee of the Peers' Budget Committee in charge of the War Department attached a *voeu*, calling upon the government to make speedy completion of the inquiry and to make clear the location of responsibility.[8]

RESIGNATION OF THE CABINET

The public demand for immediate publication of the report of the findings of the incident did not subside with the close of the Diet. Not only the *Minseito* party but several influential members of the House of Peers pressed on the government. Thus, on May 13, four members of the fourth sub-committee of the Peers' Budget Committee in the Fifty-sixth Diet[9] called on General Shirakawa, war minister, to obtain a definite reply from the latter as to the date of publishing the findings, in pursuance of the promise made by both the prime minister and the war minister in the House of Peers during the session just ended. General Shirakawa replied that the investigation by the War Department had almost been completed and the report would soon be handed over to the prime minister for appropriate action; and, therefore, he refused to engage in a frank exchange of views with the callers at this time.[10] An important cabinet meeting was called on May 14 to deliberate upon the publication of the report. At this meeting the war minister made a detailed report to his colleagues on the result of the investigation of the incident. Though there were exchanges of opinions, the cabinet did not come to any decision, and its proceedings were kept in profound secrecy.[11] Meanwhile, it was reported at this time that the genro was in favor of making public the findings of the incident in order to maintain the glory of the Japanese army and to make clear the location of responsibility. Consequently, Baron Tanaka was persuaded to follow the genro's known attitude. However, as soon as the nature of the purported report of the investigation was known, a vigorous opposition developed among high military authorities, headed by Marshal Uyehara, a supreme war councilor and a

[8]*Op. cit.*, March 16, 1929, p. 453.
[9]Egi, Ichijo, Inouye, Oi.
[10]*Tokyo Asahi*, May 14, 1929, p. 1.
[11]*Ibid.*, May 15, 1929, p. 1.

veteran member of the board of field marshals and fleet admirals, and Admiral Suzuki, Grand Chamberlain. They held that to place General Muraoka, commander of the Kwantung garrison, on the reserve list as a disciplinary measure was purely a political move on the part of the Tanaka government and consequently a threat to the maintenance of military discipline and to the honor of the imperial army.

The report prepared by the War Department was finally transmitted to the prime minister on May 22, 1929.[12] On May 24, a meeting of the Supreme War Council was called to hear the explanations of the war minister upon the nature of the report handed to Baron Tanaka. The general consensus of opinions expressed at the council meeting was that extreme caution should be taken in the matter of making it public, in view of its bearing upon military discipline.[13] The views of the Supreme War Council were conveyed to Prime Minister Tanaka immediately after the adjournment of its meeting.[14]

While placed in such an embarrassing position between the ever increasing public demand for making public the report of the incident, on the one side,[15] and the vigorous opposition in high military circles, of which Baron Tanaka himself was an influential member because of his long and brilliant military career, on the other, the political tension of the hour became increasingly tense. On June 11, Prince Ichijo (*Kayokai*), Baron Oi (*Koseikai*), Baron Inouye (*Koseikai*), and Dr. Egi (*Koseikai*), again called on the prime minister, when Baron Tanaka promised an early publication of the report. He was even reported to have made unfavorable comments upon the attitude of certain military leaders.[16] The Big Three of military circles, namely, War Minister Shirakawa, General Suzuki, chief of general staff, and General Muto, inspector general of military education, met the following day to deliberate upon the request of Prime Minister Tanaka for reconsideration of the report of the findings of the war au-

[12]*Ibid.*, May 23, 1929, p. 6.

[13]*Ibid.*, May 25, 1929, p. 1.

[14]*Ibid.*, May 25, 1929, p. 6.

[15]The liberal press demanded an immediate publication of the report to maintain the integrity and honor of Japan before the eyes of the world. *Cf.* an editorial in *Tokyo Asahi*, May 15, 1929.

[16]*Jiji Shimpo*, June 12, 1929, p. 2.

thorities concerning the incident. The Big Three took the
position that they could not be held responsible for the incident, and that the disciplinary measures should be confined
to military authorities in Manchuria.[17]

The position of the Tanaka *Seiyukai* cabinet became increasingly serious, being placed between the popular demand
for publication of the findings, thereby making public the
location of responsibility, and the stern opposition of high
military authorities. There were frequent conferences among
high personages close to the emperor—Count Makino, Lord
Privy Seal, Admiral Suzuki, Grand Chamberlain, and Prince
Saionji, the genro. On June 27, 1929, the prime minister went
to the palace to report to the emperor concerning the report
of the findings, and the next day War Minister Shirakawa
reported to the throne the details connected with the so-called
"Grave Manchurian Incident" and the disciplinary measure
to be taken in connection therewith.[18] It was reported that
there were differences in certain important respects between
the reports made by the prime minister and by the war minister, and even between the prime minister's report made on
June 27 and his previous report to His Majesty. It was believed that Admiral Suzuki, Grand Chamberlain, and Count
Makino, Lord Privy Seal, took the position that the action
taken by the government towards the commander of the
Kwantung garrison should be directed also to the war minister.[19]

Thus, Baron Tanaka was placed in an extremely delicate
position of distinguishing the dual character of the proposed
measure in connection with the death of Chang Tso Lin. To
punish the high military officers in Manchuria would be to
impair the integrity and honor of the imperial army, and to
incur a vigorous opposition by Admiral Suzuki. On the other
hand, he was questioned by Prince Saionji, the most trusted
adviser to the throne, to make clear the political responsibility for the incident, and indirectly advised to tender his
resignation. Under the circumstances, General Tanaka had
no other course but to follow the genro's advice. Consequently, an extraordinary meeting of the cabinet was called

[17]*Op. cit.*, June 13, 1929, p. 2.
[18]*Tokyo Asahi*, June 28, 1929, p. 2; June 29, 1929, p. 1.
[19]*Ibid.*, June 29, 1929, p. 2; June 30, 1929, pp. 2, 3.

on July 1, 1929, to deliberate upon the final details connected with its general resignation. It was also decided not to make public the findings of the incident. The next day, Baron Tanaka was given an audience by the emperor to present the resignation of the ministry. Thereupon, the Hamaguchi cabinet was inaugurated in less than four hours after receiving the imperial order to form a ministry. The new administration was born amid public acclaim.

THE HAMAGUCHI CABINET AND THE REPORT

This sudden collapse of the Tanaka *Seiyukai* ministry was mainly due to its incurrence of His Majesty's displeasure regarding the Manchurian incident. It had already received a severe blow at the hands of the Privy Council in connection with the Pact of Paris containing the phraseology, "in the names of their respective peoples," after a series of maladministration in domestic affairs. The Manchurian incident, however, dealt the death blow to the ministry.

In spite of its determined insistence, while in opposition, upon publication of the report of the incident, both before and after the Fifty-sixth Diet, the Hamaguchi *Minseito* cabinet did not make any effort whatever, after getting into power, to take the action it had so persistently demanded of the Tanaka *Seiyukai* government.

Naturally, the *Seiyukai* party demanded an explanation from the new *Minseito* administration for its failure to make public the report of the findings.[20] Thus, on April 30, 1930, Representative Etsujiro Uyehara declared in the Lower House that the *Minseito* used the Manchurian incident as a party issue and an instrument to bring about the downfall of the previous cabinet, and requested Prime Minister Hamaguchi to explain why the new party in power, in spite of its insistence while out of power, did not make any effort to publish the findings. To this interpellation Premier Hamaguchi calmly replied that the matter had been settled both politically and administratively under the Tanaka administration, that there was a proper time for making it public, and that a discussion of the matter at this time (Fifty-eighth

[20]The House of Representatives was dissolved on the first day after the New Year's recess, and consequently there was no occasion for the *Seiyukai* party to demand an explanation in the Diet until the Fifty-eighth session was convened.

Diet) was productive of no benefit. He further stated that it was for the cabinet to decide as to the proper time for publishing the findings of the incident.[21] The Hamaguchi cabinet pursued a similar policy in the Upper House. The Prime Minister insisted, in reply to a question by General Shimizu on May 6, that the incident was already settled politically or otherwise, and that it was not a proper time to reopen the issues. He declined to say whether the previous cabinet fell on account of the issues raised in connection with the incident or not.[22]

No report of any sort has ever been published by either the Tanaka or the Hamaguchi cabinet concerning the sudden death of Marshal Chang Tso Lin on June 4, 1928, below a railroad bridge under Japanese control. Obviously, the incident was taken advantage of by the opposition party as the lever with which to bring about the resignation of a ministry. The result of the whole episode was the downfall of the Tanaka cabinet which sought to remain in office by removing the four highest military officers in command.

[21] *Kwampo gogai*, May 1, 1930, pp. 106–110. Cf. *Japan Weekly Chronicle*, May 8, 1930, p. 478.

[22] *Kwampo gogai*, May 7, 1930, pp. 77–84; *Japan Weekly Chronicle*, May 15, 1930, p. 510. Cf. the statement by General Ugaki in the House of Peers on Feb. 5, 1931 (*Kwampo gogai*, Feb. 6, 1931, p. 120).

Chapter XXV

THE LONDON NAVAL TREATY

THE CALLING OF THE CONFERENCE

ON OCTOBER 7, 1929, Honorable Arthur Henderson, British secretary of state for foreign affairs, handed a note to His Excellency Tsuneo Matsudaira, Japanese ambassador in London, inviting the Japanese participation in the Naval Limitation Conference to be held in January, 1930.[1] The full text was published in the vernacular press on October 9.[2]

The press generally welcomed the move on the part of the British government as a timely one, expressing no surprise at the move at this time and urging a political solution of the problem. The leading press of the country emphasized the importance of appointing an influential statesman to head the delegation so that the solution of the problem of limiting naval armaments be approached from the broad standpoint of sound statesmanship rather than handled solely by technical experts.[3]

Immediately upon the receipt of the note in Tokyo, a cabinet meeting was called on October 8 when Baron Shidehara, the foreign minister, reported to his colleagues that a telegram had just been received from the British government inviting Japan's participation in a naval conference in London. At this meeting of the cabinet, the responsibility of drafting a reply to London was entrusted to the joint respon-

[1]Foreign Office Communiqué No. 9 (Oct. 9, 1929). *Cf. Tokyo Asahi*, Oct. 8, 1929, p. 2.

[2]A tentative translation of the note was released to the press by the Foreign Office at 11:00 P.M., Oct. 8 (*Jiji Shimpo*, Oct. 9, 1929, p. 2; *Tokyo Asahi*, Oct. 9, 1929, p. 2).

[3]Editorials in *Tokyo Asahi* and *Jiji Shimpo*, Oct. 9, 1929, p. 3.

sibility of Prime Minister Hamaguchi, Foreign Minister Shidehara, and Navy Minister Takarabe. At this meeting it was agreed that an influential statesman should be appointed to head the delegation.[4]

Although the acceptance of the British invitation to the London Conference was taken for granted by the public, both the *Kasumigaseki* and the Navy Department began to study the note and prepare a reply.[5] In the preparation of the reply, the Navy Department took particular care to leave its hands untied at the conference.[6]

In order to obtain a united support of the nation's leaders, both civil and military, to the claims of the Admiralty, the minister of navy invited the nation's leaders in both civil and military circles to his official residence on October 10. At this important gathering, Rear-Admiral Suetsugu, vice-chief of naval general staff, and Rear-Admiral Sakonshi explained the conditions and claims of the various naval powers concerned, while the navy minister, Admiral Takarabe, took particular pains to emphasize the indispensability of insisting upon the seventy-per-cent ratio.[7]

[4] *Tokyo Asahi*, Oct. 9, 1929, p. 2.

In anticipation of a formal call of the conference, higher officials in the military and naval circles have for some time been considering the attitude which the Japanese delegation should take at the conference. In order to determine the attitude of Japan from the standpoint of national defense, a meeting of the nation's high military and naval officers was called on Sept. 30, 1929, at the official residence of the minister of navy, Admiral Takarabe. On Oct. 5, 1929, a preparatory committee of three technical experts who served in such capacity at the Washington and Geneva conferences was appointed in the Navy Department to study the technical phase of the subject (*ibid.*, Oct. 6, 1929, p. 1). Vice-Admiral Sakonshi called on Prince Saionji, the only remaining genro, on Oct. 7, to report on the naval conference. At this interview, which lasted two hours, the vice-admiral sought to obtain the "understandings" of the genro with respect to the attitude of the Admiralty (*Jiji Shimpo*, Oct. 8, 1929, p. 2).

[5] *Jiji Shimpo*, Oct. 9, 1929, p. 1.

[6] Admiral Takarabe, the navy minister, called together the high officials of his department on Oct. 9 and ordered them to draft a reply from the standpoint of the department (*Tokyo Asahi*, Oct. 10, 1929, p. 1).

[7] The following leaders were present: Admiral Count Yamamoto, Baron Tatsuo Yamamoto, Count Makino (Lord Privy Seal), Dr. Kitokuro Ichiki (minister of the imperial household), Korekiyo Takahashi (former prime minister and a leading member of the *Seiyukai* party), Reijiro Wakatsuki, Dr. Rentaro Mizuno, Count Uchida, Dr. Kiichiro Hiranuma (vice-president of the Privy Council), Baron Shidehara (foreign minister), General Ugaki (war minister), Education Minister Kohashi, Justice Minister Watanabe, Finance Minister Inouye, Home Minister Adachi, Admiral Suzuki (Grand Chamberlain), Admiral Baron Yamashita, and others. The navy authorities were represented by Admiral Takarabe (navy minister), Ad-

While the Navy Department was studying the note and preparing a reply from its own point of view, the Foreign Office did not fail to give most careful consideration to it. Prime Minister Yuko Hamaguchi, in his address before the *Minseito* (government party) convention at Nagoya on October 13, gave the first public utterance of the government on the subject. He defined the basic attitude of the Japanese policy at the conference to be that (1) her navy should constitute no menace toward others, while, at the same time, she would tolerate no threat or insecurity from others; (2) the aim of the conference should be an actual reduction in naval armaments; (3) Japan would be willing to accept a ratio lower than that of either Great Britain or the United States provided that it be adequate for defense in any contingency.[8] The prime minister's utterances on the approaching conference were favorably received by the press throughout the country.

The ability, training, and caliber of the principal delegate constituted the most important considerations in determining the personnel of the delegation. Since there was little doubt as to both the navy minister and the Japanese ambassador in London being included, the chief interest of the public was focused upon the selection of the principal delegate. The press of the nation united in demanding a selection of a well-balanced statesman, widely experienced in the arts of politics to command the respect of those at the conference as well as those at home, one who would be counted on to arrive at a political solution of the problem. As seen in the cabinet meeting of October 8, party leaders felt that Hon. Reijiro Wakatsuki, a former prime minister and also *Minseito's* former leader, was the logical choice for the post. Responding to the general sentiment of his party as well as the general press comment, Prime Minister Hamaguchi sounded the response of his former chief through Foreign Minister Shidehara, to whom Wakatsuki was once reported to have given a rather disappointing reception and even declined the offer, urging

miral Kanji Kato (chief of naval general staff), Admirals Takeshita, Okada, Abo (supreme war councilors), Parliamentary Vice-Minister of Navy Yabuki, Admiral Yamanashi (vice-minister of navy), Admiral Suetsugu (vice-chief of naval general staff), Admiral Sakonshi, and Admiral Hori (*Tokyo Asahi, Jiji Shimpo*, Oct. 11, 1929, p. 1).

[8]Text of the address in *Tokyo Asahi*, Oct. 14, 1929, p. 2.

the foreign minister to assume the responsibility himself. Finally, however, the prime minister's personal appeal to Wakatsuki won the latter's acceptance of the responsibility on October 12 to head the delegation.[9] The announcement of the news met with favorable comment, although, as was naturally expected, leaders of the chief opposition party, *Seiyukai*, expressed keen disappointment in the failure of either the prime minister or the foreign minister to assume the responsibility.[10]

On October 14 a draft reply, prepared by the Foreign Office, was carefully scrutinized at a joint conference of high officers of both the Foreign Office and the Navy Department, and was accepted. After receiving the approval of this joint conference, Baron Shidehara invited Mr. Wakatsuki to his residence on the evening of October 14 and conferred with the latter concerning the draft reply, to which Mr. Wakatsuki gave approval. At this meeting, the foreign minister and Mr. Wakatsuki deliberated also upon the personnel of the delegation, selection of technical advisers, and other matters.[11]

The draft reply thus having been gone over by officials and organs concerned, a cabinet meeting was called on October 15 at the official residence of the prime minister to deliberate and to decide upon the draft prepared by the Foreign Office. At this meeting, Prime Minister Hamaguchi reported that he had won their former chief, Hon. Wakatsuki, to accept the post of chief of the Japanese delegation, and brought the details regarding the recommendation to the throne of three plenipotentiaries to the deliberation of the cabinet, when it promptly approved the prime minister's recommendation. Then Baron Shidehara, the foreign minister, took the floor and presented for discussion and comment the draft reply which his department had prepared, and stated that, though the wording of the draft was abstract, concrete proposals setting forth Japan's claims would be presented in preliminary negotiations, and that the government was prepared to

[9] *Op. cit.*, Oct. 13, 1929, p. 1; also *Jiji Shimpo*, Oct. 13, 1929, p. 1.

[10] *Tokyo Asahi*, Oct. 13, 1929, p. 2.

[11] *Jiji Shimpo, Tokyo Asahi*, Oct. 15, 1929, p. 2. A meeting of the parliamentary vice-ministers and councilors of various departments was held at the premier's official residence in the afternoon of Oct. 14, 1929, at which meeting Rear-Admiral Yamanashi, vice-minister of navy, made a report on the progress of negotiations (*Tokyo Asahi*, Oct. 15, 1929, p. 2).

press the fundamental policy already decided upon in this regard.[12]

At 10:30 A.M., October 16, Premier Hamaguchi was received in audience by the emperor to report upon the preliminary negotiations between Great Britain and the United States as well as Japan and these two powers. The premier obtained the imperial sanction to the draft reply and recommended for His Majesty's consideration the appointment of Reijiro Wakatsuki, Ambassador Tsuneo Matsudaira in London, and Navy Minister Takarabe. At noon, the reply to the British government as well as the personnel of the delegation was telegraphed to the Japanese embassy in London, while the publication of the reply as well as the formal appointment of the delegates was withheld until the note was received by the British foreign secretary in London.[13] The Japanese note was handed to the British foreign secretary at five o'clock the same afternoon, and the text was made public at 8:00 P.M., October 18.[14] The publication of the text met the general approval of the press.[15]

INSTRUCTIONS TO THE PLENIPOTENTIARIES

Inasmuch as the Japanese note to Secretary Henderson was worded in general terms, definite and concrete instructions had to be drawn up to guide the plenipotentiaries in preliminary negotiations as well as at the conference.

In the drafting of the instructions, setting forth the fundamental naval policy of Japan, the Admiralty took the initiative. When the Navy Department completed the draft it was submitted to a joint conference of the Navy Department and the Foreign Office. After obtaining the approval of this joint conference, the draft was submitted to the deliberations of

[12]*Tokyo Asahi*, Oct. 16, 1929, p. 1.

[13]*Ibid.*, Oct. 17, 1929, p. 1. While the prime minister was being received in audience by the emperor, a joint meeting of the naval members of the board of field marshals and fleet admirals and of the Supreme War Council was held at the official residence of the navy minister when he reported the details of the reply as well as the circumstances that led to his appointment as a plenipotentiary, and sought to obtain the "understandings" of those high officials of the Admiralty (*Jiji Shimpo*, Oct. 17, 1929, p. 1).

[14]Foreign Office Communiqué No. 10 (Oct. 18, 1929). *Cf. Tokyo Asahi*, Oct. 19, 1929, p. 2.

[15]Editorials in *Tokyo Asahi*, Oct. 19, 1929, p. 3; *Jiji Shimpo*, Oct. 19, 1929, p. 3.

the cabinet, which formally approved it on November 26, 1929.[16]

Immediately after the cabinet approved the instructions, Prime Minister Hamaguchi was received in audience by the emperor to report in detail the government's policy towards the approaching conference, the preliminary negotiations with the powers, as well as the instructions decided upon at the cabinet meeting.[17] Admiral Kanji Kato, chief of naval staff, was also given audience by the emperor to report on those items of the instructions which fell under the imperial prerogative over supreme command.[18]

Thus, the final instructions to the delegation were given on November 26, after the prime minister received the imperial sanction thereto. Though the contents of the instructions were kept under strict secrecy, essential features were allowed to be printed in the columns of the press. According to the press reports, the Japanese delegation was instructed to declare that the fundamental naval policy of the Japanese government aimed at defense and security, renouncing any intention of aggression against other powers, and to insist upon the following "three fundamental claims" deemed essential by the imperial Admiralty to defense and security: (1) to demand 70 per cent ratio with respect to the strength of the United States in 10,000-ton 8-inch gun cruisers; (2) to claim 70 per cent ratio in gross tonnage for all auxiliary craft with respect to the United States, and (3) to oppose radical reduction or abolition of submarines and to maintain the present strength of 78,500 tons, the tonnage being not below that of either Great Britain or the United States.[19] These basic claims of the Japanese stand with respect to her naval strength met the united support of the press.[20]

JAPANESE DELEGATION AT THE CONFERENCE

In order to understand the attitude of the Japanese delegates at the conference, it would be necessary to examine the personnel of her plenipotentiaries. Honorable Tsuneo Mat-

[16]*Tokyo Asahi*, Nov. 27, 1929, p. 1.

[17]*Tokyo Asahi*, Nov. 27, 1929, p. 2.

[18]*Ibid.*, Nov. 27, 1929, p. 1.

[19]*Tokyo Asahi*, Nov. 26, 1929, p. 2.

[20]For press comment see *Japan Advertiser*, Nov. 27, 1929, p. 5.

sudaira was appointed a plenipotentiary because of his post of Japanese ambassadorship at the Court of St. James's, while Admiral Takarabe was made a plenipotentiary in order to represent the Admiralty. Admiral Takarabe, being a son-in-law of Admiral Count Gombei Yamamoto, who twice held the portfolio of premiership and who is commonly regarded as the invisible chief of the naval clique, was generally considered a titular representative of the once all-powerful *Satsuma* faction of Admiralty leadership. However, he was no longer without opposition within the navy camp. This fact of internal lack of solidarity within the naval circles, as well as his disputed leadership, unlike Admiral Tomosaburo Kato at the Washington Conference, should be kept in mind when we undertake to examine his difficulties of winning his colleagues at home. Ambassador Nagai was added to the delegation on the ground that the chief delegate, Honorable Wakatsuki, was not a linguist. Mr. Reijiro Wakatsuki, being a former chief of the then all-powerful *Minseito* party and an ex-premier in whose cabinet several members of the then incumbent Hamaguchi ministry served, was naturally in position to dominate the entire delegation.

The basic policy of the Japanese delegation was to press for the "three fundamental claims," particularly to obtain the 70 per cent ratio with respect to the United States. The first public utterance of the Japanese stand by her plenipotentiaries was made in Chicago on their way to Washington. During the brief visit to Washington, Wakatsuki had several conferences with Secretary Stimson when it was reported that Wakatsuki laid particular emphasis upon the 70 per cent ratio.

On January 21, 1930, the historic London Naval Conference was officially opened, and Mr. Wakatsuki spoke on behalf of the Japanese delegation.[21] On that same day Baron Shidehara outlined the policy of the Japanese government in his address on foreign relations before the Fifty-seventh Diet in Tokyo. Outlining the policy of the government, he declared:

Our claim to a definite amount of naval strength is ... based upon the practical necessity of making our defenses secure against foreign invasion. We offer no menace to any nation; we submit to menace from none. On that fundamental principle, it is our desire

[21]Foreign Office Communiqué No. 1 (Jan. 21, 1930).

to secure a naval arrangement satisfactory to all parties concerned.[22]

The first conference between the Japanese and American delegates to discuss a concrete proposal was held on February 4, 1930, and on February 5, Senator Reed, on behalf of the American delegation, presented a concrete American proposal which, among others, sought to allot Japan 60 per cent ratio with respect to the United States in total tonnage for auxiliary craft. Upon receipt of the memorandum setting forth the terms of the American proposal, a meeting of the Japanese delegates and higher technical advisers was held at 11:00 A.M., February 5, after which the memorandum was telegraphed to Tokyo for instructions.[23]

The dispatch was received at both the Foreign Office and the Navy Department early in the morning of February 7. Thereupon, an important joint conference of high officials of the Navy Department and the naval staff[24] was held in the Navy Department to decide upon the attitude of the Admiralty, when they decided to reject the American proposal for 60 per cent ratio in respect to large cruisers. In consultation with the Foreign Office, the government instructions were dispatched to London late in the evening.[25] Thus, the Japanese policy at the conference, setting forth the "three fundamental claims," was made clear in a memorandum handed to Senator Reed on February 12 by Ambassador Matsudaira.[26]

REED-MATSUDAIRA COMPROMISE

In order to facilitate negotiations, a series of informal conferences were held between Ambassador Matsudaira and

[22]*Kwampo gogai*, Jan. 22, 1930. Cf. *Japan Weekly Chronicle*, Jan. 30, 1930, p. 94.

[23]*Tokyo Asahi*, Feb. 6, 1930, p. 2.

[24]Vice-Admiral Yamanashi (vice-minister of navy), Chief of the Bureau of Naval Affairs Hori, Vice-Chief of Naval General Staff Suetsugu, and Chief of the Bureau of Matériel Kobayashi (*ibid.*, Feb. 8, 1930, p. 1).

[25]For outlines of the instructions and the compromise proposal, see *Tokyo Asahi*, Feb. 8, 1930, p. 2.

[26]*Ibid.*, Feb. 14, 1930, pp. 1, 2. In reply to a question put to the government by Representative Shinya Uchida in the House of Representatives on April 27, 1930, Prime Minister Hamaguchi declined to elaborate upon the statement issued by Wakatsuki in London (*Kwampo gogai*, April 28, 1930, p. 60). Cf. *Tokyo Asahi*, May 1, 1930, p. 2.

Senator Reed, beginning on February 27, 1930, and by the eighth informal conference on March 10 a tentative agreement had been reached. On March 12, Mr. Wakatsuki, chief of the Japanese delegation, accompanied by Mr. Saito, chief of the intelligence bureau of the Foreign Office, held a conference with Secretary Stimson, chief of the American delegation. On this same day the ninth informal conference between Ambassador Matsudaira and Senator Reed was held. In the forenoon of March 13, Wakatsuki had a conference with Premier MacDonald, and in the afternoon Senator Reed handed to Mr. Wakatsuki a memorandum setting forth a compromise proposal which had been arrived at as a result of a series of negotiations between himself and Ambassador Matsudaira.[27]

Immediately upon receipt of the memorandum, a conference of the Japanese plenipotentiaries was called, lasting till late at night, to deliberate upon the measure to be taken concerning the proposal, in the preparation of which the Japanese delegation through Ambassador Matsudaira participated. This was followed by another conference of technical advisers in the office of Admiral Abo, a member of the Supreme War Council, and who later succeeded Admiral Takarabe in the Navy Department in the Hamaguchi cabinet. Mr. Sato, secretary general of the delegation, and Mr. Saito were also present at this conference. After long deliberation, which lasted until four o'clock the following morning, it was decided to insist upon obtaining the "three fundamental claims" and to reject the Reed-Matsudaira compromise. And consequently Admiral Abo and Vice-Admiral Sakonshi had a long conference with Mr. Wakatsuki upon the disposition to be made of the memorandum.[28]

In view of the significance of the memorandum to the fate of the conference, the plenipotentiaries, with their signatures thereon, telegraphed the memorandum, as well as a detailed report of the negotiations, to the home government in Tokyo for instructions.[29]

[27]Yasutomi, "The Government's Policy at the Conference," *Kaizo*, XII, No. 5 (May, 1930), pp. 88–91.

[28]*Tokyo Asahi*, March 15, 1930, p. 2.

[29]*Ibid.*, March 16, 1930, p. 2.

Conflict of Views among the Delegates[30]

By this time, the conflict of views among the Japanese delegates in London became apparent. The views of the Foreign Office and those of the Admiralty were not always in agreement. It was apparent that the former was eager to make the conference a success, even at the sacrifice of relinquishing the "three fundamental claims" in minor detail. On the other hand, the latter was interested in obtaining as high a ratio as possible and was determined not to relinquish any of these claims which it considered essential to defense and security. Therefore, when the American attitude was conveyed to the Japanese delegation on February 5, allotting Japan only 60 per cent ratio in big cruisers, the navy faction of the delegation was greatly disappointed and realized that there was little hope for obtaining the recognition of their claims. From this time on their attitude became decidedly negative. They offered no suggestions of their own but merely gave counter-proposals to the American group.

Under these circumstances, the technical advisers to the delegation insisted upon rejecting the Reed-Matsudaira compromise even at the risk of wrecking the conference. And this conflict of views among the delegates was brought to the open at the time of deciding the nature of the dispatch to Tokyo concerning the American proposal of March 13. The naval members of the delegation sought to regard the dispatch merely as a report of negotiations to the home government, implying room for further compromise. However, the Reed-Matsudaira compromise was a result of a series of informal negotiations and embodied compromises reached between the Japanese and American delegations, to which the British group gave hearty approval. In these circumstances, the dispatch to Tokyo of March 14 took a very dubious form, so much so that the home government had to inquire of the delegation as to whether the dispatch was to be taken as a compromise or merely as a report of negotiations.

In this connection it is interesting to inquire as to precisely

[30]The information concerning the internal conflict of views among the Japanese delegates was given to the author by a well-known press correspondent who attended the conference.

what position Admiral Takarabe took in the matter. Did Admiral Takarabe, minister of navy, appointed to represent the Admiralty point of view, attach his signature to the dispatch with his approval and of his own free accord? Was he not aware, at the time of sending the dispatch, that it represented the resulting compromise, in fact, between the Japanese and American delegations, to the contents of which the British delegation expressed approval? Was he not in full accord with, if not a champion of, the Admiralty demand for the "three fundamental claims," the full import of which was given such a wide publicity not only among the high officials but among the general public, and for the cause of which Admiral Takarabe himself sought so earnestly to obtain the "understandings" of the nation's leaders in both military and civil affairs, prior to his departure for London? And when we remember that not only the Admiralty at home but the technical advisers in London were united in opposition to the acceptance of the compromise plan, we are left at sea as to the exact circumstances which led him to attach his signature to the dispatch.

It is now an open secret that the advice of her technical staff was not sought till a compromise had been reached, while it was even reported that Admiral Takarabe was not fully consulted at all stages of the informal negotiations between Ambassador Matsudaira and Senator Reed, which resulted in the compromise proposal. When the compromise proposal was before the conference of all the plenipotentiaries for action, only two courses were open to the navy minister to take: either to attach his signature to the document signifying his approval of the compromise as a result of negotiations, or to refuse his signature. To take the former course was to acknowledge the document as a compromise between the delegations, while to choose the second course was to risk the break-up of the conference. Being unable to assume the brunt of causing the failure of the conference and of coming home without a treaty, it was believed, Admiral Takarabe was forced to choose the former course, much against his personal opinion and despite the stern opposition by the technical staff.[31]

[31]Seitoku Ito, "Disarmament Conference," *Chuo Koron*, No. 510 (July, 1930), pp. 103–114.

The Admiralty vs. the Foreign Office on Instructions

With the dispatch for instructions on the Reed-Matsudaira compromise, the scene was temporarily shifted from London to Tokyo, and on the decision of the Tokyo government hung the fate of the conference. The significance and full import of the decision to be made was fully recognized by the Hamaguchi cabinet.

Early in the morning of March 15 Vice-Admiral Yamanashi, vice-minister of navy, called on Baron Shidehara at the Foreign Office to confer on the procedure to be taken.[32] At 9:00 A.M. a joint conference of high officials of the Navy Department and the naval general staff was called to determine the attitude of the Admiralty towards the third American proposal.[33] At this conference of high naval authorities no definite decision was reached. However, it was decided to call on the foreign minister to inquire whether the *Kasumigaseki* was responsible for the report then current in certain quarters to the effect that the Foreign Office was inclined to accept the proposal, even relinquishing the "three fundamental claims" in minor detail.[34] While the conference was still on Vice-Admiral Yamanashi called on the foreign minister, when Baron Shidehara was reported to have flatly denied that his department was in any way responsible for such compromising views. With this official denial, the joint conference decided to wire the delegation in London that a compromising view was unfounded in fact.[35] In the afternoon,

[32]*Tokyo Asahi*, March 16, 1930, p. 2. We may note in this connection that Prime Minister Hamaguchi, who was the acting minister of navy, following the precedent set by Premier Hara at the time of the Washington Naval Conference, was never seen in the Navy Department during the entire conference. Nor did such civilian officers as the parliamentary vice-minister or councilor of the Navy Department take any part in the formulation of a policy. Vice-Minister of Navy Yamanashi actually performed the functions of the minister.

[33]Note that the Admiralty never admitted that this was a compromise between the delegations but regarded it as merely a third American proposal and subject to further negotiations.

[34]When it was reported that the Japanese delegation sent a dispatch to Tokyo for instructions, the press also carried a news item that the Foreign Office officials were inclined to accept the compromise in the interest of the success of the conference, to the great resentment on the part of the naval authorities (*Tokyo Asahi*, March 15, 1930, p. 2).

[35]*Ibid.*, March 16, 1930, p. 1.

both the foreign minister and the vice-minister of navy called on Prime Minister Hamaguchi to confer on the dispatch.[36]

The immediate cause for the conflict of attitudes between the Foreign Office and Admiralty concerning the Reed-Matsudaira compromise may be attributed, in the main, to a difference in the view in which the document was regarded by these two authorities. The Foreign Office regarded the document as a compromise between the delegations of Japan and the United States and not as a mere proposal on the part of the American delegation, and consequently the document was subject to no further important modifications. In Wakatsuki's report to the home government, accompanying the dispatch of March 14, it was made perfectly plain that further demand for concession on the part of the United States would result in the break-up of the conference. On the other hand, the naval authorities insisted that it was merely another American proposal, subject to further negotiations.[37]

Accordingly, after several joint conferences of the leaders of the Navy Department and the naval staff, the determined opposition of the Admiralty to the compromise became open and resulted in the so-called "Admiralty Statement" issued in the forenoon of March 17, after a conference between the chief and vice-chief of staff. The statement to the press on the part of the Admiralty at this time was considered somewhat impolitic and inopportune, the initiative for the statement having thus been taken by the naval general staff and not by the Navy Department. In the afternoon of March 17, the Admiralty telegraphed its vigorous position to Vice-Admiral Sakonshi, chief technical adviser in London, calling upon him to take a firm stand on the "three fundamental claims" as instructed prior to departure.[38]

Spurred by such telegrams, Admiral Takarabe was placed in the very delicate position of differentiating his dual position as the minister of navy on the one hand, and as a member of the delegation on the other. It was about this time that he was reported to have sent a secret telegram to the Navy Department in his capacity as navy minister, stating that the

[36]*Ibid.*, March 16, 1930, p. 1.
[37]*Gaiko Jiho*, No. 609 (April 15, 1930), pp. 175–177.
[38]*Tokyo Asahi*, March 18, 1930, p. 1.

compromise was merely another American proposal and implying further room for concession in spite of the fact that he
attached his signature to the dispatch signifying that he was
aware of the full nature and significance of the document at
the time. It was believed that this extraordinary action on the
part of a member of the delegation was taken under pressure
exerted by the technical staff.

On March 1, high officials of the naval general staff held an
important meeting lasting six hours and finally decided to
oppose the American proposal, and immediately a copy of the
proceedings of the meeting was transmitted to each member
of the Supreme War Council.[39] On the following day, Admiral
Kato of the naval staff called on Prime Minister Hamaguchi
to explain the Admiralty opposition to the American proposal.[40]

A draft note of instructions, prepared by the Navy Department, embodying the views of the Admiralty and opposing the American proposal, was transmitted to the Foreign
Office on March 22. Thereupon, the foreign minister called a
conference of the vice-minister and the chief of the European
and American Bureau to study the draft. The navy draft,
however, having been drawn up purely from a technical point
of view, totally disregarding the results of long and laborious
negotiations between the Japanese and American plenipotentiaries, could not be adopted by the *Kasumigaseki* officials *in toto* without risking the break-up of the conference.
Under the circumstances, seeing no hope for compromise with
the Admiralty, the Foreign Office had to draw up draft instructions, independent of the navy draft, embodying in
principle the compromise arrived at by the plenipotentiaries.[41]

On March 24 a joint unofficial meeting of the naval members of the board of field marshals and fleet admirals and the
Supreme War Council was called,[42] when the vice-minister of
navy made a detailed report on the negotiations in London

[39]*Op. cit.*, March 19, 1930, p. 2.

[40]*Ibid.*, March 20, 1930, p. 2.

[41]*Ibid.*, March 23, 1930, p. 2.

[42]Those present at the meeting were: Admiral Prince Fushimi, Admiral Togo,
Admiral Okada, Admiral Kato, Vice-Admiral Suetsugu, Vice-Admiral Yamanashi,
and others.

together with the contents of Wakatsuki's report of March 14, while Admiral Kato explained the position of the naval staff and Rear-Admiral Hori explained the nature of the draft instructions drawn up by the Navy Department which had just been transmitted to the Foreign Office. The conference approved the actions taken.[43] On March 27 Admiral Kato and Admiral Okada, a leading member of the Supreme War Council and a former navy minister, called on Prime Minister Hamaguchi to express the Admiralty's opposition to the relinquishment of any of the "three fundamental claims" of the navy.[44] The views of the Foreign Office and the Admiralty thus being sharply divided, the responsibility of formulating the government instructions was squarely placed in the hands of Premier Yuko Hamaguchi.[45]

APPROVAL OF THE CABINET

At the cabinet meeting of March 28, there was a free exchange of views among the members present, the majority of whom tended to avoid a measure that might bring about the break-up of the conference, but failed to reach final decision. True that the prime minister's mind had already been made up to adopt the views of the Foreign Office, but in view of the domestic as well as international significance of the steps to be taken at this time, Premier Hamaguchi called a conference of Baron Shidehara (foreign minister) and Dr. Yoku Egi (railways minister) after the cabinet meeting.[46] As a result of this conference, the premier's decision to adopt the *Kasumigaseki* plan in preference to that of the Navy Department as the basis for instructions became certain in order to bring the conference to a successful close.

[43] *Tokyo Asahi*, March 25, 1930, p. 3.

[44] *Ibid.*, March 28, 1930, p. 2.

[45] It is an open secret that, with the full approval of Mr. Wakatsuki, both Prime Minister MacDonald and Secretary Stimson transmitted representations to Tokyo through the British and American ambassadors urging an early decision on the instructions (*Tokyo Asahi*, March 21, 22, 1930, p. 2). Cf. *The Times* (London), April 2, 1930, p. 14. In reply to an interpellation in the House of Representatives on April 30, 1930, Baron Shidehara denied that any pressure was brought upon Japan in reaching a decision in Tokyo (*Kwampo gogai*, May 1, 1930, p. 108).

[46] Dr. Yoku Egi, minister of railways in the Hamaguchi cabinet, is an ex-minister of justice and commonly regarded as "the brain" of the *Minseito* cabinet.

The essential features of the instructions agreed upon at this conference were: (1) to accept the tonnage ratio of the Reed-Matsudaira compromise without any modification, and (2) to take appropriate diplomatic measure against committing Japan for the future. However, in view of its most delicate nature and significance in domestic politics, it was agreed that the greatest caution was to be taken in the wording of the instructions.[47]

During the closing days of March, strong pressures were brought to bear upon the prime minister from both the Admiralty and the Foreign Office. On March 29, the vice-minister of navy called on Premier Hamaguchi and again set forth the stand of the Admiralty, even after having been informed of the government's attitude towards the matter.[48] And, when Admiral Kato and Baron Shidehara were thrown together at the British embassy on the evening of March 29, where a farewell party was given in honor of Prince Takamatsu, the chief of naval staff was reported to have taken the foreign minister severely to task for the alleged disregard of the views of the Admiralty by the latter. Admiral Kato protested against Baron Shidehara on the ground that, when Ambassador Matsudaira reached an agreement with Senator Reed, he was acting under informal instructions from the foreign minister and that the naval authorities were not consulted in the matter. It was believed that Admiral Kato frankly explained the position of the navy and sought detailed explanation from the foreign minister.[49]

On March 30 Baron Shidehara called together Mr. Yoshida, vice-minister of foreign affairs, and Mr. Hotta, chief of the European and American Bureau, and continued the work of drafting the instructions, while at the Navy Department there was being held a joint conference of high officials of the

[47]*Tokyo Asahi*, March 29, 1930, p. 2.

[48]After a conference with Premier Hamaguchi, Vice-Admiral Yamanashi declared, in a press interview, that, although the Navy Department had so far sided with the stand of the naval general staff, it could do nothing but abide by the decision of the cabinet, it being a department of the government. He went on to declare, however, that as a naval officer he was as firmly convinced that the "three fundamental claims" represented the minimum limits commensurate with national security and that the same should be upheld in all circumstances (*Tokyo Asahi*, March 30, 1930, p. 2).

[49]*Ibid.*, March 30, 1930, p. 2.

department and the staff[50] to confer upon the matter of draft instructions then under preparation at Kasumigaseki.[51]

To reach mutual agreement over essential points and to give a finishing touch to the draft instructions, an important joint conference of the Foreign Office and the navy authorities was held at 6:30 P.M., March 31, at the official residence of the navy minister.[52] Representing the *Kasumigaseki*, Mr. Hotta stated that, according to the official report from London, it was perfectly plain that the tentative compromise plan which embodied the results of negotiations between the Japanese and American delegates represented the utmost limits of the American concession, and that to seek further concession would be certain to spell the break-up of the conference. In these circumstances, the *Kasumigaseki* spokesman contended that, in drawing up the instructions, the Foreign Office had taken special care to respect the endeavors hitherto made by the Japanese delegation, while at the same time meeting the views of the naval authorities on questions of national defense. He stated that the draft had not yet been completed, requiring further study on certain points of terminology, and therefore he indicated only the general outlines of the draft. Vice-Admiral Suetsugu of the naval staff, on the other hand, again emphasized the attitude of the Admiralty, namely, the "three fundamental claims": (1) 70 per cent ratio in regard to big cruisers, (2) 70 per cent ratio in regard to auxiliary craft as a whole, and (3) the maintenance of the present strength of the submarines. He declared that, should these basic claims of the Admiralty fail to be recognized *in toto*, he could not endorse the draft instructions. The

---

[50]The following were present at the conference: Vice-Admiral Yamanashi (vice-minister of navy), Baron Yabuki (parliamentary vice-minister of navy), Vice-Admiral Kobayashi (chief of the Bureau of Matériel of the naval general staff), Vice-Admiral Suetaugu (vice-chief of naval staff), Rear-Admiral Hori (director of the Bureau of Naval Affairs), and others.

[51]*Tokyo Asahi*, March 31, 1930, p. 2.

[52]The Foreign Office was represented by Mr. Nagai (parliamentary vice-minister of foreign affairs), Mr. Yoshida (vice-minister of foreign affairs), Viscount Oda (councilor of the Foreign Office), and Mr. Hotta (chief of the European and American Bureau), while the navy side was represented by Baron Yabuki (parliamentary vice-minister of navy), Vice-Admiral Yamanashi (vice-minister of navy), Mr. Awayama (councilor of the Navy Department), Vice-Admiral Suetsugu (vice-chief of naval staff), Vice-Admiral Kobayashi (chief of the Bureau of Matériel), and Captain Kato (chief of the first section of the naval staff).

views of the Foreign Office and the Admiralty being so far apart, this conference did not reach an agreement but ended in a mere exchange of views. Thus the final responsibility of deciding on the nature of the instructions was entirely left in the hands of the prime minister.[53]

By March 31 the premier's decision had been firmly made after mature and careful consideration of all factors involved from all possible points of view, and after having consulted such naval leaders as Admiral Togo, Admiral Count Yamamoto, Admiral Viscount Saito, Admiral Okada of the Supreme War Council, and others, as well as the views entertained among privy councilors and Prince Saionji, the genro. Therefore, it was a foregone conclusion that the cabinet meeting of April 1 would approve the Foreign Office draft instructions.

Prior to the meeting of the cabinet, however, Premier Hamaguchi invited, at 8:30 P.M., Admiral Kato, chief of naval general staff, Admiral Okada, a leading member of the Supreme War Council, and Vice-Admiral Yamanashi, vice-minister of navy, to explain the reasons for deciding to adopt the Foreign Office plan. At this conference of the Big Three of the Admiralty, Hamaguchi declared that, in reaching the decision, he had taken into careful consideration the guiding spirit of fostering international peace, the nation's economic and financial conditions, as well as the needs of national defense. He further explained that the Admiralty point of view had been given due consideration in that an appropriate diplomatic measure would be taken to insure freedom of action after 1936. Both Admiral Kato and Admiral Okada, it was reported, reiterated to the premier their opposition to any compromise which would jeopardize the "three fundamental claims," and declared that they could do nothing in the matter, inasmuch as the prime minister had decided to adopt the views of the Foreign Office.[54]

The important cabinet meeting to decide upon the draft instructions was called to order at 10:30 A.M. at the official residence of Prime Minister Hamaguchi with all the members of the cabinet, except the war minister, in attendance. In view of its particular significance, the vice-minister of navy and the

[53] *Tokyo Asahi*, April 2, 1930, p. 1.
[54] *Ibid.*, April 2, 1930, p. 1.

director of the Bureau of Naval Affairs of the Navy Department were also invited. At the outset of the meeting the prime minister explained the circumstances connected with the drafting of the instructions and briefly outlined the attitude of the government. Baron Shidehara then gave additional explanations, in which he emphasized the fact that the compromise plan was a result of a series of negotiations between the Japanese and American delegations, to which the British delegation gave hearty approval, that there was no room for further concession on the part of the United States, that, under the plan, the national security was adequately protected, and that the instructions were to indicate merely the essential outlines, the details of which were to be worked out by the delegates in London. Following Baron Shidehara, Vice-Admiral Yamanashi stated the views of the naval authorities, while Mr. Inouye, the finance minister, spoke on the financial aspect of the instructions. The draft instructions as explained by Baron Shidehara were formally approved by the cabinet, and the meeting was adjourned at 2:15 P.M., April 1, 1930.[55]

At 3:30 Prime Minister Hamaguchi was received in audience by the emperor to report the draft instructions as approved by the cabinet. With imperial sanction, the approved instructions were dispatched to Mr. Wakatsuki through the Foreign Office at 5:00 P.M., and were received in London in the evening of April 1.[56]

Admiral Kanji Kato, chief of naval staff, who had been the leading champion of the "three fundamental claims," was received in audience by the emperor at 10:30 A.M., April 2, to report to the throne concerning the attitude of the staff on the instructions just sent to London by the government. On his return to his office, Admiral Kato, in a press interview, refused to disclose the nature of his appeal, but declared that, as one who was responsible for national defense and naval

[55]*Ibid.*, April 2, 1930, p. 1. The respective views of the Foreign Office and the Admiralty are interestingly presented by two anonymous writers in *Gaiko Jiho* No. 609 (April 15, 1930), pp. 80–91.

[56]*Ibid.*, April 2, 1930, p. 2. At the cabinet meeting of April 1, the vice-minister of navy sought to commit the cabinet members to support the naval supplementary building program to be presented under the anticipated treaty, when Finance Minister Inouye expressed his willingness to give due consideration to the Admiralty demand (*Tokyo Asahi*, April 2, 1930, p. 2).

tactics, he was still unalterably opposed to the naval tonnage allotted to Japan under the American proposal.[57]

The Japanese instructions accepting the Reed-Matsudaira compromise having been received in London, the successful conclusion of a naval treaty now became a foregone conclusion. The Japanese delegation, in the evening of April 2, issued a statement declaring that instructions accepting the compromise had been received and that the Japanese government desired it to be perfectly understood that she be free to claim, upon termination of the treaty, all she should deem necessary from the standpoint of national defense as heretofore.[58]

Now the task of thrashing out minor details progressed rapidly, and the full draft of the treaty was received by the Foreign Office on April 19. Immediately upon receipt of this draft, a conference of high officials at the *Kasumigaseki* was held to go over the document, after which it was carefully examined by the foreign minister, prime minister, and the vice-minister of navy, as well as high officers of the Admiralty, and was approved without further revision. Thus, the instructions authorizing Honorable Wakatsuki to sign the treaty on behalf of the government were transmitted in the evening of April 20.[59] Accordingly, the historic London Naval Treaty was signed on April 22,[60] the text of which was made public by the Foreign Office on the same day.[61] At the same time, both the prime minister and the foreign minister issued statements in which Prime Minister Hamaguchi praised the labors of the plenipotentiaries and emphasized the important part the support of public opinion played in the success of the conference, while Foreign Minister Shidehara dwelt at length on the moral influence the treaty would exert upon the conduct of international relations.[62]

[57]*Op. cit.*, April 3, 1930, p. 1.

[58]*The Times* (London), April 2, 1930, p. 14; *ibid.*, April 3, 1930, p. 13.

[59]*Japan Weekly Chronicle*, April 24, 1930, p. 413; *The Times* (London), April 21, 1930, p. 10.

[60]Commenting upon the signing of the treaty, *The Times* (London) said, ". . . The successful negotiation of the Three-Power agreement owed much to the statesmanship and sense of reality of the Japanese Government; and it was fittingly enough the leader of the Japanese delegation who most emphatically proclaimed the success of the conference" (April 23, 1930, p. 13).

[61]*Tokyo Asahi*, April 23, 1930, p. 2.

[62]*Ibid.*, April 23, 1930, p. 3. *Cf. Gaiko Jiho*, No. 610 (May 1, 1930), pp. 174–175.

Naval Propaganda and the Press

A survey of Japan's internal negotiations among various organs concerned, resulting in the signing of the treaty after a long delay and bitter struggle, cannot be complete without a reference to the part public opinion played during the conference. We have already seen that during the entire period of the conference no voice was raised in influential quarters, either in the press or on platforms, to challenge the "three fundamental claims" of the Admiralty. Therefore, apparently the public opinion of the nation was solidly behind the navy stand. It is fair to assume, however, that there were some students of the conference who entertained grave doubt as to the wisdom of insisting upon the original navy stand at the risk of wrecking the conference, but they refrained from expressing their views publicly for fear of being charged with "disrupting the public opinion" on the matter.

It is to be noted, in this connection, that, in so far as there was a "public opinion" concerning the navy stand of "three fundamental claims," it was "formulated" by naval leaders. There seems to be little room to doubt that the systematic and organized efforts made during the conference by the naval authorities and navy reservists' associations to "educate" the public to the idea that the 70 per cent ratio contended for represented the minimum limits for national defense were a complete success. In execution of this "educational campaign," meetings were conducted throughout Greater Tokyo during March 1–10, 1930, under the joint auspices of the City of Tokyo and *Kaigun Kyokai* or the imperial marine association. They were conducted mainly in public halls and public schools. The speakers at these meetings were largely vice-admirals in active service. Ostensibly, these meetings were intended to acquaint the general public with the progress of negotiations in London, but the inevitable effect was to "educate" the public to the Admiralty stand.[63]

Moreover, such associations and societies as *Kaigun Gunshuku Kokumin Doshikai* or national association on disarmament, *Gunshuku Mondai Remmei* or association for the study of disarmament problems, *Kaigun Kyokai* or imperial marine association, and others, organized by both active and retired

[63] *Tokyo Asahi*, March 2, 1930, p. 2.

naval leaders as well as "big navy" enthusiasts, did not fail to set their well-organized, well-disciplined machines into action in support of the Admiralty. They held meetings, particularly during the closing days of March, 1930, and passed resolutions which were given wide publicity. Thus they exerted strong pressure on the Foreign Office and the delegates in London by representations and resolutions.[64]

On the other hand, during the same period, no effective efforts were made on the part of organized societies and associations interested in peace and international coöperation. For instance, no systematic efforts were made by churches and peace societies, League of Nations Association of Japan, and other groups of like character. It was reported at the time that, although the League of Nations Association of Japan passed a resolution in a meeting of its executive committee, for some unknown reasons it failed to be given publicity in the press. Thus, all the societies and associations whose *raison d'être* was given opportunity for vindication and recognition failed to function at this most crucial moment. This fact of complete failure to give expression to their *raison d'être* was due, in large measure, to the apprehension so commonly held among the people that to express even a doubt as to the wisdom of the navy stand might be interpreted as "disrupting the united opinion of the country."[65]

What attitude did the *Seiyukai*, the chief opposition party, take concerning the London Treaty during the progress of negotiations? At the outset of the Fifty-seventh Diet, Representative Inukai, leader of the party, sought to introduce a resolution on January 21, 1930, in the House of Representatives, urging upon the delegation to insist upon the "three fundamental claims." This attempt, however, was frustrated by the dissolution of the House on the same day. And the London Conference, by mutual consent, did not enter the general election of February 20 as an issue. This election resulted in an overwhelming victory for the *Minseito* party,

[64]*Op. cit.*, March 18, 1930, p. 2. *Cf. Japan Weekly Chronicle*, April 10, 1930, p. 360.

[65]It may be mentioned here that in Greater Tokyo on March 1 a two-minute period of meditation was set aside by the Christian churches which was preceded by two meetings on naval conference held under the auspices of Japan Women's Peace Society and Women's Division of the League of Nations Association of Japan, respectively (*Tokyo Asahi*, March 2, 1930, p. 3).

giving the Hamaguchi government an absolute control of the Lower House of the Diet.

On March 27 a meeting of the executive committee of the *Seiyukai* party was held, when it was decided to call on the Foreign Office for explanations regarding the progress of negotiations. This request on the part of the *Seiyukai* party was refused on the ground that the nature of negotiations was to be kept under strict secrecy. The *Seiyukai* party, through its chief secretary, issued a statement opposing any concession on the part of the delegation that might jeopardize the security of the nation.[66]

In summary, we are led to conclude that the press of the nation, irrespective of political affiliations, united in support of the navy stand during the entire conference. However, it should be noted that, with the decision of the Hamaguchi cabinet to accept the Reed-Matsudaira compromise, the leading liberal press began to support a minor modification in the interest of the conference. The publication of the treaty was received with approval, qualified by the circumstances, the consensus of press opinion being that the treaty as concluded was the best obtainable under the circumstances. From this time on, the press again took a decidedly vigorous color as to the fate of the treaty.

PARLIAMENTARY INTERPELLATIONS REGARDING THE TREATY

With the opening of the special session of the Fifty-eighth Diet on April 25, 1930, the scene of battles was now shifted to the floor of the national legislature. At the very outset of the session, Foreign Minister Shidehara delivered his customary address on foreign relations, the major portion of which was devoted to the treaty just concluded.[67] In his eloquent defense of the treaty, Baron Shidehara assured the Diet that the safety of the nation was adequately protected under the terms of the treaty and refuted his critics by declaring:

None but extreme pessimists could possibly contend that the amount of strength to be allotted to Japan during the period ending in 1936 will prove fatally short of the needs of our national security. Taking fully into consideration the views of naval experts, we

[66]*Ibid.*, March 28, 1930, p. 2; also *Kokumin Shimbun*, March 28, 1930, p. 2.
[67]Text of Baron Shidehara's address in *Kwampo gogai*, April 26, 1930, p. 13.

have finally adopted with firm conviction the decision to join in
the present Treaty.

Again, defending the freedom of action at the termination
of the treaty, he argued:

There is no occasion for the apprehension that the Treaty of
London is to bind us hand and foot for all time to come. To show
ourself unduly disturbed, under the influence of so mistaken an
impression, would be an attitude little worthy of a self-respecting
nation.

Denying the charge that Japan's decision to sign the treaty
was made under pressure from abroad, Baron Shidehara concluded his address in the following language:

In these circumstances, every fair observer will agree that the
provisions of the London Naval Treaty contain nothing to which
we ought, even at the risk of a rupture of the negotiations, to have
taken exception and that, on the contrary, the sane and proper
course for us to take was to extend our whole-hearted coöperation
in order to secure the success of the Conference. It seems that in
certain quarters rumors so utterly wide of the truth are circulated
as that the agreement was forced upon us by other Powers. I need
hardly point out the absurdity of such reports. Having carefully
weighed all considerations, not only of foreign policy, but also of
naval, financial, economic and all the other factors of national
strength, upon which the security of a nation must, in the final
analysis, depend, we were brought to the conclusion that, in accepting the terms of the agreement arrived at, we would decidedly
be serving the real interests of this Empire.

Thus, with the formal statement of the government with
reference to the conclusion of the treaty, parliamentary battles were opened on April 25. The *Seiyukai* party (opposition)
which had suffered an overwhelming defeat at the hands of
the party in power (*Minseito*) at the polls on February 20,
1930, now sought to take advantage of the situation to embarrass the cabinet, hoping that, by joining hands with the
conservative elements in the Upper House of the Diet as well
as military and naval leaders and eventually with certain influential members of the Privy Council, to which the treaty
was destined to be submitted for advice in due course of time,
it might bring about the downfall of the ministry.

Under the circumstances, the opposition's criticism of the

administration was largely concentrated upon an attack on the contents as well as on the procedure which was adopted in the conclusion of the treaty. Immediately after the addresses by the prime minister, foreign minister, and finance minister on their respective fields, Representative Inukai, president of the *Seiyukai* party, led the interpellation front upon the treaty.[68] This veteran statesman and recognized leader in the Diet boldly challenged the government's assurances as to the security of the nation, quoting the statement to the contrary issued by the chief of naval general staff on April 2. In reply, Premier Hamaguchi confidently assured the interpellator that, irrespective of the statement in question, it is the government that is responsible to the Diet for the security of national defense and reaffirmed that the defense of the shores had not been put in jeopardy by the treaty.[69]

In the same afternoon (April 25, 1930), the *Seiyukai* attack was resumed, through Representative Ichiro Hatoyama, chief secretary of the Tanaka *Seiyukai* cabinet, who contended that the conclusion of the London Treaty, in utter disregard of the views of the naval staff, charged with the responsibility of determining the nation's defense program, constituted a usurpation of constitutional powers, and that the cabinet had embarked on a political adventure by signing the treaty in defiance of the views of naval experts. Prime Minister Hamaguchi in reply stated that the government had taken the views of not only the naval general staff but also other naval experts into careful consideration, and consequently, he argued, the interpellator's contention was based on false assumption, and therefore he did not feel constrained to make any further reply.[70]

Again, in reply to a question by Representative Shinya Uchida, parliamentary vice-minister of navy under the Tanaka *Seiyukai* cabinet, Prime Minister Hamaguchi declared he could under no circumstances disclose the contents of

[68]Representatives Inukai, Hatoyama, Uchida, and Maeda led the *Seiyukai* onslaught on the treaty in the House of Representatives (*Kwampo gogai*, April 26, 28, May 1, 4, 1930, pp. 16–17, 25–27, 55–61, 108, 127–128, 133).

[69]*Kwampo gogai*, April 26, 1930, pp. 16–17. Admiral Abo reaffirmed the national security on January 23, 1931 (*ibid.*, Jan. 24, 1931, pp. 38, 40–41).

[70]*Ibid.*, April 26, 1930, pp. 25–27. This unqualified assurance on the part of the prime minister that the national defense was secure under the terms of the treaty greatly provoked the resentment of naval leaders (*Tokyo Asahi*, April 27, 1930, p. 1).

the instructions issued to the Japanese delegation, to do so not being for the best interest of the state. He declared, furthermore, that the government could be held to answer only for statements it issues with responsibility, and consequently he did not feel it necessary to reply to questions concerning the contents of the statement issued by the Japanese delegation on February 13 in London, and he did not feel constrained to reply as to the internal negotiations or exchange of views between the cabinet and naval authorities or naval general staff. He refused to divulge the nature of the appeal to the throne by the chief of naval staff, and finally stated that, although the government had taken the views of naval experts into careful consideration, he was unable to disclose the scope and extent to which their views had been accepted.[71]

Moreover, in the House Budget Committee, on April 30, 1930, several *Seiyukai* members made persistent efforts to drive the cabinet into a corner on the treaty issue, but whenever subtle constitutional points regarding the supreme command of the navy were raised, the prime minister pleaded inability to reply to abstract questions. Thus pressed to answer under which articles of the Constitution—Article XI, which provides that the emperor has the supreme command of the army and navy, or Article XII, providing for the imperial prerogative over the organization and peace standing of the army and navy—the government acted in deciding the instructions concerning the Reed-Matsudaira compromise. Premier Hamaguchi refused to reply, holding that the government would assume full responsibility under the treaty, but at the same time pointed out that there was no conflict of views between the government and the naval staff at the time.[72]

Some of the most outspoken critics of the Hamaguchi cabinet in connection with the London Treaty in the Upper House of the Diet were Baron Nagayasu Ikeda (Koseikai), General Koichiro Shimizu (Kenkyukai), and Baron Toshiatsu Sakamoto (Koseikai), who argued that matters relat-

[71] *Kwampo gogai,* April 28, 1930, pp. 55–61. This position was affirmed by Admiral Abo, who succeeded Admiral Takarabe as navy minister in the House of Peers during the Fifty-ninth session of the Diet (*ibid.,* Jan. 29, 1931, pp. 45–47). *Cf.* the interpellations in the House of Representatives on Feb. 26, 1931 (*ibid.,* Feb. 27, 1931, pp. 480–484).

[72] *Tokyo Asahi,* May 1, 1930, p. 1.

ing to national defense and strategy ought to be determined by the army and naval general staffs, that it was wrong for civilian statesmen to decide them in accordance with their political views, and that the procedure in the instance under question infringed upon Article XI of the Constitution.

In reply to the searching questions and criticisms in the Upper House of the Diet, Premier Hamaguchi vigorously defended the procedure followed in issuing the final instructions as in no way violative of the Constitution, although, as in the Lower House, he consistently refused to give explicit interpretations of the articles of the Constitution concerned, assured that the nation's defense was adequately secure and that the cabinet, including the war and navy ministers, would assume the full responsibility under the treaty.[73]

However, it is to be observed, the prime minister went a step further before the Peers than in the Lower House, where he could count on the absolute support of his followers, in explaining the constitutional basis for the procedure followed in the signing of the treaty. Thus, Hamaguchi argued before the House of Peers—whose support he could not rely upon as in the Lower House—in reply to a question asked by General Koichiro Shimizu, that the instructions issued to the delegates embodied the government plan, that it was no more a Foreign Office plan than it was an Admiralty plan, that the responsibility of the cabinet under the Treaty was clear under Article LV of the Constitution.[74] He came near to stating explicitly the constitutional justification for the cabinet's action when, in reply to a question by Dr. Takuzo Hanai on the closing day of the Diet, the prime minister called the Peers' attention to the fact that the question related to one of concluding treaties, and that the government decided upon its full responsibility after having consulted experts as to the naval strength which constituted the subject matter of the treaty.[75]

[73]*Kwampo gogai*, May 7, 1930, pp. 79–84; May 8, pp. 88–91; May 12, pp. 126–130; May 14, pp. 179–180, 183.

[74]*Kwampo gogai*, May 14, 1930, pp. 179–180.

[75]*Ibid.*, May 14, 1930, p. 183. *Cf.* the premier's reply to Dr. Takuzo Hanai in the House of Peers with his earlier admission in the Lower House that the treaty in question was concluded under the treaty-making power of the throne upon the responsible advice of the cabinet (*ibid.*, May 4, 1930, p. 133). Hamaguchi repeated the same view in the Peers' Budget Committee on May 10 (*Tokyo Asahi*, May 11, 1930, p. 1).

CONSTITUTIONAL SUBTLETIES

In the above brief survey of parliamentary debates upon the treaty immediately following its conclusion in London, we have seen that the Hamaguchi ministry succeeded in weathering the parliamentary interpellations unscathed and managed to avoid giving official answers to constitutional issues raised. Why was the cabinet so reluctant to show the constitutional basis for the procedure in concluding the treaty, in the face of persistent demands for official interpretation of the constitutional issues involved and of the pleas for constitutional government in both Houses of the Diet?[76]

Before examining some of the possible considerations that led the ministry to pursue such an evasive course—a course doing violence to fundamental principles of parliamentary system of government—we may briefly examine the views held by leading jurists on the issues of the day. Regarding the controversy on constitutional issues raised on the floor of the Diet, leading constitutional jurists, as well as the press, were united in support of the action taken by the Hamaguchi cabinet in issuing the final instructions to the delegates in London.

Professor Tatsukichi Minobe of the Imperial University of Tokyo, in a series of lucid articles in *Tokyo Asahi*, gave a juristic justification of the government's action.[77] This eminent authority on constitutional law argued that the power to determine the organization of the army and navy, that is,

[76]Representative Tetsu Katayama (Shakai Minshuto), a Social Democrat, stated that the government's action was clearly justified under Article XII of the Constitution, being within the competence of the ministers of state as provided for in Article LV (*Kwampo gogai*, May 4, 1930, p. 127). In the course of his eloquent interpellation in the Upper House, Dr. Takuzo Hanai declared that, in his opinion, the action was clearly justifiable under Article XII and did not come within the domain of supreme command as provided for in Article XI. He even declared that the premier's lack of courage to say so did little credit to a cabinet under constitutional government (*ibid.*, May 14, 1930, p. 183). Touching on the refusal of the prime minister to give explicit interpretation of Articles XI and XII of the Constitution, Baron Nagayasu Ikeda of the Upper House declared that, irrespective of differences of opinion that might exist among scholars, it is the duty of ministers of state under constitutional government to set forth their views to avoid misgivings, holding that it was in the chambers of the Diet that public discussion of the Constitution should be made (*ibid.*, May 8, 1930, p. 88).

[77]Tatsukichi Minobe, "The London Conference and the Scope of the Power of Supreme Command," *Tokyo Asahi*, May 2, 4, 5, 1930. Also Minobe, "The Relation between the Military and Naval Authorities and the Government," *Kaizo*, XII, No. 6 (June, 1930), pp. 19–26.

the power to decide the military and naval strength of the state, does not belong to the prerogative of supreme command but to the prerogative of the throne over state affairs, that it was a matter on which the cabinet, and the cabinet alone, gives responsible advice, and with which no organ under the supreme command might interfere, and that the views of the military and naval authorities were to be only advisory, having no binding force upon the cabinet.

Commenting upon the legal nature of treaties in the domestic law of Japan, Dr. Minobe contended that, irrespective of the subject matter of a treaty in question, the imperial prerogative over treaties is to be exercised solely upon the responsible advice of the cabinet. Thus, in the jurist's opinion, even in case of treaties relating to tactics and operations, the army and naval general staffs are only entitled to participate in the preliminary investigations as technical experts, it being exclusively the political organs that assume the full responsibility for concluding them. Therefore, he contended, the London Treaty being a treaty relating to the determination of the naval strength of the state, there could be no question as to the constitutionality of the procedure taken in this instance, that the views of naval experts being advisory are only entitled to respect and consideration. Thus, in Professor Minobe's opinion, the cabinet was clearly within its exclusive competence to advise the throne concerning the subject matter of the treaty, and even granting that the naval general staff had the constitutional power to advise the emperor as to the subject matter, the London Treaty being a treaty, it was within the exclusive competence of the cabinet to give responsible advice to the throne. Other leading jurists of the nation, such as Professor Soichi Sasaki of the Imperial University of Kyoto,[78] Professor Sakuzo Yoshino,[79] and others, concurred with Dr. Minobe in this controversy.[80]

The views we have examined above were supported by an

[78]Soichi Sasaki, "The Power of Supreme Command," *Osaka Mainichi*, May 1-5, 1930; also "The Relation between the Government and the Military and Naval Authorities in the Determination of the Military and Naval Strength," *Kaizo*, XII, No. 7 (July, 1930), pp. 104-126.

[79]Sakuzo Yoshino, "Controversies over the Supreme Command," *Chuo Koron*, Nos. 509, 510 (June, July, 1930), pp. 159-168, 129-140.

[80]No influential dissenting voice on this particular phase of the question was raised by any jurist during the entire controversy.

overwhelming portion of the nation's liberal press and informed public. Probably one of the most vigorous champions
of the views above expounded was the *Tokyo Asahi*. This
leading liberal daily condemned in most vigorous terms the
attitude of the *Seiyukai* party on the ground that it might be
taken as making a political football of the constitutional question, giving ground for suspicion that the party was bent on
a denial of the principles of responsible cabinet government
over national defense, and bidding favor with the common
enemy, the naval and military cliques. This daily persistently
urged upon the prime minister to make clear the constitutional issues in the interest of sound development of constitutional government.[81]

It is to be noted that the nation's leading dailies, irrespective of political inclinations, all united in their public demand
for final settlement of the constitutional subtleties which
stand today as the greatest obstacles to the establishment of
a sound system of constitutional government in Japan. Even
Seitoku Ito, a well-known editor of the *Jiji Shimpo*, whose
timely volume on *Gunshuku* or disarmament (November,
1929) is generally credited with having given the naval stand
for 70 per cent ratio a wide publicity among the general
public, declared against the encroachment of the supreme
command on the government, holding that, should it be established as a constitutional theory that the determination
of the naval strength of the state requires the consent of the
naval staff, it would be a retrogression in constitutional
government, and that it would be tantamount to granting
the taxing power to the Admiralty. He argued, therefore,
that the ultimate responsibility for determining the nation's
naval strength rests squarely upon the shoulders of the cabinet, the views of the naval general staff having only the claim
to respect and consideration at the hands of the cabinet.[82]

Having surveyed the salient features of the constitutional
issues involved in connection with the London Treaty, we
now come back to our original inquiry: Why did the cabinet
refuse to offer explicit interpretations of the constitutional

---

[81]See editorials in *Tokyo Asahi*, April 26, May 1, May 11, 1930. *Tokyo Asahi* and
its sister daily, *Osaka Asahi*, are recognized as the two foremost dailies in Japan,
having a wide circulation among the intelligentsia.

[82]Seitoku Ito in *Chuo Koron*, No. 510 (July, 1930), p. 113.

issues raised in the Diet in the face of such overwhelming support for the government's action? Our examination of the issues involved leads us to one conclusion, that the stubborn refusal on the part of the Hamaguchi cabinet, which had just won such an overwhelming victory at the polls, was forced in deference to its possible effect upon military authorities and the conservative elements in the House of Peers and the Privy Council. Had the cabinet chosen, as it was once reported to have decided at one of its meetings,[83] to state in clear and unmistakable terms its official interpretation of the constitutional subtleties, which no cabinet in the past dared to do, it was probable that the minister of war, General Ugaki, might have tendered his resignation, which, in turn, would have led to the general resignation of the entire cabinet, while enjoying the confidence of the Lower House of the Diet. Under such delicate circumstances, Prime Minister Hamaguchi had to choose the safer, though somewhat evasive, rôle in parliamentary interpellations.[84]

The Supreme War Council and the Treaty

The controversies over the delicate constitutional issues raised in the Fifty-eighth Diet became even more serious with the close of the session. From now on the fight was shifted to one between the chief of naval general staff and the government.[85]

Admiral Takarabe, the minister of navy and a plenipotentiary to London, returned to Tokyo on May 19.[86] Immedi-

[83]It was reported that the cabinet decided to state explicitly that the government's action at the time of issuing the final instructions was done under Article XII of the Constitution. However, upon being informed that, should the cabinet proceed to carry out the decision of its meeting, Minister of War Ugaki would be forced to resign, the prime minister adopted the safe policy of evading issues throughout the session of the Diet.

[84]It is apparent that, in so far as the London Treaty was concerned, the government acted upon the constitutional theory that the cabinet was to assume full and exclusive responsibility for the determination of the nation's naval strength, under Article XII of the Constitution (*Tokyo Asahi*, May 8, 1930, p. 2).

[85]Prime Minister Hamaguchi called on Admiral Togo on May 16 to ask the latter's assistance in placating the situation created by the attitude taken on the part of Admiral Kato, chief of naval general staff (*ibid.*, May 17, 1930, p. 2).

[86]At Shimonoseki station, May 18, Admiral Takarabe was presented by a youth with a dagger together with a memorial, calling upon the navy minister to commit *harakiri* to express his apology for putting the nation's defense in jeopardy (*ibid.*, May 19, 1930, p. 7).

ately upon his arrival in Tokyo an extraordinary meeting of
the cabinet was called to welcome him and to hear his report
on the conference. At this meeting of his colleagues, the navy
minister assured the cabinet members that he would fight to
the last for the ratification of the treaty and flatly denied a
report that he was contemplating resignation over the action
taken by the government in issuing the final instructions.[87]
For some days Admiral Takarabe's efforts were exerted solely
for the purpose of explaining to high authorities in navy circles his dual position at the conference as the navy minister in
the Hamaguchi cabinet and as a member of the delegation.
His efforts were directed towards obtaining the "understandings" of Admiral Kato, chief of staff, and Admiral Okada,
former navy minister and now an influential member of the
Supreme War Council.[88]

On May 29 the navy minister called an unofficial meeting
of the naval members of the Supreme War Council to make
a detailed report to the nation's highest body in naval affairs
on the conference and to explain various points requiring
further elucidation.[89] It was reported that issues regarding
the supreme command of the navy constituted the leading
topic for discussion at this meeting. According to the *Asahi*,
Admiral Kato, stating the views of the staff, expressed sincere
regret that, before signing the treaty, no perfect agreement
had been reached between the government and his office on
the determination of the naval strength, the subject matter
of the treaty. He reiterated the assertion that his staff, from
the standpoint of national defense and naval strategy, had
refused to give consent to the government plan to the last,
and that the cabinet reached its decision without the concurrence of the former. This action on the part of the government, Admiral Kato went on to declare, constituted an
infringement upon the powers of his office. He argued further
that, not only as a legal principle but from the more important point of view of the future of Japan's national defense,
Hamaguchi's procedure should be regarded in a serious light.

[87] *Op. cit.*, May 20, 1930, p. 1.

[88] *Ibid.*, May 20–27, 29, 1930, p. 2.

[89] *Ibid.*, May 30, 1930, p. 2. The following members of the Council were present:
Admiral Prince Fushimi, Admiral of the Fleet Togo, Admiral Okada, Admiral
Takarabe (navy minister), and Admiral Kato (chief of naval general staff). The
conference lasted from 10:30 A.M. to 4:20 P.M.

The Admiral contended that the reaching of a perfect agreement of views between the government and the naval staff was an absolutely necessary condition for the determination of the tonnage of her navy. Both Admiral Togo and Admiral Okada supported Admiral Kato's views as just and proper.

Regarding the same issue, Admiral Takarabe expressed his concurrence with Admiral Kato. He likewise expressed his regret for the condition which gave rise to a grave apprehension as to the existence of complete agreement between the ministry and the staff at the time of issuing instructions. Aside from the question as to how the action stood in the light of the Constitution, Admiral Takarabe continued, it was the confirmed faith of the Admiralty that there must be a "complete understanding" between the government and the staff in determining the naval strength of the state. In this respect the navy minister declared that he was in agreement with Admiral Kato.[90]

After further discussion, it was agreed that a memorandum be drawn up embodying the agreed views concerning the determination of the naval strength, and that, after joint petition to the emperor by the chief of naval general staff and the navy minister, a copy should be kept in each office to avoid future misunderstandings. In compliance with this decision, Admiral Takarabe drew up a draft memorandum on June 1 in consultation with Prime Minister Hamaguchi, and showed it to Admiral Kato, who refused to even consider it. Admiral Togo also refused to approve it. Thereupon another draft memorandum was drawn up but failed to meet the approval of the naval leaders. In these circumstances, it was reported, Admiral Kato himself drafted one on June 2, 1930, and secured the approval of Admiral Togo and Admiral Okada and other war councilors.[91] Yet, Admiral Takarabe

[90] Just before the meeting of the cabinet on May 30, the navy minister had a conference with the premier and the foreign minister concerning the discussion held at the unofficial meeting of the naval members of the Council the previous day. At the cabinet meeting Admiral Takarabe made a brief report on the conference, and, although he refused to divulge the contents of the discussion, he stated that no constitutional or political issues were discussed at the meeting (*ibid.*, May 31, 1930, p. 1).

[91] The *Yoyokai*, a society of admirals in the first and second reserve list, recorded its strong support of the stand of Admiral Kato on the contested issue of the supreme command of the navy at its meeting on June 2, 1930. A resolution was adopted strongly condemning the government's action at the time of issuing the final in-

withheld his signature to the draft memorandum drawn up by Admiral Kato while he headed the naval general staff.[92]

The conflict between the cabinet and the naval authorities became so serious over drawing up a new replenishment naval program and over the supreme command issue that the cabinet relieved on June 10 both the vice-chief of naval staff and vice-minister of navy of their posts.[93] Thereupon, Admiral Kato, chief of naval general staff, was received in audience by the emperor at 10:40 A.M., June 10, to make a detailed report on the grand naval maneuvers in the fall. The press reported that Admiral Kato took this opportunity to make further report on the details connected with the drawing up of the memorandum as well as the divergence of views between the navy minister and himself over the wording of the memorandum. He then asked the throne to relieve him of his office on the ground that he could no longer successfully discharge the duties of his office. Later, the emperor summoned Count Makino, Lord Privy Seal, for advice, whereupon he advised the throne to summon the navy minister on the ground that the matters referred to the functions of the navy

structions, insisting that the consent of the naval general staff was absolutely essential and expressing grave apprehension as to the security of the national defense under the treaty. Although the resolution was given publicity in the press, it was not presented to any officials (text in *ibid.*, June 3, 1930, p. 2).

[92]*Ibid.*, June 12, 1930, p. 2. Commenting on the reported memorandum to be drawn up as a result of the unofficial meeting of the naval members of the Supreme War Council, a leading daily declared that the memorandum was binding only upon naval organs in their mutual transaction of business and warned against its binding effect on the government or limitations upon the Constitution. It went on to argue that, to respect the views of the naval general staff should not be construed to imply the necessity of obtaining its consent prior to concluding a treaty or drafting naval appropriations. The daily emphasized the ultimate power of decision of the government and declared that both Articles XI and XII of the Constitution, like all the other prerogatives of the throne, should be exercised upon the responsible advice of the cabinet. It further called upon the Hamaguchi government to make clear the constitutional issues raised in the interest of constitutional government (*cf.* editorial in *Tokyo Asahi*, June 1, 1930, p. 3). In his fight the government was not without support from some influential navy leaders. For instance, among the most vigorous supporters of the government on this issue was Admiral Viscount Saito, governor general of Chosen, a former navy minister, and principal delegate to the Geneva Naval Conference of 1927. In a press interview, Admiral Saito expressed his disapproval of Admiral Kato's attitude and declared that the government had the ultimate power of decision, holding that the financial aspects ought to be taken into consideration in determining the naval strength (*ibid.*, June 1, 1930, p. 2).

[93]*Ibid.*, June 10, 1930, p. 1.

minister. Having conferred with Admiral Kato at 2:30 P.M., Admiral Takarabe was received in audience by the emperor at 4:25 P.M., and recommended the appointment of Admiral Kato as a war councilor and Admiral Taniguchi, commander of the Kure naval station, to succeed Admiral Kato in the naval general staff office.[94] After obtaining the advice of Admiral Prince Fushimi and Admiral Togo, the appointment was announced on June 11.[95]

This drastic measure taken towards the foes of the government policy on the part of the staff indicated the determination of the cabinet to carry out its policy, the naval replenishment program drawn up by the staff being impossible of adoption without jeopardizing the benefits under the treaty just signed. Under the circumstances it was necessary to appoint a new chief to draw up a new naval program within the letter and spirit of the treaty stipulations. We note, however, that this drastic action on the part of the government would have been impossible had it not been for the support given to its stand by Prince Saionji, the genro, Count Makino, Lord Privy Seal, Dr. K. Ichiki, minister of the imperial household, Admiral Suzuki, Grand Chamberlain, and other leading officials close to the Court.[96] Moreover, the press of the nation favorably commented upon the government measure as unavoidable under the circumstances.[97]

The immediate obstacles of major importance having been disposed of, Admiral Takarabe was now in position to draw up a memorandum. Immediately after the resignation of Admiral Kato, the navy minister called in conference Ad-

[94]*Ibid.*, June 11, 1930, p. 2.

[95]*Ibid.*, June 12, 1930, p. 2.

[96]*Ibid.*, June 11, 1930, p. 2. On June 11, Admiral Takarabe, the navy minister, called on the prime minister to assure the latter of his determination to put the treaty in effect, for the conclusion of which he shared the responsibility, and that he would not resign the post until ratification had been effected in Japan and a new naval program drawn up (*ibid.*, June 12, 1930, p. 1).

[97]Commenting upon the resignation of Admiral Kato, *Tokyo Asahi* strongly condemned a dangerous precedent being established by a chief of naval staff in making a direct appeal to the throne on a constitutional question arising out of the supreme command, thus forestalling the ministers of state. The daily went on to declare that it was to maintain military discipline that the government dismissed the vice-chief of general staff who forged a public document by issuing a so-called "Admiralty Statement" at the time of the dispatch of instructions. It called upon the opposition parties to present a united front with the government to protect the sound development of constitutional government (*Tokyo Asahi*, June 14, 1930, p. 3).

miral Yamamoto, commander-in-chief of the combined squadron, and Admiral Osumi, commander of the Yokosuka naval station, and on June 13, attached his signature to the memorandum. The contents of the memorandum were kept under strict secrecy, but, according to the press reports, it declared that matters relating to the naval strength were to be decided in accordance with the past precedents—the complete agreement of views between the navy minister and the chief of naval general staff—and that a copy of the memorandum be transmitted to the government. Approval was obtained at an unofficial meeting of the naval members of the Supreme War Council.[98]

With a new chief of staff, the task of completing a new naval defense program progressed rapidly, and on June 21, 1930, an important joint conference of high officials of both the staff and the Navy Department, including the commanders of the various naval stations and fortifications, was called at the official residence of the navy minister to deliberate upon the new naval defense program.[99] With broad outlines of the program decided upon, the task progressed more rapidly,[100] and on June 30, an agreement was reached be-

[98]To the memorandum were attached the signatures of only Admiral Takarabe the navy minister, and Admiral Taniguchi, the new chief of naval staff. A statement was inserted at the bottom of the memorandum, however, to the effect that it embodied the agreed views reached after full deliberation in the Supreme War Council. We note here that particular care was taken as to the form of the memorandum since it related to a matter upon which the emperor had not requested an advice. The memorandum was originally drawn up between Admiral Takarabe and Admiral Kato. At a cabinet meeting the navy minister made a report on the memorandum, explaining the circumstances connected with the drafting of the document as well as its contents, and sought the "understandings" of the cabinet. However, the prime minister declared that, inasmuch as the document related to the conduct of internal negotiations within the Admiralty and had no binding effect upon the government, the cabinet should take no action, either to approve or reject the document, but merely to be informed. The cabinet accepted the prime minister's suggestion (*Tokyo Asahi*, June 20, 1930, pp. 1, 2). In reply to an interpellation by General Shimizu in the House of Peers on February 4, 1931, Baron Shidehara, the acting prime minister, denied any direct connection between the government and the naval general staff. He argued that the determination of the naval strength is made, according to the present practice, by the chief of naval general staff in consultation with the navy minister (*Kwampo gogai*, Feb. 5, 1931, pp. 104-108). Admiral Abo, who succeeded Admiral Takarabe, affirmed the contents of the memorandum in the Fifty-ninth session of the Diet (*ibid.*, Feb. 13, 1931, pp. 168-169). *Cf. ibid.*, Feb. 14, 1931, p. 175.

[99]*Tokyo Asahi*, June 21, 1930, p. 2.

[100]*Ibid.*, June 22, 24, 25, 1930, p. 2.

tween the staff and the Department.[101] However, at the same time, it was rumored that Admiral Togo did not approve the new program, and, in consequence, several calls on the part of the new chief of staff were made on Admiral Togo and Admiral Kato to obtain their "understandings."[102]

A new defense program having been drawn up, the next step to be taken was the calling of either the board of field marshals and fleet admirals or the Supreme War Council to obtain the advice of the nation's highest advisory organs in military and naval affairs on the naval strength allotted by the treaty and the new naval defense program drawn up thereunder.[103] A fresh and renewed conflict of views arose between the navy minister and Admiral Kato, now a member of the Council. Admiral Kato was now determined to have the views he had unsuccessfully pressed as the head of the naval staff given official recognition by the Supreme War Council.

In order to thrash out preliminary matters relating to the exact wording of the imperial inquiry as well as to draft a report thereon, a series of conferences was held from July 5 to July 20 among the Big Four of the Admiralty: Admiral Takarabe (minister of navy), Admiral Taniguchi (chief of naval general staff), Admiral Okada (former navy minister and an influential member of the Council), and Admiral Kato (former chief of naval staff and the severest critic of the treaty).[104] The first question that had to be settled in these informal conferences of the Big Four was the precise wording the imperial inquiry should take. Admiral Kato insisted that it be very simple and definite and suggested that it should take the form of: "Is the London Treaty defective from the standpoint of national defense and naval strategy?" and that the report should be equally definite and be either completely affirmative or negative without qualifications. On the other hand, for the Supreme War Council to take such a

[101]*Ibid.*, July 1, 1930, p. 2.

[102]*Ibid.*, July 3, 4, 5, 1930, p. 1.

[103]At the time of the Washington Naval Treaty, the naval strength was referred to the board of field marshals and fleet admirals for advice, the board including both the army and navy members. In case of the London Treaty, naval leaders insisted upon calling the Supreme War Council, Admiral Togo being the only member from the navy on the board.

[104]*Tokyo Asahi*, July 6, 7, 8, 15, 16, 21, 1930, p. 2.

position on the treaty was to place Admiral Takarabe in a very embarrassing position. Under the circumstances, the new chief of the staff drew up a draft inquiry in the following terms: "What is the effect of the naval strength allotted to Japan under the treaty on naval operations and strategy?" After a long, heated discussion, it was decided to embody the following three items in the draft reply: (1) The tonnage of the navy under the treaty was defective from the standpoint of naval defense and tactics. (2) Measures, however, were possible to replenish the defective features, the treaty being for a short duration. (3) Even then, the national defense could not be made adequate from the standpoint of naval defense and tactics.

Thus on July 21, 1930, an unofficial meeting of the naval members of the War Council was called. At this meeting, Admiral Togo and Admiral Kato demanded that the navy minister give definite assurances that the government would support the new naval replenishment program, to which Admiral Takarabe was unable to give a definite reply without consulting the prime minister. Therefore the first session of the conference adjourned without coming to any decision on the matter.[105] Consequently, Prime Minister Hamaguchi called a conference of the navy, foreign, home, and railways ministers to decide upon the government attitude on this question. At this meeting Admiral Takarabe made a detailed report of the proceedings in the Council as well as the issues raised there. After some deliberation, it was decided that the cabinet would support, as far as possible, the new replenishment program drawn up by Admiral Taniguchi.[106] Thus on July 22, Admiral Takarabe was able to assure the war councilors of the government's sincerity in executing the program, and the Taniguchi draft was approved accordingly.[107]

Immediately after the adjournment of the unofficial meeting of the Supreme War Council (July 22), the chief of naval staff was received in audience to report to the throne the proceedings of the meetings of July 21 and 22 and to petition

[105]Op. cit., July 22, 1930, pp. 1, 2.

[106]Ibid., July 22, 1930, p. 2.

[107]After the close of the Council meeting, Admiral Takarabe attended a cabinet meeting, when he reported on the proceedings of the Council in strict confidence (ibid., July 23, 1930, p. 1).

the emperor to call a formal meeting of the Council. Thus, a formal meeting of the naval members of the Supreme War Council was held in the forenoon of July 23, Admiral Togo presiding. Admiral Togo handed out a copy of the imperial inquiry to each war councilor present, when Admiral Taniguchi, who had drawn up the imperial inquiry, rose to explain the naval defense program since the Washington Conference and submitted a new replenishment program as well as a draft report to the throne. Without any question or debate from the floor, Admiral Taniguchi's draft report was formally adopted by the Council.[108] According to the *Jiji Shimpo*, the report of the Council consisted of three items: (1) The national defense program approved by the throne in 1923 should not be departed from under any circumstances. The naval tonnage allotted under the London Naval Treaty was defective for executing the above program. (2) Upon ratification of the treaty, a provisional national defense program to replenish the defective features caused by the present treaty should be drawn up by means of air forces as well as new building of vessels outside the restricted categories. (3) Even if the replenishment program had to be drawn up as indicated in the preceding clause, the national defense was still defective, and therefore, the claims made in the first clause should be given recognition at the next conference.[109]

The action of the Council was immediately reported to the emperor by Admiral Togo.[110] With all the necessary prelimi-

[108]The contents of imperial inquiry as well as the report of the Supreme War Council were kept under strict secrecy. According to the *Tokyo Asahi*, however, it was: "How does the naval strength as provided for under the London Treaty affect naval armament and strategy?" and the reply was: "The naval strength allotted to Japan by the London Naval Treaty is defective in so far as naval armament and strategy are concerned. The treaty being only for a short duration, however, we are not without means to draw up a national defense program" (*ibid.*, July 23, 1930, p. 2).

[109]*Cf. Jiji Shimpo*, Sept. 15, 1930, p. 2. Production of this report of the Supreme War Council constituted one of the bitterest controversies encountered by the cabinet when the treaty was referred to the Privy Council for advice.

[110]Following the precedent set at the time of the Washington Naval Treaty, the emperor, through an imperial messenger, transmitted the report of the War Council to the prime minister the night of July 23 (*Tokyo Asahi*, July 24, 1930, p. 2; *Osaka Mainichi*, July 25, 1930, p. 1). Chief Secretary of the Cabinet Suzuki, under instructions of the prime minister, invited Vice-Minister Yoshida of the Foreign Office to the premier's residence at 2 P.M., July 24, to confer on various procedural matters relating to the treaty; at 3 P.M. he called on Dr. Yoku Egi at the Railways Department to confer with the latter on a draft reply to the emperor concerning the report

nary steps having thus been cleared away, the prime minister was now in position, after a cabinet meeting, to petition the emperor to refer the treaty to the Privy Council for advice.

SUBMISSION OF THE TREATY TO THE PRIVY COUNCIL

An extraordinary meeting of the cabinet was called at the official residence of the prime minister at 2 P. M., July 23, to deliberate upon the next formal step to be taken on the treaty. At the outset Premier Hamaguchi presented the text of the treaty, Japanese translation, explanatory report, as well as other public documents relating to the conclusion of the treaty, and reported that all the preliminary measures, both routine and political, having been completed, he was ready to report to the emperor the following day to petition the throne that the treaty be submitted to the Privy Council for advice. This was followed by Admiral Takarabe, who also made a report in strict confidence on the proceedings of the War Council held during the forenoon of the same day. After free exchange of views among the cabinet members, they decided to take immediate steps to petition the throne for submission of the treaty to the Privy Council.[111] Thus, on July 24, the treaty was formally referred to the Council for deliberation and advice, and the focus of public attention was now centered on the proceedings of His Majesty's highest advisory body in state affairs.[112]

In this connection, we may raise an interesting question as

of the War Council; and at 5 P.M., called on the navy minister to confer on the same. As a result, a draft reply was determined pledging the government's efforts to the realization of the measures of the War Council upon coming into effect of the Treaty, in consideration of the financial situation and with the consent of the Diet to the appropriations therefor (*Tokyo Asahi*, July 25, 1930, p. 2). At the cabinet meeting of July 25, the prime minister informally showed the draft reply to the throne to his colleagues to obtain their approval (*Osaka Mainichi*, July 26, 1930, p. 1). Thus, on July 26, Premier Hamaguchi presented the address to the throne concerning the report of the War Council (*Tokyo Asahi*, July 27, 1930, p. 1). The Hamaguchi address was similar to the address which was presented by Admiral Baron Kato, the then prime minister, on February 28, 1923, after obtaining cabinet approval on February 22 (*Tokyo Asahi*, July 25, 1930, p. 2).

[111] *Tokyo Asahi*, July 24, 1930, p. 2.

[112] *Osaka Mainichi*, July 25, 1930, p. 1. This cabinet decision of July 23 to petition the emperor to refer the treaty to the Privy Council, prior to the transmission of the report of the Supreme War Council to the prime minister, was held in certain quarters of the Privy Council as violating Article VII of the ordinance concerning the organization of the cabinet (*Osaka Mainichi*, July 27, 1930, p. 1).

to the legal nature of the report of the War Council. Commenting upon the binding effect of the report, Prime Minister Hamaguchi declared, in his press interview of July 20, 1930, that the action of the Council would have no legally binding effect whatsoever in taking measures to submit the treaty to the Privy Council, and that only from considerations of practical politics and expediency the government was delaying the next step until after the formal action of the War Council.[113] The prime minister's position was given a cabinet approval on July 22, when it decided that the government should not be bound by the action of the War Council, holding that it was merely a political, and not a legal, preparation for the submission of the treaty to the Privy Council.[114] The cabinet's stand on the legal effect of the action of the War Council was generally supported by the press and the informed public.

Probably one of the most eloquent and influential exponents of the cabinet stand in this regard was the *Asahi*, a leading liberal daily in Tokyo. Ever since the triumphant entry of the returning envoy, Hon. Reijiro Wakatsuki, into Tokyo on June 18,[115] it urged upon the government to take immediate measures for submission of the treaty to the Privy Council, arguing that this body was to rely upon the responsible assurance of the government in examining the document. It declared that if the Privy Council's recommendation to the throne had to be based on the national defense program of the naval authorities rather than on the assurances of the government, it would be tantamount to

[113] *Tokyo Asahi*, July 21, 1930, p. 2.

[114] *Ibid.*, July 23, 1930, p. 1.

[115] Commenting upon the spontaneous welcome extended to Japan's principal delegate to London upon his return to Tokyo, the *Tokyo Asahi* remarked that it was an expression of the great satisfaction felt by the masses for the success of the Conference, for the political solution of the armament problem. It urged the government to take immediate steps to refer the document to the Privy Council, and insisted that the memorandum between the chief of naval staff and the navy minister should not in any way modify the basic principles of the constitutional government according to which the ministers of state alone are held responsible for all matters relating to the state (editorials in *Tokyo Asahi*, June 19, 21, 1930, p. 3). On June 19 an extraordinary meeting of the cabinet was held to welcome Mr. Wakatsuki, who made a detailed report on the Conference. The following day both Mr. Wakatsuki and Admiral Takarabe were received in audience by the emperor to make a detailed report to the throne on the London Conference (*ibid.*, June 20, 21, 1930, p. 1).

placing in the hands of the Admiralty the entire responsibility for national defense and the conduct of foreign relations. It even advocated a complete change in the personnel of high naval officials to bring about its submission to the policy of the government in naval program. It declared:

Inasmuch as the determination of naval strength as well as the conclusion of treaties is within the prerogative of the throne to be exercised only upon the responsible advice of the cabinet, there could be no doubt but that it would be within the exclusive competence of the cabinet to advise the emperor on the ratification of the treaty, taking fully into consideration the recommendations of the Supreme War Council and the Privy Council, that the Privy Council is not to be bound by the recommendation of the War Council, nor is it competent to decide upon the adoption or rejection of the same.[116]

The treaty was formally referred to the Privy Council on July 24, 1930,[117] and the secretariat immediately started its preliminary investigation.[118]

The preliminary investigation of the treaty having nearly been completed, Baron Kuratomi, president of the Privy Council, called on Prime Minister Hamaguchi at 7:40 P. M., August 4, to request the transmission to the Council of the report of the Supreme War Council as a very important document for the examination of the treaty, Hamaguchi reserved his reply till after consultation with his cabinet.[119]

[116]*Tokyo Asahi*, July 4, 1930. *Cf. Osaka Asahi*, July 16, 18, 1930, p. 2.

[117]On July 24, Prime Minister Hamaguchi called on President Kuratomi of the Privy Council and requested speedy action on the treaty (*Tokyo Asahi*, July 25, 1930, p. 2). Commenting on the submission of the treaty to the Privy Council, the *Tokyo Asahi* declared that, if the action of the Council should prove to be contrary to the views of the cabinet, the latter should petition the rejection of the Privy Council recommendation, and that the approbation of the cabinet action be referred to the Diet and general election, in conformity with the fundamental principles of constitutional government (*ibid.*, July 27, 1930, p. 3).

[118]At the first meeting of the secretariat staff for preliminary investigation of the treaty held on July 26, the secretary general as well as three secretaries on the side of the Council, Mr. Matsunaga, chief of the treaty bureau, Mr. Hotta, chief of the European and American bureaus, Mr. Saito, chief of the intelligence bureau of the Foreign Office, and Captains Shimomura and Iwamura were present (*ibid.*, July 27, 1930, p. 1).

[119]*Ibid.*, Aug. 5, 1930, p. 2. Touching on this point, the *Kokumin Shimbun* said: "In demanding the production of the copy of the War Council's report to the throne, they [privy councilors] showed themselves more concerned about embarrassing the Government than about acquainting themselves with information necessary for the performance of their work" (cited in *Japan Advertiser*, Sept. 10, 1930, p. 5).

At a cabinet meeting of August 5 the premier made a brief report on his interview with Baron Kuratomi and requested a special conference of Railways Minister Yoku Egi, Foreign Minister Shidehara, Navy Minister Takarabe, and Acting War Minister Abo to confer upon the attitude of the government toward the Privy Council.[120] It was decided that, since the report in question related to the imperial prerogative over supreme command, it would be impossible to comply with the request. This position of the cabinet was strongly supported even by certain influential members of the Privy Council. On August 6, the prime minister called on President Kuratomi to inform him of the government's decision and said that, though he was permitted to see it by special imperial grace, the cabinet did not keep a copy of the report. Hamaguchi suggested at this interview that, should Baron Kuratomi desire to see it, the only course open was to petition the emperor for permission to do so, but, he added, even if such a petition could be complied with, Baron Kuratomi would be unable to disclose the contents to other members of the Council or make a copy of the same.[121]

After the interview, the prime minister sent his messengers to the genro and others close to the Court to convey the attitude of the government.[122] After consultation with Dr. Kiichiro Hiranuma, vice-president of the Council, Baron Kuratomi, on August 7, again made an unsuccessful demand for the production of the report in writing or a copy thereof because of its vital importance in determining the Council's

[120]*Tokyo Asahi*, Aug. 6, 1930, p. 1. In the evening of Aug. 5, Viscount Watanabe, minister of justice, called on the prime minister to advise the latter against complying with the demand of Baron Kuratomi on the ground that the request was clearly beyond the legitimate exercise of the powers of the Privy Council, particularly in view of the fact that a special sub-committee had not yet been appointed to examine the treaty (*ibid.*, Aug. 6, 1930, p. 2).

[121]Some members of the Privy Council were reported to have greatly resented what they considered an unwarranted action on the part of their president. The flat rejection of the request by the government, in their opinion, made the action all the more reprehensible, as it seriously impaired the dignity of the Council (*ibid.*, Aug. 7, 1930, p. 2).

[122]This action on the part of the government was based ostensibly on the legal ground that it was without jurisdiction over the document, but in fact it was a retaliatory measure against the Council's seemingly deliberate delay in the progress of investigation of the treaty, having refused to appoint a sub-committee for more than two weeks after receiving the document.

action on the treaty.[123] Thus, after several unpleasant preliminary negotiations with the government, Baron Kuratomi, on August 11, finally appointed a sub-committee to
make special examination of the London Naval Treaty.[124]

THE SUB-COMMITTEE OF INQUIRY ON THE TREATY

This important sub-committee was composed of nine
members, headed by Count Miyoji Ito, the uncrowned
leader of the Privy Council.[125] Moreover, the announcement
of the personnel of the committee was a great disappointment
to the cabinet, as it failed to include Viscount Ishii, the sole
diplomat in the Council, while the majority of the members
were reported to be adversely inclined to the procedure taken
by the government and strongly "sympathetic" towards the
Seiyukai (opposition) party.[126] In view of the distinctly unfriendly personnel of the sub-committee,[127] it was generally
expected that the cabinet would encounter some of the most
stormy sessions at the hands of this committee.[128] Under the

[123]Tokyo Asahi, Aug. 8, 1930, p. 2. From the very beginning, the government was
firmly determined to present an uncompromising front in its dealings with the
Council, being conscious of the united support of the overwhelming portion of the
public as well as high personages close to the Court (Tokyo Asahi, July 29, 1930, p. 2).

[124]Commenting upon the Council's demand for the report of the Supreme War
Council, the Osaka Mainichi declared that it was intended primarily to embarrass
the government, and the latter's stern rejection was due largely to the possible unfavorable effect it might have upon the navy minister or the cabinet (Osaka Mainichi, Aug. 9, 1930, p. 2).

[125]Both Count Ito and Viscount Kaneko, two of the surviving original drafters
of the Constitution, played very important rôles, particularly on constitutional issues raised. For brief biographical comment upon each member of the committee,
see Osaka Asahi, Aug. 13, 1930, p. 1.

[126]Regarding the appointment of the sub-committee, Tokyo Asahi expressed
confidence in the ultimate ratification of the treaty, and declared that, if the deliberations of the committee should bring out the necessity for reform of the Privy Council, the public opinion was ready to support the government. It urged upon the
government to make clear the principle that the determination of the naval strength
was within the scope of Article LV of the Constitution, thus setting at naught any
attempt to raise issues concerning the supreme command, final instructions, and
the binding effect of the report of the Supreme War Council (Tokyo Asahi, Aug. 12,
1930, p. 3).

[127]The importance and significance of the personnel of the sub-committee may be
well appreciated when we are reminded that in practice the recommendation of a
sub-committee has never been rejected in plenary session of the Council.

[128]In committee hearings, the following issues were generally thought to evoke
heated discussions: (1) the report of the Supreme War Council on the naval strength
under the pact; (2) constitutional question involving the power of supreme com-

circumstances, Count Makino, Lord Privy Seal, called on Prince Saionji, the genro, on August 13, to consult with the elder statesman as to the attitude to be taken by him in case of an anticipated deadlock between the committee and the government.[129] The leading press of the nation united in demanding a speedy action by the committee.[130]

On August 18 the first session of the committee was held at the secretariat when the members of the sub-committee deliberated upon procedure.[131] The second session of the committee was held on August 23, when Prime Minister Hamaguchi, Foreign Minister Shidehara, and Navy Minister Takarabe spoke on the treaty.[132] Speaking of the final instructions of April 1, 1930, Prime Minister Hamaguchi asserted, on this most delicate issue of the entire proceedings, that an agreement had been reached between the government and the chief of naval staff before the final instructions were telegraphed to London. No questions were asked of the government at this session.[133] At the third session, held on August 26, Viscount Kaneko led the interpellations from the floor. At this meeting Admiral Takarabe admitted that he was not satisfied with the Reed-Matsudaira compromise, but that he consented to it in the interest of the unity of the delegates. Prime Minister Hamaguchi, on the other hand, declared that the government was prepared to assume the full responsibility for the treaty signed by plenipotentiaries of the government's own selection and concluded within the

mand of the navy; and (3) adequacy of national defense under the treaty. *Cf. Tokyo Asahi*, Aug. 11, 1930, p. 2.

[129]The interview lasted more than two hours. Although the nature of the interview between these two personages closest to the Court was not divulged, it was reported that both Prince Saionji and Count Makino were favorably disposed to the ratification of the treaty (*ibid.*, Aug. 14, 1930, p. 1). It is to be remembered that Prince Saionji had been constantly kept informed of the government's attitude in this matter (*ibid.*, July 6, 1930, p. 1; July 14, 1930, p. 2).

[130]Editorial in *Osaka Mainichi*, Aug. 15, 1930, p. 2.

[131]*Tokyo Asahi*, Aug. 19, 1930, p. 2. President and vice-president of the Council as well as all the members of the sub-committee were present, while no government delegates were in attendance.

[132]Throughout the entire committee hearings only the prime minister, foreign minister, and the navy minister were invited to explain the actions of the government.

[133]In a press interview after the committee meeting of Aug. 23, the prime minister declared that the government would not modify the stand it took in the Fifty-eighth Diet and denied vigorously that it changed its views on the supreme command in the committee (*Osaka Asahi*, Aug. 25, 1930, p. 1).

scope of its instructions.[134] The diplomatic negotiations leading up to the dispatch for instructions upon the Reed-
Matsudaira compromise plan were placed under searching
scrutiny at the fourth meeting of the committee.[135]

The delicate issues in connection with the instructions of
April 1, 1930, were made subject of most searching examination at the fifth session of the committee on September 1,
when General Kawai, former chief of general staff, led the
attack upon the Hamaguchi government. In his stinging
questions of censure General Kawai cited, in support of his
attack, telegrams alleged to have been exchanged between
the chief of naval general staff, Admiral Kato, and Admiral
Takarabe in London, the famous statement issued from the
staff at the time, as well as the resignation of Admiral Kato,
in alleged protest against the government's disregard of the
views of the Admiralty. In reply, both the prime minister
and the navy minister argued that a passive consent of the
naval general staff was obtained at the time. On the specific
charge for usurpation of constitutional powers, Prime Minister Hamaguchi vigorously defended the government's action contending that the power over treaties belonged to the
prerogative of the throne under Article XIII of the Constitution to be exercised upon the responsible advice of the
cabinet, and consequently, it was proper for the government
—including the navy and war ministers—to make the final
decision as to the naval strength which constituted the subject matter of the treaty.[136] At the sixth session of the com-

[134]Osaka Mainichi, Aug. 28, 1930, p. 3.

[135]Tokyo Asahi, Aug. 29, 1930, p. 2. Towards the closing days of August, various
associations and organizations interested in the fate of the treaty began to bring
pressure to bear upon the sub-committee by resolutions, representations, and other
means. The Gunshuku Kiseikai, or association for the realization of armament
reduction, probably the most influential single organized force for the success of
the treaty and composed of 126 such liberal leaders as Representatives Ichiro
Kiyose, Kanichi Otake, Dr. Sakuzo Yoshino and others, issued a declaration on
Aug. 28 strongly advocating a speedy ratification of the treaty. On the same day
(Aug. 28) at the Peers' Club in Tokyo, a joint fellowship meeting of interested members of the House of Peers, Yoyokai (navy), and Kaikokai (army) was held when
many admirals, generals, and "big navy" enthusiasts of the House of Peers discussed ways and means for defeating the treaty (ibid., Aug. 29, 1930, p. 2).

[136]Jiji Shimpo, Sept. 2, 1930, p. 2. Prime Minister Hamaguchi refused to state the
official interpretation of Articles XI and XII, but admitted that Article XII might,
under certain circumstances, receive the effect of Article XI, although not binding
(Tokyo Asahi, Sept. 2, 1930, p. 2).

mittee the interpellations on whether there was an agreement of views between the government and the chief of naval staff continued, when Prime Minister Hamaguchi calmly repeated his former assertions,[137] and in consequence the meeting ended in deadlock.[138] Thus, the situation between the committee and the cabinet became extremely delicate through the latter's insistence upon the existence of agreement, the committee being without competence to obtain directly the proof of Admiral Kato's opposition to the instructions of April 1, or to know the nature of the direct address to the throne made by him on April 2, 1930.[139]

At the seventh meeting (September 5) no further questions were asked on the instructions. The examination was now shifted to the "three fundamental claims" of the Admiralty and the extent of tax reductions. It was requested of the government to produce a detailed supplementary naval program as well as statistical data for tax reductions, both of which Hamaguchi politely refused on the ground that the ratification of the treaty was prerequisite to drafting a definite replenishment program or determining the exact amount of tax reductions.[140] At the eighth session (September 8), the

[137]Being subjected to searching cross-examination, the prime minister declared that Admiral Kato changed his views, after the Fifty-eighth Diet, though he tacitly consented to the instructions at the time (*ibid.*, Sept. 4, 1930, p. 2). This assertion of Prime Minister Hamaguchi in the committee greatly provoked Admiral Kato, who called on the navy minister on Sept. 8 in protest against the reported statement by the premier and insisted that in his address to the throne he reported his absolute opposition to the instructions (*ibid.*, Sept. 9, 1930, p. 2).

[138]*Ibid.*, Sept. 4, 1930, p. 2. *Jiji Shimpo* expressed disappointment in the government's admission of having reached an agreement with the naval general staff (*Jiji Shimpo*, Sept. 5, 1930, p. 3).

[139]The undiplomatic suggestion on the part of Chairman Ito of the committee to request the presence of Admiral Kato, former chief of staff, to explain this point for himself, was flatly refused by the government on the ground that such an action would be contrary to Article III of *Sumitsuin Kansei* (*Tokyo Asahi*, Sept. 5, 1930, p. 2). Again, the request of the committee for submission of all documents, including telegrams, concerning the internal negotiations between the government and the naval general staff, as well as between Admiral Kato and Admiral Takarabe, met similar refusal (*Jiji Shimpo*, Sept. 5, 1930, p. 2; *Tokyo Asahi*, Sept. 5, 1930, p. 1).

[140]*Tokyo Asahi*, *Jiji Shimpo*, Sept. 6, 1930, p. 2. Commenting upon the very delicate situation created by the refusal of the Hamaguchi government to produce the requested data, the *Tokyo Asahi* warned the *Seiyukai* party against taking advantage of the situation to engage in intrigues with certain members of the committee to bring about the downfall of the cabinet. It called upon all the parties to unite in curbing the powers of the Privy Council (*Tokyo Asahi*, Sept. 6, 1930, p. 3). Under the title, "The Privy Council," *Osaka Mainichi*, another influential daily, declared

government repeated its previous position that it was impossible to show concrete data on the subject in question
prior to the ratification of the treaty.[141] However, when asked
of the "views of the highest naval authorities"[142] on national defense under the treaty, Admiral Takarabe assured
the committee that the naval defense was secure with adequate replenishment program.[143] At the ninth meeting of the
sub-committee (September 10), Premier Hamaguchi again
flatly refused to offer concrete data for tax reductions or a
new naval program. This firm position of the government
before the committee hearings of the Privy Council and the
deaf ear to the plea for documents and data, without which
the latter contended that it was powerless to decide on the
reasonableness of the treaty and to pass intelligent judgment
upon its provisions, did not fail to aggravate the already
tense atmosphere of the proceedings.[144] Now, at the tenth

that the Council was not an organ to supervise or control the cabinet, that its sole
function was to report to the emperor on matters submitted thereto for advice,
and that the inevitable tendency of the time was to reduce it to a nominal existence
as in England (Osaka Mainichi, Sept. 7, 1930, p. 2).

[141] Tokyo Asahi, Sept. 9, 1930, p. 2.

[142] The "highest naval authorities" refers to the Supreme War Council.

[143] In his reply to a question, Admiral Takarabe, by indirect reference to the report
of the War Council, made its contents known to the committee members. This interpellation was merely for the production of the report itself (Tokyo Asahi, Sept.
8, 1930, p. 2). In view of the increasingly tense situation between the government
and the committee, Dr. Yoku Egi, "brain of the cabinet," called on Prince Saionji,
in the forenoon of Sept. 7, to state the government's determination and to obtain
his "understandings." Although the nature of his visit to the genro was not disclosed, the railways minister was reported to have stated in his interview with the
elder statesman: (1) On the supreme command issue, the government was to insist
upon having obtained a tacit agreement of the chief of naval general staff. (2) Should
the committee elect to embarrass or to discredit the cabinet for ulterior motives,
the government was determined to take a decisive step. (3) Should the Privy Council recommend the rejection of the treaty or attach reservations, the government
was ready to petition the emperor to ratify the treaty as was signed. (4) Should the
committee make another request for the production of the report of the War Council, the cabinet was determined to refuse it on the ground of lack of jurisdiction over
the matter (Jiji Shimpo, Sept. 9, 1930, p. 2).

[144] Tokyo Asahi, Sept. 11, 1930, p. 2; Osaka Mainichi, Sept. 12, 1930, p. 1. After
the meeting, Count Ito, chairman of the committee, called a conference of the
members to decide upon the next measure to be taken by the committee in view of
the stubborn attitude of the government. It decided to make another request at the
following session for production of a new naval program, upon refusal of which the
committee was to recommend suspension of its deliberations till a new naval program be drawn up. The committee decided further that, should the government
insist upon the continuation of the proceedings without presenting the information

meeting (September 12), Admiral Takarabe was forced indirectly to disclose the contents of the War Council's report
to the emperor.[145] And the anticipated deadlock between the
government and the Council, which might have resulted in
the suspension of the deliberations,[146] was avoided only by
the tactful chairmanship of Count Ito, who declared the adjournment of the meetings to September 15.[147]

The final session of the committee hearings was held on
September 15, when Hamaguchi firmly asserted that the
position on the supreme command issue was unchanged
since the Fifty-eighth session of the Diet, that he could not
produce a naval replenishment program nor statistical data
for tax reductions under the treaty. He again refused to
present the report of the War Council on the plea of lack
of jurisdiction. Thus, the cabinet refused to submit all the
documents and data to the committee which the latter considered indispensable for its examination of the treaty. In
these circumstances, the final session of the committee ended
in a complete deadlock between the government and the
sub-committee of inquiry on the treaty.[148]

THE REPORT OF THE SUB-COMMITTEE

In view of the deadlock between the government and the
committee, it was generally expected that the sub-committee

demanded, it was to reach a decision immediately and report the same to the Council in plenary session (*Tokyo Asahi*, Sept. 11, 1930, p. 2). On the other hand, the
cabinet decided to petition the emperor to limit the period of deliberations, and
should the Council recommend unfavorably upon the treaty, it was to petition the
throne against the Council for ratification (*ibid*).

[145] *Tokyo Asahi*, Sept. 13, 1930, p. 2.

[146] At a cabinet meeting of Sept. 12, which was held prior to the committee meeting, Prime Minister Hamaguchi explained to his colleagues the acute situation in
the committee, and the cabinet gave him a free hand in taking appropriate actions
according to circumstances. It was reported that the premier had ordered the chief
of the Bureau of Legislative Affairs to prepare a memorandum concerning the
technical phase of petitioning the throne to limit the period of deliberations in the
Council, and even to petition ratification in case of an adverse decision by the latter
(*Jiji Shimpo*, Sept. 13, 1930, p. 2; *Tokyo Asahi*, Sept. 12, 13, 1930, p. 2).

[147] Tokyo Asahi, Sept. 13, 1930, p. 2.

[148] *Jiji Shimpo*, Sept. 16, 1930, p. 2. The press in general expressed disappointment
in the government's failure to offer all the possible facilities to the committee in its
examination of the treaty. For instance, *Jiji Shimpo* (Sept. 12) and *Chugai Shogyo*
(Sept. 11) approved the committee demand for data and information and condemned the lack of courage and political prudence on the part of the government.
Cf. *Tokyo Asahi*, Sept. 12, 1930, p. 3.

would recommend an indefinite suspension of its deliberations or even rejection of the treaty itself.[149] The *Seiyukai*,
the chief opposition party, now sought to take advantage of
the situation to wrestle the ministry from the *Minseito*
party.[150] The press of the nation, however, vigorously supported the government in its struggle against the committee.[151] The *Gunshuku Kiseikai*, a non-partisan association
supporting the ratification of the London Treaty referred to
elsewhere, at its meeting of September 16 adopted a resolution strongly censuring the attitude of the committee and
declaring that it went beyond the legitimate exercise of its
powers. It supported the cabinet in its stand on documents
and data and demanded the establishment of a political
tradition to submit treaties to the Diet for debate and discussion.[152]

It now devolved upon the government to prepare for the
eventuality of the situation. At the cabinet meeting of September 16 it was decided to maintain its firm stand for the
ratification of the treaty. After the meeting, Dr. Yoku Egi,

[149]Professor Minobe supported the cabinet's stand in this regard, holding that the
function of the Privy Council was to scrutinize the terms of the treaty and to make
its recommendation, that it could not pass judgment upon the policies under the
treaty, it being left to the Diet to do so, that to argue that the committee could not
proceed with its inquiry without information on the naval defense program was to
deny to the government the power to sign a treaty upon its own responsibility. He
further argued that the members of the committee should resign before reporting
their inability to continue deliberations on the pact (*Tokyo Asahi*, Sept. 15, 1930,
p. 3).

[150]At the *Seiyukai* convention held on Sept. 16, President Inukai declared that the
pact was meaningless and charged the Hamaguchi cabinet with usurpation of constitutional powers in connection with the instructions of April 1, 1930 (*Tokyo Asahi*,
Sept. 17, 1930, p. 2).

[151]*Osaka Mainichi* charged that the Privy Council went beyond its legitimate
powers in demanding the report of the Supreme War Council and that the action
was uncalled for (editorial, Sept. 12, 1930, p. 2). *Osaka Asahi* urged upon the government to be more courageous and frank in giving facilities to the committee and
declared that, should the Privy Council report suspension of the proceedings or
rejection of the treaty, the prime minister should petition the throne against such
recommendation, after which he should call an extraordinary session of the Diet for
a vote of confidence (editorials, Sept. 12, 13, 1930, p. 2). *Tokyo Asahi* severely criticized the attitude of the committee and declared that the competence of the Council
extended only to the examination of the formal aspect and not the substance of
the treaty (editorial, Sept. 12, 1930, p. 3). *Jiji Shimpo*, like the *Asahi*, expressed
keen disappointment at the government's lack of courage in its dealings with the
committee and branded the attitude of the committee as "unwarranted and improper" (editorials, Sept. 14, 16, 1930, p. 3).

[152]Text of the resolution in *Jiji Shimpo*, Sept. 17, 1930, p. 2.

under instructions of the premier, called on Prince Saionji
to make a report concerning the situation, to inform him of
the attitude of the cabinet, and also to seek the genro's
"understandings."[153] At the meeting of the sub-committee
on September 17, without government delegates in attendance, it was unanimously decided to recommend unconditional ratification of the treaty.[154]

The unanimous recommendation for the ratification of the
treaty, in spite of the refusal on the part of the cabinet to
present the important documents and data, was a complete
surprise to even the most optimistic observers. It was generally expected that, at best, a rider would be attached to
the committee recommendation censuring the Hamaguchi
government for its action at the time of issuing the instructions of April 1, 1930. Though this sudden surrender of the
committee before the stubborn and determined Hamaguchi
cabinet was a complete surprise to the public, there could be
little doubt as to the general satisfaction with which the
news was received by the press and the informed public,[155]
with the obvious exception of the *Seiyukai* party.[156]

What was the reaction of the more liberal portion of the
populace to this sudden change in the situation? The better
informed public was disappointed in the government's failure
to settle once and for all the "political cancer" of the Japanese cabinet system—the supreme command issue—and con-

[153]*Tokyo Asahi, Jiji Shimpo*, Sept. 17, 1930, p. 2.

[154]*Tokyo Asahi, Jiji Shimpo*, Sept. 18, 1930, p. 2. By this time, certain members
of the Council began to attack the attitude of the sub-committee as being unwarranted and improper, and Count Ito, after consultation with leading members of
the Council, became convinced of the futility of pushing his policy of suspension
to the floor of the plenary session (*Jiji Shimpo*, Sept. 14, 1930, p. 2).

[155]See editorials in *Tokyo Asahi, Jiji Shimpo, Nichi Nichi*, and *Hochi*, Sept. 18,
1930.

[156]*Cf.* a press interview of Representative Inuaki, president of the *Seiyukai* party
(*Tokyo Asahi*, Sept. 18, 1930, p. 1). *Osaka Asahi* condemned the *Seiyukai* party for
playing the rôle of an intriguer with certain members of the sub-committee instead
of fighting for the common cause of establishing constitutional government (editorial, Sept. 14, 1930, p. 2). The *Nichi Nichi* declared that the greatest loser was the
Seiyukai party. "We are sorry for Mr. Inukai, president of the *Seiyukai* party,"
said the editor. ". . . By his dealings with a body which he should have opposed
as his enemy, he threw to the wind a reputation which it has taken him more than
fifty years to establish" (editorial, Sept. 19, cited in *Japan Advertiser*, Sept. 20,
1930, p. 5). *Nichi Nichi* was so disappointed at the speech of Mr. Inukai before his
party that it even expressed doubt as to the genuineness of the speech (editorial,
Sept. 18, 1930).

demned the "hide-and-seek" politics of the *Seiyukai*, the chief opposition party, for not uniting with the *Minseito* ministry in support of the principles of constitutional government in the latter's determined fight against the Privy Council, instead of acting in apparent intrigue with certain influential members of the committee.[157] Though not satisfactory to those who are impatient with the slow progress of constitutional government, this incident set a precedent for the succeeding cabinets to follow in the future.[158]

With the decision of the sub-committee of inquiry, the deliberations of the Council over the treaty proceeded smoothly. On September 23, the report of the committee as well as a draft address to the throne was completed and transmitted to each member of the committee.[159] At the meeting of the committee on September 26, the report, drafted by Chairman Ito in consultation with Secretary General Nikami of the Privy Council, was adopted, unconditionally recommending the ratification of the treaty.[160] Baron Kuratomi, president of the Council, informally showed to the committee a draft address to be presented to the throne immediately after the plenary session of the Council to be held on October 1, 1930.[161] A copy of the report of the committee was transmitted in the afternoon of September 27 to each privy councilor and cabinet minister.[162]

[157]*Cf. Tokyo Asahi*, Sept. 18, 1930, p. 3.

[158]*Hochi* declared: ". . . The special committee's action was undoubtedly a victory to the government. . . . It was at the same time a victory to public opinion and to party government" (cited in *Japan Advertiser*, Sept. 19, 1930, p. 5).

[159]*Tokyo Asahi*, Sept. 24, 1930, p. 2.

[160]In this report, the committee stated, in connection with the instructions of April 1, 1930, that it was satisfied with the prime minister's declaration that there was an agreement of views between the government and the chief of the naval general staff and cited the navy minister's statement that a memorandum was drawn up between the Navy Department and the staff concerning the internal negotiations for the determination of naval strength. It concluded that the committee's recommendation was explicitly based upon its confidence in the good faith of the government to carry into execution the object of the treaty by an adequate replenishment naval program and substantial tax reductions (*Tokyo Asahi*, Sept. 28, 1930, p. 2).

[161]For the reported address resolution to the emperor recommending the ratification of the treaty and placing the entire responsibility upon the cabinet for the execution of the treaty, see *Osaka Asahi*, Sept. 26, 1930, p. 1.

[162]Commenting upon the report of the sub-committee, *Tokyo Asahi* expressed keen disappointment that the government gave the committee to understand that the consent of the naval staff was necessary to any decision relating to naval strength, instead of repeating its statements in the Diet (editorial, Sept. 28, 1930, p. 3).

On October 1, the Privy Council, at its plenary session with the emperor in attendance, approved unanimously the sub-committee recommendation for ratification of the treaty without any reservation or declaration.[163] Immediately following the adjournment of the session, President Kuratomi of the Council was received in audience by the emperor to submit the address recommending the ratification of the treaty. Prime Minister Hamaguchi was immediately advised of this by Baron Kuratomi.

RATIFICATION OF THE TREATY

At ten o'clock in the morning of October 2 an extraordinary meeting of the cabinet was called to draw up a petition to the emperor to ratify the treaty. At 1:45 P.M. Premier Hamaguchi was received in audience by the emperor to petition ratification, and at 2:35 P.M. he was notified by the Court of His Majesty's compliance therewith. Thus, with His Majesty's signature, the document was immediately transmitted to the cabinet.[164] With the countersignature of Foreign Minister Shidehara, the cabinet took immediate steps to transmit it to London through the Foreign Office in Tokyo. At four o'clock in the afternoon, the prime minister, foreign minister, and the navy minister each issued a statement in which they lauded the success of the treaty in the interest of world peace and reduction of taxation and pledged the best efforts on the part of the government to the execution of the treaty in letter and in spirit.

With the imperial signature to the document, Japanese ratification of the London Naval Treaty was completed[165]

[163]*Tokyo Asahi*, Oct. 2, 1930, p. 1. At the plenary session of the Council, Viscount Ishii mildly censured the president in connection with his demand for the report of the Supreme War Council. The *Gunshuku Kiseikai*, at its meeting on Oct. 2, passed a resolution demanding Baron Kuratomi's resignation (*ibid.*, Oct. 3, 1930, p. 2.)

[164]*Ibid.*, Oct. 3, 1930, p. 2.

[165]Less than twenty-four hours after the ratification of the treaty by the emperor, Admiral Takarabe, minister of navy and a plenipotentiary to the conference, tendered his resignation and was succeeded by Admiral Baron Abo, member of the Supreme War Council and a technical adviser to the delegation. Admiral Abo's appointment was regarded as a concession to the "adequate navy" group, as he unsuccessfully sought to defeat the Reed-Matsudaira compromise. The resignation of Admiral Takarabe did not create any surprise, it being generally expected after the delicate rôle he played both at the conference and after his return to Tokyo.

after what was probably the most vigorously contested battle ever fought between the cabinet and the Privy Council in the constitutional history of Japan. The incident recorded a distinct step towards the establishment of a sounder system of cabinet government in the Island Empire.[166]

Though several questions were put to the government in both Houses during the Fifty-ninth session of the Diet, the ministry, under the leadership of Baron Shidehara (acting premier), maintained the same policy of refusing to disclose the nature of instructions, internal negotiations within the Admiralty and the cabinet, and the proceedings of the Privy Council. One incident, however, deserves our special attention. Baron Shidehara's declaration, in the House Budget Committee on February 3, 1931, that the fact that the treaty had received the imperial ratification was convincing evidence that the national defense was secure under the London Treaty, resulted in practical suspension of parliamentary proceedings until he retracted the statement on February 12, 1931. The statement was seized by the opposition members as shielding a grave diplomatic blunder by dragging the throne into politics.[167]

[166]This unprecedented victory for the principle of responsible cabinet government was attributable, in the main, to: (1) the moral encouragement of the known attitude of Prince Saionji, the genro, Count Makino, Lord Privy Seal, and others close to the Court; (2) the popular support given by the press and the informed public; (3) Prime Minister Hamaguchi's firm determination, backed by the absolute majority in the Lower House, to vindicate the basic principles of responsible government.

[167]*Tokyo Asahi*, Feb. 13, 1931, p. 1. *Cf. Kwampo gogai*, Feb. 8, 1931, p. 131.

Chapter XXVI

THE MANCHURIAN CRISIS

The Background of the Mukden Incident

THAT THE OUTBREAK of the Manchurian crisis on September 18, 1931, was not an isolated incident, but that it was merely the culminating incident of a long series of events which finally set fire to the tinder box of Far Eastern politics is generally agreed.[1] Before undertaking to analyze the procedure followed in the Sino-Japanese dispute following the Mukden incident, therefore, we shall first examine briefly some of the more important forces and factors which precipitated the crisis in the fall of 1931.

An adequate understanding of the problem requires a two-fold analysis: an examination of the politico-economic situation in Manchuria preceding the crisis, and an analysis of the economic and social forces which dominated the Japanese body politic at the time, rendering a more peaceful settlement of the various questions then outstanding between Japan and China impossible.

Important as it is to have in mind all the intricate political, economic, and legal issues arising over Manchuria, which were left unsolved between Japan and China during the past thirty-odd years, it is not our purpose to narrate in detail the conflict over these issues. Suffice it here to emphasize the importance of grasping fully the psycho-historical significance of Japan's claim to a "special position" in Man-

[1] *League of Nations, Appeal by the Chinese Government, Report of the Commission of Enquiry* (Lytton Commission), Geneva, 1932, pp. 37–66 (hereafter cited as *Lytton Report*); Masamichi Royama, *Nichiman Kankei no Kenkyu* (Tokyo, 1933), pp. 1–58, 235–254; Kin Ashida, *Saikin Sekai Gaikoshi* (Tokyo, 1934), III, 1019–1031, 1075–1104.

337

churia, without which our inquiry would be devoid of reality and practical importance. Recognizing the exceptional character of Japanese rights and interests in Manchuria, a parallel to which can seldom be found in the world's history,[2] the Lytton Commission summarizes this Japanese claim in the following words:

Patriotic sentiment, the paramount need for military defence, and the exceptional treaty rights all combine to create the claim to a "special position" in Manchuria. The Japanese conception of this "special position" is not limited to what is legally defined in treaties and agreements either with China or with other States. Feelings and historical association, which are the heritage of the Russo-Japanese War, and pride in the achievements of Japanese enterprise in Manchuria for the last quarter-century, are an indefinable but real part of the Japanese claim to a "special position." It is only natural, therefore, that the Japanese use of this expression in diplomatic language should be obscure, and that other States should have found it difficult, if not impossible, to recognize it by international instruments.[3]

That the conception of a "special position" thus defined is quite contrary to what may generally be understood by the expression by Anglo-Saxon minds is perfectly clear.[4] It is equally obvious, however, that, unless one appreciates fully the psychological significance of the sentiment and feelings with which the Japanese respond to this expression, it will be impossible to understand the dynamic character of subsequent events in Manchuria and Shanghai. As was well expressed by Viscount Ishii in his recent *Memoirs*, the Japanese have always believed that their special interests in China were neither created by an international agreement, nor could they become objects of abolition, but they were based upon solid foundations of history and geography.[5] Thus it had become a national conviction that their rights and in-

[2]Thus the Commission says: "There is probably nowhere in the world an exact parallel to this situation, no example of a country enjoying in the territory of a neighbouring State such extensive economic and administrative privileges" (*Lytton Report*, p. 38).

[3]*Ibid.*, p. 39.

[4]See especially C. Walter Young's *International Relations of Manchuria* (Chicago, 1929), and also his three volumes on *Japan's Jurisdiction and International Legal Position in Manchuria* (Baltimore, 1931).

[5]*Gaiko Yoroku*, pp. 161–163.

terests in Manchuria were not a mere accumulation of those
derived from treaties and agreements, chiefly economic in
substance and in no way different from those of other powers
in character, but something far more than that.[6]

They had gradually come to regard Manchuria and Eastern
Inner Mongolia as distinct from the rest of China, and to consider the maintenance of peace and order in this region to be
peculiarly within the exclusive domain of their responsibility
and, naturally, resented any "interference" in Manchurian
affairs by "outside powers" as being an encroachment upon
their claim to a "special position" in this region. In their
insistence upon a "paramount interest" in Manchuria, the
government has always been consistent irrespective of parties
and factions in power.[7]

The gradual modernization of China, with its "rights recovery" program, its railway policy in Manchuria, its rising
tide of nationalism, its unification movement, and other factors operating in China, along with the effects of a world-
wide depression, appeared to be threatening to reduce to
naught all the vested interests of Japan in Manchuria, if
left unchecked for any length of time, and gave rise to a new
but undefinable conception of a "life line" by the end of
1930.[8] While events in Manchuria were thus moving fast

[6]We may again quote the Lytton Commission on this point: "Japanese interests
in Manchuria differ both in character and degree from those of any other foreign
country. Deep in the mind of every Japanese is the memory of their country's great
struggle with Russia in 1904–05, fought on the plains of Manchuria, at Mukden
and Liaoyang, along the line of the South Manchuria Railway, at the Yalu River,
and in the Liaotung Peninsula. To the Japanese the war with Russia will ever be
remembered as a life-and-death struggle fought in self-defence against the menace
of Russian encroachments. The facts that a hundred thousand Japanese soldiers
died in this war and that two billion gold yen were expended have created in Japanese minds a determination that these sacrifices shall not have been made in vain"
(*Lytton Report*, p. 39).

[7]*Ibid.*, pp. 38–42 *ff*. Thus the difference between the so-called "friendship policy"
of Baron Shidehara and the *Minseito* party (representing, in the main, the industrial
and trading interests) and the so-called "positive policy" of the late General Baron
Tanaka and the *Seiyukai* party (representing, among others, the agricultural and
colonial interests) existed only in regard to specific methods to be employed to
maintain and foster this common aim. The general policies of these two factions
were brought out in striking contrast during the Fifty-sixth Diet, when Baron
Shidehara put a long interpellation to General Tanaka on his China policy (*Kwampo
gogai*, Feb. 3, 1929, pp. 87–93; *ibid.*, Feb. 6, 1929, pp. 95–98).

[8]Ashida, *op. cit.*, III, 1057–1068. According to Professor Royama, the popular
notion regarding Manchuria consists of three elements: (1) Manchuria as a first
line of defense, following the Sino-Japanese War, the three-power intervention, and

towards a Sino-Japanese clash, certain internal economic and political factors were also operating to accelerate this movement. We may now turn to an analysis of these forces.

The economic aspects will receive our first attention. The panic of 1920, the earthquake of 1923, and the banking crisis of 1927,[9] all profoundly affected the entire fabric of industrial, commercial, and agricultural interests of the country, resulting in a rapid fall in commodity prices, wage levels, and trade returns, and a corresponding increase in unemployment, social insecurity, and general unrest. Moreover, the world-wide depression which swept the entire world in the fall of 1929 did not leave the Far East unaffected. The condition of farm districts, which had been hardest hit by the waves of depression, became even worse after the famine which visited the northern part of Japan the following autumn. The situation was further aggravated by the fact that the prices of agricultural products continued to decline, while no effective relief measures could be expected from the *Minseito* administration. This situation naturally intensified social unrest, particularly in the farm districts. Thus the farmers began to regard the famine and the general economic situation, not as a natural phenomenon, but as the result of social maladjustment, and to entertain serious doubts as to the efficacy of the existing economic and social system for meliorating the critical situation. They could not believe any improvement could be effected through industrial rationalization or reform of the banking system; they were now convinced that a more fundamental reorganization of the entire economic and social order must be made to meet the exigencies of the time.

Their line of thought naturally ran in the direction of a more effective control of all economic activities at home, and a more vigorous policy on the continent. Being imbedded so deeply in the life and traditions of the land, we can easily see that, to these famine-stricken farmers and nationalistic youths, Manchuria seemed to offer an immediate and in-

the Russo-Japanese War; (2) after the industrial revolution in Japan following the Russo-Japanese War, Manchuria loomed large as a possible field for continental expansion; (3) these strategic and economic elements were gradually incorporated into a new conception of a "life line," an assertion that Manchuria and Mongolia are organically bound up with Japan and defense and existence (*op. cit.*, pp. 188–193).

[9]The Wakatsuki (*Minseito*) cabinet fell in April, 1927, following the banking crisis, and was succeeded by General Tanaka's *Seiyukai* administration. The "positive policy" of Baron Tanaka held the stage until July, 1929, when it had to be replaced by a more conciliatory administration under Hamaguchi and Shidehara.

viting solution of their problem. The psychology of the time can be appreciated better when we remember that the majority of men in the army and the navy have always come from country districts, that they sacrificed most in the two wars fought on the plains of Manchuria, and consequently that, upon the least suggestion or provocation, they could be made to support any policy which might strengthen their ties with this fair land.[10]

Nor were the feelings of insecurity and restlessness confined to rural districts. Certain recent developments in Manchuria, particularly the railway politics, were creating alarm and sensation among industrial and commercial circles as well. The "draining-off policy" on the part of China through construction of parallel or competing railway lines in Manchuria was obviously aimed at reducing to naught the whole of Japanese interests on the continent. Moreover, the visit of young Marshal Chang Hsueh-liang with General Chiang Kai-shek in Nanking during November–December, 1930, created a considerable sensation not only among Japanese residents along the South Manchuria Railway but even among that portion of the populace in Japan who had shown but little concern in Manchurian developments. Thus, towards the close of the year, the press in Tokyo united in their demand for an early settlement of these railway issues. Surprised at this spontaneous press activity, the Nanking government instructed its minister about the middle of December to sound the views of Tokyo. Upon visiting the Foreign Office, however, the minister found Baron Shidehara to be extremely conciliatory, and was satisfied that Tokyo was not contemplating any "drastic measures" in connection with Manchuria.[11] The negotiations which began at Mukden the latter part of January between Director Kimura of the South Manchuria Railway Company and Marshal Chang Hsueh-liang did not make any headway. Nor was Baron Shidehara successful in bringing about a liquidation of debts.

[10]*Cf.* Ashida, *op. cit.*, III, 1087–91. For an interesting discussion on the agricultural phase of this situation, see Kiyozawa, "Social Factors in the May 15th Incident," *Kaizo*, Nov., 1933, pp. 262–71.

[11]The ever present political struggles between the *Seiyukai* and *Minseito* parties, particularly over the phraseology, "in the names of their respective peoples," in the Pact of Paris, and also over the death of Marshal Chang Tso-lin, apparently gave to the minister the impression that the condition of internal politics was such that no unanimity could be expected in support of a vigorous continental policy (see *supra*, Chaps. XXIII, XXIV).

These failures in his efforts to bring about peace with China, in turn, gave his opponents additional weapons against the Hamaguchi policy of conciliation (see note on page 490), and intensified the rapidly growing popular dissatisfaction with the so-called "negative policy" of Baron Shidehara.[12]

As the developments in Manchuria became more critical,[13] Count Uchida was appointed to head the South Manchuria Railway Company,[14] while, almost simultaneously, Admiral Saito was replaced by General Ugaki as Governor General of Chosen.[15] These two important appointments made in the early summer were generally taken to signify the importance which the government was now attaching to the Manchurian developments, and also to indicate that the actual center of authority for directing the continental policy was shifting from Tokyo to Manchuria.[16]

At this juncture, therefore, we must take up the bearings of the proposed reduction of land armaments upon the situation. We have already seen in our study of the London Naval

---

[12]Ashida, *op. cit.*, III, 1081–87. *Cf.* Sakuro Nagao, "The South Manchuria Railway Question," *Keizai Orai*, March 31, 1931, pp. 51–66; also his "Basic Issues in the South Manchuria Railway Controversy," *Gaiko Jiho*, No. 632 (April, 1931), pp. 54–63; Shimizu, "Railway Problems in South Manchuria," *Kokusaiho Gaiko Zasshi*, Vol. XXX, No. 7 (Sept., 1931), pp. 646–63; Masukichi Hashimoto, "Observations on the Manchurian Question," *Gaiko Jiho*, No. 632, pp. 54–63; also Jumpei Shinobu, "Special Position in Manchuria and the Right of Self-defence," *ibid.*, May 1, 1931, pp. 1–13.

[13]Rep. Seigo Nakano, "Reconsideration of the Sino-Japanese Relations," *Gaiko Jiho*, No. 638 (July 1, 1931), pp. 1–23; Dr. Nagao, "Railway Diplomacy in Manchuria," *ibid.*, No. 639 (July 15, 1931), pp. 28 ff.; also a series of articles on "Foundations of Our Manchurian Policy" by Dr. Ryoei Saito in *Osaka Asahi*, July 7–10, 1931, p. 1.

[14]June 13, 1931. *Cf.* an editorial, "New President of the South Manchuria Railway Company," *Gaiko Jiho*, No. 638 (July 1, 1931), pp. i–x.

[15]June 17, 1931 (*Osaka Asahi*, June 18, 1931, p. 1). *Cf.* Dr. Rentaro Mizuno, "China Policy and the Administration of Chosen," *Gaiko Jiho*, No. 640 (Aug. 1, 1931), pp. 1–8; also Count Soyeshima, "General Ugaki and the Administration of Chosen," *ibid.*, pp. 33–48.

[16]*Osaka Asahi*, June 20, 1931, p. 1. See Yoshio Nakabayashi, "A New Policy towards Manchuria," *Chuo Koron*, July, 1931, pp. 45–54; also B. Takeuchi, "New Developments in Manchuria," *Kaizo*, Aug., 1931, pp. 162–71 (English translation in *Japan Advertiser*, July 24, 1931, p. 4). On June 30, General Minami, the war minister, invited the newly appointed president and vice-president of the South Manchuria Railway Company, as well as six leading directors of the company, for luncheon, to exchange views regarding the Manchurian situation. At this conference, General Kanaya, chief of staff, General Ninomiya, vice-chief of staff, as well as other high officials of both the War Department and the General Staff Office were present (*Osaka Asahi*, July 1, 1931, p. 1).

Treaty that the Hamaguchi (*Minseito*) cabinet was able to steer that treaty to a successful conclusion only after encountering a most vigorous opposition from the Admiralty, and was able to obtain its ratification only with the general support of the public.[17] Throughout the controversy over the treaty, the army maintained an outward indifference, but this by no means indicated that it remained an impassive spectator. On the contrary, we have every reason to believe that this impasse between the cabinet and the Admiralty convinced the military circles that they were soon to face a similar ordeal and that they must be ready to resist any and all "amateur interference" in matters of land armaments.[18] However, as the depression continued to darken the financial outlook of the country, and the sufferings of the people became more acute and widespread, the question of reducing land armaments to relieve the situation became widely discussed.[19] The popular enthusiasm thus aroused was further heightened by the approaching arms conference to be held the following February at Geneva under the auspices of the League of Nations.

Meanwhile, the military authorities made it known that no reduction in armament expenditure could be expected at this time and that any funds which might be obtained by reorganization of the army must be spent in modernization of equipments, or in otherwise increasing the efficiency of the army.[20] This decision on the part of the military authorities

[17]*Supra*, Chap. XXV.

[18]*Cf.* Professor Tadao Yanaihara, *Manshu Mondai*, or the Manchurian Question (Tokyo, 1934), pp. 10–11.

[19]See especially Dr. Ichiro Kiyosé's articles on "Readjustment of Military Expenditures" in *Osaka Asahi*, May 31, June 1, 2, 1931. Here, Representative Kiyosé denounces the suggestion that national defense should be left to military men alone, and declares that questions of national defense are really political, and that it is the business of the military department of government to draw up the most efficient plan for organization, equipment, operation, and tactics in accordance with a politically determined policy for national defense and within budgets provided for. He advocates the establishment of a commission of inquiry, composed of statesmen as well as experts, with adequate authority to look into every aspect of land and sea defense.

[20]In August, 1929, an army reorganization committee was organized under the chairmanship of General Ugaki, the then war minister. Finally, on May 1, 1931, the "Big Three" of the army—War Minister Minami, Chief of Staff Kanaya, and Inspector General of Military Education Muto—held a conference to arrive at a conclusion of twenty-nine months' work. After several conferences they reached the conclusion that no reduction in armament expenditure was possible and that any amount that might be obtained by readjustments should be used to strengthen other

was disappointing to the public, particularly to the liberal elements, who entertained some hope that the army leaders would be willing to make some contribution to improve the financial condition of the nation.[21] The army's opposition to the proposed revision of pension laws, in addition to its stand on armament question, only fanned the flame of popular disfavor.[22] This, in turn, greatly incensed the military circles, particularly the young officers, who were losing their patience with what they believed to be an unjustifiable encroachment upon their domain of service by "irresponsible third parties," and who were becoming increasingly sensitive to protect the integrity of the army and to combat the rising tide of "disarmament mania."

The war minister, General Minami, took the occasion of the conference of division commanders in early August to make public this growing dissatisfaction of the army. Thus, before the conference of commanders of divisions and fortified zones, held in Tokyo on August 4, 1931, the war minister referred, in vigorous terms, to the recent developments in Manchuria and Mongolia, and broadly denounced the Shidehara policy towards the continent. Pointing out the vital importance of Manchuria and Mongolia to the life and destiny of Japan, politically, economically, and from the standpoint of national defense, General Minami appealed to every soldier in the army to show a stronger sense of loyalty and public service. Moreover, touching on the question of army reorganization, he declared that, notwithstanding the fact that the plan which the authorities had drawn up

aspects of the service, by improving equipments, etc. This decision received the approval of the Supreme War Council on July 1 (*ibid.*, May 2, 3, 4, June 25, 27, July 1, 2, 1931, p. 1).

[21]See editorials in *ibid.*, May 6, June 30, 1931, p. 2. *Cf.* also *Tokyo Asahi, Kokumin*, and *Jiji Shimpo*, as quoted in *Japan Advertiser*, July 5, July 9, 1931, p. 5.

[22]The *Osaka Asahi*, a leading liberal daily, strongly criticized the army for objecting to any modification of pension laws as in military affairs. The same paper pointed out that 53 per cent of those on the pension list had served in the army (editorials in *Osaka Asahi*, Aug. 1, 8, 1931, p. 2). The *Kaizo*, another leading liberal journal, declared that the fundamental difficulty lies in the present system, under which only a general can be the minister of war, and that the views of the army as a whole must be arrived at in joint conferences of the war minister, chief of staff, and inspector general of military education. It advocated the reduction of three or four divisions at this time to improve the finances of the nation (leading article in *Kaizo*, Aug., 1931, p. 1).

provided for minimum needs, and that the army was making heavy sacrifices in its execution, irresponsible outsiders, having no interest in national defense, were criticizing the army as though it were bent upon exorbitant demands. He charged them with spreading propaganda to discredit the army, by advocating a reduction of armaments in total disregard of the actual condition in Manchuria.[23]

This unusual address by General Minami before military leaders,[24] covering the whole field of politics, diplomacy, and national defense, created a great sensation among cabinet circles as well as among the general public.[25] The press response was immediate and overwhelming. Thus the leading journals of the nation united as one in condemning the military for their deliberate attempt to divert the attention of the public from their drive for reduction of military expenditure and to nip the movement in the bud—a movement which was fast gaining a momentum—to reduce the power and influence of the army, by emphasizing the growing gravity of Manchurian developments.[26] The public accepted this address as an open notice to the nation that the military were now

[23]Text of the address as reported in the press may be found in *Tokyo Asahi*, Aug. 5, 1931, pp. 1, 2. *Cf. Japan Advertiser*, Aug. 5, 1931, p. 1; also *Japan Weekly Chronicle*, Aug. 13, 1931, pp. 191, 192.

[24]In addition to division commanders, and contrary to precedent, the conference was attended by Generals Suzuki, Inouye, and Shirakawa, all supreme war councilors, as well as General Hayashi, commander of the Tokyo Garrison, General Kanaya, chief of staff, General Muto, inspector general of military education, and others. They were reported to have expressed a strong dissatisfaction with Shidehara's foreign policy and urged upon the war minister to present the views of the army before the cabinet (*Tokyo Asahi*, Aug. 5, 1931, pp. 1, 2).

[25]After the cabinet meeting on August 6, Baron Shidehara mildly reminded the war minister of his indiscretion in allowing his address to be made public, as it was certain to excite misgivings at home. He expressed his fear that it might also give rise to suspicion abroad, particularly in Britain, America, and in China, as to dual diplomacy at this delicate moment in Sino-Japanese relations. War Minister Minami was reported to have expressed his disagreement with the foreign minister and declared that he saw nothing wrong or improper in making public his address, and that he had no intention of venturing on dual diplomacy. The general insisted that the wishes of the army should be taken into consideration in formulating the nation's foreign policy (*ibid.*, Aug. 7, 1931, p. 1; see also *Japan Weekly Chronicle*, Aug. 13, 1931, p. 192).

[26]Ishihama, "General Minami's Address on Manchuria," *Keizai Orai*, VI, No. 9 (Sept., 1931), pp. 53–55; Yanagizawa, "General Minami's Irresponsible Address," *Kokusai Chishiki*, XI, No. 9 (Sept., 1931), pp. 58–59. *Cf.* Kurataro Hirosa, "Japan's Militarist and Fascist Revolt," *Christian Century* (Chicago), April 20, 1932, pp. 506–08.

united in demanding a more vigorous policy towards Manchuria, failing in which, they were ready to take the situation into their own hands and to seek solution in their own way.[27]

While this conflict of policies between the civilian and military arms of government was becoming more open and intense at Tokyo,[28] developments in Manchuria were taking a decidedly critical turn. By the middle of summer a series of clashes between Chinese and Japanese residents in Manchuria and Chosen, pointed to a growing and dangerous tension.[29] And therefore, when the news of the murder of Captain Nakamura, an active officer in the army, at the hands

[27]In an editorial on "The War Minister's Political Speech," the *Tokyo Asahi* said that the war minister went beyond his authority in addressing the conference of division commanders on politics and diplomacy and charged that the obvious purpose of his speech was to divert the popular attention from armament reduction to Manchuria, and to impress upon the people the necessity of expansion rather than limitation of armaments (Aug. 5, 1931). The *Jiji Shimpo* said that the war minister was concerned more with the army than with the nation (cited in *Japan Advertiser*, Aug. 6, 1931, p. 5), while the *Nichi Nichi* wondered if the military considered themselves independent of the government in the matter of finances (*ibid.*, Aug. 7, 1931, p. 5). The *Hochi* mildly took General Minami to task for his "political speech" and expressed the hope that the references to Manchuria and Mongolia were not intended to obtain the support of the public for the movement of the military against further reduction of armaments (*ibid.*). Referring to the Manchurian phase of the address, the *Miyako* declared that General Minami would not have made such a remark had he not believed war was unavoidable and concluded that he had done a great disservice to the state (*ibid.*).

[28]Throughout August, military leaders carried their case to the nation. Thus, in his address at Toyohara, Karafuto, on Aug. 12, General Kanaya, chief of staff, vigorously criticized the movement for armament reduction, and indirectly attacked the *Minseito* cabinet (*Tokyo Asahi*, Aug. 13, 1931, p. 2), while on Aug. 31, Major General Takekawa of the general staff advocated a "firm stand" regarding the murder of Captain Nakamura (*ibid.*, Sept. 2, 1931, p. 1). At inspection meetings of reservists held throughout the country in August, officers in the army openly referred to the impending crisis in Manchuria and denounced the disarmament talk. Finally, on Sept. 1, General Suzuki, president of the Imperial Ex-Soldiers' Association, issued instructions to all members of this association, numbering over 3,000,000, regarding the attitude to be taken towards the disarmament conference to be held at Geneva in the following February, saying that, "when we lack adequate armaments to support our righteous cause then an international crisis occurs and peace is disturbed" (*ibid.*, Sept. 2, 1931, p. 1, *Japan Weekly Chronicle*, Sept. 10, 1931, p. 320), while on the following day, War Minister Minami urged upon 500 reserve officers in the Tokyo district to coöperate with the central authority in "educating" the public on disarmament and Manchurian questions (*ibid.*, Sept. 2, 1931, p. 1; *Japan Weekly Chronicle*, Sept. 10, 1931, p. 323).

[29]On the Wanpaoshan affair and the anti-Chinese riots in Chosen, see *Lytton Report*, pp. 61–63; *Gaiko Jiho*, Aug. 1, 1931, pp. 174–78; *Japan Advertiser*, July 3, 7, 1931, p. 1.

of Chinese soldiers, reached the general staff in early July,[30] the popular feelings were running high, and the patience of the military was almost at the breaking point.[31] The military authorities saw in it a deliberate attempt on the part of Chinese soldiers to undermine the whole of Japanese rights and interests in Manchuria and to inflict an irreparable insult upon the Japanese army.[32] Hence they were determined to deal a crushing blow upon them and to vindicate the honor and integrity of the imperial army in the eyes of the Chinese on the one hand,[33] and of the Japanese at home, on the other, who appeared to be losing interest in Manchuria.[34] Naturally, the military authorities, who had been watching the developments with greatest anxiety and who had been making elaborate preparations for eventualities, now superseded the Foreign Office in assuming initiative and leadership in subsequent Sino-Japanese negotiations.[35] Setting aside the more conciliatory attitude of the *Kasumigaseki*,[36] the Miyakezaka

[30]For an account of this case, see *Lytton Report*, pp. 63–66; Ashida, *op. cit.*, III, 1093–96.

[31]By this time, the Shidehara policy had become a serious political issue between the *Minseito* (government) and *Seiyukai* (opposition) parties. Consult Katsuji Inahara, "Political Parties on Continental Policy," *Gaiko Jiho*, No. 640 (Aug. 1, 1931), pp. 9–32; also Cyrus H. Peake, "The Clash of Arms in Manchuria," *Current History*, Jan., 1932, pp. 507–12, 626.

[32]Tatsuo Iwabuchi, "Civilian Representatives in Manchuria and Chosen," *Chuo Koron*, Oct., 1931, pp. 146–54; Nyozekan Hasegawa, "Imperialism and the Sino-Japanese Crisis," *Kaizo*, Oct., 1931, pp. 43–53.

[33]Ashida, *op. cit.*, III, 1089–93. *Cf. Japan Weekly Chronicle*, Aug. 27, 1931, pp. 247, 254.

[34]Certain business and trade groups, particularly in Osaka, began to advocate the renunciation of their "special position" in Manchuria. According to them, the Sino-Japanese relations must be based purely on economic and trade considerations, and Japan would lose more in Shanghai and other parts of central China by insisting on political predominance in Manchuria (Bumpin Takeuchi in *Kaizo*, Aug., 1931, pp. 165–66. *Cf.* Royama in *ibid.*, March, 1935, p. 46; Dr. Shigeo Suyehiro, "Can Japan and China Live Together?" *Gaiko Jiho*, No. 644 [Oct. 1, 1931], pp. 25–38).

[35]Masamichi Royama, "Crisis in Manchuria," *Chuo Koron*, Oct., 1931, pp. 109–17.

[36]The Foreign Office sought to keep Captain Nakamura's military status secret and to present him as an agricultural expert as the passport represented him to be in negotiations with the Chinese authorities. This suggestion was rejected by the military authorities at Miyakezaka, who insisted on his military status being made public in negotiations (*Tokyo Asahi*, Aug. 18, 1931, pp. 1, 2). *Cf.* Tokuzo Komai, "Dualism in Diplomacy," *Chuo Koron*, Oct., 1931, pp. 161–70; also *Japan Advertiser*, Aug. 30, 1931, p. 5, for Ambassador Shobu Sato's reported confession that he was surprised to find a gap existing between the government and the military authorities.

ventured on a more adventurous task of solving all pending issues, if necessary by force.[37]

As the long delays in making satisfactory settlement of the Nakamura case put an ever increasing strain on the patience of the people,[38] and as opposition parties concentrated their attacks on the government,[39] Colonel Doihara, Resident Officer at Mukden, as well as Major Shibayama, an adviser to Marshal Chang Hsueh-liang, were summoned to Tokyo to confer with the central authorities on the Manchurian developments.[40] Thus, on September 15th, an important conference of War Minister Minami, Vice-Minister of War Sugiyama, Chief of Staff Kanaya, Vice-Chief of Staff Ninomiya, as well as Colonel Doihara and Major Shibayama, was held at the general staff office to reach an agreement regarding the attitude to be taken by the military towards the Manchurian situation, particularly in connection with the Nakamura case. According to the press, they agreed to wait for further developments in the negotiations then in progress through diplomatic channels, but were determined to seek the settlement by a resort to force, if satisfactory solution

[37]After the cabinet meeting of Sept. 4th, War Minister Minami declared to the reporters that he could not state in advance whether the situation should demand a resort to armed force, but that the army would act in accordance with the wishes of the people (*Tokyo Asahi*, Sept. 5, 1931, p. 2). *Cf.* Hiroo Sasa, "The Approaching Crisis in Sino-Japanese Relations," *Kaizo*, Oct., 1931, pp. 138–47.

[38]See Royama, *Nichiman Kankei no Kenkyu*, pp. 208–54; Ashida, *op. cit.*, III, 1088–90; also Nobuo Goto, "The Future of the Manchurian Question," *Kaizo*, Nov., 1931, pp. 99–109. Dr. C. T. Wang's reported statement that the rumor of Captain Nakamura's murder was without foundation inflamed the public (*Tokyo Asahi*, Sept. 4, 6, 1931, p. 2).

[39]In the course of an address at Utsunomiya on Sept. 3, President Ki Inukai of the *Seiyukai* party (opposition) referred to the Manchurian question and declared that: "For us, Japanese, who are suffering from overpopulation, to seek an outlet in neighboring regions as peaceful merchants, industrialists, and farmers will be asserting merely our minimum right to national existence" (*ibid.*, Sept. 4, 1931, p. 1). A few days later, representatives of various factions of the Upper House invited Chief Koiso of the Military Affairs Bureau of the War Department to obtain information and explanations regarding the Manchurian developments (*ibid.*, Sept. 8, 1931, p. 2). The Imperial Ex-Soldiers' Association held a district meeting in Tokyo on Sept. 14, when the reservists passed a resolution demanding a "strong and decisive" action to protect the rights and interests in Manchuria (*ibid.*, Sept. 15, 1931, p. 2).

[40]*Ibid.*, Sept. 15, 1931, p. 1. *Cf. Japan Weekly Chronicle*, Sept. 17, 1931, p. 351. At Antung, on his way to Tokyo, Colonel Doihara was reported by the press as saying that "there was no telling what might happen in Manchuria" (*Tokyo Asahi*, Sept. 9, 1931, p. 2).

could not be obtained through diplomacy at an early date.[41] With instructions thus drawn up, Colonel Doihara left Tokyo for Manchuria on the evening of the same day, prepared to press for settlement of all questions then outstanding between China and Japan.[42]

THE MUKDEN CRISIS

In the preceding section, we have narrated in some detail the growing tension between China and Japan in Manchuria, and analyzed at length certain internal forces and factors which were gradually preparing the people for a "crisis." We have seen that, as the developments in Manchuria assumed more serious proportions, the seat of authority for directing the nation's foreign policy was virtually transferred from Kasumigaseki to Miyakezaka. We have noted also that, as September wore on, events on the spot moved apparently in advance of the wishes of the authorities either at Port Arthur or Tokyo.[43] It was in these circumstances and against this background that the Mukden crisis—the most serious since the World War—became a reality on the night of September 18, 1931.[44]

Thus, following the explosion of a bomb on the tracks of the South Manchuria Railway at Liutiaohu Station north of Mukden about 10 P.M., September 18, the Japanese forces

[41]*Ibid.*, Sept. 15, 1931, p. 1. Note also War Minister Minami's statement to the press after calling on Prince Saionji on Sept. 12 (*ibid.*, Sept. 14, 1931, p. 2). The following day Baron Wakatsuki, the prime minister, also called on the genro to discuss the Manchurian developments (*ibid.*). Cf. *Japan Weekly Chronicle*, Sept. 24, 1931, p. 373.

[42]In his interview with the press, en route to Mukden, Colonel Doihara said that, if the Chinese authorities should hesitate to acknowledge several demands which would be put before them in connection with the murder of Captain Nakamura, there might be some trouble. He said that the measures to be taken by the military under certain circumstances were already determined upon, but was not sure whether the Foreign Office could support such measures wholeheartedly (*ibid.*, Sept. 16, 1931, p. 2). While Major General Tatekawa, of the general staff, was still in Chosen en route to Manchuria to caution young officers on the spot against hasty action, he received the news of the outbreak (Bunshiro Suzuki's comment in *Keizai Orai*, Nov., 1931, pp. 97–99).

[43]Prof. Y. Nakamura, "Manchurian Incident and the Independence of High Command," *Gaiko Jiho*, No. 651 (Jan. 15, 1932), pp. 13–36. Cf. Hugh Byas' cable to the New York *Times* (Sept. 20, 1931, p. 28).

[44]It is obviously beyond the scope of this chapter to narrate in detail the military operations in Manchuria and elsewhere. For narrative of events in Manchuria on and subsequent to Sept. 18, see *Lytton Report*, Chap. IV.

at Mukden, without waiting for an order from Lieutenant General Honjo, the commander-in-chief of the Kwantung army, immediately commenced their military action against the Chinese, with the swiftness and precision characteristic of a well-planned execution.[45] Within the space of a few hours they seized a half-dozen strategic points, occupied the Mukden area, including the arsenal and barracks, and disarmed Chinese troops.[46] The initiative having thus been taken by the troops on the spot, the chief of staff of the Kwantung army did not receive a telegraphic report until 11:46 P.M. from the Special Service Station at Mukden, giving details of the attack. Upon receipt of the news, however, orders were immediately sent to the troops at Liaoyang, Yingkow, and Fenghuangsheng to proceed to Mukden. The fleet was ordered to leave Port Arthur and proceed to Yingkow, and the commander-in-chief of the Garrison army in Chosen was asked to send reinforcements. Lieutenant General Honjo left Port Arthur at 3:30 A.M. and arrived at Mukden at noon.[47]

The War Department in Tokyo received the first news of what was happening from the Special Service Station at Mukden at 2 A.M., September 19, and this news was immediately conveyed to the war, navy, and foreign ministers, as well as to the premier and the chief of staff.[48] At 8:10 A.M. War Minister Minami called on Prime Minister Wakatsuki to report on the progress of operations, after which he held a conference with Chief of Staff Kanaya to confer upon the attitude of the army. At 9:30 A.M. General Minami was received in audience by the emperor to report on the situation. An extraordinary meeting of the cabinet was called at 10:30 A.M. to deliberate upon the policy of the government.

[45]Major Shigetani of the Special Service Station at Mukden declared on Sept. 19 that the military action was taken within the limits of the authority already given, and not under an order from the commander-in-chief of the Kwantung army (*Tokyo Asahi*, Sept. 19, 1931, extra edition, p. 2).

[46]Mr. Hiroo Sasa, a well-known critic, says that the outstanding facts about this incident are: (1) conflict of policy between the Japanese and Chinese military authorities; (2) instantaneous response of Japanese troops to the explosion; and (3) commencement of a general attack on Chinese troops and the attitude of non-resistance on the part of China ("Outbreak of the Mukden Crisis," *Economist* [Osaka], Oct. 1, 1931, pp. 49–51).

[47]*Lytton Report*, p. 69; *Tokyo Asahi*, Sept. 19, 1931, pp. 1, 2.

[48]*Ibid.*, Sept. 19, 1931, extra edition, p. 2. *Cf. Kaizo*, Nov., 1931, pp. 36–37.

At this important meeting the war minister made a detailed report on the causes and progress of the conflict, while Admiral Abo, the navy minister, reported that the navy department was ready to send its fleet to Manchuria upon twelve hours' notice. Baron Shidehara, who was reported to have been taken completely by surprise at the news, insisted, however, that the operations be confined within the narrowest area compatible with the circumstances.[49] After a two-hour meeting, the prime minister announced to the press, at 12:20 P.M., that the government had decided on the policy of nonaggravation and that, in accordance with this policy, instructions had already been sent to the commander-in-chief of the Kwantung army through the war minister.[50] The cabinet decision was immediately reported to the emperor by the prime minister.[51]

Immediately following the cabinet council, a conference of the "Big Three" of the army—War Minister Minami, Chief of Staff Kanaya, and Inspector General of Military Education Muto—was held to deliberate upon the scope of military operations to be taken in the future.[52] After this conference, the war minister stated to the press that the army need not consult the cabinet as to the measures to be taken to meet the exigencies of the future, but would leave it to the commander-in-chief of the Kwantung army to exercise his discretion. Referring to the reported mobilization of certain detachments in Chosen, General Minami said that he saw no necessity for dispatching additional forces to Manchuria at the present stage and hence had suspended the mobilization.[53] A strong opposition to this order was reported from Shingishu on the Korean frontier where the 39th Mixed Brigade of the 20th Division (4,000 men and artillery) had been concentrated since 10 A.M. ready to cross the Yalu River into Manchuria.[54] On the afternoon of the following day, high officials of the three departments of the army were

[49] *Ibid.*, Sept. 20, 1931, p. 1.
[50] *Ibid. Cf.* Shinnosuke Yanagizawa, "Manchurian Crisis and Diplomacy," *Gaiko Jiho*, No. 645 (Oct. 15, 1931), pp. 72–83.
[51] *Ibid.*
[52] *Ibid.*
[53] *Ibid.*, Sept. 20, 1931, p. 2.
[54] *Ibid.*, Sept. 20, 1931, extra edition, p. 2; see also *Lytton Report*, p. 71.

called together by War Minister Minami at his official residence to formulate the basic policy of the army regarding the Manchurian situation.[55] In an important statement issued to the press after the conference, setting forth the views of the military, the war minister declared that:

(1) Additional detachments would be sent to Manchuria if counter-attacks should be attempted by Chinese troops.

(2) Cabinet approval must be obtained before Japanese troops stationed in Chosen cross the Korean frontier. In case of necessity, however, leaving no time for an approval from Tokyo, commanders-in-chief of the garrison army in Manchuria and Chosen are given the authority to take appropriate measures.

(3) It would be up to the cabinet whether we should seek solution of all outstanding issues over Manchuria and Mongolia in connection with this crisis. It is the wish of the army, however, to seek settlement of these questions now outstanding between Japan and China, and hence would convey the views of the army to the cabinet through the war minister.

(4) Solution of these issues should be sought as local issues, and not as between Nanking and Tokyo.

(5) The army agrees with the government in its policy of nonaggravation, but desires to point out that the nonaggravation of the situation does not necessarily mean the nonenlargement of military operations. This point is to be made clear to the government.[56]

At 10 A.M., September 21, an extraordinary meeting of the cabinet was called at the official residence of the prime minister to decide whether the forces in Manchuria should be increased by dispatching certain detachments from Chosen across the frontier. At this meeting of his colleagues, War Minister Minami described in detail the grave situation prevailing at Chientao, Changchun, and other centers in North Manchuria, and explained the imperative necessity of dispatching from three thousand to four thousand troops from

[55]The conference was attended by General Minami (war minister), General Kanaya (chief of staff), General Muto (inspector general of military education), Lieutenant General Sugiyama (vice-minister of war), Lieutenant General Ninomiya (vice-chief of staff), Lieutenant General Araki (vice-chief of military education), and Major General Koiso (chief of military affairs bureau of the War Department).

[56]Ibid., Sept. 21, 1931, p. 2.

Chosen to Manchuria. He pointed out that the decision had already been made by the conference of the three heads of the army in the forenoon, upon incessant requests for instructions from the commander-in-chief of the Kwantung army, and said that the war authorities could carry out this decision without consulting the cabinet. He added, however, that he was seeking the approval of the cabinet as a matter of form. This proposal elicited a strong opposition from Baron Shidehara, the foreign minister, Mr. Junnosuke Inouye, the finance minister, and some other members of the cabinet, who urged greater caution in the matter, reminding the war minister of the decision already reached by the cabinet at its previous meeting to exert all its efforts to prevent further complications of the situation. They pointed out the delicate nature of international relations, and declared that, even if the proposal of the army could be carried out strictly within treaty obligations, it would be liable to be misinterpreted abroad as the dispatch of a new expedition. The meeting closed at 5 P.M. without reaching a decision on the question.[57]

While the cabinet was still deliberating upon the matter, about four thousand troops which had been concentrated at Shingishu, Chosen, since September 19, crossed the river into Manchuria, and the report from General Hayashi, commander-in-chief of the garrison army in Chosen, stating that he had dispatched certain detachments to Manchuria on his own authority without waiting for instructions from the chief of general staff at Tokyo reached the premier at 5:30 P.M., the cabinet meeting having already been adjourned. Naturally, Baron Wakatsuki expressed dissatisfaction at the dispatch of troops before the policy of the government was finally decided.[57a] The war minister, however, defended the action of General Hayashi, citing a precedent for such an action while he was commander in Chosen during Baron Tanaka's administration. The troops had crossed the river into Manchuria, and there was nothing for the prime minister to do but to accept the *fait accompli*.[58]

[57] *Ibid.*, Sept. 22, 1931, pp. 1, 2. *Cf. Japan Weekly Chronicle*, Oct. 1, 1931, pp. 405–06.

[57a] See Tamon Maeda, *Keizai Orai*, VI, No. 11 (Nov., 1931), pp. 94–95.

[58] The matter was reported to the cabinet the following day, when the already executed action of the army had to be accepted under protest (*Tokyo Asahi*, Sept. 23, 1931, p. 1). At 1:35 P.M., Sept. 21, the headquarters of the garrison army in

Meanwhile, the first news of the crisis at Mukden reached Dr. Yotaro Sugimura, then under secretary general of the League of Nations, early on the morning of September 19 (about 3 P.M., Tokyo time). Realizing the seriousness of the news, he immediately reported the matter to Mr. Kenkichi Yoshizawa, Japanese ambassador in Paris and representative on the Council. Immediately a conference of diplomats who were then at Geneva for the current session of the League was called to confer upon the matter. They decided to report to the home government the atmosphere of Geneva regarding the news of the clash and to recommend that Tokyo adopt a policy of nonaggravation of the situation. In cabling this decision of diplomatic representatives, they requested the Foreign Office to send them detailed information on the most recent developments in Manchuria. However, in view of the apparent lack of unity and coördination, not only between the government at Tokyo and the forces in Manchuria, but also between the diplomatic and military authorities on the spot, no news regarding the crisis was forthcoming for some time. The operations on the continent seemed to be in advance of any policy formulated at Tokyo, and consequently the diplomatic representatives abroad could not state the views of the government with conviction and in good faith.[59]

While the forces in Manchuria were still engaged in extensive military operations and the government at Tokyo was seeking in vain to obtain information from its representatives on the spot,[60] the Chinese government formally brought the matter before the League of Nations on September 21 under Article 11 of the Covenant, asking the Council

Chosen issued a statement declaring that the troops had started from Shingishu for Manchuria (*ibid.*, Sept. 22, 1931, p. 2; *Japan Weekly Chronicle*, Oct. 1, 1931, pp. 399, 406). It was reported at the time that Chief of Staff Kanaya supported Baron Shidehara on the nonaggravation policy of the government (see comments in *Keizai Orai*, March, 1934, p. 110; also *Seiji Keizai Jiron*, March, 1934, pp. 96–97).

[59]Sugimura, *Kokusai Gaiko Roku* (Tokyo, 1933), pp. 145–51, 443. *Cf.* Takayama, "Kasumigaseki and Miyakezaka," *Chuo Koron*, Dec., 1931, pp. 185–90. In an editorial on "The Manchurian Quarrel," the New York *Times* said, on Sept. 22: "At Tokyo we have the extraordinary spectacle of the Foreign Office and the War Office openly at odds."

[60]So unexpected was the outbreak at Mukden that Baron Shidehara's primary concern during the first few days appeared to be directed towards confining the military operations within the narrowest possible area (*Tokyo Asahi*, Sept. 22, 1931, p. 2). Accordingly, details of the incident did not reach the *Kasumigaseki* for some

to take immediate steps to prevent a further development of the situation, to reëstablish the *status quo ante,* and to determine the amount and character of such reparations as might be due to the Chinese government.[61] When the dispute was formally placed before the League the following day, the Japanese representative, Mr. Yoshizawa, warned the Council against premature intervention as "it would only have the deplorable result of needlessly exciting Japanese public opinion."[62] After further deliberation, the Council voted unanimously to authorize its president to address an urgent appeal to both governments to refrain from any act likely to aggravate the situation or prejudice the peaceful settlement of the problem. It also decided that its president should endeavor, in consultation with the Chinese and Japanese representatives, to find adequate means of enabling the two countries to withdraw their troops forthwith without compromising the security of life and property of their nationals. At the same time, the Council decided to forward to the United States the full details of its proceedings.[63] The resolution of the Council, adopted on September 22, together with Mr. Yoshizawa's report, reached the Foreign Office at Tokyo the following afternoon.[64]

By this time, however, the Japanese forces had accomplished their main objectives of operations by placing all the strategic points in Manchuria under occupation. Accordingly, high officials of the War Department and the general staff held a joint conference on the afternoon of September

time. According to an informant, Consul General Hayashi sought in vain to have an interview with General Honjo on Sept. 19 to convey the decision of the cabinet, the news having already been received by the army headquarters (Takayama, *op. cit.,* p. 185).

[61]New York *Times,* Sept. 22, 1931, p. 9.

[62]*Minutes of the Second Meeting of the Sixty-fifth Session of the Council,* p. 3. When the matter was informally discussed in the Council on Sept. 19, Mr. Yoshizawa could not give much information. He only said that, "according to information which had appeared that day in the press, an incident had occurred on the previous evening in the neighborhood of Mukden" (*Minutes of the First Meeting of the Sixty-fifth Session of the Council,* pp. 1–2).

[63]For detailed analysis of the procedure in the League from September 19 to December 10, 1931, see Quincy Wright, "The Manchurian Crisis," *American Political Science Review,* Vol. XXVI, No. 1 (Feb., 1932), pp. 45–76; Hikomatsu Kamikawa, "The Manchurian Case and the League of Nations," *Kokusaiho Gaiko Zasshi,* XXXI (April, 1932), 341–356; Ashida, *op. cit.,* III, 1116 *ff.*

[64]*Tokyo Asahi,* Sept. 24, 1931, p. 2.

23 to formulate their next move on the continent and to decide upon their attitude towards the League.[65] A cabinet
meeting was called to order at 6 P.M., September 24, to deliberate upon instructions drafted by the Foreign Office. War
Minister Minami submitted the army stand to the cabinet,
opposing any interference in this dispute either by the League
or other powers. Baron Shidehara explained the attitude of
Kasumigaseki regarding the League procedure, and finally
succeeded in obtaining the assent of the war minister to replying to the Council.[66] It was also decided at this meeting
to instruct Mr. Yoshizawa to insist upon direct negotiations
between China and Japan.[67] Following this important cabinet council, the government made public a long statement,
setting forth for the first time since the outbreak of the incident the views of Tokyo towards the Manchurian situation
and the League procedure.[68] Thus, following the lines of
policy determined upon at its meeting on September 22,[69]
the Tokyo government explained that the military action was
necessary to forestall an imminent disaster to Japanese
vested rights in Manchuria, assured that it harbored no
territorial ambition in the region, and broadly intimated that
it would insist to the end upon direct negotiations between
the two countries. It made clear the intention of Tokyo to
withdraw its troops to the railway zone in proportion as the
situation improved.[70]

[65]*Op. cit.*

[66]*Ibid.*, Sept. 24, 1931, p. 1; see also *Kaizo*, Nov., 1931, p. 37.

[67]*Ibid.*, Sept. 25, 1931, p. 2.

[68]Text of statement in *Kokusaiho Gaiko Zasshi*, Vol. XXXI, No. 4 (April, 1932),
pp. 8–11; *Tokyo Asahi*, Sept. 25, 1931, p. 2; *Minutes of the Fourth Meeting of the
Sixty-fifth Session of the Council*, p. 7.

[69]On Sept. 22 the cabinet decided to reject any proposal to settle issues between
Japan and China through mediation or third parties; it decided to deal with the
Nanking government regarding administrative and territorial questions, but with
the local authorities regarding Manchurian and Mongolian questions (Ashida,
op. cit., III, 1108).

[70]*Ibid.*, 1108–11, 1116 *ff.* As soon as the main military objectives were achieved
in South Manchuria, details of the operations were reported to the army members
of the Supreme War Council on Sept. 25 (*Tokyo Asahi*, Sept. 26, 1931, p. 1). Four
days later, War Minister Minami invited members of the Board of Field Marshals
and Fleet Admirals as well as the Supreme War Council to his official residence to
explain in detail the progress of recent developments in Manchuria and to obtain
their support of the policy of the War Department. All the highest officials of the
army and the navy were also present at this meeting (*ibid.*, Sept. 30, 1931, p. 1).

The replies of China and Japan having reached Geneva, the Council met on September 25 to continue deliberation on the dispute, and on September 30 it approved unanimously a resolution expressing satisfaction at the assurances given by Japan and China and expressing hope that the situation would not be aggravated any further. It decided to meet again on October 14 to consider the situation as it then stood.[71]

THIRTEEN vs. ONE

We have noted elsewhere that the actual authority for directing the nation's foreign policy was gradually shifting from Kasumigaseki to Miyakezaka by the middle of August, and that this tendency towards dual diplomacy became more pronounced during the first phase of the League procedure in September. Towards the beginning of October, however, even this last vestige of dual diplomacy appeared to be waning, with the Miyakezaka in firm control of the government, directing the nation's policy towards the League as well as the Manchurian developments. This dominating position of the War Department over the Foreign Office became even more pronounced following the bombardment of Chinchow, Marshal Chang Hsueh-liang's temporary capital on the Peiping–Mukden Railway, southwest of Mukden, about 1 P.M., October 8.[72]

Thus, upon request from the prime minister for views of the army, the "Big Three" of the army—Generals Minami, Kanaya, and Muto—met at 4 P.M., October 8, at the official residence of the war minister, to formulate the conditions acceptable to the army for settlement of the Manchurian affair. According to the press reports, they discussed not only

[71]Ibid., 1126–33. Cf. New York Times, Oct. 1, 1931, p. 14. After the plenary session of the Privy Council on Sept. 30, Prime Minister Wakatsuki, War Minister Minami, and Foreign Minister Shidehara explained to the councilors details connected with the Manchurian crisis and the proceedings at Geneva. It was reported that several Privy Councilors expressed strong dissatisfaction with the way the Foreign Office was conducting the nation's foreign policy. They insisted that the Privy Council should be kept informed regarding all phases of the procedure (Osaka Asahi, Oct. 1, 1931, p. 1; see also Mr. Uyeda's comment in Gaiko Jiho, Oct. 15, 1931, pp. 199–208).

[72]Osaka Asahi, Oct. 9, 1931, p. 1. For detailed description of military operations in Manchuria following the Chinchow incident, see Lytton Report, pp. 72 ff.

matters relating to future military operations on the continent but also decided to press upon the government their views on foreign relations. They were to insist, among other things, that China alone should assume the responsibility for the incident; that all the important issues, such as railway and land-lease problems, must be settled now; that the problems should be regarded as local, and hence settlement should be sought with local authorities and not with the Nanking government; that, pending establishment of a new government in Manchuria, Japan should maintain the *status quo;* and that any attempt on the part of the League at interference in the dispute must be resisted.[73] These views of the army on military affairs as well as on foreign policy were reported to the prime minister the following day.[74] In these circumstances, therefore, no suggestion was forthcoming from any member of the cabinet, at its meeting of October 9, of reprimanding General Honjo for the Chinchow affair, an incident which gave an impression at all capitals of the world that any pledge which the government at Tokyo might give to the League could be made a mere scrap of paper by the army over whose action it had no control. While this incident was viewed at Geneva as indicating the alarming possibility of an unlimited extension of Japanese operations in North China, it was regarded at Tokyo, not as an aggravation of the situation, but merely another warning to Marshal Chang Hsueh-liang that any further attempt at resumption of his former position in Manchuria was certain to meet the forceful resistance of the imperial army.[75] There is no denying, however, that the civil departments of the gov-

[73] *Tokyo Asahi,* Oct. 9, 1931, p. 2; New York *Times,* Oct. 10, 1931, p. 3. The army's demand for negotiating with the local authorities was apparently opposed by Baron Shidehara, who regarded the Nanking government as legitimate authorities with whom to deal regarding the Manchurian affair, while the insistence of the military authorities to maintain the *status quo,* pending formation of a new government, seemed to be a serious deviation from the declared policy of the cabinet (see Sasa, "Military Leadership and Shidehara Diplomacy," *Kaizo,* Nov., 1931, pp. 127–36). In this connection, we may note the significant statement made by General Honjo, commander-in-chief of the Kwantung army, on Oct. 4, expressing a strong hope that a new régime be established in Manchuria (*Tokyo Asahi,* Oct. 5, 1931, p. 2), which was mildly reprimanded by Baron Shidehara at the cabinet meeting the following day (*ibid.,* Oct. 6, 1931, p. 1).

[74] *Ibid.,* Oct. 10, 1931, p. 2.

[75] Ashida, *op. cit.,* III, 1141–46 *ff.;* see also Mr. Hugh Byas' cable to New York *Times,* Oct. 10, 1931, p. 1.

ernment were greatly disturbed by this new development at Chinchow.[76]

Meanwhile, the bombardment of Chinchow alarmed the League, and, upon Chinese request, the Council reassembled on October 13, a day earlier than the time set. Acting under instructions from Tokyo, Mr. Yoshizawa pointed out the importance of knowing the historical background of the incident and warned the Council against theoretical arguments and reiterated the necessity of finding a solution on the basis of actual realities.[77] When the Council sought to bring further pressure upon Japan by extending an invitation to the United States to send a representative to sit at the Council table as an observer, Mr. Yoshizawa, under strict instructions from Tokyo, objected to extending this invitation on legal grounds.[78] The Council's decision, on October 15, to invite an observer from the United States, a non-member of the League, greatly incensed the general public in Japan. Thus, after the meeting of the cabinet the following day, War Minister Minami declared:

> The fundamental policy of Japan to seek settlement of the Manchurian affair through direct negotiations between China and Japan cannot be modified. . . . No good can be accomplished by the intervention of the League or any third party who possesses no knowledge of the situation.[79]

The tension between Geneva and Tokyo became more strained when the Council, at its meeting on October 24,[80] voted down the Japanese substitute resolution by 13 to 1,

[76]Thus, in a round of calls on the senior statesmen and opposition leaders—Admiral Count Yamamoto, Count Kiyoura, Baron Tatsuo Yamamoto, President Inukai of the *Seiyukai* (opposition) party, Mr. Korekiyo Takahashi, and Princes Tokugawa and Konoye of the Upper House—on October 12 and 13, Prime Minister Wakatsuki sought to obtain their support of the cabinet's policy. Both Admiral Yamamoto and Count Kiyoura were reported to have urged upon Baron Wakatsuki that he maintain complete harmony between the cabinet at Tokyo and the military authorities in Manchuria, while the prime minister assured these senior statesmen that diplomatic and war authorities were now acting in harmony (*Tokyo Asahi*, Oct. 13, 14, 1931).

[77]Wright, *op. cit.*, pp. 58–60.

[78]Ashida, *op. cit.*, pp. 1148–50; *Monthly Summary of the League of Nations*, XI, No. 10 (Oct., 1931), pp. 301–302 *ff*.

[79]*Tokyo Asahi*, Oct. 17, 1931, p. 2. The Foreign Office also issued a statement criticizing the Council's action (*ibid.*).

[80]Wright, *op. cit.*, pp. 60–64; Ashida, *op. cit.*, pp. 1154–60.

and adopted, by 13 to 1, the president's resolution calling for complete withdrawal of Japanese troops to the railway zone before the next Council meeting, set for November 16.[81] The cabinet, at its meeting on October 25, decided to make public the content of the so-called "five fundamental principles."[82] Accordingly, the Foreign Office issued a long statement the following evening, reviewing at some length the intricate issues involved, and setting forth the "basic principles" which were to serve as the bases for negotiations between the two countries.[83]

Following this unprecedented deadlock in the Council, Japanese diplomatic representatives in Europe made numerous recommendations to Tokyo to ease the atmosphere. They strongly urged that the home government propose to the League that a commission of inquiry be dispatched to the Far East to obtain further information, thereby facilitating the League procedure. This recommendation was accepted by Tokyo, and was made known to League circles informally in the early part of November.[84] When the Council reassembled on November 16, therefore, it had this compromise proposal before it, and went into private session after only twenty-one minutes' deliberation.[85] Detailed instructions having reached Geneva, Mr. Yoshizawa formally proposed to the Council on November 21 that the League should send a commission of inquiry to China. He pointed out, however, that this commission was not to be empowered to intervene in the negotiations which might be initiated between the two parties, or to supervise the movements of the military forces of either party.[86] On November 25 the cabinet decided to

[81]Dr. Ashida says that the basic policy of the League began to shift from one of finding actual settlement of the dispute to that of withdrawing from the dispute without losing its face (*op. cit.*, pp. 1160–69).

[82]*Osaka Asahi*, Oct. 26, 1931, p. 1.

[83]Text in *ibid.*, Oct. 27, 1931, p. 1. See also *Kokusaiho Gaiko Zasshi*, XXXI, No. 4 (April, 1932), pp. 40–43.

[84]Sugimura, *op. cit.*, pp. 159–62.

[85]Ashida, *op. cit.*, pp. 1167–70.

[86]*Minutes of the Eighteenth Meeting of the Sixty-fifth Session of the Council*, p. 2. The reported acceptance in principle by Mr. Yoshizawa of M. Briand's proposal that all military action be suspended while the proposed commission was conducting an inquiry met vigorous opposition from military circles as well as from the Foreign Office. Baron Shidehara promptly repudiated this acceptance by Mr. Yoshizawa (*Tokyo Asahi, Nichi Nichi*, Nov. 22, 1931, p. 1).

demand elimination from the proposed draft resolution of the Council of the section advising the two governments to issue "strict instructions to their respective commanders to refrain from all positive action likely to lead to fighting or loss of life," as it contravened the Imperial Constitution. It was argued at the cabinet council that, under the Constitution, orders to military commanders emanate from the emperor, and hence, to restrain the exercise of this prerogative of the throne by a resolution of the Council of the League could not be accepted.[87] It was decided also that a proviso should be inserted in the resolution, precluding military action to protect the lives and property of Japanese residents against the activity of bandits and lawless elements. After further consultation with war authorities, instructions were dispatched to Mr. Yoshizawa late in the evening.[88]

After two weeks of private conversations, the Council unanimously voted, on December 10, to send a commission of inquiry to the Far East to make a broad survey of all matters in dispute between China and Japan in Manchuria.[88a] The passage of this resolution was hailed in Japan as a victory of her diplomacy at Geneva; the view was taken at Tokyo that the "exceptional character of the dispute" was finally recognized by the League, and that practical statesmanship had overruled theoretical arguments at the Council table.[89] Immediately after the adoption of this resolution, the Wakatsuki (*Minseito*) ministry tendered its resignation to the emperor, and upon Prince Saionji's recommendation, Mr. Inukai, president of the *Seiyukai* (opposition), formed a new cabinet on December 13.[90]

[87]See Shimizu, *Chikujo Teikoku Kempo Kogi* (Tokyo, 1933), p. 146.

[88]*Tokyo Asahi*, Nov. 25, 1931, p. 2; *Osaka Asahi*, Nov. 26, 1931, p. 1; *Japan Weekly Chronicle*, Dec. 3, 1931, pp. 713, 714.

[88a]*Monthly Summary of the League of Nations*, XI, No. 12 (Dec., 1931), pp. 333–37. Mr. Setsuichi Aoki, head of the Tokyo bureau of the secretariat of the League of Nations, said that the resolution was a great concession to Japan on the part of the League ("The Manchurian and Shanghai Incidents and the League of Nations," *Keizai Orai*, March, 1932, pp. 202–04). *Cf.* Daikichiro Tagawa, "The Manchurian Incident and the League," *Kokusai Chishiki*, XI, No. 11 (Nov., 1931), pp. 79–90; *ibid.*, XI, No. 12 (Dec., 1931), pp. 24–32; *ibid.*, XII, No. 1 (Jan., 1932), pp. 8–16.

[89]Ashida, *op. cit.*, 1167–79; Royama, *Nichiman Kankei no Kenkyu*, pp. 268–71 *ff.*

[90]*Osaka Asahi*, Dec. 12, 13, 14, 1931, p. 1.

Public Opinion and the League Procedure

When the news of the Mukden incident first reached Tokyo, the public was obviously taken by complete surprise and consequently failed to realize the full import of the crisis. As we have observed elsewhere, the immediate reaction of the public to the news was one of violent criticism of the military action. The attacks on the army were particularly vigorous among liberal circles. Their immediate concern was to prevent the extension of operations, by placing them under the strict control of the cabinet through the minister of war. It was urgently demanded that the government issue a formal statement as soon as possible and make clear why the troops had been mobilized.[91] The press criticism of the affair became restrained in a few days.[92] By far the most vigorous criticism was raised, however, among labor circles, particularly those led by Mr. Ikuo Oyama, former professor of politics at the Waseda University and for many years affiliated with the labor movement in Japan. Thus, when the central executive committee of the Rono Taishūto, a left-wing labor party, met on September 30 to formulate its policy towards the developments in Manchuria, it appointed a committee of fifteen members, under the chairmanship of Mr. Oyama, to devise ways and means of organizing an effective movement against the expedition. It also issued a statement vigorously criticizing the military action and demanding the immediate evacuation of the occupied area.[93] Under police surveillance, however, further activities of the party were ruthlessly curbed,[94] while the Shakai Minshūto

[91] See editorials of *Tokyo Asahi* on Sept. 20, 23, 1931; also *Osaka Asahi*, Sept. 20, on "Clash of Troops between China and Japan."

[92] For example, in an editorial on Sept. 24, the *Tokyo Asahi* called upon other powers to understand the "peculiar nature of the issues involved."

[93] The statement declared that: "We firmly oppose the imperialist policy—such as plans for dispatching additional forces—which the government and the military are pursuing towards China, as it is fraught with danger of another World War. We hereby advocate the immediate evacuation of the area and absolute nonintervention in the internal affairs of China. We are determined to oppose the rampancy of the army" (*ibid.*, Oct. 1, 1931, p. 2. *Cf.* Tsunao Inomata, "Monopolistic Capitalism and the Manchurian Crisis," *Chuo Koron*, Nov., 1931, pp. 2–35).

[94] See *Japan Weekly Chronicle*, Dec. 10, 1931, p. 743; *ibid.*, Dec. 17, 1931, p. 790.

(right), or Social Democrats, headed by Mr. Isoō Abé, also for many years a professor at the Waseda University, adopted a more vacillating attitude towards the Manchurian affair.[95]

During the September session of the Council, no voice was raised in influential circles against the League assuming jurisdiction over the Mukden crisis. When the Council re-assembled on October 13, following the Chinchow incident, and voted, over Japanese protest, to invite an American ob-server to be present at its deliberations,[96] sentiments began to be expressed in influential quarters favoring an early withdrawal from the League.[97] During October, however, the liberal elements in the country, counseling caution and pru-dence in criticizing the League procedure, seemed to be able to maintain the confidence of the public on their side. Thus, Professor Kisaburo Yokota, of the Tokyo Imperial Univer-sity, probably the most outspoken critic throughout the dis-pute, openly approved the action of the Council, in an article written immediately after the adoption by the Council of its first resolution on September 30, and said that it acted in strict conformity with the Covenant of the League, and hence its action should in no way be regarded as an unwar-ranted intervention. He also expressed a grave doubt as to whether the military operations of the troops during Sep-tember 18–19 could all be justified as measures of legitimate self-defense.[98] He even likened the steps taken by Japanese forces on September 18 to those of the Germans in the sum-mer of 1914, and asserted that the so-called Chinchow inci-dent was an unjustifiable interference in the domestic affairs

[95]The Shakai Minshūto soon split into two factions, one, led by Abé and Mat-suoka, still clinging to social democracy, while the other, led by Akamatsu, openly advocated state socialism and supported the military action (Akamatsu, "Starting with a Scientific Japanism," *Kaizo*, Dec., 1931, pp. 72–77; see also *Japan Chronicle*, April 17, 1932, p. 6).

[96]The government stand on the "observer question" was upheld, among others, by Viscount Ishii (*Tokyo Asahi*, Oct. 22, 1931, p. 2) and Professor Tachi, a well-known jurist of the Tokyo Imperial University ("Manchurian Dispute and the League Covenant," *Kokka Gakkai Zasshi*, XLVI, No. 1 [January, 1932], pp. 1–21), while Dr. Ashida thought this objection was poor diplomacy (*op. cit.*, p. 1150).

[97]*Tokyo Asahi*, Oct. 20, 1931, p. 1.

[98]Yokota, "The Manchurian Crisis and the League of Nations," *Teikoku Daigaku Shimbun* (Tokyo), Oct. 5, 1931, p. 3. It was reported that this article elicited a storm of protests and many threatening letters.

of a foreign state.[99] The jurisdiction of the League over the dispute under Article XI of the Covenant was also defended by Viscount Ishii,[100] Dr. Inazo Nitobé,[101] and other liberal leaders.[102]

While the liberals were thus urging caution and prudence in handling the Manchurian affair,[103] the more impatient groups were gradually gaining in influence upon public opinion. Thus, Representative Kaku Mori, a leading member of the *Seiyukai* (opposition) party, and a well-known advocate of a "positive policy," demanded in his address

[99]Yokota, "Forced National Opinion," *ibid.*, Oct. 19, 1931, p. 2. He reminded the people that Japan must make some contribution to the world peace in order to justify her position in the Council of the League. Professor Royama, also of the Tokyo Imperial University, joined with Professor Yokota in warning the public against forced public opinion (see his "Recent Situation in the Far East," *Gaiko Jiho*, No. 644 [Oct. 1, 1931], pp. 153–63). *Cf.* also editorials of *Tokyo Asahi* (Oct. 11, 13, 1931, p. 3), counseling caution in Manchuria and emphasizing the urgent necessity of close collaboration between the military and diplomatic arms of the government.

[100]Viscount Ishii, "A Brief History of Arbitration," *Kokusai Chishiki*, XI, No. 11 (Nov., 1931), pp. 4–11. In this article, the veteran statesman defends the procedure of the League under Article 11 of the Covenant as a faithful execution of the duties imposed upon it by all members of the League. He goes on to argue that he sees no reason why Japan alone, among leading powers, should hesitate to accept the optional clause of the Statute of the Permanent Court of International Justice. Dr. Yorozu Oda, former judge of the Court, and Professor Jumpei Shinobu, of the Waseda University, also expressed the same opinion (*ibid.*, pp. 23–34, 44–45).

[101]Nitobé, "League of Nations and the Manchurian Question," *Chuo Koron*, Feb., 1932, pp. 41–46.

[102]At a round table meeting in early October, Dr. Minoru Maida, of the *Tokyo Asahi* editorial staff, justified the League action, holding that measures permitted under self-defense doctrine are not unlimited. Professor Takayanagi, of the Tokyo Imperial University, agreed with Mr. Maida and said that the guiding principles of the League were not well understood by the people, and even doubted whether the leaders of the League of Nations Association of Japan were really faithful to League principles. Professor Royama thought that the incident was "inevitable," as the Japanese military were well prepared for it and considered it as one way of solving the problem. He expressed an apprehension that if the army had laid its plans along imperialist principles and was ready to fight the whole world to carry them out, it would, indeed, be a dangerous program. Mr. Kamekichi Takahashi, a leading economist, said that the recent incident was an external explosion of the army's dissatisfaction with party politics (*Keizai Orai*, Nov., 1931, pp. 50–86).

[103]Professor Hikomatsu Kamikawa, also of the Tokyo Imperial University, had advocated for some time that Manchuria be made a Japanese mandate under the League of Nations (see his "The Manchurian Question—a Study in World Politics," *Gaiko Jiho*, No. 645 [Oct. 15, 1931], pp. 1–14; also his "Whither Goes the Manchurian Question?" *Teikoku Daigaku Shimbun*, Oct. 26, 1931, p. 3). Representative Seigo Nakano (*Minseito*) also advocated a mandate system for Manchuria as a way out, in his address at the Tokyo Imperial University on October 12 (*ibid.*, Oct. 19, 1931, p. 2).

at the Tokyo Imperial University on October 8, that Japan should feel no hesitation in defending her "life line,"[104] while Major General Tatekawa, of the General Staff, openly counseled, in an address delivered at the same place the following day, a more vigorous policy of economic expansion on the continent as a means of maintaining peace in the Orient. He saw no reason why Japanese should be obliged to remain confined within such a small territory, and urged upon the people to be ready to accept, if necessary, an imperialist charge by the Chinese people.[105] After the October deadlock in the Council, the dissatisfaction with the *Minseito* policy became even more outspoken, and, on November 2, Lieutenant General Araki declared to the press that Japan should not be content with mere insistence on the preservation of her treaty rights in Manchuria but must be prepared to show her determination not to allow any further disturbance in the Far East.[106]

The *Seiyukai*, the leading opposition party, did not fail to take every opportunity to discredit the China policy of the *Minseito* administration and to exert all its influence to bring about its downfall.[107] On November 10, President Inukai, in his address before his party, vigorously criticized the Shidehara policy of "coöperation" for allowing the League to take up the dispute, for failing to take appropriate steps to make clear to the world the prevailing situation in Manchuria prior to the outbreak of the incident. He even charged the *Minseito* with giving an impression to the world that the Mukden crisis had actually been instigated by the army.[108]

Meanwhile, certain influential factions within the *Minseito* party began to voice their opposition to the administration's conduct of foreign policy. Thus, on November 21, Mr. Kenzo Adachi, home minister and a leading whip, issued

[104]*Ibid.*, Oct. 12, 1931, p. 2. *Cf.* his article, "The Approaching Crisis in Manchuria," *Keizai Orai*, Oct., 1931, pp. 84–92.

[105]*Teikoku Daigaku Shimbun*, Oct. 12, 1931, p. 2.

[106]*Tokyo Asahi*, Nov. 3, 1931, p. 1.

[107]As early as Oct. 16, Mr. Kuhara, chief secretary of the *Seiyukai* party, issued a statement to the press declaring that Japan might be compelled to withdraw from the League on the Manchurian issue (*Osaka Asahi*, Oct. 17, 1931, p. 1).

[108]*Ibid.*, Nov. 11, 1931, p. 1; see also Kumakichi Uzaki (ed.), *Inukai Ki Dan* (Tokyo, 1932), pp. 420–21.

a public statement to the press, openly advocating a "national government" in view of the delicate nature of international relations. The publication of such an important statement without consulting the prime minister or the cabinet was naturally accepted by the public as a political bomb thrown at the *Minseito* administration.[109] The struggle which ensued between opposing factions within the party finally led to the downfall of the cabinet on December 11, 1931.[110] Upon Prince Saionji's recommendation, Mr. Inukai, president of the *Seiyukai*, formed a new cabinet two days later, with Lieutenant-General Araki as minister of war, and took over the conduct of the nation's external relations.[111]

The Stimson Note of January 7, 1932

We have already observed that ever since the outbreak of the Mukden crisis on September 18, Baron Shidehara had been fighting a losing battle in his more conciliatory policy towards China and the League. We have noted also that the opposition forces, not only among *Seiyukai* leaders, military circles, and other impatient groups, but also even among his own party ranks, became so overwhelming by the middle of November that the fall of the ministry became merely a question of a few weeks. By this time, moreover, the rank and file of the people were convinced that all the operations in Manchuria had been prompted by sheer necessity of self-defense. They were now ready to support any move their

[109] *Tokyo Asahi*, Nov. 22, 1931, p. 2; also *Japan Weekly Chronicle*, Dec. 3, 1931, pp. 706, 707.

[110] *Yomiuri Shimbun*, Dec. 11, 1931, p. 2; *Osaka Asahi*, Dec. 12, 1931, p. 1.

[111] Uzaki (ed.), *op. cit.*, pp. 423–28. *Cf. Tokyo Asahi*, Dec. 13, 1931, p. 2. For accounts of the formation of the new cabinet see Baba, "From Wakatsuki to Inukai." *Chuo Koron*, Jan., 1932, pp. 153–63 (reprinted in his *Gikai Seiji Ron* [Tokyo, 1933], pp. 205–23); Nagakawa, "Formation of the Inukai Cabinet," *Kaizo*, Jan., 1932, pp. 124–30; Minobe, "Formation of the Inukai Cabinet," *Teikoku Daigaku Shimbun*, Dec. 21, 1931 (reprinted in his *Gikai Seiji no Kento* [Tokyo, 1934], pp. 273–78); M. Royama, "Parliamentary Government and Constitutional Dictatorship," *Nihon Seiji Doko Ron* (Tokyo, 1933), pp. 471–75; also an anonymous article in *Keizai Orai*, Feb., 1932, pp. 121–35. It is said that General Araki, when he accepted the war portfolio in the *Seiyukai* cabinet, expressly reserved his freedom of action regarding military operations (see Hiroō Sasa, "Mr. Inukai's New Cabinet," *Kaizo*, Jan., 1932, pp. 145–51; also an article, "General Araki: Minister for War," *Japan Chronicle*, Feb. 2, 1932, p. 4).

army might make on the continent calculated to enhance their "life line."[112]

Meanwhile, incensed by the Council's decision of October 24, the Japanese occupation of Manchuria was further extended, and, on November 27, the press reported a new drive on Chinchow.[113] Evidently, this reported advance by Japanese forces in Manchuria was quite disturbing to the State Department at Washington. Thus, on this same date, Tokyo received some alarming dispatches from Washington, which were given wide publicity in Japan. According to these dispatches, Mr. Henry L. Stimson, then secretary of state, expressed great surprise at the latest news from Manchuria and openly accused Tokyo of violating the solemn assurances which it had given America only three days earlier, through Ambassador W. Cameron Forbes. As the press reports had it, Mr. Stimson declared that he had just obtained a definite pledge from both the civil and military authorities at Tokyo that no advance on Chinchow was contemplated, and hence the latest developments around Chinchow were nothing less than a flagrant violation by Tokyo of these assurances.[114] Such remarks on the part of Mr. Stimson at this time naturally evoked a storm of protests and bitter denunciation throughout the nation.[115] The Foreign Office spokesman bitterly criticized the intemperate remarks attributed to Mr. Stimson, while the American secretary of state denied that he had made some of the remarks attributed to him. At 3 P.M, November 29, Ambassador Forbes called at the Foreign Office and expressed Mr. Stimson's regret that his recent

---

[112]Sakuzo Yoshino, "Nationality, Classes, and War," *Chuo Koron*, No. 528 (Jan., 1932), pp. 27–28; Ishihama, "The Manchurian Question," *Keizai Orai*, Dec., 1931, pp. 26–31; Dr. Minoru Maida, "The Manchurian Incident and Self-defense," *Gaiko Jiho*, No. 646 (Nov. 1, 1931).

[113]*Tokyo Asahi*, Nov. 27, 1931, extra edition.

[114]Ashida, *op. cit.*, pp. 1185–87. For complete text of the A. P. dispatch from Washington see *Japan Advertiser*, Jan. 17, 1932, pp. 1, 14. *Cf.* Mr. John W. Perry's article in *Editor and Publisher* of Dec. 5, 1931. In this connection, read Senator William E. Borah's address, delivered at the University of Idaho on Sept. 24, when he openly accused Japan of violating the Pact of Paris, the League Covenant, and the Versailles Treaty (New York *Times*, Sept. 25, 1931, p. 1). The *Times* took the chairman of the Senate Foreign Relations Committee to task for his speech, and advised the senator that the best thing he could do for peace was to hold his tongue ("The Great Friend of Peace," New York *Times*, Sept. 26, 1931).

[115]See *Tokyo Asahi*, Nov. 29, 1931, p. 2.

utterances had caused misunderstanding in Japan.[116] This incident, of course, caused a considerable sensation in military circles who felt that if, in his interview with the American ambassador on November 23, Baron Shidehara had really made a pledge to America that Chinchow would not be attacked, he was guilty of disclosing military secrets. At the cabinet council of November 30, therefore, War Minister Minami addressed some inquiries to the Foreign Minister on this point. In reply, however, Baron Shidehara denied having given such a pledge.[117] Though the tension which was created between Washington and Tokyo by this episode was cleared up by Mr. Stimson's expression of regret and denial of certain remarks, and also by the cabinet's approval, on November 30, of Baron Shidehara's proposal that the incident be dropped at this juncture, there is no denying that this incident seriously endangered the relations between the two countries.[118] This incident served to intensify the opposition within the nation and thereby hastened the downfall of the ministry.[119]

At this time, the League Council was seriously considering the Japanese proposal to dispatch a commission of inquiry to the Orient to ascertain on the spot the contentions of the two disputing parties, and Tokyo was kept in constant touch,

[116]*Osaka Asahi*, Nov. 30, 1931, p. 1.

[117]*Tokyo Nichi Nichi*, Dec. 1, 1931, p. 1; *Japan Weekly Chronicle*, Dec. 10, 1931, pp. 742, 743.

[118]It is, of course, impossible to ascertain the actual details of this episode. According to available information here, however, the facts in the case appear to be as follows. On November 23, Mr. Cameron Forbes, the American ambassador, visited the *Kasumigaseki* and inquired of the foreign minister regarding the possibility of future advances on Chinchow. Accordingly, Baron Shidehara called on War Minister Minami in the afternoon, and explained the general atmosphere at Geneva, and asked him to see that the military authorities in Manchuria did not take further action. General Minami assured the foreign minister that the war authorities had no intention of taking further action at this time. He also promised to communicate the wishes of Baron Shidehara to General Kanaya, chief of staff, and to have him convey in person the views of the general staff. Later, the chief of staff told the foreign minister over the telephone that he, like the war minister, had no intention of taking further military action, and added that, if such an action should be taken, it would be solely in self-defense. With these assurances from the responsible war authorities, Baron Shidehara stated to Mr. Forbes, when he visited the *Kasumigaseki* the following day, that the Tokyo government had no intention of making further advances on Chinchow. These assurances were, of course, immediately cabled to Washington by the ambassador.

[119]The Wakatsuki cabinet fell within a fortnight of this incident.

through its representatives at Geneva, with every important development in the Council. Naturally, the *Kasumigaseki* was most sensitive to the apprehensions widely entertained at the time in League circles regarding the latest developments around Chinchow.[120] In view of the Geneva procedure, therefore, the cabinet was anxious that no further advances on Chinchow be taken at this time, excepting in the event of extreme Chinese provocation. In accordance with the wishes of the cabinet, therefore, the war authorities decided, on November 27, that further action in Manchuria be suspended. This decision of the authorities was immediately cabled to General Honjo, commander-in-chief of the Kwantung army.[121] On the afternoon of November 28, after reporting to the emperor, General Kanaya dispatched formal instructions to General Honjo to withdraw the forces to the railway zone from the region of Chinchow.[122]

However, with the formation, on December 13, of a new ministry under Mr. Inukai, president of the *Seiyukai*, as premier, and General Araki as minister of war, the developments in Manchuria took a new turn. Thus, in view of the renewed activities of the Chinese forces under Marshal Chang Hsueh-liang, the new cabinet, at its meeting on December 17, accepted the war minister's recommendation to send reinforcements to Manchuria.[123] On December 23, Field Marshal Prince Kanin, a prince of the blood, was appointed to head the general staff.[124] On December 27 it was decided by the general staff that a mixed brigade should be dispatched from Chosen to Manchuria to assist the forces already in Manchuria in their drive against banditry there. This de-

[120]See Dr. Ito's interesting analysis of the situation in his article, "The Sino-Japanese Dispute and the League," *Keizai Orai*, Aug., 1932, pp. 130–38. *Cf.* Maida, "Why Chinchow Became an Issue," *Chuo Koron*, Feb., 1932, pp. 79–82.

[121]*Tokyo Asahi*, Nov. 28, 1931, p. 2.

[122]The War Office issued a statement, dispelling the rumor that the decision to halt military action had some connection with Mr. Stimson's statement (*Japan Weekly Chronicle*, Dec. 10, 1931, p. 747; see also *Tokyo Asahi*, Nov. 29, 1931, p. 2).

[123]*Osaka Asahi*, Dec. 18, 1931, p. 1.

[124]Prince Kanin was the third imperial prince to fill the post. The late Prince Arisugawa was appointed the first chief of staff when this office was created in 1889. He was succeeded by Prince Komatsu, but no imperial prince has been appointed to the office since 1898 (*Tokyo Asahi*, Dec. 24, 1931, p. 11; *Tokyo Nichi Nichi*, Dec. 24, 1931, p. 2; *Japan Weekly Chronicle*, Dec. 31, 1931, p. 841). *Cf.* Mr. Baba's comment in *Gikai Seiji Ron* (Tokyo, 1933), p. 230.

cision was immediately reported to General Araki, who, in turn, reported the matter to the cabinet at its meeting in the afternoon and obtained its approval. After obtaining the imperial sanction, instructions were immediately cabled to General Hayashi, commander-in-chief of the garrison army in Chosen, in the afternoon.[125] At the same time, the government issued a long statement defending the impending military action in the vicinity of Chinchow as a measure of self-defense, which was expressly reserved by its representative at Geneva on December 10.[126] With reinforcements from Chosen, the Japanese advances continued with perfect regularity, and, on the morning of January 3, 1932, Chinchow was finally occupied by Japanese troops, who continued their march right up to the Great Wall at Shanhaikwan, where they established a permanent contact with the garrison in that place.[127]

These developments alarmed the United States, and, after conferring with the British, French, and Italian ambassadors,[128] the Washington government addressed identic notes to Tokyo and Nanking on January 7, and enunciated what later came to be known as the "Stimson Doctrine." It declared that:

In view of the present situation and of its own rights and obligations therein, the American government deems it to be its duty to notify both the government of the Chinese Republic and the Imperial Japanese government that it cannot admit the legality of any situation *de facto* nor does it intend to recognize any treaty or agreement entered into between these governments, or agents thereof, which may impair the treaty rights of the United States or its citizens in China, including those which relate to the sovereignty, the independence, or the territorial and administrative integrity of the Republic of China, or to the international policy relative to China, commonly known as the Open Door Policy; and that it does not intend to recognize any situation, treaty, or agreement which may be brought about by means contrary to the

[125]*Tokyo Asahi*, Dec. 28, 1931, p. 2.

[126]Text of statement in *Kokusaiho Gaiko Zasshi*, XXXI (April, 1932), 87–89.

[127]*Lytton Report*, pp. 77–78.

[128]New York *Times*, Jan. 5, 1932, pp. 1, 12; *ibid.*, Jan. 7, 1932, p. 1. In an editorial, "The League in Manchuria," the *Times* (New York) approved the action of the Council of the League and refuted those critics who contended that the Council ought to have done more (*ibid.*, Jan. 7, 1932, p. 22).

covenants and obligations of the Pact of Paris of August 27, 1928, to which treaty both China and Japan, as well as the United States, are parties.[129]

Owing to certain internal conditions, the Japanese reply to Washington was somewhat delayed.[130] In its reply to Washington, dated January 16, 1932, the Japanese government took note of the American observations on "the legality of matters which might impair the treaty rights of the United States or its citizens or which might be brought about by means contrary to the treaty of August 27, 1928," and declared that:

It might be the subject of an academic doubt, whether in a given case the impropriety of means necessarily and always avoids the ends secured, but as Japan has no intention of adopting improper means, that question does not practically arise.

It admitted the binding character of the stipulations of the Kellogg Pact and the Nine-Power Treaty, but suggested that "the present unsettled and distracted state of China" was not in contemplation of the parties at Washington in 1922, and consequently that, "it [the unsettled condition in China] may in material respects modify their application, since they must necessarily be applied with reference to the state of facts as they exist." It reassured Washington that Japan contemplated no territorial aims or ambitions in Manchuria, and reminded the American government that "the welfare and safety of Manchuria and its accessibility for general trade are matters of deepest interest and of quite extraordinary importance to the Japanese people," and that the

[129]Text in *Kokusaiho Gaiko Zasshi*, XXXI (April, 1932), 90–91; *Tokyo Nichi Nichi*, Jan. 9, 1932, p. 1. *Cf.* Ashida, *op. cit.*, pp. 1190–95.

[130]On Jan. 8 there was an attempt on the life of the emperor by a Korean in front of the Imperial Palace. Following the tradition in such circumstances, the members of the cabinet decided to tender their resignations. Upon His Majesty's command, however, they reconsidered their decision and remained in office (*Tokyo Asahi*, Jan. 9, 1932, p. 2). Mr. Inukai was sharply criticized for his decision to remain in office (Soichi Sasaki, "The Resignation of a Cabinet under the Constitution," *Chuo Koron*, No. 530 [March, 1932], pp. 2–18; see also editorial comments of *Tokyo Asahi* for Jan. 9, and *Tokyo Nichi Nichi* for Jan. 10). Prime Minister Inukai broadly hinted in replying to parliamentary interpellations on this affair that the delicate nature of international relations at the time compelled him to reconsider his decision (*Kwampo gogai*, Jan. 22, 1932, pp. 10–11; *ibid.*, March 23, 1932, pp. 32–36, 36–37). Mr. Kenkichi Yoshizawa, Mr. Inukai's son-in-law and the Japanese representative on the Council, did not assume the *Kasumigaseki* portfolio till Jan. 14, 1932 (see Baba, "Kenkichi Yoshizawa," *Chuo Koron*, March, 1932, pp. 150–56).

very existence of the national policy of Japan was at stake, and expressed its hope that Washington would soon come to a "correct appreciation of the situation."[131] The press of the nation unanimously supported the stand taken by the new cabinet and vigorously denied the imputation that Japan violated the Pact of Paris or the Nine-Power Treaty.[132]

The basic policy of the government towards the Manchurian affair was formally set forth before the nation when the Diet met on January 21, 1932, for the first time since the outbreak of the crisis the preceding fall. After reviewing briefly the Sino-Japanese conflict in Manchuria, Prime Minister Inukai reiterated the Japanese declaration, which was contained in her reply to the Stimson note, that she entertained no territorial ambitions in China, and that she was only insisting that her treaty rights be respected and her vested interests be protected, and nothing more.[133] Foreign Minister Yoshizawa, who followed the premier, further defined the limits of the Japanese demands and emphasized the importance of recognizing the vital relations which exist between China and Japan and declared that the settlement must be sought from political angles, in view of its historical

[131]Text in *Kokusaiho Gaiko Zasshi*, XXXI (April, 1932), 93–95. It is obviously beyond the scope of this treatise to deal extensively with the legal aspects of this note and subsequent developments. For discussions of the subject from the standpoint of international law, see Professor Quincy Wright, "The Stimson Note of January 7, 1932," *American Journal of International Law*, Vol. XXVI, No. 2 (April, 1932), pp. 342–48; Professor Kisaburo Yokota, "The Manchurian Incident and the Hoover Doctrine," *Kokusaiho Gaiko Zasshi*, XXXII (1933), 46–86; "The Manchurian Incident and the Hoover Doctrine as a Rule of International Law," *ibid.*, XXXIII (1934), 711–47; "The Stimson Doctrine and the International Situation," *Chuo Koron*, May, 1933; "New Developments of the Stimson Doctrine," *Gaiko Jiho*, Vol. 70, No. 5; Sakutaro Tachi, *Jikyoku Kokusaiho Ron* (Tokyo, 1934), pp. 70–107. While Professor Tachi strongly questions the legal significance of the new doctrine, Professor Yokota, also of the Imperial University of Tokyo, notes the "revolutionary character" of the doctrine, thus agreeing with Mr. Wright. For further literature on the subject, consult Wild, "Treaty Sanctions," *American Journal of International Law*, XXVI (1932), 488, 498–500; McNair, "The Stimson Doctrine of Non-Recognition," *British Yearbook of International Law*, XIV (1933), 65–74; Sir John Fischer Williams, "Some Thoughts on the Doctrine of Recognition in International Law," *Harvard Law Review*, XLVII, No. 5 (March, 1934), pp. 776–94.

[132]See editorial comments of *Nichi Nichi*, *Yomiuri*, and *Asahi* in *Japan Advertiser*, Jan. 19, 1932, p. 5. *Cf.* Dr. H. Kamikawa's comment on the Stimson note in *Tokyo Nichi Nichi*, Jan. 11, 1932, p. 2; also Dr. S. Washio's comment in *Japan Advertiser*, Jan. 14, 1932, p. 4.

[133]*Kwampo gogai*, Jan. 22, 1932, pp. 5–6, 16.

and geographical significance in the past. He went on to argue that, but for the repeated violations of Japanese treaty rights by China, the aggravation of the situation would not have been so serious even following the incident of September 18. He also emphasized the fact that Japan was chiefly responsible for maintaining peace and order in Manchuria and asserted that this responsibility would not be diminished in the future. In conclusion, the foreign minister expressed satisfaction that the Soviet Union had maintained an attitude of impartiality and noninterference ever since the September incident.[134] As the cabinet dissolved the House of Representatives immediately after the completion of addresses by the premier, foreign minister, and finance minister, no interpellations could be put to the government on the Manchurian affair.[135]

THE SHANGHAI INCIDENT

As the army continued its operations against banditry and enlarged its area of occupation in Manchuria, the Chinese boycott of Japanese trade throughout the country brought about a sharp decline in Japanese exports to China. This, in turn, served to increase friction and tension between the two countries, particularly among Japanese residents and Chinese merchants in and around Shanghai. Disparaging remarks which appeared in several newspapers in China following an attempt by a Korean, on January 8, on the life of the emperor greatly inflamed Japanese residents, while a mob attack on Japanese monks on January 18, causing death to one and seriously wounding the rest, put further strain on relations between China and Japan. On January 21, Consul General Murai lodged a vigorous protest with Mayor Wu Tieh-cheng against the mob assault on the monks and demanded an immediate dissolution of all anti-Japanese associations.[136] Clashes between the Japanese and Chinese continued to occur, and, on January 25, Mr. Murai sent a long

---

[134] *Ibid.*, pp. 6–7, 18–21; *Japan Advertiser*, Jan. 22, 1932, p. 2.

[135] A general election was held on Feb. 20 and resulted in an overwhelming victory for the *Seiyukai* party (see Professor Minobe, "Dissolution of the Sixtieth Diet," *Teikoku Daigaku Shimbun*, Jan. 25, 1932; "The General Election of 1932," *ibid.*, Feb. 29, 1932).

[136] Ashida, *op. cit.*, pp. 1196–1200 *ff.*

cable to Tokyo, reporting in detail the results of his negotiations with Mayor Wu and asking for instructions regarding the presentation of an ultimatum.[137] Late in the evening, the *Kasumigaseki* cabled its instructions to the consul general at Shanghai approving his proposals and authorizing him to exercise his discretion in taking any appropriate action. At 8 P.M., January 27, a twenty-two-hour ultimatum was delivered to Mayor Wu, while the navy department at Tokyo issued a statement at 7 P.M., declaring that, unless the Japanese demands be accepted in time, the Imperial Navy would be forced to take an independent action to safeguard the life and property of Japanese residents there.[138] At 3 P.M., January 28, an unconditional acceptance of Japanese terms was received by the consulate general.[139] But hostilities were started[140] between Chinese troops and Japanese bluejackets about midnight of the same day.[141]

It is not our purpose to review here the large-scale hostilities which ensued, during which Japan dispatched additional gunboats and several army divisions from the home base.[142] Nor will it be necessary to recall here the universal condemnation of Japanese action around Shanghai which was poured upon Tokyo immediately following the commencement of hostilities. The press comment in Japan upon the Shanghai outbreak was extremely reticent, but it was evident that the public support of the operations in central China was not so unanimous as in the case of the Manchurian onslaught.[143]

[137]*Tokyo Nichi Nichi*, Jan. 26, 1932, p. 2.

[138]*Tokyo Asahi*, Jan. 28, 1932, p. 2.

[139]*Tokyo Nichi Nichi*, Jan. 29, 1932, p. 2.

[140]Note Foreign Minister Yoshizawa's denial of the charge that Japanese forces started the hostilities in spite of the Chinese acceptance of the ultimatum (*Kwampo gogai*, March 23, 1932, pp. 10–11).

[141]Following the army precedent, Admiral Prince Hiroyasu Fushimi, also of the Imperial Family, succeeded Admiral Taniguchi as navy's chief of staff on February 2, 1932 (*Tokyo Nichi Nichi*, Feb. 3, 1932, p. 2).

[142]Admiral Sakonshi, "The Shanghai Incident," *Kokusai Chishiki*, XII, No. 4 (April, 1932), pp. 9–17. For further discussion of the military aspects of the Shanghai incident see *Lytton Report*, Chap. V.

[143]The *Tokyo Asahi* expressed regret that the Shanghai incident unfavorably affected Japanese standing in world public opinion, and urged the government to take immediate steps to correct this misunderstanding (editorials in Feb. 3, 5, 1932, p. 3). *Jiji Shimpo* urged upon the military to exercise caution, saying: "In Manchuria, Japan may act with a certain amount of freedom. She has vast interests in that country. Besides, the territory is indispensable to her existence. Things are

The organic connection between the Manchurian developments and the Shanghai outbreak, however, was broadly
intimated by Lieutenant General Araki, the minister of war,
when he declared before the House of Representatives on
March 22:

When we study in detail the nature and history of the Manchurian and Shanghai incidents, we cannot but realize that they
not only surpass either the Siberian expedition or the Tsinan incident in importance and effects but also, when seen from certain
angles, they become even more significant than the Russo-Japanese
War.[144]

In fact, the full import of this startling declaration by General Araki, undoubtedly the most influential individual in
Japan throughout the critical period under review, is yet to
be realized with the future development of Manchukuo, and
subsequent stabilization of Far Eastern power politics under
the Japanese doctrine of territorial propinquity and special
position.

Meanwhile, on January 29, 1932, immediately following
the Shanghai outbreak, the Chinese representative at Geneva requested the Council, while continuing to examine the
Sino-Japanese dispute under Article XI, to consider it also
under Articles X and XV of the covenant. An objection to
the proposed procedure was raised by Mr. Sato, the Japanese
representative in the Council, who expressed his doubts
whether the Council could now take up the matter—which
had so far been considered under Article XI, and insisted
that the Council first consider the question of whether it was
desirable to proceed to the examination of the issue under
Article XV. In reply, M. Paul-Boncour, president of the
Council, cited the unanimous decision of the Council of
March 13, 1924, and reminded Mr. Sato that it was not for
the Council, when it received a request under Article XV,
to decide whether or not it would discuss the matter under

different in Shanghai. It is an international city, where powers have conflicting
interests. In shaping their course in dealing with the situation in Shanghai, the military authorities should not close their eyes to the fact that the interests of some of
the powers in Shanghai are more important than those of Japan" (cited in *Japan
Advertiser*, Feb. 10, 1932, p. 5). An indiscreet comparison between the Communists
and the military clique which Dr. Nitobé made in an address in February provoked
the army (*Japan Chronicle*, Feb. 24, 1932, p. 4).

[144]*Kwampo gogai*, March 23, 1932, p. 12.

that article.[145] The following day, on January 30, when the matter was taken up again in the Council, Mr. Sato declared that a very bad impression might be created in Japan if it were learned that the Council had made a decision "in such a precipitate way on a question of such extreme importance," and repeated that he was not sure that Article XV could operate automatically in the present instance. His objection was overruled, and the Council accepted the proposals of the secretary general that a commission be formed immediately at Shanghai, consisting of official representatives there of Germany, the United Kingdom, Spain, France, Italy, and Norway, to report to the Council on the Shanghai incidents, their causes and developments. The proposals were accepted by the governments concerned, while the United States also expressed its willingness to coöperate with the commission at Shanghai.[146] When the Council met on February 2,[147] Mr. J. H. Thomas, the British representative, declared that war in everything but name was in progress over a wide area round Shanghai.[148]

As the situation progressed and became more serious, the Chinese representative finally requested the Council, on February 12, to refer the dispute to the Assembly of the League of Nations, under Article XV, paragraph 9, of the Covenant. On the same day the Shanghai commission forwarded its second report, stating that since February 3 a state of open war had existed, all pretence of truce having been abandoned.[149] Disturbed by the report, members of the

[145] *Monthly Summary of the League of Nations*, XII, No. 1 (Jan., 1932), pp. 23–25. Prof. K. Yokota defended the Council's submission of the dispute to the assembly as being quite proper in the circumstances ("League Procedure under Articles XI and XV," *Gaiko Jiho*, No. 656 [April 1, 1932], pp. 38–49; also his "The Manchurian Incident and Article XV of the Covenant of the League of Nations," *Chuo Koron* January, 1933, pp. 75–83).

[146] *Ibid.*, pp. 26–27.

[147] On February 2, Admiral Prince Fushimi became the navy's chief of staff, replacing Admiral Taniguchi. Thus, within five months of the outbreak of the Manchurian incident, the general staffs of both the army and the navy were headed by imperial princes, thereby placing the imperial army and navy beyond popular criticism (see *supra*, n. 141).

[148] *Ibid.*, XII, No. 2 (Feb., 1932), p. 42. For legal aspects of the Shanghai incident see J. Shinobu, *International Law in the Shanghai Conflict* (Tokyo: Maruzen & Co., 1933); Tachi, *Jikyoku Kokusaiho Ron* (Tokyo, 1934), pp. 1–22; Q. Wright, "When Does War Exist?" *American Journal of International Law*, XXVI, No. 2 (April, 1932), pp. 362–68.

[149] *Ibid.*, p. 44.

Council (other than China and Japan) voted, on February 16, to address an appeal to Japan. In this long communication, the twelve members of the Council "appealed to Japan's high sense of honor" to be just and restrained in her relations with China, and broadly implied that Japan violated Article X of the Covenant as well as the Nine-Power Treaty of 1922.[150] As soon as the appeal to Japan from the president of the Council reached Tokyo the following afternoon, the Foreign Office proceeded to examine its text and prepare a reply.

Meanwhile the general election of February 20 resulted in an overwhelming victory for the *Seiyukai* (government) party, giving Prime Minister Inukai an absolute control of the Lower House.[151] A reply to the Council, together with a declaration to be issued and attached to the note, having been drafted by the Foreign Office, they were submitted to the cabinet on February 23 for deliberation and approval. After obtaining the imperial sanction, Foreign Minister Yoshizawa cabled the reply and the declaration to Geneva at 6:00 P.M., instructing Mr. Sato, the Japanese representative, to transmit the documents to the president of the Council. In the long communication thus sent to Geneva, couched in the most vigorous language ever used in its diplomatic correspondence since the Russo-Japanese War, the Japanese government openly repudiated the implications of the appeal. Thus, contending that "the appeal was addressed to a quarter where it was not necessary," Tokyo reminded the Council that it might have been more effectively made to China, and bluntly asserted that Japan was naturally in a far better position to appreciate the facts than any distant power. Referring to the obligations under Article X of the Covenant, Japan recalled the strong reinforcements which were dispatched to Chinese waters by other powers in 1927 to defend Shanghai and cited the bombardment of Nanking by British and American forces in the same year. It argued,

[150]*Ibid.*, pp. 44–45; *Tokyo Asahi*, Feb. 18, 1932, p. 1; Ashida, *op. cit.*, pp. 1210–14.

[151]As the result of the February 20, 1932, elections, the *Seiyukai* members in the Lower House increased from 171 to 304, while the *Minseito* decreased from 246 to 147, giving the government party a plurality of 157 members over the nearest opposition in the House of Representatives. The total membership of the Lower House is 466 (see Sasa, "The Future of the Minseito Party," *Kaizo*, April, 1932, pp. 138–47).

moreover, that it did not and could not consider that China was an "organized people" within the meaning of the Covenant of the League of Nations, and dryly suggested that, if Japan had no interests there, it might be possible for her to go on indefinitely respecting this fiction. The Tokyo government concluded the historic note by advising the powers to exert "their utmost efforts to induce the Chinese to refrain from aggressive acts such as those which have precipitated armed conflicts of the past five months."[152]

Before the arrival of the Japanese note, however, the Japanese commander at Shanghai sent an ultimatum demanding that before 5 P.M. on February 20 the Chinese forces should be withdrawn to a distance of twenty kilometers to the north, east, and west of the International Settlement, failing which he would take the necessary action. Upon receipt of the ultimatum on February 18, the Chinese representative at Geneva asked for a meeting of the Council for submitting the dispute to the Assembly. In response to this appeal, the Council met the following day, and, after heated debate between the Chinese and Japanese representatives, decided to call a special session of the Assembly to deliberate upon the matter.[153]

While steps were being taken for the meeting of the Assembly, numerous conferences were held between Ambassador Matsudaira and Sir John Simon, between Ambassador Sato and M. Paul-Boncour, and others, with a view to reaching some agreement to prevent further devastation of the Shanghai area. On February 26, the Japanese government decided to cease hostilities, and communicated this decision to its minister at Nanking as well as representatives at Geneva. Two days later, a memorandum was made public setting forth Japan's terms.[154] On the afternoon of March 3, General Shirakawa, the Japanese commander, gave the order to stop fighting, while the Chinese commander also issued a similar order the following day.[155] These gestures at

[152]Texts of the note and declaration which accompanied it in *Monthly Summary of the League of Nations*, XII, No. 2 (Feb., 1932), pp. 45–47; *Tokyo Asahi*, Feb. 24, 1932, p. 2.

[153]*Ibid.*, pp. 47–50.

[154]Ashida, *op. cit.*, pp. 1217–19.

[155]*Lytton Report*, p. 85.

Shanghai eased the atmosphere at Geneva, and on March 11, 1932, the Assembly unanimously voted a resolution,[156] saying that the provisions of the Covenant were entirely applicable to the dispute, thereby rejecting the Japanese argument for a "special character" of Manchuria. It affirmed the Stimson Doctrine and declared that, "it is incumbent upon the Members of the League of Nations not to recognize any situation, treaty, or agreement which may be brought about by means contrary to the Covenant of the League of Nations or to the Pact of Paris." It also provided for a committee of nineteen members to carry on its work.[157]

The Assembly resolution was widely denounced in Japan as making no contribution towards a permanent solution of the Sino-Japanese dispute,[158] while General Araki, minister of war, defended the decision to withdraw forces from the Shanghai area on grounds of unity and coördination between political tactics and military operations, and added that he was desirous of avoiding a general war between China and Japan.[159] On May 5, 1932, chiefly through the good offices of Sir Miles Lampson, British minister to China, an armistice was signed between China and Japan.[160] In accordance with this agreement, evacuation of the forces was completed by the end of May.[161]

Before concluding our discussion of the Shanghai incident, reference may be made to an interesting question which arose in connection with the legal character of the armistice of May 5. This agreement was signed by the military representatives of both countries, and also by the diplomatic representatives of China and Japan, as well as by the British, American, French, and Italian ministers to China.

[156]Of the forty-seven delegations present, forty-five voted in favor of the resolution, while two (China and Japan) abstained.

[157]For debate on the resolution see *Monthly Summary of the League of Nations*, XII, No. 3 (March, 1932), pp. 80–107. According to Dr. Ashida, the Assembly deliberations resulted in (1) condemnation of Japanese action, (2) adoption by the League of the Stimson Doctrine, and (3) closer coöperation between Great Britain and the United States in the dispute (*op. cit.*, p. 1225).

[158]See leading articles in *Tokyo Nichi Nichi*, March 12, 13, 1932, p. 3; also see *Tokyo Asahi*, March 13, 1932, p. 3.

[159]General Araki's statement in reply to an interpellation in the House of Peers on March 24, 1932 (*Kwampo gogai*, March 25, 1932, pp. 29–31).

[160]Text in *Tokyo Asahi*, May 6, 1932, p. 1; *Japan Chronicle*, April 29, 1932, p. 4.

[161]*Gaiko Jiho*, June 15, 1932, pp. 179–80; *Tokyo Asahi*, June 2, 1932, p. 2.

It was held among certain members of the Privy Council that this agreement was an international agreement, coming under the "treaties and agreements" clause of the Ordinance concerning the Organization of the Privy Council, and hence ought to have been submitted to its deliberation before signature. When this question was indirectly raised in the Privy Council on May 11, however, General Araki, the war minister, defended the procedure followed at Shanghai, saying that it was purely a military agreement, which need not be submitted to the Privy Council for approval prior to signature. The councilors were not satisfied with the war minister's explanations, but did not press the point further.[162]

THE INCIDENT OF MAY 15, 1932

As we have noted elsewhere,[163] the popular enthusiasm for a parliamentary system of government, which was so evident and overwhelming during 1930, soon subsided towards the summer of 1931, and, with the outbreak of the Mukden crisis, a reaction set in. This reaction against the working of the parliamentary system gained added momentum, as the impasse between Tokyo and Geneva over the Manchurian affair became more serious and the gulf between Kasumigaseki and Miyakezaka over the execution of the nation's continental policy became more pronounced. Thus, towards the close of the year, it became manifest that the very basis of democracy and the working of the parliamentary system were being subjected to searching criticism, not only in Socialist circles, but also among young officers of the army and the navy.[164]

The assassination of Mr. Junnosuke Inouye, former minister of finance and a leading *Minseito* whip, on February 9, 1932,[165] and also of Baron Takuma Dan, an outstanding

[162]*Ibid.*, May 10, 12, 1932, p. 2.

[163]*Supra*, Chap. XXV.

[164]Soichi Sasaki, "Re-examination of the Japanese Parliamentary System," *Kaizo*, XIV, No. 1 (Jan., 1932), pp. 2–40; Ikuo Oyama, "A Coalition Cabinet under Fascism," *ibid.*, pp. 131–44; Sakuzo Yoshino, "Historical Investigation of National-Socialist Movement," *Kokka Gakkai Zasshi*, XLVI, No. 2 (Feb., 1932), pp. 276–90; also a symposium on fascism by Masamichi Royama, Katsumaro Akamatsu, and Hiroō Sasa, in *Keizai Orai*, January, 1932, pp. 37–66.

[165]*Tokyo Asahi*, Feb. 10, 1932, p. 2; Shigeichi Maeda, "Mr. Junnosuke Inouye as a Statesman," *Keizai Orai*, March, 1932, pp. 136–41.

financier, on March 5,[166] created a great sensation in political and financial circles, as indicating the general trend of the day.[167] When the Sixty-first Diet was convened on March 20 to vote funds necessitated by the Manchurian crisis,[168] a chorus of criticism was raised in both Houses against the rising tide of the reactionary movement in Japan, and the government was urged to exert all its efforts in defense of the parliamentary system.[169] Prime Minister Inukai reminded the legislators, however, that they had to assume a major portion of the responsibility for the state of mind then in vogue,[170] while General Araki, minister for war, intimated that soldiers might be moved to action unless the social maladjustments were rectified so that they could devote all their thought and endeavors to military affairs.[171]

With the adjournment of the Diet on March 25, forces against the parliamentary régime became stronger and more militant,[172] and by the beginning of May they seemed to

[166]*Tokyo Asahi*, March 6, 1932, p. 1; S. Maeda, "Baron Takuma Dan," *Keizai Orai*, April, 1932, pp. 193–97.

[167]Minobe, "Parliamentary Government and Direct Action," *Chuo Koron*, March, 1932, pp. 44–47.

[168]Thus far, the financial measures needed for military and naval operations since the outbreak of the crisis had all been met by emergency imperial ordinances.

[169]Particularly Mr. Giichi Matsumura in the Upper House (*Kwampo gogai*, March 25, 1932, pp. 25–26), and Representatives Taketomi (*ibid.*, March 24, 1932, pp. 47–51) and Kamei (*ibid.*, March 25, 1932, pp. 66–70) in the Lower House.

[170]*Ibid.*, March 24, 1932, pp. 51–53.

[171]*Ibid.*, March 25, 1932, pp. 27–28.

[172]Among the most influential of the organizations advocating a "strong government" was the Kokuhonsha, or National Foundation Society. This society grew out of an organization originally established by students at the Tokyo Imperial University about 1919 to oppose the activities of the Shinjinkai, or New Men's Society, led by the late Professor Sakuzo Yoshino, a leading student of democracy in Japan. The Kokuhonsha was organized in May, 1924, by Baron Hiranuma, Admiral Kanji Kato, General Sadao Araki, Dr. Kado Hara, and others (see Kozo Ota, "The Truth about the Kokuhonsha," *Keizai Orai*, August, 1932, pp. 180–86; Kaku Seta's article on "Reactionary Organizations among Students" in *Kaizo*, May, 1932; also comments on these organizations in *Economist* [Osaka], June 1, 1932, pp. 50–51; *ibid.*, July 1, 1932, pp. 51–52). At a public meeting held in Osaka on April 21st under the auspices of the Kokuhonsha, attended by Lieutenant General Terauchi, commander of the Osaka division, business men, educators, government officials, chiefs of local ex-soldiers' associations, and chiefs of the young men's associations, General Araki, minister for war and a leading figure in the society, spoke for two hours, urging upon the people to give their wholehearted support to the army in defending Manchuria against all invaders. In the course of this address, he declared: "Let the League of Nations say whatever it pleases, let America offer

threaten an early fall of the ministry.[173] This growing un-
popularity of democracy and the parliamentary régime
naturally alarmed party leaders, who now realized the formidable proportions which the movement towards fascism
had assumed in Japan.[174] Thus, both Mr. Inukai, president
of the *Seiyukai*, and Baron Wakatsuki, head of the *Minseito*,
vigorously denounced the growing tendency towards the
denial of parliamentary government, in their addresses before
their respective parties.[175]

About 5 o'clock in the afternoon, May 15, 1932, a band of
men in military and naval uniforms suddenly attacked the
official residence of the prime minister and shot him to
death.[176] About the same time, the headquarters of the *Seiyukai* party, the home of Count Makino, Lord Privy Seal,
Metropolitan Police Board, Bank of Japan, Mitsubishi Bank,
as well as main power stations in Tokyo, were also attacked
with bombs by armed men.[177] This assassination of a prime

whatever interference, let Russia attempt to disturb peace in Manchuria as hard as
she will, and let China decry Japan's action at the top of her voice, but Japan must
adhere to her course unswervingly" (*Osaka Asahi*, April 22, 1932, p. 2; *Japan
Chronicle*, April 23, 1932, p. 4).

[173]Baba, "Mr. Inukai and the Army," *Kaizo*, June, 1932, pp. 80–85; Sasa, "A
Fascist Cabinet," *ibid.*, pp. 86–93.

[174]Advocates of a "strong government" were not confined to Kokuhonsha leaders,
but were found even among labor groups (K. Akamatsu, "Starting with a Scientific
Japanism," *Kaizo*, Dec., 1931, pp. 72–77; also "Bourgeois Democracy," *ibid.*,
June, 1932, pp. 56–61; Kenzo Asahara, "Fascism among Labor Parties," *ibid.*,
May, 1932, pp. 33–39), and the *Seiyukai* party itself (for instance, Kaku Mori,
chief secretary of the party, and his followers). *Tokyo Asahi*, May 7, 1932, p. 2;
Osaka Asahi, May 8, 1932, p. 2; *Osaka Mainichi*, May 14, 1932, p. 1. Mr. Kenzo
Adachi, former *Minseito* leader, and his followers also supported a "national fas-
cism" (see Rep. Seigo Nakano's statement in *Osaka Mainichi*, May 13, 1932, p. 1).

[175]*Japan Chronicle*, May 10, 1932, p. 4; *Tokyo Asahi*, May 12, 1932, p. 2. In an
interview on May 12, Prime Minister Inukai asserted that advocates of a fascist
régime were in the minority and that it was too hasty to conclude that the parliamentary system had become too degenerate to permit of reform. In the same interview, he strongly intimated that the Manchurian and Shanghai developments were
responsible for his failure to do more for poor relief. Referring to the Russo-Japanese
relations, he declared that neither Japan nor the Soviet Union desired war, while,
on the question of extending recognition to Manchukuo, he said that the new state
had not been fully established (*Osaka Mainichi*, May 13, 1932, p. 1).

[176]*Tokyo Asahi*, May 16, 1932; *Japan Chronicle*, May 17, 1932, p. 5.

[177]For details of the incident consult court proceedings: for military side, *Osaka
Asahi*, Sept. 20, 1933; for naval side, *Tokyo Asahi*, Nov. 9, 1933; for participants
other than military and naval officers, *ibid.*, Feb. 3, 1934. The death list of the Ket-
sumeidan, or Blood League, included Inukai, Tokonami, Suzuki (*Seiyukai*), Wakat-

minister at his official residence by a band of men wearing
military and naval uniforms was an unprecedented event in
Japanese history, and naturally threw the entire nation into
a state of indescribable confusion.[178]

Fully appreciating the gravity of the situation thus thrown
into the open by the events of May 15,[179] Prince Saionji, the
sole remaining elder statesman, who was commanded by the
emperor to recommend the succeeding prime minister, spent

suki, Inouye, Shidehara (*Minseito*), Ikeda, Dan, Go (Mitsui interests), Kakumu,
Kimura (Mitsubishi interests), Prince Saionji, Count Makino, Count Miyoji Ito,
Prince Tokugawa (privileged class), as well as one representative each of the Yasuda,
Okura, and Sumitomo interests. Of these, attempts on Mr. Inouye, Baron Dan,
and Prime Minister Inukai were successful (*ibid.*, Nov. 22, 1934, extra edition, p. 1).
No death penalty was inflicted upon any of the participants in these attacks, the
heaviest imposed being a life sentence. For personal commentaries upon leaders in
the incident see an anonymous article in *Kaizo*, Oct., 1933, pp. 190–234; S. Tanaka,
"Personalities in the May 15th Incident," *ibid.*, Nov., 1932, pp. 273–82.

[178]See brief comments by Professor Kojiro Sugimura (Waseda) and Masamichi
Royama (Imp. Univ. Tokyo) in *ibid.*, June, 1932, pp. 97–102; H. Sasa, "Japan in
Political Crisis," *ibid.*, July, 1932, pp. 44–58.

[179]It is now known that the assassinations of Mr. Junnosuke Inouye, former
finance minister and a leading *Minseito* whip, on February 9, 1932, of Baron Takuma Dan, head of the Mitsui interests and a representative financier, on March
5, and Mr. Inukai, premier and head of a political party, on May 15, were related
to each other and carried out by men of similar temper and conviction. Of the
main factors responsible for these assassinations and abortive *coup d'état* we may
cite: (1) the panic-stricken condition in farming districts; (2) failure on the part
of the government to take effective measures to relieve the situation; (3) lack of
public confidence in parliamentary system to meet the exigencies of the day due to
the Manchurian and Shanghai developments; and (4) corruptions of party politics,
particularly their reported connections with "big business" (see Minobe, "Terror-
ism and the Future of Party Politics," *Teikoku Daigaku Shimbun*, May 23, 1932;
Dr. Ichiro Kiyosé, "May 15th Incident," *Kaizo*, Nov., 1933, pp. 283–91; an anonymous article in *ibid.*, Oct., 1933, pp. 56–67; also a résumé of articles in *Japan
Chronicle*, June 4, 1932, p. 5). By a queer coincidence, both the *Tokyo Asahi* and
Osaka Mainichi, two representative dailies in Japan, discussed the prevailing attacks on "parliamentary government" in their editorial comments on May 15,
1932.

In a long speech delivered in the House of Peers on June 7, 1932, Mr. Mannoshin
Kamiyama deplored party corruptions and likened the *Seiyukai* and *Minseito* to
burglars and thieves, but defended the parliamentary régime against dictatorships,
saying: "In the absence of an assurance that we can always have enlightened monarchs and wise statesmen to rule us, a constitutional government is almost a necessity. This is why the Imperial Diet was established" (*Kwampo gogai*, June 8, 1932,
pp. 29–36, especially, p. 33). His analogy between a member of the Diet and an
article of goods and his references to our not always being assured of enlightened
monarchs and rulers were severely criticized in the Lower House, and as the result
he was obliged to withdraw these references and analogies in the Upper House (*ibid.*,
June 14, 1932, pp. 77–78). *Cf.* Rep. Kiyosé's remarks in the Lower House on Jan.
23, 1933 (*ibid.*, Jan. 24, 1933, pp. 50, 51, 55, 58).

seven days in interviewing civil and military leaders[180] before
he finally decided on Admiral Viscount Minoru Saito, former
governor general of Chosen, as the most suitable statesman
to form a new cabinet under these circumstances.[181] Admiral
Saito, a well-known administrator and a non-party man, as
the succeeding prime minister, was widely acclaimed as the
statesman best qualified to calm the tension and excitement
created by recent events.[182] Admiral Osumi was succeeded by
Admiral Okada as navy minister, while General Araki retained his portfolio at the War Department in the new cabinet.[183] Prime Minister Saito occupied the *Kasumigaseki* post
until the appointment of Count Uchida, an experienced diplomat and the then president of the South Manchuria Railway Company, on July 6, 1932.[184]

[180]Prince Saionji had interviews with Admiral Count Yamamoto (former prime
minister), Count Kiyoura (former prime minister), Baron Wakatsuki (former prime
minister and head of the *Minseito*), Mr. Korekiyo Takahashi (acting prime minister), Baron Kuratomi (president of the Privy Council), Count Makino (Lord Privy
Seal), General Nara (aide-de-camp to the emperor), Field Marshal Uyehara, Fleet
Admiral Togo, as well as General Araki (war minister) and Admiral Osumi (navy
minister).

[181]For detailed discussion of the circumstances which led the genro to recommend
Viscount Saito, instead of Dr. Kisaburo Suzuki, president of the *Seiyukai* party,
as successor to Mr. Inukai, see Minobe, "Formation of the Saito Cabinet and the
Future of Party Politics," *Teikoku Daigaku Shimbun*, June 27, July 4, 1932; "For-
mation of a National Government," *Chuo Koron*, July, 1932, pp. 30–33; Baba,
"Personalities in the Saito Cabinet," *Kaizo*, July, 1932, pp. 65–72; T. Iwabuchi,
"The Saito Government and the Army," *ibid.*, pp. 40–44.

[182]It was reported at the time that Prince Saionji originally intended to recommend Dr. Suzuki, minister for home affairs in the Inukai Cabinet and newly elected
president of the *Seiyukai*, the majority party in the House of Representatives, but
the opposition of the army to any party cabinet, which was expressed in no uncertain terms, finally led the elder statesman to abandon a party ministry in favor of a
"national government" (Hideo Nomura, "Inside Story of the Formation of the
Saito Cabinet," *Chuo Koron*, July, 1932, pp. 270–78; Royama, *Nihon Seiji Doko
Ron*, pp. 475–77).

[183]Admiral Saito selected General Hayashi, then commander of the garrison army
in Chosen, as his war minister, but military leaders in Tokyo insisted that General
Araki should remain in office to maintain discipline in the army (*Keizai Orai*,
March, 1934, pp. 108–09 *ff*). The navy and war ministers spoke before the Houses
of the Diet on June 3 regarding the assassination of Mr. Inukai (*Tokyo Asahi*,
June 4, 1932, p. 1). Admiral Okada's vigorous expression of disapproval of the incident was favorably received in the Lower House, while General Araki's address
was interrupted several times by Solons who were evidently dissatisfied with his
failure to resign as had his colleague in the Navy Department (*Kwampo gogai*,
June 4, 1932, pp. 12–13, 13).

[184]*Tokyo Asahi*, July 7, 1932, p. 1. For an interesting commentary on Count
Uchida, see Tsunego Baba, *Gikai Seiji Ron*, pp. 343–57; *Japan Advertiser*, June 25,
1932, p. 5.

The Establishment and Recognition of Manchukuo

On March 1, 1932, a declaration was issued at Mukden, in the name of an All-Manchuria Convention, expressing the joy of the thirty million inhabitants of Manchuria for the founding of a new state of Manchukuo.[185] On March 9, the former Emperor Hsuan Tung, now known by his personal name as Mr. Henry Pu-yi, was inaugurated at the new capital at Changchun as regent of the newly established state,[186] and on March 10 the principal members of the new government were appointed.[187] Two days later a notice was issued by cable to various foreign powers,[188] informing them of the establishment of Manchukuo and requesting them to recognize it as a new state.[189]

The task of formulating general principles to guide the government in its dealings with the new régime in Manchuria had been entrusted to a special committee, consisting of members representing the foreign, war, navy, finance, and overseas departments. A statement of policy, which had been drafted by this committee, headed by Mr. Kaku Mori, chief secretary of the cabinet, was submitted to the cabinet on March 11 for deliberation and approval. After a two-day conference the cabinet agreed on March 12 upon its policy towards Manchukuo. No formal statement was issued after the cabinet council, explaining details of its deliberations or the decision reached, but the press reported that, after full deliberation, the government decided to await further developments in Manchuria before extending recognition to

[185]*Tokyo Asahi*, March 2, 1932, p. 2; *Gaiko Jiho*, No. 655 (March 15, 1932), pp. 145–52.

[186]For a detailed narrative of events leading up to the establishment of Manchukuo, see *Lytton Report*, pp. 88–97; Ashida, *op. cit.*, pp. 1226–30. *Cf.* articles by Professors Tazaki, Negishi, Hashimoto, Kamikawa, and Yano in *Gaiko Jiho*, No. 656 (April 1, 1932).

[187]For a brief description of the government of Manchukuo, consult *Lytton Report*, pp. 97–116 *ff.*; Royama, "Organization of the Government of Manchukuo," *Kaizo*, July, 1932, pp. 29–43.

[188]Notice was sent to Japan, England, the United States, France, Italy, Belgium, the Netherlands, Austria, Poland, Portugal, Denmark, Czechoslovakia, Esthonia, Lithuania, Latvia, and Soviet Russia (Ashida, *op. cit.*, p. 1230).

[189]The United States did not reply to the communication, while other powers, except Japan, merely acknowledged receipt of the notice (*ibid.*, pp. 1230–31).

the new state.[190] Thus, in its note to Manchukuo, dated March 18, the Japanese government merely expressed its satisfaction at the formation of a new state and intimated that *de jure* recognition would be forthcoming as soon as the foundations of the new régime had been firmly established.[191]

Considerations of foreign policy, particularly the proceedings at Geneva, evidently played a large part in compelling the Inukai-Yoshizawa cabinet to adopt a policy of "watchful waiting" towards Manchukuo.[192] In view of the close connections between Japan and the independence movement in Manchuria,[193] however, the attitude of the cabinet was

[190]The Cabinet deliberated upon the subject on March 11 and 12 and, after a long deliberation lasting over five hours, Prime Minister Inukai was received in audience by the emperor, on the afternoon of March 12, to report the cabinet's decision upon its policy towards Manchukuo (*Tokyo Asahi, Tokyo Nichi Nichi*, March 13, 1932, p. 2).

[191]Ashida, *op. cit.*, p. 1231.

[192]Throughout the Sixty-first session of Diet, both the prime minister and foreign minister maintained this attitude. Thus, in replying to an interpellation addressed to the government by Mr. Koichiro Shimizu (Kenkyukai), Prime Minister Inukai declared that, in his opinion, it was still doubtful whether Manchukuo had been established upon firm foundations, and expressed his hope that it would make a rapid stride towards a really independent state, when Japan would be glad to recognize her as an independent state (*Kwampo gogai*, March 25, 1932, p. 29). Mr. Yoshizawa also maintained, in his reply to an interpellation by Mr. Yamaji (*Minseito*) in the Lower House, that the international situation as well as other factors had to be taken into consideration before recognition could be extended to Manchukuo (*ibid.*, March 23, 1932, p. 15; *Japan Chronicle*, March 24, 1932, p. 4).

[193]In an illuminating article, written immediately following the declaration of independence, Professor H. Kamikawa, a well-known student of international affairs, frankly admitted the close connections which existed between Japan and the independence movement and said that the movement would not have been carried through but for the presence of the Japanese troops. In the opinion of this authority, the part played by Japanese forces in Manchuria is analogous to that of the United States marines in the case of the Cuban and Panama independence, the only difference being that the part played by the former in the movement is less than that of the latter. He even suggested that there was a strong possibility that the independent "Manchukuo" might become, in fact, a Japanese protectorate, and that such an eventuality might be frustrated if opposed by the powers, particularly the United States, Soviet Russia, England, and the League of Nations ("Formation of Manchukuo: A Study in International Politics," *Keizai Orai*, VII, No. 4 [April, 1932], Supplement, pp. 1–12). Commenting on the birth of Manchukuo, he argued further that there were only two alternative courses open to Japan, namely, a mandate system for Manchukuo and the permanent neutralization of the area ("Japanese Diplomacy on the Crossroads," *Gaiko Jiho*, April 1, 1932, pp. 137–47). Professor Tadao Yanaihara endorsed the liberal stand and said that Japanese policy must not be executed in total disregard of her trade relations with China proper and the world ("The New State of Manchukuo," *Kaizo*, April, 1932, pp. 18–29).

disappointing to the more enthusiastic supporters of the movement in Manchuria and at Tokyo.[194]

With the fall of the Inukai-Yoshizawa cabinet, following the assassination of the premier on May 15, the demand for immediate recognition of Manchukuo became more pronounced.[195] Thus, on June 3, addressing the Imperial Diet as foreign minister,[196] Viscount Saito declared that it was no longer possible to ignore the existence of the new state of Manchukuo in any international readjustments which might be made with reference to the Manchurian incident, and emphasized the importance of the tranquillity of the Far East as well as of the restoration of peace and prosperity in Manchuria in order that the new state might make healthy progress.[197] On the same day Mr. Yosuke Matsuoka, former vice-president of the South Manchuria Railway Company and an influential member of the *Seiyukai*, openly advocated immediate recognition of the new state, citing the recognition of Panama by the United States in the fall of 1903.[198]

While voices were being raised in Tokyo and in the Diet chambers advocating the immediate recognition of the new régime in Manchuria, Mr. Hsieh Chieh-shih, foreign minister of Manchukuo, called on General Honjo, commander of the Kwantung army,[199] and Count Uchida, president of the South Manchuria Railway Company, and asked for early recognition by Tokyo, while several organizations in Manchuria sent their representatives to Tokyo to urge upon the government and influential leaders immediate action.[200] Finally, on June 14th, the last day of the Sixty-second Diet, the House of Representatives passed, by unanimous vote, a

[194]For representative views in military circles, see *Keizai Orai*, April, 1932, Supplement, pp. 66–110.

[195]*Cf.* an editorial, "Recognition of Manchukuo," *Tokyo Asahi*, May 6, 1932, p. 3.

[196]Admiral Viscount Saito, the new prime minister, also held the portfolio of the foreign minister until he was succeeded by Count Uchida on July 6, 1932 (*supra*, n. 184).

[197]*Japan Advertiser*, June 4, 1932, pp. 1, 2.

[198]*Kwampo gogai*, June 4, 1932, pp. 14–16. In reply, Viscount Saito expressed the government's intention to recognize Manchukuo as soon as possible (*ibid.*, p. 16).

[199]After consulting members of his staff, General Honjo sent a long telegram to army headquarters in Tokyo, on June 7, emphasizing the necessity of an early recognition of Manchukuo for unification of the territory as well as for fundamental readjustment of Japan-Manchukuo relations (*Tokyo Asahi*, June 10, 1932, p. 2).

[200]Ashida, *op. cit.*, p. 1232.

resolution calling upon the government to follow the American example regarding Panama and, without delay, accord *de jure* recognition to Manchukuo.[201]

With the arrival of the Lytton Commission in Tokyo on July 4th after several months of intensive study in China and Manchuria, and the appointment of Count Uchida as foreign minister on July 6th,[202] events moved in rapid succession.[203] Several mass meetings were organized in Tokyo to stimulate a public demand for immediate recognition of Manchukuo.[204] Two formal interviews were held between Count Uchida and the members of the commission on July 12th and 14th, when, as the press reported, Count Uchida made it plain that Japan intended to accord recognition to Manchukuo at an early date.[205] Finding no room for persuading Tokyo to modify its attitude towards Manchukuo, the commission left Tokyo for Peiping on July 16 to prepare its report to the League of Nations.[206] General Muto was appointed commander-in-chief

---

[201]Both Mr. Kodama (*Seiyukai*) and Mr. Yamaji (*Minseito*) referred to the American recognition of Panama, while Mr. Kanichiro Kamei, a Laborite, supported the resolution for considerations of "broad policy" (*Kwampo gogai*, June 15, 1932, pp. 152, 187–90; *Tokyo Asahi*, June 15, 1932, p. 2). Commenting on the resolution, Mr. Machida, head of the foreign news bureau of the *Tokyo Asahi Shimbun*, said that the formal recognition of Manchukuo was now only a question of time and argued that the government's hesitation at this hour was altogether meaningless. In his opinion, further delays in taking the next logical step could not be expected to better the Sino-Japanese relations. He reminded the people that the Manchurian crisis had been brought about by those who saw no hope of finding a solution to the situation by peaceful negotiation with China ("Observations on the Recognition of Manchukuo," *Kokusai Chishiki*, XII, No. 7 [July, 1932], pp. 13–19). In this connection, read Viscount Ishii's address of welcome at the America-Japan Society dinner on June 21 in honor of Mr. Joseph C. Grew, American ambassador in Tokyo (text in *Contemporary Japan*, I, No. 2 [Sept., 1932], pp. 345–48).

[202]On July 5 Count Uchida told the press reporters who interviewed him on the train that recognition of Manchukuo must be accorded as soon as possible (*Tokyo Asahi*, July 7, 1932, p. 1).

[203]It was about this time that Mr. Hachiro Arita, vice-minister of foreign affairs, was reported to have given word to the British ambassador in Tokyo that Japan would not recognize Manchukuo prior to the presentation of a report by the commission to the League. This news created such a sensation in diplomatic and military circles that a formal statement of denial was issued by the Foreign Office on July 6 (*Tokyo Asahi*, July 7, 1932, pp. 1, 2; Ijuin, "Mr. Akita's Reported Assurances," *Gaiko Jiho*, No. 665 [Aug. 15, 1932], pp. 112–26).

[204]*Japan Advertiser*, July 3, 1932, pp. 1, 2.

[205]*Tokyo Asahi*, July 15, 1932, p. 2; *Japan Advertiser*, July 15, 1932, pp. 1, 2.

[206]Hiroō Sasa, "Observations on the Manchurian Policy," *Kaizo*, Sept., 1932, pp. 94–103.

of the Kwantung army, governor general of the Kwantung Leased Territory, as well as special ambassador to Manchuria,[207] though not officially accredited.[208] Combining in himself the authority of a diplomatic representative, the head of the consular service, and commander-in-chief of the Kwantung army, General Muto left Tokyo on August 20 for Changchun prepared to commence negotiations for concluding a fundamental treaty between Japan and Manchukuo, thereby according a formal recognition to the new state in Manchuria.[209]

Casting off the usual conventionality of a foreign minister's remarks, Count Uchida, in his address on the foreign policy of the nation which he delivered before members of the Diet on August 25, declared in effective language that the government had decided to accord *de jure* recognition to Manchukuo in the near future and that preparations for the final step were making rapid progress. He defended the course as the only method of stabilizing the situation in Manchuria and of restoring tranquillity in the Far East; he asserted with conviction that the proposed step in no way violated either the spirit or the letter of the Pact of Paris, or the Nine-Power Treaty of 1922, saying that the Japanese action since September 18 had been prompted solely by considerations of self-defense, and that the Nine-Power Treaty did not guaran-

[207]*Osaka Asahi*, Aug. 9, 1932, p. 1.

[208]When the Chinese minister in Tokyo called on the Foreign Office on July 28 and inquired whether the dispatch of a special ambassador to Manchuria meant *de jure* recognition of Manchukuo, Count Uchida replied that the sending of a special ambassador to Manchuria did not imply formal recognition of the new régime and cited the case of Mr. Tsunetada Kato, who was sent to Siberia as special ambassador during the Siberian expedition, without implying Japanese recognition of the Omsk government (*Tokyo Asahi*, July 31, 1932, p. 2). This reported declaration by Count Uchida to the Chinese representative in Tokyo was sharply criticized by certain advocates of "immediate recognition" in military and diplomatic circles who presented a memorandum to the foreign minister, demanding that he should abide by the policy already decided upon (Sasa, *loc. cit.*; Tachi, "Concerning the Recognition of Manchukuo," *Gaiko Jiho*, May 1, 1935, p. 5).

[209]*Lytton Report*, p. 106. For press comments in Japan, see *Japan Advertiser*, Aug. 21, 1932, p. 5. On Aug. 12, Mr. Adachi and other members of the Kokumin Domei called on Prime Minister Saito, War Minister Araki, Foreign Minister Uchida, and urged upon them to extend formal recognition to Manchukuo without further delay. At the cabinet council held on the same day, Count Uchida and General Araki were reported to have expressed different views regarding the time of recognition (*Tokyo Asahi*, Aug. 13, 1932, p. 2).

tee China against "secessionist movements."[210] When asked
to state the steps to be taken by the government in case of a
deadlock with the powers over the issue, Count Uchida
tactfully declined to make a direct reply, saying that the
government was prepared to make any sacrifice to carry out
its program.[211] The firm stand thus taken by the foreign
minister was generally welcomed by the press,[212] while apprehensions were heard in liberal quarters regarding the
logical outcome of the policy so unequivocally stated by the
government.[213]

[210]*Kwampo gogai*, Aug. 26, 1932, pp. 13–14; *Gaiko Jiho*, No. 666 (Sept. 1, 1932),
pp. 205–09. For able defense of Count Uchida's thesis, see Professor Tachi, "Formal
Recognition of Manchukuo," *Chuo Koron*, Sept., 1932, pp. 2–23; also his *Jikyoku
Kokusaiho Ron* (Tokyo, 1934), Chaps. IV, VI, XII.

[211]*Ibid.*, pp. 16–18. Mr. Seigo Nakano (Kokumin Domei) made a scathing denunciation of Mr. Stimson's recent remarks, but Count Uchida refused to make
any comment on him (*ibid.*, pp. 37–40, 40–41). Throughout the Sixty-third session
of the Diet (Aug. 23–Sept. 5, 1932), no interpellations were addressed to the government by members of the Upper House regarding the foreign policy of the nation.
The clear and definite statement of policy by the foreign minister at the outset of
the session dispelled any misgivings which might have existed among the Peers (*cf.*
H. Kamikawa, "Count Uchida's Address and Its Effect upon World Politics,"
Bungei Shunju, Oct., 1932, pp. 178–83).

[212]According to the *Tokyo Nichi Nichi*, Count Uchida "not only has justified what
has already been done but also has rebutted in advance the arguments which are sure
to be voiced by the powers in opposition to the course pursued by Japan," while
Jiji Shimpo saw the focal points of the address in "the emphasis on recognition as
the only way to solve the Manchurian situation and the determination to admit
of no outside interference." The *Tokyo Asahi* was satisfied with noting that "the
premier and foreign minister only echoed the sentiment of the people as expressed
in the resolution adopted in the last session of the Diet" (cited in *Japan Advertiser*, Aug. 27, 1932, p. 5).

[213]Writing on Sept. 6, 1932, Professor Masamichi Royama frankly admitted that,
unable to withstand the overwhelming pressure of the direct diplomacy of the army
conducted on the spot, the *Kasumigaseki* had long given up its hope of maintaining
even the semblance of dual diplomacy. The House resolution of June 14, as well as
the incessant demand of the press for immediate recognition, finally led the government to take the final step unilaterally ("Observations on International Politics,"
Bungei Shunju, Oct., 1932, pp. 190–96, reprinted in his *Nihon Seiji Doko Ron*
[Tokyo, 1933], pp. 548–54). He emphasized, moreover, the importance of finding
a solution through the League and in accordance with the accepted principles of
twentieth-century diplomacy (Royama, *Nichiman Kankei no Kenkyu* [Tokyo, 1933],
pp. 266–91). Royama was supported by Takagi, who said that the Manchurian incident would have been universally approved if it had taken place during the nineteenth century. He reminded the public, however, that we are now living in a new
age when settlement of all controversies among nations is to be sought by negotiation and conference and not by armed force. He thus proposed a conference of interested powers to settle the Manchurian question. Noting the significance of this
incident in the critical period of Japanese diplomatic history, this liberal professor
of the Tokyo Imperial University did not fail to point out, at the same time, that

Preparations preliminary to the final step having been completed,[214] Admiral Viscount Saito, prime minister, and Count Yasuya Uchida, foreign minister, were received in audience by the emperor on the afternoon of September 10, when they petitioned the throne to refer the draft treaty to be concluded between Japan and Manchukuo to the Privy Council for deliberation and advice.[215] The petition was granted, and a special sub-committee of nine members under the chairmanship of Baron Kiichiro Hiranuma, vice-president of the Council, was immediately appointed to examine the draft and to inquire into details connected with the proposed treaty. After obtaining favorable action at the hands of the sub-committee of inquiry on September 11,[216] the document was submitted to the plenary session of the Council specially summoned on September 13 for formal approval of the report of its sub-committee. The necessary advice having been obtained from the Council, the cabinet formally requested the emperor soon after the meeting of the Council to sanction the procedure. With the imperial sanction,[217] Count Uchida cabled General Muto at Mukden at 4 P.M., September 13, informing him that imperial sanction of the proposed move had been obtained and instructing him

the peace structure of the world was fighting a life-or-death battle, in the success of which Japan had to assume her share of responsibility ("The Manchurian Question and the History of American Expansion," *Kaizo*, XIV, No. 9 [Sept., 1932], pp. 78–93). Dr. H. Kamikawa, also of the Imperial University of Tokyo, doubted whether all the actions taken by Japan in Manchuria since last fall could be defended *in toto* under the plea of self-defense; he noted that the right of self-defense, though generally recognized in international law, was not without restrictions. He recalled, at the same time, that Japan made no formal reservation on this point when she signed the Pact of Paris. The same authority saw no way of preventing an open clash between Japan and the League if she was to follow the course just outlined, without giving any assurances to the world as to the future of Manchukuo (read Mr. Kamikawa's remarks at a round-table conference on September 5, in *Bungei Shunju*, Oct., 1932, pp. 216–43).

[214]On Sept. 7 Viscount Saito called on Prince Saionji, the genro, to explain the proposed step (*Tokyo Asahi*, Sept. 8, 1932, p. 1), while Foreign Minister Uchida paid a similar visit to the elder statesman the following day (*ibid.*, Sept. 10, 1932, p. 1).

[215]The visit of the premier and the foreign minister to the Imperial Palace followed the receipt of a telegram from Major General Itagaki of the Kwantung army informing that the Manchukuo government was ready for recognition (*ibid.*, Sept. 11, 1932, p. 2; *Japan Advertiser*, Sept. 11, 1932, pp. 1, 2).

[216]*Tokyo Asahi*, Sept. 12, 1932, p. 2.

[217]*Ibid.*, Sept. 14, 1932, p. 1.

to proceed with the signing of the document as scheduled.[218]

At 9:10 A.M., September 15, General Nobuyoshi Muto, special ambassador to Manchuria, and Mr. Cheng Hsiao-hsu, prime minister of Manchukuo, attached their signatures to the protocol.[219] Upon receipt of a formal report from General Muto on the completion of this historic event at Changchun at 11:10 A.M., Count Uchida went to the palace to be received in audience by the emperor to report to the throne that the long pending recognition of Manchukuo by Japan had just been effected. The text of the protocol was made public simultaneously at Tokyo and Changchun at 4 P.M.[220] At the same time, the Japanese government issued a long statement disclaiming any violation of treaty obligations on the part of Tokyo in extending *de jure* recognition to Manchukuo.[221]

THE LYTTON REPORT

The commission of inquiry which was formally set up on January 14, 1932, by virtue of the Council resolution of December 10, 1931, consisted of five members.[222] After two sittings at Geneva, the commission left for the East via America. Reaching Tokyo on February 29, the commission spent

[218]*Op. cit.*, p. 2; *Japan Advertiser*, Sept. 14, 1932, pp. 1, 2. Field Marshal Prince Kanin, chief of staff, was received in audience by the emperor on September 13th to pray for his sanction of certain military matters in connection with the protocol to be signed (*ibid.*, Sept. 15, 1932, p. 1).

[219]*Ibid.*, Sept. 16, 1932, p. 1.

[220]The protocol was promulgated as Treaty No. 9, 1932, and was accompanied by an imperial edict stating that it had obtained the emperor's sanction upon advice of the Privy Council, and was countersigned by Prime Minister Saito, Foreign Minister Uchida, War Minister Araki, and Navy Minister Okada (*Kwampo gogai*, Sept. 15, 1932). For a brief account of the procedure, see Tetsuro Furugaki, "Formal Recognition of Manchukuo," *Keizai Orai*, VII, No. 11 (Oct., 1932), pp. 68–83.

[221]Professor Jumpei Shinobu defended the military clause of the protocol as not being inconsistent with Article XX of the Covenant of the League of Nations, citing the treaty between Italy and Albania signed at Tirana in November, 1926 ("Basic Conditions for the Recognition of Manchukuo," *Keizai Orai*, VII, No. 11 [Oct., 1932], pp. 93–100; also "Analysis of the Japan-Manchukuo Protocol," *Kokusai Chishiki*, Nov., 1932, pp. 2–11). *Cf.* F. L. Schuman, *International Politics* (New York: McGraw-Hill Book Co., 1933), p. 457.

[222]The membership of the commission as finally approved by the Council of the League consisted of: Lord Lytton (British), chairman, Count Aldrovandi (Italian), General Henri Claudel (French), Major General Frank R. McCoy (American), and Dr. Heinrich Schnee (German). Japan subsequently appointed Ambassador Isaburo Yoshida as her assessor, while China named Dr. Wellington Koo, formerly prime minister and foreign minister (*Lytton Report*, p. 9).

eight days in Tokyo in daily conferences with members of the government and others, including Prime Minister Inukai, Foreign Minister Yoshizawa, War Minister Araki, Navy Minister Osumi, and Viscount Ishii. Interviews were also held with leading bankers, businessmen, representatives of various organizations and others. After further conferences with representatives of the business community at Osaka, the commission left Japan for Shanghai on March 11. After three and a half months of intensive study in China and Manchuria, it made a hurried return to Tokyo, early in July, to ascertain the attitude of the new cabinet regarding the Manchurian situation before drafting its report to the League of Nations.[223] In sharp contrast with the noisy reception with which the commission was greeted by the government and people of the Island Empire only four months before, the Tokyo reception at this time was literally dry, while the press was openly hostile. Under the circumstances, the commission had to make an early departure for Peiping, without reaching any agreement or compromise with Tokyo.[224]

On October 2, 1932, an elaborate report prepared by the commission on the Sino-Japanese dispute was released for publication simultaneously at Tokyo, Nanking, and Geneva.[225] In this voluminous report (about 100,000 words), consisting of an introduction and ten chapters, the Lytton Commission surveyed in detail the prevailing conditions in China and Manchuria, analyzed the main issues involved in the Manchurian crisis, and suggested certain "principles and conditions" to guide the Council of the League for settlement of the dispute.[226] To facilitate our understanding of the subsequent procedure, a brief summary of this document is given below.[227]

Chapters I, II, and III described the background of the conflict. Thus, in Chapter I, the commission depicted China's

[223] *Ibid.*, pp. 10–12.

[224] Ashida, *op. cit.*, pp. 1240–41.

[225] *Tokyo Asahi*, Oct. 3, 1932, p. 2.

[226] *League of Nations, Appeal by the Chinese Government, Report of the Commission of Enquiry* (Lytton Commission), Geneva, October 1, 1932.

[227] A brief summary of the report may be found in *International Conciliation*, No. 286 (Jan., 1933), pp. 58–87; Schuman, *op. cit.*, pp. 787–88; also Ashida, *op. cit.*, pp. 1242–49.

affliction—war lords, banditry, factional strife, communism
—and concluded that, "so far as Japan is China's nearest
neighbor and largest customer, she has suffered more than
any other power from the lawless conditions described in this
chapter."[228] Chapter II was devoted to the description of
Manchuria's relations with the rest of China and Russia,
where the commission observed the growing political and
economic interdependence between Manchuria and the rest
of China "contributed to induce Chinese leaders, both in
Manchuria and in Nanking, to pursue an increasingly nationalist policy directed against the interests and rights acquired
by Russia or Japan."[229] The commission argued throughout
that, in spite of all its wars and periods of "independence,"
Manchuria remained an integral part of China. Chapter III
analyzed in detail the conflicting interests between China
and Japan in Manchuria before September 18, 1931.

Chapter IV narrated how the growing tension described
in the preceding chapter reached the breaking-point on the
night of September 18, and reviewed the events in Manchuria subsequent to this night. As for the military operations
of the Japanese troops on the night of September 18, the
commission boldly asserted that "they could not be regarded
as measures of legitimate self-defense," though it "did not
exclude the hypothesis that the officers on the spot may have
thought they were acting in self-defense."[230] Chapter V summarized briefly the events at Shanghai.

Chapter VI dealt at length with Manchukuo, describing
the stages in the formation of the new state, outlining the
organization of the new régime, and commenting on the attitude of the inhabitants towards the government at Changchun. After a careful analysis of the stages in the formation
of the new state, the commission concluded that the independence movement which finally led to the creation of this
state "was only made possible by the presence of the Japanese troops," and that "a group of Japanese civil and military
officials, both active and retired, who were in close touch
with the new political movement in Japan, conceived, organized and carried through this movement, as a solution
to the situation in Manchuria·as it existed after the events
of September 18th." Arguing that the Japanese general staff
"provided assistance and gave direction to the organizers

[228]*Lytton Report*, p. 23.
[229]*Ibid.*, p. 32.
[230]*Ibid.*, p. 71.

of the movement," the commission continued that the new state could not have been formed but for the presence of Japanese troops and the activities of Japanese officials, both civil and military, and concluded: "For this reason, the present regime cannot be considered to have been called into existence by a genuine and spontaneous independence movement."[231] By emphasizing the presence of Japanese officials and advisers who "possess in every contingency the means of exercising an irresistible pressure," the commission expressed a note of pessimism regarding the future of the new régime, holding that there was no indication that it could carry out many of its reforms, and that "orderly conditions and economic prosperity could not be realized in the conditions of insecurity and disturbance which existed in 1932."[232] It concluded the chapter by saying that there was no general Chinese support for the "Manchukuo government," which was regarded by the local Chinese as "an instrument of the Japanese."[233]

Chapter VII drew attention to the fact that the struggle between China and Japan was not only of a military, but also of an economic character, China using as a weapon against Japan the boycott of goods, ships, banks, etc. In the opinion of the commission, the boycott movement was both popular and organized, being directed in the main by the Kuomintang. As to the legality of the methods employed, the commission "found it difficult to draw any other conclusion than that illegal acts had been constantly committed, and that they had not been sufficiently suppressed by the authorities and the courts."[234] It went so far as to assert that the Kuomintang was the controlling and coördinating organ behind the whole movement, that it might be the maker and the master of the government, but observed: "to determine at what point the responsibility of the party ends and that of the government begins is a complicated problem of constitutional law on which the commission does not feel it proper to pronounce."[235] On the important question whether the boycott activities throughout China "were consistent with friendly relations or in conformity with treaty obligations," the commission, unlike its pronouncement on

[231] *Ibid.*, p. 97.
[232] *Ibid.*, p. 106.
[233] *Ibid.*, p. 111.
[234] *Ibid.*, p. 119.
[235] *Ibid.*, p. 120.

the events of September 18, declined to express its opinion, holding that "it was rather a problem of international law than a subject for its enquiry."[236] Chapter VIII dealt briefly with economic interests in Manchuria, especially those of China and Japan. The all-important problem at the time, in the opinion of the commission, was "the establishment of an administration acceptable to the population and capable of supplying the last need—namely, the maintenance of law and order."[237]

In Chapter IX the commission concentrated its attention on the future. It pointed out that the issues involved in the Sino-Japanese conflict were not as simple as they were often represented to be. It was not a case in which one country declared war on another country without previously exhausting the opportunities for conciliation provided in the Covenant of the League of Nations. Neither was it a simple case of violation of the frontier of one country by the armed forces of a neighboring country, because in Manchuria there were many features without an exact parallel in other parts of the world. The commission noted, however, that there was no denying the fact that "a large area of what was indisputably the Chinese territory had been forcibly seized and occupied by the armed forces of Japan and had, in consequence of this operation, been separated from and declared independent of the rest of China. The Japanese contention that all the steps by which this was accomplished had been consistent with the obligations of the Covenant of the League, the Kellogg Pact, and the Nine-Power Treaty of Washington, and that all her military operations had been legitimate acts of self-defense, the right of which was explicit in all the multilateral treaties mentioned above, and which had not been taken away by any of the resolutions of the Council of the League, the commission observed, made this particular conflict at once so complicated and so serious.[238]

As "principles and conditions of settlement," it rejected equally as unsatisfactory the restoration of the *status quo ante*, "which would be a mere invitation to repeat the trouble," or the maintenance and recognition of the Changchun régime, which did not appeal to the inquiry commission as being "compatible with the fundamental principle of existing international obligations, nor with the good under-

[236]*Op. cit.*
[237]*Ibid.*, p. 125.
[238]*Ibid.*, pp. 126–27.

standing between the two countries upon which peace in the
Far East depends."[239] As to the latter solution, the commission asserted: "It is opposed to the interests of China. It
disregards the wishes of the people of Manchuria, and it is at
least questionable whether it would ultimately serve the
permanent interests of Japan. . . . To cut off these provinces
from the rest of China, either legally or actually, would be
to create for the future a serious irredentist problem which
would endanger peace by keeping alive the hostility of China
and rendering probable the continued boycott of Japanese
goods."[240] Though it recognized that it was less of an economic consideration than anxiety for her own security which
had determined the actions and policy of Japan in Manchuria, the commission questioned "whether the military occupation of Manchuria for an indefinite period, involving, as
it must, a heavy financial burden, was really the most effective way of insuring against this external danger; and
whether the Japanese troops would be seriously embarrassed if they were surrounded by a restive or rebellious
population backed by a hostile China."[241] The commission
further declared that any solution of the Manchurian problem must also take into consideration the interests of the
Soviet Union, the disregarding of which "would risk a future
breach of the peace and would not be permanent."[242]

Finally the commission enumerated ten general principles
to which any satisfactory solution should conform: (1) Japanese and Chinese interests must be equally protected; (2)
the interests of the Soviet Union must also be considered;
(3) any solution must conform to the provisions of the Covenant of the League, the Pact of Paris, and the Nine-Power
Treaty of Washington; (4) Japanese interests in Manchuria
must be recognized; (5) the respective rights, interests, and
responsibilities of both China and Japan must be restated
in new treaties; (6) effective provisions should be made for
facilitating the prompt settlement of minor disputes which
might arise in the future; (7) Manchuria must be granted a
large measure of autonomy consistent with the sovereignty
and administrative integrity of China; (8) preservation of
internal order should be secured by an effective local gendarmerie force, while security against external aggression

[239] *Ibid.*, pp. 127–28.
[240] *Ibid.*, p. 128.
[241] *Ibid.*, p. 129.
[242] *Ibid.*, pp. 129–30.

was to be provided by the withdrawal of all armed forces other than gendarmerie, and by the conclusion of a treaty of nonaggression between the countries interested; (9) a new Sino-Japanese commercial treaty should be concluded to encourage an economic *rapprochement;* (10) a temporary international coöperation in the internal reconstruction of China, as suggested by the late Dr. Sun Yat-sen, should be extended to China as "the final requisite for a satisfactory solution."[243] The commission concluded this chapter by suggesting to Japan that, "even with her Manchurian interests as a goal, Japan might recognize and welcome sympathetically the renaissance of Chinese national sentiment, might make friends with it, guide it in her direction and offer it support, if only to ensure that it does not seek support elsewhere," and pointing out to China that "she needs, in political and economic matters, the coöperation of all the leading Powers, but especially valuable to her would be the friendly attitude of the Japanese government and the economic coöperation of Japan in Manchuria," and that "all the other claims of her newly awakened nationalism—legitimate and urgent though they may be—should be subordinated to this one dominating need for the effective internal reconstruction of the State."[244]

Chapter X, "Considerations and Suggestions to the Council," recommended that the Council should invite both China and Japan to discuss a solution of their dispute on the lines indicated above. If this invitation should be accepted by both parties, an advisory conference, which might be composed of representatives of China and Japan, as well as two delegations representing the local population, should be called to discuss and recommend a special régime for the administration of the Three Eastern Provinces. The commission finally suggested that the results of these discussions and negotiations should be embodied in four separate instruments: (1) a Chinese declaration constituting a special regime for the Three Eastern Provinces, in the terms recommended by the advisory conference; (2) a Sino-Japanese treaty dealing with Japanese interests; (3) a treaty of conciliation and arbitration, non-aggression and mutual assistance; and (4) a Sino-Japanese commercial treaty. The commission then set forth details for carrying into effect these arrangements.[245]

[243]*Op. cit.*, pp. 130–31.
[244]*Ibid.*, p. 131.
[245]*Ibid.*, pp. 132–33 *ff.*

As anticipated, the publication of the report evoked a storm of protests and denunciation on the part of the press, commentators, and responsible government officials in Japan.[246] The press of the nation was unanimous in condemning the commission for its denial of the Japanese plea for self-defense for their operations during the night of September 18, 1931, while deliberately declining to pass upon the international law aspects of the boycott question; it stoutly refuted the commission's imputation that Manchukuo "was made in Japan," and dismissed as utterly unworkable its recommendations upon maintenance of peace and order in Manchuria by a local gendarmerie force.[247]

While the press was thus unanimous, for reasons already indicated, in denouncing the report *in toto*, commentators among critics and scholars were somewhat more divided. The consensus of opinion among them was that the commission went beyond its authority when it undertook to pass upon the events of September 18, 1931,[248] while deliberately

---

[246]Retsu Kiyozawa, a well-known journalist-critic, tells an episode which throws interesting light upon Japanese journalism at the time. According to this informant, he was attending a pressmen's conference when the report was released for publication. Almost without exception, the correspondents present expressed their surprise at the completeness and objectivity with which the League commission had prepared the report in so short a period. Nothing but indignation and ridicule, however, greeted the report in their editorial comments the following morning ("Progressive and Reactionary Aspects of Journalism," *Kaizo*, March, 1934, pp. 14–23).

[247]For press comments on the report see *Japan Advertiser*, Oct. 4, 5, 1932, p. 5. The *Nichi Nichi* and *Hochi* suggested that, if the report had appeared before Japanese recognition of Manchukuo, the solution indicated in the report might have had more chance of being accepted by Nippon (*ibid.*, Oct. 4, 1932, p. 5; *cf.* Schuman, *op. cit.*, p. 789).

[248]H. Kamikawa, "The Settlement Suggested in the Lytton Report," *Kokka Gakkai Zasshi*, XLVI, No. 11 (Nov., 1932), pp. 1608–22; "Contradictions in the Lytton Report," *Keizai Orai*, Nov., 1932, pp. 1–13; "A Solution of the Manchurian Question," *ibid.*, Jan., 1933, Supplement, pp. 21–30. For juristic arguments in support of the self-defense plea, consult Sakutaro Tachi, "On Self-Defence," *Kokusaiho Gaiko Zasshi*, XXXI, No. 4 (April, 1932), pp. 315–40; "The Manchurian Incident and the Use of Armed Force," *ibid.*, XXXII, No. 1 (Jan., 1933), pp. 1–24; Akira Osawa, "Settlement of International Controversy and Protection of Nationals Abroad," *Gaiko Jiho*, May 15, 1933, pp. 1–26. Writing in May, 1931, Professor Jumpei Shinobu opposed the broad interpretation put on "self-defense" by England and the United States in connection with the Pact of Paris, saying that past wars, in nine cases out of ten, were caused by abuses of this right under international law ("Special Position in Manchuria and the Right of Self-defense," *ibid.*, May 1, 1931, pp. 1–13) while Dr. Yotaro Sugimura, writing in 1933, likewise warned against the broad interpretation of this principle ("The Right of Self-Defense in International

declining to express its opinion on the boycott question,[249] that it was more anxious to conform to certain preconceived ideas and formulæ than to find a practical solution, and consequently, that its proposed solution of the dispute was too theoretical to be put into operation.[250] Although no open concurrence in the views of the commission concerning the military operations on the eventful night of September 18 appears to have been expressed by Japanese critics, some liberal commentators contended that, had Japan followed the British and American examples at the time of the signing of the Kellogg-Briand Pact by reserving her freedom of action in Manchuria, the Island Empire could have avoided most of the misgivings and criticisms which were poured on her since the September incident.[251] Dr. Sakuzo Yoshino, for many years professor of politics in the Tokyo Imperial University and closely identified with democratic movements in Japan, went one step further on this point when he boldly suggested that the best policy for Japan to adopt on this score was to admit frankly that the steps then taken were absolutely necessary for her own existence, instead of quibbling over technicalities regarding the limits of self-defense and insisting on her exclusive right to interpret the scope of this elementary rule of international law. He noted, moreover, that the commission's contention that, without the presence of the Japanese troops in Manchuria and the positive assistance by Japanese officials, both military and civil,

Law," *Kokusaiho Gaiko Zasshi*, XXXII, No. 7 [Sept., 1933], pp. 697–720).See, in this connection, Quincy Wright, "The Meaning of the Pact of Paris," *American Journal of International Law*, XXVII, No. 1 (Jan., 1933), pp. 39–61.

[249] See especially Kenzo Takayanagi, "Boycott in the Lytton Report," *Keizai Orai*, VIII, No. 1 (Jan., 1933), Supplement, pp. 1–20.

[250] For instance, M. Royama, "Public Opinion and the Lytton Report," *Gaiko Jiho*, No. 670 (Nov. 1, 1932), pp. 1–15; Hatao Yamakawa, "On the Lytton Report," *Kokusai Chishiki*, XII, No. 11 (Nov., 1932), pp. 12–28; Takuzo Itakura, "Formal Aspects of the Lytton Report," *ibid.*, pp. 35–45. *Cf.* Ninichi Yano, "Historical Background of the Chinese Claim to Suzerainty over Manchuria," *Gaiko Jiho*, Oct. 15, 1932, pp. 54–69. The *Japan Advertiser*, a Tokyo daily, published and edited by Americans, concluded its comment on the report thus: "The report is a legal and literary masterpiece which may some day adorn the shelves or records of the League museum, but without practical value as an international instrument" (leading article, "The Lytton Report," Oct. 4, 1932, p. 4).

[251] Y. Sugimura, *Kokusai Gaiko Roku*, pp. 7–8; see also Yukio Ozaki, "Reflections on Contemporary Politics," *Kaizo*, Feb., 1935, pp. 36–37; Hiroō Sasa, "The Lytton Report," *ibid.*, Nov., 1932, pp. 233–38.

in the independence movement, the formation of the new state in Manchuria would have been impossible, was substantially correct, and declared that the Japanese stand, unless modified, was incompatible with her membership in the League of Nations.[252] On the other hand, Representative Yukio Ozaki, a veteran statesman and well-known leader of Japanese democracy, having held a seat in the Diet consecutively since its establishment in 1890, reminded the nation that it was a high act of nonsense to suggest that Manchukuo had been formed by the free will of its people.[253] That Japan should assume full responsibility for the establishment of the Changchun régime was openly advocated by several others who saw no permanent solution of the conflict except through the League and in accordance with its principles and techniques.[254]

When the cabinet met on October 4 to deliberate upon the report and to decide upon its policy towards the League, Count Uchida, the foreign minister, insisted that the maintenance of Manchukuo as an independent state should be made a basis for any solution of the dispute, while General Araki, the war minister, reported the military dissatisfaction with the report as a whole, and particularly the portion dealing with the Japanese military operations on the night of September 18, and referred to the report as "a travelogue of the commission."[255] Admiral Okada, the navy minister, also pointed out the suggestion of the commission to maintain peace and order in Manchukuo by a local gendarmerie force as being utterly unworkable as a solution to the situation. After further deliberation, the task of formulating its policy was entrusted by the cabinet to Count Uchida and General Araki, who were to make their report to the cabinet later.[256] In accordance with the decision reached at the cabinet meeting on October 7, the task of drafting Japanese observations on the Lytton Report was entrusted to a special

[252]Sakuzo Yoshino, "Reflections on the Lytton Report," *ibid.*, pp. 225–32.

[253]Yukio Ozaki, *op. cit.*, pp. 37–38.

[254]M. Royama, *Nichiman Kankei no Kenkyu,* Chap. VII. *Cf.* also Daikichiro Tagawa, "Finding Solution through the League," *Kokusai Chishiki,* XII, No. 12 (Dec., 1932), pp. 20–30.

[255]*Japan Advertiser,* Oct. 5, 1932, p. 1.

[256]*Tokyo Asahi,* Oct. 5, 1932, p. 2.

joint committee of the foreign, war, and navy ministries.[257]
Upon the completion of the draft, it was submitted to the
cabinet for approval on October 28, after which it was reported to the emperor by the foreign minister. With the
imperial sanction, the text of Japanese observations was
handed to Ambassador Yoshida, who left for Geneva on the
evening of the same day.[258]

WITHDRAWAL FROM THE LEAGUE

On November 18, 1932, the Japanese observations on the
report of the Lytton Commission were transmitted to Sir
Eric Drummond, secretary general of the League of Nations.[259] In this elaborate answer to the League commission's findings, the Japanese government reviewed the chaotic conditions in China and the background of the Mukden
incident of September 18, 1931, defended the operations
following the outbreak as measures of legitimate self-defense,
and insisted that the maintenance and recognition of Manchukuo was the sole solution to the problem, and, in consequence, that the commission's proposals for settlement were
unacceptable to Japan.[260]

When the League Council commenced its long awaited

[257]*Op. cit.*, Oct. 8, 1932, p. 2.

[258]*Ibid.*, Oct. 29, 1932, pp. 1, 2.

[259]Text of the Japanese observations on the report of the commission in *Japan
Advertiser*, Nov. 21, 1932, pp. 3–5. *Cf. Tokyo Asahi*, Nov. 21, 1932, pp. 11–12;
Ashida, *op. cit.*, pp. 1249–59. For representative views on the observations see *Osaka
Mainichi*, Nov. 19, 1932, p. 1; *Tokyo Asahi*, Nov. 21, 1932, p. 2.

[260]In his Armistice Day address over the radio (Nov. 11, 1932) Count Yasuya
Uchida, foreign minister in the Saito cabinet, reiterated the Tokyo contention that
the actualities of the situation had to be fully appreciated before any workable
solution of the problem could be drawn up ("Facing the Approaching Session of
the League," *Kokusai Chishiki*, XII, No. 12 [Dec., 1932], pp. 2–3), while Viscount
Kikujiro Ishii, privy councilor and president of the League of Nations Association
in Japan, saw room for avoiding a headlong collision with the League in the commission observation that the Sino-Japanese conflict was not a simple case of one
country declaring war on another without previously exhausting the opportunities
for conciliation provided in the Covenant of the League, nor was it a case of the
violation of the frontier of one country by the armed forces of a neighboring country.
The veteran statesman-diplomat regarded this as an admission of the Japanese
position (*ibid.*, pp. 4–12; *Lytton Report*, p. 126). Dr. Kiroku Hayashi, president of
Keio University, was more energetic in upholding the League of Nations ("How
Should We Regard the League?" *ibid.*, pp. 13–19).

consideration of the Lytton Report on November 21,[261] Mr.
Yosuke Matsuoka, in a stirring address before the Council,
took direct issue with parts of the report and outlined in
detail the Japanese stand on the Manchurian situation. His
criticisms of the commission and its report were substantially in accord with the official observations made public
the previous day, making further elaborations on the Japanese rejection of the idea of an autonomous Manchuria and
her insistence on the correctness of her action in granting *de
jure* recognition to the new state of Manchukuo as being the
only solution adapted to existing circumstances and which
would have been followed by any other power placed in a
similar position. Referring to the chaotic conditions in
China, he expressed regret that Japan was unable to share
the commission's optimism. As for the commission's statement that the damage done to the South Manchuria Railway
on the night of September 18, 1931, was insufficient to justify
military action, Mr. Matsuoka admitted that the occurrence
of the explosion, if taken only by itself, was quite insignifi-
cant, but retorted that the report failed to take fully into
account the serious background of the situation. Had the
incident occurred at another period, he declared, "when
public temper was not so great," the commission's observations might have been correct and justified. Defending the
Japanese failure to submit the Manchurian question to the
League before the outbreak of the crisis, he cited four reasons:
(1) Japanese national sentiment did not permit of outside
interference in the Manchurian question; (2) the fear of
Japanese residents in Manchuria that their position would be
seriously undermined by the delay invariably attendant
upon League procedures; (3) the Japanese had persisted,
perhaps too long, in the hope of a solution, due largely to the
difference in mentality between them and Westerners; (4) the
breaking point was reached unexpectedly, after which events
took their own natural course.[262]

After heated debate between the Japanese and Chinese

[261]Representative Yosuke Matsuoka, former vice-president of the South Manchuria Railway Company and a *Seiyukai* leader, was supported by Ambassadors
Matsudaira (London), Sato (Brussels), and Nagaoka (Paris). Ashida, *op. cit.*, p.
1272.

[262]*Ibid.*, pp. 1272–75; *Japan Advertiser*, Nov. 22, 1932, pp. 1, 2.

representatives on the report and observations,[263] the Council
of the League voted on November 28, over Japanese protests,[264] to transfer the report and its observations to the
Assembly, without taking any action.[265] When the Assembly
of the League met in special session on December 6,[266] Mr.
Matsuoka, with directness and conviction, made the clearest
statement of the Japanese case ever made by any official
since the September incident.[267] In this comprehensive address, covering all aspects of the issue, the Japanese delegate
assured the hearers that Japan "was a loyal supporter of the
League" with which she had coöperated since its establishment. Touching again on the question of why Japan did not
bring the case before the League prior to the September
outbreak, Mr. Matsuoka said that "in view of the present
structure and scope of the League" no prompt and effective
protection could be expected from that body. "In the situation that existed in Manchuria," he declared, "Japan had

[263]On Nov. 23 a delicate issue arose over the competence of the Lytton Commission before the Council deliberations. The president of the Council asked Lord
Lytton, then present at the session, whether he had any modifications or additions
to make regarding the report in the light of the observations presented and debate
ensued, when Mr. Matsuoka insisted that the work of the commission had been
completed when it presented the report, and that, if he be allowed to express his
views on the observations and debate, he would likewise reserve the right to question the commission. This controversy continued till the following day, when Lord
Lytton reported that the commission had nothing further to add to the report
(Ashida, *op. cit.*, pp. 1275–76).

[264]Though Mr. Matsuoka's objection to transferring the question from the Council to the Assembly was based on the technical grounds that the commission was
appointed by the Council, in accordance with its resolution of the previous December, and that as the report was made to the Council it should be considered by that
body only, it seems clear that the real reason behind the Japanese stand was the
fear widely entertained in Tokyo that its case might suffer more at the hands of
the Assembly where small powers dominated. For press criticisms of the Council
action see *Japan Advertiser*, Nov. 25, 29, 1932, p. 5.

[265]*Ibid.*, Nov. 29, 1932, p. 1.

[266]The Japanese government had, by this time, changed its former attitude towards the Assembly and instructed Mr. Matsuoka to be formally present at the
meeting of the Committee of Nineteen (*Tokyo Asahi*, Nov. 30, 1932, p. 2).

[267]Commenting on Mr. Matsuoka's speech on Dec. 6, the *Japan Advertiser* declared: "It is comprehensive, embracing all factors in the dispute both favorable
and unfavorable to Japan, it is dispassionate, conciliatory and, most important of
all, it is more convincing than any other statement of its kind so far made on the part
of Japan. . . . Mr. Matsuoka has made a most able presentation of the Japanese
case. But if there is a weakness in his statement, it is one of policy. It is the lack of
any concrete proposal as a basis of settlement which the League might seize upon
to extricate itself from the present impasse" (editorial, "Mr. Matsuoka's Speech,"
Dec. 8, 1932, p. 4).

to deal, first, with an imminent danger; secondly, with a country whose authority did not extend to Manchuria; and thirdly, with a government which had adopted a policy of unilateral abrogation of treaties and conventions." "In so exceptional a situation," he asked, "was it possible to expect protection from the League?" He went on to declare that any suggestion for settlement which the Assembly might decide to make must be governed by three principles, namely:

(1) The terms must be such that they can be effectively put into operation and that they will accomplish and preserve peace in the Far East.

(2) A solution must be found for the disordered conditions of China.

(3) In case any plan for settlement is found by the League, this organization must take upon itself responsibilities for its execution.

He pleaded with the Assembly to recognize the ever changing conditions in the Far East and "judiciously adjust its views and actions to them," and reminded his hearers that "as the Japanese read the League Covenant, it is not a hard and implacable instrument."[268]

Following the presentation of the Chinese and Japanese cases by their respective spokesmen, representatives of the small powers now concentrated their attacks upon Japanese action in Manchuria and demanded a sweeping censure of the Island Empire. Thus, Czechoslovakia, Spain, the Irish Free State, and Sweden introduced in the Assembly, on the first day of the session, a joint resolution, denying the Japanese plea for self-defense for her action following the outbreak of the crisis, asserting that the presence of the Japanese troops was responsible for the creation of Manchukuo, and consequently the recognition of the new régime was incompatible with existing international obligations, and calling upon the Committee of Nineteen to seek the collaboration of the Soviet Union and the United States in its deliberations.[269] On the following day, Mr. Matsuoka, the Japanese delegate, demanded, in no uncertain terms, that this resolution of censure be withdrawn, intimating that the passage of

[268]Text of his speech in *ibid.*, Dec. 7, 1932, pp. 1, 8; *Tokyo Asahi*, Dec. 7, 1932, p. 2; also see Ashida, *op. cit.*, pp. 1282–84.

[269] *Ibid.*, p. 1291.

such resolution by the Assembly would entail consequences
"which were perhaps unintended or unanticipated by the
authors of the resolution."[270] The serious nature of the resolution was soon realized by the powers which succeeded in
persuading the sponsors of the resolution to withdraw it. On
December 9 the Assembly decided to refer all material bearing on the Sino-Japanese conflict once more to the Committee
of Nineteen, instructing it to draft a program of future procedure as soon as possible.[271]

When the Committee of Nineteen met on December 12,
it elected a sub-committee of five members, consisting of
representatives of the United Kingdom, France, Czecho-
slovakia, Spain, and Switzerland, to prepare a draft report
to the Assembly.[272] The sub-committee met in executive
session on the same afternoon and decided to prepare a report, under Article XV, Clause 3, of the Covenant of the
League, adopting the findings and recommendations of the
Lytton Report as a basis for settlement.[273] Finally, on December 15, the Committee of Nineteen adopted the report of its
sub-committee, proposing to transfer the question to a conciliatory body, composed of its own members and representatives of the United States and the Soviet Union.[274] Thus the
report, as adopted, accepted the Lytton recommendation
that neither the restoration of the *status quo ante* nor the
maintenance of Manchukuo was satisfactory. The general

[270] *Japan Advertiser*, Dec. 9, 1932, pp. 1, 2. For Japanese resentment at small
powers, see *ibid.*, p. 5.

[271] *Ibid.*, Dec. 10, 1932, pp. 1, 2. *Cf.* Schuman, *op. cit.*, p. 790.

[272] Ashida, *op. cit.*, p. 1293.

[273] Under instructions from London, Ambassador Lindley called at the Foreign
Office on Dec. 12 and explained the British proposal to transfer the settlement of
the question to a conciliatory body, which was to include representatives of both the
Soviet Union and the United States, and intimated that, should the plan be unacceptable to Tokyo, the League would be obliged to abandon its efforts under
Article XV, Clause 3, of the Covenant, and proceed under Clause 4 of the same
article (*Tokyo Asahi*, Dec. 14, 1932, p. 2). After conferring with his principal subor-
dinates at Kasumigaseki on Dec. 12 and 13, Count Uchida suggested to the cabinet,
which met in the forenoon of Dec. 13, that Japan reject the application of Article
XV, and object to the proposed conciliatory committee, particularly the inclusion of
American and Soviet representatives. His suggestions were accepted by his colleagues (*ibid.*). At 3:30 P.M. the foreign minister invited the British ambassador
to his office and conveyed the decision of the cabinet, rejecting any suggestion of a
third party interference in the settlement of the dispute, and particularly objecting
to the competence of the proposed body (*ibid.*, Dec. 15, 1932, p. 1).

[274] Ashida, *op. cit.*, pp. 1294–97.

principles and programs adopted at this meeting continued to guide the subsequent procedures of the League.[275]

As soon as the draft report of the committee, accompanied by observations by the Japanese delegation at Geneva, reached Tokyo on the afternoon of December 16, bureau chiefs of the Foreign Office deliberated upon this draft report for seven hours without reaching a decision. After further study, on December 17, Tokyo sent a long cable to its representatives at Geneva the following day, instructing them to propose several amendments to the draft, rejecting the inclusion of American and Soviet representatives in the proposed conciliatory committee, and confining the function of this body to assisting in initiating direct negotiations between China and Japan, and objecting to any proposal which denied the existence of the Changchun régime.[276] Under the circumstances, the Committee of Nineteen adjourned on December 20 until January 16, 1933, hoping in the interim to find a workable formula with Tokyo.[277]

Following the adjournment of the Committee, numerous unofficial approaches were attempted on the part of Sir Eric Drummond, Secretary General of the League of Nations, to find a formula acceptable to Japan and yet sufficiently within the framework of the League and the Lytton findings, but of no avail. On the last day of the year, Sir Eric Drummond held a long conference with Sir John Simon, British foreign secretary. As a result, the British ambassador in Tokyo called on Count Uchida early in January, with a view to finding some way out of the deadlock before the meeting of the Committee of Nineteen. This also proved vain.

Meanwhile the occupation of Shanhaikwan and extended operations in Jehol[278] gave an impression to the Powers that no effort at conciliation would prove fruitful.[279] At Geneva, however, Sir Eric Drummond and Dr. Yotaro Sugimura, under secretary of the League, continued their private conversations, with a view to finding a workable plan within the

[275] *Ibid.*, p. 1297.

[276] *Tokyo Asahi*, Dec. 18, 1932, p. 1.

[277] Ashida, *op. cit.*, p. 1298.

[278] Schuman, *op. cit.*, p. 419. The press in Japan was conspicuously silent on military operations during this period.

[279] Ashida, *op. cit.*, pp. 1298–1300 *ff.*

framework of the Lytton Report and yet adapted to the existing conditions in Manchuria. The efforts at Geneva also
failed when Japan insisted upon rejecting any proposal which
postulated the participation of the United States, while
Great Britain made it plain that she could not envisage any
solution of the issue without American collaboration.[280]

In consequence, when the Committee of Nineteen reassembled on January 16, 1933, the small powers severely
censured the secretary general for "exceeding his authority"
and rejected the so-called Drummond-Sugimura plan.[281]
After cabinet approval, Count Uchida sent instructions to
Mr. Matsuoka to insist on rejecting any proposal envisaging
the inclusion of American and Russian representatives in the
proposed conciliatory committee.[282] Under these circumstances further efforts at conciliation were abandoned, and,
on January 21, the Committee of Nineteen issued a communiqué declaring that efforts at conciliation had failed and
that it would now proceed to draft a report under Article XV,
Clause 4, of the Covenant of the League of Nations.[283]

[280]Sugimura, *Kokusai Gaiko Roku*, pp. 55–69. The Drummond-Sugimura negotiations proved somewhat more fruitful. Thus, on Jan. 14, 1933, they reached a compromise. Under this plan, (1) the Committee of Nineteen was to appoint a small
committee to assist the parties to the dispute in direct negotiations; (2) this committee was empowered to extend its invitation to states not members of the League;
(3) Chapter IX of the report was to furnish a useful basis for settlement, but any
settlement which might be suggested must be adapted to the new situation in the
Far East; (4) Chapter X of the *Lytton Report* was not to be touched; (5) the explanatory statement regarding the resolution was to be issued in the form of a declaration by the president who was to refrain from any comment on either the
restoration of the *status quo ante* or the recognition of Manchukuo (Ashida, *op. cit.*,
pp. 1300–01; *Tokyo Asahi*, Jan. 13, 14, 1933, p. 2). According to an informant, Mr.
Matsuoka approved the Drummond-Sugimura proposal that the president of the
Assembly refer to the question of nonrecognition of Manchukuo, but the Japanese
representative was free to make a counter declaration. Count Uchida alone stood
firm in rejecting the proposal (Kiyozawa, "An Open Letter to Mr. Matsuoka,"
Chuo Koron, May, 1933, pp. 162–73).

[281]Ashida, *op. cit.*, pp. 1301–02.

[282]*Tokyo Asahi*, Jan. 18, 1933, p. 2; *Osaka Mainichi*, Jan. 18, 1932, p. 1. On the
inclusion of American and Russian representatives in the proposed conciliatory
committee, Japanese delegates were divided. Those who argued for the inclusion
were of the opinion that so long as no Far Eastern question could be solved without
giving due regard to the power and influence of these two powers there was no reasonable ground for objecting to the proposal (Ashida, *op. cit.*, pp. 1302–03; Kiyozawa, *loc. cit.*).

[283]*Tokyo Asahi*, Jan. 23, 1933, p. 2. Upon receipt of the news, the War Office in
Tokyo issued a statement condemning the League procedure and envisaging the
possibility of withdrawing from the League (*ibid.*).

While the events at Geneva were thus moving towards a hopeless impasse, Count Yasuya Uchida, the foreign minister in the Saito cabinet, defined the limits of Japanese concession to Geneva in his parliamentary address on foreign relations which he delivered before the Diet on January 21, 1933. In this address on the nation's foreign policy, Count Uchida reported the signing of a protocol of alliance with the Changchun régime on September 15, 1932, thereby according Manchukuo *de jure* recogniton. He argued at length that general principles and practices of international law do not apply to China without important modifications, and that the Covenant of the League was no exception. Referring to the handling of the Sino-Japanese dispute at Geneva, the foreign minister declared that any attempt to apply to the present issue a formula based upon precedents and practices of European countries would not only make the situation in the Far East worse, but would also endanger the peace of the world itself. A new advance was taken towards enunciation of a Japanese Monroe Doctrine when the foreign minister, after emphasizing the importance of giving "due and proper elasticity corresponding to the exigencies of actual conditions" in the application of the various principles and techniques of peace, and insisting that "those real forces which are actually rendering peace possible in the various parts of the world must be respected," declared:

In this sense, our government believe that any plan for erecting an edifice of peace in the Far East should be based upon the recognition that the constructive force of Japan is the mainstay of tranquillity in this part of the world.[284]

Admiral Viscount Saito, the premier, likewise defended the nation's Manchukuo policy, expressing satisfaction that the steady progress being made there justified the correctness of the steps taken during the preceding autumn.[285]

On January 23 Dr. Kin Ashida (*Seiyukai*) addressed a long

[284]Text of the foreign minister's address in *Kwampo gogai*, Jan. 22, 1933, pp. 11–13. An English translation furnished by the Foreign Office may be found in *Japan Advertiser*, Jan. 22, 1933, pp. 1, 2; *Japan Times*, Jan. 22, 1933, p. 1.

[285]Text of the premier's address on the state of the nation in *Kwampo gogai*, Jan. 22, 1933, pp. 10–11; *Japan Advertiser*, Jan. 22, 1933, pp. 1, 2; *Japan Times*, Jan. 22, 1933, p. 1.

interpellation to the government on the foreign policy of the nation, particularly in regard to China and Geneva. In this vigorous interpellation of censure, Representative Ashida, himself an experienced diplomat and a student of world politics, took the government to task for failing to show to the people any concrete and constructive policy towards China, for allowing the military party to exercise undue influence in the shaping of the nation's foreign policy, and for giving an impression to the world that there was an army diplomacy and a Foreign Office diplomacy in Japan but no national policy capable of speaking in the name of the whole nation. He shouted to the legislative chamber that such a situation was detrimental to the best interest of the state, and called upon the war minister to utilize the power and strength of national unity towards solution of the Manchurian problem instead of indulging in the idea of "an almighty army," and demanded that the foreign minister demonstrate to the world that statements and declarations emanating from *Kasumigaseki* represented, in name as well as in fact, the policy of the nation.[286] Representative Tadao Matsumoto (*Minseito*), former secretary to the late Count Komei Kato, joined his *Seiyukai* colleague in attacking the rampancy of dualism in the conduct of the nation's foreign policy, and echoed the popular feelings of apprehension regarding the diplomatic course being taken by the government. He called upon the foreign minister to follow the footsteps of the late Count Mutsu, Marquis Komura, and other predecessors in the Foreign Office in considering the future welfare of the nation before endeavoring to satisfy the popular clamor of the masses.[287] These charges of dualism in diplomacy were flatly denied by both Count Uchida[288] and War Minister Araki.[289]

These speeches by Dr. Kin Ashida and Representative Matsumoto were generally regarded in Japan as representing

[286]*Kwampo gogai*, Jan. 24, 1933, pp. 43–47; *Japan Times*, Jan. 24, 1933, pp. 1–2. *Cf.* his article, "A New Vision of International Stability," *Kaizo*, Feb., 1933, pp. 80–87.

[287]*Ibid.*, pp. 58–62.

[288]*Ibid.*, pp. 47–49, 60–61.

[289]In reply, General Araki expressed satisfaction that, during the thirty years of his service in the army, there never existed a more harmonious coöperation between the Foreign Office and the War Department than at present (*ibid.*, p. 49).

the views of the *Seiyukai* and *Minseito*, two major existing political parties, while they were interpreted at Geneva as indicating a lack of unanimous support among Japanese at home concerning the stand being taken at Geneva by their delegates. Being thus placed in an extremely embarrassing position, Mr. Matsuoka sent a cable of protest to Dr. Kisaburo Suzuki, president of the *Seiyukai* party, of which he was an influential member, asking for details. In reply, Dr. Suzuki assured Mr. Matsuoka that the *Seiyukai* party was solidly behind the stand now being taken by the delegates.[290] The news created a sensation in Tokyo, and consequently, when the House of Representatives met on January 25, Representative Kato (Kokumin Domei) took the floor of the House on a point of order and, emphasizing the importance of presenting a united front at home, suggested that the speakers might clarify the misgivings aroused by their remarks in the Diet.[291] In reply, both Dr. Ashida and Representative Matsumoto denied any intention of criticizing the foreign policy of the government or making a political football out of the situation.[292]

The last-minute efforts at conciliation having failed,[293] the Committee of Nineteen proceeded to draft its report to the Assembly under Article XV, Clause 4, of the Covenant of

[290] *Jiji Shimpo*, Jan. 26, 1933, p. 2.

[291] *Kwampo gogai*, Jan. 26, 1933, p. 95.

[292] *Ibid.*, pp. 95–96; *Tokyo Asahi*, Jan. 26, 1933, p. 2; *Osaka Mainichi*, Jan. 26, 1933, p. 1; *Japan Times*, Jan. 28, 1933, p. 3.

[293] On Jan. 28, Ambassador Lindley called on Count Uchida at the Foreign Office and inquired whether Japan was ready to accept a draft resolution, omitting any reference to the question of extending an invitation to Washington and Moscow to send representatives in the proposed conciliatory committee, while allowing Japan to make an opposing declaration on nonrecognition of Manchukuo. He pleaded with the foreign minister to suggest some formula which would save the impending impasse between Tokyo and Geneva (*Osaka Mainichi*, Jan. 29, 1933, p. 1; *Tokyo Asahi*, Jan. 30, 1933, p. 2). In view of the gravity of the situation, the matter was reported to Prince Saionji by Count Uchida on Jan. 31 (*Tokyo Asahi*, Jan. 31, 1933, p. 2; *Jiji Shimpo*, Jan. 31, 1933, p. 2), and, on the forenoon of the following day, an extraordinary meeting of the cabinet was called to decide upon the important policy of either accepting the British proposal of conciliation under Clause 3 of Article XV or, failing that, accepting an alternative course under Clause 4 of the same article. It was decided that, under any form, the independence of Manchukuo could not be denied. After obtaining the imperial sanction, the decision of the cabinet was cabled to Geneva (*Japan Times*, Feb. 1, 1933, p. 1; *Tokyo Asahi*, Feb. 2, 1933, p. 1). At 5 P.M., Feb. 1, Count Uchida invited the British ambassador to his office and conveyed the government's decision to decline the British proposal (*ibid.*, Feb. 3, 1933, p. 2).

the League.[294] On February 17, 1933, the Committee finally issued a long report reviewing the course of conflict from the beginning and recommending a settlement of the issue along the lines suggested in the Lytton Report.[295]

At an extraordinary meeting of the cabinet called to order at 4:45 P.M., the Saito government decided to instruct its principal delegate, Mr. Yosuke Matsuoka, to cast an opposing vote against the resolution when it came up for final decision in the Assembly, but failed to reach an agreement as to whether Japan should withdraw from the League when her plea had been rejected in the Assembly.[296] On February 19, the prime minister, Admiral Viscount Saito, paid a visit to Prince Saionji, the sole remaining elder statesman, and reported the situation at Geneva. Returning to Tokyo on the following day, Admiral Saito summoned his cabinet to his official residence and reported his interview with the genro. The cabinet finally decided to sever its relations with the League, should the Assembly adopt the draft resolution drawn up by its Committee of Nineteen.[297] The basic policy of the cabinet having been determined upon,[298] Prime Minister Saito requested, on February 21, an executive session of the House of Peers to report on the recent developments at Geneva and the policy of the government towards the im-

[294]Ashida cites four factors which finally led Britain and France to give up hope of finding a formula under Article XV, Clause 3, of the Covenant: (1) Japanese military operations threatened north China; (2) Japanese rejection in any form of a formula which included participation by the United States; (3) the reported lack of intention on the part of Tokyo to withdraw from the League; (4) the moral influence of the United States in any solution of a Far Eastern question (*op. cit.*, pp. 1309–10 ff.).

[295]Schuman, *op. cit.*, p. 790; Ashida, *op. cit.*, pp. 1312–17; *Tokyo Asahi*, Feb. 19, 1933, p. 5.

[296]*Ibid.*, Feb. 18, 1933, p. 2; *Jiji Shimpo*, Feb. 19, 1933, p. 1.

[297]*Osaka Asahi*, Feb. 21, 1933, p. 1; *Japan Times*, Feb. 21, 1933, p. 1; *Jiji Shimpo*, Feb. 21, 1933, p. 2. The army members of the supreme war council met in conference at the war minister's official residence at 2 o'clock, Feb. 18, when General Araki explained the recent developments at Geneva and the report drafted by the Committee of Nineteen (*Tokyo Asahi*, Feb. 20, 1933, p. 2; *Japan Times*, Feb. 21, 1933, p. 1).

[298]Until the meeting of the cabinet on Feb. 20, members of the cabinet were divided on the question of withdrawing from the League. By the middle of the month, however, General Araki (war minister) and Count Uchida (foreign minister) had become convinced that withdrawal was inevitable. Admiral Osumi (navy minister) joined this group, but Viscount Saito, the premier, reserved his decision till his call on the elder statesman on February 19 (Ashida, *op. cit.*, pp. 1318–19).

pending crisis. A similar report was also made to the Lower House on the afternoon of the same day.[299]

On February 24 the Assembly of the League of Nations adopted, by unanimous vote, the report of its Committee of Nineteen, condemning Nippon for her action since the preceding September as defying the peace structure of the world, and recommending the nonrecognition of Manchukuo as an act of public censure of the Japanese adventure.[300] In the face of this universal repudiation by the Assembly of the Japanese plea for exceptional character of the dispute and her insistence upon settlement in full appreciation of the prevailing situation, Mr. Yosuke Matsuoka and other representatives in the Assembly withdrew from the Assembly room.[301]

The government at Tokyo now proceeded to take measures for formal withdrawal from the League.[302] The draft notice of intention to withdraw from the League having been completed, Count Uchida, the foreign minister, was given audience by the emperor on March 8 to report to the throne the content of the draft and to explain the future policy of the cabinet towards the League.[303] Three days later, the Foreign Office completed its preparations for formal submission of the matter to the privy council for advice. Thus when the cabinet met in extraordinary session on March 11, Count Uchida explained to his colleagues the draft notice to the League as well as several other documents to be submitted to the council to aid its deliberation upon the procedure. At 5:40 P.M. both the premier and the foreign minis-

[299]*Kwampo gogai*, Feb. 22, 1933, pp. 153, 279; *Japan Times*, Feb. 23, 1933, pp. 1, 2.

[300]Of the 44 delegations present, only the Siamese delegation refrained from voting, while Mr. Matsuoka cast the sole negative vote. The vote was 42 to 1, instead of 13 to 1 as in Oct., 1931 (Schuman, *loc. cit.*).

[301]*Tokyo Asahi*, Feb. 25, 1933, p. 2. *Cf.* Yotaro Sugimura, "On Leaving the League of Nations," *Kokusai Chishiki*, XIII, No. 7 (July, 1933), pp. 22–41.

[302]Details of the Geneva proceedings were reported to the cabinet on Feb. 25 by the foreign minister, when members of the cabinet exchanged views with each other regarding the date of transmitting a formal notice to Geneva of its intention to withdraw from the League, the title to continue as mandatory of the North Pacific Islands, as well as the extent of coöperation with Geneva, after withdrawal, in its cultural and peace activities, such as labor, economic, and disarmament conferences (*Tokyo Asahi*, Feb. 27, 1933, p. 3).

[303]*Ibid.*, March 9, 1933, p. 2.

ter went to the palace to petition the throne to submit the draft to the privy council for advice.[304] This was granted, and, on March 13 the secretariat of the council commenced its examination of the matter.[305]

After three sittings on the proposed step,[306] the sub-committee of nine councilors[307] voted, on March 18, to recommend to the Privy Council that it approve the proposed severance of formal relations with the League of Nations as unavoidable under the circumstances.[308] On March 27 the Privy Council, with the emperor in attendance, voted unanimously to adopt the report of its sub-committee[309] and advise the throne to notify Geneva of the intention of Tokyo to sever its relations with the League of Nations.[310] After obtaining the formal approval of the cabinet and the imperial sanction, the notice of the Nipponese intention to withdraw from the League of Nations was transmitted by cable to Sir Eric Drummond at Geneva in the afternoon. At the same time, the emperor issued an imperial rescript reminding his subjects that no change would be forthcoming in the nation's continued efforts to establish a durable peace in the region of the Far East. Prime Minister Saito, Foreign Minister Uchida, War Minister Araki, as well as Navy Minister

[304]*Op. cit.*, March 12, 1933, p. 2.

[305]*Ibid.*, March 14, 1933, p. 2. Details of the Geneva proceedings were already reported to the Privy Council at its plenary session on Feb. 22 (*ibid.*, Feb. 23, 1933, p. 2).

[306]The committee held two hearings on the draft notice on March 16 and 17, when Prime Minister Saito, Foreign Minister Uchida, War Minister Araki, and Navy Minister Osumi explained the policy of the government from their respective angles. Government delegates were not present at its meeting on March 18.

[307]The committee was composed of Baron Hiranuma, vice-president of the council, as chairman, and eight councilors, namely, Arai, Kamata, Tomii, Hara, Kawai, Arima, Ishii, and Kurino (*ibid.*, March 16, 1933, p. 2).

[308]At these hearings the government delegates explained to the committee that (1) they contemplated no change in the status of Japan as mandatory over the islands; (2) they would coöperate with the powers in promoting the peace of the world; and that (3) no advance into the Peiping-Tientsin line was under contemplation at the time (*ibid.*, March 18, 1933, p. 1). For further elucidation of these points in the House Budget Committee, see *ibid.*, p. 2.

[309]In presenting the committee report, Baron Hiranuma criticized the government for allowing the content of the draft to be published in the press while the matter was still under examination (*Jiji Shimpo*, March 28, 1933, p. 1). For published text of the notice see *Tokyo Asahi*, March 15, 1933, p. 1. The cabinet was also censured for this in the House of Representatives (*Kwampo gogai*, March 25, 1933, p. 786).

[310]*Osaka Asahi*, March 28, 1933, p. 1.

Osumi, issued instructions and statements setting forth the position of the cabinet and emphasizing the significance of this event in the diplomatic history of the Island Empire.[311]

PUBLIC OPINION AND THE FINAL DECISION

When the Committee of Nineteen gave up its hope of finding a settlement of the dispute under Article XV, Clause 3, of the Covenant of the League of Nations, and proceeded, on January 21, 1933, to draw up a report to the Assembly under Clause 4 of the same article, it gave an added impetus to the popular outcry for withdrawal from the League of Nations.[312] Thus, as February wore on, advocates for immediate severance of relations from Geneva became so insistent[313] that the press of the nation, which had long ceased to be a barometer of public opinion, became even more lukewarm,[314] while leaders of political parties chose the safer alternative of refraining from expressing their views until the cabinet finally decided, at its meeting of February 20, to withdraw from the League of Nations.[315] In these circumstances, even members of the Diet had to speak with considerable restraint in their interpellations on foreign policy,[316] while freedom of

[311]The notice was published in the *Kwampo* as Foreign Office Notification No. 21, 1933, together with the imperial rescript and the instructions of the premier (*Kwampo gogai*, March 27, 1933, pp. 1-4). *Cf. Tokyo Asahi*, March 28, 1933, p. 2.

[312]*Supra, n.* 283.

[313]See K. Honda, "Our Attitude towards the League of Nations," *Gaiko Jiho*, Jan. 15, 1933, pp. 101-20; "Recovery of Our International Prestige," *ibid.*, April 1, 1933, pp. 148-59; S. Nakano, "Isolation Unafraid," *ibid.*, pp. 37-58; N. Yano, "Supporting Manchukuo's Independence," *ibid.*, 59-69; N. Matsunami, "Showing Japanism to the League," *ibid.*, pp. 87-116.

[314]The *Tokyo Nichi Nichi* and the *Osaka Mainichi*, two leading dailies under the same management, championed the popular clamor for "strong policy" throughout the conflict.

[315]*Cf.* Sakuzo Yoshino, "Political Changes and Parliamentary Government," *Chuo Koron*, Jan., 1933, pp. 59-66. Some critics attributed this silence on the part of party leaders to their opposition to withdrawal from the League (H. Sasa, "International Crisis and Political Stability," *Keizai Orai*, April, 1933, p. 146). *Cf.* a symposium on the question by Dr. Kin Ashida (*Seiyukai*), Tadao Matsumoto (*Minseito*), and Takeo Sugiura (Kokumin Domei) in *Seiji Keizai Jiron*, VIII, No. 3 (March, 1933), pp. 12-22.

[316]Reference has already been made to interpellations made by Dr. Kin Ashida and Representative Tadao Matsumoto in the Lower House on Jan. 23, 1933, and their effect upon Japanese delegates at Geneva. Viscount Toshisada Maeda declared in the House of Peers, on March 8, that the severance of relations from Geneva was a diplomatic failure (*Kwampo gogai*, March 9, 1933, p. 238).

speech and expression maintained a precarious existence.[317]

As the situation assumed more serious proportions and the impending deadlock between Tokyo and Geneva became more imminent, however, a group of liberals, representing that inarticulate minority of the public, advocated the calling of the nation's leaders to formulate a "national policy,"[318] while others urged the government to propose concrete formulæ to Geneva which, while purporting to settle the issues in dispute, nevertheless would be in line with League principles and techniques or otherwise be acceptable to world public opinion. They counseled prudence, and reminded the people that the interest of the state would in no way be enhanced by withdrawing from the League at this time. On the contrary, the severance of relations from Geneva under such circumstances would amount to an admission on the part of Nippon that her policy of peace had been universally repudiated in the eyes of the world. They pleaded with the people that the only way to obtain an international approval of the Tokyo policy towards Manchukuo and to avoid the stigma of being a "public enemy" of the world would be for the Island Empire to offer to the world some concrete formulæ towards settlement of the Chinese question.[319]

The popular excitement in Japan reached its climax when the Assembly of the League adopted, on February 24, 1933, the report of its Committee of Nineteen, openly condemning

[317]Nyozekan Hasegawa, "Japanese Reaction towards the League," *Kaizo*, March, 1933, pp. 89–95; Tamon Maeda, "Observations on the Sixty-fourth Diet," *Kokusai Hyoron*, II, No. 3 (March, 1933), pp. 55–65.

[318]In an open letter to Count Uchida, the foreign minister, R. Kiyozawa, emphasized the urgent necessity of calling a conference of the emperor's closest advisers to formulate really a "national policy" in order to regain the confidence of the world in the statements issued in the name of the Foreign Office at Tokyo. He referred to the absence of any criticism in the press on recent foreign policy and said that, in Japan, the people would not tolerate the existence of minority opinions ("An Open Letter to Count Uchida," *Chuo Koron*, March, 1933, pp. 187–96). Dr. T. Minobe also advocated the calling of a round-table conference of representatives of political parties, the army and the navy, as well as the industrial group, as well as the labor class, to formulate a "national policy" ("Japan in Crisis," *ibid.*, Jan., 1933, pp. 53–58). *Cf.* N. Hasegawa, "Continental Policy and the Future of Politics," *ibid.*, pp. 31–44; H. Asoō, "Renaissance of Bureaucracy and Military Clans," *ibid.*, pp. 47–52.

[319]M. Royama, "The Second World War and the League of Nations," *Chuo Koron*, March, 1933, pp. 111–19; R. Kiyozawa, *loc. cit.*; Sobei Mogi, "Will the Withdrawal from the League Benefit Japan?" *Kaizo*, March, 1933, pp. 81–86; Kanson Arahata, "The League and Its Recommendations," *ibid.*, pp. 86–89.

the Nipponese action in Manchuria and placing the stigma
of illegitimacy upon the new-born state of Manchukuo.
Towards the close of the month, therefore, the possibilities
of applying economic sanctions against Japan and the imminence of an open war with the entire world began to be
discussed, while advocates of an Asiatic Monroe Doctrine
became more insistent.[320] In the face of this public frenzy and
excitement, the liberal forces in the Empire concentrated
their efforts upon cautioning calm and prudence, and warning
the military against further advances into North China across
the Great Wall.[321] There appeared to be a unanimity among
commentators that no measures of a coercive character would
be attempted against Japan unless her troops crossed the
Wall into the Peiping-Tientsin area.[322] They were also united
in insisting upon maintenance and continued assistance of
Manchukuo as the sole alternative to the present impasse.
They argued that, by actually establishing a land of para-
dise in Manchukuo could the Japanese severance of relations from Geneva amid universal censure be vindicated,
and the politics of the Far East stabilized on firm foundations.[323]

[320]Cf. H. Sasa, "International Crisis and Political Stability," *Keizai Orai*, April,
1933, pp. 148–52; also H. Kamikawa, "New Policy after Withdrawal from the
League," *ibid.*, pp. 177–83. Both Sasa and Kamikawa rejected an Asiatic Monroe
Doctrine under Japanese hegemony. Professor Kamikawa proposed a regional
league of nations. *Cf.* Morinosuke Kashima, "From Geneva to Pan-Asiatic League,"
ibid., pp. 184–92; M. Royama, "A Regional League of Nations and the World
Situation," *Kokusai Chishiki*, XIII, No. 1 (Jan., 1933), pp. 22–30.

[321]I. Yasui, "Reconstruction in Japanese Diplomacy," *Kokka Gakkai Zasshi*,
XLVII, No. 4 (April, 1933), pp. 544–56; Kin Ashida, "A New Policy of Isolation,"
Keizai Orai, April, 1933, pp. 193–200.

[322]It was generally held among commentators that an effective enforcement of
economic sanctions against Japan would inevitably lead to a first-class war with
Japan (*cf.* a symposium on economic blockade in *Keizai Joho*, March, 1933, pp.
45–75; also *Kaizo*, April, 1933, pp. 158–204). See also S. Ito, "The Imperial Navy
and Economic Blockade," *Keizai Orai*, April, 1933, pp. 115–24.

[323]Professor H. Kamikawa saw no need, as a result of Japanese withdrawal from
Geneva, for a radical change in her diplomatic front, but believed that the Nipponese diplomacy would henceforth be predicated upon the maintenance and continued development of Manchukuo ("New Policy after Withdrawal from the
League," *Keizai Orai*, April, 1933, pp. 177–78 *ff.*). Dr. Kin Ashida, editor of the
Japan Times, agreed with Professor Kamikawa, and said that the present diplomatic isolation of Japan was not due to her policy towards Manchukuo, nor was it
the all of her diplomacy ("A New Policy of Isolation," *ibid.*, p. 194). According to
Dr. Y. Sugimura, former under secretary of the League, aside from the question of
justice or wisdom, the Japanese recognition of Manchukuo cannot be revoked. It

The question of whether Japan could continue to hold, as mandatory, the North Pacific Islands, after formal withdrawal from the League of Nations, according to Article XXII of the Covenant occupied a prominent place in public discussion as the severance of relations from Geneva became imminent. Japanese jurists were almost unanimous in holding that Japan obtained her title to the mandated islands by virtue of the secret treaties during the World War, of her military occupation of these islands, and of their cession to her by the Principal Allied and Associated Powers to whom Germany had ceded them by Article CXIX of the Treaty of Versailles.[324] In consequence, her withdrawal from the League of Nations would in no way affect her legal title to continue to administer these islands as mandatory.[325] They were not convinced, however, that this position would be sustained by the Permanent Court of International Justice should the issue be brought before this body for decision.[326] They were fully aware of the practical difficulties which were certain to befall Japan after severing relations from the League.[327]

is important, however, that the world must be informed of the real aims and policy of Tokyo ("Withdrawal from the League and the New National Policy," *Gaiko Jiho*, July 15, 1933, p. 97).

[324]See Quincy Wright, "Some Legal Aspects of the Far Eastern Situation," *American Journal of International Law*, XXVII, No. 3 (July, 1933), pp. 512, 514-16; "The Effect of Withdrawal from the League upon a Mandate," *British Year Book of International Law*, 1935, pp. 104-13.

[325]Sakutaro Tachi, "Mandates under the League of Nations," *Hogaku Kyokai Zasshi*, L, 1367-1411 (Aug., 1932); "The Mandates over the North Pacific Islands," *Jiji Shimpo*, Feb. 5, 6, 7, 1933, p. 3; "Legal Effect of Japan's Withdrawal from the League upon Her Title to Continue as Mandatory of the North Pacific Islands," *Kokusai Chishiki*, XIII, No. 4 (April, 1933); Ryoichi Taoka, "Withdrawal from the League and the Mandated Areas," *Gaiko Jiho*, No. 650 (Jan. 1, 1932), pp. 68-80; *ibid.*, No. 674 (Jan. 1, 1933), pp. 120-60; Jumpei Shinobu, "Sovereignty in the Mandated Areas," *ibid.*, Nov. 1, 15, 1934, pp. 1-16, 11-24. *Cf.* Luther H. Evans, "Would Japanese Withdrawal from the League Affect the Status of the Japanese Mandate?" *American Journal of International Law*, XXVII, No. 1 (Jan., 1933), pp. 140-42.

[326]Writing in December, 1931, Professor Tachi opposed the popular demand for withdrawing from the League on the ground that it would place Japan in an embarrassing position in regard to her administration of the North Pacific Mandates ("On the Proposed Demand for Withdrawal from the League," *Kokusaiho Gaiko Zasshi*, XXX, No. 10 [Dec., 1931], pp. 952-54). While he held to the condominium theory throughout the controversy, he did not change the view expressed in this article (*cf.* "Withdrawal from the League," *Kokusai Chishiki*, XII, No. 5 [May, 1932], pp. 2-10; also his *Jikyoku Kokusaiho Ron* [Tokyo, 1934], pp. 342-52).

[327]Writing in May, 1932, Professor H. Kamikawa envisaged the possibility of the League revoking the Japanese mandate and returning the islands to Germany.

These views, representing as they did the majority of Japanese jurists, did not go unchallenged by a small group of jurists and political scientists. They could not accept the majority theory that territorial rights (*imperium*) were vested in the Principal Allied and Associated Powers; that the exercise of sovereignty (*dominium*) was vested in the mandatory; and that the mandate, having the character of a treaty between the Allied Powers and the mandatory, could be changed only with the consent of each. Thus, Mr. Kisaburo Yokota, professor of international law in the Imperial University of Tokyo, admitted that none of the theories so far advanced was satisfactory, but expressed the opinion that, in view of the spirit which prompted the establishment of this novel system, sovereignty over mandates clearly resided in the League.[328] Mr. Masamichi Royama, also of the Imperial University of Tokyo, analyzed the question from the standpoint of international politics. He rejected the condominium theory as unsatisfactory, and insisted that, in order to maintain the thesis that withdrawal from the League would have no legal effect upon her title as mandatory, Japan must be able to establish not only that (1) a mandatory need not be a League member, but also that (2) the League itself did not possess the power of revoking a mandate. Arguing that the new institution of mandates should be interpreted in the spirit of the new age, he rejected both the condominium theory and that of League supremacy as equally unsatisfactory. Emphasizing the limited character of sovereignty under international law, he contended that it must be interpreted in the light of the existence of the League of Nations and its functions as an organization of peace.[329]

The question continued to occupy a prominent place in the press and learned journals for several months after Tokyo notified Geneva of the intention to terminate its relations

He admitted that such a procedure would inevitably lead to a naval conflict, but added that Japan would be treated, in the eyes of the world, as an illegal holder of the disputed areas ("Opposing Withdrawal from the League," *Kokusai Chishiki*, XII, No. 5 [May, 1932], pp. 11-20).

[328] K. Yokota, *Kokusaiho*, I, 167.

[329] M. Royama, "Sovereignty in the Mandates: A Study in International Politics," *Kaizo*, May, 1933, pp. 66-79. *Cf.* Quincy Wright, *Mandates under the League of Nations* (Chicago, 1930), Chap. IX.

with the League.[330] In the meantime, Count Yasuya Uchida resigned as foreign minister in the Saito cabinet and was succeeded by Mr. Koki Hirota in the *Kasumigaseki* portfolio on September 14, 1933.[331] The new foreign minister made his first clarifying reference to the government's attitude regarding the mandate question in the House of Peers on January 31, 1934, in reply to a question put to the government by Mr. Kenkichi Yoshizawa, former foreign minister in the Inukai cabinet. His statement closely followed the general thesis already referred to above. Thus, the foreign minister declared that the selection of Japan as mandatory for the islands was made through negotiations among the Principal Allied and Associated Powers, and consequently that it was impossible to hold that Japan ceased to have full title to these mandated islands.[332] Further elaborations on the question were made by the foreign minister in the Upper House on February 21, in reply to a question by Baron Takehiko Sonoda. Mr. Hirota reiterated the government's stand that Japan acquired the status as mandatory through a decision reached among the Principal Allied and Associated Powers and that her status thus acquired would in no way be affected by her withdrawal from the League. He added, however, that Japan did not consider the areas as Japanese territory, although she was administering them as an integral part of Japan.[333] In consequence, the foreign minister vigor-

---

[330]On Feb. 22, 1933, the Navy Department issued an "unofficial" statement declaring that sovereignty in the mandate was vested solely in Japan, and that the islands were the "life line of the Imperial Navy" (*Tokyo Asahi*, Feb. 24, 1933, p. 2). For Professor Royama's criticism of the navy stand, see *Kaizo*, May, 1933, p. 69. Mr. Royama cited the resolution of Sept. 8, 1927, adopted by the Council of the League, in which the Japanese delegate concurred (*ibid.*, pp. 68–69).

[331]*Osaka Asahi*, Sept. 15, 1933, p. 1.

[332]*Kwampo gogai*, Feb. 1, 1934, p. 61. In the House of Representatives, Mr. Kishi declared that sovereignty over mandates resided in the mandatory (*ibid.*, Feb. 7, 1934, p. 202).

[333]Dr. Cho Shimizu, until recently president of the administrative court of litigation and now a privy councilor, holds that the Japanese mandate is not a territory of Japan, but that her withdrawal from the League in no way affects her status as mandatory (*Chikujo Teikoku Kempo Kogi* [Tokyo, 1933], p. 65). Dr. T. Minobe, emeritus professor of constitutional law in the Tokyo Imperial University, says that the islands, to all intents and purposes, do not differ from a territory of Japan, differing only in legal basis (*Kempo Satsuyo* [Tokyo, 1932], pp. 138–41). He too believes that the title suffers nothing by withdrawal from the League ("On the Mission of Admiral Okada's Cabinet," *Chuo Koron*, Sept., 1934, pp. 109–10). Dr.

ously denied that the Japanese title to these islands could be altered in any way by anybody, and that it was even legal or judicial in nature. He asserted that Japan would oppose any move to submit the matter to the Permanent Court of International Justice.[334]

Recent news from Geneva indicates that Geneva has accepted the Japanese contention that a nonmember of the League could remain a mandatory under the League of Nations.[335]

Soichi Sasaki, another noted jurist of the Kyoto Imperial University, denies that the islands are a Japanese territory but says that her sovereignty is supreme and exclusive in the areas (*Nihon Kempo Yoron* [Tokyo, 1933], p. 299).

[334]*Kwampo gogai*, Feb. 21, 1934, pp. 239–42.

[335]See J. Shinobu, "League Supervision of the Mandates," *Gaiko Jiho*, Feb. 15, 1935, pp. 1–11; also Luther H. Evans, "The Japanese Naval Base Question," *American Political Science Review*, Vol. XXIX, No. 3 (June, 1933), pp. 482–87.

PART III: THE CONDUCT OF FOREIGN RELATIONS

Chapter XXVII

THE TREATY–MAKING POWER IN JAPAN

IMPERIAL PREROGATIVE OVER TREATY-MAKING

W<small>E HAVE ALREADY OBSERVED</small> elsewhere that one of the outstanding characteristics of the Japanese constitutional system is the wide scope of the imperial prerogative over the general affairs of the state.[1] And this point is brought out most strikingly in the sweeping nature of the diplomatic prerogative of the emperor. Thus, Article XIII of the Constitution provides: "The emperor declares war, makes peace, and concludes treaties." So far as the fundamental law of the land is concerned, the emperor is under no restrictions in the exercise of his prerogative over treaties. No legal limitations are placed upon either the substance or form of a treaty that may be concluded by him; his power is unhampered by the Diet, Privy Council, or any other organ of the state.

That the Constitution contemplates no restriction upon the imperial prerogative over treaty-making is evident in the language of Prince Ito, the drafter of the Constitution of 1889:

Declaration of war, conclusion of peace and of treaties with foreign countries, are the exclusive rights of the Sovereign, concerning which no consent of the Diet is required. For, in the first place, it is desirable that a Monarch should manifest the unity of the sovereign power that represents the State in its intercourse with foreign powers; and in the second, in war and treaty matters, promptness in forming plans according to the nature of the crisis,

[1]Chap. II, *supra.*

425

is of paramount importance. By "treaties" is meant treaties of peace and friendship, of commerce and of alliance. . . .

. . . In the diplomatic usage of the present day, it is a recognized principle in every country that a Minister of State should be made the channel of communication of matters relating to diplomatic affairs and to treaties with foreign powers, except in cases of the Sovereign's personal letters of congratulation or of condolence. The principal object of the present Article is to state that the Emperor shall dispose of all matters relating to foreign intercourse, with the advice of His Ministers, but allowing no interference by the Diet therein.[2]

Commentaries on the Japanese constitutional system are unanimous in their support of the unlimited character of the imperial prerogative over treaty-making. They point to the absence of any express limitations in the organic law in striking contrast to the Prussian Constitution of 1850 upon which the Japanese Constitution was modeled in many respects. They contend, however, that this imperial prerogative over treaty-making must be exercised only with the advice of the cabinet ministers who assume the entire responsibility therefor. The point to be emphasized is the formal absence of parliamentary participation in treaty-making.[3]

THE NEGOTIATION OF TREATIES

Japanese jurists indicate four methods employed by the Foreign Office in the conclusion of treaties, all of which correspond to the generally accepted rules of diplomatic usage. (1) The most formal procedure is the signing of the treaty by plenipotentiaries with the reservation that the exchange of ratifications is to be performed at a later date. By the signatures of the plenipotentiaries the treaty is considered as conditionally concluded, and its validity is finally established by the exchange of ratifications. Most of the important bilateral as well as multilateral treaties are concluded in

[2]Count Hirobumi Ito, *Kempo Gikai* (Tokyo, 1889), pp. 25–26. It is translated into English by Miyoji Ito under the title of "Commentaries on the Constitution of the Empire of Japan." The citation is taken from *Commentaries* (Tokyo, 1889), pp. 26–28. *Cf.* Prince Ito's speech regarding the nature of treaties on May 13, 1899 (Hiratsuka, *Ito Hirobumi Hiroku* [Tokyo, 1930], II, 105).

[3]Y. Hozumi, *Kempo Teiyo*, I, 766; Minobe, *Kempo Seigi*, p. 126; Ichimura, *Teikoku Kempo Ron*, p. 873; Shimizu, *Kempo Hen*, p. 1257; S. Inada, "Treaty-Making Power," *Kokka Gakkai Zasshi*, XXXVII, No. 4 (April, 1923), p. 519.

accordance with this procedure. (2) By virtue of the un-restricted character of the imperial prerogative over treaty-making, it is possible for a treaty to be brought into actual effect by the signatures of the plenipotentiaries without reservation as to subsequent ratification. Ordinarily, only routine treaties of no great political importance are nego-tiated in this manner. The treaty of annexation of Korea of 1910, however, constitutes an important exception to the general practice above indicated. In this instance speed was paramount, and consequently the sanction of both the em-peror of Japan and the king of Korea was obtained to a draft treaty prior to the signing of the document by the plenipotentiaries of these two states. It was brought into effect upon the date of promulgation. (3) The most informal method is the exchange of memoranda between the foreign ministers and plenipotentiaries. (4) Finally, the ratification of conventions negotiated by the international labor con-ferences admits of a special procedure.[4]

The initiative for treaty negotiations is usually taken by the Foreign Office. Thus, when negotiation for the revision of existing treaties or for the conclusion of new treaties is to be started, a tentative program as to the substance as well as the procedure is drawn up by the commerce bureau of the Foreign Office when the subject matter relates prima-rily to trade and commerce, by the Far Eastern bureau when it is a political treaty relating to the Asiatic continent, by the European and American bureaus, when relating to those regions, or by the treaty bureau when it relates primarily to technical problems of international law.[5] Then it is re-ferred to a special committee composed of representatives of

[4]Minobe, *Kempo Seigi*, pp. 268–269. *Cf.* Tetsu Izumi, *Kokusaiho Mondai Kenkyu* (Tokyo, 1924), pp. 31–40; Sakutaro Tachi, *Heiji Kokusaiho Ron* (Tokyo, 1930), I, 557–559.

[5]Under the revised ordinance concerning the organization of the Foreign Office, the former *Asia-kyoku*, or Asiatic bureau, was changed to *Tōa-kyoku*, or the Far Eastern bureau, while the *Ōbéi-kyoku*, or European and American bureau, was made into two new bureaus, namely, *Oa-kyoku*, or the Europe and Near East bureau, and *America-kyoku*, or the American bureau. The *Tōa-kyoku* performs the same functions as the former Asiatic bureau, namely, matters relating to Manchukuo, China, Hongkong, Macao, and Siam. The American bureau has jurisdiction over po-litical matters relating to American countries, including Canada, and their oversea territories; and the Europe and Near East bureau has charge of similar matters not covered by either the Far Eastern or the American bureau. Other bureaus re-main the same. Imperial Ordinance No. 144, 1934 (*Kwampo*, June 1, 1934, p. 1).

the various departments concerned for deliberation upon the proposed project. When a tentative outline of the program and policy is formulated, the foreign minister submits it to the cabinet for approval. When the cabinet approves the project it is referred to *Hoseikyoku*, or the Bureau of Legislative Affairs, for further examination. When the examination is completed, it is returned to the cabinet with accompanying recommendations to be resubmitted to its deliberation for appropriate action. Upon approval by the cabinet, the foreign minister formally instructs the plenipotentiaries to proceed with the negotiations.

Thus, negotiations are conducted upon cabinet approval and under instructions from the foreign minister in accordance with such action. Instances are not unknown, however, in which ministers abroad initiated negotiations upon their own initiative, without sounding the views of the home government. Such a procedure on the part of the representatives abroad may easily place the home government in an embarrassing position, whereupon it may promptly repudiate such negotiations by recalling the offending representatives.[6]

When a tentative agreement of views is reached between the plenipotentiaries and the draft treaty drawn up, the text is transmitted to Tokyo either by mail or by telegraph, depending upon the circumstances, such as distance and urgency. For instance, in case of negotiations with China, the full text of the draft treaty, together with explanatory documents describing the details of negotiations, is mailed to Tokyo. Thereupon the matter is referred to the cabinet for formal decision. When it is approved by the cabinet, the plenipotentiaries are instructed to sign the document. In

[6]As a notable instance we may cite the case of the recall of Viscount Aoki from Washington. Viscount Aoki, former foreign minister and the then ambassador in Washington, approached President Roosevelt, without sounding the views of the home government, with a view to concluding an agreement regarding the Far Eastern situation. After obtaining the general acceptance of President Roosevelt, he telegraphed Tokyo for authority to negotiate an agreement and requested the approval of the measures already taken. Count Tadasu Hayashi, Viscount Aoki's junior in the diplomatic service, was the foreign minister. The Saionji cabinet resented the steps taken by the ambassador without previous instructions or knowledge of the Foreign Office and promptly recalled him from Washington. Aoki was succeeded by Baron Takahira, who subsequently concluded the Root-Takahira agreement in accordance with the usual practice in treaty negotiations (Shinobu, *Gaisei Kantoku to Gaiko Kikan*, pp. 596-597; also his *Gaiko Sokumenshi Dan*, pp. 404-409; Yoshino [ed.], *Kyokuto no Gaiko*, p. 97).

cases of negotiations conducted in those countries too distant to allow sufficient time for dispatching all the documents by mail, the essential details of negotiations, and the full text of the agreed draft treaty are telegraphed to Tokyo. Together with such reports of the negotiations which may be sent to the Foreign Office from time to time during the negotiations, the action of the cabinet is taken as indicated above. The necessary explanations and initiatives are usually taken by the foreign minister in the cabinet, and its approval is usually a formal one. However, in matters relating to the Far East, military and naval authorities always exert considerable influence over the cabinet. The Sino-Japanese negotiations of 1915 and the signing of the Protocol of September 15, 1932, extending *de jure* recognition to Manchukuo, are more noted cases in point.[7]

The Ratification of Treaties

When a treaty is signed, under instructions from the home government, the Foreign Office prepares a draft ratification and promulgation. It also prepares a Japanese text of the treaty, in consultation with the Bureau of Legislative Affairs. When all the necessary preliminaries are completed, the foreign minister prepares an address to the throne praying for the imperial ratification. This is then again referred to the *Hoseikyoku* for further examination, and upon completion of the investigation by the bureau it is formally submitted to the cabinet for approval. After receiving the approval of the cabinet, the prime minister petitions the emperor for ratification; thereupon the treaty is submitted to the Privy Council for advice through the Lord Privy Seal.

No provisions are made in the written Constitution for the submission of treaties to the Privy Council for advice prior to ratification. However, by virtue of the ordinance concerning the organization of the Council,[8] treaties are submitted to the Privy Council for advice, and its advice has invariably been followed by the emperor. Although individual privy councilors may informally request information on the progress of treaty negotiations, whether such a request is com-

[7]Chaps. XXI, XXVI, *supra*.
[8]*Sumitsuin Kansei*, Art. 6, Cl. 4.

plied with by the ministry depends entirely upon the particular political circumstances of the time and also upon the nature of such negotiations. The recent tendency has been to avoid the interference by the Council as much as possible.

When a treaty is referred to the Council, a preliminary examination is conducted in the secretariat of the Privy Council, under the direction of the secretary general. Hence, bureau and section chiefs of the various government departments concerned are summoned to the office of the secretariat of the Privy Council to aid the latter in its examination of the treaty, article by article. In conducting the preliminary inquiry into a treaty, the secretary general actually exerts a large influence upon the action of the Council upon it. In the case of an important treaty, a special sub-committee is appointed by the president of the Council for further examination. This sub-committee conducts its own inquiry by summoning the foreign minister and other high officers of the department and not infrequently other departmental ministers affected by the treaty. These ministers are allowed to bring various technical officers to reply to detailed questions involving routine matters. However, the committee may bar all such subordinate officers at the meeting.[9]

When the sub-committee completes its hearings, it prepares a report to the Council and transmits a copy of its report to each member of the Council and of the cabinet three days before plenary session of the Privy Council. The regular meeting of the Council is held on each Wednesday. In case of special urgency, however, an emergency meeting of the Council may be summoned upon request of the cabinet without the formal report of the secretariat. The plenary session of the Council is usually held in the presence of the emperor. The prime minister and all the members of the cabinet have seats and take part in the deliberations of the Council and answer questions that may be raised by the councilors upon the treaty in question. The cabinet ministers always vote as a unit. The deliberations in the presence of the emperor usually last only a short period, main interpellations and explanations having been already completed in committee hearings. However, in some unusual instances the

[9]In this connection we may cite the examination of the London Naval Treaty in 1930.

debate in the Council in His Majesty's presence may last several hours, as in the case of the Pact of Paris. The result of the Council deliberations is reported to the emperor by the president of the Council.

The emperor has always approved the report of the Privy Council. This imperial approval, however, should not be confused with ratification. The approval of the report of the Privy Council upon a treaty merely indicates His Majesty's approval of ratification. When this approval is given, it is immediately transmitted to the cabinet, whereupon it formally votes to petition the throne for ratification. The formal text of the treaty, to which the imperial signature is to be attached, is prepared by the Foreign Office for subsequent presentation to the throne through the secretariat of the cabinet.

An interesting question may be raised at this point: What is the legal effect of the submission of treaties to the deliberations of the Privy Council for advice? Is it an essential condition for the valid conclusion of a treaty? As we have observed in our discussion of the legal significance of the advice of the Privy Council,[10] the deliberations of this body upon treaties are merely advisory, having no legal effect upon the validity of the treaties. Hence, not all treaties and agreements are submitted to the Council for advice. The practice in the past has been, however, that the *Sumitsuin* has always insisted on the submission of all treaties and agreements, under whatever name they may have been concluded, and irrespective of whether subsequent ratification has been reserved at the time of the signature or not. Thus, all the treaties reserving subsequent ratification have been submitted to the Council for advice before ratification by the emperor. On the other hand, most of the agreements having no reservation as to ratification have also been submitted to the Council for approval prior to issuing instructions to the plenipotentiaries to sign such agreements.[11]

[10]Chap. IV, *supra*.

[11]The exchange of notes, extending for one month the operation of the convention signed on Aug. 29, 1904, regarding commercial relations between Japan and India, which was to terminate on Oct. 10, 1933, pending conclusion of a new agreement, was authorized by the Saito government, after obtaining the Council's advice in the presence of the emperor, on Oct. 7, 1933. The notes exchanged on the same date between Sir John Simon, British foreign secretary, and Hon. Tsuneo Matsudaira,

There have, however, been several important agreements concluded without obtaining the formal advice of the Privy Council. The conclusion of the Anglo-Japanese Alliance in 1902 is a case in point. As we have seen in our analysis of the alliance,[12] every step in the negotiations conducted by the Katsura ministry had been reported to the emperor and his sanction obtained, and so when it was submitted to the Council later it was accompanied by an imperial message declaring: "We have commanded the ministers of state to conclude this agreement." The cabinet contended that it was not a treaty but an agreement, the real reason being to avoid any further delay and criticism at the hands of the *Sumitsuin* which might have caused the defeat of the alliance. Be that as it may, the Council had to bow before the imperial message. This episode was not discussed in the press at the time because the proceedings of the Council were kept in strictest secrecy. It is also known that the Japanese adherence in 1915 to the London Declaration of Alliance of 1914,[13] and the secret Sino-Japanese military agreement of May 16, 1918,[14] were concluded without the advice of the Privy Council. In the former instance, the Okuma cabinet contended it was an executive agreement, while in the latter, Prime Minister General Terauchi pleaded with individual privy councilors not to raise embarrassing issues on the ground that it was a wartime measure.[15]

The most noted instance was the conclusion of the Sino-Japanese postal agreement of December, 1922, which received the imperial sanction and became effective without obtaining the formal advice of the Privy Council.[16] The *Sumitsuin* took vigorous exception to the procedure, and the

Japanese ambassador at London, were published in the *Kwampo*, or official gazette, as Foreign Office Notification No. 88. No mention was made in the publication of the formal advice of the Privy Council prior to issuing instructions to London. *Kwampo*, Oct. 10, 1933, pp. 222–224. *Cf.* press account in *Jiji Shimpo*, Oct. 10, 1933, p. 2; also *Gaiko Jiho*, Oct. 15, 1933, pp. 191–192.

[12]Chap. XI, *supra*.

[13]Chap. XVI, *supra*.

[14]Signed at Peking on May 16, 1918, between the military representatives of Japan and China. Made public on March 14, 1919. Text in *Joyaku Isan* (Foreign Office, Tokyo, 1918), pp. 853–858.

[15]*Cf.* an anonymous article in *Gaiko Jiho*, XXXVII, No. 2 (Jan. 15, 1923), pp. 415–423.

[16]Chap. XXI, *supra*.

impasse which ensued for several months was finally re-
solved by imperial messages to both the Council and the
cabinet. While the cabinet was still in conflict with the
Council, the Admiral Kato cabinet made an important
statement before the budget committee of the Lower House
upon the conflict, and indicated the usual practice in regard
to postal agreements. Thus, Dr. Hatao Yamakawa, chief of
the Bureau of Legislative Affairs, in reply to an interpellation
by Representative Fujiya Suzuki, declared:

> Certain international postal conventions, such as the inter-
> national postal union convention, require ratification, after having
> been negotiated by representatives possessing full powers. But
> agreements that are administrative in character and which fall
> within the jurisdiction of the department of communications are
> concluded by delegates without full powers and bound by strict
> instructions. . . . These agreements do not require subsequent rati-
> fication. . . .[17]

The Sino-Japanese Postal Agreement of 1910 came into
force without the formal procedure of submission to the
Council, but the emperor's sanction was requested for the
agreement of December, 1922, which automatically necessitated the submission of the agreement to the Council for
advice, because of the fact that it constituted an exception
to the international postal union convention of which both
Japan and China were members.[18]

In order to circumvent a hostile Privy Council, a cabinet
may resort to methods which will ensure a *fait accompli*, as
witness the settlement of the Tsinan incident by an exchange
of notes.[19] That it was intended to avoid the possible interference by the Council in its foreign policy is evident from
the subsequent submission to it of the two agreements
settling the Hankow and Nanking incidents, which were
almost identical in substance with the settlement of the
Tsinan incident.

[17]*Dai Shijurokkai Teikoku Gikai Shugiin Iinkai Giroku*, Pt. I, No. 2, pp. 4-6
(Feb. 3, 1923). *Cf.* Dr. Yamakawa's reply to Dr. Senshi Egi in the Peers' Budget
Committee on Feb. 21, 1923, on this point (*Dai Shijurokkai Teikoku Gikai Kizokuin
Yosan Iinkai Giji Sokkiroku*, No. 4, pp. 9-10).

[18]Statement by Dr. Hatao Yamakawa in the Peers' Budget Committee on Feb.
22, 1923 (*Dai Shijurokkai Teikoku Gikai Kizokuin Yosan Iinkai Giji Sokkiroku*,
No. 5, pp. 13-14).

[19]Chap. XXII, *supra*.

The above brief survey of several instances in which important international agreements were concluded without previous submission to the Privy Council raises anew the question of drawing a line between those international commitments which require the advice of the Council prior to ratification and those which do not necessitate such a procedure. It seems reasonable to hold that only those treaties which stipulate subsequent ratification by the emperor require their submission to this body before ratification. However, when the imperial sanction is not requested to the draft agreement, or when no subsequent ratification is reserved by the plenipotentiaries, and, consequently, the agreement is validly concluded by the signatures of the plenipotentiaries possessing full powers,[20] or by an exchange of memoranda, the imperial sanction is not requested, and, consequently, there is no opportunity for the Privy Council's participation in the process.

Thus, when treaties are signed by the plenipotentiaries without any reservation as to subsequent ratification, or when ratification is not provided for, the emperor has no discretion as to giving his sanction thereto. Therefore, submission to the *Sumitsuin*, preliminary to His Majesty's sanction, is merely a matter of form and, in effect, amounts to a report of an already accomplished fact to the Council. It is the general practice, however, that treaties and agreements, irrespective of prior imperial sanction thereto, are submitted to the Privy Council prior to promulgation.[21]

THE PROMULGATION OF TREATIES

The practice in Japan indicates that treaties are regarded as constituting a part of the law of the land, though their binding effect upon the people arises only upon promulgation.

[20]The courts recognize the binding effect of international agreements, even though they have not been ratified by the emperor with the advice of the Privy Council. Thus the Supreme Court took judicial cognizance of the Sino-Japanese agreement of Nov. 2, 1911, relating to through passage of international trains. This agreement came into force upon signature, and was published in the *Kwampo*, on November 15, 1911. The judicial decision (June 16, 1933) involving the agreement is found in *Keiji Hanrei-shu*, XII, No. 8, pp. 660 ff. *Cf.* a review of this decision by Yoshio Suzuki in *Kokka Gakkai Zasshi*, XLVIII, No. 1 (Jan., 1934), pp. 119-125.

[21]Minobe, *Gendai Kensei Hyoron*, pp. 99-104. *Cf.* Izumi, *Kokusaiho Mondai Kenkyu*, pp. 41-48; also Shimizu, *Teikoku Kempo Kogi* (Tokyo, 1933), pp. 155-156.

The form of promulgation is provided for in Article 8 of the *Koshikirei*, or ordinance relating to public documents (1907), as follows:

> In making public an international treaty, promulgation is effected by an imperial edict. This imperial edict shall state that the treaty has received the advice of the Privy Council, and after personal signature by the emperor, the Privy Seal shall be placed thereon, and the minister president of state shall inscribe the date, and attach his countersignature, together with the ministers of state chiefly concerned.[22]

Before the issuance of *Kōbunshiki* on February 26, 1886,[23] treaties used to be published as *dajokan fukoku* or notifications of the chancellor of state; but, following the publication of this ordinance concerning the forms of official documents, treaties began to be published as imperial ordinances with no serial numbers. Since February 1, 1907, however, treaties have been promulgated in the treaty section of the *Kwampo*, or official gazette, with serial numbers for each year.

The promulgation of treaties is executed in one of two ways: A treaty which goes into effect as between the contracting states after an exchange of ratifications is promulgated with the following imperial edict:

> We, having received the advice of the Privy Council, ratify this treaty ... (the treaty is described by its title) signed by the plenipotentiaries of ... (names of the contracting states) at ... (date), and cause the same to be promulgated.

The above edict is attached to the text of the treaty as preamble, and to this edict is attached the signature of the emperor, countersigned by the prime minister and the foreign minister, whereas only the foreign minister countersigns the text of ratification.[24] A treaty which comes into effect upon the signatures of the plenipotentiaries is pro-

[22]The *Koshikirei* was issued on Feb. 1, 1907, as Imperial Ordinance No. 6, 1907 (text in *Horei Zensho*, 1907, *Chokurei*, pp. 7–11), and amended by Imperial Ordinance No. 145, 1921 (*Genko Horei Shuran* [1927], I, Bk. I, 45–46).

[23]Imperial Ordinance No. 1, 1886. Text in *Horei Zensho*, 1886, *Chokurei*, pp. 1–3. No provisions were made in this ordinance as to how treaties should be promulgated.

[24]Minobe, *Kempo Seigi*, pp. 280–281.

mulgated with the following imperial edict as preamble to
the text of the treaty:

We, having received the advice of the Privy Council, sanction
this treaty . . . (the treaty is described by its title), and cause the
same to be promulgated.

This imperial sanction is to be considered as merely an act
of the emperor to announce the already determined will of
the state. The will of the state in such cases has already been
determined by the plenipotentiaries who signed the documents under authority from the throne.[25]

On the other hand, many agreements are published in the
Kwampo as notifications of the Foreign Office and not as
treaties. One of the most recent instances is the Sino-
Japanese agreement of May 6, 1930, recognizing the principle of tariff autonomy of China. This agreement, though it
received the advice of the Privy Council, was published as
Notification No. 27, 1930, of the Department of Foreign
Affairs.[26] Agreements negotiated by representatives of departments, other than the Foreign Office, and administrative
in character, are often published in the *Kwampo* as notifications of such departments. Thus, the Sino-Japanese agreement of March 6, 1926, providing for the regulation of ship-
ment of salt to Japan from Tsingtao, was published as
Notification No. 29, 1926, of the Department of Finance in
the March 6, 1926, issue of the *Kwampo*. It was signed on
February 12 of the same year between Eiji Yoshida, second
secretary of the Japanese legation in Peking as the representative of the monopoly bureau of the Japanese government,
and a representative of the corresponding office of the
Chinese government. The departmental notification referred
to above was countersigned by the finance minister. This
agreement was later published in the treaty collection compiled by the treaty bureau of the Foreign Office.[27]

DOMESTIC EFFECT OF TREATIES

That the imperial prerogative over the negotiation and
ratification of treaties is absolute and exclusive, requiring no

[25]Minobe, *Kempo Satsuyo* (Tokyo, 1932), p. 552.
[26]Text in *Kwampo*, No. 1003 (May 7, 1930), pp. 163-171.
[27]*Joyakushu*, Collection IV, No. 4.

participation by other organs of the state, all the leading jurists are agreed. However, this same unanimity of views is not found among them as to the legal effect of treaties under the municipal law of Japan. Thus, two distinct camps may be noted as to whether treaties concluded by the emperor under the diplomatic prerogative of the throne are self-executing irrespective of their contents.

The more orthodox school argues for the well-known principle of international law that treaties have binding effect only upon the contracting states, and that some further action on the part of the contracting states is necessary in order to bring treaties, having stipulations regarding rights or duties of their nationals, into force within their respective territories. The late Professor Yatsuka Hozumi gave the classic exposition of this theory in the following words:

> The promulgation of a treaty does not add or subtract anything from its force; the promulgation does not give it the force of a *horei* (body of legislative enactments and ordinances). It is merely an official declaration of the existence of the treaty, allowing no one thereafter to plead ignorance of it. . . . A treaty cannot be proclaimed as *horei*, though it is possible under the constitution to establish a law or ordinance having identical contents with a treaty. . . . But the contents of a treaty relating to *rippo jiko* (matters falling under legislative competence) as enumerated in the constitution require the consent of Diet in order to have domestic effect. It is not permissible under the constitution to promulgate a treaty as law without the consent of the Diet, or as an imperial ordinance, when it concerns a matter of legislative competence under the constitution.[28]

The general thesis thus expounded by Professor Hozumi is supported by an array of such learned constitutional jurists as Uyesugi,[29] Kakei,[30] Soyejima,[31] Ichimura,[32] Sasaki,[33] as well as international lawyers, Tachi[34] and Yamada.[35]

[28]Y. Hozumi, "Some Questions Relating to Treaties," *Hogaku Kyokai Zasshi*, XXIII, No. 10, pp. 1357–1360. *Cf.* his elaborate discussion on this point in his *Kempo Teiyo*, II, 763–786; and also his article in *Kokka Gakkai Zasshi*, III, No. 27 (May, 1889), pp. 295–299.

[29]In support of Hozumi's theory, his celebrated student, Dr. Uyesugi, says: "A treaty is a contract between the Japanese sovereign and the sovereign of another state, and is not the command of the sovereign within the state. . . . A treaty is purely an international phenomenon and it is due to a misconception of its nature to argue that it has domestic effect by virtue of its international validity. It has no

There has been growing in recent years a group of jurists who give juristic justification of the uniform practice in Japan. This school holds that, in view of the unconditional prerogative of the emperor to conclude treaties, it is to be logically presumed that he likewise possesses the power to execute them. There can be no dispute as to treaties imposing obligations only upon the state, without affecting the nationals. However, a far-reaching issue is raised when a treaty stipulates legislative enactments, imposes fiscal obligations upon the state, or otherwise affects the rights and status under domestic law. If a treaty requires internal enforcement by a governmental organ, the emperor must so order, and in case a law rather than an ordinance is required, the consent of the Diet is necessary. Proclamation does not give a treaty the force as a command of the state. . . . In the case of a treaty requiring the enactment of a law for its execution, the Diet is free to deliberate upon the project of law proposed for this end and is not bound under the constitution to take any action thereon." (*Kempo Jutsugi* [Tokyo, 1927], pp. 629–630).

[30]Professor Kakei holds that a treaty relating to *rippo jiko*, or matters falling under legislative competence under the Constitution, must receive the consent of the Diet for its enforcement. He holds, however, that the Diet cannot refuse its consent to such enforcement legislation, as a treaty is superior to law (*Kokka Gakkai Zasshi*, XIX, No. 7 [July, 1905], pp. 134–144).

[31]Dr. Giichi Soyejima holds that the subject of treaty-making power is the state. According to him, therefore, Article XIII of the Constitution merely indicates that the emperor concludes treaties on behalf of the state, but it does not define the scope of such representation. Hence, the unlimited character of the emperor's treaty-making power extends only to those matters coming within his exclusive competence. It follows, therefore, by exercising his treaty power, the emperor cannot bind the state organs or his subjects if the subject matter of a treaty falls within the scope of legislative competence under the Constitution. He goes on to argue that, in concluding treaties with Japan, other states must take cognizance of this constitutional limitation upon the emperor's treaty-making power, and subsequent legisative action must always be implied as a condition to valid conclusion of such treaty. Soyejima, *Nihon Teikoku Kempo Yoron* (Tokyo, 1926), pp. 118–127. *Cf.* S. Inada, "Treaty-making Power in Japan," *Kokka Gakkai Zasshi*, XXXVII, No. 4 (April, 1923), pp. 516–533.

[32]Ichimura says that the binding effect of treaties extends only to the contracting states and not to their nationals, and that when a treaty relates to *rippo jiko* it requires the legislative consent thereto before the treaty in question be put into effect as municipal law. In deliberating upon such projects, Dr. Ichimura goes on to argue, the Diet is free to exercise its own discretion (*Teikoku Kempo Ron*, pp. 866–882).

[33]Professor Soichi Sasaki of the Kyoto Imperial University also shares the view that a treaty is a contract between states and binds only the contracting parties. He argues that a treaty as such has no force as municipal law, having no effect upon state organs or nationals. He classifies treaties in two categories, namely, those which require and those which do not require subsequent laws or ordinances for their execution. When no subsequent enactment of laws of issuance of ordinances is needed for their execution, as in the case of treaties modifying state boundaries or alliance, such treaties do not raise any constitutional issues. Many treaties, however, require subsequent laws or ordinances for their enforcement. Thus, treaties prohibit-

obligations of the nationals. This growing group of jurists argues that even in cases of treaties relating to *rippo jiko*, or matters falling within legislative competence under the Constitution, such treaties, upon ratification by the emperor, become part of the municipal law of the land and automatically bind the people. They hold that ratification indicates two distinct wills: one is the will of the state to conclude an agreement with the other contracting state, while the other is the will to establish a new rule for the nationals. The will is expressed in two directions, the one being expressed externally towards the contracting state by the exchange of ratifications, the other being expressed internally to the nationals by proclamation. By proclamation, they argue, a new law is added to *horei* in the form of *joyakuho*, or treaty law. Treaties, irrespective of their contents, thus are given the force of domestic law binding upon all the organs of the state as well as upon the nationals, upon proclamation.[36]

Dr. Tatsukichi Minobe, a leading exponent of this theory, expounds the self-executing nature of Japanese treaties in the following language:

It is an untenable thesis which holds that a treaty validly concluded by the emperor requires the enactment of a separate law

ing certain publications or determining conditions for naturalization require amendment of the existing press law or nationality law for their enforcement. In such cases, therefore, legislative enactments are necessary, in the process of which the Diet is legally free to exercise its own discretion, as in ordinary legislation. On the other hand, when treaties do not require legislative action but are put in force by *meirei* (ordinance), the imperial sanction to such treaties may be regarded as an act of the throne to establish a law of the land. Sasaki calls such treaties *juyakurei*, or treaty-ordinance. Such treaties are promulgated as *juyaku* (Sasaki, *Nihon Kempo Yoron* [Tokyo, 1933], pp. 697–702).

[34]Professor Tachi, a well-known professor of international law in the Imperial University of Tokyo, likewise holds that a treaty is a contract between states, and consequently its binding effect extends only to the contracting states. If a treaty is given effect as domestic law, it is by virtue of some affirmative provision of the domestic law of the state in which it is given such effect and is not inherent in the treaty itself (*Kokka Gakkai Zasshi*, XXXI, No. 12 [Dec., 1917], pp. 1803–1825). See also his *Heiji Kokusaiho Ron*, I, 574–575.

[35]Dr. S. Yamada (president of the Keijo Imperial University) also holds that, to avoid embarrassment, a practice should be established to make legislative consent a condition precedent to the valid conclusion of a treaty (*Kokka Gakkai Zasshi*, XIX, No. 7 [July, 1905], pp. 134–144).

[36]Minobe, "Domestic Effect of Treaties," *Kokka Gakkai Zasshi*, XIX, No. 7 (July, 1905), pp. 88–111. Reprinted in his *Kempo oyobi Kemposhi Kenkyu* (Tokyo, 1908), pp. 173–201. The late Prime Minister Kei Hara shared Minobe's view (Tanaka, *Hara Kei Zenshu*, I, 720–722).

of identical content. It goes without saying that it is the same state which concludes the treaty and enacts the law, and it is legally impossible for a state, having only one personality, to have two distinct wills. When a treaty is validly established the will of the state is thereby determined, and there cannot be at the same time another will of the state which may possibly conflict with the established will. If the contents of a treaty concern domestic law, then with the completion of the treaty, domestic law has also been completely established. . . . The Diet does not have competence even in the case of treaties that concern legislative matters. The provision of Article 5 that the legislative power is to be exercised with the consent of the Diet is not a fundamental principle that admits of no exception. On the contrary, the constitution itself recognizes many exceptions to this principle. . . . Thus, in view of the facts that, unlike the constitutions of many states, the power to conclude treaties is unconditionally vested in the emperor by Article 13 of the constitution, it is in accordance with the spirit of the constitution to consider Article 13, like Articles 8, 9, 10, as constituting an exception to the general principles of legislative power of the Diet stipulated in Articles 5 and 37. Moreover, the fact that the *Giinho*, or the Law of the Houses, has no provision for legislative deliberation upon treaties strengthens this interpretation.[37]

Professor Minobe is not alone in this field.[38] He is likewise supported by a growing group of learned jurists, including Dr. Yorozu Oda, Justice Cho Shimizu, and Baron Shigeto Hozumi.

Dr. Yorozu Oda agrees with Professor Minobe when he holds that a treaty is binding not only upon the contracting states but also upon their respective nationals, but differs

---

[37]Minobe, *Kempo Seigi* (1930), pp. 276–278. *Cf.* his *Kempo Satsuyo* (1932), pp. 545–554. Dr. Minobe, however, denies that international law and municipal law are identical in character. He admits, on the other hand, that international law is binding in interstate relations, while municipal law is operative between a state and its nationals ("Distinctions and Relations between International Law and Municipal Law," *Hogaku Kyokai Zasshi*, L [1932], 577–591, 810–838, 1005–1025). Dr. Sakutaro Tachi, the well-known professor emeritus of international law in the Tokyo Imperial University, holds that there is room for extending to promulgated treaties the same legal effect as statutes, if a rule of law, either written or customary, can be found which admits of such construction (*Heiji Kokusaiho Ron*, I, 574–575). He recently stated to the author that he does not believe such a rule of law has been established in Japan.

[38]*Cf.* Toda, "Treaties," *Kokka Gakkai Zasshi*, XI (1897), 176–182, 353–373; also Kimura, "International Treaties," *ibid.*, IX (1895), 709–731, 784–806, 906–926.

from the latter when Oda argues that, if a treaty relates to matters which, under specific constitutional mandate, necessitate statutory regulation, it cannot be placed in execution without parliamentary consent to necessary legislation. Furthermore, he contends that in such deliberations Diet is free to exercise its full discretion. Should the Diet refuse to pass the necessary legislation, he believes that the treaty, even though ratification has been effected, has no legal effect in Japan. However, when the treaty does not require any legislative enactment, it possesses a binding effect upon the nationals by its promulgation as treaty, and the Diet may not defeat it by subsequent legislation.[39] Justice Shimizu, on the other hand, is more in agreement with Professor Minobe. Thus, admitting that there exists a divergence of views among jurists on this point, Shimizu upholds the general practice of promulgating all treaties as treaties, including those relating to *rippo jiko*.[40] Baron Hozumi concurs with Minobe in holding that the treaty-making power of the emperor also comprehends the legislative power, and hence, when such treaties, even though they relate to *rippo jiko*, are promulgated, they become *joyakuho*, or treaty law, and are binding upon all organs of the state as well as the people. He differs from the latter, however, when he upholds the well-known theory that treaties and statutes are equally

[39]Yorozu Oda, "Treaties," *Hogaku Kyokai Zasshi*, XI (1893), 124–133. Dr. Oda is professor emeritus of public law in the Kyoto Imperial University and served his full term as judge of the Permanent Court of International Justice.

[40]Shimizu, *Teikoku Kempo Kogi* (Tokyo, 1933), pp. 154–158. Dr. Shimizu was chief judge of the Administrative Court of Litigation prior to his appointment as privy councilor on June 15, 1934, during Viscount Saito's administration. Shimizu held ten years ago that Article XIII of the Constitution constitutes an exception to the general principles of legislative power of the Diet, namely, that laws are to be made with the consent of the Diet. This exception was deliberately adopted, according to him, in order to avoid possible difficulties which might arise in case of conflict between the emperor and the Diet, and thus forestall all possibility of placing Japan in an embarrassing situation in executing treaty obligations with foreign countries. He opposed, however, the general practice of promulgating all treaties as *joyaku*, without regard to their content, as violative of the spirit of constitutional government. He argued then that treaties relating to *rippo jiko* must be promulgated as laws, while those falling within the ordinance power of the emperor as ordinances, to be effective under the municipal law of Japan. He saw room for publishing treaties as *joyaku* (treaty) only when they do not contain matters to be regulated either by law or by ordinance (*Kempo Hen* [1923], pp. 179–181, 1254–1269). *Cf.* his articles in *Kokka Gakkai Zasshi*, XXXIV, No. 1 (Jan., 1920), pp. 60–77; *ibid.*, XXXV, No. 9 (Sept., 1921), pp. 1205–1220.

binding, and consequently, in case of conflict between them, the later one must prevail.[41]

Thus far we have been concerned with the examination of the views of jurists who are divided upon the legal effect of treaties.[42] We may now inquire into official pronouncements upon this point. The government's interpretation of *joyakuho* was given in unmistakable language during the Forty-second session of the Diet. In reply to an interpellation put to the Hara (*Seiyukai*) government by Dr. Yoku Egi in the House of Peers on February 12, 1920, Sennosuke Yokota, chief of the Bureau of Legislative Affairs, replied:

> If a treaty stipulates an enactment of legislation, the government introduces bills in accordance therewith; but if the treaty itself affects the rights and duties of nationals, the government views such treaty provisions as treaty law and deems it unnecessary to introduce in the Diet a bill having identical content with the said treaty.[43]

Again, in answering an interpellation in the House of Representatives during the same session, Yokota continued:

> When a treaty contains provisions of legislative character, upon promulgation in accordance with the *Koshikirei*, it possesses the force of law. This is a characteristic feature of the Japanese constitution. . . . A treaty is concluded by the exercise of the imperial prerogative; it is therefore an expression of the will of the state externally towards the other contracting state. At the same time, it is an expression of the will of the state internally towards the nationals, inasmuch as the will of the state is a unity and cannot be divided. . . . All treaties, irrespective of their contents, are valid as domestic law, having an identical effect both externally and internally.[44]

[41]Hozumi, *Mimpo Soron*, or *Outlines of Civil Law* (Tokyo, 1929), I, 33–35. Baron Shigeto Hozumi, eldest son of the late Baron Nobushige Hozumi, the well-known authority on family law and former president of the Privy Council, is professor of civil law in the Imperial University of Tokyo.

[42]For brief review of these theories, see Professor Nakamura's article in *Gaiko Jiho*, No. 166 (Sept. 1, 1932), pp. 32–54. For recent semi-official commentaries, see Tokujiro Kanamori (counselor, and later chief, of the Bureau of Legislative Affairs), "Treaty as Municipal Law," *Jichi Kenkyu*, IX, No. 5 (May, 1933), pp. 15–24; also Hirobumi Terashima (secretary of the Foreign Office), "Some Questions Regarding Treaties," *Gaikko Jiho*, April 1, 1934, pp. 92–108.

[43]*Teikoku Gikaishi*, XI, 1493.

[44]*Ibid.*, XI, 1778–1779. This remarkable statement was made on Feb. 17, 1920, in reply to an interpellation by Representative Takao Saito.

That the theory thus expounded by Sennosuke Yokota has been the official interpretation of the legal effect of treaties in Japan may be surmised by a cursory review of official pronouncements in the Diet. It will be seen that the treaty law has uniformly been regarded superior to the other components of *horei*, or the entire body of law of the land. In other words, a treaty may amend or annul the effect of legislative acts or imperial ordinances, while it cannot be modified by subsequent legislation or imperial ordinances as "a treaty is a contract with a foreign state and cannot be broken by the will of one state."[45]

An interesting question is raised, however, when a treaty stipulates payment of funds or otherwise necessitates appropriations for its execution. The first instance is when payment of funds is stipulated in the treaty itself. Such expenditure comes under "the expenditures that appertain to the legal obligations of the government" and the Diet receives the restrictions imposed by Article LXVII of the Constitution. Hence the legislature is denied the right to exercise its full discretion in its deliberations upon it, and therefore it cannot reject or reduce the amount without the concurrence of the executive. However, in case the treaty necessitates certain expenditure for its enforcement, the legal situation is quite different. Until voted upon by the Diet, such expenditure for enforcement of treaty obligations does not come under the categories enumerated in the restrictive article referred to above. Consequently, the Diet is able to exercise its free discretion in voting the necessary appropriations, and hence it is possible that the government may be placed in an embarrassing position by the refusal of the legislative branch to vote the necessary funds.[46] The situation will be the same in the case of an (forcement legislation.

[45] Tsukuba, "Treaties," *Kokka Cakkai Zasshi*, VI, No. 66 (Aug., 1892), pp. 451–462. Prince Ito also emphasized the self-executing nature of treaties and declared that "the emperor makes the contract and the subjects obey it." (Midori Komatsu, *Ito Ko Zenshu* [Tokyo, 1928], III, 171, 184; also Hiratsuka, *Ito Hirobumi Hiroku*, II, 105). *Cf.* the statement by Dr. Keijiro Okano in the House of Representatives on March 10, 1906 (*Teikoku Gikaishi*, VI, 940–941).

[46] Minobe, *Kempo Seigi* (1930), pp. 693–694. He holds that expenditures due to treaty obligations should be treated as those which "appertain to the legal obligations of the government," and thus placed beyond parliamentary discretion (*Kempo Satsuyo* [1932], p. 612). Shimizu expresses a similar view (*Teikoku Kempo Kogi* [1933], pp. 500–503).

Thus, the executive may be forced to appropriate the necessary funds from outside the budget, or even resort to emergency imperial ordinances.[47]

JUDICIAL APPLICATION OF TREATIES

From what we have seen in the foregoing pages an interesting question is raised as to the part that the courts of law play in the enforcement of treaty obligations. The supreme power of interpreting treaties is vested in the Supreme Court of Japan. We have already observed that the courts take full cognizance of treaties and enforce them as other components of domestic law. Although there is no express provision in the Constitution directing the courts to recognize treaty obligations as binding upon them, nor has there been any express decision upon this point, the binding effect of treaties has always been assumed in court decisions.[48] Moreover, that treaties and international law are part of the municipal law of the land is implied in several legislative enactments, lifting the contents of treaties into the general body of domestic law.[49] When a treaty and statute relate to the same subject matter, the courts always endeavor to construe them so as to give effect to both, if this can be done without violating the express language of each.[50]

The courts have yet to determine whether they are bound to enforce a treaty when it clearly conflicts with a statute.

[47]*Cf.* the statement made by Dr. Hatao Yamakawa, chief of the treaty bureau of the Foreign Office, in the House of Peers on Feb. 18, 1922 (*Teikoku Gikaishi*, XIII, 225).

[48]Thus, in the Kim case, decided on March 5, 1908, the Supreme Court of Japan passed upon the scope of the Japanese-Korean agreement of Nov. 17, 1905 (*Hanrei Iho*, Vol. XIX, *Keiji Hanrei*, pp. 165–166). In both 1921 (*Hanrei Iho*, Vol. XXXII, *Daishinin Keiji Hanrei*, pp. 195–203) and in 1928 (*Daishinin Hanreishu*, Vol. VII, 1928, *Minji no Bu*, pp. 1128–1139), the Supreme Court passed upon the well-known principle of diplomatic immunities of diplomatic officers residing in Tokyo. *Cf.* Kisaburo Yokota, *Kokusaiho*, or *International Law* (Tokyo, 1933), I, 24–29.

[49]Minobe cites the following instances: Civil Code, Art. 2; Tariff Law, Art. 1; Law No. 70, 1899, Arts. 1, 2, 3, 6, 7; Copyright Law, Art. 28; Patent Law, Art. 33 (*Kempo Satsuyo* [1928], p. 471). As recent examples, Law No. 20, 1932 (law concerning bills of exchange and promissory notes) and Law No. 57, 1933 (law concerning cheques) may be cited. Professor S. Hozumi cites treaty law as a source of Japanese civil law (*Mimpo Soron* [1929], I, 30).

[50]Dictum in Paulhelm case, decided on July 30, 1907 (*Hanrei Iho*, Vol. XVIII, *Minji Hanrei*, pp. 383–389). *Cf.* Tachi in *Kokka Gakkai Zasshi*, XXXII, No. 8 (Aug., 1918), pp. 1116–1118.

So far, they have been able to avoid placing themselves on record on this point. Consequently, those jurists who uphold the contractual theory of treaties, which we have reviewed at length elsewhere, differ from those who uphold the self-executing nature of international commitments. Thus, the first school holds that the treaties are superior to legislative enactments between the states, but the nationals are bound only by municipal law. According to this school, therefore, the courts are bound to give effect to laws when they come in conflict with treaty stipulations.[51] The second group of jurists, on the contrary, are bound to insist that the courts must give effect to treaties under the doctrine of superiority of treaty to law.[52] They argue, however, that when a state deliberately undertakes to violate international law or treaty obligations by statutory enactment, it will give rise to a question of violation of international obligations, but the courts are bound to enforce such conflicting legislation as valid under municipal law.[53] This point, it is to be observed, still remains an academic question.

LEGISLATIVE PARTICIPATION IN TREATY-MAKING

The Imperial Diet possesses no power of direct participation in treaty-making. It plays no formal part in the initiation, negotiation, ratification, or enforcement of treaties. However, in view of the increasing scope of treaty law, or treaties affecting the rights and duties of nationals or relating to matters of legislative competence, the Diet may exert an indirect influence over treaty-making. In the early period of Japanese parliamentary history, the Diet made determined efforts to assert its power of participation in the treaty-making process, as witness the series of resolutions and addresses passed in the Lower House of the Diet in connection with the revision of unequal treaties in the 1890s, the most notable instance being the passage of a resolution in the Lower House by an almost unanimous vote, on June 1, 1894. Here, the House asserted its legislative preroga-

[51]*Ibid.*, p. 1118.

[52]Neither the Constitution nor the *koshitsuho*, or laws relating to the imperial household, may be modified by treaties (Minobe, *Kempo Satsuyo* [1932], p. 554).

[53]*Ibid.*, pp. 493–494, 569–570.

tive of participating in treaty-making process, should a
treaty relate to matters of legislative competence, namely,
the prerogative of the Diet to give its assent to the Enforcement bill.[54] Though the House never abandoned the general
thesis asserted in this classic resolution,[55] the executive uniformly ignored the stand thus taken by the House. Moreover, the Diet seems to have acquiesced in the general practice, and has not, since 1894, formally asserted by resolution,
or otherwise reiterated, the legislative prerogative over certain classes of treaties. On the contrary, the legislative branch
of government never failed to pass necessary legislation or
appropriations for the enforcement of treaties.

A reference is due at this juncture to those treaties which
do not affect directly the rights and duties of nationals or
otherwise bind administrative organs but which merely impose upon the contracting states obligations to enact certain
legislation or issue ordinances of specified content. In the
enforcement of such treaties, it is to be noted, the scope of
parliamentary discretion is at least as wide as in the ordinary
process of legislation. Thus the Diet may defeat the object
of such commitments by declining to pass the necessary
legislation.[56] The enactment of the law concerning bills of

[54]Chap. IX, n. 67, supra.

[55]This resolution was referred to by Representative Mori on March 10, 1906
(Teikoku Gikaishi, VI, 940). On Feb. 17, 1920, when a bill necessitated for the execution of the Treaty of Versailles was introduced in the Lower House, Rep. Takao
Saito called the attention of the government to the fact that the said treaty contained many matters within legislative competence, matters affecting civil law,
commercial law, and law of civil procedure. He declared that a treaty is a contract
between states and binds the parties, but that it has no binding effect upon the nationals. He said that if the treaty in question is to be enforced as municipal law,
parliamentary assent thereto must be obtained by enactment of new legislation. To
enforce the treaty without legislative consent, he argued, was a violation of the
Constitution and encroachment upon the legislative prerogative of the Imperial
Diet. He referred to the theory and practice of treaty-making in Great Britain, and
advocated that similar practice should be established in Japan, saying that such
practice was in accordance with the spirit of the Constitution, and was also conducive to developing more harmonious relations between the legislature and the
executive (ibid., XI, 1778). Dr. Soichi Sasaki holds that, by statutory mandate, the
executive may be compelled to report all treaties to the legislature after having been
concluded (Sasaki, Nihon Kempo Yoron [1933], p. 338).

[56]Professor Minobe, the leading exponent of the self-executing theory of treaties,
admits this distinction and holds that parliamentary consent is implied for valid
conclusion of such treaties. Hence, the failure on the part of the Diet to pass the
necessary legislation should not give rise to charges of breach of treaty obligations
(Kempo Satsuyo [1932], pp. 550–551).

exchange and promissory notes in 1932 and the law concerning cheques in 1933 are cases in point. For the purpose of avoiding difficulties caused by differences in the laws of countries in which bills of exchange circulate, and of giving more security and stimulus to international trade relations, a convention providing a uniform law for bills of exchange and promissory notes was signed on June 7, 1930, at Geneva.[57] As signatory to this convention, Japan assumed the obligation to introduce within her territory the Uniform Law forming Annex I of this convention.[58]

The subject matter of this Uniform Law was already covered in Part IV of the Commercial Code.[59] Hence the adoption in Japan of this convention would have meant a radical revision of that portion of the existing law relating to bills of exchange and promissory notes, a procedure necessitating a legislative action. The government, therefore, proceeded to achieve the object of this convention by legislation. A committee of experts, to which the convention was referred for appropriate action, recommended its adoption in January, 1931. In accordance therewith, a special committee of 13 members was appointed in the Justice Department to revise the existing commercial code. After prolonged deliberations, this committee drafted a new bill concerning bills of exchange and promissory notes in January of the following year for introduction in the legislature. After further deliberation, the bill was finally introduced in the Sixty-second session of the Diet by the Saito cabinet.[60] It was introduced in the House of Peers on June 4, 1932, by Hon. Matsukichi Koyama, the justice minister.[61] In introducing the bill the

[57]Japanese delegates signed the final act on June 7, 1930 (Foreign Office Notification No. 111, Dec. 26, 1933), but not the convention till Sept. 5, 1930.

[58]Article 1 of the convention provided: "The High Contracting Parties undertake to introduce in their respective territories, either in one of the original texts or in their own languages, the Uniform Law forming Annex I of the present Convention." Article 4 stipulated that instruments of ratification should be deposited with the Secretary General of the League of Nations before Sept. 1, 1932.

[59]Chapters I, II, III of Part IV of the commercial code related to rules governing bills of exchange and promissory notes, while Chapter IV covered cheques.

[60]For details of this bill as introduced in the Diet, see *Tegata Hoan Setsumeisho*, or explanatory note on the bill concerning bills of exchange and promissory notes, issued by the civil bureau of the Justice Department in June, 1932.

[61]The bill as it was introduced in the Diet was practically a verbatim translation of the convention, with only minor modification in Clause 3 of Article 44.

justice minister insisted that the government was not seeking
to obtain parliamentary assent to the convention as such,
but that its consent was needed for enforcement of the convention, as its subject matter constituted an amendment of
the commercial code, in the process of which legislative action was required.[62]

After obtaining a favorable action in the House of Peers
on June 8, the bill was introduced in the Lower House the
following day by the justice minister.[63] Replying to a long
interpellation put to the government by Representative
Fujiro Hara,[64] Justice Minister Koyama said that an argument might be advanced with the interpellator that one
way of bringing into effect the stipulations of this convention
was to promulgate it in accordance with the forms provided
for in the *Koshikirei*. He declared, however, that, in the
opinion of his government, parliamentary consent was necessary, in case it is deemed that the enforcement of certain
provisions of a treaty should be effected by municipal law
rather than a treaty. He admitted that the content of the
bill had already been established by the convention, but
pointed out the fact that, from the standpoint of municipal
law, it constituted a revision of the existing law regarding
bills of exchange and promissory notes. Thus he defended
the introduction of this bill in the Diet prior to petitioning
the emperor for ratification of the convention. As in the
Upper House, he did not deny the legislative discretion in
deliberating upon the bill, but strongly hinted that an exercise of such discretion might lead to the rejection of the convention by the emperor.[65] The bill was referred to a special
committee of eighteen members, appointed by the Speaker
of the House. On June 14 this committee made its report to

[62]*Kwampo gogai*, June 5, 1932, pp. 13–20; June 9, 1932, pp. 37–40. The bill was
referred to a special committee of nine members, appointed by the president of the
House of Peers, which held its meetings on June 6 and 7. The following day the
committee made its report to the floor, formally recommending its passage without
amendment. In making the report, the vice-chairman declared that the members of
the committee took their action with definite reservation that their legislative power
was in no wise restricted in their deliberation upon the bill. They were told, however,
that amendment or rejection of the bill by the Diet would be likely to render the ratification of the convention impossible (*ibid.*, June 9, 1932, p. 40).

[63]*Ibid.*, June 10, 1932, pp. 77–84.

[64]*Ibid.*, pp. 84–85.

[65]*Ibid.*, pp. 85–86.

the floor recommending its adoption. This was promptly complied with by the House, without debate.[66]

The legislative action necessary for the execution of the convention having been taken, the road was now open for its ratification. Thus, on July 15, 1932, the *Tegataho*, or law concerning bills of exchange and promissory notes, was promulgated,[67] and, three days later, the emperor ratified the convention with the advice of the Privy Council. Its ratification was deposited with the Secretariat of the League of Nations on August 31 of the same year.[68] The convention, however, was not promulgated till December 26, 1933,[69] along with three conventions of 1931 relating to cheques.[70] The new law concerning bills of exchange and promissory notes, as well as the law concerning cheques, became operative on January 1, 1934.[71]

Before concluding our discussion of the treaty-making power in Japan, our attention is directed to draft conventions and recommendations of the international labor conferences.[72] As to the interpretation of "authority or authorities

[66]*Ibid.*, June 15, 1932, p. 190.

[67]Law No. 20, 1932 (*Kwampo*, July 15, 1932, pp. 425–431).

[68]Foreign Office Notification No. 113, 1933 (Dec. 26, 1933).

[69]The Convention Providing a Uniform Law for Bills of Exchange and Promissory Notes was promulgated as Treaty No. 4, 1933 (*Kwampo gogai*, Dec. 26, 1933, pp. 1–66); Convention for the Settlement of Certain Conflicts of Laws in Connection with Bills of Exchange and Promissory Notes, as Treaty No. 5, 1933 (*ibid.*, pp. 69–91); and Convention on the Stamp Laws in Connection with Bills of Exchange and Promissory Notes, as Treaty No. 6, 1933 (*ibid.*, pp. 92–112). Protocols to these conventions were also published on the same date.

[70]Three conventions relating to cheques were signed at Geneva on March 19, 1931, namely, Convention Providing a Uniform Law for Cheques, Convention for the Settlement of Certain Conflicts of Laws in Connection with Cheques, and Convention on the Stamp Laws in Connection with Cheques. A bill concerning cheques, designed to carry into effect stipulations of these engagements, was introduced in the Sixty-fourth Diet (spring of 1933) by the Saito cabinet. The Diet voted favorably on the bill with only minor amendments. Thereupon, the emperor ratified these conventions on July 18, 1933, with the advice of the Privy Council. On July 29th of the same year, the Kogitteho, or law concerning cheques, was promulgated (Law No. 57, 1933. *Kwampo*, July 29, 1933, pp. 769–773). Ratifications were deposited with the Secretariat of the League of Nations on Aug. 25, 1933 (Foreign Office Notification No. 114, 1933). These conventions were published on December 26, 1933, as Treaties Nos. 7, 8, 9, 1933, respectively (*Kwampo gogai*, December 26, 1933, pp. 113–170, 171–195, 196–215).

[71]Imperial Ordinance No. 315, 1933 (*Kwampo*, Dec. 13, 1933, p. 317).

[72]*Cf.* Kenneth W. Colegrove, "Treaty-making Power in Japan," *American Journal of International Law*, XXV, No. 2 (April, 1931), pp. 291–293.

within whose competence the matter lies, for the enactment of legislation or other action" as stipulated in Article
CCCCV of the Treaty of Versailles, the government has asserted from the beginning that the "competent authority
or authorities" so far as Japan is concerned refers to the
Privy Council and not to the Imperial Diet.[73] Hence, in
spite of the repeated protests on the part of the press,[74]
jurists,[75] students of labor,[76] and members of the Diet,[77] the
government submits draft conventions to the Privy Council
for approval or for rejection. This submission of draft conventions for rejection is a unique procedure, as the cabinet
has never requested the *Sumitsuin* to reject treaties.[78] The
ministry may shift the entire responsibility for action or
non-action upon draft conventions to the Privy Council
when such a procedure is deemed expedient for political
reasons.[79] When it appears, however, that public opinion is
solidly behind the adoption of a certain draft convention,
or general sentiment favors such a legislation, the ministry
may be forced to introduce a bill designed to meet such pub-

[73]Replying to Representative Ichiro Kiyose's interpellation on this point, Baron
Shidehara, foreign minister, declared, during the Fiftieth Diet, that this provision
is to be interpreted according to the municipal law of several states and consequently
does not necessarily refer to the legislature (*Kwampo gogai*, March 27, 1925, pp.
928–929). *Cf.* Shimizu, *Teikoku Kempo Kogi* (1933), p. 158; also Professor Nakamura in *Gaiko Jiho*, Sept. 1, 1932, pp. 53–54.

[74]Leading Article, "Ratification of Draft Conventions of International Labor
Conferences," *Gaiko Jiho*, XXXVI, No. 4 (Aug. 15, 1922), pp. 437–452; also an
editorial on "Draft Conventions and Legislative Assembly," *Tokyo Asahi*, Dec. 14,
1928, p. 3.

[75]Professor Minobe holds that draft conventions and recommendations are proposals for internal legislation and hence, logically speaking, should be submitted
to the Diet for deliberation (*Kempo Seigi* [1930], pp. 271–273; also his *Kempo
Satsuyo* [1932], p. 553).

[76]*Cf.* Teijiro Uyeda, "Ratification of Draft Conventions of the Labor Conference," *Gaiko Jiho*, XXXV, No. 4 (Feb. 15, 1922), pp. 588–594. Also Junshiro Asari
(chief of Tokyo office of the International Labor Office), "Ten Years of International
Labor Organization," *Gaiko Jiho*, No. 623 (Nov. 15, 1930), pp. 166–171.

[77]Rep. Kiyose's interpellation in *Kwampo gogai*, March 27, 1925, pp. 927–928;
also Bunji Suzuki in *ibid.*, Jan. 27, 1929, pp. 91–92.

[78]Thus, at the plenary session of the Privy Council, held on March 19, 1930, in
the presence of the emperor, the Hamaguchi ministry's request for rejection of three
draft conventions, adopted in the tenth and eleventh international labor conferences,
was approved without debate (*Tokyo Asahi*, March 20, 1930, p. 1).

[79]*Gaiko Jiho*, XXXVI, No. 4 (Aug. 15, 1922), pp. 437–452.

lic demand, modifying somewhat the contents of such draft conventions or recommendations.[80]

With the gradual development of parliamentary government in Japan, it seems safe to predict the legislative participation in treaty-making will assume a broader scope by interpellations, resolutions, and other formal means of control of the executive. Though all ministries, irrespective of party affiliations, have always declined to disclose the nature of treaty negotiations or contents of treaties prior to ratification, it will be more difficult in the future to deny the indirect participation of the legislative branch of government in the making and enforcement of treaties, particularly those relating to matters of legislative competence. Hence, the Lower House may exert an increasing degree of actual control over the executive in treaty-making by resolutions, directing the ministry to start negotiations with powers regarding certain important subject matter, or expressing legislative support to the executive on the negotiations already entered into, or may exercise its legislative prerogative over appropriations by declining to vote the necessary funds for the discharge of obligations under treaties. Thus, it may be confidently expected that, with the firmer establishment of responsible cabinet government—though it appears quite afar at present—the negotiation, ratification, and enforcement of treaties in total disregard of the legislative branch of government will become a matter of political impossibility.

[80]See the introduction, in the Fifty-second session of the Diet, of the Seamen's Minimum Age bill, embodying the principles of the draft convention concerning minimum age for firemen, adopted in 1921 (*Kizokuin Gijiroku*, Jan. 25, 1927, pp. 92–93; *ibid.*, Feb. 1, pp. 182–183; *Kwampo gogai*, Feb. 6, 1927, p. 177; *ibid.*, Feb. 20, pp. 274–276).

Chapter XXVIII

THE WAR POWER

THE DECLARATION OF WAR

THE POWER to declare war on a foreign state is the prerogative of the throne, under the broad provision of Article XIII of the Constitution, which states that, "the emperor declares war, makes peace, and concludes treaties." As his prerogative over treaty-making, the emperor's war-making power under the Constitution is absolute and exclusive, requiring participation by no other organs of the state. The act of declaration of war involves two distinct aspects: (1) determination of the will of the state to commence war, and (2) manifestation of the will so determined. This act of manifestation may in turn be further divided into two separate acts: one directed towards the enemy, and the other directed towards the nationals.

The determination of the will to commence war is solely an internal act of the government, and consequently is determined by the emperor upon advice of his cabinet. The decision to commence war against a foreign state is thus made upon collective responsibility of the entire cabinet ministers. Since, however, the execution of war is largely in the hands of the military and naval authorities, upon declaration of the war the chiefs of army and naval general staffs are always consulted as to military and naval preparations, as witness the Sino-Japanese and Russo-Japanese wars. Moreover, the board of field marshals and fleet admirals and the Supreme War Council, the emperor's highest advisory bodies on national defense, are invariably brought into conference. In addition to the military and naval authorities, the genro, or elder statesmen, have also been called into the Imperial Court to advise the throne as to all state affairs relating to the outbreak of war. In fact, no war has been fought by Japan without the affirmative advice of this small group of the emperor's trusted advisers. As we have already seen in our survey of the Sino-Japanese War, the Russo-Japanese War, and the Japanese entry into the World War, the final decision has always been made in a joint conference of the genro, the cabinet, and chiefs of army and naval general staffs, held in His Majesty's presence. With the passing of the genro, and firmer establishment of the parliamentary system, the entire responsibility for the decision to commence war will be placed in fact as well as in theory in the cabinet, which is responsible to the elected "representatives" of the Diet.

In view of the dual character of the Japanese constitutional system, under which matters relating to military and naval tactics and operations are placed outside the domain of cabinet responsibility and competence and placed under the direct control of the emperor as the commander-in-chief of the nation's armed forces, lack of harmony between the cabinet and the general staffs may arise. The general staffs of the navy and the army not being under the complete control of the cabinet, it is conceivable that the staffs may exert undue pressure upon the executive to take "decisive" measures against a foreign state, or may discourage the executive from taking a more "positive" attitude in diplomatic negotiations preceding the commencement of war. For instance, there was a reported lack of harmony between the executive and the high command at the commencement of the Sino-Japanese War and in the early period of the Manchurian incident, while a complete agreement was maintained between these two organs during the Russo-Japanese War.[1]

A question may be raised here as to whether the imperial prerogative over the war power may be restricted by international treaties. The general practice as well as the views of Japanese jurists seems to support the binding effect of international treaties upon the war power in Japan. The Hague

[1]*Cf.* Makino, "The High Command and *Kasumigaseki*," *Kokusaiho Gaiko Zasshi*, XVI, No. 5 (Feb., 1918), pp. 369–376. For an exhaustive treatise on the power of supreme command, consult Dr. Tomio Nakano, *Tosuiken no Dokuritsu* (Tokyo, 1934), *passim.*

conventions thus place restrictions upon the war power of the emperor. This construction may reasonably be implied from the statement made by General Terauchi, war minister in the Katsura cabinet, during the Twenty-fifth session of the Diet. Moreover, that the Anglo-Japanese Alliance placed certain restrictions upon the war power of the emperor may be surmised from our review of parliamentary interpellations upon Japan's entry into the World War.

The Covenant of the League of Nations brought this question anew to the attention of the jurists and commentators upon the Japanese constitutional system. Dr. Tatsukichi Minobe, the well-known jurist of the Imperial University of Tokyo, again propounded his theory of treaties, and contended that the covenant, though it placed several restrictions upon the emperor in the exercise of his prerogative over foreign affairs, including treaty-making, the war power, appointment of diplomatic representatives, and preparation of the budget, nevertheless was constitutional. He cited the Anglo-Japanese Alliance as a precedent placing restrictions upon the war power of the emperor.[2] Professor Makino, another noted jurist of the same university, supported his colleague in upholding the constitutionality of the covenant. He admitted that the covenant placed limitations upon the emperor's powers over supreme command as well as the organization and peace standing of the army and navy. He upheld the covenant, however, on the ground that the emperor was assuming the restrictions of his own accord. He declared that the provisions of Article XIII of the Constitution referred to the imperial prerogative to declare war without the consent of the Diet; that the power to declare war was a power of the state, and consequently that the declaration of war made by the emperor, who is an organ of the state, must be regarded as legal under the municipal law of Japan.[3] Dr. S. Takahashi, a celebrated authority on international law, followed somewhat the same views as Dr. Makino. He likewise made the distinction between international law and constitutional law so far as the Covenant was

[2]Minobe, "League of Nations and the Constitution," *Kokka Gakkai Zasshi*, XXXIV, No. 1 (Jan., 1920), pp. 78–102; also his *Kempo Seigi*, pp. 266–267.

[3]*Kokusaiho Gaiko Zasshi*, XVII, No. 8 (April, 1919), pp. 739–741; also his article in *ibid.*, XVIII, No. 4 (Dec., 1919), pp. 319–329.

concerned. Thus, he argued that, though the emperor might receive certain restrictions under the Covenant in the exercise of his war powers, his freedom to go to war would be in nowise limited thereby. He held, therefore, that the restrictions under the Covenant would be a factor in the emperor's decision to declare war. He cited the Anglo-Japanese Alliance as a precedent, a treaty limiting the imperial prerogative on war-making yet requiring no constitutional amendment.[4]

Inasmuch as its effects under international law and municipal law are different, the decision to commence war is manifested externally through two distinct acts. Thus the declaration of war is directed towards the enemy and is made in accordance with international law. Both the Sino-Japanese War and the Russo-Japanese War were actually commenced prior to the declaration of war by the emperor. After ratification by Japan of the Hague Convention concerning the outbreak of war in 1912, however, this has not been possible,[5] and, in consequence, the Japanese declaration of war on Germany in August, 1914, was made prior to the commencement of actual hostilities. The proclamation of war, on the other hand, is directed toward its nationals and made in the form of an imperial rescript, countersigned by all ministers of state, indicating that the entire cabinet assumes the responsibility therefor.

THE EXECUTION OF WAR

We have already observed that the decision to make war is absolutely and exclusively vested in the emperor as his prerogative, allowing no participation on the part of the Imperial Diet. Accordingly, so far as the legal power is concerned, war can be declared in total disregard of the views or attitude of the legislative department. However, since the commencement of war necessitates expenditures, and the Diet's consent to necessary appropriations is required, the legislative branch, in practice, does take part in the execution

[4] S. Takahashi in *ibid.*, XVII, No. 8 (April, 1919), pp. 738–739.

[5] The convention was signed on Oct. 18, 1907, ratified by the emperor on November 6, 1911, and promulgated as Treaty No. 3, 1912 (Jan. 13, 1912). Text in *Genko Horei Shuran* (1927), I, Bk. VII, 360–364.

of war. Therefore, it is a practical impossibility for the executive to decide upon war without having a reasonable expectation that necessary appropriations are forthcoming from the
Diet, and consequently, the emperor, who acts upon the advice of the executive, receives indirect checks upon his war
power from the Diet.

As to which organ, the executive or the legislative, in practice, plays the dominant rôle in the declaration of war,
generalization is difficult to make. The executive apparently
led the legislative department in declaring war on China.
It appeared, at the time, that the measure was designed to
shift the public attention from internal politics to foreign
affairs, thereby bringing about a needed unity and harmony
among various political factions. Hence, whatever may have
been the actual motivation on the part of the executive, an
instant and overwhelming unity of the public was achieved
in this instance. The Russo-Japanese War, however, presents
a striking contrast. The executive in this case was somewhat
behind the public demand for immediate action. It would
be more difficult to conclude on this point as to the Japanese
entry into the World War. It may be submitted here that,
had a more liberal ministry been in power, Japanese entry
into the war might have been greatly delayed. It may be
noted, in this connection, however, that whoever may have
been the prime movers in those three wars, there can be little
doubt as to the spontaneous and effective achievement of
harmony and unity of all factions in voting the necessary
war appropriations for the prosecution of war. Thus, the
practice seems to indicate, whatever may be the immediate
cause for creating a condition for declaration of war against
a foreign state, the Imperial Diet is inevitably placed in a
position which renders it impossible to refuse the necessary
appropriations. Thus the Diet was convened in extraordinary
session immediately after the declaration of war in each of
these three instances, and all the political parties at once
buried their factional differences, though they did not agree
with the executive in particular policies.

With the declaration of war, the supreme command of the
armed forces on land and sea is directed from the imperial
headquarters, under the personal command of the emperor
as generalissimo, supported by the chiefs of the army and

naval general staffs.[6] As to movement of forces, objects of attacks, and similar matters relating to tactics and operations, the executive uniformly declines to disclose them to the Diet.

To meet the exigencies of the time due to the imminence of war or upon declaration of war, appropriation of funds through domestic or foreign loans, censorship of the press, restrictions upon freedom of travel, and other emergency measures may be taken by the government under Articles VIII and LXX of the Constitution. Not only may the executive take such needed measures, fiscal or otherwise, to meet the emergency situation arising out of war, but it is also empowered, under Article XXXI of the Constitution, to take all necessary emergency measures in times of war or in cases of national emergency.[7] Under this provision of the fundamental law, orders issued by the imperial headquarters may have binding effect upon the civilian population in so far as necessary for the execution of military operations. Martial law may be also be established.[8]

Hence, under the present system, the executive may completely dominate the legislative department of government in both the commencement and the execution of war. The executive may appropriate the necessary funds for initial activities of the military and naval forces from reserve funds and may further take such emergency financial measures under Articles VIII and LXX of the Constitution. True, while such emergency measures must be submitted to the following session of the Diet for parliamentary approbation, such action does not insure an effective control of the executive, since parliamentary disapproval of the measures already taken merely creates a political responsibility of the cabinet. At most it may cause resignation of the ministry so censured, but it does not invalidate the measures already taken or re-

[6]Statement by Admiral Count Yamamoto, then prime minister, to the House Budget Committee on Jan. 22, 1914 (*Dai Sanjuikkai Teikoku Gikai Shugiin Iinkai Giroku*, Pt. I, No. 1, pp. 4-6). *Cf.* Nagao Ariga, *Teishitsu Seido Kohon* (Tokyo, 1915), pp. 311-312; Minobe, *Kempo Satsuyo* (Tokyo, 1932), p. 334.

[7]Article XXXI of the Constitution provides: "The provisions contained in the present Chapter (providing for the rights and duties of subjects) shall not affect the exercise of the powers appertaining to the emperor, in times of war or in cases of a national emergency."

[8]Minobe, *Kempo Satsuyo* (1932), pp. 339-342.

lieve the national treasury from the financial obligations thus assumed. The Diet, in practice, has uniformly approved such emergency financial measures as a matter of course and has never asserted its legislative prerogative over "the purse strings" when faced with such measures.

The power to terminate war is likewise vested in the emperor exclusively, requiring no parliamentary concurrence or consent. Normally, a war is terminated by a treaty of peace, concerning which the principles and practices applicable to treaty-making apply.

THE USE OF ARMED FORCES IN FOREIGN AFFAIRS

Closely allied with the war power is the power of the emperor to dispatch forces to foreign territories with or without the consent of the latter. Jurists are divided as to whether intervention in a foreign territory is justifiable under international law. Thus Dr. Sakutaro Tachi argues for intervention under certain conditions, while Dr. Nagao Ariga refutes the arguments advanced by Professor Tachi.

Though the jurists may differ as to the technical question of whether an intervention in another state without the latter's consent constitutes a violation of international law, Japanese forces have, on several occasions, invaded foreign territories uninvited and without formal declaration of war. The Siberian Expedition during the latter days of the World War, the Shantung Expedition during the Tanaka administration, and the Manchurian (1931) and Shanghai (1932) incidents are a few of the most notable instances. On all these occasions, apparently the initiative was taken by military authorities. Thus, the decision to dispatch troops to Siberia was made in the advisory council on foreign relations presided over by General Terauchi, then the prime minister and a trusted head of the powerful *Choshu* military clique,[9] while the decision to send forces to Shantung, which occasioned the so-called Tsinan incident in May, 1928, was made by a cabinet headed by General Baron Tanaka, who was the war minister during the major portion of the Siberian Expedition. It was reported at the time that the decision to dispatch forces to Shantung was made without even the understanding

[9]Chap. XVIII, *supra.*

of the Foreign Office, and certainly without any civilian representation of the views of the *Kasumigaseki* in the cabinet. The decision in the cabinet, however, was made in full knowledge of the views of the general staffs.[10] Likewise there can be little doubt that the military and naval authorities led the civilian arm of the government throughout the trying days of delicate negotiations following the outbreak of the Sino-Japanese conflict in the fall of 1931.[11]

The dispatching of military forces or gunboats to foreign territories or foreign ports for "the protection of Japanese nationals abroad" presents another interesting problem. Such measures are often resorted to in meeting the "exigencies" arising in China. Under the Japanese doctrine of territorial propinquity and special interest in the regions of the Far East, the executive is constantly faced with the question of protecting Japanese rights and interests in China by armed forces, particularly because of the unsettled conditions on the continent. Such measures, however, involving the dispatch of forces or gunboats to a foreign territory, are always taken upon the approval of the cabinet in consultation with the war and naval authorities, through the war and navy ministers. Thus, the cabinet assumes collective responsibility for such decision to dispatch forces, but it is generally accepted that only the military and naval authorities assume the responsibility for any particular movement of forces, as witness the two notable expeditions referred to above.[12]

As to whether the diplomatic and consular representatives are superior in such cases to military or naval authorities at the spot, it is difficult to draw a line of demarcation. When an imminent danger is at hand, the consular representatives concerned wire the foreign office in Tokyo for armed protection. The matter will be immediately transmitted to the Navy or War Department, or both, whereupon it will be referred to the cabinet for decision. Upon cabinet approval, the navy minister or war minister instructs the commander of the marines or the troops, as the case may be, to offer the needed protection to the nationals, in consultation with the consular representatives. However, if the danger is so

[10]Chap. XXII, *supra.*
[11]Chap. XXVI, *supra.*
[12]*Cf.* Minobe, *Kempo Satsuyo* (1932), pp. 336-339.

imminent and instant as to allow no time for telegraphing
Tokyo for specific instructions, the consul in charge of the
region may ask for armed protection directly from the commander of forces near by, at the same time reporting the
same to the Foreign Office. The commanders of the armed
forces and the marines are under instructions to consult and
coöperate with the local representatives of the Foreign
Office but are also free to exercise their discretion in cases of
extreme emergencies. Under such circumstances, instances
may arise when the local representatives of the Foreign Office
and the military or naval forces lack harmony and coöperation in their respective activities.

Chapter XXIX

THE FORMULATION OF POLICIES

Having surveyed the Japanese theory and practice in treaty-making and in war-making in the previous two chapters, we shall now inquire into the principles and practices in the formulation of policies, with particular reference to parliamentary control of foreign relations. We shall examine only the more important questions relating to (1) the recognition of foreign states, governments, and belligerency; (2) the annexation of territory; and (3) the protection of Japanese nationals abroad.

Recognition of Foreign States, Governments, and Belligerency

The constitutional provision relating to the imperial prerogative over foreign affairs as stipulated in Article XIII of the organic law is sweeping in its scope. Although the declaration that "the emperor declares war, makes peace, and concludes treaties" refers expressly to his prerogative in treaty-making and the war power, it has been construed to extend to the entire field of foreign relations. It shows that the emperor is the sole representative of the state without parliamentary consent and that, without imperial delegation, no other person can, independent of the emperor, represent the state towards other states. It is obvious, however, that to hold that the emperor alone represents the state does not mean that every act of representing the state is done by him in person. The minister of state for foreign affairs at home and ambassadors, ministers, and consuls abroad likewise represent the state in its external relations. All these officers, how-

461

ever, are given the power of representation by the emperor and represent him directly and the state indirectly.[1]

The constitutional provision thus cited should not be regarded as restrictive. There seems to be little room for doubt, either in theory or in practice, that the full import of this article refers to the supreme power of the emperor over all the activities of the state in its external relations. To send state messages on behalf of the state to the heads of foreign states, to recognize ambassadors, ministers, and consuls sent by foreign states, to lodge diplomatic protests with foreign governments, to declare severance of diplomatic relations, to dispatch armed forces abroad, to occupy foreign territories, to recognize new states, new governments, and belligerency, are all included within the meaning and scope of the emperor's diplomatic prerogative under this article. It is needless to point out here, however, that every act of the emperor relating to foreign relations, as in other prerogatives over the general affairs of the state, must be done with the responsible advice of a minister of state.[2]

Thus, under the all-embracing imperial prerogative over foreign relations, the emperor recognizes foreign states, governments, belligerency, insurgency, and other facts in international relations, always through the Foreign Office, upon the advice of the cabinet. This is done in accordance with accepted rules of international usage, as by concluding treaties, by receiving diplomatic officers or granting exequaturs to consuls from foreign states. Moreover, the same may be done by diplomatic correspondence or exchange of notes, by formal salute of foreign flags, and other means recognized in international law. Thus, the Czechoslovak army was recognized as a belligerent army by an exchange of notes, through Ambassador Chinda in London, after authorization from the home government. The government in Soviet Russia was recognized by concluding a formal and fundamental treaty in 1925, and the Chinese Nationalist government by concluding a tariff agreement.

It will be of interest to note, in this connection, that, when questions involving civil or criminal matters are brought into court, the court examines the facts in the case and renders its

[1]Minobe, *Kempo Seigi* (Tokyo, 1930), p. 263.
[2]See our discussion on this point in Chap. II, *supra*.

judgments as to the facts of such political decision independent of the political department of government. It may inquire of the political department as to the facts, for information and reference, but is not bound by such information furnished by the latter. We shall cite only a few of the more important instances wherein the courts of law went into the details concerning the recognition of foreign states, governments, and belligerency.

In the celebrated case against one Kimura and five others who were charged with violation of Articles 148 and 162 of the Japanese Criminal Code, and Article I, Clause 1, of Law No. 66, 1905, relating to counterfeiting foreign notes, the Supreme Court of Japan had to pass upon the date of the establishment of the Chinese Republic. Here, the six persons were charged with counterfeiting notes issued by a bank established by the revolutionary force in Shanghai in November, 1911. The defendants were engaged in counterfeiting military notes which were being issued by this bank. The question before the court turned upon the issue of the date upon which the revolutionary government was actually in existence. The Supreme Court of Japan reviewed in detail the various acts of the revolutionary force and determined upon January 1, 1912, as the date of the establishment of the revolutionary government. This was the date when Dr. Sun Yat Sen became the provisional president of China, with headquarters in Nanking.[3] In the case of one Russian charged with counterfeiting the Russian forty-rouble bills, the Supreme Court of Japan likewise passed upon the question of the continuity of the state and the recognition of new governments. In this case the court recognized the continuity of the state of Russia and passed upon the recognition of the revolutionary government of March 28, 1917, and the Kerensky government of August, 1917, and declared that irrespective of the changes of governments, the Russian state continued to exist, and that the counterfeiting of Russian rouble bills was a violation of Law No. 66, 1905, relating to counter-

---

[3]"Although the recognition of the Chinese Republic by the powers was not accorded until under the Yuan Shi Kai régime, the actual establishment of the successful revolutionary government was established by Dr. Sun Yat Sen at Nanking on January 1, 1912. The Chinese Republic was established on this date." The Kimura case was decided by the Supreme Court of Japan on November 14, 1914. For text of the decision, see *Hanrei Iho*, XXVI, *Daishinin Keiji Hanrei*, 117–125.

feiting foreign money.[4] In the case against one Inouye and his associate, charged with counterfeiting notes issued by the Omsk government during April, 1919, while residing in Vladivostok, the Supreme Court again was called upon to decide whether the Japanese government had recognized the Omsk government, and declared that there was no evidence that it had, and in consequence decided that the defendants were not guilty of violating Article 162 of the Criminal Code.[5]

The above three cases indicate that the courts of law have power to inquire into political acts and to determine for themselves as to such political decisions, independent of the political department of government.

A brief inquiry should be made as to the part played by the legislative department in this regard. As in other fields of international relations, the Imperial Diet has no direct voice in the determination of the political question under review. Its participation in the process is limited primarily to interpellations and resolutions, neither one of which binds the executive department legally, although they may exert certain political influence, the precise degree of which depends largely upon the particular circumstances of the time and the general atmosphere in the legislative chamber. This topic will be discussed under our general inquiry into the parliamentary control of foreign relations.

Annexation of Territories

The Constitution does not provide for specific modes by which transfers of territory may be made. The practice prior to the promulgation of the Constitution in 1889 was not uniform. Annexations were made by imperial rescript, by ordinance, and by treaty. Thus, the recognition of the Loochoo Islands as part of the Japanese Empire was made by an imperial rescript, issued in September, 1872. The Ogasahara Island was recognized as a part of the Empire in June, 1875,

---

[4] "So long as Russia does not lose its identity as a state, the counterfeiting of roubles issued by the Russian government constitutes a violation of Law No. 66, 1905, irrespective of the downfall of the government which issued the roubles in question." Case No. 1864, 1919. Decided by the Supreme Court on November 27, 1919 (*ibid.*, XXXI, Pt. 1, *Daishinin Keiji Hanrei*, pp. 62–65).

[5] Decided on June 15, 1921. For text of the decision, see *ibid.*, XXXII, *Daishinin Keiji Hanrei*, pp. 99–115.

by dispatching resident officials, and finally, several near-by islands were incorporated in 1891 by an imperial ordinance.[6] The Japanese claim in Karafuto was ceded in favor of Russia in exchange for the Chishima Islands, by a treaty concluded between the two countries in May, 1875, followed by the addition of the Kurile Islands the same year.[7] After the promulgation of the Constitution and the establishment of a constitutional régime, the practice has been uniform. Thus, the addition of Formosa was made by treaty following the Sino-Japanese War, the southern half of Karafuto by treaty following the Russo-Japanese War, and the annexation of Korea in 1910 also by treaty. It seems reasonable to hold, therefore, that transfers of territory, either acquisition of a new territory or cession of a part of the existing territory, take place by means of treaty, without parliamentary consent or delegation.[8]

The provisions relating to the naturalization of aliens are set forth in the *Kokuseki-ho*, or nationality law, first enacted in 1899 at the time of the revision of treaties. Under the nationality law, persons possessing certain qualifications are to be naturalized, with the approval of the minister of home affairs.[9]

PROTECTION OF NATIONALS ABROAD

The protection of Japanese nationals abroad is usually effected through diplomatic means, as by presenting protests to the Foreign Office of the state in which the Japanese nationals reside. The methods employed by Japan are those recognized in general practice among nations and do not require particular emphasis at this point. The Tokyo government does not adopt diplomatic measures for protecting the rights and interest of its nationals abroad, except when questions of violation of generally accepted rules of international law or treaty obligations are involved. Thus, it declines to lodge a

[6] Imperial Ordinance No. 190, 1891 (Sept. 10, 1891).

[7] Notification No. 164, 1875 (Nov. 10, 1875).

[8] Minobe, *Kempo Satsuyo* (Tokyo, 1932), pp. 127–130. *Cf.* Ichimura, *Teikoku Kempo Ron*, pp. 373–379.

[9] For details relating to nationality, see Law No. 66, 1899. The nationality law was amended in 1924 (Law No. 19, 1924). *Cf.* Minobe, *op. cit.*, pp. 142–192; also Yamada, *Kokusai Shiho* (Tokyo, 1931), pp. 95–188.

diplomatic protest while the case in question is still pending in the court of the state concerned, or unless certain acts of a foreign state, or a public body of that state, are deemed to be violative of international law or treaty obligations. The more notable instances of protests which may be cited are those lodged with the United States government regarding the San Francisco school children incident of 1906, regarding the passage of the Alien Land Law in California of 1913, and the passage of the Immigration Law of 1924 carrying the so-called Japanese Exclusion Clause.

There is no known instance in which a Japanese minister or consul abroad instituted a suit in a foreign court to protect Japanese interests, although this power is recognized.[10]

As pointed out elsewhere, the Japanese government had often resorted to the dispatch of marines or armed forces to various regions of China for "the protection of Japanese residents there" and as a measure of "self-defense," some of the most notable instances of which had already been dealt with elsewhere. Though such measures have been confined to regions of political unrest and where the rights and interests of Japanese residents were in imminent danger, charges have sometimes been made that, in some instances, such measures were deliberately adopted from considerations of internal politics.

DETERMINATION OF FOREIGN POLICY

The minister of state for foreign affairs ordinarily plays the most important rôle in the determination of foreign policy, as head of the department and as a member of the cabinet, as well as the one who is the principal adviser to the throne on foreign affairs. Since all treaties and important questions relating to international relations must obtain the approval of the cabinet, and since the foreign minister as a member of the cabinet is responsible for offering all the necessary information as well as explanations to his colleagues before they reach an agreement, the dominant rôle of the foreign minister in cabinet decisions on foreign matters may easily be seen. Under the circumstances, if a cabinet lacks a

[10]*Cf.* the statement made by Kogoro Takahira, government delegate, in the House Budget Committee on Dec. 5, 1899 (*Dai Jushikai Teikoku Gikai Shugiin Yosan Iinkai Sokkiroku*, p. 20).

foreign minister in full charge of the *Kasumigaseki* and to represent the views of the Foreign Office in cabinet deliberations, such ministry may often lack unity and consistency in conducting foreign affairs. The *Seiyukai* cabinet under General Baron Tanaka (1927–1929), in which General Tanaka himself acted as the foreign minister throughout his administration, displayed a lack of unity and consistency in the nation's foreign policy. Deprived of its voice in the cabinet, the *Kasumigaseki* ceased, for the time being, to give to the administration the benefit of its information on world affairs in the formulation of important foreign policy. It was reported that Baron Tanaka deliberately failed to recommend a reputable statesman to head the Foreign Office and to act as the principal adviser to His Majesty on foreign affairs. His failure was, apparently, due to his determination to carry out his "positive policy" towards China, unhampered and unchecked by the staff of the Foreign Office.

The formulation of policies regarding China presents a somewhat unique picture. The general staff is represented by numerous agents throughout China and is thus able to command more reliable information concerning the political, economic, military, and other matters relating to her external as well as internal affairs, than the Foreign Office. Moreover, the military and naval authorities entertain particular concern and feel peculiar responsibility concerning the future of China, and consequently the Foreign Office feels the strongest pressure from military circles in this regard. The formulation of general policies in regard to China is, therefore, always conducted with full participation of the military and naval authorities. This preponderant military and naval influence over the Foreign Office in the formulation of general policies concerning China has come to be more pronounced since the Russo-Japanese War.

Throughout the last forty years of Japanese parliamentary history which is covered in the present study, general policies have been formulated by the cabinet, usually upon the initiative of the Foreign Office and in consultation with other departments concerned, but final decisions upon such questions of high politics have almost invariably been reserved to joint conferences of the genro and the cabinet. Ordinarily such conferences were held in the presence of the emperor. On these occasions the emperor's highest personal advisers joined his constitutional advisers in the formulation of important policies, such as the conclusion of important treaties, the initiation of diplomatic negotiations, the severance of diplomatic relations, the conduct of war, the conclusion of peace, and other questions of high policy. In our detailed analysis of several diplomatic incidents in Part II of this treatise, we have examined in detail this general practice in operation. Not infrequently the foreign minister exerted no greater influence than a secretary general of such conferences. Such was the case with Foreign Minister Hayashi in the formulation of the Manchurian policy following the Russo-Japanese War,[11] and Foreign Minister Motono in the Terauchi cabinet in the formulation of the Japanese policy towards Siberia.[12]

This general practice of formulating important foreign policies in joint conferences of the genro and the cabinet is fast becoming a thing of the past. Thus, at present, all important political decisions are made in the cabinet upon its own responsibility. This does not imply, however, that Prince Saionji, the sole remaining genro, is not consulted. On the contrary, the cabinet always sounds the wishes and views of this liberal elder statesman, as witness the recent conclusion of the London Naval Treaty. The position of the genro is being taken over by the Lord Privy Seal and other high personages close to the emperor.[13] The army and the navy still exercise a large and often controlling influence upon the cabi-

[11]An important joint conference of high officials and advisers was held on May 22, 1906, to formulate a general policy to be pursued in Manchuria. At this conference, the following were present: Prince Ito, resident general in Korea and genro; Prince Yamagata, president of the Privy Council and genro; Prince Saionji, prime minister and quasi-genro; Marquis Matsukata, privy councilor and genro; Marquis Inouye, genro; General Terauchi, minister of war; Admiral Saito, minister of navy; Yoshiro Sakatani, finance minister; Count Tadasu Hayashi, foreign minister; General Prince Katsura, former prime minister, who conducted the Russo-Japanese War; Admiral Count Yamamoto, navy minister during the war; General Kodama, chief of general staff. As the "explainers for the Foreign Office," Viscount Chinda, vice-minister of foreign affairs, and Enjiro Yamaza, chief of political affairs bureau of the Foreign Office, were also invited (Hiratsuka, *Ito Hirobumi Hiroku*, I, 391–409).

[12]Chap. XVIII, *supra*.

[13]This tendency is particularly noticeable since the formation of the present ministry in July, 1934 (Minobe, "Formation of the Okada Cabinet," *Keizai Orai*, IX, No. 8 [Aug., 1934], pp. 78–85; also his article, "Mission of the Okada Cabinet," *Chuo Koron*, No. 562 [Sept., 1934], pp. 108–115; Moriguchi, "Formation of a New Cabinet and the Future of Political Parties," *ibid.*, No. 561 [Aug., 1934], pp. 19–26; Baba, "Admiral Okada's Cabinet," *ibid.*, pp. 179–187).

net in regard to naval and land defenses. This is possible under the present constitutional system whereby the task of drawing up the program for national defense is left in the hands of the chiefs of the army and naval general staffs, and the cabinet's control is confined largely to its deliberations upon the budget necessary for the realization of the programs thus drawn up. In view of the dual character of the war and the navy ministers in the constitutional system, which we have discussed in detail elsewhere, the cabinet is placed under heavy pressure to accept the general program presented thereto by the military and naval authorities. The significance of the naval general staff was demonstrated in the conclusion of the London Naval Treaty, and there is reason to expect even greater opposition from the military circles for any attempt to reduce land defense either by domestic re-organization or by international agreement.

Parliamentary Control of Foreign Relations

Broadly stated, the general modes of parliamentary control of the executive in the conduct of foreign relations are the same as those relating to other aspects of the administration. Thus, the legislative control of foreign affairs may be comprehended under the following three heads: legislative power, fiscal power, and the general supervisory power.

We have observed elsewhere that the scope of legislative control of the executive over foreign relations is greatly limited under the present practice of regarding treaties, even those affecting the rights and duties of the nationals, as being effective under municipal law without further parliamentary action thereon. We have noted, however, that, with the gradual establishment of the parliamentary system, the actual legislative control may be increased by means of its legislative power to enact tariff laws, to regulate the ownership of land by aliens, to prescribe the conditions for naturalization, and other legislative matters. Thus, by invoking its right to refuse to enact legislation needed for the enforcement of treaties, to decline to vote the necessary funds for the execution of treaties, or to refuse to appropriate funds for the establishment of diplomatic or consular agencies abroad, a hostile Diet may seriously embarrass the executive in the conduct of foreign relations. It will be of interest to point out in this connection, however, that the Diet has never refused to pass needed enforcement legislation. In only one instance, during the past forty years of its existence, did the Diet fail to pass appropriations necessary to support an executive policy in foreign relations. The Forty-sixth Diet refused to appropriate 110,000 yen asked for by the executive for establishing a diplomatic mission at the Papal Court, and thereby refused to sanction the executive program.[14] No other instance of similar importance is known. This power over the "purse strings" may thus be invoked to block important programs and policies of the executive.

However, the fiscal power of the Diet over the Foreign Office is further restricted in that it has no competence over the nature of the use to which the unusually large secret service fund is put either before or after the money has been appropriated. It may be used for any purpose whatever when deemed advisable for the interest of the state in its dealing with other powers, and under the discretion of the foreign minister. Thus, the members of the Diet are even denied, on grounds of diplomatic secrecy, the right to inquire as to the use of this fund, which looms so large in the Foreign Office annual expenditures.

Finally, it is to be observed that the Imperial Diet does not feel it worth while to scrutinize the relatively small budget allotted to the Foreign Office. On the contrary, the opposition members find it more effective and advantageous, as a means of legislative supervision of the executive or of embarrassing the ministry in power, to bring departments with larger budgets into scrutiny and criticism.

The third and perhaps the most effective means of legislative control of foreign relations is found in parliamentary interpellations and resolutions. By means of interpellations, the entire field of foreign relations may be brought within the scope of parliamentary criticism and discussion. To such interpellations and questions, however, the cabinet has al-

---

[14]See the statements issued by the Foreign Office on Jan. 24, and Feb. 1, 1923 (cited in Shinobu, *Gaisei Kantoku to Gaiko Kikan*, pp. 412–416). *Cf.* parliamentary interpellations on this question during the session (*Kwampo gogai*, Feb. 21, 1923, pp. 333, 345–347); also Yoshino, "Diplomatic Representative to the Papal Court," *Kokusai Chishiki*, III, No. 3 (March, 1923), pp. 23–28.

ways adopted, irrespective of parties in power, the policy of avoiding, as much as possible, parliamentary interpellations or engaging in debates upon diplomatic issues. Thus, the ministry has uniformly declined to disclose the existence or contents of secret treaties, agreements, or other international commitments, confidential documents, the subject matter of negotiations still in progress, and diplomatic policies to be pursued in the future, when put in form of hypothetical questions. Moreover, the government always declines to state its position as to bills pending in foreign legislatures, or its views upon political conditions existing in foreign countries, or to state its interpretation of foreign constitutions and laws.

The cabinet may, however, take advantage of an interpellation to state its position on pending diplomatic issues with a foreign state, thus avoiding a direct statement to such state. Foreign Minister Shidehara cast a veiled criticism upon the Soviet's attitude on international obligations in the course of his celebrated pronouncement upon the doctrine of the continuity of foreign policy, in reply to a question addressed to him in the Lower House on July 1, 1924. He declared, in the course of his reply, that the means of executing diplomatic policies might change, and even the policies themselves may differ according to the changing circumstances of the time, but the obligations of a state towards other states, whether by treaties or otherwise, must be carried out, irrespective of the changes in government.[15]

The power of the Houses of Diet to pass resolutions is often resorted to as a means of expressing the will of the House on particular issues in diplomatic affairs. It may be used as a means of expressing want of confidence in the cabinet in conducting particular diplomatic relations, and consequently such resolutions may be of greatest political significance, as witness the various resolutions passed in the Lower House during its struggle for parliamentary participation in foreign relations in the 1890s, particularly concerning the revision of treaties. Such resolutions were likewise introduced, but always defeated, during the subsequent years, following the close of the Sino-Japanese War, on the conclusion of the "dis-

[15] *Kwampo gogai*, July 2, 1924, pp. 8–9. *Cf.* Matsubara, "Continuity of Diplomatic Policy," *Gaiko Jiho*, XL, No. 5 (Sept. 1, 1924), pp. 81–95; Shinobu, *Gaisei Kantoku to Gaiko Kikan*, pp. 216–218.

honorable peace treaties," on the Siberian Expedition, on the "grave Manchurian incident," and on other occasions.

On the other hand, resolutions may be passed expressing the views of the legislative branch of government on any important pending questions of foreign policy. Thus, the Nagano Resolution of March 20, 1923, introduced in the House of Representatives, urging immediate recognition of the Soviet government and calling upon the government to formulate a definite policy towards Russia, sought to bring political pressure upon the executive for a definite action.[16] Likewise, the House of Representatives passed, by a unanimous vote, a resolution in the Sixty-second Diet demanding an early recognition of Manchoukuo.[17] On the other hand, the passage of resolutions in both Houses of the Diet, almost identical in content, on July 1, 1924, strongly condemning the American immigration law carrying the objectionable exclusion clause, intended to express the sentiments of the legislative chambers upon a legislative act of a foreign state. The fact that the resolutions were passed unanimously in both Houses tends to show that they had the whole-hearted support of the ministry, though the foreign ministry declined to state precisely the position of the cabinet.[18]

In recent years several unsuccessful attempts were made by members of the Lower House to create special committees of inquiry to investigate specific diplomatic issues, such as the Nikolaevsk incident and the Paris Peace Conference, but the government in power always opposed such a move, as we have observed in our analysis in Part II of this treatise, on the ground that the creation of a parliamentary committee of inquiry on foreign policy would be an encroachment upon the cabinet and an invasion upon its peculiar prerogative, and that it would seriously embarrass the ministry in the conduct of foreign relations. The creation of such a committee in the Lower House to act as a liaison between the cabinet and the people and to discharge the parliamentary supervision of the executive on foreign affairs with more intelligence

16*Kwampo gogai*, March 21, 1923, pp. 803–815.

17*Ibid.*, June 15, 1932, pp. 187–190. See also *Tokyo Asahi*, June 15, 1932, p. 2.

18For the House resolution, see *Kwampo gogai*, July 2, 1924, pp. 11–15. For the Peers' resolution, see *Dai Shijukukai Teikoku Gikai Kizokuin Giji Sokkiroku*, July 1, 1924, pp. 27–31.

and corresponding effectiveness had long been advocated by several leading students of Japanese diplomacy.[19] The advisory council of foreign relations created in 1917 included two influential members of the Lower House, the primary purpose being not to ensure full and extended discussion in the Diet, but to circumvent such parliamentary criticism and scrutiny by committing the leaders of two powerful parties to the government policy in advance, thereby inevitably tampering with the subsequent parliamentary criticism of foreign relations.[20]

POPULAR CONTROL OF FOREIGN RELATIONS

Closely related to the subject of parliamentary control of foreign relations is the problem of participation in the formation, execution, and supervision of foreign policies by the general public. This control by the public of the conduct of foreign relations may be exercised largely by means of the press, the speech, and the association. Here again no substantial progress has been made in the last four decades of Japanese constitutional history. Questions relating to diplomacy or to national defense have always been regarded by the executive as excluded from popular participation and as peculiarly within the exclusive domain of the executive, and the general public has acquiesced in this general assertion on the part of the executive. Hence, as we have observed in Part II, the cabinet has been consistent, irrespective of the party in power, in disclosing as little as possible to the "representatives of the people" on matters relating to the conduct of foreign relations or national defense. Moreover, the executive branch has uniformly taken the position that such questions relating primarily to the external relations of the state should be placed outside the domain of partisan politics, and this plea has been generally accepted by the public.

[19]Mochizuki, "Reform of Diplomatic Organs," *Chuo Koron*, No. 267 (June, 1911), pp. 40–47; Shinobu, "Committee on the Reform of Diplomatic System," *Gaiko Jiho*, XXX, No. 10 (Nov. 15, 1919), pp. 962–967; Royama, "Parliamentary Committee on Foreign Relations," *ibid.*, XXXVI, No. 4 (Aug. 15, 1922), pp. 453–463; Morishima, "Foundations of People's Diplomacy," *Kokusai Chishiki*, VI, No. 6 (June, 1926), pp. 12–22; also Professor Nakamura, "Popular Control of Foreign Policy," *Gaiko Jiho*, No. 671 (Nov. 15, 1932), pp. 1–26.

[20]Chap. V, *supra*.

Important exceptions, however, should be noted. We have observed elsewhere that political parties, particularly in recent years, have not failed to resort to questions of foreign policy for attacking the ministry in power, as witness the *Minseito* onslaught upon the *Seiyukai* ministry in connection with the publication of the report upon the death of Marshal Chang Tso Lin and the phraseology "in the names of their respective peoples" in the Pact of Paris. We have already seen that these attacks were used as political footballs rather than motivated by sincere conviction. The point to be emphasized is that foreign policy has come to play an ever increasing rôle in the working of the parliamentary system in Japan in recent years.

A serious hindrance, however, to the development of an effective control by the general public over foreign policy is found in the general lack of knowledge and information on the part of the public regarding current problems of foreign policy. This is due, in the first instance, to the absence of adequate facilities to convey information from those in charge of the conduct of foreign relations. The Foreign Office, as we have seen on numerous occasions, has been very reluctant, with the possible exception of the Sino-Japanese crisis arising out of the Manchurian incident, to furnish the press with information on current diplomatic questions. The *Kasumigaseki* publishes only the treaties and agreements, and a few journals of little importance. The official publications thus issued by the Foreign Office are limited in scope, the major portion being devoted to the reports of consuls abroad, translations of the foreign press, and other matters largely routine in character. The Foreign Office does, however, furnish the public with press releases on important diplomatic issues, which may find wide circulation in the press as "official information." In spite of this, the news that is allowed to be printed is often perfunctory and general, and it has often been charged that important information on international questions is more often obtained from abroad as dispatches from foreign capitals than from the *Kasumigaseki* intelligence bureau. This has often been true of diplomatic negotiations.

Under the restrictions placed upon the press under the Press Law and the Publication Law, the freedom of the press is greatly restricted, and the temporary suspension of papers

deemed "contrary to the public interest" or "relating to diplomatic or military secrets" is common. Moreover, under the ordinance power of the ministers of foreign affairs, of navy, and of war, further restrictions may be placed upon the press, as we have already observed, particularly while the country is engaged in war or military operations, or while important diplomatic negotiations are in progress.

Important restrictions upon academic freedom are to be found in the fact that professors of all imperial universities and other government institutions of higher learning are civil officers and, therefore, are subject to the restrictions of various ordinances relating to civil service officers, particularly the disciplinary ordinances. The most notable instance known is the celebrated case of the forced retirement of Dr. Tomizu of the Imperial University of Tokyo in connection with his activities during the Russo-Japanese War. Dr. Tomizu, a professor in the faculty of law of the university, throughout the Russo-Japanese negotiations and the war advocated a "strong policy" towards Russia and vigorously condemned in the press and on the platform any move to terminate the war abruptly. In consequence, he was suddenly placed on the retired list on August 24, 1905. This aroused an instant resentment on the part of the entire faculty of law, which finally resulted in the reappointment of Dr. Tomizu as lecturer, and the resignation of the minister of education and the president of the university. In this fight for academic integrity and freedom of expression, the law faculty of the Kyoto Imperial University joined its sister institution in Tokyo.[20]

In brief summary, it is to be observed that the general center of the control of foreign relations is shifting from the absolute and autocratic executive department under the direction and effective "supervision" of the genro to a more democratic control by the legislative body, through a firmer establishment of a parliamentary régime. At present, however, it appears safe to submit that the most effective pressure upon the executive comes directly from the Privy Council because of its advice to the throne on the ratification of treaties, and secondly, from the military and naval circles in matters relating to national defense and to China. The once all-

[21]Kudo, *Teikoku Gikaishi*, III, 527–529. *Cf. Tokyo Asahi*, Aug. 26, 1905, p. 2; also *ibid.*, Oct. 6, 1905, p. 3.

controlling influence of the council of elder statesmen is fast declining as a real factor in the conduct of foreign relations, and the press bids well in the immediate future to become the most powerful barometer of public opinion on foreign policies as well as on domestic questions. With more adequate information available to the public on foreign relations, and with the establishment of a standing parliamentary committee on foreign relations, working hand in hand with a smoothly functioning parliamentary system, the actual center of control over foreign relations may, in course of time, be found in the House of Representatives, the "representative chamber of public opinion."

APPENDIX

THE CONSTITUTION OF THE EMPIRE OF JAPAN[1]

Preamble

HAVING, by virtue of the glories of Our Ancestors, ascended the Throne of a lineal succession unbroken for ages eternal; desiring to promote the welfare of, and to give development to the moral and intellectual faculties of Our beloved subjects, the very same that have been favoured with the benevolent care and affectionate vigilance of Our Ancestors; and hoping to maintain the prosperity of the State, in concert with Our people and with their support, We hereby promulgate, in pursuance of Our Imperial Rescript of the 12th day of the 10th month of the 14th year of Meiji, a fundamental law of State, to exhibit the principles, by which We are to be guided in Our conduct, and to point out to what Our descendants and Our subjects and their descendants are forever to conform.

The rights of sovereignty of the State, We have inherited from Our Ancestors, and We shall bequeath them to Our descendants. Neither We nor they shall in future fail to wield them, in accordance with the provisions of the Constitution hereby granted.

We now declare to respect and protect the security of the rights and of the property of Our people, and to secure to them the complete enjoyment of the same, within the extent of the provisions of the present Constitution and of the law.

The Imperial Diet shall first be convoked for the 23rd year of Meiji and the time of its opening shall be the date when the present Constitution comes into force.

When in the future it may become necessary to amend any of the provisions of the present Constitution, We or Our successors shall assume the initiative right, and submit a project for the same to the Imperial Diet. The Imperial Diet shall pass its vote upon it, according to the conditions imposed by the present Constitution,

[1] Text as in Ito, *Commentaries.*

and in no otherwise shall Our descendants or Our subjects be permitted to attempt any alteration thereof.

Our ministers of State, on Our behalf, shall be held responsible for the carrying out of the present Constitution, and Our present and future subjects shall forever assume the duty of allegiance to the present Constitution.

CHAPTER I

THE EMPEROR

Article I.—The Empire of Japan shall be reigned over and governed by a line of Emperors unbroken for ages eternal.

Article II.—The Imperial Throne shall be succeeded to by Imperial male descendants, according to the provisions of the Imperial House Law.

Article III.—The Emperor is sacred and inviolable.

Article IV.—The Emperor is the head of the Empire, combining in Himself the rights of sovereignty, and exercises them, according to the provisions of the present Constitutions.

Article V.—The Emperor exercises the legislative power with the consent of the Imperial Diet.

Article VI.—The Emperor gives sanction to laws and orders them to be promulgated and executed.

Article VII.—The Emperor convokes the Imperial Diet, opens, closes and prorogues it, and dissolves the House of Representatives.

Article VIII.—The Emperor, in consequence of an urgent necessity to maintain public safety or to avert public calamities, issues, when the Imperial Diet is not sitting, Imperial Ordinances in the place of law.

Such Imperial Ordinances are to be laid before the Imperial Diet at its next session, and when the Diet does not approve the said Ordinances, the Government shall declare them to be invalid for the future.

Article IX.—The Emperor issues or causes to be issued, the Ordinances necessary for the carrying out of the laws, or for the maintenance of the public peace and order, and for the promotion of the welfare of the subjects. But no Ordinance shall in any way alter any of the existing laws.

Article X.—The Emperor determines the organization of the different branches of the administration, and salaries of all civil and military officers, and appoints and dismisses the same. Exceptions especially provided for in the present Constitution or in other laws, shall be in accordance with the respective provisions (bearing thereon).

Article XI.—The Emperor has the supreme command of the Army and Navy.

Article XII.—The Emperor determines the organization and peace standing of the Army and Navy.

Article XIII.—The Emperor declares war, makes peace, and concludes treaties.

Article XIV.—The Emperor declares a state of siege. The conditions and effects of a state of siege shall be determined by law.

Article XV.—The Emperor confers titles of nobility, rank, orders and other marks of honor.

Article XVI.—The Emperor orders amnesty, pardon, commutation of punishments and rehabilitation.

Article XVII.—A Regency shall be instituted in conformity with the provisions of the Imperial House Law.

The Regent shall exercise the powers appertaining to the Emperor in His name.

CHAPTER II

Rights and Duties of Subjects

Article XVIII.—The conditions necessary for being a Japanese subject shall be determined by law.

Article XIX.—Japanese subjects may, according to qualifications determined in laws or ordinances, be appointed to civil or military or any other public offices equally.

Article XX.—Japanese subjects are amenable to service in the Army or Navy, according to the provisions of law.

Article XXI.—Japanese subjects are amenable to the duty of paying taxes, according to the provisions of law.

Article XXII.—Japanese subjects shall have the liberty of abode and of changing the same within the limits of law.

Article XXIII.—No Japanese subject shall be arrested, detained, tried or punished, unless according to law.

Article XXIV.—No Japanese subject shall be deprived of his right of being tried by the judges determined by law.

Article XXV.—Except in the cases provided for in the law, the house of no Japanese subject shall be entered or searched without his consent.

Article XXVI.—Except in the cases mentioned in the law, the secrecy of the letters of every Japanese subject shall remain inviolate.

Article XXVII.—The right of property of every Japanese subject shall remain inviolate.

Measures necessary to be taken for the public benefit shall be provided for by law.

Article XXVIII.—Japanese subjects shall, within limits not prejudicial to peace and order, and not antagonistic to their duties as subjects, enjoy freedom of religious belief.

Article XXIX.—Japanese subjects shall, within the limits of law, enjoy the liberty of speech, writing, publication, public meetings and associations.

Article XXX.—Japanese subjects may present petitions, by observing the proper forms of respect, and by complying with the rules specially provided for the same.

Article XXXI.—The provisions contained in the present Chapter shall not affect the exercise of the powers appertaining to the Emperor, in times of war or in cases of a national emergency.

Article XXXII.—Each and every one of the provisions contained in the preceding Articles of the present Chapter, that are not in conflict with the laws or the rules and discipline of the Army and Navy, shall apply to the offices and men of the Army and of the Navy.

CHAPTER III

THE IMPERIAL DIET

Article XXXIII.—The Imperial Diet shall consist of two Houses, a House of Peers and a House of Representatives.

Article XXXIV.—The House of Peers shall, in accordance with the Ordinance concerning the House of Peers, be composed of the members of the Imperial Family, of the orders of nobility, and of those persons who have been nominated thereto by the Emperor.

Article XXXV.—The House of Representatives shall be composed of Members elected by the people, according to the provisions of the Law of Election.

Article XXXVI.—No one can at one and the same time be a Member of both Houses.

Article XXXVII.—Every law requires the consent of the Imperial Diet.

Article XXXVIII.—Both Houses shall vote upon projects of law submitted to it by the Government, and may respectively initiate projects of law.

Article XXXIX.—A Bill, which has been rejected by either the one or the other of the two Houses, shall not be again brought in during the same session.

Article XL.—Both Houses can make representations to the Government, as to laws or upon any other subject. When, however, such representations are not accepted, they cannot be made a second time during the same session.

Article XLI.—The Imperial Diet shall be convoked every year.

Article XLII.—A session of the Imperial Diet shall last during three months. In case of necessity, the duration of a session may be prolonged by Imperial Order.

Article XLIII.—When urgent necessity arises, an extraordinary session may be convoked, in addition to the ordinary one.

The duration of an extraordinary session shall be determined by Imperial Order.

Article XLIV.—The opening, closing, prolongation of session and prorogation of the Imperial Diet, shall be effected simultaneously for both Houses.

In case the House of Representatives has been ordered to dissolve, the House of Peers shall at the same time be prorogued.

Article XLV.—When the House of Representatives has been ordered to dissolve, Members shall be caused by Imperial Order to be newly elected, and the new House shall be convoked within five months from the day of dissolution.

Article XLVI.—No debate can be opened and no vote can be taken in either House of the Imperial Diet, unless not less than one third of the whole number of the Members thereof is present.

Article XLVII.—Votes shall be taken in both Houses by absolute majority. In the case of a tie vote, the President shall have the casting vote.

Article XLVIII.—The deliberations of both Houses shall be held in public. The deliberations may, however, upon demand of the Government or by resolution of the House, be held in secret sitting.

Article XLIX.—Both Houses of the Imperial Diet may respectively present addresses to the Emperor.

Article L.—Both Houses may receive petitions presented by subjects.

Article LI.—Both Houses may enact, besides what is provided for in the present Constitution and in the Law of the Houses, rules necessary for the management of their internal affairs.

Article LII.—No Member of either House shall be held responsible outside the respective Houses, for any opinion uttered or for any vote given in the House. When, however, a Member himself has given publicity to his opinions by public speech, by documents in print or in writing, or by any other similar means, he shall, in the matter, be amenable to the general law.

Article LIII.—The Members of both Houses shall, during the session, be free from arrest, unless with the consent of the House, except in cases of flagrant delicts, or of offenses connected with a state of internal commotion or with a foreign trouble.

Article LIV.—The Ministers of State and the Delegates of the Government may, at any time, take seats and speak in either House.

CHAPTER IV

The Ministers of State and the Privy Council

Article LV.—The respective Ministers of State shall give their advice to the Emperor, and be responsible for it.

All Laws, Imperial Ordinances and Imperial Rescripts of whatever kind, that relate to the affairs of the State, require the counter-signature of a Minister of State.

Article LVI.—The Privy Councillors shall, in accordance with the provisions for the organization of the Privy Council, deliberate upon important matters of State, when they have been consulted by the Emperor.

CHAPTER V

The Judicature

Article LVII.—The Judicature shall be exercised by the Courts of Law according to law, in the name of the Emperor.

The organization of the Courts of Law shall be determined by law.

Article LVIII.—The judges shall be appointed from among those who possess proper qualifications according to law.

No judge shall be deprived of his position, unless by way of criminal sentence or disciplinary punishment.

Rules for disciplinary punishment shall be determined by law.

Article LIX.—Trials and judgments of a Court shall be conducted publicly. When, however, there exists any fear that such publicity may be prejudicial to peace and order, or to the maintenance of public morality, the public trial may be suspended by provision of law or by the decision of the Court of Law.

Article LX.—All matters that fall within the competency of a special Court shall be specially provided for by law.

Article LXI.—No suit at law, which relates to rights alleged to have been infringed by the illegal measures of the administrative authorities and which shall come within the competency of the Court of Administrative Litigation specially established by law, shall be taken cognizance of by a Court of Law.

CHAPTER VI

Finance

Article LXII.—The imposition of a new tax or the modification of the rates (of an existing one) shall be determined by law.

However, all such administrative fees or other revenue having the nature of compensation shall not fall within the category of the above clause.

The raising of national loans and the contracting of other liabilities to the charge of the National Treasury, except those that are provided in the Budget, shall require the consent of the Imperial Diet.

Article LXIII.—The taxes levied at present shall, in so far as they are not remodelled by a new law, be collected according to the old system.

Article LXIV.—The expenditure and revenue of the State require the consent of the Imperial Diet by means of an annual Budget.

Any and all expenditures overpassing the appropriations set forth in the Titles and Paragraphs of the Budget, or that are not provided for in the Budget, shall subsequently require the approbation of the Imperial Diet.

Article LXV.—The Budget shall be first laid before the House of Representatives.

Article LXVI.—The expenditures of the Imperial House shall be defrayed every year out of the National Treasury, according to the present fixed amount for the same, and shall not require the consent thereto of the Imperial Diet, except in case an increase thereof is found necessary.

Article LXVII.—Those already fixed expenditures based by the Constitution upon the powers appertaining to the Emperor, and such expenditures as may have arisen by the effect of law, or that appertain to the legal obligations of the Government, shall be neither rejected nor reduced by the Imperial Diet, without the concurrence of the Government.

Article LXVIII.—In order to meet special requirements, the Government may ask the consent of the Imperial Diet to a certain amount as a Continuing Expenditure Fund, for a previously fixed number of years.

Article LXIX.—In order to supply deficiencies, which are unavoidable, in the Budget, and to meet requirements unprovided for in the same, a Reserve Fund shall be provided in the Budget.

Article LXX.—When the Imperial Diet cannot be convoked, owing to the external or internal condition of the country, in case of urgent need for the maintenance of public safety, the Government may take all necessary financial measures, by means of an Imperial Ordinance.

In the case mentioned in the preceding clause, the matter shall be submitted to the Imperial Diet at its next session, and its approbation shall be obtained thereto.

Article LXXI.—When the Imperial Diet has not voted on the Budget, or when the Budget has not been brought into actual existence, the Government shall carry out the Budget of the preceding year.

Article LXXII.—The final account of the expenditures and revenue of the State shall be verified and confirmed by the Board of Audit, and it shall be submitted by the Government to the Imperial Diet, together with the report of verification of the said Board.

The organization and competency of the Board of Audit shall be determined by law separately.

CHAPTER VII

Supplementary Rules

Article LXXIII.—When it has become necessary in future to amend the provisions of the present Constitution, a project to the effect shall be submitted to the Imperial Diet by Imperial Order.

In the above case, neither House can open the debate, unless not less than two-thirds of the whole number of Members are present, and no amendment can be passed, unless a majority of not less than two-thirds of the Members present is obtained.

Article LXXIV.—No modification of the Imperial House Law shall be required to be submitted to the deliberation of the Imperial Diet.

No provision of the present Constitution can be modified by the Imperial House Law.

Article LXXV.—No modification can be introduced into the Constitution, or into the Imperial House Law, during the time of a Regency.

Article LXXVI.—Existing legal enactments, such as laws, regulations, Ordinances, or by whatever names they may be called, shall, so far as they do not conflict with the present Constitution, continue in force.

All existing contracts or orders, that entail obligations upon the Government, and that are connected with expenditure, shall come within the scope of Art. LXVII.

BIBLIOGRAPHY

DOCUMENTS

CHIHO GYOSEI GAKKAI, *Dai Nippon Teikoku Gikaihsi,* or Parliamentary Record of Japan (Tokyo, 1926–1930). 13 Vols.

HOSOKAI, *Hanrei Iho,* or Compilation of Court Decisions (Tokyo, 1894–   ).

Daishinin Hanrei-shu, or Compilation of the Supreme Court Decisions (Tokyo, 1922–   ).

JAPAN, *Dai Nippon Teikoku Tokei Nenkan,* or Statistical Yearbook of Japan (Tokyo, 1890–   ).

Gaiko Iho, or Foreign Office Reports (Tokyo, 1920–   ).

Gaimusho Kohyoshu, or Compilation of Foreign Office Releases (Tokyo, 1922–   ).

Genko Horei Shuran, or Compilation of Laws and Ordinances in Force (Tokyo, 1927). 3 Vols.

Horei Zensho, or Compilation of Laws and Ordinances (Tokyo, 1890–   ).

Joyaku Isan, or Compilation of Treaties and Conventions (Tokyo, 1908, 1913, 1918, 1926).

Kizokuin Giji Sokkiroku, or Record of the Proceedings of the House of Peers (1890–   ).

Kizokuin Iinkai Giji Sokkiroku, or Record of the Proceedings of the Committees of the House of Peers (Tokyo, 1890–   ).

Kwampo, or Official Gazette (Tokyo, 1890–   ).

Kwampo gogai, or Official Gazette, extra edition (Tokyo, 1890–   ).

Shugiin Giji Sokkiroku, or Record of the Proceedings of the House of Representatives (Tokyo, 1890–   ).

Shugiin Iinkai Giji Sokkiroku, or Record of the Committees of the House of Representatives (Tokyo, 1890–   ).

LEAGUE OF NATIONS, *Appeal by the Chinese Government, Report of the Commission of Enquiry* (Geneva, 1932).

485

BOOKS

ARIGA, NAGAO, *Kinji Gaikoshi,* or *Recent Diplomatic History* (Tokyo, 1910).

ASHIDA, KIN, *Saikin Sekai Gaikoshi,* or *Diplomatic History of Recent Times* (Tokyo, 1934). 3 Vols.

ASO, DAISAKU (ed.), *Kato Komei Den,* or *Biography of Komei Kato* (Tokyo, 1928).

BABA, EIICHI, *Kempo Seiji no Riron to Jissai,* or *Principles and Practices of Constitutional Government* (Tokyo, 1926).

BABA, TSUNEGO, *Gikai Seiji Ron,* or *Commentaries on Parliamentary Government* (Tokyo, 1933).

DENNETT, TYLER, *Roosevelt and the Russo-Japanese War* (New York, 1925).

FUKUSHIMA, YASOROKU (ed.), *Kaikoku Gojunenshi,* or *Fifty Years of New Japan* (Tokyo, 1908). 2 Vols.

HANAI, TAKUZO, *Shotei Ronso: Kokumin Taikai Jiken,* or *Commentaries on Court Debates: National Peoples Mass Meeting Incident* (Tokyo, 1930).

HIRATSUKA, ATSUSHI, *Ito Hirobumi Hiroku,* or *Secret Memoirs of Prince Ito* (Tokyo, 1929).

HIROTA, NAYE, *Naikaku Kotetsu Gojunenshi,* or *Fifty Years of the Japanese Cabinet* (Tokyo, 1930).

HOZUMI, YATSUKA, *Kempo Teiyo,* or *Principles of Constitutional Law* (Tokyo, 1910). 2 Vols.

ICHIMURA, KOKEI, *Teikoku Kempo Ron,* or *Imperial Constitutional Law* (Tokyo, 1926).

ICHIJIMA, KENKICHI (ed.), *Okumako Hachijugonenshi,* or *Eighty-five Years of Marquis Okuma* (Tokyo, 1926). 3 Vols.

ISHII, VISCOUNT KIKUJIRO, *Gaiko Yoroku,* or *Diplomatic Memoirs* (Tokyo, 1930).

ITO, COUNT HIROBUMI, *Kempo Gikai,* or *Commentaries on the Constitution of the Empire of Japan* (Tokyo, 1889).

ITO, SEITOKU (ed.), *Kato Komei,* or *Life and Letters of Count Komei Kato* (Tokyo, 1929). 2 Vols.

IZUMI, TETSU, *Kokusaiho Mondai Kenkyu,* or *Studies in International Law* (Tokyo, 1924).

KOMATSU, MIDORI (ed.), *Ito-ko Zenshu,* or *Life and Letters of Prince Ito* (Tokyo, 1928). 3 Vols.

KUDO, TAKESHIGE, *Teikoku Gikaishi,* or *Parliamentary History of Japan* (Tokyo, 1901–06). 3 Vols.
    Yosan Seido Ron, or *The Budgetary System* (Tokyo, 1910).
    Meiji Kenseishi, or *Constitutional History of Japan during the Meiji Era* (Tokyo, 1914–22). 2 Vols.

Taisho Kenseishi, or *Constitutional History of Japan during the Taisho Era* (Tokyo, 1927).

MINOBE, TATSUKICHI, *Kempo oyobi Kempo Shi Kenkyu*, or *Studies in Constitutional Law and History* (Tokyo, 1908).

Gyoseiho Satsuyo, or *Principles of Administrative Law* (Tokyo, 1928). 2 Vols.

Kempo Seigi, or *Commentaries on the Constitution* (Tokyo, 1928).

Gendai Kensei Hyoron, or *Commentaries on the Contemporary Parliamentary Government* (Tokyo, 1930).

Kempo Satsuyo or *The Law of the Japanese Constitution* (Tokyo, 1932).

Gikai Seiji no Kento, or *Studies in Parliamentary Politics* (Tokyo, 1934).

MORIGUCHI, SHIGEJI, *Kensei no Genri to sono Unyo*, or *Principles and Practices of Constitutional Government* (Tokyo, 1929).

MYOGA, FUSAKICHI, *Nippon Seito no Gensei*, or *Contemporary Political Parties in Japan* (Tokyo, 1929).

NISHIKAWA, TORAJIRO, *Siberia Shussei Hishi*, or *Secret History of the Siberian Expedition* (Tokyo, 1925).

NISHINO, GEN, *Yosan Gairon*, or *Introduction to the National Budget* (Tokyo, 1926).

NOMA, GOZO, *Rippo Ichigen Ron*, or *Unitary Theory of Legislation* (Tokyo, 1926–27). 2 Vols.

ODA, YOROZU, *Gyseiho Kogi*, or *Lectures on Administrative Law* (Tokyo, 1924). 3 Vols.

ONO, HIDEO, *Nippon Shimbun Hattatsushi*, or *History of the Development of the Press in Japan* (Tokyo, 1924).

ONOZUKA, KIHEIJI, *Gendai Seiji no Shokenkyu*, or *Studies in Contemporary Politics* (Tokyo, 1926).

OTSU, JUNICHIRO, *Dai Nippon Kenseishi*, or *Constitutional History of Japan* (Tokyo, 1927). 8 Vols.

ROYAMA, MASAMICHI, *Nichiman Kankei no Kenkyu*, or *Studies in the Japanese-Manchurian Relations* (Tokyo, 1933).

Nihon Seiji Doko Ron, or *Trends in Japanese Politics* (Tokyo, 1933).

SAITO, RYOYEI, *Kinsei Toyo Gaikoshi Josetsu*, or *Recent Diplomatic History of the Orient* (Tokyo, 1928).

SAKAMOTO, KIZAN, *Gensui Koshaku Yamagata* or *Field-Marshal Prince Yamagata* (Tokyo, 1922).

SASAKI, SOICHI, *Nihon Kempo Yoron*, or *Introduction to Japanese Constitution* (Tokyo, 1933).

SHIMIZU, CHO, *Kempo Hen*, or *Principles of Constitutional Law* (Tokyo, 1923).

Teikoku Koho Taii, or *Introduction to Japanese Public Law* (Tokyo, 1926).

Chikujo Teikoku Kempo Kogi, or *Commentaries on the Constitution* (Tokyo, 1933).

SHINOBU, JUMPEI, *Gaiko Kantoku to Gaiko Kikan*, or *Control of Foreign Relations and the Organs for the Conduct of Foreign Affairs* (Tokyo, 1926).

Taisho Gaiko Jugonenshi, or *Fifteen Years of Diplomatic History during the Taisho Era* (Tokyo, 1927).

Meiji Hiwa: Nidai Gaiko no Shinso, or *Two Leading Diplomatic Episodes during the Meiji Era* (Tokyo, 1928).

Mammo Tokushu Ken Ron, or *Special Rights and Interests in Manchuria and Mongolia* (Tokyo, 1932).

International Law in the Shanghai Conflict (Tokyo, 1933).

SUGIMURA, YOTARO, *Kokusai Gaiko Roku*, or *Reflections on International Politics* (Tokyo, 1933).

TACHI, SAKUTARO, *Heiji Kokusaiho Ron*, or *International Law of Peace* (Tokyo, 1930).

Senji Kokusaiho Ron, or *International Law of War* (Tokyo, 1931).

Kokusai Remmei Kiyaku Ron or *Commentaries on the Covenant of the League of Nations* (Tokyo, 1932).

Jikyoku Kokusaiho Ron, or *Contemporary Issues and International Law* (Tokyo, 1934).

TANAKA, ASAKICHI (ed.), *Hara Kei Zenshu*, or *Life and Letters of Kei Hara* (Tokyo, 1929). 2 Vols.

TAOKA, RYOICHI, *Kokusaihogaku Taiko*, or *International Law*, Vol. I (Tokyo, 1934).

TOKUTOMI, CHOICHIRO, *Koshaku Katsura Taro Den*, or *Biography of Prince Taro Katsura* (Tokyo, 1917).

UYESUGI, SHINKICHI, *Teikoku Kempo*, or *Imperial Constitution* (Tokyo, 1924).

Kempo Jutsugi, or *Commentaries on the Constitution* (Tokyo, 1927).

YOKOTA, KISABURO, *Kokusaiho*, or *International Law*, Vol. I (Tokyo, 1933).

YOSHINO, SAKUZO, *Nisshi Kosho Ron*, or *Sino-Japanese Negotiations* (Tokyo, 1915).

Niju Seifu to Iaku Joso, or *Dual Government and the Supreme Command* (Tokyo, 1922).

Gendai Kensei no Unyo, or *Observations on Contemporary Parliamentary Government* (Tokyo, 1930).

MAGAZINES AND PERIODICALS

American Journal of International Law.
American Political Science Review.
Bungei Shunju, or *Literary Review.*
Chuo Koron, or *Central Review.*
Contemporary Japan.
Gaiko Jiho, or *Revue Diplomatique.*
Hogaku Kyokai Zasshi, or *Journal of the Judicature Society.*
Hogaku Shimpo, or *Journal of Law.*
Kaizo, or *Reconstruction.*
Kokka Gakkai Zasshi, or *Journal of Political and Social Science.*
Kokusaiho Gaiko Zasshi, or *Journal of International Law and Diplomacy.*
Kokusai Chishiki, or *International Understanding.*
Kokusai Hyoron, or *International Review.*
Taiyo, or *The Sun.*

NEWSPAPERS

Japan Advertiser.
Japan Chronicle.
Japan Weekly Chronicle.
Japan Times.
Jiji Shimpo.

Osaka Asahi.
Osaka Mainichi.
Tokyo Asahi.
Tokyo Nichi Nichi.

For details, see Mr. George E. Sokolsky's volume, *The Tinder Box of Asia* (New York, 1933), chaps. V, VI, VIII, especially pp. 211–14. A most stringent criticism of Baron Shidehara's China policy was offered by Mr. Yosuke Matsuoka, former vice-president of the South Manchuria Railway Company (who became its president in August, 1935) and a leading member of the *Seiyukai* party. Thus, in his interpellation on foreign affairs on January 23, he vigorously defended what he termed a "life-line theory" of the Manchurian situation, saying that the issue over Manchuria and Mongolia was not a mere matter of 200,000 Japanese residents, nor one of certain mileage of railroads. He characterized Baron Shidehara's policy towards China and Manchuria as one of an endless series of concessions and withdrawals. He bluntly charged that the railway negotiations just started at Mukden were motivated solely by considerations of domestic politics. He contended that what Japan was demanding in Manchuria was the assurance of the minimum right to existence as a nation, and urged upon the government that the hour had come to act more decisively (*Kwampo gogai*, Jan. 24, 1931, pp. 48–50). Baron Shidehara replied to Mr. Matsuoka the following day and flatly denied the interpellator's charges (*ibid.*, Jan. 25, 1931, pp. 51–52, 52–54). Replying to Mr. Takeji Kawamura in the Upper House on February 2, the foreign minister said that the main cause for the sharp decline in the railway income was directly traceable to the falling prices of soya beans, and not to the so-called parallel railway lines (*ibid.*, Feb. 3, 1931, pp. 89–92, 92–93, 99). Replying to another member of the House of Peers on March 9, he pleaded with the Peers to show more patience in dealing with Chinese authorities. Referring specifically to the question of liquidating the outstanding unsecured or inadequately secured debts in arrears, Baron Shidehara admitted negotiations were then in progress with Nanking and that the Chinese proposal was not such as to be unacceptable as a basis for further negotiations (*ibid.*, March 10, 1931, pp. 374, 374–82). See also a Shanghai dispatch on March 6 regarding this item in *Osaka Asahi*, March 7, 1931, p. 7. There were, of course, students of Japan's continental policy who sought to assist Baron Shidehara in his policy of conciliation. Writing in February, 1931, for instance, Professor Shinobu reminded the public of the growing menace to peace in Manchuria, and counseled the people against violation of the territorial integrity of China. To resort to force even in defence of our special rights and interests in Manchuria, he argued, was a clear case of appealing to "war as an instrument of national policy," and as such, incompatible with obligations we had assumed under the Kellogg Pact. He advocated the early establishment of a standing commission of conciliation to which such issues might be referred for settlement ("Sino-Japanese Relations," *Gaiko Jiho*, Feb. 1, 1931, pp. 1–19).

INDEX

Abé, Mr. Isoo, 363.

Abei, Rep. Bankon, 101, 102.

Abo, Admiral: at London naval conference, 291; rôle of, during Manchurian crisis, 351.

Adachi, Mr. Kenzo, 365.

Administrative Court, 18.

Advisory Council on Foreign Relations: establishment of, 43–45; organization and functions of, 45–46; purposes, 46, 473; persons composing, 46n.; constitutionality of, discussed, 46; decline of, 47–48; rôle in discussion of the Siberian expeditions, 205–208, 210; deliberates on Japanese policy at Paris Conference, 221; secrecy of, 221; considers Paris peace treaty, 224; considers participation in Washington naval conference, 231–232; rôle during Washington naval conference, 233–234.

Akiyama, Rep. Teisuke, 146–147.

Anglo-Japanese Alliance, 244; negotiation of, 124, 128; renewal of (1905), 128–129, 157; renewal of (1911), 129; termination of (1921), 130–131; Kato on applicability of to U. S., 185; relation to Declaration of London, 197.

Anglo-Japanese treaty of commerce and navigation (1894), 105–106.

Annexation of territories, 464–465.

Antung-Mukden Railway, 185.

Aoki, Mr. Shuzo, 70; vice-minister of foreign affairs, 71; becomes foreign minister, 98; refuses to answer questions of Diet, 98–99; resigns from Foreign Office (1891), 99.

Arai, Rep. Shogo, 98.

Araki, Lieutenant General, 365, 369, 370; on Manchurian and Shanghai incidents, 375; defends withdrawal from Shanghai, 379–380; helps draft reply to Lytton Report, 401–402; rôle in Japanese withdrawal from League, 412n., 414f.

Argentina, 77.

Arisugawa, Prince, 111.

Army: attitude of, toward occupation of Weihawei, 124–125; rôle of officers in negotiations with China, 116; urges peace with Russia, 149, 154; advocates seizure of Saghalien, 152; officers of, take part in discussion of peace terms with Russia, 151, 153; part of, in Korean negotiations (Nov., 1905), 161; chief of staff of, confers on demands to be presented to China, 190; attitude on Chinese question, 191; army expansion bill in Thirty-fifth Diet, 194–195; rôle of officers in controversy over Siberian expeditions, 207–209; accusations of disharmony between, and Foreign Office, made in Diet (1920), 211; popular beliefs about the influence of military cliques and financiers, 214–215, 217–218; chief of staff of, confers on defense program after Washington Conference, 236–238; representatives of, confer on Seiyukai Chinese policy, 248; rôle of officers of, in bringing about Tsinan incident, 248–251; conduct of officers during scandal following assassination of Chang Tso Lin, 277–282; effect on, of contest between naval clique and cabinet, 343; attack of General Minami on disarmament advocates, 345; rôle in precipitating Manchurian crisis, 345f.; views of, on Manchurian situation, stated by War Minister Minami, 351–352; independent action of, during development of Manchurian crisis, 349, 353, 354; views of, concerning settlement of Manchurian crisis, 357–359, 365; coöperation with, of Inukai ministry, 369; accused in Diet of imposing a dual foreign policy on Japan, 409–411; initiative of, in Japanese military activity, 458–459; agents of, in China, 467; interest of, in Chinese affairs, 467; rôle in foreign

491